Fodor's 93
Mexico

W9-BIM-692

Fodor's Travel Publications, Inc.
New York • Toronto • London • Sydney • Auckland

Fodor's Mexico

Editor: Carolyn Price
Contributors: Jim Budd, Barbara Franco, Marian Goldberg, Edie Jarolim, Andrea Lehman, David Lida, Wendy Luft, Maribeth Mellin, Eleanor Morris, Marcy Pritchard, Linda K. Schmidt, Frank Shiell
Researcher: Mary Ellen Schultz
Creative Director: Fabrizio La Rocca
Cartographer: David Lindroth
Illustrator: Karl Tanner
Cover Photograph: Andy Caulfield/Image Bank

Design: Vignelli Associates

Special Sales

Fodor's Summer Travel Promotion Official Order Form

4.) Mail this Official Order Form (no photocopies or facsimilies accepted), your dated register receipt showing proof of purchase during the stated promotion period, plus a check for $1.50 [U.S.] shipping and handling made out to "Random House, Inc." to:

Fodor's AudioBook Promotion
P.O. Box 100
400 Hahn Road
Westminster, MD 21158

5.) Please send my tape to:

Name _____

Address _____Apt. _____

City _____State _____Zip_____

All Order Forms must be postmarked by September 15th, 1993. Limit: one order per customer. Offer good while supplies last. Substitutions may be made by Fodor's if chosen title is no longer available. Please allow four weeks for delivery.

Fodor's Summer Travel Promotion Official Order Form

Follow these simple steps to receive your Random House AudioBook:

1.) Buy any Fodor's travel guide (not including Fodor's Flashmaps and Pocket Guides) between May 15th and August 15th, 1993 and keep your dated store receipt as proof of purchase.

2.) Select tape by checking off <u>one</u> choice below.

____ **"A" is for Alibi** (Sue Grafton) 0-394-57977-1 ($15.95 value)

____ **The Accidental Tourist** (Anne Tyler) 0-394-55673-9 ($16.00 value)

____ **Chesapeake** (James Michener) 0-394-55695-X ($15.95 value)

____ **The General's Daughter** (Nelson DeMille) 0-679-41599-8 ($16.00 value)

____ **Interview with the Vampire** (Anne Rice) 0-394-55617-8 ($16.00 value)

3.) Fill out legibly all the information requested on the back of this form. (Over)

Contents

Maps and Plans

Foreword

We would like to express our gratitude to Lic. Victor Hugo Becerra Femal, State Director of Tourism for the State of Zacatecas and Arq. Luis Castro Pardo, Federal Delegate of Tourism in the State of Zacatecas, and their staffs; Aurora Lopez de Ortigoza and staff of the Paraiso Radisson Hotel; Adolfo Salido in Hermosillo and Modesto Lozano in Guaymas, both at the Secretaría de Fomento al Turismo, Sonora; and Victor Barriguete, Felipe Valdez, Katherine Renpenning, and Guadalupe Terrazas at the Gobierno del Estado, Departamento de Comercio y Turismo in Chihuahua.

While every care has been taken to ensure the accuracy of the information in this guide, the passage of time will always bring change and, consequently, the publisher cannot accept responsibility for errors that may occur.

All prices and opening times quoted here are based on information supplied to us at press time. Hours and admission fees may change, however, and the prudent traveler will avoid inconvenience by calling ahead.

Fodor's wants to hear about your travel experiences, both pleasant and unpleasant. When a hotel or restaurant fails to live up to its billing, let us know and we will investigate the complaint and revise our entries where the facts warrant it.

Send your letters to the editors of Fodor's Travel Publications, 201 E. 50th Street, New York, NY 10022.

Highlights'93 and Fodor's Choice

Highlights '93

Having launched a massive highway improvement program, made unleaded gasoline available throughout the country, and opened its borders to American tour coaches, Mexico may well reach its goal of attracting 10 million international travelers annually by the middle of the decade.

Yucatán/ Quintana Roo The Yucatán peninsula is undergoing two opposing trends that mirror what is happening in other tourism destinations worldwide: a continued explosion of development and a growing concern for the environment. **Tour operators** are capitalizing on these trends by selling packages that focus on the Mayan ruins, wildlife, and natural beauty for which the peninsula is famous.

Almost since its inception, Cancún has been Mexico's most popular destination, hosting more than 1.8 million foreign visitors in 1990. Judging by the numbers of package-tour takers, college students, and weekend vacationers who flock to its white Caribbean beaches and warm turquoise waters, Cancún is now almost synonymous with Mexican tourism.

The devastation caused by Hurricane Gilbert in 1988 is far in the past. Countless hotels have been made over, and new ones are springing up, although as the authorities become more concerned that Cancún is approaching the saturation point, the growth rate is slowing down. Among the deluxe international properties to have opened recently are the **Conrad Cancún** and the **Marriott Casa Magna.** The **Ritz Carlton** and the **Aoki-Westin** will round out the list of new openings by 1993. The all-inclusive fad has also arrived at Cancún, offering yet another alternative vacation concept.

As the hotel inventory plateaus, however, **time-share condominiums** are going up at a feverish pitch—not just in Cancún, but all along the Caribbean coast and on Isla Mujeres as well. In an effort to keep pace with the nearly constant flow of visitors, the vast majority of whom are North Americans, **charter airlines** have been boosting their service to Cancún and Cozumel from a growing number of gateways.

To attract a more diversified clientele, in 1991 Cancún launched an annual **Jazz Festival** that attracted names like Wynton Marsalis and Gato Barbieri. At press time, the '92 lineup has been set, and the '93 schedule in the works. The **Cancún Convention Center,** the original venue for the area's cultural events, is being rebuilt (Hurricane Gilbert razed it) and is scheduled to reopen by 1993. In addition, two megaprojects—comprising an "eco-archaeological" park, aquariums, yacht marinas, golf courses, hotels, and commercial space—are in the works in and around Cancún.

The offshore island of Cozumel, Mexico's largest cruiseship port and a favorite among honeymooners and scuba divers, is taking steps to curb progress' toll on the environment. Development of several deluxe hotels has been halted; the island museum has embarked on a serious save-the-turtle campaign; and Isla de Pasión—a tiny island off the west coast, previously used for picnic cruises—has been made into a state reserve. Cozumel's hotels—which together offer about 3,500 rooms—hope to boost the ranks of foreign visitors, who numbered more than 137,000 in 1990.

Fans of Isla Mujeres (on offshore island much smaller and less developed than Cozumel) can be reassured that it has seen relatively little change, either physically or temperamentally. A quiet place with beaches and fishing similar to Cozumel's, Isla Mujeres has only about 600 hotel rooms. Still, there have been some new additions, including the **Condominio Playa Norte Nautibeach,** the **Cristalmar** condohotel, and the cozy little **Na-Balam,** as well as the scheduled opening in the spring of 1992 of an all-inclusive resort, **Costa Club,** as the island's largest hotel property. The **Cabañas María del Mar** and the **Mesón del Bucanero** have also been renovated and expanded.

Although there is talk of rebuilding the town dock to accommodate cruise ships and of operating an air charter service to Florida, Mérida, Chichén Itzá, and the Guatemalan ruins of Tikal, actual planning has not begun. In the meantime, Isla remains a backwater, beloved by backpackers and other budget travelers.

Mérida, the charming and understated capital of the State of Yucatán, will not soon become a mass-tourism destination. But **Progreso,** a town on the Gulf of Mexico and Mérida's closest access to the sea, is another story. Hotel development near Progreso, at **Yucalpetén** and **Nuevo Yucatán,** proceeds at a steady pace. The face of northern Yucatán is also being altered by the proliferating in-bond (foreign-owned assembly plants) manufacturing plants and the burgeoning offshore oil industry. And if Cuba succeeds in garnering international tourists, many of them will pass through Mérida, a gateway for flights to Havana.

Amateur archaeologists are now able to visit the Mayan site of **Oxkintok,** about 51 kilometers (31 miles) south of Mérida, though the ruins are still buried in the jungle and just barely excavated. A display at the **Mérida Museum of Anthropology and History,** of the artifacts found at Oxkintok provides an overview of the current work being done at the site.

The Caribbean coast is attracting growing numbers of independent travelers. **Ecotourism** is on the rise here as well, thanks to the exotic birds, marine life, and lagoons of the **Sian Ka'an Biosphere Reserve.** The Boca Paila peninsula, virtually all of which is contained in that reserve, is earning a glowing reputation for flatfishing, fly-fishing, and bone-fishing. Small resorts catering to scuba divers and fisher-men are gaining in popularity along the **Xcalak peninsula** at the southern base of the Quintant Roo coast, near the Be-lize border. The final frontier of this vast, sparsely inhab-ited, and beautiful region, Xcalak has miles and miles of deserted, undeveloped beaches (though rumors of im-pending construction abound). The northern part of the Caribbean coast—generally known as the Cancún-Tulum Corridor—has undergone the most dramatic transforma-tion along the coast, as resorts and time-share communities multiply and sprawl in competition for the time-share dollar. The changes are particularly visible at **Puerto Aventuras,** a 900-acre development with marinas, a golf course, hotels, condos, and all the trappings of a self-con-tained resort.

A similar project is under way at Playacar in **Playa del Carmen,** where the arrival of cruise ships and the develop-ment of first-class resorts have altered the town's appear-ance and character. A long-time favorite of budget travelers looking for isolated beaches and low-cost accom-modations, Playa is gradually becoming a paradise for in-vestors with visions of luxury condos and limitless profits. Time-share and resort developments are under way all along the corridor, where the government is building a four-lane highway for easy access from Cancún to Tulum.

Also of interest to amateur archaeologists is ongoing prog-ress on the **Ruta Maya,** a five-country venture geared at de-veloping impoverished regions and promoting low-impact tourism to the Mayan sites in Mexico, Belize, Guatemala, Honduras, and El Salvador. Funding from the European Economic Community will enable the countries to embark on promotions, archaeological excavations, and market studies; the project will be headed by Mexico. Several tour companies have begun offering Ruta Maya trips of the more accessible sites on Mexico's Yucatán peninsula and in Gua-temala and Belize.

Central Mexico and Mexico City With the new free trade agreements between the United States and Mexico, the capital city is, more than ever, a des-tination for business as well as vacation travelers. To fill the demand, the following hotels are under construction or on the drawing boards at press time. Scheduled for completion at the end of 1992 is a **Hotel Royal** (part of a Mexican-owned chain) at the south end of the city. Especially for business travelers, a **Radisson Sierra** is under construction on Cam-pos Elíseos (near the Stouffer Presidente and the Nikko). The foundation is being laid for a **Four Seasons** on the Reforma, across from the street from the new Marquis Reforma. The **Ritz Carlton** plans a hotel and office tower on the Reforma at Tiber. In the planning stages are a Lufthansa-owned **Eurobuilding** hotel-office building on the Reforma at Havre and a **Hilton** on the property owned by that company on the Reforma at Mississippi. And, finally, the ruins of the deceased, classic Presidente Zona Rosa, still looming on the horizon ever since the 1985 earthquake, are being restored.

Acapulco Work is completed on a new highway between Acapulco and Mexico City that will cut the driving time to 3½ hours (a good portion is already open), more stoplights and telephone booths have been installed along the Costera Miguel Alemán, and the streets seem to be cleaner. The city and state governments have also built several large garages and parking lots in town to handle the expected increase in tourists arriving by automobile.

Long-distance calls can be made from many of the phones—some of them even take credit cards. In an effort to get the hawkers off the streets and beaches, the government has built open-air markets at strategic points throughout the city. The municipal beaches look a lot cleaner and new restrooms and showers have been installed, but pollution in Acapulco Bay remains a sore point. Swimmers should stick to the hotel pool.

Other Pacific Coast Resorts Development at Huatulco—the newest of Mexico's planned beach resorts, located on the Pacific in the state of Oaxaca—has been slower than anticipated. **Marriott** plans a property at some point in the future.

Baja California and Mazatlán The northern third of the Baja California peninsula from Tijuana to Ensenada continues to undergo unprecedented development. In Tijuana, an unusual attraction called **Mexitlan** opened in 1991. An open-air museum with miniature replicas of Mexico's archaeological sites, colonial churches, and historic buildings, Mexitlan presents an immersion in the cultures of Mexico with music and dance performances, restaurants serving Mexican cuisine, and galleries carrying high-quality folk art.

Time-share and condominium resorts and hotels and restaurants continue to rise along the oceanfront hills on the coastal corridor from Tijuana to Ensenada. Several major projects including marinas, golf courses, and residences are in the planning stages.

Loreto, in the state of Baja California Sur on the Sea of Cortés, continues to grow at a more leisurely pace. The overall resort development—planned by FONATUR for the area—includes the town of Loreto, where a new *malecón* (boardwalk) was constructed in 1991; Nopoló Bay, where the impressive 18-hole Loreto-Nolpoló Club de Golf opened in 1991; and Puerto Escondido, where a full-scale marina attracts boaters cruising the Baja coast.

As to the twin resorts of Cabo San Lucas and San José del Cabo, a new 241-room Conrad Los Cabos was scheduled to open in late 1992, and three new golf-oriented resorts are under construction. The highway between the two towns is slowly being widened to four lanes, though construction is expected to last several years.

The mainland beach resort of Mazatlán, just across the Sea of Cortés from the southern tip of the Baja peninsula, boasted the highest hotel occupancy rates of the entire Mexican Riviera in 1990. Also in northern Mexico, the country's second largest city, Monterrey, welcomed a new hotel in late 1990: the 307-room **Fiesta Americana Monterrey,** a 12-story, *gran turismo* property geared to business travelers and located in the spiffy San Agustín residential area.

Air Transportation From New York, Mexicana has inaugurated first-class service to Mexico City. Airlift from the West Coast of the United States was boosted by Alaska Airlines' service to Los Cabos and other Pacific Coast destinations; by Continental Airlines' flights from Los Angeles and Phoenix to Mexico City; by Aeromexico's expanded schedule between Los Angeles and Puerto Vallarta, Mazatlán, Guadalajara, and Mexico City; and by Aerocalifornia's addition of service between Los Angeles and Los Cabos.

Mexicana's 1990 acquisition of the regional carriers Aerocaribe and Aerocozumel has made it vastly easier for passengers to book flights from the United States to various gateways in southeastern Mexico. Several Guatemalan airlines have also entered the fray in that region by connecting Cancún to Flores, the closest airport to the superb Mayan ruins of Tikal.

Ground Transportation Independent travelers who like to explore Mexico in their own automobiles will find this mode of travel considerably simplified by the new availability of **unleaded gas.** Pemex, the state-owned oil company, announced in 1990 that its "Magna Sin" would be sold at stations along 11 major tourist highways.

And for those who enjoy touring by **motorcoach,** the likelihood of a bilateral free-trade agreement has encouraged the U.S. and Mexican governments to sign a memorandum of understanding that will facilitate border crossings by bus tours and charters.

A new first-class train service, the **División del Norte,** has made the experience of rail travel between Mexico City and Ciudad Juárez more palatable. These renovated American Pullman sleeping cars—either with one- or two-bed roomettes or four-bed *alcobas*—are complemented by dining cars only between Zacatecas and the capital. Zacatecas is about 603 kilometers (375 miles) north of Mexico City, or a

14-hour ride; for the other 22 hours of the journey, passengers must make do with box lunches and breakfasts. Still, for touring the northern states of Aguascalientes, Zacatecas, and Chihuahua, the División del Norte represents a welcome new option. One-way fares start at $100, about 40% less than the airfare between the two points.

Tour Programs As more and more North Americans visit Mexico, the country's tour operators are coming up with increasingly creative and adventurous options to cater to the sophisticated, upscale end of the market. Among them: The **Foundation for Field Research** (Box 2010, Alpine, CA 92001, tel. 619/445–9264) runs a series of scientific expeditions for which volunteers are sought. Current Mexico projects include taking a census of the rare bird life in Chiapas; restoring colonial mansions in Alamos, Sonora; photographing the aboriginal arts of the Mayo tribe in Sonora; and saving the caguama sea turtles in Baja and the giant leatherback turtles in Michoacán. Nature and birding are the focus of **Clipper Cruise Line's** two-week cruises to Western Mexico and the Sea of Cortés (tel. 314/727–2929). **Maya-Caribe Travel** (87 Wolfs Lane, Pelham, NY 10803, tel. 800/223–4084 or 914/738–8254) offers a "hands-on Mexico" series of regional arts, crafts, and folklore classes for small groups. The courses, which last seven to 10 days, are taught by locals, and include black clay ceramics, glass-blowing, archaeology, weaving, folkloric dance, and Mexican cuisine.

Risks of Mopeds, Although such incidents do not often reach the internation-
Scuba Diving al press, travelers should be aware of the high rate of accidents—many of them fatal—caused by moped driving and scuba diving in Mexico and other places where such sports are practiced by large numbers of tourists. Many of these accidents are suffered by neophytes, who are lulled by assurances of how simple it is to ride a moped or dive, and are insufficiently instructed in proper safety precautions to avoid harm.

If you have never driven a moped, you need to understand certain mechanical basics, such as continued throttling of the engine, correct use of the brakes, and how to maneuver turns and hills. Ask for instruction, and stay off highly trafficked streets. Experts also recommend wearing helmets, long sleeves, long pants, gloves, goggles, and high-top athletic shoes.

Neophyte scuba divers should have a complete physical exam before undertaking a dive, as many diving deaths are caused by cardiovascular problems, asthma, seizure disorders, and diabetes. Drinking before diving is one of the major culprits behind scuba accidents on Cozumel. Cozumel, incidentally, is quite strict about scuba; a diver must carry a Certification Card or complete a resort course. Neophytes simply will not be provided with equipment. Finally, if you have travel insurance that covers evacuation, make sure the policy applies to scuba-related injuries, as not all the companies provide this coverage.

Fodor's Choice

No two people will agree on what makes a perfect vacation, but it's fun and helpful to know what others think. We hope you'll have a chance to experience some of Fodor's Choices yourself while visiting Mexico. We have tried to offer something for everyone and from every price category. For more information about each entry, refer to the appropriate chapters (listed in the margin) within this guidebook.

After Hours

Guadalajara	Factory, Aranzazu Hotel
	Lobby Bar, Fiesta Americana
	Plaza Tapatía
Yucatán	Carlos 'n' Charlie's, Cancún and Cozumel
	Christine's or La Boom disco, Cancún

Art Festivals

Heartland	Festival Cervantino, Guanajuato
Mexico City	Ballet Folklórico de México
	Carnaval, Tepoztlán
Oaxaca	Guelaguetza
Yucatán	Maya dances, reenacted sacrifice, Tulipanes, Mérida
	Mexican fiesta nights

Buildings and Monuments

Guadalajara	Centro Cultural Cabañas
Heartland	Zacatecas Cathedral
Mexico City	Casa de los Azulejos
	Chapultepec Castle
	Palacio de Bellas Artes
	Palacio de Iturbide
Oaxaca	Church of Santo Domingo

Day Trips

Chiapas/Tabasco	Lagos de Montebello
Mexico City	Puebla/Cholula
	Teotihuacán pyramids

	Tepotzotlán
	Valle de Bravo
Oaxaca	San Bartolo Coyotepec, Teotitlán del Valle

Museums

Chiapas/Tabasco	CICOM, Villahermosa
	Na-Bolom, San Cristóbal de las Casas
Heartland	Rafael Coronel Museum of Masks, Zacatecas
Mexico City	Franz Mayer Museum
	Frida Kahlo Museum
	Museo del Templo Mayor
	National Museum of Anthropology

Bars and Nightlife

Mexico City	Nueva Opera
	Plaza Garibaldi
	Up and down the Zona Rosa

Off the Beaten Track

Chiapas/Tabasco	Yaxchilán
Guadalajara	Tequila
Heartland	*Lavandería*, San Miguel de Allende
	Paricutín volcano
Yucatán	Flamingo preserves during spring nesting season, Ría Lagartos
	Maya caves at Loltún, Balankanche, and Bolonchén
	Boca Paila and Xcalak peninsulas

Parks and Gardens

Guadalajara	El Jardín
Mexico City	Alameda Park
	Bosque de Chapultepec
	Plaza San Jacinto

Shopping

Chiapas/Tabasco	Calle Real de Guadalupe, San Cristóbal de Las Casas
Mexico City	Bazar Sábado
	Fonart stores

La Ciudadela market

Bazaar del Centro

Oaxaca Daily markets

Archaeological Sites

Chiapas/Tabasco Palenque

Mexico City Templo Mayor

Oaxaca Mitla

Monte Albán

Yucatán Chichén Itzá

Tulum

Uxmal

Special Moments

Baja Whale-watching from Hotel Finisterra, Cabo San Lucas

Chiapas/Tabasco Firewalk on Carnival Tuesday, San Juán Chamule

Guadalajara Basílica of Zapopán on October 12

Saturday evening on the Plaza de Armas

Heartland Sunset boat trip, Janitzio

Yucatán *Calesa* (horse-drawn carriage) ride through Mérida

Diving near coral formations, Cozumel

Snorkeling in natural aquarium, Xel-Há Lagoon

Spinnaker sailing off Cancún

Sunset on Isla Mujeres

Watching Kukulcán slither down the Castillo at Chichén Itzá on the equinoxes

Taste Treats

Baja Fresh dorado, wahoo, and lobster

Guadalajara Crepes at St. Michael's

Huasteca Country Shrimp

Oaxaca Mole

Yucatán Cochinita píbil

Fresh corn tortillas

Montejo, León Negro, and Carta Clara beers

Tik-In-Chik

Towns and Villages

Chiapas/Tabasco	San Cristóbal de las Casas
	San Juan Chamula
Heartland	Zacatecas
	Pátzcuaro
Mexico City	Coyoacán

Views

Chiapas/Tabasco	Río Grijalva from CICOM complex, Villahermosa
	San Cristóbal de las Casas from the hill of the Church of Guadalupe
Heartland	Zacatecas from the city's aerial tramway
Mexico City	Popocatépetl and Ixtaccíhuatl volcanoes from the air

Works of Art

Mexico City	Cacaxtla murals, Tlaxcala
	Diego Rivera murals

Hotels

Very Expensive	Camino Real, Cancún (Yucatán)
	Casa de Sierra Nevada, San Miguel de Allende (Heartland)
	Mesón de Santa Rosa, Querétaro (Heartland)
	Palmilla, San José del Cabo (Baja)
	Quinta Real (Guadalajara)
	Stouffer Presidente, Cozumel (Yucatán)
	Villa Montana, Morelia (Heartland)
Expensive	Chan Kah, Palenque (Chiapas and Tabasco)
	Fiesta Americana (Guadalajara)
	Posada de Don Vasco, Pátzcuaro (Heartland)
	Virrey de Mendoza, Morelia (Heartland)
Moderate	Calinda Roma (Guadalajara)
	Playacar, Playa del Carmen (Quintana Roo)
	La Mansión del Bosque, San Miguel de Allende (Heartland)
	Na-Bolom, San Cristóbal de las Casas (Chiapas and Tabasco)

Rincón del Arco, San Cristóbal de las Casas (Chiapas and Tabasco)

Inexpensive López, Campeche (Yucatán)

Restaurants

Very Expensive Hacienda de los Morales (Mexico City)

La Vianda (Guadalajara)

Expensive El Jardín, Morelia (Heartland)

La Cava, Guanajuato (Heartland)

Restaurante Josecho, Querétaro (Heartland)

Stouffer Presidente (Oaxaca)

Moderate El Rey Tacamba, Morelia (Heartland)

Fonda La Mesa del Matador, San Miguel de Allende (Heartland)

Parrilla Tarasca, Uruapan (Heartland)

Inexpensive Fonda El Mesón (Mexico City)

Fonda La Trattoria (Guadalajara)

Jardines de Chiapa, Chiapa de Corzo (Chiapas and Tabasco)

La Habichuela, Cancún (Yucatán)

La Mansión, Cancún (Yucatán)

Los Almendros, in Mérida, Cancún, and Ticul (Yucatán)

Normita, San Cristóbal de las Casas (Chiapas and Tabasco)

Restaurant Hotel Posada La Basílica, Pátzcuaro (Heartland)

Restaurante Mamucas, Mazatlán (Pacific Coast Resorts)

Restaurante Polanco (Mexico City)

Rincón Maya, Cozumel (Yucatán)

La Bella Epoca, Mérida (Yucatán)

Mexican States and Capitals

CALIFORNIA

Mexicali ★

ARIZONA

NEW MEXICO

BAJA
CALIFORNIA
NORTE

Golfo

de

Hermosillo ★

SONORA

CHIHUAHUA

Chihuahua ☆

BAJA
CALIFORNIA
SUR

California

COAHU

SINALOA

La Paz ★

Culiacán ★

DURANGO

Durango ★

ZACATECAS

Zacatecas
★

AGUASCALIENTES

Tepic
★

Aguascalientes ★

NAYARIT

Guanajua

Guadalajara ★

GUANAJUA

JALISCO

Colima ★

Morelia ★

COLIMA

MICHOACAN

GUERRE

PACIFIC OCEAN

N

0   200 miles

0   300 km

World Time Zones

Numbers below vertical bands relate each zone to Greenwich Mean Time (0 hrs.).
Local times frequently differ from these general indications,
as indicated by light-face numbers on map.

Introduction

By Erica Meltzer

Free-lance writer Erica Meltzer lived in Mexico City for three years, working as a writer, translator, meeting planner, and teacher. She is now based in New York and visits Mexico frequently.

He who has been touched by the dust of Mexico will never again find peace in any land, says an old Mexican proverb. This is not hyperbole. I first went to Mexico when I was 15. I spend several summers there and eventually lived in Mexico City for three years. But I can't stay away.

Gringos have always had complex relationships with this country. Graham Greene wrote a cranky book about his travels in Mexico in the 1930s and finally had to admit that "it was as if Mexico was something I couldn't shake off, like a state of mind." Malcolm Lowry was "afflicted" with Mexico and insisted that he would prefer to die there, yet the Mexicans in his *Under the Volcano* are sinister and manipulative, or hopelessly passive. D.H. Lawrence made "noble savages" of the Indians, and both B. Traven and Katherine Anne Porter wrote compassionately of the downtrodden peasants.

Explaining one's obsession with a place is a monumental and painful task. I remember how strange and glorious it felt as a 15-year-old first-timer to Mexico to see the Maya ruins at Kabah in Yucatán: a gold and amber haze enshrouded the fluted columns and marred friezes, the stillness shattered only by the rustling of iguanas in the tall grasses. And I remember the heat, that throbbing sun, which dampened the mossy, claustrophobic walls in the subterranean vault at Chichén Itzá.

In Mexico City, my friends and I spent all our taco money on booklets at the Museum of Anthropology, then got sick on fresh peanuts in the shell from the marketplace. In Zihuatanejo resident hippies offered us drug-spiked oranges. Everywhere we were followed by young men who knew enough English to tell us what beautiful eyes we had; soon we were able to appreciate the Spanish-language version of those compliments.

When I went to live in the capital in 1979, I resided in four different middle-class neighborhoods not far from the Paseo de la Reforma. It was easy to live there on a limited budget. Eight *tacos al pastor* cost a couple of dollars, and we expatriates were fond of going into the markets to find inexpensive but pretty trinkets for decorating our apartments. There were petty problems to deal with, like having to buy stock in the phone company to get a phone, then waiting as long as six weeks for it to be installed; most people simply "bought" the phone and line from previous tenants so as not to bother with getting their own listing.

Sunday mornings we'd go biking in Chapultepec Park, where ventors sold paprika-covered white jicamas on sticks, like Popsicles, then have brunch in Polanco. We jogged in the Parque México, in Colonia Condesa, then sat on benches chatting with aging refugees from the Spanish Civil War and World War II. We prided ourselves on knowing the most obscure cantinas downtown and on enduring 12-hour bus rides—sometimes standing room only—to the beaches. It's a mild form of that expatriate malady known as "going native."

Mexico's intellectual and artistic life is fascinating. In the 1920s and 1930s, the country had a literary circle as prestigious and incestuous as Virginia Woolf's Bloomsbury or the Paris of Gertrude Stein. B. Traven palled around with Mexico's most famous cinematogorapher, Gabriel Figueroa, and was godfather to his son. They all knew Diego Rivera, who shared the favors of Tina Modotti with Edward Weston. Rivera and his wife, Frida Kahlo, persuaded President Lázaro Cárdenas to give asylum to Leon Trotsky. Trotsky lived in Coyoacán, a colonial village, with Riviera and Kahlo. He had a brief fling with Kahlo before his assassination.

In the 1980s Mexico's tradition of an intellectual elite and of glaring class disparities lives on. Just as during the 300 years of Spanish rule when the "pure-blooded" children of the Spaniards, the Creoles, imposed their sense of superiority on the mixed-blood *mestizos*, so Creoles dominate Mexican cultural and political life today. Many of their parents came to Mexico to escape Franco's Spain, and even their last names give them away: The names are originally Basque, or they boast the aristocratic "de" (as in President Carlos Salinas de Gortari or his immediate predecessor, Miguel de la Madrid Hurtado). This class is collectively personified by the "Thousand Families," and they virtually run the country's media, banking, real estate, industrial, tourism, and public sectors. Their children study in Europe and eschew the United States; a strong anti-Americanism runs through their politics. Mexican friends have told me, with absolute conviction, that the United States is refusing to bail Mexico out of its $105 billion debt dilemma in order to annex Baja California. They never forget that America appropriated two-fifths of their national territory in 1847, and they deride American intervention in Central America while remaining silent on their own country's record of human-rights abuses and abysmal treatment of Guatemalan refugees.

Malinchismo—Mexico's hatred of things Mexican and love of things foreign—is more evident among the middle and lower classes. Thousands of unemployed laborers flood the United States border each week. Their better-off compatriots flock to the Galleria in Houston on weekends to bring home American appliances, designer labels, and gourmet food, or buy condos in San Diego and Colorado. They cultivate friendships with Americans and struggle to learn English. Women lighten their hair with henna, and TV commercials always feature blondes; one would never know this was a country of dark-skinned mestizos and Indians. Presidential prospects are limited for anyone with the misfortune to "look" Indian, and the word *indio* itself is derogatory; the correct neutral term is *indigena*.

The Indians, who account for about 10% of the total population of 85 million, cannot read of their plight in the nation's print media. Besides the fact that many of the Indians are illiterate and do not understand Spanish, the news media are muzzled. And yet the Indians have not always been passive. There were violent uprisings in the state of Chiapas in 1712 and again in 1869; some 200,000 died in the Yucatán Caste Wars in the 1840s. The Indian community of San Juan Chamula, Chiapas, threw out the local priest in the early 1980s, along with hundreds of their own numbers who had converted to fundamentalist Portestant sects.

Pre-Columbian religious traditions are clung to fiercely. I once visited a *curandero* (shaman) near San Miguel de Allende who broke raw eggs over us to purge the evil spirits. In the church in San Juan Chamula, there are no pews and no altar. The "worship" I witnessed consisted of a man wringing a chicken's neck while his family drank Coca-Cola and burned candles on the floor in front of "Christian" idols. The Day of the Dead ceremonies enacted at candlelit cemeteries in the state of Michoacán, where families place food on the graves of their dead, are rooted in ancient forms of ancestor worship and appeasement of bloodthristy deities. Mexico's relationship with the Catholic Church has not been a peaceful one: Two periods of violent anticlericalism (in the 1850s and 1920s and '30s) resulted in rioting, the demolition of churches and convents, and the persecution and murder of priests. Even today the church is not allowed to own land, and the government does not officially recognize its existence. Yet 93% of the people are baptized Catholics. Religious people are married in two ceremonies: by the state, because civil marriages are the only legally binding ones, and again by the church.

Violence is undeniably a part of Mexican life. Politicans are kidnapped, guerrilla groups hide out in the mountains, labor unions and students demonstrate, sometimes met by police repression. Drunken brawls are common in this country of high alcoholism.

On the other hand—and there *is* always an other hand in Mexico, this country of eros and thanatos, love and death, running madly together—I have had fatherly taxi drivers advise me not to be out on the streets so late and not to trust them by leaving my luggage unattended in the cab. There was the woman in Zihuatanejo who soothed a bad sunburn with a rubdown of crushed tomatoes. One good friend even lent me money, explaining that Mexicans never did that for each other. Students threw parties for me and sent me to their relatives when I traveled in the country. Mexican *pachangas*—celebratory, frequently tipsy, parties—are peerless.

Speaking Spanish is a definite advantage in Mexico. It is the most populous Spanish-speaking country in the world, and it has its own richly expressive vocabulary, a hybrid of Castilian, Indian, and English. I still say *¡híjole!* when something upsets or disgusts me, although I haven't been able to trace its etymology. There are dozens of exclamatory words: *¡Qué caray! ¡Aguas! ¡Chispas!* Let those roll off your lips and you feel a satisfaction no Anglo-Saxon word can give. Then there are the derogatory adjectives applied with robust enthusiasm to people and situations: *pinche* (damned), *naco* or *mensa* (stupid), and *pendejo* (also stupid, but rather vulgar). Mexicans say *sí, no?* (yes, no?) to mean something like, "it's true, isn't it?" They deride motherhood with *me vale madre* (I couldn't care less) and extol fatherhood with *qué padre* (how wonderful). And there is that ubiquitous little word, so infinite in its uses: *ya*, which translates variously as "already," "yet," and—when used alone as an exclamation—"enough already!" A close friend is a *cuate*, which has a deliciously cozy feel to it that "buddy" cannot possibly duplicate. People's personalities really do change when they speak another language.

Business correspondence seems flowery when compared with North American efficiency, and politeness—not always sincere—is an art. *Mi casa es su casa* (my house is your house) is one of the most-used Mexican expressions of hospitality, but do not take it seriously: I had a long and warm correspondence with one of my Mexican teachers who kept telling me I must come and stay with her, but when I phoned on arrival in Mexico City, she recommended a hotel.

Let a modicum of annoyance or impatience appear in your voice, and you will see how quickly Mexicans take offense. Possibly this tendency arises more often with foreigners than with other Mexicans—proof of that underlying animosity—but I have seen how angry Mexicans can be with one another over a perceived slight or wrong.

Machismo has to be addressed. When I lived in Mexico I learned to lower my eyes on the street and camouflage my anatomy. I got so used to the unsolicited male attention that on visits back to the United States, I wondered what was wrong with the men.

Tourism and development are transforming Mexico and its people to the point where the government has admonished the residents of Puerto Vallarta with a wall sign saying, VIVIMOS DEL TURISMO, NO DEL TURISTA (we live off tourism, not off the tourist). And the small colonial towns and fishing villages, such as San Miguel de Allende, Zihuatanejo, and Puerto Escondido, which are often described as "charming" and "typical," are now full of Americans. San Cristóbal de las Casas, however, is not likely to lose its charm for at least 10 years. I imagine that when I go back to Paricutín, the volcano near Uruapan, I will still be able to ride a mule to the lava-covered church spires of the town buried by its last eruption in 1943. I will still enjoy picnics in utter isolation on the banks of Lake Avándaro and buy herbal medicines in the market at Valle de Bravo. Sunny breakfasts at a small hotel in Taxco, overlooking that completely colonial city, will still be possible, as will a night in a dingy has-been hotel of "traditional" or downtown Acapulco. In Mexico City, I can still walk by my apartment building in the Zona Rosa and appreciate its faintly neglected look. For the best buildings in Mexico are *not* the modern ones; in the capital, at least, the modern ones were the first to fall in the 1985 earthquake. No, it's the slightly dilapidated walk-up flats, furnished 50 years ago with genteel lace, sturdy wooden chairs, and yellowing paintings of the Madonna, that I delight in—down to the last plastic flower and brown clay salsa bowl.

1 Essential Information

Before You Go

Government Tourist Offices

For a current calendar of events, train schedules and fares, brochures and other general information about travel in Mexico, contact the nearest **Mexican Government Tourism Office.**

In the U.S. 405 Park Avenue, Suite 1402, New York, NY 10022, tel. 212/755–7261; 1911 Pennsylvania Avenue NW, Washington, DC 20006, tel. 202/728–1750; 128 Aragon Avenue, Coral Gables, FL 32134, tel. 305/443–9160; 70 E. Lake Street, Suite 1413, Chicago, IL 60601, tel. 312/565–2786; 2707 N. Loop West, Suite 450, Houston, TX 77008, tel. 713/880–5153; Center Plaza Building, 45 NE Loop 410, Suite 125, San Antonio, TX 78216, tel. 512/366–3242; 10100 Santa Monica Boulevard, Suite 224, Los Angeles, CA 90067, tel. 213/203–8191. If there is no office near you, call 800/262–8900.

In Canada 1 Place Ville Marie, Suite 2409, Montreal, Quebec H3B 3M9, tel. 514/871–1052; 2 Bloor Street W., Suite 1801, Toronto, Ontario M4W 3E2, tel. 416/925–0704 or 416/925–1876.

In the U.K. 60–61 Trafalgar Square, London WC2N 5DS, tel. 071/734–1058.

Tour Groups

Mexico is a genuine travel bargain. The combination of a weak peso and the buying power of tour operators creates some attractively priced packages. In the resort areas, independent packages are a good choice: The beach and other attractions are nearby and usually easy to reach. Group tours are more common for exploring Mexico's interior or pursuing such special interests as archaeology and Mayan or Aztec culture. Below is a sampling of available packages.

When considering a tour, find out: exactly what expenses are included—particularly tips, taxes, side trips, additional meals, and entertainment; government ratings of all hotels on the itinerary and the facilities they offer; cancellation policies for both you and the tour operator; the number of travelers in your group; and, if you are traveling alone, the cost of the single supplement. Most tour operators request that bookings be made through a travel agent—in most cases there is no additional charge for doing so.

General-interest **American Express Vacations** (300 Pinnacle Way, Norcross, GA
Tours 30093, tel. 800/241–1700; in GA 800/421–5785) has a vast array of tours; if you don't see a package you like, one can be designed for you. **Friendly Holidays** (1983 Marcus Ave., Suite C130, Lake Success, NY 11042, tel. 516/358–1200 or 800/221–9748) is one of the largest wholesalers to Mexico. **GoGo Tours** (69 Spring St., Ramsey, NJ 04476, tel. 201/934–3500 or 800/821–3731) offers a wide selection of tours at an equally wide range of prices. **Mexico Travel Advisors** (1717 N. Highland Ave., Suite 1100, Los Angeles, CA 90028, tel. 213/462–6444 or 800/876–6824) has been leading tours to Mexico for over 60 years. **Gadabout Tours** (700 E. Tahquitz Canyon Way, Palm Springs, CA 92262, tel. 619/325–5556 or 800/952–5068) has a motorcoach and fly-in available for tours to the Copper Canyon, Baja, Cabo San Lucas, the

Colonial cities, Veracruz, and the Yucatan Peninsula, as well as a Mexico Riviera Cruise and a Baja Adventure Tour. **American Leisure** (9800 Center Pkwy., Suite 800, Houston, TX 77036, tel. 800/777–1980; in TX, 713/988–6098), **Cartran Tours** (1334 Parkview Ave., Suite 210, Manhattan Beach, CA 90266, tel. 800/422–7826), and **Travel Impressions** (465 Smith St., Farmingdale, NY 11735, tel. 516/845–8000 or 800/284–0044) are three other leading tour operators to Mexico.

Special-interest Tours

Adventure If lying motionless on a beach for a week is your idea of the perfect vacation, don't call **Mountain Travel-Sobek** (6420 Fairmount Ave., El Cerrito, CA 94530, tel. 800/227–2384). Mexican outings include rafting on the Usumacinta River on the Mexico/Guatemala border and volcano climbing near Mexico City. **Baja Expeditions** (2625 Garnet Ave., San Diego, CA 92109, tel. 619/581–3311 or 800/843–6967), the oldest and largest adventure travel outfitter in Baja, Mexico, schedules sea kayaking, mountain biking, whale watching, and scuba diving expeditions plus natural history cruises. The **Sierra Club** (Outings Department, 730 Polk St., San Francisco, CA 94109, tel. 415/923–5630) offers various adventure tours of Mexico's Baja region.

Archaeology **Sanborn Tours** (Box 749, Bastrop, TX 78602, tel. 512/321–1131 or 800/531–5440) and **Armadillo Tours** (4301 Westbank Drive, Bldg. 360, Austin, TX 78746, tel. 512/328–7800 or 800/284–5678) explore the Mayan ruins of Yucatán, Chichén Itzá, and Uxmal. Sanborn also has tours to Aztec ruins in central Mexico and various Mexican colonial towns. Offering trips ranging in length from 5 to 12 days, they will even arrange specific tours upon request. **Mexico Travel Advisors** (*see* General-interest Tours, *above*) has trips to the ancient remains of Monte Albán, outside of Oaxaca and Palenque, in Chiapas. **Maya-Carib** (87 Wolf Lane, Pelham, NY 10803, tel. 800/223–4084) has unique archaeological and learning vacations in the Yucatán and elsewhere in Mexico. Customized itineraries are also available.

Copper Canyon Four times the size of the Grand Canyon, Copper Canyon can be toured by rail. Both **Sanborn Tours** and **Armadillo Tours** (*see* Archaeology, *above*) offer rail trips through the canyon that start in Chihuahua in the north and end at the Sea of Cortés city of Los Mochis. That the train can ride along and through the canyon is a major feat of engineering; luxuries, however, are limited.

Fishing **Sanborn Tours** (*see* Archaeology, *above*) also offers deep-sea fishing packages using Cabo San Lucas or Mazatlán as a base.

Natural History **Questers Worldwide Nature Tours** (257 Park Ave. S, New York, NY 10010, tel. 212/673–3120) doesn't just visit the great pre-Columbian ruins, it also takes nature lovers to a monarch butterfly reserve and a flamingo colony.

Sailing **Oceanic Society Expeditions** (Fort Mason Center, Bldg. E. Suite 230, San Francisco, CA 94123, tel. 415/441–1106 or 800/326–7491) sails for Baja in ships that accommodate 15 to 25 passengers for whale-watching, encounters with other sea life, and snorkeling. A portion of the trip fee aids conservation efforts.

Shopping **Gray Line Tours** (Box 2422, South Padre Island, TX 78597, tel. 512/943–2144 or 800/321–8720) runs five-hour shopping tours for $15 from border towns in Texas to Mexico.

Package Deals for Independent Travelers

All the general-interest tour operators above also offer air/hotel packages, some including such options as half-day sightseeing tours and discounted car rental. You can also try **Asti Tours** (21 E. 40th St., New York, NY 10016, tel. 800/327–4390 or, in NY, 800/535–3711). Many airlines also feature packages: **American Fly AAway Vacations** (800/321–2121), **Continental Grand Destinations** (tel. 800/634–5555 or 800/284–0303), **Delta Airlines** (tel. 800/872–7786), and **United Vacations** (tel. 800/328–6877).

Tips for British Travelers

Tourist Information Contact the **Mexican National Tourism Office** (60–61 Trafalgar Sq., London WC2N 5DS, tel. 071/734–1058) for brochures and tourist information.

Passports and Visas You will need a valid, 10-year passport (cost £15) and a tourist card to enter Mexico.

Customs Entering Mexico, you may bring (1) 200 cigarettes, or 50 cigars, or 250 grams of tobacco; (2) up to 2 liters of wine or spirits; (3) one still camera and one 18mm film or video camera and 12 rolls of film each; and (4) gift items not exceeding a combined value of $300. You are not allowed to bring meat, vegetables, plants, fruit, or flowers into the country. Returning to the United Kingdom, you may bring home, if you are 17 or older: (1) 200 cigarettes, or 100 cigarillos, or 50 cigars, or 250 grams of tobacco; (2) two liters of table wine and (a) one liter of alcohol over 22% by volume (most spirits) or (b) two liters of alcohol under 22% by volume (fortified or sparkling wine); or (c) two more liters of still table wine; (3) 60 milliliters of perfume and 250 milliliters of toilet water; and (4) other goods up to a value of £32, but not more than 50 liters of beer or 25 lighters.

Insurance We recommend that you insure yourself against sickness and motoring mishaps with **Europ Assistance** (252 High St., Croydon, Surrey CR0 1NF, tel. 081/680–1234). It is also wise to take out insurance to cover the loss of luggage (although check that such loss isn't already covered in any existing homeowner's policies you may have). Trip-cancellation insurance is another wise buy. **The Association of British Insurers** (51 Gresham, London EC2V 7HQ, tel. 071/600–3333, fax 071/696–8999) gives comprehensive advice on all aspects of vacation insurance.

Tour Operators Among the many companies offering packages to Mexico are the following:

Bales Tours (Bales House, Junction Rd., Dorking, Surrey, RH4 3HB, tel. 0306/76881) offers a 2½-week escorted tour that visits archaeological sites in central Mexico and the jungles of Yucatán. Optional extensions include Cozumel or Palenque.

British Airways Holidays (Atlantic House, Hazelwick Avenue, Three Bridges, Crawley, W. Sussex RH10 1NP, tel. 0293/611611) offers a 14-day "Mexican Discovery" tour that ends in Cancún, with an optional four-night extension there.

Cosmosair (Ground Floor, Dale House, Tiviot Dale, Stockport, Cheshire SK1 1TB, tel 061/480–5799) offers holiday packages to the United States with extensions to Mexico.

Kuoni Travel (Kuoni House, Dorking, Surrey RH5 4AZ, tel. 0306/740–888) offers 7- to 14-day tours including "Mexican Highlights" to Mexico City, Taxco, and Acapulco; and "Mexican Panorama" to Mexico City, Mérida, Villahermosa, Oaxaca, and Cancún. Also available are a "Two Center Holiday" tour, covering Mexico City and Acapulco, and a Cancún-only tour. Prices vary greatly but include airfare, hotels, and transfers but no meals.

Mexican Holidays (23 Eccleston St., London SW1 9LX, tel. 071/730–8640) will custom-design a holiday in any part of Mexico.

Airlines and Airfares **British Airways** has a direct flight to Mexico City. Other airlines flying to Mexico, with brief stops en route, include **Continental** (via Houston), **American** (via Dallas), **KLM** (via Amsterdam), **Air France** (via Paris), **Delta** (via Miami), **United** (via Chicago or Washington, Dulles), **Lufthansa** (via a German city), and **Iberia** (via Madrid). Mexicana Airlines, which operates domestic routes within the country, also offers flights to Mexico from Miami and New York City. A standard return APEX fare to Mexico City from London at press time ranged from £500 in low season to £600 in high season. Check *Time Out* and the Sunday papers for charters and discount flights.

When to Go

In terms of climate, the dry season—October through May—is the best time to see Mexico. Rain can fall daily during the peak of the rainy season (June–September), when it frequently lasts for hours. Even if it is not raining, much of the country is overcast—a less than perfect condition for a beach vacation.

During the North American winter, December through February, the Mexican resorts—where the vast majority of tourists go—are the most crowded and therefore the most expensive. To avoid the masses, the highest prices, and the worst rains, visit Mexico during October, April, or May. Hotel rates at the beach resorts can be cut by as much as 30% in the shoulder season, 50% in the off-season.

Mexicans travel during traditional holiday periods: Christmas/New Year's, Semana Santa (Holy Week, the week before Easter), and school vacations in the summertime, as well as over extended national holiday weekends, called *puentes* (bridges), and during festivals (*see* Festivals and Seasonal Events, *below*). If your trip coincides with these times, reserve both lodgings and transportation well in advance. For flights within Mexico, remember to get to the airport early: Airlines in Mexico have a practice, especially during heavy travel periods, of bouncing ticket holders who haven't checked in at least one hour before flight time.

Climate The variations in Mexico's climate are not surprising considering the size of the country. The coasts and low-lying sections of the interior are often very hot if not actually tropical, with temperatures ranging from 24° to 31°C (75° to 88°F) in winter and well above 32°C (90°F) in summer. A more temperate area ranging from 16° to 21°C (60° to 70°F) is found at altitudes of 1,220–1,830 meters (4,000–6,000 feet). In general, the high central plateau on which Mexico City, Guadalajara, and many of the country's colonial cities are located is springlike year-round.

Acapulco	**Jan.**	88F	31C	**May**	90F	32C	**Sept.**	90F	32C
		72	22		77	25		77	25
	Feb.	88F	31C	**June**	90F	32C	**Oct.**	90F	32C
		72	22		77	25		77	25
	Mar.	88F	31C	**July**	91F	33C	**Nov.**	90F	32C
		72	22		77	25		75	24
	Apr.	88F	31C	**Aug.**	91F	33C	**Dec.**	88F	31C
		72	22		77	25		73	23

Cozumel	**Jan.**	82F	28C	**May**	89F	32C	**Sept.**	89F	32C
		68	20		73	23		75	24
	Feb.	84F	29C	**June**	89F	32C	**Oct.**	87F	31C
		68	20		75	24		73	23
	Mar.	86F	30C	**July**	89F	32C	**Nov.**	84F	29C
		69	21		75	24		71	22
	Apr.	89F	32C	**Aug.**	91F	33C	**Dec.**	84F	29C
		71	22		75	24		68	20

Ensenada	**Jan.**	64F	18C	**May**	70F	21C	**Sept.**	77F	25C
		45	7		54	12		61	16
	Feb.	66F	19C	**June**	72F	22C	**Oct.**	73F	23C
		46	8		57	14		55	13
	Mar.	66F	19C	**July**	75F	24C	**Nov.**	72F	22C
		46	8		61	16		48	9
	Apr.	68F	20C	**Aug.**	75F	24C	**Dec.**	66F	19C
		52	11		63	17		46	8

Guadalajara	**Jan.**	75F	24C	**May**	88F	31C	**Sept.**	79F	26C
		45	7		57	14		59	15
	Feb.	77F	25C	**June**	84F	29C	**Oct.**	79F	26C
		46	8		61	16		59	15
	Mar.	82F	28C	**July**	79F	26C	**Nov.**	77F	25C
		48	9		59	15		48	9
	Apr.	86F	30C	**Aug.**	79F	26C	**Dec.**	75F	24C
		54	12		59	15		46	8

La Paz	**Jan.**	72F	22C	**May**	88F	31C	**Sept.**	92F	33C
		57	14		64	18		76	24
	Feb.	74F	23C	**June**	92F	33C	**Oct.**	89F	32C
		56	13		69	21		71	22
	Mar.	80F	27C	**July**	95F	35C	**Nov.**	81F	27C
		56	13		75	24		66	19
	Apr.	83F	28C	**Aug.**	93F	34C	**Dec.**	74F	23C
		60	16		76	24		59	15

Mexico City	**Jan.**	70F	21C	**May**	79F	26C	**Sept.**	72F	22C
		41	5		52	11		52	11
	Feb.	73F	23C	**June**	77F	25C	**Oct.**	72F	22C
		45	7		54	12		52	11
	Mar.	79F	26C	**July**	73F	23C	**Nov.**	72F	22C
		48	9		52	11		52	11
	Apr.	81F	27C	**Aug.**	73F	23C	**Dec.**	70F	21C
		50	10		52	11		43	6

Monterrey	Jan.	68F	20C	May	88F	31C	Sept.	88F	31C
		48	9		68	20		70	21
	Feb.	73F	23F	June	91F	33C	Oct.	81F	27C
		52	11		72	22		63	17
	Mar.	79F	26C	July	91F	34C	Nov.	75F	24C
		55	13		72	22		55	13
	Apr.	86F	30C	Aug.	93F	34C	Dec.	70F	21C
		64	18		72	22		50	10

Puerto Vallarta	Jan.	84F	29C	May	91F	33C	Sept.	93F	34C
		63	17		68	20		73	23
	Feb.	86F	30C	June	93F	34C	Oct.	93F	34C
		61	16		73	23		73	23
	Mar.	86F	30C	July	95F	35C	Nov.	91F	33C
		63	17		73	23		68	20
	Apr.	88F	31C	Aug.	95F	35C	Dec.	86F	30C
		64	18		73	23		64	18

San Miguel de Allende	Jan.	79F	26C	May	91F	33C	Sept.	82F	28C
		48	9		61	16		61	16
	Feb.	82F	28C	June	91F	31C	Oct.	82F	28C
		52	11		63	17		61	16
	Mar.	88F	31C	July	84F	29C	Nov.	81F	27C
		55	13		61	16		52	11
	Apr.	90F	32C	Aug.	84F	29C	Dec.	77F	25C
		59	15		61	16		48	9

Current weather information for foreign and domestic cities may be obtained by calling The Weather Channel Connection at 900/WEATHER from a touch-tone phone. In addition to the weather report, The Weather Channel Connection offers local time and travel tips as well as hurricane, foliage, and ski reports. The call costs 95¢ per minute.

Festivals and Seasonal Events

Mexico has a full calendar of national holidays, saints' days, and special events; below are some of the most important or unusual ones. For further information and exact dates, contact the Mexican Government Tourism Office (*see* Government Tourist Offices, *above*).

Jan. 1: New Year's Day is a major celebration throughout the country. Agricultural and livestock fairs are held in the provinces; in Oaxaca, women display traditional *tehuana* costumes.
Jan. 6: Feast of Epiphany is the day the Three Kings bring gifts to Mexican children.
Jan. 17: Feast of San Antonio Abad honors animals all over Mexico. Household pets and livestock alike are decked out with flowers and ribbons and taken to a nearby church for a blessing.
Jan.: Feast of the Immaculate Conception is a religious celebration in which lights and flowers transform Morelia.
Feb.: Día de la Candelaria, or Candlemas Day, means fiestas, parades, bullfights, and lantern-decorated streets. Festivities include a running of the bulls through the streets of Tlacotalpan, Veracruz.
Feb.–Mar.: Carnival is celebrated throughout Mexico, but

most notably in Mérida and Veracruz, where there are parades with floats and bands.

Mar. 21: Benito Juárez's Birthday is a national holiday that is most popular in Guelatao, Oaxaca, where Juárez, the beloved 19th-century president of Mexico and champion of the people, was born.

Mar.–Apr.: Holy Week or (Semana Santa) is observed throughout the country with special passion plays during this week leading up to Easter Sunday.

Apr.: International Horse Fair is an event held in Texcoco, Estado de México.

Apr.–May: San Marcos National Fair, held in Aguascalientes, is one of the country's best fairs. It features native *matachnes* (dances performed by grotesque figures), mariachi bands, and bullfights.

May 1: Labor Day is a day for workers to parade through the streets.

May 5: Cinco de Mayo marks the anniversary of the French defeat by Mexican troops in Puebla in 1862.

May 15: Feast of San Isidro Labrador is celebrated nationwide with the blessing of new seeds and animals.

June 1: Navy Day is commemorated in all Mexican seaports and is especially colorful in Acapulco.

June: Feast of Corpus Christi is celebrated in different ways. In Mexico City, children are dressed in native costumes and taken to the cathedral on the *Zócalo* (main square) for a blessing. In Papantla, Veracruz, the Dance of the Flying Birdmen, a pre-Hispanic ritual to the sun, is held throughout the day.

June 24: Saint John the Baptist Day is a popular national holiday, with many Mexicans observing a tradition of tossing a "blessing" of water on most anyone within reach.

July 16: Feast of the Virgen del Carmen is a celebration, with fairs, bullfights, fireworks, sporting competitions, even a major fishing tournament.

July: Guelaguetza Dance Festival is a Oaxacan affair that dates to pre-Columbian times.

Late July: Feast of Santiago is a national holiday that features *charreadas*, Mexican-style rodeos.

Aug. 15: Feast of the Assumption of the Blessed Virgin Mary is celebrated nationwide with religious processions. In Huamantla, Tlaxcala, the festivities include a running of the bulls down flower-strewn streets.

Aug. 25: San Luis Potosí Patron Saint Fiesta is the day the town honors its patron, St. Louis, with traditional dance, music, and foods.

Sept. 15–16: Independence Day is when all of Mexico celebrates independence with fireworks and parties that outblast New Year's Eve. The biggest celebrations take place in Mexico City.

Sept. 29: San Miguel Day honors St. Michael, the patron saint of all towns with San Miguel in their names, with bullfights, folk dances, concerts and fireworks.

Oct.: October Festivals means a month of cultural and sporting events in Guadalajara.

Oct. 4: Feast of St. Francis of Assisi is a day for processions dedicated to St. Francis in various parts of the country.

Oct. 12: Columbus Day is a national holiday in Mexico.

Oct.–Nov.: International Cervantes Festival, in Guanajuato, is a top cultural event that attracts dancers, singers, and actors from a number of different countries.

Nov. 2: All Soul's Day or **Day of the Dead** is when Mexicans remember the departed in an oddly merry way, with candy skulls sold on street corners and picnickers spreading blankets in cemeteries.

Nov. 20: Anniversary of the Mexican Revolution is a national holiday.

Nov.–Dec.: National Silver Fair is an annual Taxco event in which silver is exhibited and sold.

Dec. 12: Feast Day of the Virgin of Guadalupe is the day on which Mexico's patron saint is feted with processions and native folk dances, particularly at her shrine in Mexico City.

Dec. 16–24: Christmas is the day for *posadas* (processions) that lead to Christmas parties and to *piñatas* (decorated, suspended hollow balls) that are broken open to yield gifts. Mexico City is brightly decorated, but don't expect any snow.

What to Pack

Pack light: Though baggage carts are available now at airports, luggage restrictions on international flights are tight. Also, you'll want to save space for purchases. Mexico is filled with bargains on clothing, leather goods, arts and crafts, and silver jewelry.

Clothing   What you bring depends on your destination. For the resorts, bring lightweight sports clothes, bathing suits, and cover-ups for the beach. Bathing suits and immodest clothing are inappropriate for shopping and sightseeing, both in cities and beach resorts. Mexico City is a bit more formal than the resorts and highly elevated, therefore cooler. Men will want to bring lightweight suits or slacks and blazers for fancier restaurants; and women should consider packing tailored dresses. Many restaurants require jacket and tie. Jeans are acceptable for shopping and sightseeing, but shorts are frowned upon for men or women. You'll need a lightweight topcoat for winter and an all-weather coat and umbrella for sudden summer rainstorms.

Resorts, such as Cancún and Acapulco, are both casual and elegant; you'll see high-style designer sportswear, tie-dyed T-shirts, cotton slacks and walking shorts, and plenty of colorful sundresses. The sun can be fierce; bring a sun hat (or buy one locally) and sunscreen for the beach and for sightseeing. You'll need a sweater or jacket to cope with hotel and restaurant air-conditioning, which can be glacial. Few restaurants require jacket and tie.

Miscellaneous   Bring a spare pair of eyeglasses and sunglasses and an adequate supply of prescription drugs. You can probably find what you need in the pharmacies, but you may need a local doctor's prescription. You are allowed to bring one regular and one movie camera (or video camera), with eight rolls of film for each; bring the limit because film is expensive in Mexico. Also bring a plastic water bottle for carrying your own supply on the road, insect repellent, especially for the beach resorts, and a small flashlight.

Carry-on Luggage   Passengers on U.S. airlines are limited to two carry-on bags. For a bag you wish to store under the seat, the maximum dimensions are 9 × 14 × 22 inches. For bags that can be hung in a closet or on a luggage rack, the maximum dimensions are 4 × 23 × 45 inches. For bags you wish to store in an overhead bin, the maximum dimensions are 10 × 14 × 36 inches. Any item that exceeds the specified dimensions may be rejected as a carryon and checked. Keep in mind that an airline can adapt the rules to the circumstances, so on an especially crowded flight don't be surprised if you are allowed only one carry-on bag.

In addition to the two carryons, you may bring aboard a handbag (pocketbook or purse); an overcoat or wrap; an umbrella; a camera; a reasonable amount of reading material; an infant bag; and crutches, a cane, braces, or other prosthetic devices. Infant/child safety seats can also be brought aboard if parents have purchased a ticket for the child or if there is space in the cabin.

Foreign airlines have different policies. In tourist class they generally allow only one piece of carry-on luggage in addition to handbags and bags filled with duty-free goods. Passengers in first and business classes are allowed to carry on one garment bag as well. It is best to call your airline to find out its current policy.

Checked Luggage U.S. airlines generally allow passengers to check two or three suitcases whose total dimensions (length × width × height) do not exceed 62 inches and whose weight does not exceed 70 pounds.

Rules governing foreign airlines can vary, so before you go, check with your travel agent or the airline itself. All airlines allow passengers to check in two bags. In general, expect the weight restriction on the two bags to be not more than 70 pounds each, and the size restriction to be not more than 62 inches total dimension on each bag.

Taking Money Abroad

Traveler's checks and all major U.S. credit cards are accepted in most tourist areas of Mexico. The large hotels, restaurants, and department stores accept cards readily. Some of the smaller restaurants and shops, however, will only take cash. Credit cards are generally not accepted in small towns and villages, except in tourist-oriented hotels. When shopping, you can usually get much better prices if you bargain with dollars.

Although you won't get as good an exchange rate at home as in Mexico, to avoid long lines at airport currency exchange booths, it's wise to change a small amount of money into pesos before you go. Many U.S. banks will change your money into pesos. If your local bank can't provide this service, you can exchange money through **Thomas Cook Currency Services Inc.** To find the nearest office, contact Thomas Cook at 630 Fifth Avenue, New York, NY 10011, tel. 212/757–6915.

It's always wise to carry some traveler's checks. All major ones are accepted. The most widely recognized are **American Express, Barclays, Thomas Cook,** and those issued through major commercial banks such as **Citibank** and **Bank of America.** Some banks will issue the checks free to established customers, but most charge a 1% commission. Buy some of the traveler's checks in small denominations to cash toward the end of your trip. This will save you from having to cash a large check and ending your stay with more pesos than you need. Remember to take the addresses of offices in Mexico where you can get refunds for lost or stolen traveler's checks.

The best place to change money are at banks and *casas de cambio* (exchange houses). Banks give the best rate of exchange. Most airports have money exchanges that give the same rate as banks. You can usually get more pesos for your dollars at Mexican airports or banks than at U.S. airports. Hotels will also change money, but they give the poorest rates.

Getting Money from Home

There are at least three ways to get money from home:

1) Have it sent through a large commercial bank with branches in Mexico. The only drawback is that you must have an account with the bank; if you don't, you will have to go through your own bank, and the process will be slower and more expensive.

2) Have money sent through **American Express.** If you are a cardholder, you can cash a personal check or a counter check at an American Express Office; the amount varies with the type of card you have. If you have a personal (green) card, you can cash a check for up to $1,000; $200 will be in cash and $800 in traveler's checks. Generally there is a 1% commission on the traveler's checks. You can also get money through **American Express MoneyGram.** Through this service, you can receive up to $1,000 per person, per day, for a total of $10,000; minimum purchase $100. You simply call home and ask someone to go to an American Express office or an American Express MoneyGram agent located in a retail outlet and fill out an American Express MoneyGram. It can be paid for with cash or with any major credit card. The person making the payment is given a reference number and telephones you with that number. The American Express MoneyGram agent calls an 800 number and authorizes the transfer of funds to an American Express office or participating agency in Mexico. There are two categories of service. **Immediate Service** (10-minute service) is available at American Express offices in major cities only. You can receive a minimum of $100 to a maximum of $10,000, in $50 increments, payable in U.S. dollars, traveler's checks, or pesos. When paying in cash, the fee is $35 for sending $300; $175 for $5,000. When paying by credit card, expect a $5 added charge. The fees are cheaper for **Next Day Service** (24-hour service), available at "Banamex" (Banco Nacional de Mexico) branches throughout Mexico, but money will only be delivered in pesos. At press time, the fee for $1–$50 was $12; for $50.01–$300, $15; for $300.01–$500, $30. You pick it up by showing identification and giving the reference number. Fees vary according to the amount of money sent. For the American Express MoneyGram location nearest your home and the location of offices in Mexico, call 800/543–4080. You do not have to be a cardholder to use this service.

3) Have money sent through **Western Union.** The U.S. number is 800/325–4176. If you have a MasterCard or Visa, you can have money sent for amounts up to your credit limit. If you do not have those credit cards, have someone take cash or a certified check to a Western Union office. The money will be delivered to a bank in Mexico within one business day. Fees vary with the amount of money sent. For $500, the fee is $34; for $1,000, $48. Credit card fees are higher. For $500, the fee is $50; for $1,000, $60.

Mexican Currency

The unit of currency in Mexico is the peso, subdivided into 100 centavos. Mexicans use the dollar sign, often accompanied by the initials M.N. (for *moneda nacional*, or national currency), although banks and international financiers favor the prefix "P$." Because of inflation, centavos are rarely used; bills are issued in denominations of 1,000, 2,000, 5,000, 10,000, 20,000, and 50,000 pesos. Coins come in 1-, 5-, 10-, 20-, 50-, 100-, 200-, 500-, 1,000-, and 5,000-peso denominations. The peso is devalued daily to keep pace with inflation. At press time (January 1991), the official exchange rate was 2,980 pesos to the U.S. dollar, 2,574 pesos to the Canadian dollar, and 5,242 pesos to the pound sterling.

Dollars are widely accepted in many parts of Mexico, particularly near the border and in Cozumel, a free port. Many tourist shops and market vendors take them as well.

What It Will Cost

Mexico has a reputation for being inexpensive, particularly compared with other North American vacation spots such as the Caribbean islands. Actual costs will vary with the when, where, and how of your travel in Mexico. "When" is discussed in When to Go, above. As to "how," tourists seeking a destination as much as possible like home, who travel only by air or package tour, stay at international hotel chain properties, eat at restaurants catering to tourists, and shop at fixed-price tourist-oriented malls may not find it such a bargain. Anyone who wants a closer look at the country and is not wedded to standardized creature comforts can spend as little as $30 a day on room, board, and local transportation. Speaking Spanish is also helpful in bargaining situations and when asking for dining recommendations. As a general rule, the less English is spoken in a region, the cheaper things will be (*see also* Language, *below*).

Cancún, Puerto Vallarta, Mexico City, Acapulco, and Ixtapa and to a lesser extent Mazatlán, Manzanillo, and the created resorts of Huatulco and southern Baja California are the most expensive places to visit in Mexico. Taxis charge fixed rates to and from the airport and between hotels and beaches or downtown. To avoid being taken, compare the zoning regulations with your map, settle on a rate before you get in the cab, and always count your change. Water sports can cost as much as they do on the Caribbean islands. All the beaches, however, offer budget accommodations, and the smaller, less accessible ones are often more moderately priced, examples being the Gulf Coast and northern Yucatán, parts of Quintana Roo, Puerto Escondido, and the beaches of Chiapas.

Average costs in the major cities vary, although less than in the past because of the increase in business travelers. A stay in one of Mexico City's top hotels, and dinner at one of its finest restaurants, can cost $150 and $35, respectively—as much as at the coastal resorts. As with beach resorts, more modest alternatives can always be found.

Probably the best value for your travel dollar is found in the smaller inland towns, such as San Cristóbal de las Casas, Mérida, and Oaxaca, where tourism is less developed. Although Oaxaca lodging can run as high as $70 a night, colonial-style hotels with adequate accommodations for under $25 can be found, and tasty, filling meals are rarely more than $10.

Taxes Mexico has a value-added tax of 10% called I.V.A. *(impuesto de valor agregado)*, which is occasionally (and illegally) waived for cash purchases. Other taxes and charges apply for phone calls, dining, and lodging. An airport departure tax of U.S. $12 or the peso equivalent must be paid at the airport for international flights from Mexico. Traveler's checks and credit cards are not accepted.

Sample Costs Cup of coffee: P$2,000
Bottle of beer: P$4,000
Plate of tacos: P$5,000
2-km taxi ride: P$5,000
Double room in Mexico City or Cancún—Very Expensive: over P$200,000; Expensive: P$150,000–P$200,000; Moderate: P$60,000–P$150,000; Inexpensive: under P$60,000.

Passports and Visas

Americans U.S. citizens can enter Mexico with a tourist card and proof of citizenship. The only acceptable proof of citizenship is either a valid passport or an original birth certificate plus a photo ID. Tourist cards can be obtained from a travel agent, an airline agent at the airport, or from local Mexican consulates. They are also often given out on to your plane. Be sure to hold on to your receipt because you must hand it in upon departure, and if you lose it you will be inconveniently detained. A tourist card is valid for a single entry of up to six months. For stays beyond 90 days, it is best to get permission at the border or at your local Mexican consulate. To obtain a new passport, apply in person; renewals can be obtained in person or by mail. First-time applicants should apply to one of the 13 U.S. Passport Agency offices at least five weeks in advance of their departure date. In addition, local county courthouses, many state and probate courts, and some post offices accept passport applications. Necessary documents include: (1) a completed passport application (Form DSP-11); (2) proof of citizenship (certified birth certificate issued by the Hall of Records of your state of birth, or naturalization papers); (3) proof of identity (valid driver's license or state, military, or student ID card with your photograph and signature); (4) two recent, identical, 2-inch-square photographs (black-and-white or color head shot with white or off-white background); and (5) a $65 application fee for a 10-year passport (those under 18 pay $40 for a five-year passport). You may pay with a check, money order, or exact cash amount; no change is given. Passports are mailed to you in about 10–15 working days. To renew your passport by mail, you'll need to send a completed Form DSP-82, two recent, identical passport photographs, your current passport (if less than 12 years old and issued after your 16th birthday), and a check or money order for $55. For further information, contact the Mexican Consulate, 2827 16th St. NW, Washington, DC 20009, tel. 202/736–1000.

Canadians Canadian citizens can enter Mexico with a tourist card and proof of citizenship. The only acceptable proof is a valid passport or your original birth certificate plus a photo ID. The tourist card can be obtained from travel agents, airlines, or local Mexican consulates. To acquire a passport, send a completed application (available at any post office or passport office) to the Bureau of Passports, Suite 215, West Tower, Complexe Guy-Favreau, 200 boul. René Lévesque O., Montréal, Québec H2Z 1X4. Include $25, two photographs, a guarantor, and proof of Canadian citizenship. Applications can be made in person at regional passport offices in many locations, including Edmonton, Halifax, Montreal, Toronto, Vancouver, and Winnipeg. Passports are valid for five years and are nonrenewable.

Britons All British subjects require a valid 10-year passport (cost £15) and a Mexican tourist card to enter Mexico. Passport applications in the United Kingdom are available through travel agencies or a main post office. Send the completed form to a regional passport office or to the Passport Office (Clive House, 70 Petty France, London SW1H 9BR, tel. 071/279–3434 for recorded information, or 071/279–4000). The Mexican tourist card is free from the airline or the Mexican Embassy (8 Halkin St., London SW1X 7DW, tel. 071/235–6393).

Customs and Duties

On Arrival Upon entering Mexico, you will be given a baggage declaration form and asked to itemize what you're bringing into the country. You are allowed to bring in two liters of spirits or wine for personal use; 200 cigarettes, 50 cigars, or 250 grams of tobacco; a reasonable amount of perfume for personal use; one movie camera and one regular camera and 12 rolls of film for each; and gift items not to exceed a total of $300.

There are no restrictions or limitations on the amount of cash, foreign currencies, checks, or drafts that can be imported or exported by visitors.

On Departure If you are bringing any foreign-made equipment into Mexico, such as cameras, it's wise to carry the original receipt with you or register the equipment with U.S. Customs before you leave (Form 4457). Otherwise you may end up paying duty on your return.

U.S. Residents You may bring home duty-free up to $400 of foreign goods, as long as you have been out of the country for at least 48 hours and you haven't made an international trip in the past 30 days. Each member of the family is entitled to the same exemption, regardless of age, and exemptions may be pooled. For the next $1,000 worth of goods, a flat 10% rate is assessed; above $1,400, duties vary with the merchandise. Included in the allowances for travelers 21 or older are one liter of alcohol, 100 cigars (non-Cuban), and 200 cigarettes. Only one bottle of perfume trademarked in the United States may be imported. There is no duty on antiques or works of art over 100 years old. Anything exceeding these limits will be taxed at the port of entry and may be taxed additionally in the traveler's home state. Gifts valued at under $50 may be mailed duty-free to friends or relatives at home, but you may not send more than one package per day to a single addressee and packages may not include perfumes costing more than $5, tobacco, or liquor.

Since Mexico is considered a "developing" country, it is listed under the U.S. Customs Service's GSP (Generalized System of Preferences) program, and many arts and handicrafts may be brought back into the United States duty-free. You will still need to declare the items and state their value and use, but it won't count against your $400 limit. For a list of exempt items, write to the U.S. Customs Service (Box 7404, Washington, DC 20044). Ask for a copy of *GSP and the Traveler*, a brochure listing exempt items.

Canadian Residents Exemptions for returning Canadians range from $20 to $300, depending on length of stay out of the country and how often you have used your personal exemption. For the $300 exemption, you must have been out of the country for one week. In any given year, you are only allowed one $300 exemption. You may bring in duty-free up to 50 cigars, 200 cigarettes, 2.2 pounds of tobacco, and 40 ounces of liquor, provided these are declared in writing to Customs on arrival and accompany you in hand or checked-through baggage. Personal gifts should be mailed labeled "Unsolicited Gift—Value under $40." For further details, call Canadian Customs general information (tel. 416/973–8022) or obtain a copy of the Canadian Customs brochure "I Declare."

British Residents *See* Tips for British Travelers, *above*.

Traveling with Film

If your camera is new, shoot and develop a few rolls before leaving home. Pack some lens tissue and an extra battery for your built-in light meter. Invest about $10 in a UV or skylight filter and screw it onto the front of your lens. It will protect the lens and also reduce haze.

Film doesn't like hot weather. If you're driving in summer, don't store film in the glove compartment or on the shelf under the rear window. Put it behind the front seat on the floor, on the side opposite the exhaust pipe.

On a plane trip, never pack film or videocassettes in checked luggage; if your bags are X-rayed, your picture may be ruined. Always carry undeveloped film with you through security, and ask to have it inspected by hand. (It helps to isolate your film in a plastic bag, ready for quick inspection.) Inspectors at American airports are required by law to honor requests for hand inspection; abroad, you'll have to depend on the kindness of strangers.

The old airport scanning machines—still in use in some countries—use heavy doses of radiation that can turn a family portrait into an early morning fog. The newer models—used in all U.S. airports—are safe for anything from 5 to 500 scans, depending on the speed of your film (fast film is more easily damaged). The effects are cumulative: You can put the same roll of film through several scans without worry. After five scans, though, you're asking for trouble.

If your film is fogged and you want an explanation, send it to the **National Association of Photographic Manufacturers** (550 Mamaroneck Ave., Harrison, NY 10528, tel. 914/698–7603). They will try to determine what went wrong. The service is free.

Language

Spanish is the official language of Mexico, although Indian languages are spoken by approximately 20% of the population, many of whom speak no Spanish at all. Basic English is widely understood by most people employed in tourism; less so in the less developed areas. At the very least, shopkeepers will know the numbers for bargaining purposes.

As in most foreign countries, knowing some words and phrases in the mother tongue has a way of opening doors. Unlike some other nationalities, Mexicans are not scornful of visitors' mis-pronunciations and grammatical errors; on the contrary, they welcome even the most halting attempts to use their language. For a rudimentary vocabulary, featuring many terms travelers are likely to encounter in Mexico, *see* Spanish Vocabulary and Menu.

The Spanish most Americans learn in high school is based on Castilian Spanish, which is as different from Latin American Spanish as British English—or Continental French—is from North American English or French. In terms of grammar, Mexican Spanish ignores the *vosotros* form of the second person. As to pronunciation, the lisped Castilian "c" or "z" is un-known in Mexico. The most obvious differences are in vocabulary: Mexican Spanish has thousands of Indian words, and the use of *¿mande?*—instead of *¿cómo?* (excuse me?) is a dead give-away that one's Spanish was acquired in Mexico. Words or phrases that are harmless or everyday in one Spanish-speaking country can take on salacious or otherwise offensive meanings in another. Unless you are lucky enough to be briefed on these nuances by a native coach, the only way to learn is by trial and error.

Staying Healthy

The two health risks associated with travel to Mexico are the severe air pollution in Mexico City and the possibility of con-tracting malaria or dengue fever if you stray from the beaten path. The sheer number of people in the capital, thermal inver-sions, and the inability to process sewage have all contributed to the high levels of lead, carbon monoxide, and other pollu-tants in the atmosphere in Mexico City. Though the long-term effects are not known, children, the elderly, and those with res-piratory problems are advised to avoid jogging, outdoor sports, and being outdoors more than necessary.

If you plan to travel outside the major cities and tourist resorts of Mexico, you should consider taking precautions against ma-laria or dengue fever. Check with your physician or call the **U.S. Public Health Quarantine Station** nearest you for informa-tion on vaccination requirements and recommendations. In Mexico you can purchase malaria-preventive Aralen tablets without a prescription. To be effective, the tablets must be tak-en before entering a malarial region. Dengue fever—a viral disease transmitted by mosquitoes and characterized by high fever, severe headaches, and joint and muscle pain—is becom-ing more prevalent in parts of Mexico. No specific treatment exists, so take proper precaution: Remain in well-screened are-as, wear clothing that covers your arms and legs, and use mos-quito repellent.

Many travelers are eventually hit with an intestinal ailment known facetiously as Montezuma's Revenge or the Aztec Two-Step. Generally, it lasts only a day or two. A good antidiarrheal agent is paregoric, which dulls or eliminates abdominal cramps. You will need a doctor's prescription to get it in Mexico. The National Institute of Health recommends Pepto-Bismol and loperamide (Imodium) for mild cases of diarrhea. Lomotil is no longer recommended because it usually prolongs the infection. If you come down with it, rest as much as possible, drink lots of fluids (such as tea without milk) or, in severe cases, rehydrate yourself with a salt-sugar mixture added to water. The best defense against food and waterborne diseases is a smart diet. Stay away from unbottled or unboiled water, ice, raw food, unpasteurized milk, and milk products.

If you have a health problem that might require purchasing prescription drugs while in Mexico, have your doctor write a prescription using the drug's generic name (brand names vary widely from country to country).

The **International Association for Medical Assistance to Travelers (IAMAT)** is a worldwide organization offering a list of English-speaking doctors whose training meets British and American standards. For a list of physicians in Mexico who are part of this network, contact IAMAT (417 Center St., Lewiston, NY 14092, tel. 716/754–4883; in Canada: 40 Regal Rd., Guelph, Ontario N1K 1B5, tel. 519/836–0102; in Europe: 57 Voirets, 1212 Grand-Lancy, Geneva, Switzerland). Membership is free.

Emergencies **Air Evac International** (8665 Gibbs, Suite 202, San Diego, CA 92123, tel. 619/292–5557 or 800/854–2569) provides evacuation for the sick or injured out of Mexico. Call for a free brochure and details about the service.

Insurance

Travelers may seek insurance coverage for such areas as health and accident, lost luggage, and trip cancellation. Your first step should be to review your existing health and homeowner's policies; some health insurance plans cover medical expenses incurred while traveling, some major medical plans cover emergency transportation, and some homeowner's policies cover luggage theft.

Health and Accident Several companies offer coverage designed to supplement existing health insurance for travelers:

Access America (Box 11188, Richmond, VA 23230, tel. 800/284–8300 or 800/334–7525) provides medical insurance and coverage for medical evacuation and travel accidents.

Carefree Travel Insurance (Box 310, 120 Mineola Blvd., Mineola, NY 11501, tel. 516/294–0220 or 800/323–3149) provides coverage for emergency medical evacuation and accidental death and dismemberment. It also offers 24-hour medical advice by phone.

International SOS Assistance (Box 11568, Philadelphia, PA 19116, tel. 215/244–1500 or 800/523–8930), a medical-assistance company, provides emergency-evacuation services, worldwide medical referral, and optional medical insurance.

Travel Guard International, underwritten by Transamerica Occidental Life Companies (1145 Clark St., Stevens Point, WI 54481, tel. 715/345–0505 or 800/782–5151), offers reimbursement for medical expenses with no deductible or daily limit, and emergency evacuation services.

Wallach and Company, Inc. (107–3 West Federal St., Middleburg, VA 22117, tel. 703/687–3166 or 800/237–6615) offers comprehensive medical coverage, including emergency evacuation services worldwide.

Lost Luggage Luggage loss is usually covered as part of a comprehensive travel insurance package that includes personal accident, trip cancellation, and, sometimes, default and bankruptcy insurance. Companies that offer comprehensive policies include:

Access America, Inc., a subsidiary of Blue Cross–Blue Shield (*see* Health and Accident Insurance, *above*); **Carefree Travel Insurance** (*see* Health and Accident Insurance, *above*); **Near Services** (450 Prairie Ave., Suite 101, Calumet City, IL 60409, tel. 708/868–6700 or 800/654–6700); **Travel Guard International** (*see* Health and Accident Insurance, *above*).

Luggage Insurance On international flights, airlines are responsible for lost or damaged property only up to $9.07 per pound (or $20 per kilo) for checked baggage and up to $400 per passenger for carry-on baggage. If you're carrying valuables, either take them with you on the airplane or purchase additional coverage from companies such as **Tele-Trip** (tel. 800/228–9792), a subsidiary of Mutual of Omaha, and **The Travelers Insurance Corporation** (Ticket and Travel Dept., 1 Tower Sq., Hartford, CT 06183–5040, tel. 203/277–0111 or 800/243–3174). Tele-Trip operates sales booths at airports and also issues insurance through travel agents. Tele-Trip will insure checked or hand luggage for up to $500 per individual or $1,000 per family (husband, wife, and minor children). Luggage insurance must be purchased in conjunction with a larger travel insurance package, and rates vary depending upon the length of trip and the particular package chosen.

Before you go, itemize the contents of each bag in case you need to file an insurance claim. Be certain to put your address on and in each piece of luggage, including carry-on bags. If your luggage is stolen and later recovered, the airline will deliver the luggage to your home or hotel free of charge.

Trip Cancellation and Flight Insurance Consider purchasing trip-cancellation insurance if you are traveling on a promotional or discounted ticket that does not allow changes or cancellations. You are then covered if an emergency causes you to cancel or postpone your trip. Trip-cancellation insurance is usually included in combination travel insurance packages available from most tour operators, travel agents, and insurance agents.

Flight insurance, which covers passengers in the case of death or dismemberment, is often included in the price of a ticket when paid for with American Express, MasterCard, or other major credit cards.

Car Rentals

When considering this option, remember that Mexico is still a developing country. Acquiring a driver's license is more a question of paying someone off than of tested skill, and Mexican men have a tendency to show off on the road—often at the expense of other vehicles and pedestrians. The highway system is very uneven: in some regions, modern, well-paved super highways prevail; in others, particularly the mountains, potholes and dangerous, unrailed curves are the rule.

Driving in Mexico City can be especially hellish. To begin with, the city is a maze. Add to that the lack of clearly marked lanes and directional signs, traffic jams, freely honking horns, non-functional traffic lights, the practice of ripping off license plates and breaking into parked cars, children jumping onto car hoods to perform unsolicited windshield washing, and the irritating tendency of policemen to stop motorists and demand bribes—even if you have done nothing wrong—and you have a driving situation suited only for the steely nerved.

To rent a car in Mexico you need a valid driver's license from your country of residence. Mexican rental agencies are more familiar with U.S. and Canadian licenses than with the international driver's licenses issued by the American Automobile Association, which must be obtained before you leave home. You will need to leave a deposit—the most acceptable being a blank, signed credit card voucher. Without a credit card, you may not be able to rent a car.

Mexican auto insurance is imperative, if inadequate, as deductibles can be exceedingly high. The largest U.S. rental car agencies are represented in Mexico, which also has its own national and local firms (their rates are frequently less expensive). It is always best to book in advance from home. This will give you an American reservation number, and the price will be substantially less. For example, a Ford Taurus costs about $70 (300,000 pesos) when reserved in advance. When rented in Mexico, it costs about $150 per day (about 650,000 pesos). One important thing to keep in mind, however, if you are booking in advance, is that you cannot always count on getting the make and model of your choice upon arrival. The least-expensive rental car—a Volkswagen sedan—may be unavailable, and you might have to settle for a larger, more costly model. Manual transmission cars are more common than automatics.

Daily rates vary from about $50 for unlimited mileage on a manual Volkswagen Beetle without air-conditioning to $95 for a mid-size automatic with unlimited mileage. You can find cheaper rates than this, but they will have a per kilometer charge that can augment your rental bill substantially. Also not included in the daily rate are insurance, gasoline, and 10% tax. Weekly package rates for the same models, including unlimited free mileage, cost about $200 and $450, respectively. Weekly rates always offer a much better deal.

Think twice before you rent a car in one location and drop it off at another: Drop-off charges can be hefty—about 33¢ per kilometer between rental city and drop-off city—and in some places drop-off is not possible at all.

For day trips and local sightseeing, engaging a car and driver (who often acts as a guide) for a day can be a hassle-free, more economical way to travel. Hotel desks will know which taxi companies to call, and you can negotiate a price with the driver.

Car rental reservations can be made by calling: **Avis** (tel. 800/331-1084 in the U.S., 800/879-2847 in Canada); **Budget** (tel. 800/472-3325 in the U.S. and Canada); **Dollar** (tel. 800/800-4000 in the U.S. and Canada); **Hertz** (tel. 800/654-3001 in the continental U.S., 800/654-3131 in AK and HI, 800/263-0600 in Canada); and **National** (tel. 800/328-4567).

Student and Youth Travel

The **International Student Identity Card (ISIC)** entitles students to special fares on local transportation and discounts at museums, theaters, sports events, and many other attractions. If the ISIC is purchased in the United States, the $14 cost also includes $3,000 in emergency medical insurance, plus hospital coverage of $100 a day for up to 60 days. With the card, students are also provided with a phone number to call collect in case of emergency. Apply to the **Council on International Educational Exchange** (CIEE, 205 E. 42nd St., New York, NY 10017, tel. 212/661–1414). In Canada, the ISIC is available from Travel Cuts (187 College St., Toronto, Ont. M5T 1P7, tel. 416/979–2406).

Council Travel, a CIEE subsidiary, is the foremost U.S. student travel agency, specializing in low-cost charters and serving as the exclusive U.S. agent for many student airfare bargains and student tours. CIEE's 72-page *Student Travel Catalog* and "Council Charter" brochure are available free from any Council Travel office in the United States (enclose $1 postage if ordering by mail). In addition to the CIEE headquarters at 205 East 42nd Street (tel. 212/661–1450) and a branch office at 35 West 8th Street (tel. 212/254–2525) in New York City, there are Council Travel offices in Tempe, AZ; Berkeley, La Jolla, Long Beach, Los Angeles, San Diego, San Francisco, and Sherman Oaks, CA; Boulder, CO; New Haven, CT; Washington, DC; Atlanta, GA; Chicago and Evanston, IL; New Orleans, LA; Amherst, Boston, and Cambridge, MA; Ann Arbor, MI; Minneapolis, MN; Durham, NC; Columbus, OH; Portland, OR; Providence, RI; Austin and Dallas, TX; Seattle, WA; and, Milwaukee, WI. Offices also exist in Britain, France, Germany, and Tokyo. The London office is located by Oxford Circus, at 28A Poland St., London, W1 (tel. 071/437–7767).

The **Educational Travel Center** (438 N. Frances St., Madison, WI 53703, tel. 608/256–5551) is another student travel specialist worth contacting for information on student tours, bargain fares, and bookings.

Students who would like to work abroad should contact **CIEE's Work Abroad Department** (205 E. 42nd St., New York, NY 10017, tel. 212/661–1414). The council arranges paid and voluntary work experiences overseas for up to six months. CIEE also sponsors study programs in Latin America and Asia and publishes many books of interest to the student traveler. These include *Work, Study, Travel Abroad: The Whole World Handbook* ($12.95 plus $1.50 book-rate postage or $3 first-class postage) and *Volunteer! The Comprehensive Guide to Voluntary Service in the U.S. and Abroad* ($8 plus $1.50 book-rate postage or $3 first-class postage).

The Information Center at the **Institute of International Education** (IIE, 809 UN Plaza, New York, NY 10017, tel. 212/883–8200) has reference books, foreign-university catalogues, study-abroad brochures, and other materials that may be consulted free of charge by students and nonstudents alike. The Information Center is open weekdays 10–4.

IIE administers grant and study programs offered by U.S. and foreign organizations and publishes a well-known annual series of study-abroad guides, including *Academic Year Abroad, Va-*

cation Study Abroad, Study in the United Kingdom and Ireland, and *Management Study Abroad.* The institute also publishes *Teaching Abroad,* a book of employment and study opportunities overseas for U.S. teachers. For a current list of IIE publications, prices, and ordering information, write to Institute of International Education Books (809 UN Plaza, New York, NY 10017). Books must be purchased by mail or in person; telephone orders are not accepted. General information on IIE programs and services is available from regional offices in Atlanta, Chicago, Denver, Houston, San Francisco, and Washington, DC.

Traveling with Children

Getting There All children, including infants, must have proof of citizenship for travel to Mexico. Children traveling with a single parent must also have a notarized letter from the other parent stating that the child has his or her permission to leave the country. (For more information, *see* Passports and Visas, *above.*)

On international flights, children under age 2 not occupying a seat pay 10% of adult fare. Various discounts apply to children age 2–12. Infant travel on U.S. carriers is more a matter of airline policy than federal regulation. If you want to ensure your infant's safety, purchase a separate ticket and bring his or her car seat. Since some infant car seats are not allowed, check with the airline in advance or order the Federal Aviation Administration booklet "Child/Infant Safety Seats Acceptable for Use in Aircraft" (APA–200, 800 Independence Ave. SW, Washington, DC 20591, tel. 202/267–3479). Some airlines allow infants to travel in their own car seat at no charge if an extra airline seat is available; otherwise the seat will be stored and the infant must travel on the parent's lap. If you opt to do this, keep the child outside of the seatbelt so he or she won't be crushed in case of a sudden stop. When contacting the airline, inquire about special children's meals or snacks. The February 1990 and 1992 issues of *Family Travel Times* include "TWYCH's Airline Guide," which contains a rundown of the children's service offered by 46 airlines. (*See* Publications, *below,* for ordering information.)

Publications **The Family Travel Guides Catalogue,** edited by Carole Meyers and updated annually, is the only catalogue that lists and describes current books covering the area of family travel (Carousel Press, P.O. Box 6061, Albany, CA 94706–0061, tel. 510/527–5849). Send $1 for postage and handling.

Family Travel Times is an 8- to 12-page newsletter published 10 times a year by TWYCH (Travel with Your Children, 45 W. 18th St., 7th floor tower, New York, NY 10011, tel. 212/206–0688). A $35 subscription includes access to back issues and twice-weekly opportunities to call in for specific information. Send $1 for a sample issue.

Kids and Teens in Flight is a brochure developed for young travelers by the U.S. Department of Transportation. To order a free copy, call 202/366–2220.

Hints for Disabled Travelers

The **Information Center for Individuals with Disabilities** (Fort Point Place, 27–43 Wormwood St., 1st Floor, Boston, MA

02110–1606, tel. 617/727–5540) offers useful problem-solving assistance, including lists of travel agents who specialize in tours for the disabled.

Moss Rehabilitation Hospital Travel Information Service (1200 W. Tabor Rd., Philadelphia, PA 19141–3099, tel. 215/456–9600; TDD 215/456–9602) provides information on tourist sights, transportation, and accommodations in destinations around the world.

Mobility International USA (Box 3551, Eugene, OR 97403, tel. 503/343–1284) is an international organization with 500 members. For a $20 annual fee it coordinates exchange programs for disabled people around the world and provides information on accommodations and organized study programs.

The **Society for the Advancement of Travel for the Handicapped** (347 Fifth Ave., Suite 610, New York, NY 10016, tel. 212/447–7284, fax 212/725–8253) offers access information. Annual membership costs $45, $25 for senior travelers and students. Send $2 and a self-addressed envelope for information on a specific destination.

Publications *The Itinerary* (Box 2012, Bayonne, NJ 07002, tel. 201/858–3400) is a bimonthly travel magazine for the disabled. Call for a subscription ($10 for one year, $20 for two); it's not available in stores.

Hints for Older Travelers

The **American Association of Retired Persons** (AARP, 601 E St. NW, Washington, DC 20049, tel. 202/434–2277) administers a Purchase Privilege Program through which independent travelers can get discounts on hotels, airfare, car rentals, and sightseeing. AARP members must be at least 50 years old. Annual dues are $5 per person or per couple. The **AARP** also arranges group tours, cruises, and apartment living all over the world through "AARP Travel Experience from American Express" (400 Pinnacle Way, Suite 450, Norcross, GA 30071, tel. 800/927–0111).

If you're planning to use an AARP or other senior-citizen identification card to obtain a reduced hotel rate, mention it at the time you make your reservation rather than when you check out. At participating restaurants, show your card to the maître d' before you're seated; discounts may be limited to certain set menus, days, or hours. Your AARP card will identify you as a retired person but will not ensure a discount in all hotels and restaurants. For a free list of hotels and restaurants that offer discounts, call or write the AARP and ask for the "Purchase Privilege" brochure or call the AARP Travel Service. When renting a car, be sure to ask about special promotional rates, which may offer greater savings than the available discount.

National Council of Senior Citizens (1331 F St. NW, Washington, DC 20004, tel. 202/347–8800) is a nonprofit advocacy group with some 5,000 local clubs across the country. Annual membership is $12 per person or couple. Members receive a monthly newspaper with travel information and an ID for reduced-rate hotels and car rentals.

Mature Outlook (6001 N. Clark St., Chicago, IL 60660, tel. 800/336–6330), a subsidiary of Sears, Roebuck, & Co., is a travel club for people over 50. It offers discounts at Holiday Inns and a bimonthly newsletter. Annual membership is $9.95 per couple. Instant membership is available at participating Sears stores and Holiday Inns or by calling the 24-hour, toll-free number.

Elderhostel (75 Federal St., Boston, MA 02110–1941, tel. 617/426–7788) is an innovative, low-cost educational program for people 60 or over (only one member of a traveling couple needs to qualify). Participants live in dorms and other accommodations on some 1,600 campuses around the world. Mornings are devoted to lectures and seminars, afternoons to sightseeing and field trips. The price includes room, board, tuition (in the United States and Canada), and round-trip transportation (overseas).

Publications *Travel Tips for Older Americans* (Dept. of State Publication 8970, revised 1990) is available for $1 from the Superintendent of Documents (U.S. Government Printing Office, Washington, DC 20402-9325, tel. 202/783–3238).

The Mature Traveler (GEM Publishing Group, Box 50820, Reno, NV 89519, tel. 702/786–7419) is a monthly newsletter for the over-49 traveler. An annual subscription costs $23.50.

Get Up and Go, by Gene and Adele Malott, editors of *The Mature Traveler* newsletter (*see above*), is a complete handbook for those over 49. The 325 pages of tips and deals sells for $10.95 plus $1.75 postage.

The International Health Guide for Senior Citizen Travelers, by Dr. W. Robert Lange, MD, is available for $4.95 plus $1.50 for shipping from Pilot Books (103 Cooper St., Babylon, NY 11702, tel. 516/422–2225).

Further Reading

The best nonfiction on Mexico blends history, culture, commentary, and travel description. The works below are categorized, but by no means mutually exclusive.

History For decades, the standard texts written by scholars for popular audiences have been *A History of Mexico,* by Henry B. Parkes; *Many Mexicos,* by Lesley Byrd Simpson; and *A Compact History of Mexico,* an anthology published by the Colegio de México. Two journalists recently have made important contributions to the literature on historical and contemporary Mexico: Alan Riding's *Distant Neighbors: A Portrait of the Mexicans,* and Jonathan Kandell's *La Capital: The Biography of Mexico City.* Works focusing on the ancient Mexican Indian cultures include *The Maya* and *Mexico,* by Michael D. Coe; *The Last Lords of Palenque,* by Victor Perera and Robert D. Bruce; and *The Blood of Kings: Dynasty & Ritual in Maya Art,* by Linda Schele and Mary Ellen Miller, a handsome coffee-table book that summarizes ground-breaking work in our understanding of the ancient Maya.

Culture/Ethnography Excellent ethnographies include Oscar Lewis's classic works on the culture of poverty (*The Children of Sanchez* and *Five Families); Juan the Chamula,* by Ricardo Pozas, about a small village in Chiapas; *Mexico South,* by Miguel Covarrubias, which discusses Indian life in the early 20th century; Gertrude Blom's *Baring Witness,* on the Lacandones of Chiapas; and *Ma-*

ria Sabina: Her Life and Chants, an autobiography of a shaman in the state of Oaxaca.

Food You may learn as much about Mexican culture in Patricia Quintana's *The Taste of Mexico*, a lushly photographed cookbook, as you would in a first-rate sociological study. At the very least, the perfect margarita will be within your grasp.

Travelogues Two of the more straightforward accounts from the early 19th century are the letters of Fanny Calderón de la Barca *(Life in Mexico)* and John Lloyd Stephens's *Incidents of Travel in Central America, Chiapas and Yucatán*. Foreign journalists have described life in Mexico during and after the revolution: John Reed *(Insurgent Mexico)*; John Kenneth Turner *(Barbarous Mexico)*; Aldous Huxley *(Beyond the Mexique Bay)*; and Graham Greene *(The Lawless Roads*, a superbly written narrative about Tabasco and Chiapas, which served as the basis for *The Power and the Glory)*. In much the same vein, but more contemporary, are works by Patrick Marnham *(So Far from God)*, about Central America and Mexico, and Hugh Fleetwood, whose *A Dangerous Place* is informative despite its cantankerousness. The newest travelogue on Mexico (published October 1991) is Alice Adams' *Mexico: Some Travels and Some Travelers There*, which includes an introduction by Jan Morris. Probably the finest travelogue-cum-guidebook is Kate Simon's *Mexico: Places and Pleasures*.

Mexican Literature Poet/philosopher Octavio Paz is the reigning dean of Mexican intellectuals. His best works are *Labyrinth of Solitude*, a thoughtful, far-reaching dissection of Mexican culture, and the biography of Sor Juana Inés de la Cruz, a 17th-century nun and poet. Latin American literature is increasingly being translated into English. Among the top authors are Carlos Fuentes *(The Death of Artemio Cruz* and *The Old Gringo)*, Juan Rulfo *(Pedro Páramo)*, Jorge Ibarguengoitia, and Elena Poniatowska. Recent biographies of the artist couple Frida Kahlo and Diego Rivera (by Hayden Herrera and Bertram D. Wolfe, respectively) provide glimpses into the Mexican intellectual and political life of the '20s and '30s.

Foreign Literature D. H. Lawrence's *The Plumed Serpent* is probably the best-known foreign novel about Mexico, although its noble savage theme is considered slightly offensive today. Lawrence recorded his travels in Oaxaca in *Mornings in Mexico*. A far greater piece of literature is Malcolm Lowry's *Under the Volcano*. The mysterious recluse B. Traven, whose fame rests largely on his *Treasure of the Sierra Madre*, wrote brilliantly and passionately about Mexico in *Rebellion of the Hanged* and *The Bridge in the Jungle*. Also noteworthy is John Steinbeck's novel *The Sea of Cortez*.

Arriving and Departing

From the United States by Plane

Airports and Airlines The number of airlines serving Mexico from the United States is constantly changing as the two nations continue to revise their bilateral agreements. The bankruptcy and later revival of Aeroméxico in 1988 contributed to even more confusion in the air situation. Since 1986, however, Mexico has been opening the way for more charter flights, an increasingly popular option for

inexpensive air service. The country's two major carriers—
Aeroméxico and Mexicana—are being supplemented by several smaller airlines serving domestic destinations and a new
charter company, Latur. Significantly lower airfares can frequently be had by flying into Tijuana from southern California
and then catching a domestic flight to your final destination.

As with all air travel, a number of fare types and booking restrictions apply; consult a travel agent. Sometimes it is also
worth investigating package tours for flights even if you do not
wish to use a tour's other services (hotels, meals, transfers,
etc.). Because a packager can book seats by blocks, a flight-plus-lodging package can sometimes be less than the cost of
airfare that is booked separately.

Airports with frequent direct (although not always nonstop)
service to the United States are Acapulco, Cancún, Cozumel,
Guadalajara, Ixtapa, Mazatlán, Mérida, Mexico City, Puerto
Vallarta, and San José in Los Cabos.

Airlines specifically serving Mexico from major U.S. cities include **Aero California** (tel. 800/258–3311) from Los Angeles;
Aeroméxico (tel. 800/237–6639) from Houston, Los Angeles,
Miami, New York, and Tucson; **American** (tel. 800/433–7300)
from Chicago, Dallas/Fort Worth, Miami, and Raleigh–Durham; **Continental** (tel. 800/525–0280) from Houston and Newark, NJ; **Delta** (tel. 800/241–4141) from Atlanta, Dallas/Fort
Worth, Los Angeles, New York, and Orlando; **Lufthansa** (tel.
800/645–3880) from Dallas/Fort Worth; **Mexicana** (tel. 800/
531–7921) from Chicago, Dallas, Denver, Los Angeles, Miami,
New York, San Antonio, San Francisco, and San Jose; **Northwest** (tel. 800/447–4747) from Memphis to Cancún; and **United**
(tel. 800/538–2929) from Dulles/Washington, Chicago, Orlando, and San Francisco.

Flying Time Flight times to Mexico City are: from New York, 4.5 hours;
from Chicago, 4.25 hours; from Los Angeles, 3.5 hours. Flight
times to Cancún are: from New York, 4 hours; from Chicago, 3.5
hours; from Los Angeles, 5 hours. Flight times to Acapulco are:
from New York, 6 hours; from Houston, 2 hours; from Los Angeles, 3 hours.

Enjoying the Flight If you can sleep on a plane, it makes sense to fly at night. Unless
you are flying from Europe, jet lag won't be a problem, as there
is little or no time difference between the United States and
Canada and most parts of Mexico. Sleepers usually prefer window seats to curl up against; those who like to move about the
cabin should request an aisle seat. Bulkhead seats (located in
the front row of each cabin) have more legroom, but seat trays
are attached rather awkwardly to the arms of your seat. Bulkhead seats are generally reserved for the disabled, the elderly,
or passengers traveling with infants.

Discount Flights If you have the flexibility, you can sometimes benefit from last-minute sales that tour operators have to fill a plane or bus. A
number of brokers specializing in such discount sales also have
sprung up. Another option is to join a travel club that offers
special discounts to its members. The following charge about
$20–$50 annually: **Moment's Notice** (40 E. 49th St. New York,
NY 10017, tel. 212/486–0503), **Discount Travel International**
(114 Forrest Ave., Suite 203, Narberth, PA 19072, tel. 215/668–
7184), **Travelers Advantage**, CUC Travel Service, (49 Music Sq.
W, Nashville, TN 37203, tel. 800/548–1116), and **Worldwide**

Discount Travel Club (1674 Meridian Ave., Miami Beach, FL 33139, tel. 305/534–2082), which gives out a toll-free number upon joining. Sometimes tour and charter-flight operators advertise in Sunday travel supplements as well. Try to find out whether the tour operator is reputable, and specifically, whether you are tied to a precise round-trip or whether you will have to wait until the operator has a spare seat to return.

Smoking   While all Mexican airlines allow smoking aboard and United States Federal Law permits smoking on international flights, many U.S. and all Canadian airlines have their own nonsmoking policies to Mexico. If, however, you are flying an American carrier on which smoking is permitted and the airline tells you that no seats are available in the nonsmoking section, insist on one. Department of Transportation rules apply to all domestic carriers on international routes and the airline must find seats for all nonsmokers, provided they meet check-in restrictions. DOT regulations do not apply, however, to foreign carriers traveling out of or into the United States. On foreign carriers, ask for a seat far from the smoking section.

From the United States by Car

There are two absolutely essential things to remember about driving in Mexico. First and foremost is to carry Mexican auto insurance, which can be purchased near border crossings on either the U.S. or Mexican side. If you injure anyone in an accident, you could well be jailed—whether it was your fault or not—unless you have insurance. Guilty until proven innocent is part of the country's *Code Napoleon*.

The second item is that if you enter Mexico with a car, you must leave with it. The fact that you drove in with a car is stamped on your tourist card, which you must give to immigration authorities at departure. If an emergency arises and you must fly home, there are complicated customs procedures to face. The reason is that cars are much cheaper in the United States, and you are not allowed to sell your vehicle in Mexico.

Insurance   Remember that the domestic insurance on your car is not valid in Mexico. Purchase enough Mexican automobile insurance at the border to cover your estimated trip. It's sold by the day, and if your trip is shorter than your original estimate, a prorated refund for the unused time will be issued to you upon application after you exit the country. *Dan Sanborn's Insurance* (Headquarters, McAllen, TX, tel. 512/686–0711) and *Seguros Atlántico* (AllState reps) have offices in most border cities. Also, you might try *Instant Mexico Auto Insurance*, in San Ysidro, California (tel. 619/428–2221). All three are experienced and reliable.

Highways   There are several major highways into Mexico from the U.S. border. From California, at Tijuana, a good highway (Mex. 1) runs more than 1,610 kilometers (1,000 miles) down the length of Baja California, with ferries to the mainland at Santa Rosalia, La Paz, and Los Cabos. From Nogales, Arizona, Mex. 15 follows the Gulf of California coast on the mainland for 1,208 kilometers (750 miles) to Mazatlán on the Pacific, then turns gradually inland to Guadalajara. From Texas, starting in El Paso, Mex. 45 runs between Mexico's two great northern mountain ranges, the Sierra Madre Occidental and Sierra Madre Oriental. This road leads to the cities of Chihuahua, Torreón, Durango, and Zacatecas on the central highland, 1,208 kilometers (750 miles) from the Texas border. In northeastern Mexico, two main highways head south, one (Mex. 57) from Piedras Negras to Saltillo and the other, the Pan-American Highway (Mex. 85), from Laredo to Monterrey. From Saltillo, you can head to Durango, Zacatecas, or San Luis Potosí, which is just about at the geographical center of the country. From Monterrey, the Pan-American Highway drops south through Ciudad Victoria and Mante down to Pachuca and then Mexico City. At Mante, Mex. 80 branches off toward Tampico and the Gulf Coast. The Sierra Madre Occidental's ruggedness prevents any highway from crossing it north of the spectacular Durango–Mazatlán road (Mex. 40). The farther south you get, the more east–west links exist, tying together the major north–south arteries. In 1990 the Mexican government instituted a Northern Border Program to improve highway safety and make road travel more convenient at the U.S.-Mexican border. Additional vehicles have been added to the government's "Green Angels" roadside patrol force (*see* Getting Around by Car, in Staying in Mexico, *below*); unleaded gasoline, previously difficult to find, is becoming readily available; and lots of clean rest stops are popping up along newly repaved and upgraded roadways.

From the United States by Train, Bus, and Ship

By Train Rail service from the U.S. border at Nuevo Laredo (across from Texas's Laredo) to Mexico City has become a great deal more pleasant since the 1988 introduction of *El Regiomontano*, which covers the 1,210-kilometer (750-mile) trip in 18 hours. The train stops in Monterrey, Saltillo, and San Luis Potosí; private rooms with bath and one or two berths are available. For service to the U.S. side of the border, call **Amtrak** (tel. 800/872–7245). Information and schedules on Mexican trains are available from **Mexico By Rail** (tel. 800/228–3225) in the United States or at local railroad stations in Mexico.

By Bus Getting to Mexico by bus is no longer for just the adventurous or budget-conscious. In the past, bus travelers were required to change to Mexican vehicles at the border, and vice versa. Now, however, in an effort to bring more American visitors and their tourist dollars to off-the-beaten-track markets and attractions, the Mexican government has removed this obstacle and a growing number of trans-border bus tours are available.

In addition, gateway cities such as El Paso, Del Rio, Laredo, McAllen, Brownsville, and San Antonio, Texas, and Tijuana are served by several small private bus lines as well as by **Greyhound Lines.** (Check your telephone book for the local number that will connect you with the national switchboard. The Laredo Station number is 512/723–4324.)

Gray Line Tours (tel. 512/943–2144 or 800/321–8720) runs five-hour- to seven-day-long bus tours, including shopping tours, across the border. Prices range from $15 for a five-hour excursion to $99 for three-day packages including hotel and transportation, and $249 for seven-day inclusive packages.

Alamo Coaches of San Antonio's (tel. 512/923–8222 or 800/527–3453) trans-border trips include festival trips, such as their tour to Monterrey, commemorating the holiday of Our Lady of Guadalupe, Mexico's patron saint.

Tour Masters of Los Angeles (tel. 213/386–1698 or 800/992–8877) runs more than six different trans-border tours.

By Ship Many cruise lines include Mexican ports on their cruise itineraries. Most originate from across the Gulf of Mexico, usually at Miami, stopping in Key West, Cancún, and Cozumel. Others sail from Los Angeles along the Pacific coastline. Still others include both coastlines, passing through the Panama Canal. Many large travel agencies, especially **Empress Travel** (tel. 800/468–4748), organize cruise packages from major U.S. ports, especially Miami, Fort Lauderdale, and San Diego.

Celebrity Cruises (tel. 800/437–3111) offers a five-night cruise aboard the SS *Britanis*, starting in Miami and visiting Key West, Playa del Carmen, and Cozumel before returning to Miami, for $449–$999 per person, double occupancy depending on accommodations and season.

Commodor/Bermuda Star Line (tel. 800/237–5361) has a similar cruise from New Orleans on *The Enchanted Seas*, stopping at Playa del Carmen, Cozumel, and Grand Cayman, while *The Enchanted Isle* sails from San Diego to the Mexican Riviera—Cabo San Lucas, Mazatlán, and Puerto Vallarta. Prices for these seven-day cruises start at $995, although they can be much higher depending on season and accommodations.

Holland American Line (tel. 800/426–0327) will begin 15-day cruises from Los Angeles to Fort Lauderdale via the Mexican Riviera, the Panama Canal, and Costa Rica in the fall of 1992. Prices including airfare will start at $2,900 per person, double occupancy. The line also operates a seven-day Caribbean cruise on the *New Amsterdam* that makes a ½-day stop in Cozumel.

Other cruise lines with Mexican stops include **Carnival Cruise Line** (tel. 800/432–5424), **Epirotiki** (tel. 212/599–1750), **Norwegian Cruise Lines** (tel. 800/327–7030), **Princess Cruises** (tel. 800/421–0522), **Royal Caribbean Cruise Line** (tel. 800/327–6700), **Royal Viking Line** (tel. 800/422–8000), and **Society Expeditions** (tel. 800/426–7794).

For details on the possibility of freighter travel to or from Mexico, consult **TravLtips Inc.** (Box 188, 16307 Depot Rd., Flushing, NY 11358, tel. 718/939–2400 or 800/872–8584).

Staying in Mexico

Getting Around

By Plane While **Mexicana** and **Aeroméxico** provide the bulk of air service within Mexico, connections among the smaller cities have been severely cut back. Fortunately, regional airlines have filled in most of the gaps. **Aerocaribe** serves the Yucatán and the Southeast; **Aeromar** serves central Mexico; **Aerocozumel** flies between Cozumel and Cancún; and **Aerovías Oaxaqueñas** flies between Oaxaca and Puerto Escondido and Salina Cruz. Reservations for these carriers can be made in the United States via **Mexicana. Aero California** also flies within Mexico, serving Guadalajara, Loreto, Los Mochis, Hermosillo, and Tijuana. Call them directly. **International Airlines** offers connecting service between the large beach resorts and Mexico City. Remember to arrive one hour before your internal flight, as overbooking is common. Collect and recheck your baggage with each plane change to decrease the chances of loss. Be prepared to pay a departure tax on some Mexican domestic flights.

Both Aeroméxico and Mexicana have air-hotel packages, called V.T.P., which stands for *viaje todo pagado* (all-inclusive trip). Certain discounts on these carriers may apply for flights originating in the United States.

By Train Since 1987 the **Ferrocarriles Nacionales de México** (Mexican National Railways, tel. 52–5–547–1084) has been putting luxury trains into service around the country, with upgraded dining and club cars, air conditioning, first-class service, and several with sleeping cars. These services, however, are still available only on certain designated trains. *El Constitucionalista* runs between Mexico City and Querétaro, Irapuato, and San Miguel Allende. *El Jarocho* commutes overnight between the capital and Veracruz, and there are also overnight trains from Mexico City to Guadalajara *(El Tapatío)* and Oaxaca *(El Oaxaqueño)*. Two other trains go as far north as León, Aguascalientes, and Zacatecas. Service to Yucatán, Chiapas, and to Michoacán has not yet been refurbished. The *Expreso del Mar* runs between Nogales (across from Arizona) and Guaymas. There is also an antique narrow-gauge train that runs between Mexico City and Cuernavaca on weekends. Whichever train you take, be prepared for a relatively slow ride and bring a snack. The meals are less than appetizing.

One of the newest and most popular tourist trains coasts alongside the Copper Canyon from Chihuahua to Los Mochis on the Pacific Coast (tel. 52–14–16–1657). Other railways include the **Chihuahua-Pacific Railway** (tel. 52–5–54–5325), the **Pacific Railway** (tel. 52–5–547–2019), and the **Sonora-Baja California Railway** (tel. 52–5–657–2386).

Primera especial (special first-class) tickets on overnight trains entitle passengers to reserved, spacious seats that turn so traveling companions can face each other. *Primera regular* (regular first-class) service is also available on many trains. Second-class coaches are less comfortable.

Sleeping accommodations consist of *camarines* (private rooms with bath and one lower berth), *alcobas* (same as *camarines*, but with an upper and a lower berth), and couchettes.

Train tickets must be purchased at least one day in advance, from Mexico City's Buenavista Station, local stations, or local Mexican travel agents, who will, of course, charge you extra. You can also reserve tickets in advance (15 to 30 days is recommended) from the United States by calling **Mexico by Rail** (tel. 800/228–3225) or your travel agent. Plans are also under way to hook up Mexico's rail services with satellite reservation systems, as well as to begin "auto train" service for transporting vehicles and buses. For further information contact Mexico by Rail offices in the United States and Mexico.

By Bus Mexican buses run the gamut from comfortable air-conditioned coaches with bathrooms on board (deluxe and first-class) to dilapidated "vintage" buses (second- and third-class) on which pigs and chickens travel and stops are made in the middle of nowhere. While a lower-class bus ride can be interesting if you are not in a hurry and want to see the sights and experience the local culture, these fares are only about 10% less than first-class. Therefore, travelers planning a long-distance haul are well advised to buy the first-class ticket, which, unlike the other classes, can be reserved in advance.

The Mexican bus network is extensive, far more so than the railroads, as buses are the poor man's form of transportation. In deciding between bus and train travel, your choice will often be determined by availability and flexibility: buses go where trains do not, service is more frequent, tickets can be purchased on the spot (except during holidays and on long weekends, when advance purchase is crucial), and first-class buses can be almost as comfortable as trains. Bring something to eat on all overnight bus rides in case you don't like the restaurant where the bus stops, and bring toilet tissue, as rest rooms vary in cleanliness. Smoking is permitted on all Mexican buses.

In the large cities, bus stations are located a good distance from the center of town, which can be inconvenient. Some towns have different stations for each bus line, but fortunately there is a trend toward consolidation. Bus service in Mexico City is well organized, operating out of four terminals. **Central de Autobuses** (Plaza del Angel, Londres 161, tel. 52–5–533–2047), a travel agency in the capital, will make reservations and send bus tickets to your hotel for a small fee. The best first-class lines include **ADO,** serving Yucatán, Palenque, Villahermosa, and Veracruz from the Eastern Bus Terminal (tel. 52–5–542–7192) and Matamoros, Pachuca, and Tampico from the Northern Bus Terminal (tel. 52–5–567–8455); **Cristóbal Colón,** which goes to Chiapas and the Guatemala border from the Eastern Bus Terminal (tel. 52–5–542–7263); and **Transportes del Norte,** which goes up to the U.S. border from the Northern Bus Terminal (tel. 52–5–587–5511).

By Car
Road and Traffic
Conditions

There are several well-kept toll roads in Mexico—primarily of the two-lane variety—covering mostly the last stretches of major highways *(carreteras)* leading to the capital. (*Cuota* means toll road; *libre* means no toll, and such roads are usually not as smooth.) Approaches to most of the other large cities are also in good condition, and the new Northern Border Program (*see* from the United States by Car, in Arriving and Departing, *above*) will be cleaning up some of the ubiquitous potholes. In rural areas, roads are quite poor: Caution is advised, especially during the rainy season, when rock slides are a problem. Driving in Mexico's central highlands may also necessitate adjustments to your carburetor. Generally, driving times are longer than for comparable distances in the United States. *Topes* (road cops, or bumps) are also common; it's best to slow down when approaching a village.

Driving at night is not recommended because of poor visibility (Mexicans tend to drive with no headlights), the difficulty of getting assistance in remote areas, and the risk of banditry. Popular lore has it that such incidents occur primarily in the long, desolate stretches of Baja California and northern Mexico, although they can occur anywhere. Common sense goes a long way in this regard: If you have a long distance to cover, start out early and fill up on gas. Allow extra time for unforeseen occurrences as well as for the trucks that seem to be everywhere. During the day, be alert to animals, especially cattle and dogs. (The number of dead dogs lying beside—and in the middle of—Mexican highways is appalling.)

Traffic can be horrendous in the cities, particularly in Mexico City. As you would in big cities anywhere, avoid rush hour (7–9 AM and 5–7 PM) and lunchtime (1–3 PM). Signage is not always adequate in Mexico, so if you are not sure where you are going, travel with a companion and a good map. Always lock your car, and never leave valuable items in the body of the car (the trunk will suffice for daytime outings).

The Mexican Tourism Ministry publishes a good general road map, available free from its offices. PEMEX, the state-owned oil company, has an excellent, highly detailed road atlas *(Atlas de Carreteras)*; Guía Roji puts out current city, regional, and national road maps. PEMEX and Guía Roji publications are available in bookstores; gas stations generally do not carry maps.

Rules and Safety Regulations   Illegally parked cars are not treated lightly. Cars are either towed or their license plates removed, which requires a trip to the traffic police headquarters for payment of a fine. When in doubt, avoid street parking and look for a parking lot, where your car is likely to be safer.

If an oncoming vehicle flicks its lights at you in daytime, slow down: it could mean trouble ahead. When approaching a narrow bridge, the first vehicle to flash its lights has right of way. One-way streets are common in many communities. One-way traffic is indicated by an arrow; two-way, by a two-pointed arrow. A circle with a diagonal line superimposed on the letter *E* (for *estacionamiento*) means "no parking." Other road signs follow the now-widespread system of international symbols, a copy of which will usually be provided when you rent a car in Mexico.

Speed Limits   Mileage and speed limits are given in kilometers: 100 kph and 80 kph (62 and 50 mph, respectively) are the most common maximum speeds. A few of the newer toll roads allow 110 kph (68.4 mph). In cities and small towns, observe the posted speed limits, which can be as low as 30 kph (18 mph).

Fuel Availability and Costs   PEMEX franchises all the gas stations in Mexico. Stations are located at most road junctions, cities, and towns, but do not accept credit cards or dollars. Fuel prices, however, are the same at all stations and about the same as in the United States. Unleaded gas is becoming more common, and the government is now trying to distribute it throughout the country.

At the gas stations, keep a close eye on the attendants, and if possible, avoid the rest rooms: They're generally filthy.

National Road Emergency Services   The Mexican Tourism Ministry operates a fleet of almost 250 pickup trucks to render assistance to motorists on the major highways, known as the *Angeles Verdes*, or Green Angels. The bilingual drivers provide mechanical help, medical first aid, radio-telephone communication, basic supplies and small parts, towing, tourist information, and protection. Services are free, and spare parts, fuel, or lubricants are provided at cost. Tips are always appreciated.

The Green Angels patrol fixed sections of the major highways twice daily from 8 AM to 8 PM. If you break down, pull off the road as far as possible, lift the hood of your car, hail a passing vehicle, and ask the driver to notify the patrol. Most bus and truck drivers will be quite helpful. The Green Angels' 24-hour, nationwide hot line is 250–4817.

If you witness an accident, do not stop to help but instead locate the nearest official.

By Taxi Taxis in Mexican cities are the best alternative to public transportation, which, though inexpensive, is slow and sometimes rife with pickpockets. Always establish the fare beforehand, and always count your change. When taking a taxi from the airport, be sure to take a government-subsidized cab. These cabs accept the taxi vouchers that can be purchased at stands outside the airport. This will ensure that your fare is established beforehand. Be careful, however. Even these cab companies may overcharge you at the ticket counter. Prepare yourself by locating the taxi zone of your destination on a map and make sure the counter clerk sells you a properly zoned ticket. For example, you may unknowingly buy a ticket from zone one to zone four, when you only need a ticket from zone three to zone four. Regardless, the rates for non-government-subsidized cabs will still routinely exceed the official taxi rate. In most of the beach resorts, there are inexpensive fixed-route fares, but if you don't ask, or your Spanish isn't great, you may get taken. In the cities, and especially the capital, meters do not always run, and if they do, their rates have usually been updated by a chart posted somewhere in the cab. For distances more than several kilometers, negotiate a rate in advance; many drivers will start by asking how much you want to pay to get a sense of how street-smart you are.

Taxis are available on the street, at taxi stands *(sitios)*, and by phone. Street taxis—usually Volkswagen Beetles—are subsidized cabs and are always the cheapest; large limousines standing in front of hotels will charge far more. Never leave luggage unattended in a taxi.

In addition to private taxis, many cities operate a bargain-price collective taxi service using VW minibuses, both downtown and at the airports. The vehicle itself is called a *combi;* the service, *colectivo* or *pesero*. Peseros run along fixed routes, and you hail them on the street and tell the driver where you are going. The fare—which you pay before you get out—is based on distance traveled. (For information on taxis in Mexico City, *see* Chapter 3.)

Telephones

The Mexican telephone system is antiquated. Lines are frequently tied up, the number of digits varies from city to city, obtaining information from the operator is not always possible, and public phones are often out of order. Pay phones in Mexico City have been free since the earthquake of 1985; elsewhere you must carry a good selection of coins. Long-distance calls can be made from public phones only if they are collect.

Local and long-distance calls can also be made from telephone company offices, specially marked shops (usually with a telephone symbol hanging out front), and hotels, although the last place an excessive surcharge on top of the phone tax and value-added tax, which comes to about 58%. For international calls, call collect whenever possible; there is often a charge whether or not the call is completed. Direct dial to the United States is available from most luxury hotels, but if you must go through an operator, expect a long wait to be connected. International operators speak English. Dial 09 to place international calls; 02 for long-distance calls; 04 for local information; 01 for long-distance information. To reach Mexico City from the United States you must dial 011–52 (country code) and 5 (city code) and the local number. The area code 905 is no longer being used.

The Secretaria de Turismo (SECTUR) operates a 24-hour hot line in Mexico City with multilingual experts providing information on the capital and the entire country. You can also call collect from anywhere in Mexico by adding the prefix 91–5 to the following numbers: 250–0123, 250–0151, or 545–4306.

Mail

The Mexican postal system is notoriously slow and unreliable; *never* send, or expect to receive, packages, as they may be stolen (for emergencies, use a courier service or the new express-mail service, with insurance). There are post offices *(oficinas de correos)* even in the smallest villages, and numerous branches in the larger cities. Always use airmail for overseas correspondence; it will take anywhere from 10 days to two weeks or more, where surface mail might take three weeks to arrive. Service within Mexico can be equally slow. Airmail rates are P$2,000 for a letter (up to 10 grams) or postcard to the United States, and P$3,000 to the United Kingdom.

To receive mail in Mexico, you can have it sent to your hotel or use *poste restante* at the post office. In the latter case, include the words "a/c Lista de Correos" (general delivery) and the zip code. A list of names for whom mail has been received is posted and updated daily by the post office. American Express cardholders or traveler's check holders can have mail sent to them at the local American Express office. For a list of the offices worldwide, request a copy of *Traveler's Companion* from American Express (Box 678, Canal Street Station, New York, NY 10013).

Addresses

The Mexican method of naming streets is exasperatingly arbitrary. Streets in the centers of many colonial cities (those built by the Spaniards) are laid out in a grid surrounding the zócalo and often change names on different sides of the square; other streets simply acquire a new name after a certain number of blocks. The naming system for numbered streets is identical to the American habit of designating numbered streets as either "north/south" or "east/west" on either side of a central avenue. Streets with proper names, however, can change mysteriously from Avenida Juárez, for example, to Calle Francisco Madero, without any way of knowing where one begins and the other ends. On the other hand, blocks are often labeled numerically, according to distance from a chosen starting point, as in "la Calle de Pachuca," "2a Calle de Pachuca," etc.

Many Mexican addresses have "s/n" for *sin número* (no number) after the street name. This is common in small towns where there are fewer buildings on a block. Similarly, many hotels give their address as "Km 30 a Querétaro," which indicates that the property is on the main highway 30 kilometers from Querétaro.

As in Europe, addresses in Mexico are written with the street name first, followed by the street number. The five-digit zip code *(código postal)* precedes, rather than follows, the name of the city. "Apdo." *(apartado)* means "post office box number."

Veteran travelers to Mexico invariably make one observation about asking directions in the country: Rather than say they do not know, Mexicans tend to offer guidance that may or may not be correct. This is not out of malice, but out of a desire to please. Therefore, patience is a virtue when tracking down an address.

Tipping

When tipping in Mexico, remember that the minimum wage is the equivalent of $4 a day and that the vast majority of workers in the tourist industry live barely above the poverty line. However, there are Mexicans who think in dollars and know, for example, that in the United States porters are tipped about $1 a bag; many of them expect the peso equivalent from foreigners (P$2,980 at press time) but are happy to accept P$1,000 from Mexicans. They will complain either verbally or with a facial expression if they feel they deserve more—you and your conscience must decide. Overtipping, however, is equally a problem. Following are some general guidelines, in pesos:

Porters and bellboys at airports and at moderate and inexpensive hotels: P$2,000 per bag
Porters at expensive hotels: P$4,000 per bag
Hotel room service: P$700 *(Expensive);* P$400 *(Moderate* and *Inexpensive)*
Maids: P$2,000 per night (all hotels)
Waiters: 10%–20% of the bill, depending on service (make sure a 10%–15% service charge has not already been added to the bill, although this practice is not common in Mexico)
Taxi drivers: no tip unless they have done something extraordinary
Gas station attendants: P$500
Children (windshield-wiping, car-watching, etc.): P$100
Parking attendants and theater ushers: P$300

Opening and Closing Times

Banks are open weekdays 9 AM–1:30 PM. In some larger cities, a few banks also open weekdays 4–6 PM, Saturday 10 AM–1:30 PM and 4–6 PM, and Sundays 10 AM–1:30 PM. Banks will give you cash advances in pesos (for a fee) if you have a major credit card. Traveler's checks can always be cashed (for less favorable exchange rates) at hotels, airports, *casas de cambio* (exchange houses), shops, and restaurants. Stores are generally open weekdays and Saturdays from 9 or 10 AM to 7 or 8 PM; in resort areas, they may also be open on Sundays. Business hours are 9 AM–7 PM, with a two-hour lunch break (siesta) from about 2 to 4 PM. Government offices are usually open 8 AM–3 PM. All government offices, banks, and most private offices are closed on national holidays. Museums and most archaeological zones close Mondays, with few exceptions.

Shopping

Mexico is one of the best countries in the world to purchase *artesanía* (handicrafts), and many items are exempt from duty (*see* Customs and Duties, in Before You Go, *above*). The work is varied, original, colorful, and inexpensive, and it supports millions of families who are carrying on ancient traditions. Though cheap, shoddy merchandise—masquerading as "native handicraft"—is on the rise, careful shoppers who take their time can come away with real works of art.

At least three varieties of outlets feature Mexican crafts: indoor and outdoor municipal markets; government-run shops (known as *Fonart*); and tourist boutiques in the towns, shopping malls, and hotels. By shopping in the municipal shops or markets you can avoid the VAT and you'll be able to pay in pesos or dollars, but be prepared to bargain. The boutiques are overpriced but convenient, and they usually accept credit cards if not dollars. (You may be asked to pay up to 10% more on credit-card purchases; savvy shoppers with cash have greater bargaining clout.) The 10% tax (I.V.A.) is charged on most purchases but is often disregarded by eager or desperate vendors.

It is not always true that the closer you are to the source of an article, the better the selection and price are likely to be. Mexico City, Oaxaca, and San Miguel de Allende have some of the best selections of crafts from around the country, and if you know where to go, you will find bargains. As a general rule, prices are always higher at the beach resorts.

Bargaining is accepted in most touristy parts of Mexico and is most common in the markets. Start by offering no more than half the asking price and then come up very slowly, but do not pay more than 70%. Always shop around. In major shopping areas like San Miguel, shops will wrap and send purchases back to the United States via a package delivery company. In some areas you will be able to have items such as *huaraches* (leather sandals), clothing, and blankets tailor-made. If you are buying anything made of wood, freeze or microwave it to avoid termite infestation. Keep in mind that items made from tortoiseshell and black coral will not be allowed back into the United States.

Mexican craftspeople in given regions excel in ceramics, weaving and textiles, silver, gold, and semiprecious stone jewelry, leather, woodwork, and lacquerware. A short guide to what to buy and where follows:

Ceramics Blue talavera (Puebla); black (Oaxaca); masks and figurines (Michoacán); also in Jalisco, Taxco, Valle de Bravo, Tlaquepaque, and Chiapas.

Jewelry Silver (Taxco, San Miguel, and Oaxaca; be sure purchases are stamped "925," which means 92.5% pure silver); gold filigree (Oaxaca, Guanajuato); semiprecious stones (Puebla, Querétaro).

Leather Yucatán, Chiapas, Oaxaca, and Jalisco.

Metalwork Copper (Santa Clara del Cobre in Michoacán); tin (San Miguel de Allende).

Weavings and Textiles Shawls and blankets (Oaxaca, Jocotopec, near Guadalajara, and Pátzcuaro); *huipiles*, *guayaberas*, and embroidered clothing (Yucatán and Michoacán); henequen hammocks and baskets (Yucatán); reed mats (Oaxaca, Valle de Bravo); also in the Mezquital region east of Querétaro.

Woodwork Masks (Guerrero, Mexico City); *animalitos* (painted wooden animals, Oaxaca); furniture (Guadalajara, Michoacán, San Miguel de Allende, and Cuernavaca); lacquerware (Uruapan, Michoacán, and Olinalá, Guerrero); guitars (Paracho, Michoacán).

Sports and Outdoor Activities

Hunting, Fishing, and Bird-watching The best area for these activities is Baja California and the Sea of Cortés. For information on hunting and the hunting calendar, contact the Dirección General de Area de Flora y Fauna Silvestres (Dirección General de Conservación Ecológica de los Recursos Naturales, Río Elba 20, Col. Cuauhtémoc, 06500 México, D.F., tel. 52-5-553-5545). Licenses can be obtained from Mexican consulates in Texas, California, New Mexico, and Arizona, or in Mexico from the Secretaría de Desarrollo Urbano y Ecología. For information on fishing and mandatory permits, contact the Secretaría de Pesca (Alvaro Obregón 269, 06700 México, D.F., tel. 52-5-211-0063).

Tennis and Golf Most major resorts have lit tennis courts, and there is an abundance of 18-hole golf courses in Mexico, many of them designed by such noteworthies as Percy Clifford, Larry Hughes, and Robert Trent Jones. Contact the Federación Mexicana de Tenis (Durango 225-301, México, D.F., tel. 52-5-514-3759) and the Federación Mexicana de Golf (Cincinati 40, 02710 México, D.F., tel. 52-5-563-9194 or 52-5-563- 9195) for information. At private golf and tennis clubs, you must be accompanied by a member to gain admission. Hotels that do not have their own facilities will often secure you access to ones in the vicinity. Many deluxe international hotel chain properties also feature extensive health-club facilities.

Mountain Climbing, Camping, Hiking Mountain climbing centers on the volcanoes outside of Mexico City—Ixtaccíhuatl and Popocatépetl—and on Mt. Orizaba in the state of Veracruz (at 5,750 meters or 18,851 feet, it is one of the highest in the world). Climbing experience is advised, and ropes and crampons are recommended. Avoid climbing during the rainy season. For information and guides, contact the Club de Exploraciones de México (Juan Mateos 146, México, D.F., tel. 52-5-578-5730).

Like mountain climbing, camping is not a particularly popular pastime among the Mexicans. Though many national parks provide free camping facilities, most camping takes place outside them. Camping is best on the Pacific Coast and in Baja, which is endowed with forests of pine, granite formations, and lagoons. An hour out of Mexico City, you can camp and hike at Cumbres de Ajusco, Desierto de los Leones, and La Marquesa. The Chiapas lakelands at Lagunas de Montebello are one of the least explored and most beautiful parts of the country.

Horseback Riding Horseback riding is a sport the Mexicans love. The dry ranchlands of northern Mexico have countless stables and dude ranches, particularly in San Miguel de Allende and Querétaro, in the Heartland. Horses can be rented by the hour at all the beaches, and horseback expeditions can be arranged to the Copper Canyon in Chihuahua and the forest near San Cristóbal, Chiapas. A new horse ranch, Taballo del Mar, just opened in Huatulco near Baya Conejos just a short taxi ride from the Huatulco Sheraton (tel. 52–9–581–0055, ext. 784). The Sheraton's travel agency will make arrangements at your request.

Hot Springs Mexico is renowned for its *balnearios* (mineral bath springs), which today are surrounded by a cluster of spa resorts and ha-cienda-type hotels. Most of the spas are concentrated in the center of the country, in the states of Aguascalientes, Guana-juato, México, Morelos, Puebla, and Querétaro.

Spectator Sports

Charreada This Mexican rodeo is a colorful event involving elegant flour-ishes and maneuvers, handsome costumes, mariachi music, and much fanfare. There are charreadas most Sunday mornings at Mexico City's Rancho del Charro; inquire at the tourist office or a travel agency.

Soccer As in Europe, this is Mexico's national sport (known as *futból*). It is played almost year-round at the *Estadio Azteca* in Mexico City as well as in other large cities.

Jai alai, horse racing, dog racing, cockfights, boxing, and bull-fights are practiced all over Mexico. Again, ask at the tourist office, travel agencies, and hotels, or pick up the local newspa-per.

Beaches

Beaches are the reason most tourists visit Mexico. Generally speaking, the Pacific is rougher and the waters less clear than the Caribbean; consequently there is better snorkeling and scuba diving at the latter. Beaches on the Gulf of Mexico are often covered with tar. In Chiapas, the largely undeveloped beaches are covered with hot black sand. Deep-sea fishing is particularly renowned off the northern Pacific and in the Sea of Cortés, between Baja California and Mazatlán. The Acapulco waters are so polluted that swimming is not advised, but there is no problem at the other Pacific resorts. All beach resorts of-fer a variety of water sports, including waterskiing, windsurf-ing, parasailing, and if the water is clear enough, snorkeling and scuba diving. Surfers favor Puerto Escondido, near Huatulco, and Santa Cruz, near San Blas. Sailing is delightful at Mexico's inland lakes, including Avándaro (near Valle de Bravo), Chapala, Pátzcuaro, and Tequesquitengo.

Caution is advised when venturing out in the Mexican sun. Sunbathers lulled by a slightly overcast sky or the sea breezes can be burned badly with as little as 20 minutes' exposure. Use strong sunscreens, and avoid the peak sun hours of noon to 2 PM.

Dining

Mexican cooking is developing an international reputation and popularity. It is not subtle. It is spicy, varied, and exotic. The poor subsist on staples of rice, bean, and tortillas, which form the basis for creative variations on sophisticated national dishes.

Seafood is abundant, not just on the coasts but also in the lake regions around Guadalajara and in the state of Michoacán. *Ceviche*—raw fish and shellfish *(mariscos)* marinated in lime juice and topped with *cilantro* (coriander), onion, and chili—is almost a national dish, though it originated in Acapulco. It is worth trying, but make sure it's fresh. Shrimp, lobster, and oysters can be huge and succulent, but when ordering oysters, bear in mind the folk adage about eating oysters only in months with names that contain the letter *r*. Other popular seafood includes *huachinango* (red snapper), abalone, crab, turtle steak, and swordfish.

Mexicans consume lots of beef, pork, and barbecued lamb *(barbacoa)*, with a variety of sauces. Chicken and other poultry tend to be dry and stringy, but when drenched in sauces or disguised in *enchiladas, tacos,* or *burritos,* they are quite palatable. Chicken *mole* can be especially tasty. Regional variations are described in the appropriate chapters.

Maize was sacred to the Indians, who invented innumerable ways of preparing cornmeal, from the faithful tortilla to the *tamal* (cornmeal wrapped in banana leaves or corn husks), *tostada* (lightly fried, open tortilla heaped with meat, lettuce, etc.), and simple *taco* (a tortilla briefly heated, filled, and wrapped into a slim cylinder; one variation on this is called *flauta,* or flute).

Fresh fruits and vegetables are another Mexican forte. Jicama, papaya, mamey, avocado, mango, guayaba, peanuts, squash, and tomatoes are just some of the produce native to Mexico. (All fresh produce should be washed or peeled before eating, however, because bacteria exist in Mexico to which foreigners may not have been exposed.)

Other Mexican specialities less common abroad are *antojitos* or *botanas* (appetizers), *chilaquiles* (a rich breakfast made with chile, tortilla, tomatoes, onions, cream, and cheese), and *chile nogado* (a large chile pepper stuffed with pork, raisins, onion, olives, and almonds and covered with heavy cream, walnuts, and pomegranates). Soups are rich—particularly the pork-based *pozole, sopa azteca* (avocado and tortilla in a broth), and *sopa de flor de calabaza* (squash-flower soup). But this barely touches on the plenitude and diversity of Mexican cuisine, which also encompasses an astonishing assortment of breads, sweets, beers, wines (which are fast improving), and cactus-based liquors. Freshly squeezed fruit juices and fruit shakes *(licuados)* are safe to drink and taste heavenly; coffee varies from standard American-style and Nescafé to espresso and *café de jarra,* which is laced with chocolate and served in a coarse clay mug. Imported liquor is very expensive; middle-class Mexicans stick with the local rum.

A word on hygiene: Most travelers to Mexico are only too familiar with the caveat "Don't drink the water" (*see* Staying Healthy, in Before You Go, *above*). Stick to bottled waters and soft drinks, and when ordering cold drinks, skip the ice *(sin hielo)*. Hotels with purified water systems will post signs to that effect in the rooms. *Tacos al pastor*—thin pork slices grilled on a spit and garnished with the usual cilantro, onions, and chile—are delicious but dangerous. Be wary of Mexican hamburgers, because you can never be certain what meat they are made with (horsemeat is very common). And if you're not keen on spiciness, ask that a dish be served *no muy picante*.

Mexican restaurants run the gamut from humble hole-in-the-wall shacks, street stands, and chairs and tables in the markets to *taquerías*, American-style fast-food joints, and internationally acclaimed gourmet restaurants. Prices, naturally, follow suit. One bargain found everywhere in Mexico is the fixed-menu lunch known as *comida corrida*, which is served between 1 and 4 PM. Generally, this type of cooking is uninspired and oily but reliably filling.

Lunch is the big meal; dinner is rarely served before 8 PM. There is no government rating of restaurants, but you'll know which ones cater to tourists simply by looking at the clientele and the menu (bilingual menus usually mean slightly higher prices than at nontourist restaurants). Credit cards—especially MasterCard (Banamex and Carnet) and Visa (Bancomer)—are increasingly accepted. For a list of Mexican menu terms, *see* Menu Guide.

Lodging

The price and quality of accommodations in Mexico vary about as much as the country's restaurants, from super-luxurious, international-class hotels and all-inclusive resorts to modest budget properties, seedy places with shared bathrooms, *casas de huéspedes* (guest houses), youth hostels, and *cabañas* (beach huts).

More and more of the international hotel chains are moving into Mexico, and some of them are adding budget lines to the existing upscale products. Since many are franchises, service standards vary, but travelers can count on a certain standardization of rooms, English-speaking staff, guaranteed dollar rates, and toll-free reservation numbers in the United States. Companies with several Mexican properties include Best Western (tel. 800/334–7324), Club Med (tel. 800/CLUB MED), Conrad International and Hilton Hotels (tel. 800/HILTONS), Hyatt International (tel. 800/228–9000), Marriott (tel. 800/ 228–9290), Posadas de México (Hoteles Fiesta Americanas, tel. 800/FIESTA–1; Holiday Inn, tel. 800/HOLIDAY), Princess (tel. 800/223–1818 or in NY, 800/442–8418), Quality Inn (Hoteles Calinda, tel. 800/228–5151), Radisson (tel. 800/333–3333), Sheraton (tel. 800/325–3535), Stouffer Presidente (tel. 800/ GRACIAS), and Westin (Hoteles Camino Real, tel. 800/582– 8100). A good Spanish-owned chain is Grupo Sol's Melia Hotels (tel. 800/336–3542). Good Mexican-owned chains include Krystal (tel. 800/231–9860) and Misión (tel. 52–5–525–0393).

Hotel rates are subject to the 10% value-added tax, and service charges and meals are generally not included. The Mexican government categorizes hotels, based on qualitative evaluations, into *gran turismo* (super-deluxe hotels, of which there are only about 20 nationwide); 5-star down to 1-star; and economy class. Keep in mind that many hotels that might otherwise be rated higher have opted for a lower category to avoid higher interest rates on loans and financing.

High- versus low-season rates can vary significantly (*see* When to Go, in Before You Go, *above*). Hotels in this guide have air-conditioning and private bathrooms, unless stated otherwise, but bathtubs are not common in inexpensive hotels and properties in smaller towns.

Mexican hotels—particularly those owned or managed by the international chains—are always being expanded. In older properties, travelers may often have to choose between newer annexes with modern amenities and rooms in the original buildings with possibly fewer amenities and—equally possible, but not certain—greater charm.

Reservations must be made in advance if you are traveling during high season or holiday periods. Overbooking is a common practice in some parts of Mexico, such as Cancún, and there is little you can do to avoid this. Travelers to remote areas will encounter little difficulty in obtaining rooms on a "walk-in" basis. If you arrive in Mexico City without a reservation, the Mexican Hotel and Motel Association operates a booth at the airport that will assist you (tel. 52–5–286–5455).

One last note of advice: If you are particularly sensitive to noise, you should call ahead and find out if your hotel of choice is located on a busy street. You might also request a room situated well away from the lobby bar, which could easily entertain clientele until the wee hours of the morning. Many of the most engaging accommodations in Mexico are often situated on downtown intersections that experience heavy automobile and pedestrian traffic, and large hotels are known to feature lobby bars with live music in the middle of an open-air atrium leading directly to rooms. What is fun and diverting for one traveler could prove irritating to the next, so plan *before* you go if you want your own vacation to suit your own tastes.

Villa Rentals **At Home Abroad, Inc.** (405 E. 56th St., Suite 6H, New York, NY 10022, tel. 212/421–9165) has properties in Acapulco and Puerto Vallarta.

Hideaway International (Box 1270, 15 Goldsmith St., Littleton, MA 01460, tel. 508/486–8955) handles rentals in Acapulco, Cancún, Cozumel, Puerto Vallarta, and San Miguel de Allende.

Villas and Apartments Abroad (420 Madison Ave., Room 305, New York, NY 10017, tel. 212/759–1025) can set you up in a villa in Acapulco or Puerto Vallarta.

Villas International (605 Market St., San Francisco, CA 94105, tel. 415/281–0910 or 800/221–2260) can find villa rentals in Acapulco, Akumal, Cancún, Cozumel, Manzanillo, and Puerto Vallarta.

Credit Cards

The following credit card abbreviations are used throughout this guide: AE, American Express; DC, Diners Club; MC, MasterCard; V, Visa.

Personal Security and Comfort

Many Americans are aware of Mexico's reputation for corruption. The patronage system is a well-entrenched part of Mexican politics and industry, and workers in the public sector—notably policemen and customs officials—are notoriously underpaid. Everyone has heard, at least secondhand, a horror story about foreigners (not to mention the Mexicans themselves) languishing away in Mexican jails; highway assaults, pickpocketing, and the preponderance of bribes.

Use common sense, as you would anywhere. Wear a money belt; make use of hotel safes; and carry your own baggage whenever possible. Don't bother going to the police to report a crime unless you speak excellent Spanish and have a great deal of patience.

Women traveling alone in Mexico are likely to be subjected to *piropos* (catcalls). Avoid direct eye contact with men on the street, as it invites further acquaintance. Don't wear tight clothes if you don't want to call attention to yourself. If you speak Spanish, pretend you don't and ignore would-be suitors or say "no" to whatever they say. Don't enter street bars or cantinas unaccompanied.

2 Portraits of Mexico

Mexico at a Glance: A Chronology

Pre-Columbian Mexico

c. 50,000 BC Asian nomads cross land bridge over the Bering Strait to North America, gradually migrate south

c. 5000–1500 BC Archaic period: beginnings of agriculture, village life

c. 1500–200 BC Formative or Pre-Classic period: development of pottery, incipient political structures

c. 800–400 BC Olmec culture, the "mother culture" of Mexico, flourishes along gulf coast

c. 200 BC–AD 900 Classic period (Golden Age, AD 200–800): height of pre-Columbian culture. Three centers at Teotihuacán (near Mexico City), Monte Albán (Oaxaca), and Mayan culture in the far south. Peaceful, priest-run city-states produce impressive art and architecture

AD 650–900 Decline of Classic cultures: fall of Teotihuacán c. 650 leads to competition among other city-states, exacerbated by migrations of northern tribes

c. 900–1521 Post-classic period: rule passes to military; war and war gods gain prominence

c. 900–1150 Toltecs, a northern tribe, establish a flourishing culture at their capital of Tula under the legendary monarch Topiltzin-Quetzalcóatl

c. 1200 Rise of Mixtec culture at Zapotec sites of Monte Albán and Mitla; notable for production of picture *codices*, which include historical narratives

c. 1000–1450 Mayan culture, declining in south, emerges in the Yucatán; under Toltec rule, Chichén Itzá dominates the peninsula

1111 Aztecs migrate to mainland from island home off the Nayarit coast. Vulgar and partial to human sacrifice, they are not welcomed by the peoples of central Mexico

1150–1350 Following the fall of Tula, first the Chichimecs, then the Tepanecs assert hegemony over central Mexico. The Tepanec tyrant Tezozómoc (1320–1426), like his contemporaries in Renaissance Italy, establishes his power with murder and treachery

1376 Tezozómoc grants autonomy to the Aztec city of Tenochtitlán, built in the middle of Lake Texcoco

1420–1500 Aztecs extend their rule to much of central and southern Mexico. A warrior society, they build a great city at Tenochtitlán

1502 Moctezuma II assumes throne at the height of Aztec culture and political power

1517 Spanish expedition under Francisco Hernandez de Cordoba lands on Yucatán coast

1519　Hernán Cortés lands in Mexico, founds Veracruz, determines to conquer. Steel weapons, horses, and smallpox, coupled with a belief that Cortés was the resurrected Topiltzin-Quetzalcóatl, minimize Aztec resistance. Cortés enters Tenochtitlán and captures Moctezuma

The Colonial Period

1520–1521　Moctezuma is killed; Tenochtitlán falls to Cortés. The last Aztec emperor, Cuauhtemoc, is executed

1528　Juan de Zumarraga arrives as bishop of Mexico City, gains title of "Protector of the Indians;" native conversion to Catholicism begun

1535　First Spanish viceroy arrives in Mexico

1537　Pope Paul III issues a bull declaring that native Mexicans are indeed human and not beasts. First printing press arrives in Mexico City

1546–48　Silver deposits discovered at Zacatecas

1547　Spanish conquest of Aztec Empire—now known as "New Spain"—completed, at enormous cost to native peoples

1553　Royal and Pontifical University of Mexico, first university in the New World, opens

1571　The Spanish Inquisition established in New Spain; it is only abolished in 1820

1609　Northern capital of New Spain established at Santa Fe (New Mexico)

1651　Birth of Sor (Sister) Juana Inés de la Cruz, greatest poet of colonial Mexico (d. 1695)

1718　Franciscan missionaries settle in Texas, which becomes part of New Spain

1765　Charles III of Spain sends José de Galvez to tour New Spain and propose reforms

1769　Franciscan Junipero Serra establishes missions in California, extending Spanish hegemony

1788　Death of Charles III; his reforms improve administration, but also raise social and political expectations among the colonial population, which are not fulfilled

1808　Napoleon invades Spain, leaving a power vacuum in New Spain

The War of Independence

1810　September 16: Father Miguel Hidalgo y Costilla preaches his *Grito de Dolores*, sparking rebellion

1811　Hidalgo is captured and executed; leadership of the movement passes to Father José Maria Morelos

1813　Morelos calls a congress at Chilpancingo which drafts a Declaration of Independence

1815　Morelos is captured and executed

The Early National Period

1821 Vicente Guerrero, a rebel leader, and Agustín de Iturbide, a Spanish colonel converted to the rebel cause rejuvenate the Independence movement. Spain recognizes Mexican independence with the Treaty of Córdoba

1822 Iturbide is named Emperor of Mexico, which stretches from California through Central America

1823 After ten months in office, Emperor Agustín is turned out

1824 A new constitution creates a federal republic, the Estados Unidos Mexicanos; modeled on the U.S. Constitution, the Mexican version retains the privileges of the Catholic Church and gives the president extraordinary "emergency" powers

1829 President Vicente Guerrero abolishes slavery. A Spanish attempt at reconquest is halted by General Antonio López de Santa Anna, already a hero for his role in the overthrow of Emperor Agustín

1833 Santa Anna is elected president by a huge majority; he holds the office for 11 of its 36 changes of hands by 1855

1836 Although voted in as a liberal, Santa Anna abolishes the 1824 constitution. Already dismayed at the abolition of slavery, Texas—whose population is largely American—declares its independence. Santa Anna successfully besieges the Texans at the Alamo. But a month later he is captured by Sam Houston following the Battle of San Jacinto. Texas gains its independence as the Lone Star Republic

1846 The U.S. decision to annex Texas leads to war

1848 The treaty of Guadalupe Hidalgo reduces Mexico's territory by half, ceding Texas, New Mexico and California to the U.S.

1853 Santa Anna agrees to the Gadsden purchase, ceding a further 30,000 square miles to the U.S.

The Reform and French Intervention

1855 The Revolution of Ayutla topples Santa Anna and leads to the period of The Reform

1857 The liberal Constitution of 1857 disestablishes the Catholic Church among other measures

1858–1861 The civil War of the Reform ends in liberal victory. Benito Juárez is elected president. France, Spain and Britain agree jointly to occupy the customs house at Veracruz to force payment of Mexico's huge foreign debt

1862 Spain and Britain withdraw their forces; the French, seeking empire, march inland. On May 5, General Porfirio Díaz repulses the French at Puebla

1863 Strengthened with reinforcements, the French occupy Mexico City. Napoleon III of France appoints Archduke Ferdinand Maximilian of Austria as Emperor of Mexico

1864 Maximilian and his empress Charlotte, known as Carlota, land at Veracruz

1867 With U.S. assistance, Juárez overthrows Mexico's second empire. Maximilian is executed; Carlota, pleading his case in France, goes mad

1872 Juárez dies in office. The Mexico City-Veracruz railway is completed, symbol of the new progressivist mood

The Porfiriato

1876 Porfirio Díaz comes to power in the Revolution of Tuxtepec; he holds office nearly continuously until 1911. With his advisors, the *cientificos*, he forces modernization and balances the budget for the first time in Mexican history. But the social cost is high

1890 José Schneider, of German ancestry, founds the Cerveceria Cuauhtemoc, brewer of Carta Blanca

1900 Jesús, Enrique, and Ricardo Flores Magón publish the anti-Díaz newspaper *La Regeneración*. Suppressed, the brothers move their campaign to the U.S., first to San Antonio, then to St. Louis

1906 The Flores Magón group publish their Liberal Plan, a proposal for reform. Industrial unrest spreads

The Second Revolution

1910 On the centennial of the Revolution, Díaz wins yet another rigged election. Revolt breaks out

1911 Rebels under Pascual Orozco and Francisco (Pancho) Villa capture Ciudad Juárez; Díaz resigns. Francisco Madero is elected president; calling for land reform, Emiliano Zapata rejects the new regime. Violence continues

1913 Military coup; Madero is deposed and murdered. In one day Mexico has three presidents, the last being General Victoriano Huerta. Civil war rages

1914 American intervention leads to dictator Huerta's overthrow. Villa and Zapata briefly join forces at the Convention of Aguascalientes, but the Revolution goes on

1916 Villa's border raids lead to an American punitive expedition under Pershing. Villa eludes capture

1917 Under a new constitution, Venuziano Carranza, head of the Constitutionalist Army, is elected president. Zapata continues his rebellion, which is brutally suppressed

1918 CROM, the national labor union, is founded

1919 On order of Carranza, Zapata is assassinated

1920 Carranza is assassinated; Alvaro Obregón is elected president, beginning a period of reform and reconstruction. Schools are built and land is redistributed. In the next two decades, revolutionary culture finds expression in the art of Diego Rivera and José Clemente Orozco, the novels of Martin Luis Guzmán and Gregorio Lopez y Fuentes, and the music of Carlos Chavez

1923 Pancho Villa is assassinated. The U.S. finally recognizes the Obregón regime

1926–1928 Catholics react to government anticlericalism in the Cristero Rebellion

1934–1940 The presidency of Lázaro Cárdenas leads to the fullest implementation of revolutionary reforms

1938 Cárdenas nationalizes the oil companies, removing them from foreign control

Post-revolutionary Mexico

1951 Mexico's segment of the Pan-American Highway is completed, confirming the industrial growth and prosperity of post-war Mexico. Culture is increasingly Americanized; writers such as Octavio Paz and Carlos Fuentes express disillusionment with the post-revolution world

1968 The Summer Olympics in Mexico City showcase Mexican prosperity, but massive demonstrations indicate underlying social unrest

1981–1982 Recession and a drop in oil prices severely damage Mexico's economy. The peso is devalued

1985 Thousands die in the Mexico City earthquake

1988 American-educated economist Carlos Salinas de Gortari is elected president; for the first time since 1940, support for the PRI, the national political party, seems to be slipping

Talking Mexican

By Kate Simon

Bronx native Kate Simon is the author of nine travel books, including Mexico: Places and Pleasures, *which remains a classic after 28 years.*

"Talking Mexican" is excerpted from her book Never Say Ahoritita Again.

Mexicans still cherish an art once highly prized among us (think of Emerson, of Melville, of Hawthorne): conversation. They know it takes two to make a good talker—the confident speaker and the eager listener. A Mexican tête-à-tête—except among the dour mountain people, who prefer long, motionless silences—is a graceful act. The talker, carried away by his own mellifluous sounds, often repeats himself. His listener seems to find him fascinating. His eyes glow, he smiles, he melts, he frowns, he is delighted, he is appalled; he is completely immersed in the words and their passion and keeps them going with a gamut of encouragements: *"Claro, pues si"* ("Of course, obviously"), *"Qué bueno"* ("How nice"), *"Qué lindo"* ("How lovely"), *"¡No me digas!"* ("Don't tell me!"), and, as a sorrowful cadence, *"Ai lástima"* ("What a pity").

Spanish isn't absolutely essential in large centers, although all sorts of doors and amiabilities will open for the traveler who conquers a few Spanish words of greeting and politesse. The Mexican is so delighted with the *"americano"* who tries even a little that he will, with a peculiar delicate empathy, help shape the words you need. A sympathetic Mexican can make you feel that you know Spanish; it's your tongue that is stupid.

Like other languages, but more so, Spanish is heavily embroidered with diminutives. Usually endearments, they also have other uses. They serve as intensifiers of meaning: *Chico* means "small"; *chiquito*, "very small"; and *chiquitito*, "almost invisible." A diminutive also suggests doubt, skepticism. *Hay sol* means that the sun is out, but if you are in an excursion boat under a cloudy sky and the boatman hopefully says there is *solecito*, beg to be taken ashore before the descent of a storm that maddens the lake. An important early lesson in Spanish is the use of *ahora*, meaning "now," which when spoken straight out usually denotes an intention of getting something done reasonably soon. The addition of one diminutive bit—*ahorita*—stretches the distance between promise and deed; *ahoritita* carries us into improbability; *ahorititita* becomes a piece of silliness.

The curious impersonal reflexive *se* conjures up a bewildering world of small satanic forces. One doesn't break a glass. *Se me rompió*—it broke itself, no fault of mine. If you bargain with a market woman, she will not say, "I can't," but *"No se puede"*—"one (little *se*) cannot." A lost object—even my own bag—lost itself, and it wasn't *I* who caused me to be late, but that mischievous bit of fate, *se*.

This deference to unpredictable external powers may bespeak a fatalism whose reverse side is bright casualness. A

Mexican will warmly, charmingly, and with—at the moment—complete sincerity declare his affection, admiration, and profound need to see you again, very soon. Unaccustomed to such quick warmth, you settle into this cozy nest of love, this having been accepted by Mexico. Time passes, nothing happens. You have been forgotten. You feel unlovely, unwelcome, the contemptible "big foot" who ate up vast Texas, responsible for all the world's messes and of course "Yankee imperialism." But it's only *se* that intervened and manipulated your friend's life in some unexpected way that was more attractive, more novel, than the prospect of another encounter with you.

A people who arrange a highly ornamented holiday for their dead and hold in awe the death dance of the bullfight are not inclined to respect precise dates, neat boxes of time. Anything is at any time likely to happen—a flat tire, a nearby fiesta, a change of mood—to be enjoyed *si Dios nos presta el tiempo* ("if God lends us the time"). Another imposing fact about the language is that the word for "to expect" (*esperar*) is identical with that for "to await" and "to hope." You might witness this miracle of linguistic transmutation at a rural train station as your assured expecting melts into vague awaiting and then vaporizes into humble hope—hope that some train that pertains to you will show up, sometime.

One of the pleasant quirks of the language is the big, baroque, generous phrase that can't mean what it says. Someone gives you his address and adds, "*Esta es su casa*" or "*Aquí tiene su casa*" ("Consider this your home"), or "*Mi casa es su casa*" ("My house is your house")—obviously ridiculous and yet frequently said as proof of boundless, aristocratic generosity (a Don Quixote touch?). Clearly, the only person in Mexican history who took such statements seriously was Cortés, the conquistador who took not only the house and treasures of Moctezuma but the whole of his host's empire. Admire an object and you may be told it is yours. Smile and without making a move say, "Thank you," to which the answer may be, "To serve you" ("*A su servicio*"). "At your command" ("*A sus órdenes*") often acknowledges a formal introduction. These phrases are not servile or meant to buy favor, but express the courtliness of old Spain.

On the other hand, Spanish can be direct and even harsh. Observe the park signs, which say flatly, "This is yours, take care of it" ("*El parque es suyo, cuídelo*").

In other areas the touch is delicate, even elegant. One doesn't hit a man with "He is disagreeable," but, instead, one dismisses him as "little amiable." "*Venga por favor tempranito*" takes the pressure off the necessity to be absolutely on time (*temprano*). No one wants to rush you, you must understand, but try to be nice and come on time, mollified and seduced by little *ito*, the most persuasive of Mexican persuasions.

In the wide world of *amor* anything goes; the limits are wide and brilliant, painting the conversational sky with dazzling rainbows. Shelley's "I die! I faint! I fail!" are pale mutterings compared with Mexican strophes of romantic love. A woman must have quite a bit of Spanish to appreciate the flowers of words thrown at her feet. But even a little helps. Not necessarily very young or lovely, she might still have the word *guapa* ("handsome woman") wafted toward her, or if she's fair-haired, like the *Yanquis* from north of the border, she could be called *güerita* ("blondie"). Her lack of response (and there shouldn't be any unless she's ready to face the consequences) might evoke something like "Can't you even say thanks, for God's sake?" ("*¿No puedes decir gracias, por Dios?*"), and this, too, might amuse her if she happens to understand what's going on.

A knowledge of Spanish enables one to discern nuances of class in certain areas of speech. The courtliness of "*hágame el favor*" ("please do me the kindness") moves downward into the middle class with "*por favor*," then becomes the cajoling peasant phrase "*por favorcito*."

Perhaps most important, it lets one sample the wilder pleasures of Mexican radio, such as its ads for Pepsi-Cola. An old feeble female voice pleads, "Buy me a taco." Old feeble male voice: "Sure, they're delicious." Strong radio voice out of seemingly unrelated space: "Delicious? Pepsi-Cola is more delicious. Drink Pepsi!" This is followed by a female voice shrieking, "I can't stand it anymore. *You* pay the household bills; I can't seem to manage on the money you give me." This time the out-of-the-blue voice says gently, "Calm yourself. Have a Pepsi." Then a siren's voice, quite dulcet, with a tiny rasp of passion: "Darling, please buy me another diamond." Her lover's rich voice: "What? So that you can be even more delicious?" Voice from the blue: "More delicious? Pepsi-Cola is more delicious." Without Spanish and the radio, how could one be grateful for the sponsorship of "*Mox Foctorr de Hawlywoot, naturalmente*"?

Fiesta

By Octavio Paz

Poet, essayist, and diplomat, Octavio Paz is one of Mexico's most prominent spokesmen. This essay is excerpted from his best-known work, The Labyrinth of Solitude, *originally published in 1962.*

The solitary Mexican loves fiestas and public gatherings. Any occasion for getting together will serve, any pretext to stop the flow of time and commemorate men and events with festivals and ceremonies. We are a ritual people, and this characteristic enriches both our imaginations and our sensibilities, which are equally sharp and alert. The art of the fiesta has been debased almost everywhere else, but not in Mexico. There are few places in the world where it is possible to take part in a spectacle like our great religious fiestas with their violent primary colors, their bizarre costumes and dances, their fireworks and ceremonies, and their inexhaustible welter of surprises: the fruit, candy, toys, and other objects sold on these days in the plazas and open-air markets.

Our calendar is crowded with fiestas. There are certain days when the whole country, from the most remote villages to the largest cities, prays, shouts, feasts, gets drunk and kills, in honor of the Virgin of Guadalupe or Benito Juárez. Each year on the fifteenth of September, at eleven o'clock at night, we celebrate the fiesta of the *Grito*[1] in all the plazas of the Republic, and the excited crowds actually shout for a whole hour . . . the better, perhaps, to remain silent for the rest of the year. During the days before and after the twelfth of December,[2] time comes to a full stop, and instead of pushing us toward a deceptive tomorrow that is always beyond our reach, offers us a complete and perfect today of dancing and revelry, of communion with the most ancient and secret Mexico. Time is no longer succession, and becomes what it originally was and is: the present, in which past and future are reconciled.

But the fiestas that the Church and State provide for the country as a whole are not enough. The life of every city and village is ruled by a patron saint whose blessing is celebrated with devout regularity. Neighborhoods and trades also have their annual fiestas, their ceremonies and fairs. And each one of us—atheist, Catholic, or merely indifferent—has his own saint's day, which he observes every year. It is impossible to calculate how many fiestas we have and how much time and money we spend on them. I remember asking the mayor of a village near Mitla, several years ago, "What is the income of the village government?" "About 3,000 pesos a year. We are very poor. But the Governor and the Federal Government always help us to meet our expenses." "And how are the 3,000 pesos spent?" "Mostly on

---

[1] *Padre Hidalgo's call-to-arms against Spain, 1810.—Tr.*
[2] *Fiesta of the Virgin of Guadalupe,—Tr.*

fiestas, señor. We are a small village, but we have two patron saints."

This reply is not surprising. Our poverty can be measured
by the frequency and luxuriousness of our holidays.
Wealthy countries have very few: There is neither the time
nor the desire for them, and they are not necessary. The
people have other things to do, and when they amuse themselves they do so in small groups. The modern masses are
agglomerations of solitary individuals. On great occasions
in Paris or New York, when the populace gathers in the
squares or stadiums, the absence of people, in the sense of a
people, is remarkable: There are couples and small groups,
but they never form a living community in which the individual is at once dissolved and redeemed. But how could a
poor Mexican live without the annual fiestas that make up
for his poverty and misery? Fiestas are our only luxury.
They replace, and are perhaps better than, the theater and
vacations, Anglo-Saxon weekends and cocktail parties, the
bourgeois reception, the Mediterranean café.

In all of these ceremonies—national or local, trade or
family—the Mexican opens out. They all give him a
chance to reveal himself and to converse with God, country, friends, or relations. During these days the silent
Mexican whistles, shouts, sings, shoots off fireworks,
discharges his pistol into the air. He discharges his soul.
And his shout, like the rockets we love so much, ascends to
the heavens, explodes into green, red, blue, and white
lights, and falls dizzily to earth with a trail of golden
sparks. This is the night when friends who have not ex-
changed more than the prescribed courtesies for months
get drunk together, trade confidences, weep over the same
troubles, discover that they are brothers, and sometimes,
to prove it, kill each other. The night is full of songs and
loud cries. The lover wakes up his sweetheart with an orchestra. There are jokes and conversations from balcony to
balcony, sidewalk to sidewalk. Nobody talks quietly. Hats
fly in the air. Laughter and curses ring like silver pesos.
Guitars are brought out. Now and then, it is true, the hap-
piness ends badly, in quarrels, insults, pistol shots, stab-
bings. But these too are part of the fiesta, for the Mexican
does not seek amusement: He seeks to escape from himself,
to leap over the wall of solitude that confines him during the
rest of the year. All are possessed by violence and frenzy.
Their souls explode like the colors and voices and emotions.
Do they forget themselves and show their true faces? Nobody knows. The important thing is to go out, open a way,
get drunk on noise, people, colors. Mexico is celebrating a
fiesta. And this fiesta, shot through with lightning and delirium, is the brilliant reverse to our silence and apathy, our
reticence and gloom.

According to the interpretation of French sociologists, the
fiesta is an excess, an expense. By means of this squander-

ing the community protects itself against the envy of the gods or of men. Sacrifices and offerings placate or buy off the gods and the patron saints. Wasting money and expending energy affirms the community's wealth in both. This luxury is a proof of health, a show of abundance and power. Or a magic trap. For squandering is an effort to attract abundance by contagion. Money calls to money. When life is thrown away it increases; the orgy, which is sexual expenditure, is also a ceremony of regeneration; waste gives strength. New Year celebrations, in every culture, signify something beyond the mere observance of a date on the calendar. The day is a pause: Time is stopped, is actually annihilated. The rites that celebrate its death are intended to provoke its rebirth, because they mark not only the end of an old year but also the beginning of a new. Everything attracts its opposite. The fiesta's function, then, is more utilitarian than we think: Waste attracts or promotes wealth and is an investment like any other, except that the returns on it cannot be measured or counted. What is sought is potency, life, health. In this sense the fiesta, like the gift and the offering, is one of the most ancient of economic forms.

This interpretation has always seemed to me to be incomplete. The fiesta is by nature sacred, literally or figuratively, and above all it is the advent of the unusual. It is governed by its own special rules that set it apart from other days, and it has a logic, an ethic, and even an economy that are often in conflict with everyday norms. It all occurs in an enchanted world: Time is transformed to a mythical past or a total present; space, the scene of the fiesta, is turned into a gaily decorated world of its own; and the persons taking part cast off all human or social rank and become, for the moment, living images. And everything takes place as if it were not so, as if it were a dream. But whatever happens, our actions have a greater lightness, a different gravity. They take on other meanings and with them we contract new obligations. We throw down our burdens of time and reason.

In certain fiestas the very notion of order disappears. Chaos comes back and license rules. Anything is permitted: the customary hierarchies vanish, along with all social, sex, caste, and trade distinctions. Men disguise themselves as women, gentlemen as slaves, the poor as the rich. The army, the clergy, and the law are ridiculed. Obligatory sacrilege, ritual profanation is committed. Love becomes promiscuity. Sometimes the fiesta becomes a Black Mass. Regulations, habits, and customs are violated. Respectable people put away the dignified expressions and conservative clothes that isolate them, dress up in gaudy colors, hide behind a mask, and escape from themselves.

Therefore the fiesta is not only an excess, a ritual squandering of the goods painfully accumulated during the rest of the year; it is also a revolt, a sudden immersion in the formless, in pure being. By means of the fiesta, society frees itself from the norms it has established. It ridicules its gods, its principles, and its laws: It denies its own self.

The fiesta is a revolution in the most literal sense of the word. In the confusion that it generates, society is dissolved, is drowned, insofar as it is an organism ruled according to certain laws and principles. But it drowns in itself, in its own original chaos or liberty. Everything is united: good and evil, day and night, the sacred and the profane. Everything merges, loses shape and individuality and returns to the primordial mass. The fiesta is a cosmic experiment, an experiment in disorder, reuniting contradictory elements and principles in order to bring about a renascence of life. Ritual death promotes a rebirth; vomiting increases the appetite; the orgy, sterile in itself, renews the fertility of the mother or of the earth. The fiesta is a return to a remote and undifferentiated state, prenatal or presocial. It is a return that is also a beginning, in accordance with the dialectic that is inherent in social processes.

The group emerges purified and strengthened from this plunge into chaos. It has immersed itself in its own origins, in the womb from which it came. To express it in another way, the fiesta denies society as an organic system of differentiated forms and principles, but affirms it as a source of creative energy. It is a true "re-creation," the opposite of the "recreation" characterizing modern vacations, which do not entail any rites or ceremonies whatever and are as individualistic and sterile as the world that invented them.

Society communes with itself during the fiesta. Its members return to original chaos and freedom. Social structures break down and new relationships, unexpected rules, capricious hierarchies are created. In the general disorder everybody forgets himself and enters into otherwise forbidden situations and places. The bounds between audience and actors, officials and servants, are erased. Everybody takes part in the fiesta, everybody is caught up in its whirlwind. Whatever its mood, its character, its meaning, the fiesta is participation, and this trait distinguishes it from all other ceremonies and social phenomena. Lay or religious, orgy or saturnalia, the fiesta is a social act based on the full participation of all its celebrants.

Thanks to the fiesta, the Mexican opens out, participates, communes with his fellows and with the values that give meaning to his religious or political existence. And it is significant that a country as sorrowful as ours should have so many and such joyous fiestas. Their frequency, their brilliance and excitement, the enthusiasm with which we take part, all suggest that without them we would explode. They free us, if only momentarily, from the thwarted impulses, the inflammable desires that we carry within us. But the Mexican fiesta is not merely a return to an original state of formless and normless liberty: The Mexican is not seeking to return, but to escape from himself, to exceed himself. Our fiestas are explosions. Life and death, joy and sorrow, music and mere noise are united, not to re-create or recognize themselves, but to swallow each other up. There is nothing so joyous as a Mexican fiesta, but there is also nothing so sorrowful. Fiesta night is also a night of mourning.

If we hide within ourselves in our daily lives, we discharge ourselves in the whirlwind of the fiesta. It is more than an opening out: We rend ourselves open. Everything—music, love, friendship—ends in tumult and violence. The frenzy of our festivals shows the extent to which our solitude closes us off from communication with the world. We are familiar with delirium, with songs and shouts, with the monologue . . . but not with the dialogue. Our fiestas, like our confidences, our loves, our attempts to reorder our society, are violent breaks with the old or the established. Each time we try to express ourselves we have to break with ourselves. And the fiesta is only one example, perhaps the most typical, of this violent break. It is not difficult to name others, equally revealing: our games, which are always a going to extremes, often mortal; our profligate spending, the reverse of our timid investments and business enterprises; our confessions. The somber Mexican, closed up in himself, suddenly explodes, tears open his breast and reveals himself, though not without a certain complacency, and not without a stopping place in the shameful or terrible mazes of his intimacy. We are not frank, but our sincerity can reach extremes that horrify a European. The explosive, dramatic, sometimes even suicidal manner in which we strip ourselves, surrender ourselves, is evidence that something inhibits and suffocates us. Something impedes us from being. And since we cannot or dare not confront our own selves, we resort to the fiesta. It fires us into the void; it is a drunken rapture that burns itself out, a pistol shot in the air, a skyrocket.

3 Mexico City

Introduction

By Erica Meltzer

Updated by
Pancho Shiell

Mexico City is loved and hated as much as any world capital. It's complex, and emphatically not the kind of place one falls casually in love with; *that* process takes time. Most travelers to Mexico skip it altogether, heading instead to the beaches and ruins. Those who do spend a few days can easily tally a list of its shortcomings: the ugliness, the pollution, the crime, the poverty.

But there's a passionate core beneath the battle scars and pockmarks. In this Latin metropolis of 20 million people, life takes place on the streets and in the leafy plazas, where its denizens buy, sell, cook, eat, quarrel, make love, and celebrate. *Chilangos* (as Mexico City residents are called by other Mexicans, with a hint of distaste) excel in the social arts, be it at cafés or in the markets. Their politeness is impeccable, even unbearable to often ungracious Westerners, and yet they are demons behind the wheel. Seeming apathy or cynicism is matched by volubility on political subjects. They simultaneously love—and despise—gringos.

And vice versa. The capital has a huge expatriate community: 30,000 Americans at last count, not to mention large numbers of Britons and other Europeans, Japanese, and Central and South Americans. Young Americans go to study Spanish and end up teaching English as well—illegally, for the most part, but then, the city needs English teachers. They stay at first because it's an inexpensive place to live, because there's an easy camaraderie among people like themselves, and simply because it's a challenge. But for many, the city grows on them. It's chaotic, unwieldy, an architectural hodgepodge in which four color schemes prevail: the earthy browns, reds, and grays of colonial stone (more than 1,400 buildings from that era have been declared historical monuments); the chalky blue and rose-pink pastels of wealthy, neo-Aztec stucco homes; the national colors of red, white, and green; and the steely haze of the skyscrapers—and the polluted, sun-blocked skies.

The social contrasts are unimaginable: downcast Indian children beg barefoot on the street . . . wizened old women slap cornmeal into tortillas and roast them in oil-filled caldrons over open fires . . . millionaires impress one another in lavish homes, country clubs, and restaurants.

There is another clue to the magnetism of the place: Writers and artists "do time" in Mexico City, apparently captivated by its relentless and uncanny stimulation of the senses. Stephen Crane came through town, as did John Dos Passos. The poet Langston Hughes shared a flat with photographer Henri Cartier-Bresson near La Lagunilla market. Somerset Maugham met D. H. Lawrence, whom he despised, at a dinner party in Mexico City. B. Traven, the reclusive author of *Treasure of the Sierra Madre* and many lesser-known novels about Mexico, lived on Rio Misisipi from 1957 until his death in 1969; his widow lives there still. During the Mexican Revolution and through much of the 1920s, Katherine Anne Porter made her home in the former suburb of Mixcoac; Hart Crane was often a guest. Hemingway stopped by in 1941 to check out the bullfights. William S. Burroughs accidentally killed his wife in the city while cleaning his gun, Norman Mailer spent summers there in the 1950s, and Saul Bellow wrote about Trotsky's assassination there. Malcolm Lowry, Graham Greene, Aldous Huxley,

Evelyn Waugh, Jack Kerouac, and Lawrence Ferlinghetti are only a few more of the literary set who have lived there.

Some of the statistics of life in Mexico City are overwhelming, if not appalling, and they affect travelers, whether or not they venture away from the tourist zones. The current population of about 20 million represents about one-fourth of the country's population; that figure could reach 36 million by the turn of the century. Immigrants from impoverished rural areas flood in at the rate of 3,000 a day, probably unaware that 5 million people live in outrageous poverty, without such basics as running water or electricity. The presence of 4 million vehicles makes for horrendous traffic and exacerbates the smog due to thermal inversion. The air quality is so poor that schools were closed for a month in early 1989. Breathing in Mexico City has been equated with smoking two packs of cigarettes a day.

Drainage and flooding have been problems since Aztec days, as the city was built on a swamp and gets torrential rains between May and September. Mexico City is 2,241 meters (7,350 feet) above sea level; many visitors are prone to altitude sickness, and both physical exertion and alcohol consumption should be kept to a minimum.

The world's largest city is the oldest capital in North and South America, having been built by the Aztecs, or Mexicas, in 1325. They called it Tenochtitlán, and eventually it became the chief city of the largest empire in pre-Columbian Mesoamerica, extending from Texas to Honduras. Early European visitors compared its magnificence to Venice; vestiges of that splendor are evident at a few sites within the city limits.

The Aztec city was a network of islands linked by bridges and canals across Lake Texcoco, with satellite settlements in the surrounding Valle de Anáhuac (Valley of Mexico). At the time of the conquest (1521), the area's population numbered anywhere from 500,000 to 2 million. Cortés got wind of Tenochtitlán's existence—and wealth—from other Mexican tribes anxious to have their overlords toppled. Emperor Moctezuma's gold offerings to the conquistador only whetted his voracious appetite. Moctezuma received Cortés as a god—the vanished Quetzalcóatl, or Feathered Serpent, who had sailed east, promising to return. With great dispatch Cortés proceeded to charm him, imprison him, and murder him. The Spanish soldiers built Mexico City with the stones from Aztec temples, massacring thousands in the process and decimating the rest of the population with European diseases. Next came priests, monks, and friars, who zealously enslaved the remaining Indians in order to build several hundred churches and convents, about 50 of which survive.

The 300 years of the colonial and viceregal eras still breathe through architectural relics. Modernism—and sheer necessity—has encroached on this legacy. But large, distinctive pockets of the city, particularly the downtown area and the southern suburbs of San Angel and Coyoacán, are still rich with warm red and quarried stone, curving facades, and cobblestones. The Spaniards were fond of mansions and fountains, inner courtyards and ironwork balconies, and they excelled in blending Baroque and Moorish flourishes. Quite a few of the city's 70 museums are housed in such surroundings.

The great eras and events in Mexican history are all encapsulated in the city. The Spaniards were sent packing in 1821, to be followed 26 years later by the Americans. Two decisive battles of the Mexican-American War were fought at Chapultepec Castle and the Ex-Convent of Churubusco. The French intervention of 1864–1867—headed by ineffectual Austrian emperor Maximilian—left Parisian embellishments along the broad boulevard of Paseo de la Reforma. The dictatorship of Porfirio Díaz (1876–1911) resulted in another wave of Francophilia, from the neoclassical Fine Arts Palace to Art Nouveau gaslights, etched-glass walls, and quaint little streetcars. Díaz's reign marked the 19th-century apogee of foreign investment in Mexico: Under his sponsorship the railroads, agriculture, mining, construction, and the oil industry were developed, and a new class of wealthy Mexicans emerged.

Nearly 2 million Mexicans died in the streets of the capital during the Mexican Revolution of 1910–20. La Ciudadela (the fortress), now an outdoor handicraft market, was the arsenal and headquarters for the rebels' stand against the liberal Madero government. With the return of stability, a new architectural hybrid was born: Colonial facades were refaced with ocelotshape gargoyles, and cornices were adorned with plumed serpents. But the city's growth accelerated, both upward and outward, in the postwar years, sweeping up and to some extent homogenizing the outlying villages. The architecturally innovative National Autonomous University opened in 1953, and a subway system that now covers 111 kilometers (69 miles) was inaugurated in 1969. Unchecked growth and prosperity were followed by unbridled spending, debt, aggravated class differences, and social unrest.

Hundreds of student demonstrators were shot to death in 1968 by federal troops in the northern section of Tlatelolco, the site of the Aztecs' last battle. That same year the Summer Olympics were held in Mexico City. Periodic earthquakes have leveled parts of the city; the catastrophic 1985 quake took at least 10,000 lives.

The physical setting for all this is the 918-square-kilometer (570-square-mile) Valle de Anáhuac, most of which is occupied by the greater metropolitan area. The valley—more accurately, a basin—sits on the Central Plateau, completely surrounded by mountains and two extinct volcanoes. Because the city was built on the dried beds of Lake Texcoco, much of the subsoil is soft, and it is slowly sinking.

"El D.F."—for *Distrito Federal* (Federal District), which is comparable to the District of Columbia—has come to be the abbreviation for the city proper and for the outlying areas it is slowly encompassing. But the city is also called, simply, "Mexico," not unlike "New York" for New York City. Its residents are envied and resented. Envied because they are in the national limelight and their standard of living is (often erroneously) perceived to be higher; resented because they monopolize government services, the media, commerce, finance, and education.

It's easy to lose sight of the immensity of this city when you live there. Every city has residents whose lives are confined to one or two neighborhoods. But the majority of chilangos (Mexico

City residents) spend many hours in vehicular transit; Mexico City is not particularly a walker's city.

Short-term visitors will be quite overwhelmed by the capital's size. There are infinite demands on one's attention; all the senses are gripped. One-legged beggars on church steps hold out their hands. Fire-eaters eke out a living by doing stunts at traffic lights. In almost any public building you'll be confronted by the pageantry of Mexican history in murals both savage and tender, idealistic and iconoclastic. The markets are redolent of tree-ripened papayas, mangoes, pineapples; from *tortillerías* and *taquerías* emanate the fresh, wistful odors of cornmeal and sizzling oil.

There are the sounds, too: rude car horns and blasting radio salsa, but also mariachis and children's off-key songs and the sometimes sensual, sometimes strident conversational tones of Mexican Spanish. And there is jostling. Mexicans do not always adhere to Western ideas about lining up and waiting their turn, and there is less prudishness about personal space. They smoke and drink about as much as Europeans do, so boisterousness is commonplace. And though Mexican men will stare and call after *güeras*—fair-skinned women—they generally keep their hands to themselves.

Try not to limit yourself to the upscale Zona Rosa (Pink Zone), which is as "typical" of Mexico City as Fifth Avenue is of Manhattan. Certainly, the capital has fancy restaurants, world-class hotels, touristy but high-quality crafts shops and boutiques, arts and nightlife. But it's also a Third World metropolis—exasperating, endearing, moving, riveting, and most of all, engaging.

Give it more than a few days, and it will work its strange magic. Follow the locals' example, and wind down for a weekend in one of the colonial towns—Cuernavaca, Puebla, or Valle de Bravo—a two- or three-hour drive from the capital. Then come back into town. Mexico City takes patience and a sense of humor; it demands open eyes, yet one must take certain things about it on faith. This is its modest promise: It cannot possibly leave you indifferent.

Essential Information

Arriving and Departing by Plane

Airports and Airlines All roads (and flights) lead to Mexico City. **Aeroméxico** (tel. 800/237–6639) serves Mexico City daily from Houston, Los Angeles, Miami, New Orleans, New York, and Tucson; at press time additional cities were being planned. Aeroméxico offers special low joint fares with certain U.S. airlines for connections from throughout the United States to Mexico's gateway cities. The airline serves some 35 cities within Mexico, and its domestic subsidiary, **Aeroliteral,** serves another 15 locations. **Mexicana** (tel. 800/531–7921) has regular service from Chicago, Dallas/Fort Worth, Denver, Los Angeles, Miami, New York, San Antonio, and San Francisco. It has direct or connecting service at over 30 locations throughout the country, and its subsidiary, **Aerocaribe,** serves the Yucatán area.

U.S. carriers serving Mexico City include **American, Continental, Delta,** and **United.** From Canada there are flights on **Iberia** (from Montreal). Other international carriers serving Mexico City include **Air France, Aeroflot, Aerolíneas Argentinas, Aeroperú, Avensa, Avianca, Japan Air Lines, KLM, Lufthansa,** and **Taca.**

Promotional fares in an almost endless variety frequently are available. Tour and charter packages usually include substantial airfare and hotel discounts. Considerable savings can often be had by flying from border points within Mexico. Airline tour packages purchased within Mexico can also be quite attractive. If you purchase tickets in Mexico for domestic flights (other than to border cities) you will be charged 10% sales tax (IVA). Also, bear in mind that on some domestic flights no-shows or those who cancel less than 45 minutes before their Mexican domestic flight may be charged up to 20% of the ticket price in penalties.

Between the Airport and Center City Taxis are available at both the domestic and international arrival areas. Purchase your ticket at the **Transportación Terrestre** (ground transportation) counters located in the baggage carousel area or just outside at the curb. (Avoid *pirata* taxi drivers offering their services.) Government-controlled fares are based on which *colonia* (neighborhood) you are going to and are usually less than $8 to most hotels. A 10% tip is enough for airport drivers. All major car rental agencies have booths at both arrival areas, but renting a car is not recommended unless you are heading out of town or know Mexico City *very* well.

Porters and carts are available in the baggage retrieval area. Just outside is a bank where you can exchange dollars for pesos at a rate more favorable than you'll get at your hotel. (To speed up your arrival even more, bring $50–$75 in pesos with you.) The Mexico City Tourist Office and the Hotel Association both have stands in the arrival areas that can provide information and find visitors a room for the night.

Customs procedure is unique: On the plane, you are handed a declaration form to fill out. Present it with your baggage to the customs inspector, who will ask you to press a button on a post with two lights that looks just like a traffic signal. If the green light flashes, you pass right through; if it's red, your baggage is examined. With this random system, your chance of getting green is, unofficially, about 15-to-1 in your favor.

Arriving and Departing by Car, Train, and Bus

By Car Proof of vehicle ownership *must* be shown at the Mexican border. Either the title or a letter from a bank giving permission to take the car out of the United States is necessary. Moreover, only the person whose name appears on the Mexican import permit is allowed to drive said vehicle in Mexico. *Always* purchase Mexican car insurance at the border, since uninsured drivers responsible for accidents can wind up in jail.

Highways range from toll, four-lane divided superhighways, to two-lane highways, and you have the option of taking more scenic paved country roads (watch out for meandering livestock). Maximum speed limit on major highways is 140 kph (86.9 mph). Obey lower posted speed limits on smaller roads and in populated areas. In remote regions where distance between towns is considerable, it is wise to fill up at every opportunity. Eighty-seven octane unleaded gasoline, called *Magna Sin*, is now available throughout most of the Republic. During daylight hours highways and major roads are patrolled by the *Angeles Verdes* (Green Angels), whose green trucks are well equipped to provide mechanical assistance to motorists in distress at no charge, courtesy of the Mexican Government. It is advisable not to drive at night, especially in mountainous areas.

Throughout Mexico City, a new and *strictly enforced* law, *"Un Día Sin Auto"* (One Day Without a Car), applies to all private vehicles, including your own. One of several effective measures to reduce smog and traffic congestion, this law prohibits every privately owned vehicle (including out-of-state, foreign, and even rental cars) from being used on one designated weekday. Cars in violation are refused service by parking garages and gas stations, and are inevitably impounded by the police. Expect a hefty fine as well. The weekday is specified by the last numbers or letters of the license plate. To find out which is your day without a car, contact the Mexican Government Tourism Office nearest you, and by all means plan your schedule accordingly.

No matter where you cross the border, you almost certainly will approach Mexico City via Querétaro on Highway 57, a toll expressway that passes through miles of suburbs. Turn off at the Reforma-Centro ("centro" means downtown) exit and you will be headed for the heart of the Capital.

By Train Mexico's National Railways have improved dramatically, with modern streamliners such as the *Regiomontano*, which runs daily from Nuevo Laredo, at the Texas border, to Mexico City. It has private cabins with toilet and also "First-Class Special" cars with airplane-style seats. Waiters serve hot meals at the seats or in the dining car, and there is also an observation car with bar. The scenic trip takes 18¼ hours.

By Bus Reserved seating is available on first-class Mexican bus lines which depart throughout the day from major border cities to Mexico City. You can purchase your tickets on the U.S. or Mexican side of the border. If you plan stopovers en route, make sure your ticket is to that stopover city; you can reserve a seat to continue on your journey when you arrive at that point. In Mexico, platform announcements are in Spanish only. From Matamoros, the trip to Mexico City takes about 14 hours; from Laredo, 15 hours; from Ciudad Juárez (El Paso), 24 hours; from Nogales, 40 hours; from Tijuana, 44 hours.

Getting Around

By Bus The Mexico City bus system is used by hundreds of thousands of commuters daily because it's cheap—400 pesos (less than 15 cents)—and goes everywhere. Hence, expect to be jostled and be wary of pickpockets, who sometimes work in teams. In Mexican Spanish, the word for bus and truck is the same: *camión*. One of the principal bus routes runs along Paseo de la Reforma, Avenida Juárez, and Calle Madero, connecting Chapultepec Park with the *Zócalo* (main plaza). Stops are clearly indicated by shelters, signs, and often lines of waiting passengers. A bus also may be taken along Avenida Insurgentes Sur to San Angel and University City or along Avenida Insurgentes Norte to the

Guadalupe Basilica. You can get virtually anywhere in the city by bus; call 5/525–9380 for route information (in Spanish).

Intercity bus tickets can be purchased at **Mexicorama** (tel. 5/525–2050) in the Plaza del Angel arcade in Zona Rosa. The staff speaks English. The arcade has two entrances, one on Londres and the other on Hamburgo, both between Florencia and Amberes.

Buses to other Mexican cities depart from four outlying stations: North, Río Cién Metros 4907; South, Taxqueña 1320; East, Zaragoza 200; and West, Río Tacubaya and Sur 122. The metro connects with these terminals, but passengers cannot bring luggage on the metro.

By Car Millions of intrepid drivers brave Mexico City's streets every day and survive, but for out-of-towners the experience can be traumatic. Streets are confusing, rush-hour traffic is nightmarish, and parking places can be hard to come by. Police tow trucks haul away illegally parked vehicles, and retrieving them requires fluency in Spanish, detectivelike skills, and the patience of Job (call 5/658–1111 to begin your quest). Visitors can hire a chauffeur for their cars through a hotel concierge or travel service such as American Express. An automobile will come in handy if you plan to explore the nearby communities of Cuernavaca, Taxco, Pachuca, Puebla, and Tehuacán (*see* Excursions, *below*), but don't forget the "Day Without A Car" program (*see* Arriving and Departing by Car, *above*).

By Pesero Originally six-passenger sedans, then vans, and now minibuses with stereo music, *peseros* operate on a number of fixed routes and charge a flat rate (a peso once upon a time, hence the name). Peseros offer a good alternative to buses and taxis. Likely routes for tourists are along the city's major west-east axis (Chapultepec Park/Reforma/Avenida Juárez/Zócalo) and north-south along Insurgentes, between the Guadalupe Basilica and San Angel/University City. Just stand on the curb, check the route sign on the oncoming pesero's windshield, hold out your hand, and it will pick you up. Tell the driver where to stop, or press the button by the door. At press time (January 1991), the fare ranges from 500 pesos for up to five kilometers to 1,000 pesos for over 17 kilometers.

By Subway Transporting 5 million passengers daily, Mexico City's metro is one of the world's best, busiest, and cheapest transportation systems—the fare is the same as for buses, about a dime. The impeccably clean marble and onyx stations are brightly lit, and modern French-designed trains run quietly on rubber tires. Lines 1, 2, and 3 operate from 5 AM to 12:30 AM on weekdays, 6 AM to 1:30 AM Saturdays, and 7 AM to 12:30 AM Sundays and holidays. Lines 4, 5, 6, 7, and 9 operate 6 AM–12:30 AM, 6 AM–1:30 AM, and 7 AM–12:30 AM, respectively. Trains are least crowded between 10 AM and 4 PM. During rush hours, men use separate cars from women and children. There are eight continuously expanding lines covering over 160 kilometers (100 miles): numbers 1 through 7 and the new number 9. A new line under construction at press time will soon bear the number 8. Color-keyed signs are posted all around, and maps and assistance are provided at information desks. At the southern edge of the city, the Taxqueña station connects with the new electric train (*Metro Ligero*) that continues south to Xochimilco. To the southeast, the new Metro Ligero from the Pantitlán station has a projected route all the

Mexico City Subways

6 7 El Rosario

5 Politécnico

3 Indios Verdes

Martín Carrera

Tezozomoc
Azcapotzalco
Ferrería
Vallejo
Lindavista

Aquiles
Serdán
Norte 45
**Instituto
del Petróleo**
Basílica
La Villa
4 6

Camarones

Autobuses del
Norte
Potrero
Talismán

Refinería

La Raza

Misterios
Bondojito

Panteones
Tacuba
Cuitláhuac
Valle Gómez
Consulado

**2 Cuatro
Caminos**
Popotla
Eduardo
Molina
San Juan
de Aragón

San Joaquín
Colegio Militar
Tlatelolco
Canal del
Norte
Oceanía

Normal
Guerrero
Morelos

Polanco
San Cosme
Revolución
Hidalgo
Bellas Artes
Allende

Insurgentes
Juárez
Zócalo
San Lázaro
Terminal Aérea

Auditorio
Chapultepec
Sevilla
Balderas
Salto del
Agua
Moctezuma
Balbuena

Cuauhtémoc
I. la
Católica
**Pino
Suárez**
Candelaria
Hangares

Constituyentes
Juanacatlán
Niños
Héroes
San
Antonio
Abad
Fray
Servando
Aeropuerto
Pantitlán
1 5 9

**Centro
Médico**
Hospital
General
Gómez
Farías
Metro Ligero

Tacubaya
9
Chabacano
Jamaica
Mixihuca
Velódromo
Cd. Deportiva
Zaragoza
Puebla

Patriotismo
Chilpancingo
Lázaro Cárdenas
Viaducto
Santa Anita
4
TOWARD PUEBLA

1 Observatorio
Etiopía
Xola

San Pedro de
los Piños
Eugenia
Villa de Cortés

San Antonio
División del
Norte
Nativitas

Mixcoac
Zapata
Portales

7
Coyoacán
Ermita

**Barranca del
Muerto**
Viveros

M.A. de Quevedo
General Anaya

Copilco
2 Tasqueña

Metro Ligero

3 Universidad
TO XOCHIMILCO
(under construction)

N

way to Puebla. The metro is well attended and safe. Some stations, such as Insurgentes, are shopping centers. Even if you don't take a ride, visit the Zócalo station, which has large models of central Mexico City during three historic periods. The Bellas Artes station has replicas of archaeological treasures on exhibit, and inside the Pino Suárez station is a small Aztec pyramid, uncovered during construction.

By Taxi The Mexico City variety comes in several colors and sizes. Large, unmarked *turismo* sedans with hooded meters are usually stationed outside major hotels. The drivers are almost always English-speaking guides and can be hired for sightseeing on a daily or hourly basis (always negotiate the price in advance). *Sitio* taxis operate out of stands, take radio calls, and are authorized to charge a small premium. Among these, **Servi-Taxis** (tel. 5/516–6020) and **Super-Taxis** (tel. 5/566–0077) offer 24-hour service. Taxis that cruise the streets range from sedans to Volkswagen Beetles—the latter with the front passenger seat removed for more legroom. They are available either when the *libre* (free) light is on or when the windshield sign is displayed. Since taxi meters are no longer adjusted to keep pace with inflation, the driver will use a posted rate sheet to compute the fare from the meter. Meter rates don't necessarily apply at night and on Sundays, so it's best to negotiate the fare before entering the taxi (never "cab"). Taking a taxi in Mexico City is extremely inexpensive and tips are not expected unless you have luggage, when 10% is sufficient.

Important Addresses and Numbers

Tourist Information The **Mexico City Tourist Office,** (Departamento de Turismo del Distrito Federal) maintains information booths at both the international and domestic arrivals area at the airport, the Buenavista Train Station, Fonart (Av. Júarez 89), as well as on highways leading into the city. In town, information, brochures and assistance are available in the lobby of its main office at Amberes 54 at the corner of Londres in the Zona Rosa. For tourist information and advice by phone, dial INFOTUR (tel. 5/525–9380, 5/525–9381, 5/525–9382, 5/525–9383, or 5/525–9384) from 9 AM to 9 PM daily. Operators are multilingual and have access to an extensive data bank. The **Secretariat of Tourism (SECTUR)** operates a 24-hour multilingual hot line providing information on both Mexico City and the entire country (tel. 5/250–0123, 5/250–8419, or 5/250–8601). Don't be discouraged, as lines are usually busy. You can also call collect from anywhere in Mexico by dialing the prefix 91 and any of the above numbers. SECTUR operates a Tourist Information Center at Presidente Masaryk 171 (in Polanco), open Monday–Friday, 8 AM–8 PM.

A new city-government entity, **Agencia del Ministerio Publico Para Turistas,** has been set up exclusively to assist tourists with legal advice. It has two offices: in the Zona Rosa (Florencia 20, corner of Hamburgo, tel. 5/625–8761), and in the Downtown Historic Center (Argentina corner of San Idelfonso, tel. 5/789–0833). A central phone number for both (tel. 5/625–8618) answers 24 hours a day, 365 days a year.

Consulates and Embassies The **U.S. Embassy** (Paseo de la Reforma 305, tel. 5/211–0042) is open weekdays 8:30–5:30 but is closed for American and Mexican holidays. The **Canadian Embassy** (Schiller 529, tel. 5/254–

3288) is open weekdays 9–4 and is closed for Canadian and Mexican holidays. The **British Embassy** (Lerma 71, tel. 5/207–2449) is open weekdays 9:30–1 and 4–7 PM.

Emergencies
Police

Dial 06 for police, Red Cross, ambulance, fire, or other emergency situation. If you are not able to reach an English-speaking operator, call the SECTUR hot line (*see* Tourist Information, *above*). For missing persons or cars, call LOCATEL at 5/658–1111.

Hospital

American British Cowdray Hospital (Observatorio and Sur 136, tel. 5/515–8359 or 5/277–5000).

English-language
Bookstores

Sanborns—a mini-department store chain with branches all over town, including three along Paseo de la Reforma, one on Niza in the Zona Rosa, and one downtown on Calle Madero in the House of Tiles—carries U.S. newspapers and magazines, paperbacks, and guidebooks. The **American Book Store** at Calle Madero 25 has an even more extensive selection. *The News*, a daily English-language newspaper, available at hotels and on newsstands in the tourist areas, provides a summary of what is happening in Mexico and the rest of the world with cultural and entertainment listings, daily stock market reports, and a Sunday travel supplement.

Telephones

Thanks to the privatization of *Telefónos de México* in late 1991, the country's exasperatingly inefficient phone service is being gradually overhauled. It will take time, however, and meanwhile public phone procedures prove confusing at best.

Public phones include the regular black "pay phones," which have been free for local calling ever since the 1985 earthquake. Ignore the signs saying to deposit a 20-centavo coin, which has been obsolete for years. If you find one that works, after three minutes a recorded voice may announce *tiempo transcurrido* (time's up) and abruptly disconnect you; just redial. You can also call long distance *por cobrar* (collect) by dialing the operator: 02 for within Mexico and 09 for international. International operators speak English, and you can use the international number on your AT&T credit card to call the United States. New, blue, push-button coin-slot phones with digital screens all appear to be identical, but they are not. On some, when you pick up the receiver the screen announces *solo para emergencia* (free emergency calls only), although they don't indicate the emergency numbers, and coins drop through to the return slot. On others, the screen tells you to insert a minimum of 100 pesos, and it will swallow thousands; you can even chance dialing long distance direct, but you can't dial the operator. Don't be misled by the signs on these blue phones giving explicit instructions for inserting a credit card in the vertical slot indicated by an arrow, because there are no slots. Also new are cream-and-brown digital phones. These do indeed have credit card slots at the bottom, which, for now, accept only Visa or MasterCard for long-distance calls but will not connect to the operator. Dial 04 for information. For residential listings, as with the telephone directory, you need to know *both* surnames of the individual, unless it's a gringo with only one. Be patient, as it usually takes some time for the operators to answer, if they do at all. Small businesses are often listed under the owner's name.

Many bars, restaurants, and shops have regular phones that customers can use for dialing only within Mexico City, either at no charge or by paying the proprietor just a few cents.

From business or residential phones, and from deluxe hotels equipped with long distance direct dial (called *LADA*), you can dial long distance direct within the republic (91 + area code + number) or to the United States (95 + city area code + number). LADA codes for Mexican cities and other countries are listed in the telephone directory. Use this same direct dialing advantage from the new public phones that are marked "LADATEL." They have a different type of card slot that accepts special plastic bar-coded LADATEL cards. These can be purchased at prices varying from 5,000 to 50,000 pesos, depending on your needs, and are available at tourist offices and at certain stores displaying the LADATEL sign. The phone displays the "countdown" in pesos, and when the cards are used up they are discarded. Keep in mind that it is much more expensive to call from Mexico to the United States than from the United States to Mexico. Also, hotels add a hefty surcharge and tax on all international calls. The cheapest way to call the United States is through the 09 operator, using the international number on your AT&T or local phone company credit card whenever possible. For now, the only AT&T "USA Direct" dedicated-line phones in Mexico City are at the airport, upstairs outside the immigrations area. A major breakthrough is direct access from most of the new push-button public phones in Mexico City to AT&T "USA Direct" operators in the United States for placing collect and credit card calls. Simply touch "**01." No coins are necessary. For a charge payable by AT&T credit card, the AT&T operator can also connect you with U.S. 800 numbers.

The modernization of the phone system also includes new toll-free 800 phone numbers for calling *within Mexico* (although comparable, they are not linked with U.S. 800 numbers). This service is now being offered by some Mexican hotel chains for reservations and by the airlines Aeroméxico and Mexicana. Separately, some U.S.-based companies such as Radisson Hotels are introducing international 800 numbers for calling toll-free from Mexico to their reservation centers in the United States.

Rotary lines are scarce, except for those at airlines, big hotels, or major companies, so you may be given several phone numbers for the same place. If one is busy, try another.

With the increasing installation of new phone and fax lines in Mexico City, many phone numbers have been or are in the process of being changed. If you dial a changed number, a recording will intercept with the new number, so it is worthwhile to know the numbers 1 through 9 in Spanish.

Guided Tours

Mexico City has no dearth of tour operators eager to show you around the capital. You can book tours through the travel desk at most hotels or contact the following reputable tour operators, which can arrange half- and full-day tours or one involving a special interest: **American Express** (Paseo de la Reforma 234, tel. 5/533–0380), **Mexico Travel Advisors (MTA)** (Génova 30, tel. 5/525–7250), and **Línea Gris** (Londres 166, tel. 5/533–1540).

Orientation The basic city tour ($15) lasts four hours and takes in the Zócalo, Palacio Nacional, Catedral Metropolitana, and Bosque de Chapultepec. A four-hour pyramid tour costs around $12 and covers the Basílica de Nuestra Señora de Guadalupe and the major ruins at Teotihuacán. The six-hour, light-and-sound version of the pyramid tour is run mid-October through May and costs $16.

Special-interest
Cultural The seven-hour tour ($32) is run on Sunday mornings only and includes a performance of the folkloric dances at the Palacio de Bellas Artes, a gondola ride in the canals of Xochimilco's floating gardens, and a visit to the modern campus of the National University.

Bullfights Also on Sundays only are trips to the bullring with a guide who will explain the finer points of this spectacle. This four-hour afternoon tour ($15) can usually be combined with the Ballet Folklórico–Xochimilco trip.

Nightlife These are among the most popular tours of Mexico City. The best are scheduled to last five hours and include transfers by private car rather than bus, dinner at an elegant restaurant (frequently Del Lago), a drink and show at the Plaza Garibaldi, where mariachis play, and a nightcap at Gitanerías, which features Spanish flamenco performances. Nightlife tours begin at $50.

Walking Huge as it is, Mexico City is not difficult to negotiate. Both the downtown historic section and Zona Rosa are compact and easily walkable.

Exploring

Orientation

Most of Mexico City is aligned around two major thoroughfares: Paseo de la Reforma and Avenida Insurgentes. Administratively, the city is divided into 16 *delegaciones* (districts) and about 400 colonias each with street names fitting a given theme, such as rivers, philosophers, doctors, or revolutionary heroes. The same street can change names as it goes through different colonias, making finding an address a bit more difficult. Hence most street addresses include the colonia they are in.

The principal sights of Mexico City are organized into three tours. You need a full day to cover each thoroughly, though each can be done at breakneck speed in four or five hours. Tour 1, Zócalo and Alameda Park, concentrates on a relatively compact area that can be seen on foot. Its focus is historical, since the Zócalo and Alameda Park were the heart of both the Aztec and the Spanish cities. The second tour, taking in Reforma, Zona Rosa, and Chapultepec Park, will necessitate some form of transportation if done in its entirety, but strong walkers can cover most of it on their own. Exploring San Angel and Coyoacán, two suburbs in southern Mexico City, will also require a taxi ride or two. These pretty colonial towns within the city will be of interest to those seeking the tranquillity and atmosphere of the "lost" Mexico City.

Highlights for First-time Visitors

Bellas Artes, Tour 1
Castillo de Chapultepec, Tour 2
Museo de Antropología, Tour 2
Museo Frida Kahlo, Tour 3
Palacio Nacional, Tour 1
Plaza Hidalgo, Tour 3
Plaza San Jacinto, Tour 3
Teotihuacán, Excursions
Zona Rosa, Tour 2

Tour 1: Zócalo and Alameda Central

Numbers in the margin correspond to points of interest on Zócalo and Alameda Central map.

The **Zócalo** (formal name: **Plaza de la Constitución**), or main square, of Mexico City was built by the Spaniards on the site of the main temple complex of Tenochtitlán, the capital of the Aztec Empire. Throughout the 16th, 17th, and 18th centuries, the Spaniards and their descendants constructed elaborate churches and convents, elegant mansions, and stately public edifices, many of which have long since been converted to other uses. There is an air of Old Europe to this section of the city, which, in its entirety (the *Centro Histórico*), is a national monument that has recently undergone a major refurbishing. Imposing buildings are constructed with the ubiquitous blood-red volcanic *tezontle* stone and the quarry stones that the Spaniards recycled from the rubble of the Aztec temples they razed. Throngs of small shops, eateries, cantinas, and street vendors contribute to an inimitably Mexican flavor, even an exuberance.

The downtown area is also consistently filled with people. Travelers should be alert to pickpockets, especially on crowded buses, and should avoid dark streets at night.

The Zócalo is an enormous paved square, the largest in the Western Hemisphere; it and the surrounding structures rose on the Aztec ceremonial center, which once comprised 78 buildings. *Zócalo* means pedestal or base: In the mid-19th century an independence monument had been envisioned for the spot to replace the overcrowded market stalls that once filled it, but the monument was never built. The term stuck, however, and now the word *zócalo* is applied to the main plazas of most Mexican cities. Mexico City's Zócalo (since it's the original it is always capitalized) is used for government rallies and festive events. It is also the focal point for Independence Day celebrations on the eve of September 16, and is spectacularly festooned during the Christmas–New Year holiday season. The changing of the guard takes place daily in the late afternoon.

❶ Around the square are the two most important symbols of church and state in Mexico. On the north side is the **Catedral Metropolitana** (Metropolitan Cathedral), which, over the centuries, has sunk noticeably into the spongy subsoil. Its lopsidedness is evident when viewed from across the square, but an engineering project to stabilize the structure was completed in early 1991. Construction on the oldest and largest cathedral in Latin America began in 1573 and continued intermittently over the next three centuries. The result is a medley of Baroque and neoclassical touches. Inside are four identical domes, their airiness made earthbound by rows of supportive columns. There are five altars and 14 chapels, mostly in the fussy, Churrigueresque style, an extremely decorative form of Spanish Baroque from the mid-17th century. Like most Mexican churches, the cathedral is all but overshadowed by the innumerable paintings, altarpieces, and statues—in graphic color—of Christ and the saints. *Open daily 8–6.*

Adjacent to the Cathedral, the comparatively small 18th-century **Sagrario Church,** also tilted, has an elaborate Churrigueresque facade.

Turn left as you leave the cathedral and walk one block north on
❷ Seminario to view the excavated ruins of the **Templo Mayor** (Great Temple of the Aztecs). It was unearthed accidentally in 1978 by electric company repairmen and has since been turned into a vast and historically significant archaeological site and museum. The temple depicts the myth of the goddess Coyolxauhqui (the moon), who was killed, decapitated, and dismembered by her brother, Huitzilopochtli (the sun), for trying to persuade her 400 other brothers to murder their mother. (Coyolxauhqui's only crime was to become pregnant by touching a feather to her breast.) Captives from rival tribes—as many as 10,000 a year—were sacrificed here to the bloodthirsty Aztec deities, as suggested by the seven rows of leering stone skulls adorning one side of the structure.

The adjacent **Museo Templo Mayor** contains 3,000 pieces, including ceramic warriors, stone carvings and knives, skulls of sacrificial victims, a rare gold ingot, models and scale reproductions, a room on the destruction of Tenochtitlán by the Spaniards, and the centerpiece, an eight-ton stone disk of the goddess. *Corner of Guatemala and Argentina. Small admission fee. Open Tues.–Sun. 9–5. Call 5/542–1717 to reserve English-language tours.*

Returning to the Zócalo on Seminario, the first building on
❸ your left is the **Palacio Nacional,** or National Palace, which was initiated by Cortés on the site of Moctezuma's home and remodeled by the viceroys; its current form dates to 1693, although a third floor was added in 1927. Now the seat of government, it has always served as a public function site. In fact, during colonial times, the first bullfight in "New Spain" took place in the inner courtyard.

Diego Rivera's sweeping, epic murals on the second floor of the main courtyard have the power to mesmerize. For more than 16 years (1929–45), he and his assistants mounted the scaffolds day and night, perfecting techniques adapted from Renaissance Italian frescoes. The result, nearly 1,200 square feet of vividly painted wall space, is grandiosely entitled *Epic of the Mexican People in Their Struggle for Freedom and Independence.* The larger-than-life paintings represent two millennia of Mexican history, as seen from the artist's Marxist stance. The innocence of pre-Hispanic times is portrayed by idyllic, almost sugary scenes of Tenochtitlán. Only a few vignettes—a lascivious woman baring her leg in the marketplace, a man offering a human arm for sale, and the carnage of warriors—acknowledge other aspects of ancient life. As you walk around the floor, you pass images depicting the savagery of the conquest and the hypocrisy of the Spanish priests, the noble Indepen-

San Angel and Coyoacán

Zócalo and Alameda Central

Alameda Central, **12**
Casa de los Azulejos, **8**
Catedral Metropolitana, **1**
Dirrección General de Correos, **9**

La Iglesia de San Francisco, **6**
Monte de Piedad, **4**
Monumento a Benito Juárez, **13**
Museo Franz Mayer, **11**

Palacio de Bellas Artes, **10**
Palacio de Iturbide, **5**
Palacio Nacional, **3**
Templo Mayor, **2**
Torre Latinoamericana, **7**

dence Movement, and the bloody revolution. Marx appears amid scenes of class struggles, toiling workers, industrialization (which Rivera idealized), the decadence of the bourgeoisie, and nuclear holocaust. The murals are among Rivera's finest works, equal in genius and craftsmanship to works by Da Vinci and Michelangelo. They are also the most accessible and probably the most visited of the artist's paintings. The palace also houses two minor museums—dealing with 19th-century president Benito Juárez and the Mexican Congress—and the liberty bell rung by Padre Hidalgo to proclaim independence in 1810 hangs high on the central facade. It chimes every eve of September 16 while, from the balcony below, the president repeats the historic shout for independence known as *el grito. Admission free. Open daily 9–5. Closed holidays.*

④ Turn left and then right onto the south side of the Zócalo, which is occupied by the twin buildings of **Ayuntamiento** (City Hall). The arcade of the western structure is decorated with colonial tiles of the coats of arms of Cortés and other conquistadores. Complete your tour of the square by heading north, through the arcade, on 5 de Febrero. The **Monte de Piedad** ("Mountain of Piety") will be on your left, at the far northwest corner of the Zócalo. It was built in the late-18th century on the site of an Aztec palace to help the poor and currently houses the National Pawn Shop, which sells jewelry, antiques, and other pawned goods. *Open Mon.–Sat. about 10–7.*

Time Out At Cinco de Mayo 10 is one of Mexico City's most venerable and atmospheric cantinas, **Bar la Opera** (tel. 5/512–8959). The bar/restaurant has two claims to fame: Pancho Villa supposedly rode his horse into the place and demanded service by shooting a hole in the ceiling (you can still see it); and it was one of the first cantinas to allow women. Stop in for a drink or a snack.

There are two notable sites on Calle Tacuba: the **Palacio de Minería,** a 19th-century architectural landmark; and the neoclassical **Museo Nacional de Arte** (National Art Museum), which contains a superb collection of pre-Hispanic, religious, and contemporary artwork. *The museum is at Calle Tacuba 8, tel. 5/521–7320. Small admission fee. Open Tues.–Sun. 10–5.*

⑤ From Calle Tacuba, walk one block south to Calle Madero, one of the city's busiest and most typical streets in terms of its architectural variety. On the south side of Calle Madero, between Bolívar and Gante, is the **Palacio de Iturbide** (Emperor Iturbide's Palace), which has been converted into a branch of Banamex (Banco Nacional de México). This handsome Baroque structure—note the imposing door and its carved stone trimmings—was built in 1780 and became the residence of Iturbide in 1822. One of the heroes of the Independence Movement, the misguided Iturbide proclaimed himself emperor of a country that had thrown off the imperial yoke of the Hapsburgs only a year before; his empire, needless to say, was short-lived. Major cultural exhibitions are held in the atrium. *Calle Madero 17. Admission free. Inner atrium open weekdays 9–6, and on weekends during exhibitions.*

⑥ **La Iglesia de San Francisco,** built on the site of Mexico's first convent (1524), is located a block west of the palace, on the same side of Calle Madero. Moctezuma's zoo was supposed to have stood on the site in Aztec times. The present 18th-century

French Gothic church is one of the newest buildings on the street. The beautiful ceiling paintings are being restored. *Admission free. Open daily.*

⓻ In stark contrast to the church is the **Torre Latinoamericana** (Latin American Tower), once the tallest building in the capital. This 47-story skyscraper was built in 1956, and on clear days the observation deck and restaurant on the top floors afford fine views of the city. *Calle Madero and Eje Central Lázaro Cárdenas. Small admission fee. Observation deck open daily 10 AM–11:30 PM.*

⓼ Three other interesting buildings are off Eje Central Lázaro Cárdenas, a main thoroughfare. The 17th-century **Casa de los Azulejos** (House of Tiles) is catercorner from the tower, on the north side of Calle Madero at the corner of Callejón de la Condesa. Its well-preserved facade of white, blue, and yellow tiles, iron grillwork balconies, and gray stonework make it among the prettiest Baroque structures in the country. Currently occupied by Sanborns, a chain store/restaurant, it was built as the palace of the Counts of the Valle de Orizaba, an aristocratic family from early Spanish rule. Inside are a Moorish patio, a monumental staircase, and a mural by Orozco. *Calle Madero 4. Open daily 8 AM–10 PM.*

⓽ Continue north on Callejón de la Condesa to the **Dirección General de Correos** (General Post Office) at the corner of Calle Tacuba and Eje Central Lázaro Cárdenas. This neo-Renaissance building (1908) epitomizes the grand imitations of European architecture common in Mexico during the Porfiriato, or dictatorship of Porfirio Díaz (1876–1911). On the upper floor, the **Museo de la Filatelia** exhibits the postal history of Mexico. *Open Mon.–Sat. 8 AM–midnight, Sun. 8–4. Museum open weekdays 9–7.*

⓾ The most celebrated public building of the Díaz period is the **Palacio de Bellas Artes** (Fine Arts Palace), which is diagonally across from the post office, at the corner of Lázaro Cárdenas and Avenida Juárez and abutting Alameda Park. It was constructed as an opera house between 1904 and 1934, with time out for the revolution. In addition to being a handsome theatrical venue (the Ballet Folklórico de México performs here, as do other national and international artists), it is renowned both for its architecture—by the Italian architect Adamo Boari, who also designed the post office—and for its paintings by several celebrated Mexican artists, including Rufino Tamayo and Mexico's trio of muralists: Rivera, Orozco, and Siqueiros. In the palace, Rivera reconstructed his mural, *Man in Control of His Universe*, which was commissioned for and then torn down from Rockefeller Center in New York City, because of its political message (epitomized by the face of Lenin). The marble palace contains a Tiffany stained-glass curtain depicting the two volcanoes outside Mexico City and also houses temporary art exhibits. *Tel. 5/510–1388. Open Tues.–Sun. 10:30–6:30.*

⓫ Aficionados of colonial Spanish decorative and applied arts should detour at this point to visit the **Museo Franz Mayer.** Located one block west of the rear of the Palace on Avenida Hidalgo (in the Plaza Santa Veracruz), the museum opened in 1986 in the 16th-century Hospital de San Juan de Dios. Exhibits include wooden chests inlaid with ivory, tortoiseshell, and ebony; tapestries, paintings, and lacquerware; rococo clocks, glassware, architectural ornamentation; and an unusually large assortment of *talavera* ceramics and tiles. Wall plaques explain in detail the history of tiles (*azulejos*), a technique carried from Mesopotamia and Egypt to the Persians, Arabs, and Spaniards, who brought it to Mexico. The museum building is faithfully restored, with pieces of the original frescoes peeking through; classical music plays in the background. *Av. Hidalgo 45, at the Plaza Santa Veracruz, tel. 5/518–2265. Small admission fee except on weekends. Open Tues.–Sun. 10–5. Call ahead for an English-speaking guide.*

12 **Alameda Central** (Alameda Park), across Avenida Hidalgo from the Plaza Santa Veracruz, has been one of the capital's oases of greenery and a gracious center for festivities since Aztec times. The Indians held their *tianguis* (market) on the site. In the early days of the Viceroyalty, it was where victims of the Inquisition were burned at the stake. National leaders, from 18th-century viceroys to Emperor Maximilian and President Díaz, clearly envisioned the park as a symbol of civic pride and prosperity: Over the centuries, it has been endowed with fountains, railings, a Moorish kiosk imported from Paris, and ash, willow, and poplar trees. Its most conspicuous man-made **13** structure is the white marble semicircular **Monumento a Benito Juárez** (monument to Juárez) on the Avenida Juárez side of the park. It is a fine place for strolling and listening to live music on Sundays and holidays.

Fonart, the government-owned handicrafts chain, has a store at Avenida Juárez 89, just west of the park (*see* Shopping, *below*). At the far western side of the Alameda is **Museo Mural Diego Rivera,** built to display Diego Rivera's controversial mural, *Sunday Afternoon Dream in the Alameda Park*. The mural was done in the Hotel Del Prado in 1947–48. The controversy was due to Rivera's inscription, "God does not exist," which he later replaced with the bland "Conference of San Juan de Letrán." The mural—one of Rivera's most gentle and poetic—was relocated following the hotel's destruction in the 1985 earthquake. *Museo Mural Diego Rivera, at Calles Balderas and Colón. Admission free. Open Tues.–Sun. 10–6.*

Tour 2: Reforma, Reforma, Zona Rosa, and Chapultepec Park

Numbers in the margin correspond to points of interest on the Chapultepec Park, Reforma, Zona Rosa, and Downtown Historic Section map.

The Paseo de la Reforma was built by Emperor Maximilian in 1865 to connect the Palacio Nacional with his residence, the Castillo de Chapultepec. It was modeled after the Champs-Elysées in Paris. Reforma is 30 blocks long, so public transportation is recommended if you want to cover all the sights described. Begin at Reforma's northern end, about 2 kilometers (1.2 miles) north of Bellas Artes, in the area known as **Tlatelolco** (Tla-tel-**ohl**-coh). Before the conquest, Tlatelolco and Tenochtitlán were sister cities, and the domain of Cuauhtémoc, the last Aztec emperor. In modern times its name makes residents shudder, because it was here that several hundred protesting students were massacred by the National Guard in 1968. The 1985 earthquake destroyed an entire housing complex in Tlatelolco, in which hundreds perished.

① The center of Tlatelolco is the **Plaza de las Tres Culturas,** so named because Mexico's three cultural eras—pre-Hispanic, colonial, and modern—are represented on the plaza in the form of the small ruins of a pre-Hispanic ceremonial center (visible from the roadway); the **Iglesia de Santiago Tlatelolco** (1609) and **Colegio de la Santa Cruz de Tlatelolco** (1535–36); and the ultra-contemporary **Ministry of Foreign Affairs** (badly damaged by the earthquake and still undergoing repairs). The church contains the baptismal font of Juan Diego, the Indian to whom the Virgin of Guadalupe appeared in 1531. The Colegio (college) concentrates on studies of Indian language and culture. *The plaza is bounded on the north by Manuel González, on the west by Av. San Juan de Letrán Norte, and on the east by Paseo de la Reforma, between Glorieta de Peralvillo and Glorieta Cuitláhuac.*

The plaza itself can be seen in passing, but nearby are several other points of interest: the **Mercado de Tepito,** the **Mercado de ③ la Lagunilla,** and **Plaza Garibaldi.** Tepito is a typical market selling tools and used clothing, but it is situated in the midst of some of the worst tenements in the city, at the corner of Aztecas and Héroes de Granaditas. Walk six blocks east on the latter street—you are now back at the northern part of the centro—and between República de Chile and Allende you come to Mercado de la Lagunilla, known affectionately as the Thieves' Market. Go on Sundays, when it is busiest, and watch your money: Here, along with the usual flea-market fare, you can find antiques (some of them fake), toys, secondhand books and clothes, semiprecious stones, art, and some handicrafts.

Plaza Garibaldi is Mexico City's mariachi square (*see* Nightlife, *below*). Head here at night, when it resounds with music and festivity until the wee hours, especially on weekends. One warning: Late at night things can get a bit raucous. Choose a cantina, order a tequila; the musicians will be around shortly to serenade you (tipping is essential). On the north side of the square is the Mercado de San Camilito, where typical Mexican food is served. The plaza and its surrounding area have recently been refurbished. *Just east of Av. Lázaro Cárdenas, between República de Honduras and República de Perú.*

Return to Paseo de la Reforma where it intersects Avenida Juárez and Bucareli and head west (left) down Reforma. Porfirio Díaz had a number of statues to illustrious men erected along this stretch, including Simón Bolívar, Columbus, Pasteur, and Cuauhtémoc. The most famous of these statues is used by locals as a geographic point of reference: it is the *Monumento a la Independencia,* a Corinthian column topped by a gold angel (thus the more common "the Angel"). Beneath the pedestal lie the remains of the principal heroes of the Independence Movement, and an eternal flame burns in their honor.

④ The Angel marks the western midpoint of the **Zona Rosa** (Pink Zone), which for years has been the one part of the city in which tourists have felt most comfortable because of the plethora of restaurants, cafés, art galleries, hotels, discos, and shops. It is also an affluent residential neighborhood, populated by foreign diplomats and businesspeople (the American Embassy is just across Reforma).

The architecture in the Zona Rosa is appealing. Most buildings, two or three stories high, were originally private homes built in

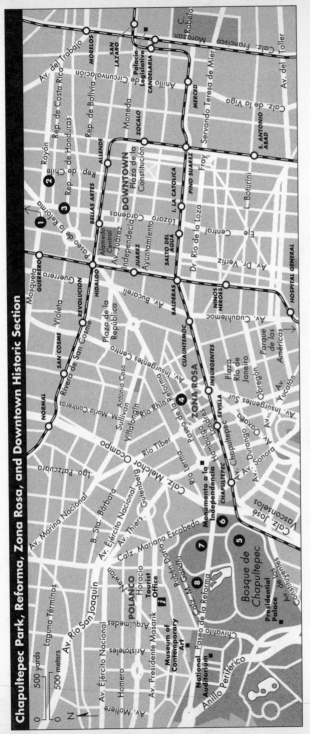

Chapultepec Park, Reforma, Zona Rosa, and Downtown Historic Section

81

Castillo de
Chapultepec, **5**
Mercado de la
Lagunilla, **2**
Museo de Arte
Moderno, **6**

Museo Nacional de
Antropología, **8**
Museo Tamayo, **7**
Plaza de las Tres
Culturas, **1**
Plaza Garibaldi, **3**
Zona Rosa, **4**

the 1920s for the wealthy. All the streets are wistfully named after European cities; some, such as Genova, are garden-lined pedestrian malls. The appellation Zona Rosa was supposedly applied to lend credence to the neighborhood's aristocratic pretensions.

To enjoy the Zona Rosa, just walk the lengths of Hamburgo and Londres and follow some of the side streets, especially Copenhague—a veritable restaurant row. The large handicrafts market on Londres is officially **Mercado Insurgentes,** though most people call it either **Mercado Zona Rosa,** or **Mercado Londres** (*see* Shopping, *below*). Just opposite the market's Londres entrance is **Plaza del Angel,** a small shopping mall where a *mini-tianguis* (native market) specializes in antiques and curios on Saturdays and Sundays.

Time Out Stop for tea and pastries at one of two tea shops on Hamburgo: **Duca d'Este** on the southeast corner of Florencia (164–B Hamburgo, tel. 5/525–6374) or **Salón de Té Auseba** (159–B Hamburgo, tel. 5/511–3769).

The third area of Reforma covers most of the first of three sections of **Bosque de Chapultepec** (Chapultepec Park). The main entrance to the park lies four blocks southwest of the Zona Rosa. The 1,600-acre park functions as a "green space" for families on weekend outings, cyclists, joggers, and museum-goers. It is also one of the oldest parts of Mexico City, having been inhabited by the Mexica tribe as early as the 13th century. The Mexica poet-king Nezahualcoyotl had his palace here and ordered construction of the aqueduct that brought water to Tenochtitlán. Ahuehuete trees (Moctezuma cypress) still stand from that era, when the woods were used as hunting preserves.

The entrance to the park is guarded by the *Monumento a los Niños Héroes* (Monument to the Boy Heroes), consisting of six marble columns adorned with eaglets. In it are buried the six young cadets who wrapped themselves in the Mexican flag and then jumped to their deaths from the ramparts during the U.S. invasion of 1847. (That war may not take up much space in American textbooks, but to the Mexicans it is still a troubling symbol of their neighbor's aggressive dominance: The war cost Mexico almost half its national territory—the present states of Texas, California, Arizona, New Mexico, and Nevada.)

⑤ The **Castillo de Chapultepec,** like the Palacio Nacional, witnessed the turbulence and grandeur of all Mexican history. In its earliest permutations, its home on the Cerro del Chapulín (Grasshopper Hill) was a Mexica palace, where the Indians made one of their last stands against the Spaniards; later it was a Spanish hermitage, gunpowder plant, and military college. Emperor Maximilian used the castle (parts of which date to 1783) as his residence, and his example was followed by various presidents from 1872 to 1940, when Lázaro Cárdenas decreed that it be turned into the **National History Museum.**

Displays on the museum's ground floor cover Mexican history from the conquest to the revolution; the bathroom, bedroom, tea salon, and gardens were used by Maximilian and his wife, Carlotta, during the 19th century. The ground floor also contains works by 20th-century muralists O'Gorman, Orozco, and Siqueiros, whereas the upper floor is devoted to temporary exhibits, Díaz's malachite vases, and religious art. Because it is situated on top of a hill, the Castillo is accessible by car, on foot (10 minutes), or by a free but unreliable shuttle bus and elevator. *Tel. 5/553–6242. Small admission fee. Open Tues.–Sun. 9:30–5.*

Just down the hill from the Castillo is the **Museo Galeria de la Lucha del Pueblo Mexicano por su Liberatad,** which goes by the more fanciful **Museo del Caracol** (Museum of the Snail), because of its spiral shape. The museum concentrates on the 400 years from the Viceroyalty to the Constitution of 1917, using dioramas and light-and-sound displays that children can appreciate. *Tel. 5/553–6285. Admission free. Open Tues.–Sun. 9–5.*

❻ The **Museo de Arte Moderno** (Museum of Modern Art) is just north of the Castillo on the south side of Reforma. Two rooms are devoted to plastic arts from the 1930s to the 1960s; a third focuses on the past 20 years; and a fourth room and annex house temporary exhibits of contemporary Mexican painting, lithography, sculpture, and photography. *Tel. 5/553–6211. Small admission fee. Open Tues.–Sun. 10–6.*

The private collection of painter Rufino Tamayo now has a permanent home in the sleek and austere **Museo Tamayo.** Tamayo's **❼** unerring eye for great art is evidenced by paintings and sculptures by such contemporary masters as Picasso, Miró, Warhol, and Henry Moore. *In Chapultepec Park, on the north side of Paseo de la Reforma and west of Gandhi, tel. 5/286–6519. Small admission fee. Open Tues.–Sun. 10–6.*

The greatest museum in the country—and arguably one of the **❽** finest archaeological museums anywhere—is the **Museo Nacional de Antropología** (National Museum of Anthropology), just west of the Museo Tamayo. Even its architectural design (by Pedro Ramírez Vázquez) is distinguished. The collection is so extensive—covering some 100,000 square feet—that four hours are barely adequate to see it. However, bilingual guides take you through the highlights in two-hour tours. English guidebooks are available in the bookshop.

Begin in the Orientation Room, which traces the course of Mexican prehistory and the pre-Hispanic cultures of Mesoamerica. There are 12 rooms on the ground floor, including preclassical cultures, Teotihuacán, the Toltecs, Oaxaca, the Maya, and the north and west of Mexico. The so-called Aztec calendar stone and profusely feathered Aztec headdresses, reconstructed Mayan temples, and reproductions of the Mayan paintings from the ruins of Bonampak are just some of the highlights. (The gold diadem from Palenque and other priceless relics, stolen from the museum in the early 1980s, were recovered in June 1989.) Statuary, jewelry, weapons, clay figurines, and pottery evoke the brilliant, quirky, and frequently bloodthirsty civilizations that peopled the subcontinent during Europe's Dark Ages. The nine rooms on the upper floor contain faithful ethnographical displays of current indigenous peoples, using maps, photographs, household objects, folk art, clothing, and religious articles. *Tel. 5/553–6266. Small admission fee. Open Tues.–Sat. 9–6, Sun. and holidays 10–6.*

Other sights in the first section of Chapultepec Park include three small boating lakes; the Casa del Lago, a cultural center and fancy restaurant; a botanical garden; archaeological excavations (visitable by appointment); and the zoo housing Mexico's pandas, gifts from China. **Los Pinos,** the residential palace of the president of Mexico, is located on the park's southern boundary, at Avenida Constituyentes and Parque Lira. It is heavily guarded and cannot be visited. The less crowded second and third sections contain amusement parks (*see* What to See and Do with Children, *below*), the national cemetery, and the **Lienzo Charro** (rodeo).

Time Out After visiting the museums, take a five-minute taxi ride just north of the park to Colonia Polanco, which is quickly upstaging the Zona Rosa as the chic place for shopping and dining. The outdoor tables at **Sanborcito's,** also known as **Restaurante Polanco,** are usually filled by the residents of this well-heeled, tranquil neighborhood. It has a small but moderately priced menu and is especially good for brunch. *Emilio Verde at Julio Castelar, overlooking a lovely park with a statue of Lincoln.*

Reforma wends its leisurely way west into the wealthy neighborhoods of Lomas de Chapultepec, where most of the houses are hidden, fortresslike, behind stone walls.

Tour 3: San Angel and Coyoacán

Numbers in the margin correspond to points of interest on the San Angel and Coyoacán map.

To explore the southern part of the city—which until 50 years ago was separate suburbs—take a taxi or pesero down Avenida Insurgentes. At 34 kilometers (21 miles), the longest avenue in the city, Insurgentes did not exist as such before the 1920s. It is blaring and unabashedly commercial, epitomizing the functional ugliness of much of Mexico City.

❶ Get off at Avenida La Paz. On the east side of Insurgentes is a bizarre monument to revolutionary leader and onetime president Alvaro Obregón. The gray granite *Monumento al General Alvaro Obregón* marks the spot where the national hero Obregón was gunned down in a restaurant in 1928, and the centerpiece inside is none other than Obregón's hand and forearm—eerily preserved in formaldehyde—which he lost in a 1915 battle.

❷ To make the most out of your visit to the next site, try to come on a Saturday, when the indoor and outdoor handicrafts market known as **Bazar Sábado** (Saturday Bazaar) is operating. Cross Avenida Insurgentes on Avenida La Paz, then take the southern fork off Avenida La Paz (Calle Madero) until you come to the **Plaza San Jacinto.** You are now in San Angel, a little colonial enclave of cobblestone streets, gardens drenched in bougainvillea, stone walls, and pastel houses.

Plaza San Jacinto is interesting in its own right. In 1847 about 50 Irish soldiers of St. Patrick's Battalion—who had sided with the Mexican side in the Mexican–American War—had their foreheads branded here with the letter *D* (for deserters) and were then hanged by the Americans. These men had been enticed to swim the Rio Grande and desert the ranks of U.S. General Zachary Taylor by pleas to the historic and religious ties between Spain and Ireland; as settlers in Mexican Texas, they felt their allegiance lay with Mexico, and they were among the bravest fighters in the war. They met their end when the American flag flew over Chapultepec Castle after the death of the *niños héroes* (*see* Tour 2, *above*). A memorial plaque at No.

85

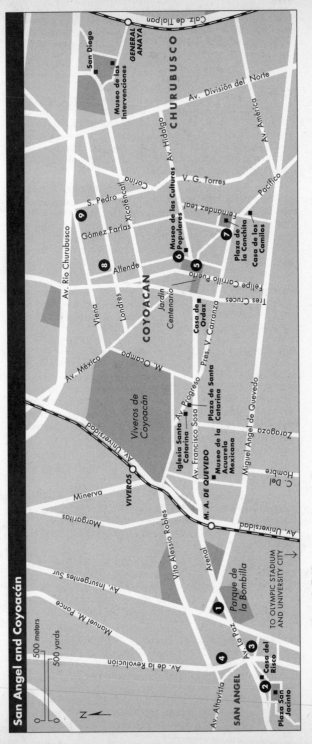

San Angel and Coyoacán

Bazar Sábado, **2**
Casa de la Malinche, **7**
Convento e Iglesia del
Carmen, **3**
*Monumento al General
Alvaro Obregón,* **1**
Museo Alvar y Carmen
T. de Carrillo Gil, **4**

Museo de Frida
Kahlo, **8**
Museo de Leon
Trotsky, **9**
Palacio de Cortés, **6**
Parroquia de San Juan
Bautista, **5**

23 listing their names and expressing Mexico's gratitude for their help in the "unjust North American invasion" now stands in the plaza, where each September a ceremony is conducted in their honor.

One of the prettiest houses on the plaza—and also open to the public—is the **Casa del Mirador** or **Casa del Risco**. It dates from the 18th century, and fountains situated in the patio and abutting the eastern wall explode with broken porcelain, tiles, shells, and mosaics. The **Museo de la Casa del Risco** houses a splendid collection of 14th- to 18th-century European and colonial Mexican paintings as well as period furnishings. *Plaza de San Jacinto 5 & 15, tel. 5/548–2329. Small admission fee. Open weekdays 9–3, Sat. 10–3. Closed Sun.*

The Bazar Sábado is held off to one side of the plaza and specializes in unique high-quality handicrafts at excellent prices. Outside, vendors sell embroidered clothing, leather goods, wooden masks, beads, *amates* (bark paintings), and other trinkets. The better-quality—and higher-priced—goods are found inside, including *animalitos* (painted wooden animals from Oaxaca), glassware, pottery, jewelry, and papier-mâché flowers. There is an indoor restaurant as well. *Open Sat. 10–7.*

After strolling around San Angel, retrace your steps along Calle Madero to Plaza del Carmen, at the corner of Avenida La Paz and Avenida Revolución. The **Convento e Iglesia del Carmen** (Carmelite Convent and Church) were erected by Carmelite friars with the help of an Indian chieftain in 1617; the tile-covered domes and fountains, gardens, and cloisters make these the most interesting examples of colonial religious architecture in this part of the city. The church still operates, but the convent is now the **Museo Regional del Carmen,** with a fine collection of 18th-century religious paintings, icons, mummified corpses, and pre-Hispanic handicrafts. *Av. Revolución 4 at Av. de la Paz. Tel. 5/548–5312. Small admission fee. Open Tues.–Sun. 10–5.*

One of the largest selections of Mexican folk art is on sale at the Fonart branch at Avenida La Paz 17, almost at the corner of Avenida Revolución.

❹ Take Avenida Revolución one block north to the **Museo Alvar y Carmen T. de Carrillo Gil.** This private collection contains murals by Orozco, Rivera, Siqueiros, and other modern artists. *Av. Revolución 1608 at Desierto de los Leones. Tel. 5/548–6467. Open Tues.–Sun. 10–6.*

The next part of the tour is set in Coyoacán, a village that extends east of Avenida Insurgentes and about 1 kilometer (less than a mile) from San Angel. Consider taking a taxi to the Plaza de Santa Catarina on Avenida Miguel Angel Quevedo, about halfway into the center of Coyoacán, as the tour involves a lot of walking.

Coyoacán means "Place of the Coyotes," and according to local legend, a coyote used to bring chickens to a friar who had saved the coyote from being strangled by a snake. Coyoacán was founded by Toltecs in the 10th century and later was settled by the Aztecs, or Mexica. Bernal Díaz Castillo, a Spanish chronicler, wrote that at the time of the conquest there were 6,000 houses. Cortés set up headquarters in Coyoacán during his siege of Tenochtitlán and at one point considered making it his capital. He changed his mind for political reasons, but many of the Spanish buildings left from the two-year period it took to build Mexico City still stand.

Contemporary Coyoacán exudes charm. The village has had many illustrious residents from Mexico's rich and intellectual elite, including Miguel de la Madrid, president of Mexico from 1982 to 1988; Orozco, the muralist; Gabriel Figueroa, cinematographer for Luis Buñuel and John Huston; the film star Dolores del Río; El Indio Fernández, a film director; and writers Carlos Monsivais, Elena Poniatowska, and Jorge Ibargüengoitia. While superficially it resembles San Angel, Coyoacán has a more animated street life.

Most of the houses, if not actually colonial, honor the traditions of colonial Mexican architecture, and the village is very well kept. As you walk east on Avenida Francisco Sosa, a block to your left is the **Viveros de Coyoacán** (Nurseries of Coyoacán), an expansive, tree-filled park. On one side of the Plaza Santa Catarina is the **Iglesia Santa Catarina,** a pretty 16th-century church; in the plaza there is a bust of Mexican historian Francisco Sosa, who lived here and wrote passionately about Coyoacán. Stop in at Avenida Francisco Sosa 202, the **Casa de Jesús Reyes Heroles,** home of the late minister of culture. It is a fine example of 20th-century architecture on the colonial model and is now used as a cultural center. Continuing along Avenida Francisco Sosa, you will pass the 17th-century **Casa de Diego de Ordaz** at the corner of Tres Cruces, a *mudejar* (Spanish-Arabic) structure adorned with inlaid mortar.

You now stand before the portals of the heart of Coyoacán, its main square (Plaza Hidalgo). The adjacent **Jardín Centenario** is a large park, surrounded by two important colonial buildings and outdoor cafés. Small fairs and amateur musical performances are frequent occurrences. The **Parroquia de San Juan Bautista,** one of the first churches to be built in New Spain, lies directly opposite the garden. It was completed in 1582, and its door is decorated with a baroque arch. Perpendicular to the church, on the north side of the garden, sprawls the **Palacio de Cortés,** where Cuauhtémoc was held prisoner. An 18th-century building, it is supposed to have been erected by one of Cortés's descendants from the stones of his original house and is now used as Coyoacán's City Hall.

One of the most powerful symbols of the conquest is located in Coyoacán but, significantly perhaps, is not even marked. This is the **Casa de la Malinche,** the beautiful, red stone house of Malinche, Cortés's Indian mistress and interpreter, whom the Spaniards called Doña María and the Indians called Malintzín. Malinche was instrumental in the conquest by enabling Cortés to communicate with the Náhuatl-speaking tribes he met en route to Tenochtitlán. Today she is a much-reviled Mexican symbol of a traitorous xenophile, hence the term *malinchista,* used to describe anything tainted by foreign influences. The legends say that Cortés's wife died in this house, poisoned by the conquistador; they also say he wrote his famous letter to Emperor Charles V in the house. Mysterious noises are said to destroy the peace of the present inhabitants. The house faces a pretty little square, in the center of which lies an 18th-century church. *Two blocks east of Plaza Hidalgo on Calle Hidalgo, at the corner of Vallarta.*

Time Out   Return to the main square for some refreshments before em-
barking on the next part of the tour. **La Guadalupana,** at the
corner of Higuera and Caballocalco, is a popular cantina from
the 1920s with snacks (such as shrimp broth and *totopos con frijoles,* a kind of corn tortilla with beans), and one of the few in
Mexico City where women can feel comfortable. The
quesadillas served in the little restaurants on Higuera have at-
tained citywide fame.

From the plaza, walk five blocks north on Allende to the corner
of Londres. Remodeled in early 1992, the bright blue adobe
8 house—the **Museo de Frida Kahlo**—is where the painter Frida
Kahlo was born and lived with Diego Rivera from 1929 until
their respective deaths in 1954 and 1957. Kahlo has become
quite a cult figure in recent years, not only because of her paintings—which consist almost entirely of self-portraits, many of
them rather morbid—but because of her bohemian lifestyle
and flamboyant individualism. As a child Kahlo was crippled by
polio, and several years later she was impaled on a tramway
rail; she spent much of her life in casts and excruciating pain.
She had countless operations, including the amputation of a
leg; was addicted to alcohol and drugs; had affairs with Leon
Trotsky and several women; and married Rivera twice and
stuck with him, despite his philandering (including an affair
with her own sister). Kahlo's astounding vitality and originali-
ty are reflected in this house, from the giant papier-mâché skeletons outside and the painted tin retablos on the staircase to
the gloriously decorated kitchen, the wheelchair and paint-
brushes set up at her easel, and the childlike bric-a-brac in her
bedroom. Even if you know nothing about Kahlo, a visit to the
museum—filled also with letters, diaries, clothes, and paintings by Kahlo and other great moderns, including Klee and
Duchamp—will leave you with a strong, visceral impression of
this early feminist. *Londres 127, tel. 5/554–5999. Admission
free. Open Tues.–Sun. 10–6.*

Leon Trotsky lived, was murdered, and his ashes were kept a
short walk away. Go five blocks east on Londres and then two
blocks north on Av. Río Churubusco; his house is at the corner
9 of Viena. From the outside, the **Museo de Leon Trotsky** resembles an anonymous and forbidding fortress, with turrets for
armed guards; it is difficult to believe that it is the home and
final resting place of one of the most important figures of the
Russian Revolution. But that fact only adds to the allure of the
house, which is owned by Trotsky's grandson.

Ring the bell to get in. A volunteer will take you through this
modest, austere dwelling—anyone taller than five feet must
stoop to pass through doorways—to Trotsky's bedroom (with
bullet holes in the walls from the first assassination attempt, in
which the muralist Siqueiros was implicated), his wife's study,
the dining room, and the study where Ramón Mercader finally
drove an ice pick into Trotsky's head. (On his desk, cluttered
with writing paraphernalia and an article he was revising in
Russian, the calendar is open to the fateful day of August 20,
1940.) The volunteers will tell you how Trotsky's teeth left a
permanent scar on Mercader's hand; how he clung to life for 26
hours; what his last words were; and how his death was spon-
sored by the United States. Not all of the volunteers, however,
speak English. *Av. Río Churubusco 410, tel. 5/554–0687. Admission free. Open Tues.–Sun. 10–5.*

What to See and Do with Children

The best place to take children in Mexico is the parks, particularly Chapultepec. It has a **children's zoo** with a miniature railroad for viewing the animals, picnic grounds, and a boating lake. Youngsters can play with the animals, ride ponies, and climb tree houses. *First section of Chapultepec Park. Admission free. Open daily 8–6.*

An amusement park and roller coaster called the **Montaña Rusa** (Russian Mountain) is located in the third section of the park, along with a man-made lake, restaurant, and cafeteria.

Reino Aventura is a 100-acre theme park on the southern edge of the city, comprising six "villages": Mexican, French, Swiss, Polynesian, American, and Children's World. Shows include performances by trained dolphins. *Carretera Picacho a Ajusco, Km 1.5. Admission: about $12, includes entrance and all rides (discounts for senior citizens and children). Open Tues.–Fri. 10–6, weekends 10–8.*

Off the Beaten Track

Colonia Condesa (full name: Hipódromo de la Condesa) is a residential zone with an oval-shape park, the Parque Mexico, which used to be the Hippodrome or racetrack, and around which runs Calle Amsterdam on three sides. The colonia was built in 1902–1903 on the site of a former hacienda, named for a 17th-century countess (*condesa*), and by 1910 the local Jockey Club had opened the Hippodrome, later used for car races and air stunts. During the late 1920s and 1930s, when post-Revolutionary Mexico was returning to stability, a building boom saw the addition of many architecturally similar Art Deco, neo-Hollywood, and neocolonial houses to the neighborhood, giving a pleasant uniformity to the streets.

In the 1940s, Condesa was still an elegant residential community, but by the 1950s and 1960s, formerly one-family dwellings were being converted into multifamily apartments. The colonia lost its cachet, and nowadays it is inhabited by many older Jews and Spanish Civil War refugees of more modest means. Because of this European slant, it is not surprising that the neighborhood is one of the few where bagels are sold and where there are several good German restaurants. It's about a 15-minute walk southeast along Sonora from the *Monumento a los Niños Héroes*, or two blocks west of Avenida Insurgentes on Teotihuacán.

Shopping

Native crafts and specialties from all regions of Mexico are available in the capital, as are designer threads and modern art. The best, most concentrated shopping area is the **Zona Rosa**, an 18-square-block area bounded by Reforma on the north, Havre on the east, Chapultepec on the south, and Varsovia on the west. The neighborhood is chock-full of boutiques, jewelry stores, leather-goods shops, antiques stores, and art galleries, as well as dozens of great little restaurants and coffee shops. Day or night, the Zona Rosa is always lively.

Mexico City Shopping

Acapulco Joe's, **13**

Aero Boutiques, **42**

Antil, **17**

Aries, **9, 39**

Arte en Plata, **19**

Artes Popular en Miniatura, **30**

Bazaar del Centro, **52**

Bazaar Sábado, **38**

Cartier, **12**

Celaya, **45**

Centro Artesanal Buenavista, **54**

Ciudadela Market, **46**

Class, **3**

El Aguila Descalza, **32**

El Palacio de Hierro, **14**

El Puerto de Liverpool, **1**

Feders, **41**

Fiorucci, **24**

Flamma, **16**

Flato, **10**

Fonart, **25, 47**

Gaitán, **33**

Galería Circulo, **29**

Ginatai, **35**

Girasol, **31**

Gucci, **21**

Jardín de Arte, **43**

Joyas de Plata, **32**

Juan Martín Gallery, **11**

La Lagunilla, **48**

La Patty's Boutique, **23**

La Rosa (arcade), **27**

Liverpool, **5, 36**

Los Castillo, **26**

Mercado Insurgentes (Mercado Londres or Mercado Zona Rosa), **20**

Mercado San Juan (Centro Artesanal), **49**

Mexican Opal Company, **8**

Muller's, **15**

Museo de Artes Populares, **50**

Perisur Shopping Center, **40**

Plaza del Angel, **18**

Plaza Polanco, **4**

Portales de los Mercaderes, **51**

Ralph Lauren, **10**

Rubén Torres, **13**

Sanborns, **2, 7, 34, 44**

Suburbia, **6, 37**

Tamacani, **28**

Tane, **22**

Tardán, **53**

Polanco, a choice residential neighborhood along the northeast perimeter of Chapultepec Park, is blossoming with fine shops and boutiques, many of which are branches of Zona Rosa or downtown establishments. Many are located in malls like the huge ultramodern **Plaza Polanco** (Jaime Balmes 11).

There are hundreds of equally good shops spread out along the length of Avenida Insurgentes, as well as along Avenida Juárez and in the old downtown area. The major department store chains are **Liverpool** (at Av. Insurgentes Sur 1310, Mariano Escobedo 425, and in the Plaza Satélite and Perisur shopping centers), **Suburbia,** which is the new name for **Paris Londres** (at Horacio 203, Sonora 180, Av. Insurgentes Sur 1235, and also in Plaza Satélite and Perisur), and **El Palacio de Hierro** (at the corner of Durango and Salamanca), which is noted for fashions by well-known designers at prices now on par with those found in the United States. The posh and pricey shopping mall **Perisur** is out on the southern edge of the city near where the Periférico Expressway meets Avenida Insurgentes. **Plaza Satélite,** an ultramodern mall, is at the city's northern edge on the Anillo Periférico. Department stores are generally open Mondays, Tuesdays, Thursdays, and Fridays from 10 AM to 7 PM, and on Wednesdays and Saturdays from 10 AM to 8 PM.

Sanborns is a minidepartment store chain with 19 branches in Mexico City alone. Those most convenient for tourists are at Madero 4 (its original store in the House of Tiles, downtown); on the Reforma, one at the Angel monument and another at the Diana Fountain; and in the Zona Rosa, corner of Niza and Hamburgo. They feature a good selection of quality ceramics and handicrafts (they can ship anywhere), and most have restaurants or coffee shops, a pharmacy, and periodical and book departments carrying English-language publications.

Under the auspices of the National Council for Culture and Arts, **Fonart** (National Fund for Fomenting Handicrafts) operates six stores in Mexico City and others around the country. The most convenient locations are at Londres 136, 2nd floor, Zona Rosa, and at Juárez 89, downtown just west of Alameda Park. Prices are fixed, and the diverse, top-quality folk art and handcrafted furnishings from all over Mexico represent the best artisans. Major sales at near wholesale prices are held at the main store-warehouse (Av. Patriotismo 691, Col. Mixcoac) during the second half of March, June, September and November.

A Saturday "must" for shoppers and browsers is a visit to the **Bazaar Sábado** (Saturday Bazaar) at Plaza San Jacinto in the southern San Angel district (*see* Tour 3, *above*). Inside a converted 18th-century mansion, dozens of fine shops sell handicrafts and regional clothing; an art show and handicraft stands are set up in the adjacent square. On Sundays, over 100 artists exhibit and sell their paintings and sculptures at the **Jardín del Arte** (Garden of Art) in Parque Sullivan, just northeast of the Reforma-Insurgentes intersection. Along the west side of the park, a colorful weekend *mercado* (market) with scores of food stands is also worth a visit.

The following list will get you started. As you explore, you will find hundreds more.

Zona Rosa

Arcades **La Rosa,** a sparkling, new shopping arcade between Amberes and Génova, opened in 1991 and houses 72 prestigious shops and boutiques. It spans the entire depth of the block from Londres to Hamburgo with entrances on both streets. The pink neo-colonial **Plaza del Angel** (Londres 161) has a *Centro de Antigüedades* (antiques center) with several fine shops. On Saturday, together with other vendors, they set up a flea market in the arcades and patios. On Sunday, bibliophiles gather here to sell, peruse, and buy collectors' books and periodicals.

Clothing **Acapulco Joe's** (3 locations: Amberes 9, also in Polanco at Mazaryk 310 and 318) has great T-shirts, beachwear, and hip unisex sportsclothes. **Rubén Torres** (Amberes 9) has a wide selection of sportswear, from jerseys and jumpsuits to T-shirts and shorts, all nicely designed and well made. **Guess** (Amberes 17) features chic denim sportswear for guys and gals. **Fiorucci** (Londres 138 at Amberes) features famous Italian designer funwear for daytime or evening, activewear, beachwear, T-shirts, and sweaters. Next door at Londres 140, **La Patty's Boutique,** open Sundays, has two floors replete with top Mexican-label casuals for guys and gals.

Designers **Cartier** (Amberes 9, Zona Rosa, and the lobby of the Stouffer Presidente in Polanco) sells genuine designer jewelry and clothes, under the auspices of the French Cartier. However, **Gucci** (Hamburgo 136) has no connection with the European store of the same name; nevertheless, it has a fine sellection of shoes, gloves, and handbags. **Ralph Lauren** (Amberes 21) is the home of Polo sportswear made in Mexico under license and sold at Mexican prices.

Galleries The **Juan Martín Gallery** (Amberes 17) is one of the city's best avant-garde studios. **Galería Círculo** (Hamburgo 112) displays and sells the works of such contemporary artists as Climent and Tamayo, as well as prints by Dalí, Picasso, Miró, and others.

Jewelry The owner of **Los Castillo** (Amberes 41) developed a unique method of melding silver, copper, and brass, and is considered by many to be Taxco's top silversmith. The exclusive **Flato** (Amberes 21) sells original pieces by the internationally known jeweler Paul Flato, who specializes in gold. Taxco silver of exceptional style is sold at **Arte en Plata** (Amberes 24 and Londres 162) with many designs inspired by pre-Hispanic art. **Pelletier** (Amberes 15) sells fine jewelry and watches. **Tane** (Amberes 70, Zona Rosa; Edgar Allan Poe 68, in Polanco; and other locations) is a treasure trove of superb silver works—jewelry, flatware, candelabra, museum-quality reproductions of antique pieces, and bold new designs by young Mexican silversmiths. The **Mexican Opal Company** (Hamburgo 203) is run by Japanese who are very big on opals. They sell set and loose stones as well as a selection of jewelry in silver and gold.

Leather For leather goods you have more than a few choices in Mexico City. **Ginatai** (Niza 46) stocks excellent leather suits, boots, and purses; and **Gaitán** (Copenhague 32, corner of Hamburgo) features an extensive array of leather coats, luggage, golf bags, and saddles. **Aries** (Florencia 14 and Plaza Polanco) is Mexico's finest purveyor of leather goods, with a superb selection of clothes, shoes, and accessories for both men and women. The prices are high. Just down the street, **Antil** (Florencia 22) also specializes in high-quality leather goods.

Mexican Handicrafts The **Mercado Insurgentes** (also called **Mercado Zona Rosa**) is an entire block deep, with entrances on both Londres and Liverpool (between Florencia and Amberes). This is a typical neighborhood public market with one big difference: Most of the stalls (222 of them) sell crafts. You can find all kinds of handmade items—including serapes and ponchos, baskets, pottery, silver, and onyx, as well as regional Mexican dresses and costumes.

Girasol (Génova 39) has a whimsical selection of hand-loomed fabrics and delightful hand-embroidered gowns and skirts. Handwoven wool rugs, tapestries, and fabrics with original and unusual designs can be found at **Tamacani** (Amberes 38).

The Unusual **Arte Popular en Miniatura** (Hamburgo 130) is a tiny shop filled with tiny things, from dollhouse furniture and lead soldiers to miniature nativity scenes. **Flamma** (Hamburgo 167, at the corner of Florencia) is a town house that sells a beautiful array of handmade candles. **Muller's** (Florencia 52, corner of Londres) has just about everything that can be made from Puebla onyx from jewelry to dining tables.

Downtown

The Zócalo and Alameda Park areas have interesting markets for browsing and buying handicrafts and curios; polite bargaining is customary. The biggest is the **Centro Artesanal Buenavista** (Aldama 187, by the Buenavista Central Train Station). **La Lagunilla** market attracts antique hunters who know how to determine authenticity, and also coin collectors. The best day is Sunday when flea market stands are set up outside (on Libertad, just east of Paseo de la Reforma Norte), with everything from collectibles, to interesting knickknacks, to junk. Within the colonial walls of **La Ciudadela** market (Balderas, about 4 blocks south of Avenida Juárez) are 344 artisans' stalls selling a variety of good handicrafts from all over the country.

Museo de Artes Populares (Museum of Arts and Crafts) could well be a museum, but is in fact a large store displaying and selling an array of folk art and handicrafts—pottery, ceramics, glassware, textiles, etc.—from practically every region of the country. Housed in an early 18th-century convent (across the street from Alameda Park and the Juárez Monument, at Juárez 44), it is open 7 days a week.

Bazaar del Centro (downtown, at Isabel la Católica 30, just below Madero) is a restored late-17th-century noble mansion built around a garden courtyard that houses several chic boutiques, top-quality handicraft shops, and prestigious jewelers such as Aplijsa, known for its fine gold, silver, pearls, and gemstones. Other shops sell Taxco silver, Tonalá stoneware, and Mexican tequilas and liqueurs. It is elegant, worth a visit, and also has a congenial bar.

Portales de los Mercaderes (Merchants' Arcade) has attracted merchants since 1524. The arcade extends along the entire west side of the Zócalo, between Madero and 16 de Septiembre avenues. Today it is lined with jewelry shops, selling gold (sometimes by the gram) and authentic Taxco silver at prices lower than in Taxco itself where the overhead is higher. In the middle of the arcade (Plaza de la Constitución 17) is **Tardán,** an unusual shop specializing in fine quality and fashionable men's hats of every imaginable type and style.

Celaya (Cinco de Mayo 13) in the downtown historic section, is a decades-old haven for those with a sweet tooth. It specializes in candied pineapple, papaya, guava, and other exotic fruits, almond-paste, candied walnut rolls, and *cajeta*, a typical Mexican dessert of thick caramelized milk.

Feder's (2 locations: the factory at Mérida 90 in Colonia Roma and a booth at Bazar Sábado, Plaza San Jacinto 11, San Angel) has great hand-blown glass, Tiffany-style lamps, and artistic wrought iron.

At the Airport

For truly last-minute shopping, **Aero Boutiques** at the Benito Juárez Airport (upstairs, just after you complete immigration departure procedures) is a comprehensive duty-free store selling, among the usual imports, a fine selection of tequila, Mexican rums and liqueurs, Cuban cigars, and some Mexican handicrafts. Have your passport and boarding pass handy to show the cashier; all major credit cards are accepted.

Sports

Bullfights

The main season is the dry season, around November through March, when celebrated *matadores* appear at **Plaza México,** the world's largest bullring, which seats 40,000. Gray Line Tours offers bullfight tour packages (*see* Guided Tours in Essential Information, *above*), or tickets, which range from about $2 to $25, can be purchased at hotel travel desks. Try the bullring ticket booths on Saturdays between 11 AM and 2 PM or Sundays between 11 AM to 3:30 PM for tickets as well. The ring is located next to the Cuidad de Deportes sports complex, and the show goes on at 4 PM. *Calle A. Rodín s/n, Col. Nápoles, tel. 5/ 563–3959.*

Golf

The major hotels should be able to arrange guest privileges at the five private 18-hole courses around Mexico City, except on weekends, when tee times are at a premium. The fashionable **Club Campestre de la Ciudad de México** (Mexico City Country Club) has a golf course, pool, gym, and tennis and fronton courts. Tourists are admitted to these and other private clubs so bring your Tourist Card. *Calzada Tlalpan 1978, tel. 5/549– 3040.*

Horse Racing

The season at the beautiful **Hipódromo de las Américas** lasts from mid-January through December, when thoroughbreds run daily except Mondays and Wednesdays. Betting is pari-mutuel. The races are especially enjoyable to watch from the swank Derby or Jockey Club restaurants. Tickets can be purchased at hotel travel desks or at the track, which is located in the northwest section of the city near the Querétaro Highway. *Av. Conscripto y Av. Periférico, tel. 5/557–4999.*

Jai Alai

You can watch and bet on men playing this lightning-fast Basque-style handball game at **Frontón México** (on the northwest corner of the Plaza de la República), daily except Fridays and Sundays, 6 PM–1 AM. Women's matches are played at **Frontón Metropolitano** (Bahía de Todos los Santos 190), daily except Sundays, 4 PM–10 PM. Betting, which goes on while the games are being played, is a fascinating skill in itself; instructions on the betting sheets are in Spanish and English.

Jogging

There are jogging tracks in Chapultepec Park and at the *Villa Olímpica* (Olympic Village). Another joggers' favorite is along the pastoral paths of the Coyoacán Nurseries by the Viveros Station of the #3 metro line. Early morning runners will probably see young novice bullfighters there going through their training maneuvers. Keep in mind, by the way, that air quality is often poor and this is the highest city in North America—7,349 feet/2,240 meters above sea level—so take it easy until your heart and lungs become accustomed to the altitude.

Tennis

Tennis buffs should consider staying at one of the hotels (*see* Lodging, *below*) that have courts on site. **Club Reyes,** three blocks from Bosque Chapultepec (tel. 5/277–2690), is open daily from 7 AM to 9 PM. Call ahead for reservations. Facilities of the **Club Deportivo Chapultepec** (Chapultepec Sports Club) include a swimming pool, gym, horseback riding, and tennis courts. The Davis Cup matches are played here. *Mariano Escobedo, across from the Hotel Camino Real, tel. 5/589–1200.*

Water Sports

The best place to swim is at your hotel pool. There are numerous public swimming pools in the city, and the vast **Cuemanco** sports park (Canal de Cuemanco, on the way to Xochimilco) has an immense pool as well as facilities for every imaginable kind of sport, including an artificial lake for canoeing. Rowers can ply their sport in the lakes of Chapultepec Park. Rentals are nearby.

Near Mexico City are many outdoor sporting opportunities. You can enjoy boating, freshwater fishing, swimming and water sports on Lake Tequesquitengo and Lake Zempoala (near Cuernavaca), Lake Avándaro (Valle de Bravo) and Valsequillo Dam (near Puebla). Take up tennis, horseback riding, or golf in Cuernavaca, Tehuacán, Puebla, Valle de Bravo, and other cities and towns.

Dining

By Frank (Pancho) Shiell

Frank Shiell has lived in Mexico so long he forgets he's not Mexican.

Mexico City has been a culinary capital ever since the time of Moctezuma. Chronicles tell of the daily banquet extravaganzas prepared for the slender Aztec emperor by his palace chefs. Over 300 different kinds of dishes were served for every meal, comprising vast assortments of meats and fowls seasoned in dozens of ways; limitless fruits, vegetables, and herbs; and freshwater fish and fresh seafoods that were rushed to Tenochtitlan from both seacoasts by sprinting relay runners.

Until the 15th century, Europeans had never seen indigenous Mexican eatables such as corn, chiles of all varieties, tomatoes, potatoes, pumpkin, squash, avocado, turkey, cacao (chocolate), and vanilla. In turn, the colonization brought European gastronomic influence and ingredients—wheat, onion, garlic, olives, citrus fruits, cattle, sheep, goats, chickens, pigs (and lard for frying)—and ended up broadening the already complex pre-Hispanic cuisine into one of the most multifaceted and exquisite in the world: traditional Mexican.

Mexico's food, like Mexican art, is just as diverse and abundant as its geography. Distinct regional specialties typify each of the republic's 32 states and even the different provinces within the states. Fresh ingredients are bountiful, recipes are passed down through generations, and preparation requires much loving care, and a lot of patience. (Mexican gastronomes are dismayed by foreigners' glaring misconceptions of Mexican food as essentially tacos, enchiladas and burritos; they are bewildered by "Tex-Mex," and appalled by Taco Bell.)

Today's cosmopolitan Mexico City, with some 15,000 restaurants, is a gastronomic melting pot. Here you can find establishments ranging from simple family-style eateries to five-star world-class restaurants. In addition, there are fine international restaurants specializing in cuisines of practically every foreign culture. Among them, the most prevalent are Spanish and haute-cuisine French—France also invaded Mexico and influenced its eating traditions.

In the past decade a renaissance of Mexican cooking has brought about a new wave known as *cocina mexicana moderna* (modern Mexican cuisine), which is featured in many Mexico City restaurants. Emphasis is on the back-to-basics, delicate tastes of traditional regional dishes served in smaller portions with refined aesthetic presentation. Also significant in this modern trend is the revival of ancient indigenous cuisine, when frying and cholesterol were nonexistent, and foods, especially fish, were baked, grilled, or steamed in leaves.

Mexico City mealtime hours are 7–11 AM for breakfast (*desayuno*), 1–4 PM for lunch (*comida*), and 7 PM–midnight for dinner (*cena*). At deluxe restaurants, dress is formal (coat and tie), and reservations are required as noted below. For tourists on the run there are American-style coffee shops (VIPS, Denny's, Shirley's, and Sanborns) all over the city; many are open 24 hours.

The following selection of recommended restaurants is organized by cuisine and price range. Those highly recommended (regardless of price range) are indicated by a star ★.

Category	Cost*
Very Expensive	over $45
Expensive	$30–$45
Moderate	$15–$30
Inexpensive	under $15

per person, excluding drinks, service, and sales tax (10%)

French

After Mexican and international, French restaurants are the most popular in Mexico City and exist in all price categories.

Very Expensive   **Fouquet's de Paris.** Don't be put off by the dazzling rug in the lobby of the Camino Real hotel. Enter the restaurant and you'll find a haven of peace and tranquility. The atmosphere tends to be impersonal, however, and the service formal and sedate. It's worth reserving a window table for a view of the attractive patio. The dining room, while elegant, won't win any prizes for interior design. The best pâtés in Mexico and tender and juicy lamb chops are part of the diverse and stylish menu. Fouquet's is a pioneer in presenting international cooking festivals, when visiting chefs raise the standards a notch or two. The desserts are in a class all their own. Outstanding are the sorbets, such as delicately flavored passion fruit and *guayaba* (guava). The mousses, cakes, and pastries are light and delicious. *Hotel Camino Real, tel. 5/203–2121. Reservations advised. Jacket and tie required. AE, DC, MC, V. No lunch weekends.*

Expensive
★   **Champs Elysées.** On the corner of Amberes and Reforma, commanding an impressive view of the Independence (Angel) monument, is one of the bastions of haute cuisine in Mexico City. Champs Elysées is never far from the the top of any list of the best restaurants in the capital. The variety of sauces served with both meat and fish dishes is impressive, with the Hollandaise sauce over sea bass or red snapper probably taking top honors. Regulars find either the roast duck (carved at your table) or the pepper steak hard to resist. Vegetables are all steamed to perfect firmness and, of particular note, is the fulsome cheese board. The price of a meal is above average, but the investment will be well worth it. *Amberes 1, Zona Rosa, tel. 5/514–0450. Reservations advised. Jacket preferred. AE, DC, MC, V.*

Villa Reforma. Six years ago Nick Noyes and Philippe Gerondeau took over an ailing restaurant on Paseo de la Reforma and turned it into a delightful French provincial restaurant. The house and grounds are attractively laid out with two floors of dining areas decorated in peaches and yellows. Downstairs is a windowed terrace and a row of five bricked arches that are overgrown with ivy. The cuisine is fussier than provincial French, but not quite haute. The chef (formerly of Fouquet's de Paris) produces some innovative specialties: cream of artichoke soup, duckling in strawberry sauce, turkey steak in lemon sauce, and red snapper in avocado sauce. The vegetable dishes are admirable. Eggplant with a basil sauce, ratatouille, and a *jardinière de légumes dauphinois* (broccoli, asparagus, and cauliflower in a Hollandaise sauce) can all be enjoyed with the main dish or as a vegetarian option. Villa Reforma bakes its own breads and pastries and is a very popu-

Mexico City Dining

Los Irabien, **32**
Maxim's de Paris, **9**
Prendes, **26**
Restaurante
Tandoor, **11**
San Angel Inn, **31**
Suntory, **24**
Villa Reforma, **2**

lar breakfast spot; a sumptuous brunch is served on Sunday. *Paseo de la Reforma 2210, Lomas de Chapultepec, tel. 5/596–0123 or 5/596–4355. Reservations advised. Jacket and tie required for dinner. AE, DC, MC, V.*

Moderate   **La Petite France.** Located in the Mediterranean-looking Pasaje de Polanco, this could be on the Côte d'Azur. Tables under a canopy stretch out onto the street, while the yellows and greens of the decor, the many hanging plants, and the white cast-iron furniture suggest dining in a garden. The menu is strong on imagination, with such specialties as fish soup with Pernod and roast lobster with basil. The chicken-liver mousse is a delicate alternative to coarser pâtés such as duck. The stuffed mushrooms and *moules Provençales* (mussels Provençale) are typically Mediterranean dishes that rely on mixed herbs for flavor. Fish dishes loom large with *truite meunière* (trout, lightly fried and served with lemon), a giant prawn brochette, and deep-fried sea bass claiming most attention. The lamb chops are tender, although the mint sauce is an alarming shade of electric green. Beautifully garnished and presented, the dishes catch the eye with a colorful, good selection of steamed vegetables. *Av. Presidente Masaryk 360, Col. Polanco, tel. 5/250–4470 or 5/548–3918. Reservations accepted. Dress: informal. AE, DC, MC, V. No dinner Sun.*

Inexpensive   **El Buen Comer.** One of the more original Polanco eating spots, El Buen Comer (eating well) consists of not more than 20 tables in the front yard and garage of a private house. It is so popular at lunchtime that reservations are essential. The entrance is discreet and can easily be missed; indeed, the atmosphere inside is more that of a large private lunch party than a restaurant. Oysters are meticulously cleaned and scrubbed before opening and then are left in their own water, not washed under the faucet, as is the usual Mexican habit. They are served with an unusual vinegar and chopped shallot sauce, but are so tasty they can be savored with just a squeeze of lime. The four house pâtés are excellent. A favorite main course of the habitués is quiche Lorraine, cooked to order in an individual dish. The quiche royale with shrimps is a must for seafood lovers. The fondues are exquisite. Whole steaks can be served to order with fine herbes, pepper, tartar, or shallots, which are a rare commodity in Mexico. The clientele consists of people from the business community who insist on eating well but don't want a heavy or complicated meal. El Buen Comer makes a great stop after shopping in Polanco. *Edgar Allan Poe 50, Col. Polanco, tel. 5/203–5337 or 5/545–8057. Reservations required at lunch. Dress: casual. No credit cards. Closed Sun. and daily at 5 PM.*

Indian

Moderate   **Restaurante Tandoor.** There is much cause for rejoicing, now that a respectable Indian restaurant has come to town. Owner Niaz Ahmad Siddiqui makes regular tours to the subcontinent to forage for dishes that can successfully be transplanted to Mexico. The venue is a small house in Polanco. The front room can seat about 30 people. The furnishings are makeshift, but no one seems to care; the satisfied customers who line up outside at lunchtime certainly don't. Everything here is homemade in the traditional Indian way. Curries are superlative and you can choose the desired spiciness. Rave reviews for the chicken and almond curry, which retains its delicate nutty flavor while still having its full spicy impact, and for the mutton *gosht,* a mix of large chunks of mutton cooked with spinach in a mild but complex sauce. All the *vindaloos* (a typical, very hot curry) are mouth searing, and the kitchen even manages a good chicken tandoor. The rice is excellent, made with a selection of sumptuous spices, such as cardamom, caraway, and saffron. Breads such as nan, chapatis, and papadums are also available. *Lope de Vega 341a, Col. Polanco, tel. 5/203–0045. Reservations advised. Dress: informal. AE, DC, MC, V.*

International

Very Expensive **Estoril.** Now in two locations: Rosa Martin runs the establishment occupying a refurbished 1930's house in fashionable Polanco; her daughter Diana manages the original Estoril in an elegant Zona Rosa townhouse. Both use only the very best ingredients and serve international cuisine with a Mexican flair; their forte, however, is traditional Mexican. The *perejil* frito (fried parsley) is a popular starter. The smoked oyster mousse and cold avocado soup are delicate, while the *caldo de gallina con cognac* (chicken broth with cognac) and *crepas de chicharrón con salsa verde* (fried pork rinds with green sauce) are distinctive. The main dishes offer some unusual taste combinations: giant prawns in chablis or curry sauces and sea bass in fresh coriander sauce. To finish, try either the delicious *tarte tatin* (an upside-down apple tart with caramel) or the homemade sorbets, especially the refreshing mint flavor. *Zona Rosa: Genova 75, tel. 5/511–3421. Polanco: Alejandro Dumas 24, Col. Polanco, tel. 5/531–4896. Reservations advised. Jacket and tie required. AE, DC, MC, V.*

★ **Hacienda de los Morales.** This is a Mexican institution and a fine example of a hacienda-turned-restaurant. The original building dates from the 16th century. The atmosphere is colonial Mexico in the grand style—huge spaces of terra-cotta and luxuriant green, with dark wood beams. One can just glimpse a bygone world in places such as these. The menu combines both international and Mexican cuisine with some imaginative variations on both. The *sopa de mariscos del Golfo* weighs in as a substantial seafood soup. The walnut soup is served either hot or cold and is a delicate and unusual specialty. Attention to detail is shown in the choice of cured hams—Parma or Serrano—with melon slices. Fish is seemingly unlimited, with a rainbow trout meunière (lightly sautéed in butter, served with lemon juice and parsley), sea bass *marinière* (in a white wine sauce), and a mixed seafood gratin. The charcoal-broiled grain-fed chicken has a distinct flavor, and the paillarde is always of the highest quality. Vegetables are ordered separately, and the sautéed string beans, broccoli, and spinach all arrive lightly cooked with their natural goodness intact. The Hacienda de los Morales is regularly hired for functions, so don't be surprised if there's a lot of activity. *Vázquez de Mella 525, Col. Los Morales, tel. 5/540–3225. Reservations necessary. Dress: jacket advised. AE, DC, MC, V.*

★ **Les Célébrités.** In addition to superb French fare, this elegant restaurant also serves the best in Mexican cuisine. When the Nikko Hotel opened in 1987, Chef Joel Roubenchon, one of the creators of nouvelle cuisine in France, came to Mexico to set up this restaurant off the hotel lobby. With him came the ultimate in restaurant technology and a policy of using only the very finest ingredients. He organized an Annual Gastronomy Festival, held in the fall, featuring the creative modern Mexican cuisine of celebrity Mexican chef-author-painter Marta Chapa, whose original work-of-art dishes are now permanently on the menu: medallion of lobster in *guayaba* (guava) sauce; salmon roll stuffed with lemon mousse in grapefruit sauce; and, for dessert, pomegranate sherbet or red and green prickly pear sherbet. *Hotel Nikko, Campos Elíseos 204, Col. Polanco, tel. 5/ 203–4020. Reservations required. Dress: jacket and tie required for dinner. AE, DC, MC, V. Open Mon.–Fri. 6:30 AM– 11 PM. Dinner only Sat. Closed Sun.*

★ **Maxim's de Paris.** Here you can enjoy the best French food anywhere and, better yet, nouvelle Mexican cuisine prepared by the creative hands of Chef Yves Ferrer. His pre-Hispanic *crepas de huitlacoche* (crepes of corn fungus) are a modern delicacy. Inspired by Mexico's great wealth of foodstuffs, Ferrer has conceived original dishes such as fillet of sea bass in jellied sauce of beef bone marrow. Operated under the auspices of the original Maxim's in Paris—the menu has the same design— this spacious but intimate restaurant is located in the Hotel Stouffer Presidente. Decor is Parisian art deco under a stained-glass ceiling; the wine cellar is nonpareil, and the service impeccable. *Hotel Stouffer Presidente, Campos Elíseos 218, Col. Polanco, tel. 5/254–0033. Reservations required. Dress: jacket and tie required. AE, DC, MC, V. Lunch and dinner Mon.–Fri. Dinner only Sat. Closed Sun.*

Moderate– Expensive **Bellinghausen.** This is one of the most pleasant lunch spots in the Zona Rosa. The partially covered summery courtyard at the back, set off by an ivy-laden wall, is a magnet at lunchtime for executives and tourists alike. A veritable army of waiters, in striped blue-and-white jackets, scurry back and forth serving such tried-and-true favorites as *sopa de hongos* (mushroom soup); a delicious chicken broth served à la Mexicana with rice, raw onion, avocado, and a coriander garnish; and a *filete chemita* (broiled steak with mashed potatoes). The *higaditos de pollo* (chicken livers) with a side order of sauteed spinach is another winner. Sometimes it even has *charalitos* (tiny fish from Lake Patzcuaro), which are a must if available. Other specials include *gusanos de maguey* (worms from the maguey cactus), *cabrito* (baby goat), roast lamb, and Spanish paella. *Londres 95, Zona Rosa, tel. 5/511–9035 or 5/511–1056. Reservations advised. Dress: informal. AE, DC, MC, V. Closed Sun.*

Inexpensive **Andersons.** Mexico is a city of institutions: Andersons is one of its most lighthearted. This is the headquarters of a chain (some branches are called Carlos 'n' Charlies) with outlets in Acapulco, Cancún and Ixtapa, among other cities. The decor is all card-table green and white. Photographs and paraphernalia of patrons past and present adorn the walls. The menu is international with a dash of Mexican. The place is well known for its multiple varieties of cooked oysters and *ostiones 444* (12 oysters baked with bacon, garlic, and cheese toppings). Other successes include Oriental chicken, which comes in a tangy sweet-and-sour sauce, and the *puntas de filete à la Mexicana* (tender and piquant sirloin tips). On the fish side, the *huachinango* (white-fleshed ocean fish) in green sauce is an unusual creation. Tables are rather cramped and the service can be fast and furious to the point of being hyper, so don't come if you want a romantic dinner. *Paseo de la Reforma 382, Col. Juárez, tel. 5/525–1006. No reservations. Dress: casual. AE, DC, MC, V.*

Italian

Moderate **La Lanterna.** The Petterino family has run this two-story restaurant in the same building for 20 years. The downstairs has the rustic feel of a northern Italian trattoria, with the cramped seating adding to the intimacy. Upstairs is more spacious. All the pastas are made on the premises, and the Bolognese sauce, in particular, is a local favorite. The management is especially proud of its *osso buco à la milanaise* (the real bone and not the knuckle, which is often passed off as such). Other dishes worth trying include a raw artichoke salad, *conejo al Salmi* (rabbit in a wine sauce), *filete al burro nero* (steak in black butter), and *saltimbocca à la Romana* (veal and ham in Marsala sauce). *Paseo de la Reforma 458, Col. Cuahtémoc, tel. 5/207–9969. No reservations. Dress: casual but neat. MC, V. Closed Sun.*

Japanese

Very Expensive **Suntory.** With restaurants in Boston, Singapore, Paris, and São Paulo, the Suntory name has become synonymous with the best in Japanese dining. As you enter, by way of three rocks in a bed of well-raked sand, you are transported into a small-town patio in a dense green garden. In this enchanted world you are not absolved of the difficulty of choice. Is it the teppanyaki room to watch your fresh meat or fish prepared with a variety of vegetables? Or perhaps the shabu-shabu room beckons with wafer-thin sashimi and a copper pot of steaming vegetable broth in which to cook elegant slices of beef? If you are a raw-fish enthusiast, perhaps the sushi bar? Prices are high, especially for Mexico, but the argument holds that raw materials of the highest quality will always cost, wherever you decide to eat. *Torres Adalid 14, Col. Del Valle, tel. 5/536–9432. Reservations advised. Dress: neat but casual. AE, DC, MC, V.*

Mexican

Very Expensive **Isadora.** Some of Mexico City's most inventive and exciting cooking takes place in this converted private house in Polanco. The three smallish dining rooms have a 1920s feel but are uncharacteristically ascetic—pale walls dabbed with modern-art squiggles. The management sponsors "cooking festivals," and virtually every month the kitchen produces dishes from a different country. The basic menu changes six times a year, and over that same period it will include three Mexican food fests. What might be called the set menu features coarse duck pâté and excellent seafood pasta, with no holding back on the juicy prawns, shellfish, and squid. Ice creams, meringues, and chocolate cake for dessert benefit from the addition of the chef's delicate, pale green mint sauce. *Molière 50, Col. Polanco, tel. 5/520–7901. Reservations necessary. Jacket and tie required. AE, DC, MC, V. Closed Sun.*

★ **Los Irabien.** This beautiful dining area filled with leafy plants and the owner's impressive art collection is a worthwhile stop for the gourmet and culture hound alike. Chef Enrique Estrada, who trained at the Waldorf Astoria in New York, is one of Mexico's finest exponents of nouvelle cuisine à la Mexicaine. His *ensalada Irabien* triumphs as a mixture of smoked salmon, abalone, prawn, quail eggs, lettuce, and watercress; and his *ensalada Valle de Bravo* is no less impressive, with Serrano ham, apple, quail eggs, mushrooms, Gruyère, and walnuts. Two outstanding entrées include the nopal cactus stuffed with fish fillet in garlic and the fillet steak in strawberry sauce *à la pimienta*. Less exotic dishes, such as a juicy prime rib of beef, are also available, and lavish care in preparation and presentation is evident in all courses. Los Irabien is one of the city's breakfast spots par excellence. Where else could one be tempted by *huevos de codorniz huitzilopochtli* (quail eggs with tortilla on a bed of *huitlacoche* in a squash-blossom sauce)? *Av. de la Paz 45, Col. San Angel, tel. 5/660–2382. Reservations advised. Jacket and tie required. AE, DC, MC, V.*

San Angel Inn. If architectural style and natural setting were everything, the San Angel Inn would consistently head the list. In the south of the city, this magnificent old hacienda and exconvent, with its elegant grounds and immaculately tended gardens, is both a joy to the eye and an inspiration to the palate. Whether you're enjoying a quiet aperitif on the cool patio or seated in the exquisitely decorated dining room, the San Angel Inn will claim the full attention of all your senses. The dark mahogany furniture, crisp white table linens, and beautiful blue-and-white Talavera place settings all combine to touch just that right note of restrained opulence. There are many dishes to be recommended, especially the *crepas de huitlacoche* (corn-fungus crepes) and the *sopa de tortilla* (tortilla soup). The *puntas de filete* (sirloin tips) are liberally laced with chili, as they should be, and the *huachinango* (red snapper) is offered in a variety of ways. Desserts—from light and crunchy meringues to gâteaux bulging with cream—can be rich to the point of decadence. *Calle Palmas 50, Col. San Angel Inn, tel. 5/548–4514 or 5/548–6840. Reservations necessary. Jacket required. AE, DC, MC, V.*

Expensive **Lincoln.** Lincoln, with its portrait of the great statesman in the entrance, is reminiscent of a New England club—leather upholstery, discreet dining booths, and plenty of dark wood to provide a serious, rather disciplined atmosphere. Fish is the main draw, although the traditional Mexican menu does offer some meat dishes. The salsa verde, with large chunks of cheese, onion, and *perejil* (parsley), is an ideal complement to the appetizers. From there the range and choice are impressive. Soups include such delicacies as *sopa de almeja* (clam soup), and a thick crab soup. Among the main dishes, the *huachinango a la Veracruzana* is notable. A common dish in Mexico, it is here distinguished by its extraordinary freshness and its sauce, which avoids being watery, a common pitfall in other establishments. The typical *albóndigas en chipotle* (meatballs in hot chile sauce) is another favorite. Desserts are not designed to be stunning; *arroz con leche* (something like a rice pudding) or *natilla* (liqueur-flavored custard) are an acceptable way to round off a meal. *Revillagigedo 24, Col. Centro, tel. 5/510–1468. Reservations accepted. Dress: casual but neat. AE, DC, MC, V.*

Prendes. This downtown institution, first opened in 1892, is back in business under new ownership after having been closed down due to earthquake damage. In fact, the building is still tilted. There is an air of history and legend—the President of Mexico dines here, as did his predecessors. Trotsky ate here with Ramón Mercader, who axed him to death two days later. The decor is minimal but is highlighted by the famous Prendes murals, which depict such celebrities as Gary Cooper and Walt Disney dining here. Prendes features some traditional Mexican dishes, but emphasis is now on delicate and decorative nouvelle Mexican cuisine. Oysters, *ceviche* (raw fish marinated in lime juice, tomatoes, onions, and chile) or a cream of maize soup are typical starters. The *filete chemita* (fillet of beef) with some delicious mashed potatoes and the fillet of fish meunière with nuts are two popular main courses. It's a good spot to try when exploring the downtown area. *16 de Septiembre 10, Col. Centro, tel. 5/512-7517. Reservations required. Dress: jacket and tie required. AE, DC, MC, V.*

Villa Reforma. Occupying a converted house in the exclusive Lomas de Chapultepec residential area, this secluded restaurant is very popular for lunch on the terrace, candlelight dinner, breakfast at 8—try the *jugo de tuna* (prickly pear juice)—or sumptuous Sunday brunch with music. Previously known for its French provincial fare, Villa Reforma now features innovative nouvelle Mexican cuisine: *sopa "Maria Candelaria"* (squash blossom soup with corn kernels), *huevos a la poblana* (poached eggs on a tortilla topped with cream cheese and slices of poblano chile), duckling in strawberry sauce, turkey steak in lemon sauce, and *huachinango* (red snapper) in avocado sauce. Villa Reforma is also famed for its home-baked breads and pastries. *Paseo de la Reforma 2210, Lomas de Chapultepec, tel. 5/596-0123 or 5/596-4355. Reservations advised. Dress: jacket and tie required for dinner. AE, DC, MC, V.*

Moderate–Expensive
El Arrollo. More than just a restaurant, this dining complex is a famous attraction in itself, complete with its own bullring. Located at the south end of town near the beginning of the highway to Cuernavaca, it was founded over 50 years ago by the Arrollo family and is now run by jovial Jesús ("Chucho") Arrollo. His loyal following includes celebrities, dignitaries and bullfighters, and the place is also enjoyed by families, tourists, and groups (generous menus are available for 15 or more and 100 or more). Over 2,600 people can dine simultaneously in a labyrinth of 11 picturesque dining areas. Typical Mexican specialties—roast baby lamb wrapped in maguey leaves, chicken mole, a dozen types of tacos and much more—are prepared in open kitchens where the copper and ceramic casseroles are big enough to swim in. There's mariachi music galore and the full gamut of Mexican drinks including pulque. The small bullring is the setting for bullfights with audience participation and not-very-brave bulls, as well as for special banquets and lively fiestas. Breakfast starts at 8 AM and lunch is served until 7 PM. *Insurgentes Sur 4003, Col. Tlalpan, tel. 5/573-4344. Reservations recommended, required for groups. Dress: casual. AE, DC, MC, V. Open daily.*

★ **Fonda El Refugio.** Since it opened in 1954, this fine Zona Rosa restaurant has been internationally known for its exquisite Mexican cuisine that delights even the most delicate palates. A habitual dining place for local devotees, it also offers a delightful introduction to Mexican gastronomy. The first thing you see upon entering this converted two-story town house is a mouthwatering display of homemade cream-pudding desserts. Atmosphere is casual yet classy in the intimate colonial-decor dining rooms. The menu varies daily with a selection of appetizers, soups, and regional dishes such as chicken mole, assorted *chiles rellenos*, grilled pork chops, and *albóndigas en chile chipotle* (meat balls in chile chipotle sauce). In the fall, their *chiles en nogada* are famous. This traditional dish displays the colors of the Mexican flag—green baked chiles stuffed with ground meat, walnuts, and rice, topped with white cream and red pomegranate seeds. To make selection easy, there is also a set house specialty for each day of the week. Whichever day it is, start with a plate of *botanas* (hors d'oeuvres) and, in addition to tequila with *sangrita*, try the refreshing *aquas* made with *chía* (sage seeds), *jamaica* (hibiscus), or *tamarindo*. After dessert, try *café de olla* (cinnamon-flavored coffee boiled in a clay pot and sweetened with brown sugar). *Liverpool 166, Zona Rosa, tel. 5/528–5823. Reservations recommended. Dress: casual but neat. AE, DC, MC, V. Closed Sundays and holidays.*

Las Palomas. In a residential neighborhood not far from the Zona Rosa, this is a congenial meeting place, delightfully decorated with colorful hand-painted tiles, wrought-iron grillwork, flowers, foliage, and art. Socialite-owner-hostess Lila Briones attends loyal customers, who even include some of her rival restaurateurs and chefs, as well as noted journalists, authors, and other cognoscenti in the field of Mexican gastronomy. Lila is faithful to the recipes she inherited from the days of her great-grandmother's country hacienda, such as homemade *tinga* (shreds of beef in a sauce of a blend of chiles of various flavors) and sensational homemade green chicken mole. Her brother Miguelangel barrel-pickles a coveted appetizer of chiles jalapeños with cauliflower, carrots, radish, onion, and squash. Other specialties include *huachinango* (red snapper) in homemade avocado sauce, *chochinita pibil* (baby pig Yucatecan style), and *bacalao* (codfish Spanish-style, with red and green bell peppers). Among desserts: homemade rice pudding and *natillas* (Spanish-style custards). A folkloric trio and guitarist-balladeer add to the talented milieu. *Cozumel 37, Col. Roma, tel. 5/553–7084. Reservations suggested. Dress: casual but neat. AE, MC, V. Open daily for lunch and dinner.*

Moderate **Focolare.** Among the prettiest places to eat in the Zona Rosa, Focolare's dining area is a covered patio with a fountain in the middle and a high roof attractively decorated with hanging wicker baskets. At the far end, a double blue-tile staircase leads to the second floor and adds to the feeling of spaciousness. This is a great breakfast spot. The buffet caters to the Mexican taste (red-hot chili first thing in the morning), but it also has less violent ways to start the day. Dishes are organized by region; if you are a fan of Oaxaca's chocolate mole sauce, you can enjoy a different one here every day of the week. Yucatecan dishes figure strongly at Focolare. Particularly worthwhile is the *cochinita pibil* (strips of pork in a heavy sauce). In fact, if you wanted to do a gastronomic tour of Mexico, Focolare would be a good guide as to which places should be given priority. From Puerto Angel, for example, it does a delicious *calamares* dish in a delicate mandarin sauce, supposedly typical of this tiny port on the Oaxacan coast. Another highlight is *cuete de res*, which is a special cut of beef prepared in a sumptuous almond sauce. Service is attentive and one can either eat quickly and be gone or linger over a meal. On Sundays, a healthy brunch is served, accompanied by a live band. *Hamburgo 87, Zona Rosa, tel. 5/511–2679 or 5/511–4236. No reservations. Dress: casual. AE, DC, MC, V.*

Fonda del Recuerdo. A solid family restaurant, the *fonda* (inn) has an enviable reputation among tourists and visitors. Every day from 2 to 10, five different groups from Veracruz and the north provide music that creates a festive atmosphere. A traditional Mexican menu features excellent seafood, meat, and *antojitos* (Mexican hors d'oeuvres). Mixed fish-and-seafood platters for two, four, or eight people, and whole fish or fillets (grilled with garlic or served with tomatoes, onions, and chile) are recommended. Meat from the kitchen's own *parillas* (grills) is always first-rate. The fonda is renowned for its gigantic portions, so you may find there's no room for dessert. If the appetite is willing, however, the *crepas de cajeta al tequila* (crepes with burned goat's milk and tequila) are worth trying. The continual party atmosphere and good Mexican cooking from Veracruz make this an excellent dining spot to enjoy with friends. *Bahía de las Palmas 39, Col. Anzures, tel. 5/545-1652. Reservations advised. Dress: informal. AE, DC, MC, V.*

Fonda Don Chón. This simple family-style restaurant, deep in downtown, is famed for its pre-Hispanic (indigenously Mexican) dishes. "This highly nutritious cuisine of our ancestors before the discovery of the Americas is also food of the future," says chef-owner Alonso Reyes, son of the founder. This restaurant is for the adventurous, although some pre-Hispanic delicacies, such as corn fungus, are featured at some of Mexico's most elegant restaurants. A knowledge of zoology, Spanish, and Nahuatl helps to decipher the menu, which changes daily. A gamut of products from throughout the Republic are prepared fresh every day, and no processed foods are used. *Escamoles de hormiga* (red ant roe), 97% protein, is known as the "caviar of Mexico" for both its deliciousness and costliness. Another delicacy, also served in small portions, is *gusanos de maguey* (maguey cactus worms) worth $100 a kilo and seen in some tequila bottles, served in tacos or with guacamole. Among exotic entrées are armadillo in sesame mole sauce, iguana soup, and snake (boa or rattle) steak. More traditional specialties include *mixiote de carnero* (barbecued lamb in maguey leaves). The coconut cake dessert is excellent, and live music adds to the atmosphere. *Regina 159, Col. Centro, tel. 5/522-170. No reservations. Dress: casual. AE, MC, V. Open daily 10 AM-7 PM.*

Fonda El Mesón. Located near Fonda Don Chón, on a pleasant pedestrian square, this unpretentious restaurant also specializes in pre-Hispanic cuisine. Well-known veteran chef Fortino Rojas keeps a watchful eye over the kitchen, which is on view from the spacious dining room, and he personally serves unique fare to an assortment of loyal customers—workers, gourmands, and the mayor of Mexico City and his colleagues. Fortino prepares *chapulines tostados al comal* (toasted grasshoppers), *ahuautli* (dried larva of river flies) served with red mole sauce, and entrées of wild boar in pumpkin seed sauce. There's more: manta ray in tomato sauce, pheasant in rose petal sauce, puma in garlic sauce, followed by homemade *flan* (custard) and other treats. Owner Alberto Alcázar plans on changing the restaurant's name to something more befitting— perhaps *La Mesa de Moctezuma* (Moctezuma's Table). He says that with over 2,000 dishes to choose from, the Aztec king was probably the best nourished of any ruler in history. *Plaza Juan José Baz 7, Col. Centro, tel. 5/542-9563. No reservations. Dress: casual. AE, MC, V. Open daily 1 PM-7 PM.*

Las Mercedes. Styled as a *restaurant de epoca*, Las Mercedes specializes in traditional Mexican food with some ancient recipes that have stood the test of time. The decor is modern rustic, with furniture from Michoacán and a pleasant terra-cotta and coffee color scheme. Enjoy the variety of fresh-fruit and seed juices (known as *aguas*) and some *sopecitos* (chicken and chorizo on flat tortillas) before beginning your meal in earnest. Both the *sopa de fideos con albondigitas* (pasta soup with meatballs) and the *sopa de tortilla* make excellent starters. The *lomo de cerdo en salsa de huitlacoche* (pork in a sauce made from the corn-husk fungus) is exceptional. The *plato Mercedes*, a sampling of both the old and the new Mexican cuisines, is highly recommended. Las Mercedes is a good choice for breakfast when such delicacies as eggs with shrimp, oysters, and asparagus are offered. *Rio Guadalquivir 91, Col. Cuauhtemoc, tel. 5/208-7369. Reservations accepted. Dress: informal. AE, DC, MC, V.*

Inexpensive **Café de Tacuba.** This typically Mexican restaurant is an essential breakfast, lunch, dinner, or snack stop for those exploring the city's downtown historic district. Since it opened in 1912, in a section of an old convent, it has charmed locals and visitors with its warm colonial decor and traditional Mexican fare. Colorful hand-painted Talavera tiles from Puebla line the walls. In the rear dining room, huge 18th-century oil paintings depict the historic invention of *mole poblano*, one of Mexico's most original dishes with a sauce of countless ingredients including a variety of chiles and chocolate. The complex recipe was created by the nuns in the Santa Rosa Convent of Puebla. Of course, mole poblano is on the menu here, as are delicious tamales made fresh every morning—Oaxaca style with black mole and banana leaf or a fluffy Mexico City version. Enjoy pastries galore. *Tacuba 28, Centro, tel. 5/518-4950. No reservations. Dress: casual. MC, V. Open daily.*

★ **Las Cazuelas.** Traditional Mexican cooking at its best is on tap at one of the most famous of the downtown fondas. The open view kitchens are kept immaculately clean, and diners often take a peek at the bubbling *mole* and *pipian* sauces before being seated. (*Mole* is a chocolate-based chile sauce with many other spices; *pipian* is a lightly *picante*, sesame-flavored sauce from the Yucatan, which is often served with poultry.) The large dining area is brightened by hand-painted chairs from Michoacán and by the crisp green-and-white table linen. An ideal first course to share is the *entremés ranchero de carnitas, chicharrón y quesadilla* (mixed Mexican hors d'oeuvres). All the ingredients, and especially the *chicharrón* (fried pork rinds), are the *de primera* (the best quality available). Main courses center around various moles or pipian sauces with pork or chicken. If you like the slightly bitter but spicy, hot taste of the *pasilla chile*, try the *hongos en salsa de pasilla con carne de puerco* (mushrooms with pork). Finish with a *café de olla* (cinammon coffee in a jug) and a domestic brandy, then enjoy some fine mariachi singing from a talented and professional group (from 4 to 6 daily). *Rep. de Colombia 69, Col. Centro, tel. 5/522-0689. No reservations. Dress: casual. AE, MC, V.*

Spanish

Expensive **El Parador de Manolo.** A period two-story house was remodeled into this Spanish restaurant in fashionable Polanco. The Bar Porrón on the ground floor serves a variety of Spanish tapas, including an excellent prawn mix in a spicy sauce. In the brasserie-style dining room upstairs, choose from a Spanish menu or from the list of the chef's recommendations. The specially cured Serrano ham is possibly the best in the city, while the *calamares fritos* (fried squid) or the *crepas de flor de* *calabaza al gratin* (squash-blossom crepes) make other fine starters. Fish dishes are the most appealing for a main course, although the chateaubriand Parador for two (in a black corncob sauce) is truly original. Desserts cater to the Spanish sweet tooth and are less notable. Wines are on display downstairs, as are the fresh fish of the day. *Presidente Masaryl 443, Polanco, tel. 5/545–7723. Reservations accepted. Dress: informal. AE, MC, V.*

Moderate **Babieca.** Almost hidden in the growing Lomas shopping complex, the Babieca, despite its rustic decor, could not really be anything other than Spanish (the name is taken from El Cid's horse, and the decor has strong equestrian overtones). This is a wonderful place to eat *tapas* (little dishes—appetizers), especially if you don't want a heavy meal. There could be nothing more Spanish than the tapas served here: *tortilla de patata, abulón* (abalone), *chorizo con chistorra* (dried meats and sausage), *morcilla* (black pudding), and *gambas al ajillo* (prawns in garlic) are all exquisite. If a full meal beckons, try the *setas a la Provençale* (wild mushrooms in butter, wine, parsley and garlic) to start, then move on to a brochette of giant prawn with a Gruyère gratin. The dessert truffles are superlative, the meringues in chocolate sauce are downright sinful, and the date-and-nut tart is both sticky and irresistible. *Bosques de Duraznos 187, Col. Bosques de las Lomas, tel. 5/596–4601 or 5/596–2625. Reservations advised. Dress: informal. AE, DC, MC, V.*

Lodging

As might be expected of a megalopolis, Mexico City has 17,000 hotel rooms—enough to accommodate every taste and budget. Those with prior reservations are likely to obtain rooms at their desired price and location. Demand for rooms is unpredictable, but if you arrive without a reservation, it is wise to take the best available accommodation for the first night and hunt for something more appropriate the following day. Be sure to confirm your reservations.

Though Mexico City is huge and spread out, most hotels are located within the districts listed below, which are not far from each other. Chapultepec Park and the swank Polanco neighborhood are on the west side of the city. Paseo de la Reforma runs from Chapultepec, northeast through "midtown", and intersects with Avenida Juárez at the beginning of the downtown area. Juárez becomes Avenida Madero which continues east to the downtown historic district and its very core, the Zócalo. The Zona Rosa, replete with boutiques, cafés, restaurants, and night spots, is just south of Reforma in the western midtown area.

The following selection is organized by the major areas of the city and then by price. Highly recommended lodgings are indicated by a star ★.

Category	Cost*
Very Expensive	over $100
Expensive	$80–$100

Moderate	$50–$80
Inexpensive	under $50

*All prices are for a standard double room, excluding service
charge and sales tax (10%).*

Airport

Expensive **Fiesta Americana Aeropuerto.** Opened in 1985 and expanded
since, this deluxe hotel is located over a short footbridge from
the airline terminal, making it convenient for those who arrive
late and have an early-morning flight. For this convenience you
pay a price. Day rates (9–6) are available at about half the full
rates. *Benito Juárez Airport, 15620, tel. 5/762–0199 or 800/
223–2332. 340 rooms and suites. Facilities: all rooms have climate control, satellite color TV, radio, minibar, purified water, 24-hr room service; restaurant, coffee shop, lobby bar,
nightclub, pool, health center with sauna, valet, shops, car rental, garage, facilities for the handicapped. AE, DC, MC, V.*

Alameda Central

Moderate **Hotel de Cortés.** This delightful small hotel is housed in a coloni-
★ al building (1780) designated a national monument. A major
renovation in 1990 has given luster and luxury to the colonial-
decor rooms and added two lovely soundproofed suites overlooking Alameda Park. The new restaurant also views the park,
and a friendly bar opens to the tree-shaded central courtyard
and fountain, a lovely setting for tea or cocktails. Every Saturday evening (8–10 PM), a mariachi festival entertains guests and
visitors. The Franz Mayer Museum is just a block away, and it's
an easy walk to the Zócalo. Loyal guests make reservations
through Best Western many months in advance. *Av. Hidalgo 85,
tel. 5/518–2181 or 800/334–7234. 29 rooms and suites. Facilities: climate control, soundproofing, remote-control color satellite TV, radio, minibar, automatic safe, bathroom
amenities, restaurant, bar. AE, DC, MC, V.*

Chapultepec Park and Polanco

Very Expensive **Camino Real.** Super luxurious and immense—about the size of
★ the Pyramid of the Sun in Teotihuacan—this city within a city
hosts heads of state and celebrities as well as business and
pleasure travelers. Impressive works of art embellishing the
endless corridors and lounges include Rufino Tamayo's mural
of *Man Confronting the Universe, Sighs* by painter Pedro
Coronel, and an imposing sculpture by Calder. As a result of
recent renovation, 100 enlarged rooms with extra-deluxe
amenities now compose the fifth-floor Executive Level.
Foquet's de Paris restaurant holds French culinary festivals,
and the airy Azulejos features Mexican cuisine and special Sunday buffet brunches. The only drawback: It's easy to get lost
in the endless corridors of this architectural masterpiece.
*Mariano Escobedo 700, 11590, tel. 5/203–2121 or 800/228–
3000. 713 rooms and suites. Facilities: gardens, 1 heated pool
for general use, 2 pools provided exclusively for suites, 4 tennis
courts, health club, 10 bars and restaurants, disco, fully bilingual business center. AE, DC, MC, V.*
Hotel Nikko Mexico. One of the city's newest hotels (1987), and

part of the Japanese Nikko chain, this property occupies a prime position adjacent to Chapultepec Park and Paseo de la Reforma, and just a five-minute walk to the Anthropology Museum. The four "Fountain Club" executive floors have better rooms and extra facilities. Three top restaurants excel in their gastronomic specialties: Les Celébrités (French), Teppan Grill (Japanese), and El Jardín (Mexican). *Campos Elíseos 204, 11560, tel. 5/203–4800 or 800/NIKKO–US. 771 rooms and suites. Facilities: all rooms and suites feature air-conditioning, 24-hr room service, color TV with US Cablevision, refrigerator, radio, phone with message service; 3 restaurants, bar, 2 pools (1 heated), health club with Nautilus equipment, 3 tennis courts, shopping arcade, travel agency. AE, DC, MC, V.*

Expensive **Stouffer Presidente México.** Formerly called El Presidente Chapultepec and still referred to as such, this 42-story business/convention hotel is, like its next door neighbor, the Nikko, adjacent to Chapultepec Park and the posh Colonia Polanco. The dramatic five-story lobby is a hollow pyramid of balconies, with music presented daily at the lively lobby bar. The rooms are immense and those on the top two floors afford views of two snow-capped volcanoes. There are a number of smart stores and no fewer than six eateries on the premises, including a branch of Maxim's of Paris. *Campos Elíseos 218, 11560, tel. 5/250–7700, 800/472–2427, or 800/433–5456; 800/843–9633 in CA. 877 rooms and suites. Facilities: all rooms have air-conditioning, color TV, FM radio, work area, 24-hr room service; 5 restaurants, lobby bar, coffee shop, shopping arcade, baby-sitting service, underground parking garage. AE, DC, MC, V.*

Moderate **Park Villa Motel.** This two-story colonial hacienda, in a tranquil
★ residential setting, is ideal for travelers with a car. Overlooking its pretty garden is the Restaurant Jardín del Corregidor, which serves authentic Spanish cuisine. If you are driving, you'll need to get directions to its secluded site near the southeast side of Bosque de Chapultepec (Chapultepec Park). The nearest subway stop is Juanacatlán. *Gómez Pedraza 68 (enter at Constituyentes), 11850, tel. 5/515–5245. 45 rooms. Facilities: color TV. No credit cards.*

Zócalo

Moderate **Gran Hotel Howard Johnson.** The name was changed, but locals still refer to this establishment by its original (and more appropriate) name: *Gran Hotel de la Ciudad de México*. Ensconced in what was formerly a 19th-century department store, this older, more traditional hotel has contemporary rooms. Its central location—adjacent to the Zócalo and near the Templo Mayor—makes it the choice of serious sightseers. And its distinctive Belle Epoque lobby is worth a visit in its own right, with a striking stained-glass Tiffany dome, chandeliers, singing canaries in gilded cages, and 19th-century wrought-iron elevators gliding smoothly up and down. For breakfast (7–11 AM), the fourth-floor Mirador overlooks the Zócalo. The Del Centro restaurant/bar is run by Delmónicos, one of Mexico City's best. Recent correspondence from our readership indicates a need for some hotel refurbishment. *16 de Septiembre 82, 06000, tel. 5/510–4040, 800/221–6509, or 800/654–2000. 125 rooms. Facilities: all rooms have minibar, phone, satellite color TV; 2 restaurants, bar, concierge, travel agency, a Mexicana Airlines ticket office, parking. AE, DC, MC, V.*

Mexico City Lodging

Majestic Best Western. The atmospheric, colonial-style Hotel Majestic was built in 1937. Its location is perfect for anyone interested in exploring the downtown historic district: it is right on the Zócalo at the corner of Madero. The seventh-floor dining room and terrace—which feature international and Mexican specialties—have marvelous panoramas of the entire Zócalo. Breakfast is served at 7:30, and the Sunday buffet (1–5 PM) features live Mexican music. It is worth a visit just to see the view, and nonguests are welcome. Rooms are comfortable, and the service is efficient and courteous. Colorful hand-painted ceramic tiles and potted plants decorate the public areas. *Madero 73, 06000, tel. 5/521–8600 or 800/528–1234. 85 rooms. Facilities: climate control, color TV, minibar. AE, DC, MC, V.*

Inexpensive **Catedral.** Located just one block from the Catedral and Templo Mayor, this older, well-maintained hotel is situated in the heart of the downtown historic district. Rooms are comfortable, and the service is friendly. *Donceles 95, 06000, tel. 5/521–6183. 116 rooms. Facilities: room service, bar, restaurant, travel agency, free parking, laundry. AE, MC, V.*

Zona Rosa

Very Expensive **Clarion Reforma Suites.** Opened in 1988, this all-suite deluxe
★ hotel caters to the business traveler. Facilities include a heliport, limousine service, and free car wash. The exclusive Executive Suites feature either a sauna or Jacuzzi, and the even-more-deluxe Clarion Suites have both. The Bellini Restaurant serves international cuisine with Italian accents. The 22-story hotel is located between the Zona Rosa and Chapultepec Park. *Paseo de la Reforma 373, 06500, tel. 5/207–8944 or 800/228–5151. 81 suites. Facilities: air-conditioning, cable TV with movies, 24-hr room service, concierge, valet parking. AE, DC, MC, V.*

Expensive– **Marco Polo.** Posh and right in the center of the Zona Rosa, this
Very Expensive deluxe, small, yet ultramodern all-suite hotel offers the ameni-
★ ties and outstanding personalized service often associated with a small European property. Rooms on the top floor facing north have excellent views of Paseo de la Reforma, and the U.S. Embassy is close by. In the street-level Marco Polo Restaurant and Bar you can listen to sophisticated live jazz at lunch, over cocktails, and at dinner. *Amberes 27, 06600, tel. 5/207–1893. 60 rooms and 4 penthouse suites with Jacuzzi and terrace. Facilities: climate control, color cable TV, FM radio, minibar, kitchenettes, valet parking, multilingual secretarial service. AE, DC, MC, V.*

Expensive **Aristos.** This 15-story hotel is on the busy Paseo de la Reforma, in front of the U.S. Embassy and the Mexican Stock Exchange. All 360 rooms are well furnished and feature the hues of the decade: peach and mauve, with brass and wood accents. The business center has a bilingual staff and a message service. *Paseo de la Reforma 276, 06600, tel. 5/211–0112 or 800/5–ARISTO. 360 rooms and suites. Facilities: all rooms have 2 phones, radio, color TV, alarm clock; sun deck, sauna, gymnasium, travel agency, unisex beauty parlor. AE, DC, MC, V.*
Century. This zebra-stripe high rise stands out in the middle of the Zona Rosa. Rooms have round Roman-style marble baths, round beds, and semi-circular private balconies. Violins add a romantic touch at the rooftop Regine restaurant, and the

street-level Petit Pois serves a good breakfast and luncheon buffet. The large penthouse suites are superb. *Liverpool 152, 06600, tel. 5/584–7111 or 800/221–6509. 143 rooms. Facilities: all rooms have marble bath, color satellite TV, FM radio, minibar, carpeting, private balcony; restaurant, bar, disco, heated swimming pool, sauna, massage, car rental, currency exchange, baby-sitting, parking. AE, DC, MC, V.*

★ **Galería Plaza.** A Westin Hotel and part of the prestigious Camino Real chain, the Plaza is convenient for shopping and dining out in the elegant Zona Rosa. It has faultless rooms, service, and facilities, but once inside it's hard to remember that you are in Mexico. Advantages include cable TV from the United States, the 24-hour restaurant, and a secure underground parking lot. *Hamburgo 195 at Varsovia, 06600, tel. 5/211–0014 or 800/228–3000. 434 rooms and suites. Facilities: all rooms are air-conditioned and have minibar, color satellite TV and radio, 24-hr room service; rooftop pool with sun deck, shops, concierge, valet parking. AE, DC, MC, V.*

Holiday Inn Crowne Plaza. Well organized for business travelers and large groups, this establishment has an ample selection of bars, restaurants, and entertainment, including the lively Stelaris rooftop nightclub. There is not much Mexican atmosphere, but even if the sun doesn't shine, you can get a good tan in the solarium. *Paseo de la Reforma 80, 06600, tel. 5/705–1515 or 800–HOLIDAY. 583 rooms. Facilities: phones, minibars, refrigerators in all rooms; restaurant, concierge, bar. AE, DC, MC, V.*

Imperial. Opened in 1990, the Hotel Imperial occupies a stately, turn-of-the-century European-style building, right on the Reforma alongside the Columbus Monument. Quiet elegance and personal service are keynotes of this Spanish-owned property, which is part of the prestigious HUSA chain. *Reforma 64, 06600, tel. 5/705–4011. 70 rooms, junior and master suites. Facilities: cable TV, automatic-dial telephones, air-conditioning, minibar, automatic safe, bathroom amenities in all rooms; restaurant, café, bar, room service, travel agency, secretarial service. AE, DC, MC, V.*

Krystal Rosa. Part of the Mexican Krystal Hotel chain, this superbly run, recently remodeled high-rise hotel is centrally located and has an excellent view of the city from the pool terrace. All rooms have telephones, minibars, and color TVs with satellite transmission. *Liverpool 155, 06600, tel. 5/211–0092 or 800/231–9860. 330 rooms. Facilities: restaurant, bar, nightclub, heated pool, business center. AE, DC, MC, V.*

Plaza Florencia. This is a modern hotel on a smart shopping street. Rooms are well furnished, cheerfully decorated, and soundproofed against the location's heavy traffic noise; the higher floors have views of the Angel monument. Some large family suites are available. *Florencia 61, 06600, tel. 5/211–0064. 140 rooms, including 10 suites. Facilities: all rooms have air-conditioning, heat, color TV and phone; coffee shop, restaurant, and bar, nightclub. AE, DC, MC, V.*

Sevilla Palace. A glistening new showplace with five panoramic elevators to its 23 floors and 414 rooms, a covered rooftop pool with Jacuzzi, health club, terraced rooftop lounge with a city view, restaurants, a top-floor supper-club with entertainment, and convention halls with capacities up to 1,000. Well-located near the Columbus traffic circle. *Paseo de la Reforma 105; tel. 5/566–8877. 414 rooms. Facilities: all rooms have climate con-*

trol, color satellite TV, automatic telephones; concierge, valet parking. AE, DC, MC, V.

Moderate   **Calinda Geneve.** A Quality Inn, this friendly, centrally located hotel features a remarkable gallery, the Salón Jardín, containing more plants than a greenhouse and a remarkable stained-glass ceiling. It attracts guests and nonguests alike for cocktails and dining, and a Mexican buffet luncheon is served daily, accompanied by live Mexican music. Colonial-style carved chairs and tables furnish the hotel's pleasant lobby, and the rooms are adequate if a little cramped. The clientele is almost exclusively non-Mexican. El Jardín restaurant serves wursts and sausage to the accompaniment of American jazz. *Londres 130, 06600, tel. 5/211–0071 or 800/228–5151. 347 rooms. Facilities: all rooms are air-conditioned and have phone, minibar, room service, color cable TV; travel agency, boutique, grill restaurant, bar with nightly entertainment. AE, DC, MC, V.*

★   **María Cristina.** Full of Old World charm, this Spanish Colonial–style gem is a Mexico City classic. Impeccably maintained since it was built in 1937, the peach-color building surrounds a delightful garden-courtyard that is the setting for its El Retiro bar and Río Nansa restaurant. A 1990 refurbishment has resulted in three new, tastefully decorated apartment–style master suites, complete with Jacuzzis. Located in a quiet residential setting near Sullivan Park, the hotel is just a block from Reforma, and close to the Zona Rosa. *Río Lerma 31, 06500, tel. 5/566–9688. 156 rooms and suites. Facilities: color cable TV, minibar, safe, minibar room service; travel agency, boutique, beauty parlor, valet parking. DC, MC, V.*

Inexpensive   **Hotel Misión México.** A part of the Misión chain, this very comfortable hotel is well placed for shopping and sightseeing. *Nápoles 62, tel. 5/533–0535. 50 rooms. Facilities: All rooms are air-conditioned and have color TV and phones; coffee shop, lobby bar. AE, MC, V.*

The Arts and Nightlife

Mexico City has a rich cultural scene and nightlife, with something for virtually every taste. Good places to check for current events are the Friday edition of *The News*, a daily English-language newspaper, and *Tiempo Libre*, a weekly listing of activities and events in Spanish. Both are available at newsstands. Free concerts are given Sundays at 1 PM at Chapultepec Castle.

The Arts

Dance   The world-renowned **Ballet Folklórico de México,** directed by Amalia Hernández, offers a stylized presentation of Mexican regional folk dances and is one of the most popular and spectacular shows in Mexico. Performances are given on Sundays at 9:30 AM and 9 PM and Wednesdays at 6 and 9 PM at the Palace of Fine Arts (Av. Juárez and Eje Central Lázaro Cárdenas, tel. 5/512–3633). Hotels and travel agencies can secure tickets.

Not to be confused with the above is the **Ballet Folklórico Nacional de Mexico,** directed and choreographed by Silvia Lozano. The company performs authentic regional folk dances regularly at the Teatro de la Ciudad, also known as the Mexico City Opera House (Donceles 36, tel. 5/510–2197).

The **National Dance Theater,** a component of the National Auditorium complex in Chapultepec Park, and the **Dance Center** (Campos Elíseos 480, tel. 5/520–2271) frequently sponsor modern dance performances.

Music The primary venue for classical music is the **Palace of Fine Arts** (Av. Juárez and Eje Central Lázaro Cárdenas, tel. 5/512–3633), which has a main auditorium and the smaller Manuel Ponce concert hall. The National Opera has two seasons at the Palace: January–March and August–October. The National Symphony Orchestra stages classic and modern pieces at the palace in the spring and fall.

Another top concert hall is **Ollin Yolitzli** (Periférico Sur 1541, tel. 5/655–3611), which hosts the Mexico City Philharmonic several times a year. The State of Mexico Symphony performs at **Nezahualcóyotl Hall** in University City (tel. 5/655–6511). The **Teatro de la Ciudad** (Donceles 36, tel. 5/510–2197) is also a popular site for a number of musical programs, both classical and popular, year-round. And the **Sala Chopín** (Alvaro Obregón 302, tel. 5/533–1380) presents a number of free musical events throughout the week.

Theater Visitors with a grasp of Spanish will find a wide choice of theatrical entertainment, including recent Broadway hits. Prices are reasonable compared with stage productions of similar caliber in the United States. Though Mexico City has no central theater district, most theaters are a 15- to 30-minute taxi ride from the major hotels. The top theaters include **Hidalgo** (Av. Hidalgo 23, tel. 5/521–3859), **Julio Prieto** (Nicolás San Juan at Zola, tel. 5/543–3478), **Insurgentes** (Av. Insurgentes Sur 1587, tel. 5/660–2304), and **San Rafael** (Virginia Fábregas 40, tel. 5/ 592–2142).

Nightlife

Night is the key word to understanding the timing of going out in Mexico City. People generally have cocktails at 7 or 8 PM, take in dinner and a show at 10 or 11, head to the discos at midnight, and then find a spot for a nightcap somewhere around 3 AM. The easiest way for the non-Spanish-speaking visitor to do this is on a nightclub tour (*see* Guided Tours, in Essential Information, *above*). However, those who set off on their own should have no trouble getting around. For starters, Niza and Florencia streets in the Zona Rosa are practically lined with nightclubs, bars, and discos that are especially lively on Friday and Saturday nights. The big hotels offer both bars and places to dance or be entertained, and they are frequented by locals. Outside of the Zona Rosa, Paseo de la Reforma, Avenida Juárez and Insurgentes Sur have the greatest concentration of night spots. Remember that the capital's high altitude makes liquor extremely potent, even jolting. Imported booze is very expensive, so you may want to stick with what the Mexicans order: tequila, rum, and *cerveza* (beer).

Dinner Theater The splashiest shows are found in the big hotels and in Zona Rosa clubs. **El Patio** (Atenas 9, tel. 5/535–3904) is a classic, old-style nightclub with tiny tables, surly waiters, and poor food; go there only if you must see one of the headliners, such as Julio Iglesias or Vicky Carr. **El Gran Caruso** (Londres 25, on the edge of the Zona Rosa, tel. 5/545–1199) is where the waiters sing arias between courses. In the Crowne Hotel Plaza, **Stelaris**

(Paseo de la Reforma 80, tel. 5/566–7777) has top entertainers (performing Mon.–Sat. at midnight), good food, and music for dancing. Strolling violinists serenade the patrons of **Regine** (Hotel Century, Londres at Amberes, tel. 5/584–7111). **La Veranda** (María Isabel Sheraton, Paseo de la Reforma 325, tel. 5/211–0001) serves dinner while international-caliber stars perform; afterward the dance floor is open. Mexican headliners perform at **Maquiavelo** (Hotel Krystal Rosa, Zona Rosa, tel. 5/211–0092) Mon.–Sat. at 11 PM and 1 AM.

Discos Dance emporiums in the capital run the gamut from cheek-to-cheek romantic to throbbing strobe lights and ear-splitting music. Most places have a cover charge, but it is rarely more than $10. **Lipstick** (Hotel Aristos, Paseo de la Reforma 274, tel. 5/211–0112) is a longtime favorite where the action begins nightly at around 10. **Cero Cero** (Camino Real, Mariano Escobedo 700, Polanco, tel. 5/545–6560) has live bands as well as tapes and is open every night 9 PM–4 AM. **Le Chic** (Hotel Galería Plaza, Hamburgo at Varsovia, Zona Rosa, tel. 5/211–0014) is small, elegant, with stuffed chairs, and deafening modern sounds. It's open Mon.–Sat. 9 PM–3 AM. The emphasis is on romantic mood music and touch dancing at **Valentino's** (Florencia 36, Zona Rosa, tel. 5/525–2020), which is open Mon.–Sat. 9 PM–4 AM.

Hotel Bars The lobby bars in the **María Isabel Sheraton** (Reforma 325), **Stouffer Presidente México** (Campos Elíseos 218, Polanco), and **Camino Real** (Mariano Escobedo 900, Polanco) are all good bets for a sophisticated crowd and lively music, usually until around midnight.

After Midnight **Afro Tramonto** features a raunchy, but not overly rowdy, show that appeals to gentlemen, though escorted ladies are welcome. *Av. Insurgentes and Sullivan, on the north side of Paseo de la Reforma, tel. 5/546–8807. Cover: $4. Open Mon.–Sat. 10 PM–4 AM.*

Much more sophisticated since its complete remodeling in 1990, **Gitanerías** continues to be an authentic Spanish flamenco nightclub (*tablao*). Now, in addition to a fiery flamenco show featuring dancers, singers and guitarists, there is also disco dancing to flamenco and Latin rhythms. Only light supper and drinks are served, and the first show starts at midnight. *Oaxaca 15, Col. Roma, tel. 5/208–2264. Closed Mon.*

The traditional last stop for nocturnal Mexicans is **Plaza Garibaldi** (Rep. de Honduras just off Eje Central Lázaro Cárdenas), where exuberant mariachis gather to unwind after evening performances—by performing even more. They play in the square and inside the cantinas and clubs surrounding it; the better ones are **Guadalajara de Noche** (tel. 5/526–5521) and **Tenampa** (tel. 5/526–6176). If the extroverted singer-musicians focus on you, a friendly smile and a tip are expected. *Open daily until 4 AM and even later on Fri. and Sat.*

Excursions

Xochimilco, Cuernavaca, and Tepoztlán

This excursion to the south and southwest of Mexico City begins in Xochimilco (So-chee-**meel**-co), famous for its floating gardens, where visitors can take rides in gondolalike boats and get a fleeting sense of pre-Hispanic Mexico City. Beyond Xochimilco, in the neighboring state of Morelos, lies Cuernavaca, a weekend retreat for wealthy chilangos and foreigners. The climate in Cuernavaca, just 85 kilometers (53 miles) and an altitude descent of almost 2,500 feet from Mexico City, changes dramatically to lush, semitropical. The city is known for its many Spanish-language schools, the beautiful Borda Gardens, and Diego Rivera murals in the Palacio de Cortés (Palace of Cortés). An overnight stay is recommended. From Cuernavaca we suggest a detour to Tepoztlán, which features a 16th-century Dominican convent.

Tourist Information The **Morelos State Tourist Office** in Cuernavaca is located on the south side of the Borda Gardens. *Morelos Sur 802, tel. 73/14–38–60. Open weekdays 9–8, Sat. 9–6, Sun. 9–3.*

Guided Tours All the major Mexico City tour operators can arrange trips to Xochimilco, Cuernavaca, and Tepoztlán (*see* Guided Tours in Essential Information, *above*).

Getting Around To reach Xochimilco by car, take Periférico Sur to the extension of División del Norte; an alternate route is from Calzada de Tlalpán to Calzada México Xochimilco and then Calzada Guadalupe Ramírez. Xochimilco is 21 kilometers (13 miles) from the Zócalo in Mexico City; the trip should take between 45 minutes and 1 hour, depending on traffic. If Xochimilco is your final destination, you are probably better off taking a taxi. By public transportation, take Metro Line 2 to Taxqueña and then any bus marked "Xochimilco."

To continue south by car, return to Periférico Sur, turn left (south) on Viaducto Tlalpan, and watch for signs to Cuernavaca. The *cuota* or toll road (Rte. 95D) is much faster than the *carretera libre*, or free road (Rte. 95). Route 95D will take you about 1½ hours to cover 85 kilometers (53 miles).

Tepoztlán is 26 kilometers (16 miles) east of Cuernavaca, via Route 95D. Buses also run every 20 minutes.

Exploring Xochimilco According to legend, the Xochimilcas were the first of the seven Náhuatl tribes to leave Aztlán, the mythical Aztec homeland in the north. Reaching Xochimilco ("the place where flowers are planted") between AD 900 and 1200, they devised a system of *chinampas* (floating gardens) to grow and transport food along the canals of Tenochtitlán. Originally, the gardens were anchored with roots, poles, and mud; as they grew, and the waters receded, they became permanently affixed to the lakebed. Canoes carried the flowers and produce to the capital.

Today Xochimilco is the only place in Mexico where the gardens still exist. Go on a Saturday, when the *tianguis* (market) is most active, or on a Sunday. (Note that Xochimilco is a popular destination for families on Sundays.) On weekdays the place is practically deserted, so it loses much of its charm. Hire a *trajinera* (flower-covered launch); an arch over each launch spells out its name—usually a diminutive for a woman's name—in flowers. As you sail through the canals, you'll pass mariachis and women selling tacos in other launches.

Exploring Cuernavaca Downtown Cuernavaca is fairly compact. The most attractive sights are the mansions of the wealthy weekenders set in the hills on the edge of town, but you have to be a guest to get in. The four main sites are located near the main square. The **Palacio de Cortés**—Cortés's palace-cum-fortress—now houses the **Museo de Cuauhnáhuac** (Museum of Cuauhnáhuac, the Indian name for Cuernavaca), which focuses on Mexican history before and after the conquest. On permanent exhibit is a collection of some of Diego Rivera's finest murals, which, like those of Mexico City's National Palace, dramatize the history and the horrors of the conquest, colonialism, and the revolution. The beautiful and spacious **Jardín Borda** (Borda Gardens), three blocks west, was designed in the late 18th century by one member of the Borda family (rich miners of French extraction) for his relative; Maximilian and Carlotta visited the gardens frequently, and novelist Malcolm Lowry turned them into a sinister symbol in *Under the Volcano*. Opposite the gardens is the **Catedral de la Asunción,** an architecturally eclectic structure noteworthy for its 17th-century Japanese wall paintings. Diagonally opposite the cathedral is the **Palacio Municipal;** the paintings inside depict life in the city before the Spaniards.

Exploring Tepoztlán This tiny village is best known for its pyramid, and for the dances held here during Carnival, when celebrants don bright masks depicting birds, animals, and Christian figures. Anthropologists Robert Redfield and Oscar Lewis both did fieldwork here in the 1950s. The landmark is the multibuttressed Ex-Convent (1559), with fine paneled doors adorned with Indian motifs.

Cholula, Puebla, and Tehuacán

The three major destinations on this excursion are located in the state of Puebla. The capital city, also called Puebla, is a good 1½ to 3 hours by car southeast of Mexico City, depending on whether you use the toll highway or the more scenic road. You can detour along the way to see the volcanoes, Popocatépetl and Ixtaccíhuatl, up close. On your return to the capital, consider a stop in Tlaxcala, with its rare church and ex-convent of San Francisco. Cholula, one of the most sacred spots in ancient Mexico, has scores of churches and a pyramid that is considered the largest in the world in terms of volume, consisting of several layers built on top of one another over the centuries. The pyramid was an important ceremonial center during pre-Hispanic times; subsequently, the Spaniards built a large church on top of it. Puebla, another well-preserved colonial city only 8 kilometers (5 miles) east of Cholula, was the center of the Spanish tile industry; and the town of Tehuacán, another 115 kilometers (71 miles) southeast, was a thermal spa before Columbus's time. Mexico's best brands of mineral water are bottled there.

Tourist Information The **Puebla Tourist Office** can supply information. *3 Sur 1501*, *tel. 22/37–50–13. Open daily 10–2 and 4–7.*

Guided Tours All the major Mexico City tour operators can arrange trips to Cholula, Puebla, and Tehuacán (*see* Guided Tours in Essential Information, *above*).

Getting Around From Mexico City, head east toward the airport and turn onto Calzada Zaragoza, the last wide boulevard before arriving at the airport; it becomes the Puebla Highway at the toll booth. Route 190D is the toll road straight to Puebla; Route 150 is the free road. To go directly to Cholula, take the exit at San Martín Texmelucan and follow the signs. From Puebla, Cholula is a couple of kilometers west. To stop at the volcanoes, take the free road 33 kilometers (20 miles) to Chalco. From there it is four kilometers (2.5 miles) to the Amecameca-Chalco sign, from which you continue 22 kilometers (13.6 miles) on Route 115 to Amecameca. To Tehuacán, follow Route 150 from Puebla for 115 kilometers (71 miles).

Exploring Cholula As you leave Mexico City—if the smog is not too thick—the **volcanoes** will be visible to the south. "Popo" is 5,455 meters (17,887 ft) high. To see it up close you should exit at either of the main highways at Chalco and follow the signs to the Parque Nacional. Popo last erupted in 1802. The legend states that Popocatépetl, an Aztec warrior, had been sent by the emperor—father of his beloved Ixtaccíhuatl—to bring back the head of a feared enemy in order to win Ixtaccíhuatl's hand. He returned triumphantly only to find that Ixtaccíhuatl had killed herself, believing him dead. The grief-stricken Popo laid out her body on a small knoll and lit an eternal torch that he watches over, kneeling. Each of the four peaks composing the volcano is named after different parts of her body—hence its nickname "The Sleeping Lady." (In addition, the silhouette of the volcano resembles the figure of a reclining woman.) Climbing Popo or "Ixta" is for serious mountaineers, but the park, a verdant pine forest, makes a good spot for a picnic.

Most of the 40 colonial churches in Cholula are in poor condition. One of the two most stunning and well-preserved churches is 6.4 kilometers (4 miles) south of town, in **San Francisco Acatepec.** Completely covered with Puebla tiles, it has been called the most ornate Poblano rococo facade in the country. Equally unusual is the interior of the church in **Santa María Tonantzintla,** 3.2 kilometers (2 miles) toward Cholula. Its polychrome wood-and-stucco carvings—inset columns, altarpieces, and the main archway—are the epitome of Churrigueresque. Set off by ornate gold-leaf figures of vegetal forms, angels, and saints, the carvings were done by native craftsmen.

Closer to town, the **Great Pyramid** was the centerpiece of a Toltec and then Aztec religious center and consists of seven superimposed structures connected by tunnels and stairways. The Spaniards, as they often did, built a chapel to **Nuestra Señora de los Remedios** (Our Lady of the Remedies) on top of it. Behind the pyramid is a vast temple complex of 43 acres, once dedicated to Quetzalcóatl. *Small admission charge. Open daily 10–5.*

Exploring Puebla Maize was first cultivated in the Tehuacán Valley; later, the region was a crossroads for many ancient Mesoamerican cultures, including the Olmecs and Totonacs. The town of Puebla is notable for its idiosyncratic Baroque structures that are built of red brick, gray stone, white stucco, and the beautiful Talavera tiles produced from local clay. The Battle of May 5, 1862—resulting in a short-lived victory against French invaders—took place just north of town. The national holiday, Cinco de Mayo, is celebrated yearly on that date in its honor.

While in Puebla, don't miss the **Cathedral.** Onyx, marble, and gold adorn the high altar, designed by Mexico's most illustrious colonial architect, Manuel Tolsá.

The colonial **Convento de Santa Rosa,** now a ceramics museum, contains the intricately tiled kitchen where Puebla's renowned mole sauce was invented by the nuns as a surprise for their demanding gourmet bishop. Puebla is also famous for *camote,* a popular candy made from sweet potatoes and fruit. La Calle de las Dulces (Sweet Street) is lined with shops competing to sell a wide variety of freshly made camote.

Exploring Tehuacán Tehuacán is a good place to stop and relax for a night or two on your way to or from Oaxaca. The principal sight is the **Museo de la Valle de Tehuacán (the Ex-Convento del Carmen),** with exhibits on the development of agriculture. The appeal of "taking the waters" has faded over time, though there are several mineral-water swimming pools at ex-haciendas outside of town.

Exploring Tlaxcala Capital of the tiny state of the same name, Tlaxcala (Tlas-**ca**-la) will interest church lovers. (At Carnival time, it also hosts some spectacular dances.) The **monastery complex of San Francisco** (1537–1540), which stands atop a hill one block from the handsome main square, was the first permanent Catholic edifice in the New World. The most unusual feature of the church is its wood ceiling beams, carved and gilded after the Moorish fashion. (Moorish or *mudejar* architecture appeared in Mexico only during the very early years after the conquest, when Spain was still close enough in time to the Moorish occupation to be greatly influenced by Arabic architectural styles.) The austere convent, now a museum of history, boasts 18th-century religious paintings and a small collection of pre-Columbian pieces. Near the convent is a beautiful outdoor chapel whose symmetrical rear arches show Moorish and Gothic traces.

The **Palacio de Gobierno** (Government Palace), which occupies the north side of the Zócalo, was built about 1550. Inside are vivid epic murals of Tlaxcala before the conquest, painted in the 1960s by local artist Desiderio Hernández Xochitiotzin.

About 1 kilometer (less than a mile) west of Tlaxcala is the large, ornate **Sanctuary of Ocotlán.** It dates from the 18th century ánd was built on the site of a miracle performed by the Virgin. (In 1541, during a severe drought, she answered the prayers of an Indian by causing water to flow from the ground.) Noteworthy are the Churrigueresque, white plaster facade, which conjures up images of a wedding cake; the two Poblano (red-tile) towers; and, inside, the brilliantly painted and gilded Camarín chapel.

Off the Beaten Track **Cacaxtla.** The deep red and blue frescoes at the ruined ceremonial center of Cacaxtla were painted by a Mayan group from Campeche between AD 600 and 900. Discovered in 1975 (excavations are ongoing), the murals are among the best-preserved in Mexico.

Toluca and Valle de Bravo

This excursion to the west of Mexico City encompasses Toluca, capital of the state of Mexico and renowned for its Friday market but not much else, and Valle de Bravo, a lovely lakeside village popular with vacationing chilangos that because of its lush, green setting is often called Mexico's Switzerland. We suggest a brief stop en route at Desierto de los Leones, a forested national park whose centerpiece is an intriguing Carmelite monastery.

Tourist Information The **Mexico State Tourist Office** in Toluca is located at Edificio Plaza Toluca. *Av. 5 Lerdo de Tejada Pte. 101, tel. 721/4–10–99. Open weekdays 9–8, Sat. 9–3.*

Guided Tours All the major Mexico City tour operators can arrange tours to Toluca, with a stop at the Desierto de los Leones (*see* Guided Tours in Essential Information, *above*).

Getting Around By car, take Boulevard López Mateos to Calzada al Desierto de los Leones if you are going to the park. To go straight to Toluca, follow Paseo de la Reforma all the way west (it eventually merges with the Carretera a Toluca). Buses depart Terminal Poniente every 20 minutes. There are two choices for getting to Valle de Bravo: the winding but scenic route, which you pick up 3.2 kilometers (2 miles) west of Zincantepec, or Route 15. The former takes twice as much time to drive to but is worth it if you have the time and enjoy unspoiled mountain scenery.

Exploring Toluca On your way to Toluca, consider a brief stop at the **Desierto de los Leones**, a 5,000-acre national park 30 kilometers (18.6 miles) west of Mexico City. Deer and armadillos roam in the pine forest, and there are several walking trails. The focal point is the ruined 17th-century Carmelite ex-monastery, strangely isolated amid so much greenery. Guides will point out the incongruous torture chambers. The park played a significant role during the War of Independence: At a spot called Las Cruces, the troops of Father Hidalgo trounced the Spaniards but resolved not to go on and attack Mexico City, an error that cost the insurgents 10 more years of fighting.

The capital of the state of Mexico, Toluca is an industrial town. Go only on a Friday (market day); but before venturing into the market, stop at the **Casa de Artesanías** on Paseo Tollocán to get a feel for the prices. Specialties in the market come from surrounding villages and include serapes, rebozos, coarse wool sweaters, pottery, and cotton cloth.

Time Out If you fancy a picnic and don't mind a bit of a drive, make a 44-kilometer (27-mile) detour south of Toluca on Route 130 to **Nevado de Toluca Park**. At 4,691 meters (15,390 feet), the Nevado de Toluca, a now-extinct volcano, is Mexico's fourth-largest mountain; on clear days, its crater affords wonderful views of the valley. Picnickers might also enjoy a stop at **Parque de los Venados** (Park of the Deer).

Exploring Valle de Bravo Valle de Bravo is colonial, with white stucco houses trimmed with red balconies, tile roofs, and red-potted succulents cluttering the doorways. The town is hilly, many of the streets are unpaved, and beyond it lies Lake Avándaro, which is surrounded by pines and mountains. Valle was founded in 1530. There are no historical monuments to speak of, but plenty of diversions: boating, waterskiing, and swimming in the lake and its waterfalls, and the more sociable pleasures of the Sunday market, where exceptionally good pottery is the draw. Although Valle is an enclave for artists and the wealthy, it attracts inhabitants who prefer a low profile.

Teotihuacán, Tula, and Pachuca

Hugging the roads to the north of Mexico City are several of the country's most celebrated pre-Columbian and colonial monuments. The Basílica de Guadalupe, a church dedicated to Mexico's patron saint, and the pyramids of Teotihuacán make an easy day tour, as does the combination of the ex-convent (now a magnificent museum of the viceregal period) at Tepotzotlán and the ruins at Tula. Pachuca, however, is farther north and is more comfortably visited as part of an overnight excursion.

Tourist Information The **Hidalgo State Tourist Office** in Pachuca can help you. *Allende 406, tel. 771/3-95-00. Open weekdays and Sat. morning.*

Guided Tours All the major Mexico City tour operators can arrange trips to Teotihuacán, Tula, and Pachuca (*see* Guided Tours in Essential Information, *above*).

Getting Around To reach La Villa de Guadalupe by car, take Avenida Insurgentes Norte to the Pachuca toll road (Rte. 85); the side road for Acolmán is 3 kilometers (1.9 miles) after the toll booth. Buses run every half hour from the Central de Autobuses del Norte to Teotihuacán, and the trip takes about one hour. Pachuca is a good 77 kilometers (48 miles) beyond Teotihuacán and can be reached either by doubling back to Route 85 or along the old road to Pachuca, via Epazoyucán.

To get to Tepotzotlán from Mexico City, follow Periférico Norte out to the Carretera a Querétaro. After 41 kilometers (25.4 miles) there is a detour for Tepotzotlán. Tula is about 8 kilometers (5 miles) north of Teotihuacán off Route 57D. Buses to Tula leave Mexico City every 20 minutes; from Pachuca, every 15 minutes.

Exploring La Villa de Guadalupe "La Villa"—more formally known as La Villa de Guadalupe, the site of the two Basilicas of the Virgin of Guadalupe—is technically within the northern limits of Mexico City (The #3 Metro line goes from downtown to the **Basílica** stop). Also, it can easily be visited in combination with the pyramids of Tenochtitlán, farther north. From here the Spaniards laid siege to Tenochtitlán in 1521, and in 1867 La Villa served as Porfiro Díaz's headquarters for the ousting of Emperor Maximilian. But the area's symbolic importance derives from the miracle that transpired here on December 12, 1531, when an Indian named Juan Diego received from the Virgin a cloak permanently imprinted with her image so he could prove to the priests that he had indeed had a holy vision. On that date each year, millions of pilgrims arrive, many crawling on their knees for the last few hundred meters, and praying for cures and other divine favors. The **Basílica Vieja** (Old Basilica) dates to 1536, although various additions were made during the intervening centuries; the altar was executed by sculptor Manuel Tolsá. The basilica now houses a museum of ex-votos (votive offerings) and popular religious art, painting, sculpture, and decorative and applied arts from the 15th to the 18th century.

Because of increasing numbers of pilgrims, the old church is no longer large enough to accommodate all worshipers. In 1976 the government erected the **Basílica Nueva** (New Basilica), a grotesque and most unchurchlike mass of steel, wood, resinous fibers, and polyethylene designed by Pedro Ramírez Vázquez, who is also the architect of the Museum of Anthropology. It holds 10,000 people; the famous cloak is enshrined in its own altar and can be viewed from a moving sidewalk that passes below it.

Exploring Teotihuacán Most tour buses to the ruins stop briefly in **Acolmán** to see the outstanding Gothic church and ex-convent, now a museum. The original Augustinian church (1539) is noteworthy for its vaulted roof and pointed towers; the ornate cloister and Plater-

Teotihuacán

0 — 400 meters
0 — 400 yards

N

Palace of the Jaguar
Pyramid of the Moon
Temple of the Plumed Conch Shells
Plaza of Columns
Avenue of the Dead
Pyramid of the Sun
Viking Group
Rio San Juan
The Citadel
Museum
Temple of Quetzalcóatl

esque facade, set off with candelabralike columns, were added a century later by the monks.

The monumental place occupied by Teotihuacán in early Mexican history is described in Chapter 13, The Yucatán Peninsula. That statue is easily matched by the physical grandeur and scale of the site itself: The **Pyramid of the Sun** extends over 4,640 square feet and has 248 steps to climb. (Bring comfortable walking shoes, sunscreen or visored hat; women should wear slacks.) Only the pyramids of Cholula and Cheops (Egypt) are larger.

Climbing one pyramid is probably enough for most people; in any event you will have a good view of the smaller **Pyramid of the Moon** at the northern end of the Street of the Dead. Since the entire site encompasses 13 square kilometers (8 square miles), you may actually end up visiting only one or two of the 15 or so complexes. Note the abundant carvings of Quetzalcóatl, the plumed serpent, and Tlaloc, the god of rain, on the Temple of Quetzalcóatl, and the blood-red traces of ancient murals in the Palace of the Jaguar and the Temple of the Plumed Conch Shells.

The artifacts uncovered at Teotihuacán are on display at the Museum of Anthropology in Mexico City. The on-site museum contains only scale models and chronological charts. A light-and-sound show is performed at the site nightly October–May, Tuesday–Sunday at 7 PM.

Seeing the ruins will take two to four hours, depending on how taken you are with the place (or when your tour bus leaves).

Exploring Pachuca Capital of the state of Hidalgo, Pachuca was founded by the Spaniards in the early 16th century. The town grew quickly once silver was discovered in the area. It is situated high up in the Sierra Madres and is more appealing for its vaguely colonial ambience than for any individual sight. Among the structures from the viceregal era, see the **Casa de Caja** (1670), built to house the "king's fifth" of all silver mined, which was destined for the Spanish crown. Also downtown is the **Casa Colorada,** the red stone home of the Counts of Regla. The **Museo Nacional de la Fotografía** is housed in the 17th-century Ex-Monastery of San Francisco and specializes in rare photographic archives from the revolution. Pachuca is belatedly waking up to tourism by closing some streets to vehicular traffic and putting up murals of the local Otomi Indians.

Exploring Tepotzotlán The **church** and **monastery of San Francisco Javier** at Tepotzotlán rank among the masterpieces of Mexican Churrigueresque architecture. The unmitigated Baroque facade of the church (1682) is the first thing to catch the eye, but inside and out, every square inch has been worked over, like an overdressed Christmas tree. Note especially the gilded, bemirrored Chapel of the Loreto.

After centuries of abandon—the Jesuits were expelled from New Spain in 1767—the religious complex at Tepotzotlán has been designated for a new use. The government turned the adjacent monastery (1584) into the **Museo del Virreinato** in 1964. It contains a magnificent collection of vestments, paintings, *retablos* (altarpieces), chalices, and jewels.

Exploring Tula Tula, capital of the Toltecs (its original name was Tollán), was founded in about AD 1000 and abandoned two centuries later. The Toltecs were a northern, warlike tribe who expanded as far as Yucatán to the east (parts of Chichén Itzá show a strong Toltec influence), Guatemala to the south, and Chihuahua and southern New Mexico to the north. Quetzalcóatl was originally a Toltec deity; the tribe is also thought to have introduced ball courts to Mesoamerica.

It is the 4.5-meter (15-foot) warrior statues (called *atlantes*), rather than the ruins themselves, that give Tula its fame. These basalt figures tower over Pyramid B, their harsh geometric lines looking vaguely like totem poles. Crocodiles, jaguars, coyotes, and eagles are also depicted in the carvings and represent the various warrior orders of the Toltecs.

4 Baja California

Tijuana

Introduction

By Maribeth Mellin

A former senior editor of San Diego Magazine, *Maribeth Mellin is a San Diego–based free-lance writer and photographer. She has been making regular forays to Mexico for the past 10 years.*

Just 29 kilometers (18 miles) south of San Diego lies Tijuana, Mexico's fourth-largest city. A metropolis, Tijuana can no longer be called a border "town." The official language is Spanish, but many speak "Spanglish," a mix of Spanish and English. Residents come from throughout Mexico and Central America; visitors come from throughout the world. Tijuana's promoters like to call it "the most visited city in the world." The border crossing at Tijuana is the busiest in the United States. Tijuana has served as a gigantic recreation center for southern Californians since the turn of the century. Before then it was a ranch, populated by a few hundred Mexicans. In 1911, a group of Americans invaded the area and attempted to set up an independent republic; they were quickly driven out by Mexican soldiers. When Prohibition hit the United States in the 1920s, Tijuana boomed. The Agua Caliente Racetrack and Casino opened in 1929. Americans seeking alcohol, gambling, and more fun than they could find back home flocked across the border, spending freely, which fueled the region's growth. Tijuana became the entry port for what some termed a "sinful, steamy playground," frequented by Hollywood stars and the idle rich. Then Prohibition was repealed, Mexico outlawed gambling, and Tijuana's fortunes dwindled. The Agua Caliente Resort fell into ruin and has never been revived.

The flow of travelers from the north slowed to a trickle for a while, but Tijuana still captivated those in search of the sort of fun that was illegal and frowned upon at home. The ever-growing numbers of servicemen in San Diego kept Tijuana's sordid reputation alive. Before the toll highway to Ensenada was finished in 1967, travelers going south drove straight through downtown Tijuana, stopping along Avenida Revolución and its side streets for supplies and souvenirs.

The city's population has mushroomed—from 300,000 in 1970 to more than 1.5 million today. The city has spread into canyons and dry riverbeds, over hillsides, and onto ocean cliffs.

Tourism creates jobs and bolsters Tijuana's fragile economy. The city's leaders realize this and have worked hard to attract visitors. Avenida Revolución, the main street that was once lined with brothels and bars, has undergone tremendous rehabilitation. Today the avenue is lined with shops and restaurants, all catering to tourists. Park benches and shade trees on brick paths winding away from the traffic encourage tourists to rest and watch the scenery. Many tourists are regulars, with favorite shops and restaurants. San Diegans often travel south of the border just for dinner and become neighbors of sorts, making friends with the locals.

Tijuana's tourist attractions have remained much the same throughout the century. Gambling on horses and greyhounds is legal and popular at the recently renovated Agua Caliente Racetrack. El Palacio Frontón (Jai Alai Palace), where betting is also allowed, is equally popular with its fast-paced games, cheering fans, and palatial edifice.

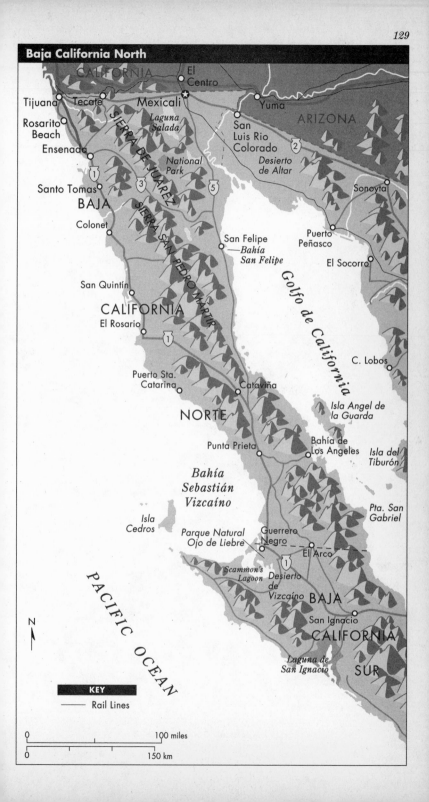

Baja California North

California
El Centro
Tijuana Tecate Mexicali Yuma
Rosarito Beach
Ensenada *Laguna Salada* San Luis Rio Colorado ARIZONA
SIERRA DE JUAREZ
Santo Tomas *National Park* *Desierto de Altar*
BAJA ③ ⑤
Colonet Sonoyta
SIERRA SAN PEDRO MARTIR
San Felipe Puerto Peñasco
—*Bahía San Felipe*
San Quintín El Socorro
CALIFORNIA
El Rosario ①
Golfo de California
Puerto Sta. Catarina Cataviña C. Lobos
NORTE *Isla Angel de la Guarda*
Punta Prieta Bahía de Los Angeles *Isla del Tiburón*
Bahía Sebastián Vizcaíno
Isla Cedros Pta. San Gabriel
Parque Natural Ojo de Liebre Guerrero Negro
El Arco
Scammon's Lagoon *Desierto de Vizcaíno* BAJA
PACIFIC OCEAN San Ignacio
CALIFORNIA
Laguna de San Ignacio SUR

N

KEY
— Rail Lines

0 _____ 100 miles
0 _____ 150 km

Baja California South

Isla Angel de la Guarda

Isla del Tiburón

Hermosillo

Mazatán

San Rafael

Pta. San Gabriel

Cieneguita

Tecoripa

El Arco

1

Guaymas

15

San Ignacio

Santa Rosalía
Mulege

Isla Lobos

Ciudad Obregón

Navajoa

Pta. Concepción

1

Laguna de San Ignacio

Bahía Concepcion

Huatabampo

15

BAJA

Rosarito

Golfo de California

Mision San Javier

Loreto

La Poza

Isla Carmen

Las Grullas Márgen Derecha

CALIFORNIA

Puerto Escondido

SIERRA GIGANTA

TO LOS MOCHIS

Insurgentes

Constitución

SUR

Isla San José

Isla Partida

Santa Rita

1

Bahía de la Paz

Isla Santa Margarita

Isla Cerralvo

TO MAZATLÁN

N

La Paz

PACIFIC OCEAN

Ensenada de los Muertos

El Triunfo

SIERRA DE SAN LAZARO

Todos Santos

Los Barriles

Santiago

9

1

Cabo Pulmo

Cabo San Lucas

San José del Cabo

KEY
— Rail Lines
🚢 Ferry Lines

0   100 miles

0   150 km

Some of Spain's and Mexico's greatest bullfighters appear at the oceanfront and downtown bullrings; some of Latin America's most popular musicians and dancers perform at the Cultural Center; and there are an extraordinary number of restaurants. Eating and drinking well are among Tijuana's greatest attractions.

Shopping is one of Tijuana's other main draws. From the moment you cross the border, people will approach you or call out and insist that you look at their wares. If you drive, workers will run out from auto-body shops to place bids on new paint or upholstery for your car. All along Avenida Revolución and its side streets, shops sell everything from tequila to Tiffany lamps; serious shoppers can spend a full day searching and bargaining for their items of choice. If you intend to buy food in Mexico, get the U.S. customs list of articles that are illegal to bring back, so your purchases won't be confiscated.

The Río Tijuana area, called the Zona Río, is quickly becoming the city's glamorous zone. The area is not far from the border, just past the dry riverbed of the Tijuana River along Paseo de los Héroes. This boulevard is one of the city's main thoroughfares, with large statues of historical figures, including one of Abraham Lincoln, in the center of the *glorietas* (traffic circles). The Plaza Río Tijuana, built on Paseo de los Héroes in 1982, was Tijuana's first major shopping center. Pueblo Amigo, a shopping and entertainment complex at the north end of the Zona Río, just 300 meters (328 yards) from the border, has a pedestrian walkway that leads from the border and through the plaza to Boulevard Paseo de los Héroes.

Arriving and Departing by Plane

Mexicana (tel. 800/531–7921), **Aeroméxico** (tel. 800/237–6639), and **Aero California** (tel. 800/237–6225) serve many cities in Mexico, with fares that are often lower than those for flights from the United States. No U.S. carriers fly into Tijuana. The airport is located on the eastern edge of the city, near the Otay Mesa border crossing. The cab fare from the San Ysidro border is about $8 per person; from the Otay Mesa border, about $10. Shuttle services operate Volkswagen vans *(combis)* from the airport to downtown and the borders.

Arriving and Departing by Car, Trolley, and Bus

By Car U.S.-5 and I-805 end at the border crossing in San Ysidro; Highway 905 leads from I-5 and I-805 to the border crossing at Otay Mesa, near the Tijuana airport. Day-trippers often prefer to park their cars on the U.S. side and walk across the border. There are acres of parking lots by the border, charging from $5 to $10 per day. It's worth the extra money to park at a guarded lot, since break-ins are common. Those driving into Tijuana should purchase Mexican auto insurance, available at many stands along the last exit before the border crossing. On holidays and weekends, there can be a wait at the border when traveling into Mexico. The wait to get back into the United States can be up to two hours, though lines are usually shorter at the Otay Mesa crossing.

By Trolley The **San Diego Trolley** (tel. 619/231–1466) travels from the Santa Fe Depot, at Kettner Boulevard and Broadway, to within

100 feet of the border every 15 minutes during the day (every 30 minutes after 7:30 PM). The 45-minute trip costs $2.

By Bus **Greyhound** (tel. 619/239–3266 or 800/528–0447) serves Tijuana from San Diego several times daily. **Mexicoach** (tel. 619/232–5049) has several departures from the Santa Fe Depot to Tijuana. **Baja California Tours** (tel. 619/454–7166) has daily buses to Tijuana. Within Mexico, **Turisticos de Baja California** (Av. Madero and Calle Mexico, tel. 66/88–3981) has charter buses and vans for trips into Baja and is planning to offer tourist buses with air-conditioning and other creature comforts for trips throughout Baja. **Autotransportes de Baja California** (tel. 66/85–8472) links Tijuana with other points in Baja; **Tres Estrellas de Oro** (tel. 66/86–9186) travels into mainland Mexico, and **Autotransportes del Pacífico** (tel. 66/86–9045) has service to the Pacific Coast. The Tijuana Central Bus Station is at Calz. Lázaro Cárdenas and Blvd. Arroyo Alamar (tel. 66/80–9060).

Getting Around

Because of the long lines to reenter the United States, those spending just a day in Tijuana are advised to park on the U.S. side of the border and walk across the border, then take a taxi to their destinations. There is a large lot with scores of taxis just the other side of the border; from there you can reach the airport, the Cultural Center, the Río area, or Avenida Revolución for under $10. The 2-kilometer (1¼-mile) walk to Avenida Revolución is an easy one through Viva Tijuana, an open-air shopping mall completed in 1991. A walkway leads from the border to the Zona Río; follow the signs to Pueblo Amigo on your immediate right after you cross the border.

By Car There are plenty of signs at the border to lead you to main highways and downtown, but once you hit the streets, Tijuana can be very confusing. There are parking lots along Avenida Revolución and at most major attractions; it is advisable to leave your car in a guarded lot. If you park on the street, pay attention to the signs. Your license plates will be removed if you park illegally.

Avis is the only major U.S. company that allows its cars to be driven into Mexico, and then only as far as Guerro Negro. **Courtesy Rentals** in San Diego (tel. 800/252–3756 or 800/252–9756 in CA) allows their cars to be taken as far as Ensenada. The larger U.S. rental agencies have offices at the Tijuana International Airport. Offices in town include **Avis** (Av. Agua Caliente 3310, tel. 66/86–4004); **Budget** (Paseo de los Héroes 77, tel. 66/84–0253); and **National** (Av. Agua Caliente 5000, tel. 66/86–2103).

By Taxi Taxis in Tijuana are both plentiful and inexpensive. Fares to all parts of the city are under $10 per person. Be sure to agree on the price before the car starts moving.

By Bus The downtown bus station is at Calle 1a and Avenida Madero (tel. 66/86–9515). Most city buses at the border will take you downtown; the bus to the border from downtown departs from Calle Benito Juárez, also called Calle 2a, between Avenidas Revolución and Constitución. All buses marked "Centro Camionera" go through downtown.

Important Addresses and Numbers

Tourist Information The **Tijuana Chamber of Commerce** is the best source of tourist information. *Av. Revolución and Calle 1, tel. 66/85–8472. Open daily 9–7.*

Baja Information (7860 Mission Center Court, Suite 202, San Diego, CA 92108, tel. 619/298–4105; in the U.S. 800/225–2786; in CA 800/522–1516) handles reservations for many Baja hotels and arranges a variety of package deals.

There is a tourism office directly across the border with maps, newspapers and English-speaking clerks. Tourist information booths are located at the foot of Calle 1, just after the pedestrian overpass across the border at the airport, and at the intersection of Avenida Revolución and Calle 4. *Tel. 66/83–1310. Open daily 9–5.*

Emergencies **Police** (tel. 134); **Red Cross** (tel. 132); **Fire** (tel. 136); **U.S. Consulate** (tel. 66/86–3886).

Guided Tours

San Diego Mini-Tours (837 47th St., San Diego, CA 92113, tel. 619/234–9044) has hourly departures from San Diego hotels to Av. Revolución in Tijuana and back, and connections with a Mexican-operated trolley tour of Tijuana.

Exploring

Numbers in the margin correspond to points of interest on the Tijuana map.

 At the **San Ysidro Border Crossing,** a pedestrain walkway travels through the Viva Tijuana dining and shopping center and an adjacent lineup of stalls filled with the full spectrum of souvenirs, and then goes up Calle 2 into the center of town.

Mexitlan (Av. Ocampo between Calles 2 and 5, tel. 66/38–4101), a fascinating combination of museum and entertainment/shopping center, opened in 1991, after several years of planning and construction. Designed by architect Pedro Ramírez Vásquez, Mexitlan has scale models of all the major architectural and cultural landmarks throughout Mexico and is an exciting addition to Tijuana. *Admission $10. Open Wed.–Mon. 10–10.*

2 Calle 2 intersects **Avenida Revolución,** now lined with designer clothing shops and restaurants, all catering to tourists. Shopkeepers call out from their doorways, offering low prices for an odd assortment of garish souvenirs. Many shopping arcades open onto Avenida Revolución; inside the front doors are mazes of small stands with low-priced pottery and other handicrafts.

3 **El Palacio Frontón (Jai Alai Palace)** is on Avenida Revolución between Calles 7a and 8a. The Moorish-style palace is a magnificent building and an exciting place to watch and bet on fast-pace jai alai games.

Time Out Among the many restaurants along Avenida Revolución, **La Especial** (Av. Revolución 718, tel. 66/85–6654) is a favorite for Mexican food that hasn't been fancied up for the tourists. Head to the **Hotel Caesar** (Av. Revolución 827, tel. 66/88–0550) for Caesar salad, which was invented here.

At Calle 11a, Avenida Revolución becomes Boulevard Agua Caliente and passes by **El Toreo de Tijuana,** where bullfights are held from May to September. A few blocks farther is the **Hipódromo de Agua Caliente,** or **Agua Caliente Racetrack.** Since 1985, some $14 million has been spent on renovations and the building of a Jockey Club and Turf Club. In the Foreign Book area, bettors can wager on races televised via satellite from California. Nearby are the two gleaming, mirrored towers of the **Hotel Fiesta Americana**—Tijuana's glamour spot.

Between Boulevard Agua Caliente and the border is the **Río Tijuana** area, running parallel to the river. With its impressive Cultural Center and shopping complex, this zone, along Avenida Paseo de los Héroes, is fast becoming Tijuana's Zona Rosa.

The **Cultural Center** was designed by architects Manuel Rosen and Pedro Ramírez Vásquez, who also created Mexico City's famous Museum of Anthropology. The Cultural Center's exhibits of Mexican history are a perfect introduction for the thousands of visitors whose first taste of Mexico is at the border. Some rotating exhibits focus on specific regions and cultures; others highlight the works of present-day artists. An important part of the center is the Omnimax Theater, with its curving 180-degree screen. *El Pueblo del Sol (People of the Sun)* is a cinematic tour of Mexico. Guest artists appear at the Cultural Center regularly. The center's bookstore has an excellent selection on Mexican history, culture, and arts in both Spanish and English. *Paseo de los Héroes and Av. Independencia, tel. 66/84–1111. Admission to the Omnimax Theater: $4.50. Open daily 9–8:30;*

the English-language version of the film El Pueblo del Sol *is presented daily at 2 PM.*

⑨ Plaza Río Tijuana, the area's largest shopping complex, is next door to the Cultural Center on Paseo de los Héroes. It is enormous, with good restaurants, department stores, and hundreds of shops. The plaza has become a central square of sorts, where holiday fiestas are held. This stretch of Paseo de los Héroes has been landscaped with shade trees and flowers, and there are long, wide sidewalks leading from the shopping complex to the Cultural Center.

Time Out   The restaurant inside the Cultural Center serves fairly good Mexican food throughout the week. It's a good place for just sitting to relax and absorb all you've seen. **Panadería Suzette,** in the Plaza Río shopping center, has an array of Mexican and French pastries; coffee is free with your selection.

⑩ Playas Tijuana along the oceanfront is slated for development in the near future. Now the area is a mix of modest and expensive residential neighborhoods, with a few restaurants and hotels. The beaches, which are long and pleasant, are visited **⑪** mostly by locals. The "Bullring by the Sea," **Plaza de Toros Monumental,** is at the northwest corner of the beach area, right by the border. Bullfights are held here on alternate Sunday afternoons from May through September (El Toreo de Tijuana hosts bullfights every second Sunday). Admission to bullfights varies, depending on the fame of the matador and where you sit.

Shopping

The traditional shopping strip is Avenida Revolución, between Calles 1 and 8. The avenue is lined with shops and arcades that display a wide range of crafts and curios. Sellers yell to shoppers in the streets, promising low prices. Bargaining is expected on the streets and in the arcades, but not in the finer shops. **Sanborns** (Av. Revolución and Calle 9) is a nice addition to the strip, with beautiful crafts from throughout Mexico, an excellent bakery, and chocolates from Mexico City. The **Drug Store, Maxim's, Dorian's** and **Sara's** have good selections of clothing and imported perfumes. **Tolan,** across from the Jai Alai Palace at Avenida Revolución 111, has an impressive variety of high-quality crafts. **Benetton, Guess, Eduardo's** (Av. Revolución 1105), and **Maya de México** (Av. Revolución 816) have sportswear and resortwear, as does **Ralph Lauren Polo** (Calle 7). **La Gran Bota** on Avenida Revolución has great cowboy boots; **Espinosa,** with branches on Avenida Revolución and in the Cultural Center, has fine silver, brass, and gold jewelry.

The Avenida Revolución shopping area has spread down Calle 1 to the foot of the pedestrian walkway leading from the border. The shops in Plaza Revolución, at the corner of Calle 1 and Avenida Revolución, stock quality crafts. If you're spending a day shopping in Tijuana it makes sense to begin shopping at the arcades at the end of the pedestrian border-crossing walkway, gauging prices as you travel toward Avenida Revolución. You may find that the best bargains are closer to the border, and you won't have to carry your rugs and piñatas around all day long.

Shopping Centers **Plaza Río Tijuana** is described in Exploring Tijuana, *above.* **Pueblo Amigo** on Boulevard Paseo de los Héroes is a fanciful pseudopueblo with colonial-style adobe buildings painted in bright blues, greens, and yellows. **Ley,** a gourmet grocery that sells salad by the pint and hard-to-find Mexican delicacies such as fresh mole sauce and pickled carrots and cauliflower, is one of the center's best shops. **Mexitlán,** on Avenida Ocampo, stocks high-quality folk art from throughout Mexico. **Plaza Fiesta,** on Paseo de los Héroes across from Plaza Río Tijuana, has a collection of boutiques, jewelry stores and stained-glass shops. Next door, the **Plaza de los Zapatos** has more than a dozen stores selling designer shoes imported from throughout the world; **La Herradura de Oro** sells fine hand-tooled saddles.

Participant Sports

Golf The **Tijuana Country Club** (Blvd. Agua Caliente, east of downtown, tel. 66/81–7855) is open to guests of some hotels. It provides rental clubs, electric and hand carts, and caddies for the 18-hole course.

Spectator Sports

Bullfights Bullfights, considered artistic spectacles, not sporting events, feature skilled matadors from throughout Mexico and Spain. They are held at **El Toreo de Tijuana** (Av. Agua Caliente just outside downtown) on Sunday at 4, during May through September. They are also held at the **Plaza de Toros Monumental.** *Playas Tijuana area, Ensenada Hwy., tel. 66/85–2210. Admission varies. Sunday at 4, July–Aug.*

Jai Alai This ancient Basque sport is played in the Moorish-style **Palacio Frontón,** or **Jai Alai Palace,** which is worth seeing even if you don't attend the games. *Av. Revolución and Calle 8, tel. 66/88–0125. Admission $2. Closed Thur.*

Horse and At the **Hipódromo de Agua Caliente** the horses race Friday and
Greyhound Races Saturday at 1:15, and the dogs race nightly at 7:45 and at 2 on Sunday and Monday afternoons. The track's new Jockey Club and restaurant, which are open to the public for $10, are lavish. In the Foreign Book area, gamblers can bet on races taking place in California and shown at Caliente on TV monitors. *Bd. Agua Caliente at Salinas, tel. 66/81–7811; in San Diego, tel. 619/231–1919.*

Charreadas Amateur cowboy associations compete at one of several rings
(Mexican Rodeos) around town on Sundays. Call 66/84–2126 for information.

Beaches

The **Playas Tijuana** area south of Ensenada (the toll road) has been under development for years but as yet has no major hotels and few restaurants. The beaches are frequented primarily by locals.

Dining

There is no shortage of good eating in Tijuana, from *taquerias* (taco stands) to gourmet and Continental restaurants. The seafood is unbeatable; beef and pork are excellent, both grilled and marinated. Pheasant, quail, rabbit, and duck are popular in the more expensive places. Puerto Nuevo–style lobster and shrimp (grilled and served with beans, rice, and tortillas) are fixtures in restaurants modeled after those at the popular seaside fishing village of Puerto Nuevo south of Rosarito. Some restaurants add a 15% service charge to the bill.

A few of the best restaurants from the '20s and '30s still attract a steady clientele with their excellent international cuisine and reasonable prices. On the more moderate scale, there are scores of seafood restaurants and kitchens that serve great Mexican food, unadulterated for foreign tastes. Avenida Revolución resembles one long food court with places for every taste and budget. At night the street life often becomes rowdy, with tourists demonstrating the effects of potent Mexican margaritas. Highly recommended restaurants are indicated by a star ★.

Category	Cost*
Expensive	over $15
Moderate	$10–$15
Inexpensive	under $10

per person excluding drinks, service, and sales tax (10%)

Expensive

★ **Alcázar del Río.** Nouvelle cuisine amid mirrors has hit Tijuana with this upscale, see-and-be-seen restaurant. Patrons are the city's success stories—the casually elegant, sophisticated elite. There's a bit of everything considered to be exotic in Tijuana—smoked salmon with capers, Australian lamb, Serrano ham with sweet cantaloupe, cherries jubilee. The halibut with pine nuts is sublimely simple, and the wine list is excellent. *Bd. Paseo de los Héroes 56–5, tel. 66/84–2672. Reservations suggested. Jacket and tie suggested. AE, MC, V.*

★ **Cilantro's.** This restaurant in the newly opened Viva Tijuana center is one of the best places to sample Mexico's regional dishes. *Ceviche* (marinated fish cocktail), *huachinango* (red snapper) with Yucatán herbs, and a rich mole sauce are all expertly prepared. The menu also features burritos and enchiladas for the less adventurous diner. Colorful posters by Mexican artists adorn the dining room, which looks out onto the shopping plaza. An adjoining disco, XS, provides post-dining entertainment. *Paseo Tijuana 406, tel. 66/82–8340. Dress: casual. AE, MC, V. Open Tues.–Sun. noon–11.*

★ **Pedrín's.** One of Tijuana's best seafood restaurants overlooks the Jai Alai Palace from a second-story garden room. Meals include deep-fried fish appetizers, fish chowder, salad, an entrée, and a sweet after-dinner drink of Kahlua and cream. Recommended dishes include *rajas shrimp*, covered with melted cheese and green chilies, and grilled lobster. *Av. Revolución 1115, tel. 66/85–4052. Reservations accepted. Dress: casual. AE, MC, V.*

Moderate

★ **La Leña.** The sparkling clean white dining room in La Leña (there are two restaurant locations) faces an open kitchen where chefs grill unusual beef dishes, such as *Gaonera*, a tender fillet of beef stuffed with cheese and guacamole. The owner often visits with his guests, asking their opinion on the menu and offering samples of tripe—only for the strong of stomach. *Bd. Agua Caliente 4560, tel. 66/86–2920; also at Av. Revo-*

lución between Calles 4 and 5. Reservations accepted. Dress: casual. AE, MC, V. Open daily noon–10 PM.

La Taberna Española. The mainstay of Plaza Fiesta's multiethnic cafés, this Spanish tapas bar attracts a youthful, sophisticated crowd. The tapa (appetizer) menu is printed in Spanish, but with a bit of imagination you should be able to select a representative sampling, including octopus in its own ink, a plate of spicy sausages, a wedge of Spanish tortilla with potatoes and eggs, and a bowl of fava beans. The interior café is smoky, fragrant, and invariably crowded; sit at the outdoor tables for a better view of the crowd waiting in line. *Plaza Fiesta, Paseo de los Héroes 10001, tel. 66/84–7562. No reservations. Dress: casual. No credit cards.*

Margarita's Village. Those who love margaritas have their choice of 14 flavors at this restaurant, which also specializes in *cabrito* (baby goat, usually roasted) and other Mexican dishes. Singing waiters hold forth in the large indoor dining room and on the outdoor second-story patio overlooking Avenida Revolución. *Av. Revolución at Calle 3, tel. 66/85–7362. No reservations. Dress: casual. AE, DC, MC, V.*

★ **Tía Juana Tilly's.** Popular with both tourists and locals looking for revelry and generous portions of Mexican specialties, this is one of the few places where you can get *cochinita píbil*, a Yucatecan specialty made of roast pig, red onions, and bitter oranges; or the traditionally bitter and savory chicken mole. Part of the same chain is Tilly's Fifth Ave., catercorner to the original on Avenida Revolución. *Av. Revolución at Calle 7, tel. 66/85–6024. Reservations accepted. Dress: casual. AE, DC, MC, V.*

Inexpensive **Carnitas Uruapan.** A large, noisy restaurant where the main attraction is *carnitas* (marinated pork) sold by weight and served with homemade tortillas, salsa, *cilantro* (coriander), guacamole, and onions. Patrons mingle at long wood tables in rustic surroundings, toasting with chilled *cervezas* (beer). *Bd. Díaz Ordaz 550, tel. 66/81–6181; also at Paseo de los Héroes at Av. Rodriguez, no phone. No reservations. Dress: casual. No credit cards. Open daily noon–midnight.*

★ **La Especial.** Located at the foot of the stairs leading to an underground shopping arcade, this restaurant attracts diners in search of home-style Mexican cooking at low prices. There's nothing fancy about the seemingly endless basement room—which is never empty. *Av. Revolución 718, tel. 66/85–6654. No reservations. Dress: casual. No credit cards.*

Señor Frog's. Heaping plates of barbecued chicken and ribs and buckets of ice-cold bottles of cerveza are the mainstay at this fun and festive formula eatery, one of many in the Carlos Anderson chain. The loud music and laughter make for a raucous atmosphere, and the food is consistently good. *In the Pueblo Amigo center, Paseo Tijuana, no phone. Dress: casual. AE, MC, V. Open daily noon–2 AM.*

Lodging

Tijuana's hotels are clustered downtown, along Avenida Revolución, near the country club on Boulevard Agua Caliente, and in the Río Tijuana area on Paseo de los Héroes. There are ample accommodations for all price levels, and a number of new hotels are under construction. **Baja Information** can reserve hotel rooms (*see* Important Addresses and Numbers, *above*).

Baja Lodging Services (4659 Park Bd., San Diego, CA 92116, tel. 619/491–0682) makes hotel, condo, and private-home reservations throughout Baja. Highly recommended lodgings are indicated by a star ★.

Category	Cost*
Expensive	over $50
Moderate	$25–$50
Inexpensive	under $25

All prices are for a standard double room, excluding service charge and sales tax (10%).

Expensive **Fiesta Americana.** The two mirrored towers of the hotel are
★ Tijuana's most ostentatious landmarks, signs of prosperity and faith in the economic potential of this lucrative border town. The Fiesta Americana often hosts receptions and parties for Tijuana's elite, and is considered by many to be the city's most glamorous place for a drink or meal. *Bd. Agua Caliente 4558, tel. 66/81–7000 or 800/223–2332. 422 rooms with bath. Facilities: nightclub, restaurant, health club, tennis courts, pool, travel agency. AE, DC, MC, V.*

★ **Lucerna.** This is one of the most charming hotels in Tijuana, with lovely gardens, a large swimming pool surrounded by palms, and comfortable rooms with tiled baths. The hotel's travel agency is particularly helpful with planning trips into Mexico. *Bd. Paseo de los Héroes and Av. Rodríguez, tel. 66/34–2000. 170 rooms and 9 suites with bath. Facilities: pool, restaurant, coffee shop, nightclub, travel agency. AE, DC, V.*

Moderate **Corona Plaza.** Though the exterior of this hotel resembles a nondescript office building, the interior is surprisingly pleasant. Rooms, which are filled with handsome bleached wood furnishings, overlook an atrium lobby and restaurant. For less noise and more air, ask for a second- or third-floor room near the pool. The bullring is within walking distance; other attractions are just a short cab ride away. *Blvd. Agua Caliente 1426, tel. 66/81–8183. Facilities: swimming pool, restaurant. AE, MC, V.*

La Mesa Inn. This recently renovated Best Western hotel/motel has a small, shaded pool and rooms you could find anywhere, with tan walls, brown carpet, earthtone decor, and no charm. Stay away from the rooms by the street and pool. *Bd. Díaz Ordaz 50, tel. 66/81–6522 or 800/528–1234. 125 rooms. Facilities: pool, coffee shop, bar. MC, V.*

★ **La Villa de Zaragoza.** A fairly new brown stucco motel with a good downtown location near the Jai Alai Palace, La Villa is one block from Revolución. In this price range it has the nicest rooms downtown. *Av. Madero 1120, tel. 66/85–1832. 42 rooms. Facilities: restaurant, parking. MC, V.*

Inexpensive **CREA Youth Hostel.** The hostel is set in a quiet, peaceful park and is part of a sports complex. The 20 beds are in same-sex dorms, and there is a cafeteria. *Av. Padre Kino, tel. 66/84–2523 or 66/84–7510. No credit cards.*

Léon. This downtown hotel just off Revolución is clean and in the middle of the action, but a bit less noisy than hotels on

Revolución. *Calle 7 and Av. Revolución, tel. 66/85-7330. 40 rooms. No credit cards.*

The Arts and Nightlife

Tijuana has toned down its Sin City image; much of the action now takes place at the **Jai Alai Palace** and the racetrack. Several hotels, especially the **Lucerna** and **Fiesta Americana**, feature live entertainment. The hippest club is **Iguanas** (Bd. Paseo de los Héroes, tel. 66/82-4967), at the Pueblo Amigo shopping center. An 18-and-over club with appearances by new wave and rock artists, Iguanas draws as many patrons from San Diego as from Tijuana. Cover charge varies with the group.

The **Odyssey** (Av. Revolución between Calle 2 and Calle 3, tel. 66/87-2477), a watering hole and disco, has a fifth-story terrace overlooking the action on Revolución. For total immersion in the flashy, high-tech disco scene try **OH! Laser Club** (Paseo de los Héroes 56, tel. 66/84-0267), **Heaven & Hell** (Paseo de los Héroes 10501, tel. 66/84-8484), **The News** (Pueblo Amigo, tel. 66/82-3387), and **Baby Rock** (1482 Diego Rivera, tel. 66/84-0440). Tijuana's discos are elegant and sophisticated, and usually have strict dress codes, with no T-shirts, jeans, or sandals allowed. Stick to high heels and spandex.

Rosarito Beach

Introduction

Not long ago, Playas de Rosarito (Rosarito Beach) was a small seaside community with virtually no tourist trade. Part of the municipality of Tijuana, it was an overlooked suburb on the way to the port city of Ensenada. Rosarito now has 80,000 residents and is an important resort area undergoing massive development. Within the next decade Rosarito should gain municipality status, with a local government overseeing a rapidly growing population of Mexicans and transplanted Americans.

Juan Machado was Rosarito Beach's first developer. In 1827, the governor of Baja California granted him 407,000 acres of Baja's coastline, called El Rosario. Machado converted the crumbling Misión del Descanso, near Cantamar, into a rambling ranch. In 1920, 14,000 of those acres were sold to a group of investors headed by Los Angeles attorney Jacob Morris Danziger. Four years later, Danziger began advertising El Rosario Resort and Country Club in California newspapers. A man of generous imagination, he lured tourists with claims of good roads, fishing, camping, bathing, and picnic grounds. In reality, the area was primitive, with no roads to speak of, and no gas, oil, or other essential creature comforts.

Danziger began to build facilities in earnest to compete with the new Agua Caliente resort in Tijuana. He claimed that his resort would be finished by 1926 and include a casino, golf course, ballroom, and guest houses, all available through private membership in his Shore Acres Country Club. But when Danziger was hit with a series of lawsuits for back pay and other outstanding bills, he had to sell his shares in Shore Acres. At that point, the resort consisted of a 10-room hotel with one bathroom.

In the early 1930s, Manuel P. Barbachano bought the hotel and surrounding acreage. The '30s were an exciting time in northern Baja—gambling, horse racing, and a continuous flow of alcohol attracted thousands of glamorous Americans eager to escape the restrictions of Prohibition. Barbachano was instrumental in getting electricity and telephone service throughout northern Baja. This further encouraged tourism, and smaller hotels and watering holes opened up along the rough road from Tijuana to Ensenada. The end of Prohibition in the United States and the outlawing of gambling in Mexico brought a halt to the weekly migration of Hollywood stars in search of liquor and fun.

As the roads improved, and particularly after completion of Baja's Transpeninsular Highway in 1973, Rosarito Beach boomed. Vacation suites were added along the beach, and timeshare and condo units were put up. As recently as 1980, the Rosarito Beach Hotel was still the only major resort in the area.

The '80s brought an amazing building boom to Rosarito. The main street, alternately known as the Old Ensenada Highway and Boulevard Benito Juárez, is packed with restaurants, bars, and shops. With the completion of a major shopping and convention complex in 1987, Rosarito Beach hit the big time.

Still, it is a relaxing place to visit. Southern Californians have practically made Rosarito (and much of Baja Norte) a weekend suburb. Surfers, swimmers, and sunbathers come here to enjoy the beach, one of the longest in northern Baja, an uninterrupted stretch of sand from the power plant at the far north end of town to below the Rosarito Beach Hotel, about 8 kilometers (5 miles) south. Horseback riding, jogging, and strolling are popular along this strand. Whales pass not far from shore on their winter migration; dolphins and sea lions sun on rocks jutting out from the sea. Rosarito has always attracted a varied crowd. Today's group is no exception—an assemblage of prosperous young Californians building villas in vacation developments, retired Americans and Canadians homesteading in trailer parks, and travelers of all ages from everywhere.

Hedonism and health have equal billing in Rosarito. One of the area's major draws is its seafood, especially lobster, shrimp, and abalone. The visiting Americans act as if they've been dry for months—margaritas and beer are the favored thirst-quenchers. People throw off their inhibitions here, at least to the degree permitted by the local constables. A typical Rosarito day might begin with a breakfast of eggs, refried beans, and tortillas, followed by a few hours of horseback riding on the beach. Lying in the sun or strolling through the shops takes care of midday. Siestas are imperative and are usually followed by more shopping, strolling, or sunbathing before dinner, dancing, and sleep.

Arriving and Departing

Rosarito Beach is 29 kilometers (18 miles) south of Tijuana, on the Pacific coast. There is no airport, but **Tres Estrellas de Oro** (tel. 66/88–9186 in Tijuana) has service between Tijuana and

Ensenada, stopping at the bus terminal in Rosarito on Avenida Benito Juárez across from the Rosarito Beach Hotel.

The easiest way to get to Rosarito Beach is to drive. Once you cross the border, follow the signs for Ensenada Cuota, the toll road that runs south along the coast. Take the Rosarito exit, which leads to what is alternately called the Old Ensenada Highway and Boulevard Juárez in Rosarito. The tolls from Tijuana to Rosarito have become exorbitantly high, running close to $10 on the toll road. While the alternate free road—Ensenada Libre—has been vastly improved, it is difficult for the first-timer to navigate, but here are directions if you want to try: In Tijuana, drive south on Avenida Revolución to Boulevard Fundadores and bear right. You'll discover that the free road and toll roads merge just north of Rosarito.

Getting Around

Most of Rosarito proper can be explored on foot, which is a good idea on weekends, when Boulevard Juárez has bumper-to-bumper traffic. To reach Puerto Nuevo and points south, continue on Boulevard Juárez, also called Old Ensenada Highway and Ensenada Libre, through town and head south. There is a tremendous amount of construction taking place along this stretch of road, incidentally, with time-share communities and resorts popping up side-by-side along the oceanfront cliffs. Taxis travel this stretch regularly. Settle the fare before departing. Buses from Tijuana and Ensenada stop across the street from the Rosarito Beach Hotel; if you wish to stop at other beach areas along the way, take a local rather than an express bus.

Important Addresses and Numbers

Tourist Information
The tourist information office (Bd. Juárez, south of La Quinta del Mar Hotel, tel. 661/2–0396 or 2–0200) has brochures from several hotels and restaurants and copies of the *Baja Times*, a handy tourist-oriented, English-language newspaper. The staff speaks English and is extremely helpful.

Emergencies
Police (tel. 134); **Fire** (tel. 135); **Red Cross** (tel. 132).

Exploring

Rosarito Beach has no historic or cultural attractions, beaches and bars being the main draws. Sightseeing consists of strolling along the 5-mile beach or down Boulevard Benito Juárez. Street numbers and addresses are meanwhile changing along Juárez. To reduce confusion, ask for landmarks when getting directions.

An immense PEMEX gasoline installation and electric plant anchor the northern end of Boulevard Juárez, which then runs along a collection of new shopping arcades, restaurants, and motels. The eight-story **La Quinta del Mar** hotel is the first major landmark, followed by the **Quinta Plaza** shopping center, which has a car wash, pharmacy, bakery, specialty shops, restaurants, and the **Centro de Convenciones**, a 1,000-seat convention center. Across the street is the **San Fernando Shopping Center.** The **tourism office** is in front of the shopping center.

Rodríguez Park, on the beach at the end of Calle Rene Ortíz, about midway between La Quinta del Mar and the Rosarito Beach hotels, has barbecue pits, picnic tables, and a nice lawn.

Time Out The long glassed-in bar that sits on a little hill between the pool and the beach at the **Rosarito Beach Hotel** (tel. 661/12–1106) is the best place to absorb the hotel's ambience. You'll have a view of the tiled roof, white adobe balconies, and flowered courtyard around the pool to one side, and the horseback riders, sunbathers, and ocean to the other. The margaritas are a potent reminder that you're in Mexico, and the nachos are fairly good. Have Sunday brunch ($15) in the dining room, overlooking the pool.

Off the Beaten Track

The most popular side trip from Rosarito Beach, if you go by sheer numbers alone, is **Puerto Nuevo** (Newport) at Kilometer 44 on the old highway. A few years ago, the only way you could tell you'd reached this fishing community was by the huge painting of a 7-Up bottle on the side of a building. You'd drive down the rutted dirt road to a row of restaurants—some just a big room in front of a family's kitchen—where you were served the classic Newport meal: grilled lobster, refried beans, rice, homemade tortillas, butter, salsa, and lime. The meal became a legend, and now at least 30 restaurants in rows in a field on the top of a cliff serve the identical meal. Try one of the family-run places, like Ponderosa (*see* Dining, *below*). The restaurants no longer serve lobster caught in local waters, which have become polluted of late. Instead, the lobster is frozen and imported from elsewhere.

Two new hotels have opened adjacent to Puerto Nuevo, and several spectacular condo and time-share developments have made this a high-rent district. The old highway merges with the new, then reappears off and on as you head south. Interesting stops along the way suit eclectric tastes: **Cantamar,** where off-road bike enthusiasts practice their driving skills on the sand dunes; a garden of archaeological reproductions that sits atop a cliff, offering a scenic rest stop just south of the Plaza del Mar hotel; and, finally, an exit from the toll road for the lookout point at Salsipuedes (which means "get out if you can"), where the view of waves crashing against the cliffs can inspire the most jaded traveler.

Shopping

The two major resort hotels have shopping arcades with laundromats, taco stands, and some good crafts stores. The **Calimax** grocery store on Boulevard Juárez is a good place to stock up on necessities.

Sticks and Stones, a pottery and furniture yard at the north end of Juárez, has an unusual selection of terra-cotta statues and fountains. The shopping arcade near La Quinta del Mar Hotel has many worthwhile shops. **La Casa del Arte** has wicker and willow furniture, large woven rugs, and hand-carved antique furniture. **Tienda González** carries fine wool serapes and rugs. **Muebles Rangel** sells carpeting and wicker furniture; **Oradia Imports** specializes in French perfumes. **Taxco Curios**

has a good selection of silver jewelry, and the last shop in the arcade, **Interios los Ríos,** has custom-designed furniture and Michoacán pottery. **Santa Fe,** across Juárez from Quinta del Mar, was one of the first shops in town featuring handcrafted rustic furniture. Now several like-minded shops have opened, meeting the demand from the many new vacation home owners in the area wishing to furnish their homes in the Mexican style. Equally popular are the handpainted tiles featured at **Artesanias Hacienda** (Bd. Juárez 2500).

Panaderia La Espiga is an excellent bakery with several branches along Juárez. At **Casa Torres,** in the arcade at the Rosarito Beach Hotel, you can purchase high-quality French perfumes for about one-third less than you would pay in the United States.

Sports and Outdoor Activities

Fishing There is a small fishing pier at Kilometer 33 on the Old Ensenada Highway; surfcasting is allowed on the beach. There is no place in Rosarito that issues fishing licenses, but tourism officials say licenses are not necessary if you fish from shore. Unfortunately, due to ongoing construction and inadequate sewage facilities, the ocean tends to be polluted, especially in residential areas—it is not a good idea to eat fish caught close to shore.

Horseback Riding Horses can be rented at the north and south ends of Juárez and on the beach for $10 per half hour. Check the horses carefully; some are pathetically thin. The number of horses on the beach is now restricted, and the horses are better cared for.

Surfing The waves are particularly good at **Popotla,** Kilometer 33, **Calafía,** Kilometer 35.5, and **Costa Baja,** Kilometer 36, on the Old Ensenada Highway.

Spectator Sports

Charreadas (Mexican Rodeos) Charreadas are held on summer Sundays at the **Lienzo Tapatío Charro Ring** south of town and at the new **Ejido Mazatlán Charro Ring** on the east side of the toll road. Call 661/84–2126 for dates and times.

Dining

Nearly all of Rosarito's restaurants feature the same items— lobster, shrimp, fresh fish, and steak—at nearly the same prices. A lobster, shrimp, or steak dinner costs about $15. Some restaurants tack a 15% service charge on to your bill. Highly recommended restaurants are indicated by a star ★.

Category	Cost*
Expensive	over $15
Moderate	$10–$15
Inexpensive	under $10

per person excluding drinks, service, and sales tax (10%)

Expensive ★ **Dragon del Mar.** This elegant Chinese restaurant is decorated with furniture and paintings imported from China. A miniature waterfall greets guests in the marble foyer and a pianist plays relaxing music. Partitioned with movable carved wooden panels, the expansive dining room still creates an intimate dining experience. The food is exquisitely prepared and appealing to the eye as well as the palate. *Blvd. Juárez 20, tel. 661/2–0604. AE, MC, V.*

La Fachada. A quiet place by Rosarito standards, La Fachada is preferred by more subdued diners. The food is good, and the atmosphere is authentic Mexican. At night a guitarist and pianist perform soothing ballads. *Blvd. Juárez 317, tel. 661/2–1785. MC, V.*

★ **La Leña.** The cornerstone restaurant of the Quinta Plaza shopping center, La Leña sits on such a high rise that you can see the ocean from the window tables. La Leña specializes in beef grilled in full view of the diners. The dining room is spacious, with the tables spread far enough apart for privacy. Try any of the beef dishes, especially the tender *carne asada* (grilled strips of beef with tortillas and guacamole). *Quinta Plaza, tel. 661/2–0826. Reservations accepted. Dress: casual. MC, V.*

La Misión. A lovely, quiet restaurant, La Misión has white adobe walls, carved wood statues in niches, and high-beamed ceilings. Gourmet seafood and steak dishes are the specialties. La Misión has patio dining in its enclosed courtyard. *Blvd. Juárez 182, tel. 661/2–0202. Reservations accepted. Dress: casual. MC, V.*

Moderate **El Nido.** A dark, woodsy restaurant with leather booths, this is one of the oldest eateries in Rosarito. It's popular with those who are unimpressed with the newer, fancier establishments. Steaks are grilled over mesquite, and the large central fireplace is a cozy touch. *Blvd. Juárez 67, tel. 661/2–1430. Reservations accepted. Dress: casual. MC, V.*

La Flor de Michoacán. *Carnitas* (marinated pork) roasted over an open pit, Michoacán style, served with homemade tortillas, guacamole, and salsa are the house specialty. The tacos, *tortas* (marinated pork kebabs roasted on skewers), and tostadas are great. The surroundings are simple but clean. Takeout is available. *Blvd. Juárez 146, no phone. No credit cards.*

Mariscos Mazatlan. You can't miss this bright blue building on the west side of Juárez, and you'll be delighted you stopped in for some of the best seafood in town. Try the seven-seas soup, a spicy chowder filled with chunks of fish and shellfish. *Blvd. Juárez, no phone. Dress: casual. No credit cards.*

★ **René's.** One of the oldest restaurants in Rosarito (1924), René's features *chorizo* (Mexican sausage), quail, frogs' legs, and lobster. There's an ocean view from the dining room, a lively bar, and mariachi music. *Blvd. Juárez south of the Rosarito Beach Hotel, tel. 661/2–1020. No reservations. Dress: casual. MC, V.*

Rosarito Village Cafe. Inexpensive margaritas, mariachis, and takeout Mexican food make this restaurant a popular watering hole and a good place for U.S.-style breakfasts. *Next to Rosarito Beach Hotel. Blvd. Juárez 777, no phone. No reservations. Dress: casual. MC, V.*

Vince's Lobster Trap. This seafood restaurant, fish market, and deli is popular with expatriate Americans—they swear Vince's has the best lobster in town. *Blvd. Juárez 39, tel. 661/2–1253. No reservations. Dress: casual. No credit cards.*

Inexpensive **Azteca.** The enormous dining room at the Rosarito Beach Hotel
★ has a view of the pool and beach area. Visitors come to the hotel regularly just for the lavish Sunday brunch, where margaritas

are the drink of choice. Both Mexican and American dishes are offered, and the portions make up for the erratic quality of the food. *Rosarito Beach Hotel, Blvd. Juárez, tel. 661/2–1106. Reservations accepted. MC, V.*

Juice'n Juice. Rosarito's health-food restaurant is a no-frills lunch counter with lots of salads, juices, yogurt, and granola. But you can also order burgers and fries. *Blvd. Juárez 14, tel. 661/2–0338. No credit cards.*

Los Arcos. Next to the Rosarito Beach Hotel, this café serves home-style Mexican food and offers open-air dining in summer. *Blvd. Juárez 29, tel. 661/2–0491. No credit cards.*

South of Rosarito Beach
Expensive

Calafía. This eccentric cliff-top restaurant serves up a terrific ocean view with its food. You can dine indoors or sit outside at tables that perch on terraces down the side of the cliff. Dance floors inside and at the bottom of the cliff are ideal. *Km 35.5 on the Old Ensenada Hwy., tel. 661/2–1581. MC, V.*

La Fonda. At this popular restaurant you can sit on an outdoor patio overlooking the beach and sip potent margaritas served with greasy nachos and hot salsa. Fresh lobster, grilled steaks, prime rib, and traditional Mexican dishes are accompanied by a delicious black-bean soup. The bar is usually crowded, and the patrons boisterous. *Km 59 on the Old Ensenada Hwy., no phone. No credit cards.*

Moderate

Puerto Nuevo. Newport is a village of 25 to 30 restaurants that serve the same dishes—grilled lobster or shrimp, Spanish rice, refried beans, and homemade tortillas with melted butter, lime, and hot sauce. Some places have full bars, others serve only wine and beer. **Ortega's,** with at least three branches in Newport and one in Rosarito, is the most crowded; **Ponderosa** is smaller and quieter and is run by a gracious family; **Costa Brava** is newer and more elegant, with tablecloths and an ocean view. Lobsters in most places are priced as small, medium, and large—medium is about $15. Rows of artisans' stands have opened around the restaurants and along the road near Puerto Nuevo, offering pottery, baskets, tacky T-shirts, and a bizarre assortment of souvenirs. *Km 44 on the Old Ensenada Hwy., no phones. Most places are open for lunch and dinner. Some take credit cards.*

Lodging

Though Rosarito is in the middle of a resort building boom, there is still a room shortage in town. Several agencies in the United States book reservations at Rosarito hotels and at nearby condo and time-share resorts, which are a great alternative that may actually be less expensive than hotel rooms if you are traveling with a group of five or more. For information contact **Baja Information** (tel. 619/298–4105; in the U.S., tel. 800/225–2786; in CA, tel. 800/522–1516), **Baja Lodging Services** (tel. 619/491–0682), or **Baja California Tours** (tel. 619/454–7166). Reservations are a must on holiday weekends. Many hotels require a minimum two-night stay for a confirmed reservation, and inexpensive rooms are hard to find. Highly recommended lodgings are indicated by a star ★.

Category	Cost*
Expensive	over $50
Moderate	$25–$50
Inexpensive	under $25

All prices are for standard double room, excluding service charge and sales tax (10%).

Expensive

★ **Quinta del Mar.** This large resort complex has three types of accommodations: moderately priced rooms, expensive town houses near the beach, and high-rise condominiums with ocean views (by far the best). Some rooms have been remodeled; ask to see a selection of rooms if you're not pleased with what you've been given. The oceanfront houses with fireplaces, patios, and barbecues are a great option for groups. *Bd. Juárez 25500, tel. 661/2–1301; reservations in the U.S.: Box 4243, San Ysidro, CA 92073, tel. 800/228–7003. 143 rooms. Facilities: pool, beach access, 3 restaurants and bars, whirlpool, steam bath, tennis, basketball, volleyball. AE, MC, V.*

★ **Rosarito Beach Hotel.** Dating to the Prohibition era, this resort is beginning to show its age, but it's still a charmer, with huge ballrooms, tiled public rest rooms, and a glassed-in pool deck overlooking a long beach. Rooms and suites in the low-rise buildings that face the beach are modern, though somewhat sterile. Accommodations in the original building surrounding the swimming pool have been overhauled and have more character. The hotel has a good restaurant with a lavish Sunday brunch and powerful margaritas. *Bd. Juárez at the south end of town, tel. 661/2–1106 or 800/343–8582; reservations: Box 430145, San Diego, CA 92143-0145. 70 rooms, 80 suites. Facilities: beach, tennis courts, pool, health club, bar, restaurant. MC, V.*

Moderate

Los Pelicanos Hotel. Completed in 1990, this beach hotel has prices that vary depending on location of rooms and whether they have a balcony with an ocean view. All rooms have access to the beach. *At the end of Calle Ebano, tel. 661/2–0445; U.S. mailing address: Box 3871, San Ysidro, CA 92073. 39 rooms. Facilities: restaurant, bar. MC, V.*

Motel Quinta Chica. This motel at the south end of town has little character but comfortable beds. Rooms in the front face the free road and have ocean breezes; those in the back have the constant roar of traffic on the toll road. *Km 26.8 on the Old Ensenada Hwy., no phone; reservations in the U.S.: tel. 800/ 228–7003. 90 rooms. Facilities: restaurant and bar across the street. MC, V.*

Inexpensive

Baja Village. Completed in 1989, this motel is on the main boulevard, which is very noisy during the day. Rooms are carpeted and some have color TV. Restaurants, stores, and the beach are all within walking distance. *Blvd. Juárez 228 at Via Las Olas, tel. 661/2–0050. U.S. mailing address: Box 309, San Ysidro, CA 92073. 21 rooms, 3 suites. Facilities: parking, restaurant, bar. MC, V.*

Cupalas del Mar. Opened in 1991, this small hotel is between Juárez and the beach, and is quieter than most, with sunny clean rooms and satellite TV. *Calle Guadalupe Victoria 9, tel. 661/2–2490, fax 661/2–2494. 39 rooms. Facilities: pool, parking, hot tub. No credit cards.*

South of Rosarito **Hotel New Port Baja.** Within walking distance of the lobster
Expensive restaurants at Puerto Nuevo, this large hotel sprawls over a
clifftop in a horseshoe shape that gives most rooms a great
view. Rooms do not have air-conditioning, and the noise from
the pool can be annoying when your windows are open. The patio restaurant is quite good. *Km. 45 on the Old Ensenada
Hwy., tel. 661/4–1166. Reservations in the U.S.: Box 2776,
Chula Vista, CA 92012-2776, tel. 619/422–6918 or 800/678–
7244. 147 rooms. Facilities: pool, restaurant, meeting rooms.
MC, V.*

★ **La Fonda.** A longtime favorite with beachgoers, La Fonda has a
few older rooms, decorated with carved wood furniture and folk
art, with great views of the ocean. The restaurant and bar are
immensely popular. If you plan on getting any sleep, ask for a
room as far away from the bar as possible. *Km 59 on the Old
Ensenada Hwy., no phone; reservations in the U.S.: Box 268,
San Ysidro, CA 92073. 18 rooms. Facilities: beach, restaurant,
bar. No credit cards.*

Las Rocas. This is an elegant addition to the strip of older hotels perched on cliffs above the ocean. The blue and purple
scheme stands out against the surroundings, and the rooms
have coffee makers and microwaves. The pool and whirlpool
seem to spill over the cliffs into the ocean. *Km. 37 on the Old
Ensenada Hwy., tel. 661/2–0653. 34 rooms. Facilities: pool,
whirlpool, restaurant, bar. No credit cards.*

Plaza del Mar. This hotel, spa, and oceanfront resort is set beside an archaeological garden, which is open to the public. The
garden's Aztec and Maya ruins are replicas of the faded and
overgrown originals. Accommodations are in long Quonset hut-
like buildings clustered around courtyards. *Take the La Mision
exit from the toll road and go north 1 mile. Km 58 on the Old
Ensenada Hwy., tel. 661/5–9152; reservations in the U.S.: tel.
800/762–6380. 180 rooms. Facilities: pool, hot tub, tennis
courts, shuffleboard, restaurant, bar. MC, V.*

Nightlife

The many restaurants in Rosarito Beach keep customers entertained with live music, piano bars, or *folklórico* (folk music and
dance) shows; the bar scene is also active. Drinking and driving
laws are stiff—the police will fine you no matter how little
you've had. If you plan to drink, take a cab or assign a designated driver.

Bar La Quinta (Quinta Del Mar Hotel, Bd. Juárez 25500, tel.
661/2–0016) offers live music Wednesday through Sunday
night, recorded disco music other nights, and a large dance
floor.

Beachcomber Bar and Salón Mexicano (Rosarito Beach Hotel,
Bd. Juárez, tel. 661/2–1106). The Beachcomber overlooks the
ocean and has live piano music, plus a Mexican fiesta on Friday
nights. The cavernous disco has a live band and dancing.

Calafia (Km 35.5 Old Ensenada Hwy., tel. 661/2–1581) has live
music and dancing Friday through Sunday afternoon and evening, with a great view of the ocean.

El Torito (Blvd. Juárez 318, no phone) has live music for dancing on weekends until 2 AM.

Rene's (Bd. Juárez south of town, tel. 661/2–1061) is a rowdy place with a live dance band, mariachis, and wide-screen satellite TV.

Rosarito Vice has rock music, a rowdy atmosphere, and a second-story dance floor. For those who prefer a more subdued ambience, **Las Olas** (Blvd. Juárez, upstairs) has tropical music for weekend dancing.

Ensenada

Introduction

Ensenada is a major port 104 kilometers (65 miles) south of Tijuana on Bahía de Todos Santos. The paved highway (Mexico Route 1) between the two cities often cuts a path between low mountains and high oceanside cliffs; exits lead to rural roads, oceanfront campgrounds, and an ever-increasing number of resort communities. The Coronado Islands can be clearly seen off the coast.

The small fishing communities of San Miguel and El Sauzal are off the highway just north of Ensenada. The smell of fish from the canneries lining the highway can be overpowering at times. The beach-side strip between San Miguel and Ensenada has long been a haven of moderately priced oceanfront motels and trailer parks.

Although Ensenada has grown incredibly since 1984, it remains charming and picturesque. Juan Rodríguez Cabrillo first discovered Ensenada, which means "bay" in Spanish, in 1542. Sebastián Vizcaino named the region Ensenada-Bahía de Todos Santos (All Saints' Bay) in 1602. Since then, Ensenada has drawn a steady stream of discoverers and developers. First, ranchers made their homes on large spreads along the coast and up into the mountains. Gold miners followed, turning the area into a boomtown during the late 1800s. After the mines were depleted, the area settled back into pastoral peace. The harbor gradually grew into a major port for shipping agricultural goods from the surrounding ranches and farms. Now it is one of Mexico's largest seaports and has a thriving fishing fleet and fish-processing industry.

Ensenada is a popular weekend destination for southern Californians. There are no beaches in Ensenada proper, but beaches north and south of town are satisfactory for swimming, sunning, surfing, and camping. During the week, Ensenada is just a normal, relatively calm port city, with a population of about 150,000. On weekends, when the young, rowdy crowd spreads from the cantinas (bars) into the streets, it turns into a party town.

For decades, most hotels and bars have catered to groups of young people intent on drinking and carousing. But now there is a concerted effort to attract conventioneers and business travelers. A group of civic boosters has renovated the Riviera del Pacifico, the grand old gambling hall turned civic center that is Ensenada's most stately edifice. The waterfront area has been razed and rebuilt, with taco stands replaced by shopping centers, hotels, and a massive Plaza marina, scheduled to open by 1993. Cruise ships anchor regularly offshore. Ensenada's first full-scale members-only resort is completed at Punta Banda, 29 kilometers (18 miles) south of town. The **Baja Beach and Tennis Club** is built on the ruins of another resort that was started in the 1960s, when it was rumored that gambling would again become legal in Baja. The rumors were false, and for 20 years the shell of a grand casino sat half buried by sand on a desolate point. Now developers have poured close to $15 million into a marina, beachfront casitas, and a large health club.

Ensenada is the last major city for hundreds of miles if you are traveling south on Mexico Highway 1 or the Transpeninsular Highway. **San Quintín,** 184 kilometers (115 miles) south of Ensenada, is an agricultural community said to be the windiest spot in Baja. Fishing and hunting are the draws here. **Cataviña** has a gas station and a few small hotels. Farther south are turn-offs for a dirt road to **San Felipe** and a paved road to **Bahía de los Angeles.** At the end of Baja Norte, 595 kilometers (372 miles) from Ensenada, stands a steel monument in the form of an eagle, 42 meters (138 feet) high. It marks the border between the states of Baja Norte and Baja Sur. The time changes from Pacific to Mountain time as you cross the 28th parallel. Guerrero Negro, Baja Sur's northernmost town, with hotels and gas stations, is 2 kilometers (1¼ miles) south.

Arriving and Departing by Plane

Airport and Airlines Ensenada has only a small airstrip, **Aeropuerto el Cipres** (tel. 667/6–6301), for private planes. The bureaucratic shuffling that would allow pilots to clear customs in Ensenada is under way, and there are plans to allow regional airlines to use the airport. Most people who visit Ensenada drive. Tourist cards are required only if you are traveling south of Ensenada or staying longer than 72 hours.

Arriving and Departing by Bus, Ship, and Car

By Bus Ensenada can be reached by bus from Tijuana, Mexicali, and Mexico City. **Autotransportes de Baja California** and **Tres Estrellas de Oro** travel throughout Baja, linking all the major cities. The bus station is at Avenida Riveroll between Calles 10 and 11, tel. 667/8–2322.

By Ship Ensenada is a year-round port for **Carnival Cruise Lines** (tel. 800/232–4666), which sails from Los Angeles twice each week. **Admiral Cruises** (tel. 800/772–7272) has three- and four-night cruises from Los Angeles. **Starlite Cruises** (tel. 800/488–7827) has one-day cruises from San Diego, with gambling on board ship. The **Ensenada Express** (tel. 619/232–2109) will have ferry service from San Diego to Ensenada, using high-speed hydrofoils. Service is expected to start in 1992.

By Car Mexico Highway 1, called Ensenada Cuota, is a toll road that runs along the coast from the Tijuana border to Ensenada. The toll booths along the road accept U.S. and Mexican currency; tolls are usually about $2.50. The road is excellent, though it has some hair-raising curves atop the cliffs and is best driven in daylight. The free road, called Ensenada Libre, runs parallel to the toll road off and on, cutting east of the low hills along the coast. Although free, the road doubles your traveling time and is very rough in spots.

Getting Around Ensenada

Most of Ensenada's attractions are situated within five blocks of the waterfront; it is easy to take a long walking tour of the city. A car is necessary, though, to reach La Bufadora, the Chapultepec Hills, and most of the beaches. Buses travel the route from Ensenada through Guerrero Negro at the border between Baja Norte and Baja Sur and on down to the southernmost tip of Baja. Addresses can be confusing within the city, particularly along the waterfront, where the road is called Boulevard Costera, Gral. Lázaro Cárdenas, Alternate Highway 1, and Carretera Transpeninsular.

By Bus **Tres Estrellas de Oro** and **Autotransportes de Baja California** cover the entire Baja route and connect in Mexicali with buses to Guadalajara and Mexico City.

By Taxi There is a *sitio* (central taxi stand) on Avenida López Mateos by the Bahía Hotel (tel. 667/8–3475). Be sure to set the price before the taxi starts moving. Destinations within the city should cost less than $10.

By Car Ensenada is an easy city to navigate; most streets are marked. If you are traveling south, you can bypass downtown Ensenada on the Highway 1 truck route down Calle 10. To reach the hotel and waterfront area, stay with alternate Highway 1 as it travels along the fishing pier and becomes Boulevard Costero, also known as Lázaro Cárdenas. This road ends at Calle Agustín Sangines, also known as Calle Delante, which leads out to Highway 1 traveling south. The parking meters along Ensenada's main streets are patrolled regularly; parking tickets come in the form of either a boot on the car's tires or confiscated license plates. Parking has become horrendous as new shopping centers arise on former parking lots. The new Plaza Marina at the beginning of Blvd. Costero will have paid parking, which may be your best option.

Ensenada Rent-a-Car (tel. 667/8–1896) has an office on Avenida Alvarado between Lázaro Cárdenas and López Mateos.

Important Addresses and Numbers

Tourist Information The **State Tourist Commission** office (Av. López Mateos 1305, tel. 667/6–2222) is open weekdays 7–7, Saturday 9–1, Sunday 10–1. The **Convention and Visitors Bureau** (tel. 667/8–2411) has a stand with pamphlets and brochures on Boulevard Costera at the waterfront.

Emergencies **Police** (Ortíz Rubio and Libertad, tel. 134); **Hospital** (Av. Ruíz and Calle 11, tel. 667/8–2525); **Red Cross** (tel. 132).

Air Evac International (tel. 619/425–4400) is an air ambulance service that travels into Mexico from San Diego to bring injured tourists back to the United States.

Language Classes A great way to get to know Ensenada and improve your Spanish simultaneously is to attend weekend or week-long classes at the **International Spanish Institute of Ensenada** (tel. 667/6–0109 or 619/472–0600 in CA).

Guided Tours

Baja California Tours offers comfortable, informative bus trips throughout Baja and can arrange special-interest tours. Vans depart daily from San Diego to Ensenada; midweek transportation-and-hotel packages are a real bargain. *6986 La Jolla Blvd., #204, La Jolla, CA 92037, tel. 619/454-7166, fax 619/454-2703.*

Las Bodegas de Santo Tomás (Av. Miramar 666, tel. 667/8–3333), Baja's oldest winery, offers tours and tastings daily at 11 AM, 1 PM, and 3 PM and costs $2. Group tours should be arranged in advance.

Gordo's Sportfishing (Sportfishing Pier, tel. 667/8–2190) operates whale-watching trips from December through February. The half-day trip goes to La Bufadora and Isla Todos Santos and costs $25 per person.

Exploring

Numbers in the margin correspond to points of interest on the Ensenada map.

The city of Ensenada, the third largest in Baja, hugs the harbor of **Bahía de Todos Santos.** If you have access to a car, begin your tour of Ensenada by driving north up Calle 2 or east on the Mexico Highway 1 bypass around town into the **Chapultepec Hills** to **El Mirador** (The Lookout). From here one can see the entire Bahía de Todos Santos, from the canneries of San Miguel south to the towns of Punta Banda and La Bufadora.

To tour the waterfront and downtown, you'll be better off on foot. As Highway 1 leads into town from the north, it becomes Boulevard Costero, running past shipyards filled with massive freighters. To the right, between the water and the street, the massive Plaza Marina shopping-and-dining complex is scheduled to open by 1993. At the northernmost point at the water's edge sits an indoor/outdoor **Fish Market,** where row after row of counters display piles of shrimp as well as tuna, dorado, marlin, snapper, and dozens more species of fish caught off Baja's coasts. Outside, stands sell grilled or smoked fish, seafood cocktails, and fish tacos. Browsers can pick up some standard souvenirs, eat well for very little money, and take some great photographs. The hot-pink Plaza de Mariscos, which blocks the view of the traditional fish market from the street, is a comfortable place to eat. **Boulevard Costera** runs along the waterfront from the market and the **Sportfishing Pier** past new mini-malls designed to keep tourists by the waterfront. Many of these half-finished buildings lack tenants thus far, as locals and investors adjust to the rapid changes along the waterfront. At the intersection of Boulevard Costera and Avenida Riveroll is the **Plaza Cívica,** with sculptures of Benito Juárez, Miguel Hidalgo, and Venustiano Carranza. Cruise ships dock offshore from here, and passengers are ferried to the pier, where they can walk to a shopping center called **Centro Artesenal de Ensenada.**

Time Out You can't visit the fish market without trying at least one fish taco. Strips of fresh snapper, halibut, or other freshly caught fish are dipped in batter and deep-fried, then wrapped in fresh corn tortillas. Choose your topping—cilantro, salsa, tomatoes, onions, pickled carrots—from an array of dishes set out on the counter.

Boulevard Costera becomes Boulevard Lázaro Cárdenas at Avenida Riviera, site of the **Riviera del Pacífico.** This rambling white adobe hacienda-style mansion was built in the 1920s with money raised on both sides of the border. An enormous gambling palace, hotel, restaurant and bar, the Riviera was a glamorous place frequented by wealthy U.S. citizens and Mexicans, particularly during Prohibition. When gambling was outlawed in Mexico and Prohibition ended in the United States, the palace lost its raison d'être. In 1977, the Tourism and Convention Bureau began refurbishing the palace and its lavish gardens. During daylight, visitors can now tour the elegant ballrooms and halls, which host occasional art shows and civic events. Riviera del Pácifico is now officially called the Centro Social, Civico y Cultural de Ensenada (Social, Civic and Cultural Center of Ensenada), and there are plans for including it in a major convention-center complex along the waterfront. *Bd. Costera and Av. Riviera, tel. 667/6-4310. Admission free. Open daily 9-5.*

Ensenada's traditional tourist zone is centered one block east of the waterfront along **Avenida López Mateos.** High-rise hotels, souvenir shops, restaurants, and bars line the avenue from its beginning at the foot of the **Chapultepec Hills** for eight blocks south to the dry channel of the Arroyo de Ensenada. South of the riverbed is a row of inexpensive motels, across the street from the **State Tourist Office, Fonart** government crafts store, and the **Caliente Foreign Book** (corner of Av. López

Mateos and Castillo, tel. 667/6–2133), where horse-racing fans can place their bets on races televised via satellite. **Avenida Juárez** is Ensenada's downtown area where the locals shop for ⑩ furniture, clothing, and other necessities. **Parque Revolución,** ⑪ near the north end of Avenida Juárez at the **Mother's Monument**—a tall, bronze mother holding a child—is the prettiest of the city's parks, with a bandstand, a children's playground, and plenty of comfortable benches in the shade. The city's largest cathedral, **Our Lady of Guadalupe,** is at Avenida Floresta ⑫ and the south end of Juárez.

Off the Beaten Track

The hillsides and valleys outside Ensenada are known for their grapes and olives; many of the wineries have tours that can be arranged through hotels in Ensenada. The **Cetto Winery** (tel. 66/88–2581 in Tijuana) is located in the Guadalupe Valley, on Highway 3, north toward Tecate. The valley is about a 30-minute drive from Ensenada on a paved highway that runs up into the hills past cattle ranches and orchards.

La Bufadora is an impressive blowhole in the coastal cliffs at Punta Banda, off Highway 1 at Maneadero, about 15 minutes south of Ensenada. The drive, 19 kilometers (12 miles) west on Highway 23, is a slow and somewhat risky trip (don't attempt it at night), but the scenery along the coast is worth the effort. Legend has it that the spray from La Bufadora's geyser comes from a whale that was trapped in the rocks as a calf and couldn't escape when it grew to its full size. Viewers gather on a concrete platform at the edge of the cliffs and take their chances with the water's spray. Large and small seafood restaurants, taco stands, and souvenir shacks line the road's end.

Shopping

Most of the tourist shops are located along Avenida López Mateos beside the hotels and restaurants. There are several new two-story shopping arcades with brand-name sportswear stores. Dozens of curio shops line the street, all selling similar selections of pottery, woven blankets and serapes, embroidered dresses, and onyx chess sets.

La Rana (Av. López Mateos 715) has a wide selection of beach attire and surfing supplies. **Originales Baja** (Av. López Mateos 623) sells large brass and copper birds, wood carvings, and glassware. **Artes de Quijote** (Av. López Mateos 503) has an impressive high-quality selection of carved wood doors, huge terra-cotta pots, crafts from Oaxaca, and large brass fish and birds. **Artesanias Castillo** (Av. López Mateos 656) has an impressive array of silver jewelry from Taxco. The government craft store, **Fonart** (Av. López Mateos 1303) is filled with excellent indigenous crafts. **Plaza Hussong's** (Av. Ruiz 337 at Av. López Mateos) is a classy two-story mall completed in early 1992; tenants include a large **Benetton** store and **Lofino's Imports,** displaying European china and crystal. **Avila Imports,** across the street from Hussong's, sells French perfumes, Hummel statues, and crystal. **Librería Banuelos** (Av. Ruíz 370) and **El Spaña** (Av. Ruíz 217) have a good selection of English-language magazines and books. **El Pegaso** (Obregón and Calle

Segunda) carries clothing, jewelry, furniture, and crafts from
throughout Mexico.

Centro Artesenal de Ensenada, a shopping center on the waterfront, caters to cruise-ship visitors. The best shop by far is
Unique Art Center (tel. 619/497–1529); it carries museum-quality pottery and varied folk art by the indigenous peoples of
northern Mexico.

Sports and Outdoor Activities

Hunting and fishing are popular sports around Ensenada,
which calls itself the "Yellowtail Capital of the World."

Sportfishing   Fishing boats leave the **Ensenada Sportfishing Pier** regularly.
The best angling is from April through November, with bottom
fishing good in the winter. Charter vessels and party boats are
available from several outfitters along Avenida López Mateos,
Boulevard Costera, and off the sportfishing pier. Trips on
group boats cost about $35 per day. Licenses are available at
the tourist office or from charter companies.

Ensenada Clipper Fleet (pier, tel. 667/8–2185) has charter and
group boats.

Gordo's Sportfishing (*see* Guided Tours, *above*), one of the oldest sportfishing companies in Ensenada, has a motel on the waterfront, charter boats, group boats, and a smokehouse.

El Royal Pacifico (26651 Naccome Dr., Mission Viejo, CA
92691, tel. 714/859–4933) offers advance-sale tickets and reservations on sportfishing boats in Ensenada from its U.S. office.

Golf   **Bajamar** (tel. 667/8–1844 or 619/298–4105 in CA) is an excellent
18-hole course 32 kilometers (20 miles) north of Ensenada at
the Bajamar condominium and housing resort. The **Baja Country Club** (tel. 667/3–0203, 800/564–2253, or 619/420–8533 in
CA) opened in 1991 with 18 holes of golf at a secluded 300-acre
course south of Ensenada near Maneadero.

Tennis   **Bajamar** (*see* Golf, *above*) and the **Baja Tennis Club** (San Benito
123, no phone) have public courts.

Spectator Sports

There is no racetrack in Ensenada, but horse-racing fans can
place bets and watch televised races from Tijuana's Agua Caliente Racetrack and Los Angeles's Santa Anita and Hollywood
tracks at the **Caliente Foreign Book** (Av. López Mateos, behind
the Riviera del Pacifico Building, tel. 667/6–2133). A second
Caliente establishment is scheduled to open in the Plaza Marina.

Charreadas   Rodeos are scheduled sporadically at the ring (Av. Alvarado
and Calle 2, tel. 667/4–0242).

Beaches

Since the waterfront in Ensenada proper is taken up by fishing
boats, the best swimming beaches are south of town. **Estero
Beach** is long and clean, with mild waves. Surfers populate the
beaches off Highway 1 north and south of Ensenada, particularly at **San Miguel, California, Tres Marías** and **La Joya**
beaches; scuba divers prefer **Punta Banda,** by La Bufadora.

Lifeguards are rare; swimmers should take caution. The tourist office in Ensenada has a map that shows safe diving and surfing beaches.

Dining

Some restaurants add a service charge of 10% to 15% to your bill in addition to the 15% tax. Highly recommended restaurants are indicated by a star ★.

Category	Cost*
Expensive	over $15
Moderate	$10–$15
Inexpensive	under $10

per person, excluding drinks, service, and sales tax (10%)

Expensive
★ **El Rey Sol.** A family-owned French restaurant over 40 years old, El Rey Sol is in a charming building with stained-glass windows, and is decorated with wrought-iron chandeliers and heavy oak tables and chairs. Specialties include French and Mexican presentations of fresh fish, poultry, and vegetables grown at the owner's farm in the Santo Tomás Valley. Appetizers come with the meal; the excellent pastries are baked on the premises. *Av. López Mateos 1000, tel. 667/8–1733. Reservations accepted. Dress: casual, though jackets and ties are common. AE, MC, V.*

La Casa del Abulón. The former Kiki's restaurant has been given a face-lift with bouquets of silk flowers, bright pink table linens, and wall murals depicting Neptune and other legends of the sea. But the best additions are a new chef and an ambitious menu featuring abalone prepared several ways, along with quail, prime rib, and a superb calamari steak rolled and stuffed with lobster. The menu also has less-expensive Mexican dishes and burgers. The restaurant has a less-than-perfect ocean view—rock jetties and rusted boats detract from the natural beauty—but in the evening, candlelight and live dance music make it a romantic spot. *Blvd. Costero at Ave. Sangines, tel. 667/6–5785. Reservations accepted. Dress: casual. AE, MC, V.*

La Cueva de los Tigres. This dining room on the beach, with sliding glass windows, is especially nice at sunset. The enduring specialty, abalone in crab sauce, has won numerous international awards. Though the prices for seafood are higher here than elsewhere, the preparation is so consistently excellent that patrons regularly drive down from southern California just for dinner. *Km 112 at Playa Hermosa, tel. 667/6–4650. Reservations accepted. Dress: casual. AE, MC, V.*

Moderate
★ **Casamar.** A long-standing, dependable restaurant, Casamar is known for its wide variety of excellent seafood. Large groups, families, and couples fill the main dining room. Lobster and shrimp are prepared in several ways but seem the freshest when grilled *con mojo y ajo* (with garlic and butter). The upstairs bar has live jazz on weekend nights. *Bd. Lázaro Cárdenas 987, tel. 667/4–0417. No reservations. Dress: casual. MC, V.*

El Toro. An old favorite with a new location on the main drag, this large adobe and red-tile restaurant is considered *the* place in town for grilled meats—steak, lamb, and quail—by candlelight. *Bd. Costero 1790, tel. 667/6–0834. No reservations. Dress: casual. MC, V.*

Taberna Española. Owner Fernando Ullate has created a warm, comfortable tapas bar and restaurant that has become one of Ensenada's most popular restaurants among locals and visitors alike. The paella alone makes a visit worthwhile; when combined with a pitcher of fruity sangria and a basket of crusty bread it becomes a memorable feast. Ask about the daily specials. If you're not in the mood for a full meal or want a late-night snack, dine on a combination of tapas, or appetizers, including cheeses, sausages, and garlicky olives. *Blvd. Costero 1982, tel. 667/6–0767. Reservations accepted. Dress: casual. MC, V.*

Inexpensive **Cafe Au Lait.** This pretty little French café is a popular lunch spot for fresh sandwiches on pita bread or baguettes, crepes, or baked potatoes smothered with butter and cheese. The pastry counter displays a tempting selection of apple strudel, carrot cake, and a sinful linzer torte, served with cappuccino, espresso, or simple fresh-brewed coffee or teas. The café is a good spot for an afternoon or after-dinner snack as well. *Ave. Ruiz 153, tel. 667/4–6647. No credit cards.*

Plaza Mariscos. Several taco stands fill this bright pink plaza in front of the fish market. One way to choose which place to eat is by checking out the bowls of condiments arrayed on picnic tables between the stands—if the salsa, onions, cilantro, and pickled vegetables look good you're bound to like the tacos as well. Most stands serve *ceviche*, seafood cocktails, and fish tacos; a couple have beef tacos as well. Mariachis stroll between the tables—if you request a song, you're expected to give the musicians a tip. The stands at the front of the plaza look out to the street; those in the back have a view of the goings-on at the fish market. *Blvd. Costero, no phone. No credit cards.*

Lodging

Ensenada has become a major resort town, with prices to match. Low-cost places are hard to find, and reservations are a must on holiday weekends, when rates increase as much as 25%. **IMPA/Mexico Information** (7860 Mission Center Ct., Suite 202, San Diego, CA 92108, tel. 619/298–4105, in CA 800/522–1516, elsewhere in U.S. 800/522–1516) handles hotel reservations, tourist information and group tours, and often has special packages and rates for Baja hotels. **Baja Lodging Services** (4659 Park Bd., San Diego, CA 92116, tel. 619/491–0682) makes hotel, condo, and private-home reservations throughout Baja. Highly recommended lodgings are indicated by a star ★.

Category	Cost*
Expensive	over $55
Moderate	$25–$55
Inexpensive	under $25

All prices are for a standard double room, excluding service charge and tax (10%).

Expensive **Corona.** The only hotel on the waterfront, the Corona has one completed hotel building and plans for two more, plus condos and a marina. The building is tastefully done, with white towers and peaks rising over the red-tile roof, resembling a little castle by the sea. The rooms have bleached-wood furnishings, beige carpeting, tiled baths, and balconies facing the water or downtown. The hotel is almost always full on weekends. Reservations are essential. *Blvd. Costero 1442, tel. 667/6–4023; reservations in the U.S.: 482 San Ysidro Blvd., Suite 203, San Ysidro, CA 92173. 93 rooms. Facilities: pool, restaurant, bar, marina, MC, V.*

★ **Las Rosas.** This pink palace just north of town is by far the most modern hotel in the area, with an atrium lobby and a green-glass ceiling that glows at night. All rooms face the ocean and pool. The hotel is elegant, with marble floors, mint green and pink upholstered couches facing the sea, and lots of glass. Some rooms have fireplaces and Jacuzzis. Even the least expensive rooms are lovely. The hotel is booked solid most weekends; make reservations far in advance. *Mexico Hwy. 1 north of town, tel. 667/4–4310; reservations in the U.S.: tel. 800/225–2786. 32 rooms and suites. Facilities: pool, hot tub, restaurant, cocktail lounge, jewelry shop, gallery. AE, MC, V.*

Punta Morro. For seclusion and the sound of crashing surf you can't beat this all-suites hotel 2 miles north of town beside the university campus. The three-story tan building faces the north end of the bay; the restaurant sits on rock pilings over the waves. Studios and one-, two-, and three-bedroom suites have terraces facing the ocean, kitchenettes, and seating areas; some also have fireplaces. The large rectangular hot tub is the place to mingle and enjoy the scenery, while the wooden deck that juts out from the cliffs is the spot to go for solitude. Stairs lead down to a rocky beach, and the surf is usually too rough for swimming. *Mexico Hwy. 1, 2 mi north of town, tel. 667/8–3507 or 800/726–6426; reservations in the U.S.: Box 434263, San Diego, CA 92143-4263. 30 suites. Facilities: restaurant, bar, pool, hot tub, beach. MC, V.*

★ **San Nicolás.** This is a private place that doesn't look like much from the street but is actually a massive resort behind cement walls painted with Indian murals. The San Nicolas is 20 years old, but much of it has been refurbished. The suites boast tiled hot tubs; living rooms with deep green carpeting, mauve furnishings, and beveled glass doors; and mirrored ceilings in the bedrooms. The less extravagant rooms are comfortable and decorated with folk art. There is a waterfall over the pool and a good restaurant overlooking the gardens. *Av. López Mateos and Av. Guadalupe, tel. 667/6–1901; reservations in the U.S.: Box 4C, San Ysidro, CA 92073, tel. 800/225–2786. 150 rooms and suites. Facilities: 2 pools, hot tub, restaurant, cocktail lounge, disco, convention facilities, shops, cable TV. AE, MC, V.*

Moderate **Misión Santa Isabel.** Ensenada's only colonial-style hotel has a central courtyard and pool area, tiled hallways, and carved wood furniture in the rooms. *Av. López Mateos at Av. Castillo, 667/8–3616. 52 rooms, 6 junior suites. Facilities: pool, restaurant, bar, tour desk. MC, V.*

★ **Quintas Papagayo.** A bungalow and low-rise seaside establishment opened in 1947, Quintas Papagayo is a place where couples honeymoon and come back each year for their anniversaries. The accommodations are far from spectacular—rustic and homey are better descriptions—but you feel as if you've discovered a special hideaway where everyone remembers your name. Fireplaces, kitchens, patios, and decks are available. *Mexico Hwy. 1 north of town, tel. 667/4–4980 or 667/ 4–4155; reservations: Box 150, Ensenada, Baja CA, or tel. 619/ 491–0682 in the U.S. 50 rooms. Facilities: pool, restaurant, bar, tennis courts, beach. MC, V.*

Inexpensive   **Joker Hotel.** A bizarre, brightly colored mish-mash of styles makes it hard to miss this hotel, conveniently located for those traveling south of Ensenada. Spacious rooms have private balconies, satellite TV, and phones. *3 mi south of Ensenada on Hwy. 1, tel. 667/6–7201; reservations in the U.S.: 800/678– 7244. 20 rooms. Facilities: pool, whirlpool. MC, V.*

Nightlife

Ensenada is a party town for college students, surfers, and young tourists. **Hussong's** and **Papa's and Beer** on Avenida Ruíz are rowdy at night. Most of the expensive hotels have bars and discos that are less frenetic.

La Taberna Espanola (Blvd. Costero 1982) is a great place to gather for a night-long feast of tapas and sangria and a flamenco show. **Tortilla Flats,** on the harbor and with a view of the fishing boats, has dining and dancing of a more mellow sort. **Smitty González,** on Avenida Ryerson, attracts devoted disco dancers. **Joy's Discotheque** at Avenidas López Mateos and Balboa is popular with the locals, as is **Xanadu Disco** on Avenida Ejercito Nacional.

Northeast Baja: Mexicali, Tecate, and San Felipe

Introduction

Mexicali, the capital of Baja California Norte, shares the Imperial Valley farmland and the border crossing with Calexico, a small California city. Mexicali is an expanding city. New neighborhoods (called *colonias*) crop up steadily in the far-reaching suburbs. Massive new government buildings and sprawling shopping centers appear throughout the city. *Maquiladoras* (manufacturing plants operated by companies from the United States and Japan) bring new jobs for the steady stream of workers from mainland Mexico. The current population of Mexicali is estimated to be 800,000. As a capital city, Mexicali sees a great deal of government activity. In the southern part of the city, a Civic and Commercial Center has been built with a hospital, government offices, and shopping center. Though water is scarce in these largely desert lands, the Mexicali area is blessed with some of the world's richest topsoil, and agriculture is the primary source of income in this section of Mexico.

The construction of the Imperial Canal in 1902 brought an influx of Chinese immigrants to the region. Their presence is strongly seen in the faces of many inhabitants; Mexicali is a good place to sample Chinese cuisine, and Chinese imports fill the curio shops. After the completion of the Imperial Canal, Mexicali began its prodigious growth, transformed forever from the small mining outpost it had been for years.

During Prohibition, Mexicali earned a reputation as a seamy border town; liquor was plentiful and gambling and prostitution were common. The first highway to Tijuana—an impressive engineering feat in itself—was financed from taxes imposed on these activities. Since 1935, when gambling was outlawed, the town has toned down considerably.

Mexicali is a place to do business and serves as a stopover on the way to the mainland. A train that reaches points throughout Mexico originates in Mexicali. Sometimes referred to as "The Gateway to the Sea of Cortés," Mexicali is the port of entry for travelers to the beaches of San Felipe.

At the end of Highway 5, traveling 200 kilometers (125 miles) south of Mexicali along solitary stretches of desert and salt marshes, lies the fishing village of **San Felipe** on the Sea of Cortés. San Felipe has been a popular getaway spot for years, a place where hardy travelers in recreational vehicles and campers hide out for weeks on end. It is gradually gaining in popularity with those seeking hotels, swimming pools, and good restaurants and has recently gained the attention of developers seeking to build resort communities.

Not until 1948, when the first paved road from the northern capital was completed, did San Felipe become a town of permanent residence. Now it is home to an impressive fishing and shrimping fleet. The largest boats are docked 5 kilometers (3 miles) south of town within a man-made breakwater enclosure. A hurricane nearly destroyed San Felipe in 1967, but residents rebuilt most of the town, and since then it has grown steadily. Today San Felipe boasts an international airport and an increasing number of hotels. On the way into town there are at least a dozen campgrounds on the beach. These are quite popular and fill up quickly during the winter and spring holidays. Dune buggies, motorcycles, and off-road vehicles abound. On weekends, San Felipe can be boisterous.

San Felipe draws many fishermen, especially in the spring. Launches, bait, and supplies are readily available. Game wardens regularly check for valid fishing licenses, which are available through fishing charters and Mexicali travel agencies. Bahía San Felipe has dramatic changes in its tides. The tides crest at 6 meters (20 feet), and since the beach is so shallow, the waterline can move in and out up to 1 kilometer (about ½ mile). The local fishermen are well aware of the peculiarities of this section of the Sea of Cortés. Many of them visit the shrine of the Cerro de la Virgen (Virgin of Guadalupe) before setting sail. This shrine sits high on a hill at the north end of the bay and offers a view of the town and the desert mountains behind it.

Tecate is about 144 kilometers (90 miles) west of Mexicali on Highway 2. It is a quiet community, a typical small Mexican town that happens to be on the border. Tecate never offered the vice on which many other border towns thrive. So incidental is the border to local life that its gates are closed from midnight until 7 AM. More than 70,000 people live in and around Tecate, yet despite its relatively small size, the town is known throughout Mexico for the beer that bears its name.

Although the brewery is the biggest industry, farming is also good in this area. A bit farther south, the valleys of Guadalupe and Califia boast some of Mexico's lushest vineyards. Olives and grain are also grown in profusion. Indians thrived in this area before the settlers drove them out, and a few tribes still inhabit the land south of town. The government strives to protect these tribes, mostly by not interfering in their affairs. It is rare for anyone to be allowed access to their communities.

Tecate's main tourist draw is Rancho la Puerta, a fitness resort that caters to well-heeled southern Californians.

Arriving and Departing by Plane

There are no flights from the United States to the Mexicali International Airport, but flights within Mexico are available on **Mexicana** (tel. 800/531–7921), **Aeromexico** (tel. 800/237–6639), and regional carriers.

San Felipe has an international airport, but no regular commercial flights thus far. Private and charter planes are landing there.

Arriving and Departing by Car, Bus, and Train

By Car Mexicali is located on the border, opposite Calexico, California, approximately 184 kilometers (115 miles) east of San Diego and 88 kilometers (55 miles) west of Yuma, Arizona. Tecate lies on the border between Tijuana and Mexicali on Highway 2. The 134-kilometer (84-mile) journey from Tecate east to Mexicali on La Rumorosa, as the road is known, is as exciting as a roller-coaster ride, with the highway twisting and turning down steep mountain grades and over flat, barren desert. San Felipe is 200 kilometers (125 miles) on the coast south of Mexicali via Highway 5. Visitors in this area will not need tourist cards but should purchase Mexican car insurance at agencies near the border.

By Bus Four Mexican bus lines run out of the Mexicali Station: **Tres Estrellas de Oro** goes through Tecate on its way to Tijuana; **Transportes del Pacifico** goes to Mexico City and other points on the mainland; **Transportes Norte de Sonora** frequents border towns in Baja and on the mainland; and **Autotransportes de Baja California** goes to San Felipe, Tijuana, and Ensenada. It is possible to purchase reserved seats the day before departure, but only at the bus station (Av. Independencia, tel. 65/67–2410 or 65/67–2420).

Mexicali **Central Bus Station** (Centro Cívico, Av. Independencia, tel. 65/67–2451).

San Felipe **Autotransportes de Baja California** (Av. Mar de Cortés, tel. 657/7–1039).

Tecate **Central Bus Station** (Av. Benito Juárez and Calle Abelardo Rodríguez, tel. 665/4–1221).

By Train Although there is no train service available through Baja, El Tren del Pacífico (Estación de Ferroccarril, Box 3–182, Mexicali, Baja California, Mexico, tel. 65/7–2386) runs from Mexicali to points south in the mainland interior. The station is located at the south end of Calle Ulises Irigoyen, a few blocks north of the intersection of Avenida López Mateos and Avenida Independencia. Trains leave twice daily. The first is the express with sleeping and dining cars; the other is the local, coach only. The fares are reasonable, and there are several different travel options for which you may make advance reservations.

Getting Around

By Car The ideal way to see the northeastern part of Baja is to drive your own car or rent one in Mexicali. Most U.S. car-rental agencies do not allow their cars to be taken into Mexico. Be sure to buy Mexican auto insurance before driving into Baja.

Four major rental agencies operate out of the Mexicali airport: **Avis** (tel. 800/331–1212), **Budget** (tel. 800/527–0700), **Hertz** (tel. 800/654–3131), and **National** (tel. 800/227–7368).

By Taxi Taxis are easy to find in downtown Mexicali, especially around the intersection of Avenidas Azueta and Reforma. Negotiate your fare before you start the trip. Taxis are less available in Tecate and San Felipe, but your hotel should be able to arrange one for you if you wish to explore outside the town.

Important Addresses and Numbers

Tourist Information Information is available at the **Tourist Commission** and **Mexicali Chamber of Commerce** offices (Blvd. Lopez Mateos and Calle Camelias, tel. 65/52–9795). In Tecate, the **State Tourism Office** (1305 Libertad Alley, tel. 665/4–1095) has a full array of pamphlets and an English-speaking clerk; the office is open Monday–Friday 9–7, Saturday 9–3, Sunday 10–2. The **San Felipe State Tourism Office** (Av. Mar de Cortés, tel. 657/7–1155) is open weekdays 9–7, weekends 10–2.

Emergencies Mexicali **Police** (Centro Cívico, tel. 65/2–4443); **Hospital** (Durango and Salina Cruz, tel. 657/5–1666).

San Felipe **Police** (Ortiz Rubio and Libertad, tel. 657/7–1006); **Hospital** (tel. 657/7–1001).

Tecate **Police** (Liberated Alley, tel. 665/4–1176 or 134); **Red Cross** (tel. 132); **Fire** (tel. 136).

Guided Tours

VTC Tours (237 Rockwood Dr., Suite 210, Calexico, CA 92231, tel. 619/357–0342) offers one-day and overnight tours of Mexicali and San Felipe; the two-day tour of Mexicali is $89 per person, including hotel.

Baja California Tours offers comfortable, informative bus trips through all of Baja and can arrange special-interest tours. Vans depart daily from San Diego to San Felipe; midweek transportation and hotel packages are a real bargain. *6986 La Jolla Blvd., #204, La Jolla, CA 92037, tel. 619/454–7166, fax 619/454–2703.*

Exploring

Mexicali's sights are few and far between, and most visitors are in Mexicali for business. A tourist-oriented strip of curio shops and sleazy bars is located along Avenida Francisco Madero, one block south of the border. **El Antiguo Palacio de Gobierno,** the former capitol building, is closer to the center of town, almost two blocks from the border, at the intersection of Avenida Obregón and Avenida E; it often exhibits paintings and sculptures. The **Regional Museum,** which is administered by the Autonomous University of Baja California (UABC), provides a comprehensive introduction to the natural and cultural history of Baja. *Av. Reforma 1998, near Calle L, tel. 65/62–5717. Admission free. Open Tues.–Sat. 9–6.*

Parque Obregón at **Avenida Reforma and Calle Irigoyen,** and **Parque Constitución** at Avenida México and Zuazua, are the only two parks in downtown Mexicali. Parque Obregón is one street away from the border, next to the House of Culture; Parque Constitución is farther into the downtown area, built around a large music pavilion. The **Mexicali Zoo** is in the City Park, **Bosque de la Ciudad,** south of town; the entrance is at the south end of Calle Victoria, between Cárdenas and Avenida Independencia. Adjoining this park is the **Xochimilco Lagoon** (the Mexicali reservoir), where there are picnic facilities and pedal-boat rentals.

If you allocate an hour for exploring **Tecate,** you'll be hard put to fill your time. **Parque Hildalgo,** in the center of town, is a typical Mexican village plaza, with a small gazebo and a few wrought-iron benches. **Parque López Mateos,** on Highway 3 south of town, is the site for dance and band concerts on summer evenings.

San Felipe is the quintessential dusty fishing village, with one main street (two, if you count the highway into town). The *malecón* (waterfront boardwalk) is little more than a cement sidewalk beside a seawall, with a collection of fishing pongas clustered at one end. The only landmark in town is the **shrine of the Virgin of Guadalupe,** at the north end of the malecón on a hill overlooking the Sea of Cortés and San Felipe Bay.

Shopping

Baldini Importers in Mexicali (Calle 7 and Av. Reforma) offers a nice selection of imported items. Two outdoor markets sell produce in Mexicali—one at Calle Obregón and Calle del Comercio and the other at the end of Calle Aldama, a block south of Parque Constitución. In Tecate, a large artisan's market is located just off the Tecate-Ensenada highway. In San Felipe, there's the typical array of sombreros, sundresses, and T-shirts, and a large supply of fireworks. **Curios Oaxaca** has some nicer rugs and dresses from Oaxaca, and **Roberta's** is a small store where you can get supplies and souvenirs.

Sports and Outdoor Activities

Mexicali
Golf

Golf is played at the **Mexicali Campestre Golf Course** (Km 11.5 on Hwy. 5 south of town, tel. 65/61–7130), which stays open Tuesday through Sunday. The 18-hole course is open throughout the year. Although this is a private club, anyone can use the course. Greens fees are around $10.

San Felipe
Fishing

The Sea of Cortés offers plentiful sea bass, snapper, corbina, halibut, and other game fish. Most hotels can arrange fishing trips. Licenses and trips can also be arranged at the **Fishing Cooperative** office on Calle Zihuatanejo and at the bright blue ramshackle house at the north end of the malecón. Clamming is good as well.

Tony Reyes (tel. 714/538–8010) offers six-day fishing trips on a converted shrimp boat. The cost, including meals and beer or sodas, is $575 per person.

Baja Fishing Tours (2143 San Diego Ave., San Diego, CA 92110, tel. 800/832–BAJA) runs fishing trips down from the border in May and June. Six-day fishing trips on shrimp boats are $525 per person, or $575 per person on a new, air-conditioned boat.

Dining

Northeast Baja is not known for fine dining, but there are several good Chinese restaurants in Mexicali. Your best bet in San Felipe is seafood, especially fresh shrimp. Highly recommended restaurants are indicated by a star ★.

Category	Cost*
Expensive	over $15
Moderate	$10–$15
Inexpensive	under $10

per person, excluding drinks, service, and sales tax (10%)

Mexicali
Expensive
★
La Misión Dragón. With its eclectic landscape, this restaurant resembles a combination of a mission house and a Chinese palace. Behind its gates are fountains, a garden, and Asian and Mexican artifacts. The locals hold large dinner celebrations here, and the Chinese food is top-notch. *Av. Lázaro Cárdenas 555, tel. 65/66–4320 or 65/6–4451. No reservations. Dress: casual. MC, V.*

Moderate
★
Cenaduría Selecta. This charming restaurant has been serving traditional Mexican food since 1945. The waiters are formal and efficient, the menus come in wooden folders, and the rows of booths always seem filled with locals enjoying themselves. *Av. Arista and Calle C 1510, tel. 65/62–4047. No reservations. Dress: casual. MC, V.*

Chu-Lim. This spacious yet quiet Chinese restaurant is a welcome haven from the bustle of downtown shopping. The walls and ceilings are decorated in detailed Oriental-style paneling. *Morelos 251, tel. 65/62–8695. No reservations. Dress: casual. MC, V.*

Inexpensive
★
Casita de Pátzcuaro. A good place for tacos and burritos, this is a favorite with regulars headed for San Felipe. *Av. López Mateos 648, tel. 65/62–9707. No reservations. Dress: casual. No credit cards.*

Las Cazuelas. A nice, clean restaurant, Las Cazuelas serves traditional Mexican dishes and good combination meals. *Av. Benito Juárez 56, tel. 65/64–0649. No reservations. Dress: casual. No credit cards.*

San Felipe
Expensive
★
Alfredo's. Located in La Trucha Vagabunda Hotel, Alfredo's is run by the daughter of Mexico City restaurateur Alfredo Bellinghieri. With its crystal chandeliers, the dining area resembles a large ballroom. The fettuccine Alfredo and lasagna are first-rate, and the tender, tasty *carne asada Siciliano* (grilled beef) is marinated in olive oil and oregano. *Calle Mar Báltico, tel. 657/7–1333. No reservations. Dress: casual. No lunch. MC, V.*

Moderate
Rubens. This trailer-park restaurant is a popular hangout for regulars who return to San Felipe year after year. The Coco Loco, a blend of liquors and coconut milk, is reason enough to

return, and the shrimp omelette receives high marks. *North of town on Ave. Golfo de California, tel. 65/7–1091. No reservations. Dress: casual. MC, V.*

Inexpensive **Tacos La Gaviota** and **Tacos La Bonita,** both in the downtown area, serve tacos filled with fish, clam, shrimp, or pork at outdoor stands. Straddle a stool at the counter, order one of each, and enjoy a $2 feast. *Av. Mar de Cortés, no phone. No credit cards.*

Tecate **El Passetto.** This could be the best Italian restaurant in all of
Moderate Baja, with superb garlic bread and homemade pasta. The proprietor makes his own wines, which are pretty good. Live music on the weekends. *Callejón Libertad 200, tel. 665/4–1361. MC, V.*

El Tucán. By Tecate standards, this steakhouse is fancy. It is four blocks from the border. *Av. Juárez 1100, tel. 665/4–1102. No reservations. Dress: casual. MC, V.*

Inexpensive **Le Jardine.** The setting is plain and the food simple Mexican fare, but the café tables outside offer a gratifying view of the plaza. *Libertad Alley 274, no phone. No credit cards.*

Lodging

Hotels are abundant in Mexicali, but scarce in San Felipe and Tecate. Rates are lower than in the rest of Baja, and accommodations, as a rule, are modest and plain. Highly recommended lodgings are indicated by a star ★.

Category	Cost*
Very Expensive	over $100
Expensive	$45–$100
Moderate	$20–$45
Inexpensive	under $20

*All prices are for a standard double room, excluding service charge and sales tax (10%).

Mexicali **Holiday Inn.** This is the perennial favorite of those doing busi-
Expensive ness in the city, with standard rooms and services and no surprises. *Av. Benito Juárez 2220, tel. 65/66–3801; reservations in the U.S.: 800/465–4329. 173 rooms. Facilities: pool, coffee shop, restaurant, bar. AE, MC, V.*

★ **La Lucerna.** The prettiest hotel in Mexicali, La Lucerna has lots of palms and fountains around the pool. *Av. Benito Juárez 2151, tel. 65/66–1000; reservations in the U.S.: Box 2300, Calexico, CA 92231. 200 rooms. Facilities: pool, restaurant, coffee shop, bar. MC, V.*

Moderate **Castel Calafía.** One of the newest hotels in town, with plain, clean, and comfortable rooms. *Justo Sierra 1495; tel. 65/68–3311 or 800/927–2402. 173 rooms. Facilities: pool, restaurant, bar. MC, V.*

San Felipe **Las Misiones.** A pretty oasis of blue pools and green palms by
Expensive the beach, this resort is popular with group tours. Las Misiones is a good choice for travelers who want to get away from it all, but if you want to feel like you're actually in Mexico, you're better off at a hotel in town. The rooms are in various

stages of renovation. *Av. Misión de Loreto 130, tel. 657/7–1280 or 800/336–5454. 241 rooms. Facilities: restaurant, bar, 3 pools, tennis courts. MC, V.*

Moderate
★
El Cortés. Probably the most popular hotel in San Felipe, El Cortés has a lively bar, a long, clean beach, and a small pool and hot tub. Some of the rooms have beachfront patios. *Av. Mar de Cortez, tel. 657/7–1055; reservations in the U.S.: Box 1227, Calexico, CA 92231, tel. 706/566–8324. 90 rooms. Facilities: pool, beach, restaurant, bar, boat launch. MC, V.*

La Trucha Vagabunda. On a hill overlooking the town and beaches of San Felipe, this pretty blue-and-white hotel is quickly becoming the favored place to stay. The rooms are white, airy, and impeccably clean, and the restaurant is exceptionally good. *Av. de los Cedros Sur, tel. 657/7–1333; reservations in the U.S.: Box 5484, Calexico, CA 92231, tel. 619/ 298–4105 or 800/522–1516 in CA, 800/225–2786 elsewhere in the U.S. 45 rooms. Facilities: pool, restaurant, bar, disco. MC, V.*

Inexpensive
El Capitán. This two-story brick and adobe motel is across the street from the beach and is popular with families. The rooms are basic, and the small grounds are nothing more than a parking lot. *Av. Mar de Cortés 298, tel. 657/7–1303. 40 rooms. Facilities: pool, laundry room. MC, V.*

Tecate
Expensive
Hacienda Santa Veronica. Billed as an off-road and dirt-racing country club, the Hacienda is a pretty countryside resort featuring rooms furnished with Mexican colonial beds, bureaus, and fireplaces. Bulls are raised on the 5,000-acre ranch, and guests can watch matadors train in *pachangas*, or bloodless bullfights. The off-road raceway is set far enough away from the rooms to keep the noise of revving engines from disturbing the guests, and a number of trails for horseback riding traverse the property. *Hwy 2, 2 mi east of Tecate; reservations in the U.S.: tel. 619/341–9811. 87 rooms. Facilities: restaurant, pool, bar, tennis courts, horseback riding, RV park. MC, V.*

Rancho Tecate. A family winery has been converted into a peaceful country resort with casitas and a main guest house. A golf course is under construction, with a few holes ready for play. *Hwy 3, 5 mi south of Tecate, tel. 665/4–0011. 37 rooms. Facilities: restaurant, bar, tennis, golf. MC, V.*

Health Spas

Tecate
Very Expensive
Rancho la Puerta. For those who can afford $1,500 or more a week, Rancho la Puerta is a peaceful, isolated health spa and resort 5 kilometers (3 miles) west of Tecate. Spanish-style buildings with red-tile roofs and modern glass-and-wood structures are spread throughout the sprawling ranch. Hiking trails lead off into scrub-pine hills surrounding the resort, and a large bright-blue pool is the central gathering spot for guests intent on relaxation. Guests stay in luxurious private cottages, and usually check in for a week or more, taking advantage of the special diet and exercise regimen to lose weight and get in shape. *Hwy. 2, tel. 65/4–1005, or 619/744–4222 in CA. Facilities: health club, massage, beauty salon, pool, tennis courts, restaurant. AE, MC, V.*

The Arts and Nightlife

Mexicali   **Teatro del Estado** (tel. 65/64–0757) is on Calle López Mateos near the government center. Stage hits from Mexico City are often presented, and dance troupes and musical groups, both classical and modern, are often featured.

There is nightly entertainment in the **Lucerna** (tel. 65/6–1000) and **Holiday Inn** (tel. 65/6–1300).

San Felipe   The bar at the **El Cortez Hotel** (tel. 657/7–1055) is always crowded. **Hotel Las Misiones** (tel. 657/7–1280) has live music and dancing on weekend nights.

Guerrero Negro and Scammon's Lagoon

Humans aren't the only travelers who migrate below the border for warmth in the winter months. Every winter thousands of great gray whales swim south from the Bering Sea off Alaska to the tip of the Baja Peninsula. Just over the state line between Baja Norte and Baja Sur, at the 28th parallel, they stop to give birth at Scammon's Lagoon. Up to 6,000 whales show up each year, stopping not far from shore for the calves to be born. Far from diminutive, the newborns weigh about one-half ton and drink nearly 50 gallons of milk each day.

If it weren't for the whales, and for the Transpeninsular Highway, which runs near town, few travelers would venture to **Guerrero Negro** (Black Warrior) 720 kilometers (450 miles) south of Tijuana. Guerrero Negro is near the Vizcaíno desert, on the Pacific Ocean. The area is best known for its salt mines, which produce one-third of the world's salt. Salt water collects in over 780 square kilometers (300 square miles) of sea-level ponds and evaporates quickly in the desert heat, leaving huge blocks of pure white salt.

Guerrero Negro received its name from a whaling ship that ran aground in nearby Scammon's Lagoon in 1858. The town's population is 10,000, with many employed by the salt company. Each year, from January to March, the whales and the tourists arrive. The rest of the year, Guerrero Negro is a way station along the highway, a place to stop for gas and supplies, and maybe a meal.

Scammon's Lagoon is about 27 kilometers (17 miles) south, down a sand road that crosses the salt flats, which is passable but rough. The lagoon got its name from U.S. explorer Charles Melville Scammon of Maine. In the mid-1800s, he discovered the lagoon in Bahía Sebastián Vizcaíno, off the coast of Baja. The whales and their calves that visited these waters were a much easier and plentiful prey for the whalers than the great leviathans swimming in the open sea. On his first expedition to the lagoon, Scammon and his crew collected over 700 barrels of valuable whale oil, and the whale rush was on. Within 10 years, nearly all the whales in the lagoon had been killed, and it took almost a century for the whale population to increase to what it had been before Scammon arrived. It wasn't until the 1940s that the U.S. and Mexican governments took measures to protect the whales and banned the whalers from the lagoon.

Today even whale-watching boats must have permission from the Mexican government to enter Scammon's Lagoon, known in Mexico as Laguna Ojo de Liebre (Hare's Eye Lagoon). The area around the lagoon is now a national park, Parque Natural de Ojo de Liebre (Rabbit's Eye Natural Park). Whale-watching from the shores of the lagoon can be disappointing without binoculars. But it is still an impressive sight to see the whales spouting water high into the air, and their 12-foot-wide tails smashing into the water.

At **Laguna de San Ignacio,** about 100 kilometers (62 miles) south, fishermen will take you out in their boats to get closer to the whales. But for a better view, and an easier stay in this rugged country, travel with an outfitter who will arrange your travel to Guerrero Negro, your accommodations, and your time on the water. The whales will come close to your boat, rising majestically from the water, and sometimes swim close enough to be petted on their crusted backs.

Arriving and Departing

By Plane The closest international airport to Guerrero Negro is in La Paz, 800 kilometers (500 miles) southeast; there is a small airstrip in town.

By Car and Bus Guerrero Negro is just south of the Baja Norte/Baja Sur state line, about 720 kilometers (450 miles) from the Tijuana border. **Tres Estrellas de Oro** (tel. 682/2–3063 in La Paz) has buses to Guerrero Negro from La Paz.

Guided Tours

The best way to see the whales is with a tour company that's familiar with the area. **Baja Expeditions** (2625 Garnet Ave., San Diego, CA 92109, tel. 619/581–3311; outside CA 800/843–6967) has whale-watching trips on boats and kayaks and is the premier Baja adventure operator in the United States. Their adventure tours span the peninsula and the Sea of Cortés. **Baja Discovery** (Box 152527, San Diego, CA 92115, tel. 619/262–0700 or 800/829–BAJA) operates a whale-watching camp at Laguna San Ignacio south of Guerrero Negro, with tent camping on an island in the lagoon, and boat trips among the whales.

Dining The best restaurant in town is **Malarrimo,** at a trailer park near the entrance to town. Seafood is the specialty, and though the prices have climbed to the high–moderate range the food is still worth the cost. **Mario's,** by El Morro hotel, is good for seafood and Mexican dishes.

Lodging

There are five hotels in Guerrero Negro, with a total of 100 rooms. Double-occupancy rooms cost from about $15 to $70 per day; rates tend to increase during peak whale-watching times from December through February. Credit cards are not normally accepted, but the hotels do take traveler's checks.

El Morro. A small inn on a more primitive scale, El Morro has rooms with private baths and hot showers. *Bd. Zapata, no phone.*
La Pinta. Part of a small chain of hotels in Baja, this motel has clean, spacious rooms. It is a few kilometers outside town, look-

ing like an oasis of palms in the desert. *Reservations in the U.S.: tel. 800/336–5454. 26 rooms. Facilities: coffee shop.*
Malarrimo. This popular trailer park and restaurant has a six-room motel, with private baths and TV. *At entrance to town, no phone.*

Loreto

Introduction

The original capital of the Californias, Loreto now aspires to be simply a "capital" resort area. In 1976, when the coffers were full of oil revenue, the government tapped the Loreto area for development. Streets were paved in the dusty little village, and telephone service, electricity, potable water, and sewage systems were installed in both the town and the surrounding area. The town of 8,000 even got an international airport. One luxury hotel was built, as was a championship tennis center, where John McEnroe was signed as a touring pro.

Then everything came to a halt. No new hotels have opened since 1980. The Loreto Tennis Tournament, where McEnroe puts in an appearance, moved to Ixtapa. Today Loreto, with a population of 15,000, is a good place to escape the crowds, relax, and go fishing. The town has always been a favorite getaway for a few knowing sports enthusiasts. Their fears that it would be spoiled have thus far been largely unfounded, though the residential trailer parks are filling up and private homes are clustered in secluded enclaves. Loreto is much the way it was decades ago, except that now it is more accessible.

Located on the Sea of Cortés, some 1,200 kilometers (750 miles) south of the U.S. border in California, Loreto's setting is truly spectacular. The gold and green hills of the Sierra Gigante seem to tumble into the cobalt sea. Rain is rare. According to the local promoters, the skies are clear 360 days of the year. There aren't even any bugs—or at least very few—to plague vacationers. The dry, desert climate is not one in which insects thrive.

Loreto was the site of the first California mission. Jesuit priests Eusebio Kino and Juan María Salvatierra settled the area in the 1680s and work began on the mission buildings in 1697. It was from Loreto that Father Junípero Serra, a Franciscan monk from Mallorca, Spain, set out in 1769 to found missions from San Diego to San Francisco—in the land then known as Alta California.

Mexico won its independence from Spain in 1821, and the missions gradually were abandoned. The priests, who were often from Spain, were ordered to return home. Loreto had been the administrative as well as the religious center of the Californias, but with the withering of the mission and the 1829 hurricane that virtually destroyed the settlement, the capital of the Californias was moved to La Paz. A severe earthquake struck the Loreto area in 1877, further destroying the town.

For a century the village languished. The U.S. fishermen who rediscovered the town were a hearty breed who flew down in their own aircraft and went after marlin and sailfish in open launches. Loreto's several small hotels were built to serve this rough-and-ready set; most of the properties were built before 1960, when no highway came down this far and there was no airport worthy of the name.

Fonatur, the government tourism-development agency, is a more recent arrival. Its projects take in not only the village, but some 24 kilometers (15 miles) of coastline. An area known as Nopoló, for example, currently installed a golf course and is slated to be the address of swank hotels. Puerto Escondido is the site of a large marina, but planned hotels have yet to be constructed. The little town is destined to be a bedroom community for all the people who will work at the hotels, shops, and restaurants that have yet to be built. The infrastructure has been completed, and Loreto sits waiting.

Arriving and Departing by Plane

Aero California (tel. 800/258–3311) has daily flights from Los Angeles and La Paz to Loreto's airport, which is 7.2 kilometers (4.5 miles) southwest of town.

Arriving and Departing by Car and Bus

Loreto is 1,200 kilometers (750 miles) south of the U.S. border via Highway 1. Early starts are recommended to avoid nighttime driving. **Tres Estrellas de Oro** (tel. 662/6–1146 in Tijuana) provides bus services along this route.

There is a car-rental agency at the airport and in the **Stouffer Presidente** (tel. 683/3–0700), but only a few vehicles (all with standard shift) are available. There are two gas stations in Loreto; be sure to fill your tank before heading out on any long jaunts.

Getting Around

By Taxi Taxis are in good supply, and fares are inexpensive. It is wise to establish the fare in advance.

Important Addresses and Numbers

Tourist Office (Calle Salvatierra across from the mission, tel. 683/3–0035; closed Sun.); **Police,** who may not speak English (tel. 683/3–0035).

Guided Tours

Picnic cruises to Isla Coronado, excursions into the mountains to visit the San Javier Mission and view prehistoric rock paintings, and day trips to Mulege can be arranged through hotels. The local tour operator is **Turismo los Candeleros** (tel. 683/3–0700).

Exploring

One could allocate 15 minutes for a tour of downtown Loreto and still have time left over. The renovated malecón, built in 1991, has turned the waterfront into a pleasant place for a stroll: A marina houses the panga fleet and private yachts; the adjoining beach is a popular gathering spot for locals, especially on Sunday afternoons; and, the beach playground has a great assortment of play equipment for kids. The small **zócalo** (main square) and town center is one block west on Calle Salvatierra. The church, **La Misión de Nuestra Señora de Loreto,** the first of the California missions, is the only historic sight. Founded in 1697 by Jesuit Father Juan María Salvatierra, the church was the first mission in the Californias, the beginning of a chain of missions that eventually stretched as far as San Francisco and Sonoma in what is now the United States. The carved stone walls, wood-beam ceilings, gilded altar, and primitive-style portraits of the priests who have served there are worth seeing. The **Museum of Anthropology and History,** also called **El Museo de los Misiones,** next door to the church, contains religious relics, tooled leather saddles used in the 19th century, and displays of Baja's history. The museum is open Wednesday through Sunday from 9 to 4. Adjacent to the church is a new shopping complex with boutiques that sell fine silver and crafts.

Nopoló, where the luxury resorts are scheduled to go up, is about 8 kilometers (5 miles) south of town. Already in operation is the five-star Stouffer Presidente, and across the way is a nine-court tennis complex. A spectacular 18-hole golf course designed by Desmond Muirhead opened in 1991 after years of construction. The course sits between the highway and Nopoló Bay.

According to Fonatur's plans, there will be 5,700 hotel rooms in the Nopoló area, along with about 1,000 private homes and condo units within 10 years. For now sidewalks and concrete foundation slabs run through fields of weeds and shrubs.

More progress has been made 16 kilometers (10 miles) down the road in **Puerto Escondido,** where the marina, still under construction in the harbor, already contains 100 boat slips. Nearby is a recreational vehicle park, **Tripui,** where new hotel rooms are under construction. Facilities for motorists and sailors include a snack shop, a bar and restaurant, stores, showers, a laundry, a pool, and tennis courts. A boat ramp has been completed at the marina; just ask around for David Hernández, the port captain, to pay your fees and get permission to launch your boat. **Isla Danzante,** 5 kilometers (3 miles) southeast of Puerto Escondido, has good diving and reefs.

Picnic trips to nearby **Coronado Island** may be arranged in Loreto, at Nopoló, or in Puerto Escondido. The island is inhabited only by sea lions. Snorkeling and scuba diving opportunities are excellent.

Off the Beaten Track

A longer excursion involves driving 134 kilometers (84 miles) north on Highway 1 to **Mulege,** an old mission that was frequented by U.S. sportsfishermen long before the current building boom. Mulege is a tropical town in the Sea of Cortés, with beaches along Bahía Concepción, the largest protected bay in Baja.

Santa Rosalia, 64 kilometers (40 miles) north, is known for its **Iglesia Santa Barbara,** a prefabricated iron church designed by Alexandre-Gustave Eiffel, creator of the Eiffel Tower.

Shopping

There are few opportunities for shopping in Loreto. **Kino's** and **La Choya,** near each other on the waterfront, handle an assortment of handicrafts, including ceramics, sweaters, and serapes. Resortwear is also available. A smaller selection is to be found in the shop at the **Stouffer Presidente** (tel. 683/3–0700), which also stocks reading material in English. **El Alacran** and **Pintado a Mano,** in the small shopping complex behind the church on Calle Salvatierra, have the best selection of folk art, jewelry, and souvenirs in town. Groceries and ice are available at **Plaza Focardi,** on Calle Salvatierra, easily spotted because of its six shades of pink.

Sports and Outdoor Activities

Fishing Fishing put Loreto on the map, especially for the American sports enthusiast. Cabrillo and snapper are caught year-round; yellowtail in the spring; and dorado, marlin, and sailfish in the summer. Visitors who plan to fish should bring tackle with them because the tackle that is available locally is likely to be primitive and worn. All Loreto-area hotels can arrange fishing, and many own skiffs; the local fishermen congregate with their small boats on the beach at the north end of town. **Alfredo's Sportfishing** (tel. 683/3–0016) takes anglers out and has good guides. **Sportsman's Tours** (2945 Harding St., Ste. 211, Carlsbad, CA 92008, tel. 619/630–BAJA or 800/234–0618, fax 619/720–0528) has fishing trips to Loreto and other spots in Baja.

Sailing The best sailing is off the beach by the Stouffer Presidente on Nopoló Bay. Hobie Cats and similar craft may be rented at the hotel (tel. 683/3–0700).

Scuba Diving The coral reefs off Coronado and Carmen islands are an undersea adventure. The scuba specialist is **Fantasia Divers** (tel. 683/3–0700).

Tennis The **Loreto Tennis Center** (tel. 683/3–0700), adjoining the Stouffer Presidente in Nopoló, 8 kilometers (5 miles) south of Loreto, is open to the public.

Beaches

All Loreto-area hotels are on the waterfront, but the beaches are disappointing, being more stones than sand.

Dining

There aren't many restaurants in Loreto, but the seafood is excellent no matter where you go. Reservations are not required and the dress is casual.

Category	Cost*
Expensive	over $10
Moderate	$5–$10
Inexpensive	under $5

**per person, excluding drinks, service, and sales tax (10%)*

Moderate–Expensive **Cesar's.** One block east of the church sits the best restaurant in town, with good seafood and traditional Mexican dishes. Try the giant shrimp stuffed with cheese, wrapped with bacon, and grilled. The most expensive dinner won't be more than $10. *Calle Salvatierra at Zapata, tel. 683/3–0203. MC, V.*

Moderate **Tripui.** The recreational vehicle park in Puerto Escondido is the best place outside Loreto for seafood. *At the RV park, tel. 683/3–0818. MC, V.*

Inexpensive **Café Olé.** The best taquería in town also offers good burgers and delicious chocolate shakes. *Calle Francisco Madero, tel. 683/3–0496. No credit cards.*

Lodging

The choices are good, but limited. The most luxurious hotels are out of town and isolated. Highly recommended lodgings are indicated by a star ★.

Category	Cost*
Very Expensive	over $150
Expensive	$50–$150
Moderate	$40–$50
Inexpensive	under $40

All prices are for a standard double room, excluding service charge and sales tax (10%).

Very Expensive ★ **Stouffer Presidente Loreto.** Across from the Loreto Tennis Center on Nopoló Beach is this three-story all-inclusive resort. Remodeled in 1988, all guest rooms have a color TV, an FM radio, and a balcony or terrace overlooking the Sea of Cortés. Besides all meals and drinks, a stay at this lavish property includes one day of fishing, Spanish and scuba-diving lessons, bullfights, biking, horseback riding, tennis, a full spectrum of water sports—water skiing, windsurfing, sailing, snorkeling—and all taxes and tips. El Cimarrón serves fresh fish and steaks, and there's nightly entertainment in the lobby bar. *Blvd. Misión de Loreto s/n, 23880, tel. 683/3–0700; 800/843–9633, in CA; 800/GRACIAS. 258 rooms and suites. Facilities: sportfishing fleet, 2 pools (1 with swim-up bar), restaurant, lobby bar, disco, 10 lit tennis courts and pro shop (at tennis center), laundry, newsstand, shops, parking, car rental. AE, DC, MC, V.*

Moderate **La Pinta.** Part of a chain of Baja California hotels, this property is a much-remodeled fishing camp on the beach. It has its own fleet of launches. *Blvd. Misión de Loreto, tel. 683/3–0025; reservations in the U.S.: tel. 800/678–7244. 48 rooms. Facilities: pool, 2 tennis courts. MC, V.*

Misión. An old favorite, this is the only hotel right in Loreto. It has a view of the water beyond the seawall. The beach across the street is stony, but most guests come to fish; arrangements for fishing can be made at the hotel. *Calle de la Playa, 23880 in town, tel. 683/3–0048. 54 rooms. Facilities: pool, restaurant, bar. MC, V.*

★ **Oasis.** This is one of the original fishing camps and a favorite with those who want to spend as much time as possible on the water. Many of the rooms, set amid a tropical oasis of palms, have a view of the water. The hotel has its own fleet of skiffs. *Loreto Beach, tel. 683/3–0112; reservations in the U.S.: tel. 619/491–0682. Facilities: pool, tennis, fishing, boats. MC, V.*

Inexpensive **Serenidad.** Some 128 kilometers (80 miles) north of Loreto, this
★ hotel is worth the trip. The rooms have fireplaces (nights can be chilly), and the Saturday barbecue is a Baja institution. *Mulege, tel. 685/3–0111; reservations in the United States: Box 520, Corona, CA 91720, tel. 714/735–8223. 27 rooms. Facilities: pool, restaurant, airstrip. MC, V.*

Nightlife

After-dark entertainment is pretty much limited to the lobby bar and disco at the **Stouffer Presidente;** this is also the only place with TVs in the rooms and a satellite dish to pick up U.S. programs. The bars at the other hotels usually attract a congenial crowd, but the fisherfolk drawn to the Loreto area turn in early.

La Paz

Introduction

La Paz is one of those cities that make you wish you'd been here 20 years ago. In the slowest of times, in late summer when the heat is oppressive, you can easily see how it must have been when it was a quiet place, living up to its name—"Peace." Today the city has a population of 170,000. It was commerce that first attracted Hernán Cortés and his soldiers in 1535—the beautiful bay was rich with oysters and pearls. In 1720, the Jesuits arrived to civilize and convert the Indians. Instead, the missionaries inadvertently decimated the local populace by introducing smallpox. Within 30 years, there was no one left to convert.

While the rest of Mexico was being torn apart by revolution, a permanent settlement was established in 1811. La Paz became a refuge for those escaping the mainland wars. In 1829, after then-capital Loreto was leveled by a hurricane, La Paz became the capital of the Californias. Troops from the United States occasionally invaded the capital, but sent word to Washington that the Baja Peninsula was not worth fighting for. In 1853, a different group of invaders arrived from the United States. Led by William Walker, these Southerners were intent on making La Paz a slave state. The Mexicans quickly banished Walker from La Paz. Peace reigned for the next century. In 1940, disease wiped out the oyster beds, and with the pearls gone, La Paz no longer attracted prospectors and was left in peace.

La Paz officially became the capital of Baja California Sur in 1974 and is now the state's largest settlement. It is the site of the power plant for all the state, a fleet of cruise ships, the ferry to Mazatlán, the state bureaucracy, the governor's home, and the state jail. It is the stop-off for fishermen and divers headed for Cerralvo, La Partida, and Espiritu Santo islands, where parrotfish, manta rays, neons, and angels blur the clear waters by the shore, and marlin, dorado, and yellowtail leap out of the deep, dark sea.

La Paz's charm is evident in the early morning. The dull brown hills surrounding the sprawling city turn golden amber; the sea turns aqua blue. The waterfront plaza is empty except for foraging kittens, a half-dozen joggers, and a trickle of workers. In downtown's plaza, Jardín Velazco (Velazco Garden), the pink quartz gazebo shines in the sunlight, and dense trees and blooming hibiscus shade the freshly swept tile paths. Bells ring in the Catedral de Nuestra Señora de La Paz, and children wearing school uniforms stroll to class arm in arm. At sunset the city grows calm, and Los Pacenos (the peaceful ones), as the residents are called, pause at the waterfront on their way home to watch the sea grow dark again.

Arriving and Departing by Plane

The La Paz airport, about 16 kilometers (10 miles) north of town, is home to **Aero California** (tel. 682/2–1113, 800/258–3311), which flies from Los Angeles, Aguascalientes, Culiacán, Guadalajara, Loreto, Los Mochis, Mexico City, and Tijuana to La Paz. **Aeroméxico** (tel. 800/237–6639, 682/2–0091, or 682/2–0093) flies in from Tijuana, Guadalajara, Puerto Vallarta, Mexico City, Culiacán, Guaymas, Los Angeles, and Tuscon.

Arriving and Departing by Car, Bus, and Ferry

By Car   La Paz is 1,474 kilometers (921 miles) south of the U.S. border at Tijuana on the Transpeninsular Highway, and 211 kilometers (132 miles) north of Los Cabos at the southern tip of the peninsula.

By Bus   **Tres Estrellas de Oro** (tel. 682/2–6476) operates buses along the Transpeninsular Highway to the border and Los Cabos.

By Ferry   The ferry system connecting Baja to mainland Mexico has been privatized and is constantly undergoing changes in rates and schedules. Currently there are ferries from La Paz to Mazatlán and La Paz to Topolobampo. The ferry office is at the dock on the road to Pichilingue (tel. 682/5–3833). Go to the office and purchase your ticket personally in advance of your trip, and expect confusion. **Baja Express** is a new ferry system using hydrofoils, or fast catamarans, for daily departures from La Paz to Topolobampo/Los Mochis. Future plans include ferries to Los Cabos, Guaymas, and Santa Rosalia. In La Paz, purchase tickets from the Baja Express office on the Malecón at Calle 16 de Septiembre (tel. 682/5–6311 or 682/5–6313). Reservations can be made in the U.S. by calling 800/829–0510, 800/828–3242, or 800/876–3942.

Getting Around

By Rental Car   A car is not necessary if you plan to stay in town, since taxis are readily available. But if you'd like to explore the more remote beaches, a car is a must. Rental is about $70 per day for a Volkswagen Beetle, with insurance and unlimited mileage. If you want a sedan or air-conditioning, call ahead to reserve a car. Rental agencies include **Budget** (Paseo Obregón at Hidalgo, tel. 682/2–1097), **Hertz** (tel. 682/2–0919) and **Avis** (tel. 682/2–2651), both at the airport, and **Servitur Autorento** (5 de Febrero at Abasolo, tel. 682/2–1448).

By Taxi Taxis are inexpensive, but be sure to set the price with your driver before the cab gets going.

Important Addresses and Numbers

Tourist The main tourism office is on the malecón near Calle 16 de
Information Septiembre (tel. 682/2–1199, 682/2–1190, 682/2–7975, or 682/ 2–5939).

Emergencies **Police** (682/2–6610); **Fire** (682/2–0054); **Red Cross** (682/2–1111); **Clínica La Paz** (Revolución 461, tel. 682/2–0685; 682/2–2800) has English-speaking doctors on staff.

Guided Tours

Travel agencies in the hotels and along the boardwalk offer tours of the city, day-long trips to Los Cabos, sportfishing, and boating excursions.

Exploring

Numbers in the margin correspond to points of interest on the La Paz map.

The Malecón The **malecón** is La Paz's boardwalk, tourist zone, and main
❶ drag rolled into one. As you enter town from the north, you can tell that the main waterfront street, **Paseo Alvaro Obregón**, has become the malecón (wharf or waterfront boardwalk) when funeral parlors and auto-parts stores are replaced by hotels and boutiques. By mid-1993, there is supposed to be a more official
❷ entry point to the city—the 500-acre **Fidepaz Marina,** 10 blocks
❸ north of the current center of activity. The **State Tourism Department** headquarters is across from the marina.

Time Out If you begin your tour in the evening and can handle frenetic
❹ activity, have your first margarita and some nachos at **La Paz-Lapa.** The portions are gargantuan, and the quality is consistently good. *Paseo Obregón at León, tel. 682/2–6025. Open noon–1 AM. MC, V. Closed Tues.*

❺ La Paz's only true colonial Mexican hotel is **Los Arcos** (Paseo Obregón 498, tel. 682/2–2744). The center courtyard has a fountain surrounded by flowers and is a pleasant place for a short quiet rest, if no one is playing ping-pong nearby.

Shops carrying the predictable assortment of sombreros, onyx chess sets, and painted plaster curios line the next few blocks. Wander through **Artesanías la Antigua California** (Paseo Obregón 220, tel. 682/5–5230) for a sampling of better Mexican crafts—colorful woven baskets from Michoacán and carved masks from Guerero.

❻ **La Perla Hotel** has the best seats on the malecón for watching the steady stream of teens cruising through town in their cars, red and yellow lights twinkling around their license plates, and the latest U.S. hits blaring on their radios. *Paseo Obregón 1570, tel. 682/2–0777.*

A white arch over the street at the foot of Calle 16 de Septiembre marks the entrance to the center-city area. Across
❼ the street, a two-story white gazebo is the focus of the **Malecón Plaza.** Military bands and mariachis play in the gazebo on

weekend nights, when you can barely make it through the crowd of children chasing balloons and young men eyeing the parade of young women in miniskirts.

Central La Paz   This downtown district is where the travelers from mainland Mexico do their shopping. Though the imported goods are no bargain for those from the United States, browse through **Dorian's,** a large chain department store at the corner of Avenidas Septiembre and Agosto to see what the mainlanders buy.

⑧ **La Catedral de Nuestra Señora de La Paz** (Our Lady of La Paz Cathedral) is downtown's big attraction. It was built in 1860 near the site of La Paz's first mission, which was established in 1860 by Jesuit Jaime Bravo. It faces the zócalo, which also goes **⑨** by the names **Plaza Constitución** and **Jardín Velazco.**

⑩ On the opposite end of the plaza is the **Biblioteca de las Californias,** a library specializing in the history of Baja California, with reproductions of the local prehistoric cave paintings, oil paintings of the missions, and the best collection of historical documents on the peninsula. *Madero at Cinco de Mayo, tel. 682/2–2640. Open by appointment.*

⑪ One gets an excellent sense of La Paz's culture and heritage at the **Museum of Anthropology,** constructed in 1983 at the corner of Altamirano and Cinco de Mayo. Exhibits include re-creations of Comondo and Las Palmas Indian villages, photos of cave paintings found in Baja, and copies of Cortés's writings on first sighting La Paz. Many of the exhibit descriptions are written only in Spanish, but the museum staff will help translate for you. *Ignacio and Cinco de Mayo, tel. 682/2–0162. Admission free. Open daily 8–6.*

The museum's original building at the corner of Avenidas Altamirano and Constitución, on the same block as the muse-⑫ um, is now the **Biblioteca Justo Sierra,** a children's library. *Av. Altamirano at Av. Constitución, tel. 682/2–2852. Admission free. Open weekdays 8–8, Sat. 9–2.*

Pichilingue South of town Paseo Alvaro Obregón, or the malecón, becomes what is commonly known as the Pichilingue Road, which curves north along the bay about 16 kilometers (10 miles) to the terminals where the ferries from Mazatlán arrive, and many of the sportfishing boats depart. Just outside town the road divides, with outgoing traffic climbing up a steep cliff overlooking de-⑬ serted beaches. The road passes over **Playa Coromuel,** with its bright-blue water slide.

A few kilometers south is the most deluxe resort in town, La ⑭ Concha. Next door is the **Governor's House,** surrounded by guards and gates, the largest and most impressive home in the ⑮ area. The scenery is less inviting as you pass the **Ferry Terminal,** where warehouses serve as waiting rooms. Roadside stands serving oysters and grilled fish line the highway across the street from the terminal.

Since the time of pirate ships and Spanish invaders, ⑯ **Pichilingue** was known for its preponderance of oysters bearing black pearls. In 1940, an unknown disease killed off all the oysters, leaving the beach deserted. Now Pichilingue is a pleasant place to sunbathe and watch the sportfishing boats bring in their haul.

Time Out Two large palapas serve cold beer and oysters *diablo*, raw oysters steeped in a fiery hot sauce. The palapas are open from sunrise to sunset and serve some of the freshest and least expensive grilled fish in town—a full meal with drinks won't cost more than $5. The palapas are unnamed, and there are no phones on the point, but any taxi driver will know what you're talking about if you say you want oysters *diablo* in Pichilingue.

Off the Beaten Track

The workshop of weaver **Fortunada Silva** (Abasolo 3315, tel. 682/2–4575) sits on a dirt lot just outside town, on the way to the airport. Silva, an elderly gentleman who speaks no English, demonstrates his craft in a large workroom filled with looms and spinning wheels. His siblings and offspring (some of whom speak English) weave the yarn into simple rugs, place mats, and tablecloths that are sold in a small shop at the front of the workshop.

Shopping

Soko's (corner Avenidas Obregón and 16 de Septiembre next to the arch) has rooms filled with curios of the velvet-painting genre. **Bazar del Sol,** the next block north, has a more imaginative selection, with brightly painted *animalitos* (small wood animals) from Oaxaca and pastel-glazed pottery from Guanajuato. **Artesanías la Antigua California** (Av. Obregón 220) has more imports from the mainland, with pottery from Guadalajara, carved and painted gourds from Olinala, and replicas of Aztec and Mayan artifacts arranged gallery style. **Curios La Carretera** (Av. Obregón between Av. Muelle and Av. Tejada) has three large showrooms with carved wood tables and chairs, heavy blue and purple glassware, and an excellent selection of English-language books on Baja.

Sports and Outdoor Activities

Diving Popular diving spots include the white coral banks off Isla Espíritu Santo, the sea lion colony off Isla Partida, and the seamount 14 kilometers (9 miles) farther north.

Scuba Aguilar gives windsurfing and sailing lessons, rents equipment, and operates dives and excursion tours to Espíritu Santo and the wreck of the *Salvatierra,* a sunken ferry boat. *Independencia 107, Box 179–B, tel. 682/2–0719. 2-tank dive trips: $55. Open daily 9:30–1:30 and 4:30–7:30.*

Fishing and Boating The considerable fleet of private boats in La Paz now has more room for docking at two marinas, the **Fidepaz** at the north end of town, and the **Hotel Palmira marina** south of town. Fishing is a big draw in La Paz, and several U.S. and Mexican companies run long-range and one-day fishing charters from La Paz. Most hotels have fishing operations. The **Dorado Velez Fleet** (Box 402, La Paz 23000, tel. 682/2–2744, ext. 637, or 682/5–2816), operated by Jack Velez in the Los Arcos hotel, has cabin cruisers, which can be chartered for about $200 per day. **Sportsman's Tours** (2945 Harding St., Ste. 211, Carlsbad, CA 92008, tel. 619/630–BAJA or 800/234–0618, fax 619/720–0528) has fishing trips to Loreto and other spots in Baja.

Spectator Sports

The town turns out as fleets of yachts go by during races from Southern California to Los Cabos and up the Sea of Cortés to La Paz in the spring. Fishing tournaments are held in August and November, and the Baja 1,600-kilometer (1,000-mile) road race in November creates a mighty roar.

Beaches

Swimming and snorkeling are best south of town, on the way to Pichilingue. Near the La Concha resort is **Playa el Coromuel,** home of the bright blue El Torrero (The Bullfighter), a gigantic water slide that seems at least five stories high and ends in the ocean—best to try it when the tide is in, or you'll end up scraping your bottom in the sand. There's a U-turn just north of the beach that will lead you back to the entrance.

Playa de Pichilingue, between the ferry landing and the end of the point, has plenty of private space and two palapa restaurants that serve cold drinks and fish. Beyond the palapas, off a dirt road, is **Punta Balandra,** with scores of secluded coves and the popular **Playa Tecolote** and **El Coyote,** where campers in Volkswagen buses stay put for days, watching the lights of the city from across the water.

Dining

Some restaurants, particularly in the hotels, add a service charge of 10% to 15% to your bill. Highly recommended restaurants are indicated by a star ★.

Category	Cost*
Expensive	over $15
Moderate	$10–$15
Inexpensive	under $10

*per person excluding drinks, service, and sales tax (10%)

Expensive

★ **El Bismark.** You've got to wander a bit out of your way to reach El Bismark, where locals go for good, home-style Mexican food. Specialties include the *cochinita pibil* (marinated pork chunks) served with homemade tortillas; *carne asada* (marinated, grilled steaks), served with beans, guacamole, and tortillas; and enormous grilled lobsters. You'll see families settle down for hours at long wood tables, while waitresses divide their attention between the patrons and the soap operas on the TV above the bar. *Santos Degollado and Av. Altamirano, tel. 687/2–4854. MC, V.*

Las Brisas. The palapa theme is upscale here, with linen tablecloths, leather chairs, and candles in hurricane lamps. The fresh salsa with chunks of onion and tomato and lots of pungent cilantro is a sign of good things to come. Try a plate filled with fresh *cabrillo* (sea bass) grilled over mesquite, crusted with toasted garlic, and served with steak fries, homegrown tomatoes, and a basket of homemade tortillas. *Paseo Obregón at Colegio Militar, no phone. AE, MC, V.*

Moderate

La Paz-Lapa. The noise level here is deafening, but it's a fun place, with wide-screen TV in the bar and waiters so jolly you expect them to break into song. The sunset view of the ocean is great, and you're sure to make friends with fellow diners. The food, your basic beef, chicken, fish, and Mexican selections, is tasty and plentiful. *Paseo Obregón at León, tel. 682/2–6025. AE, MC, V. Open noon–1 AM; closed Tues.*

Restaurante Yate. The location—on the waterfront beside the Malecón Plaza—is ideal. One of a score of palapas on the malecón, the Yate is distinguished by its first-rate cappuccino—a rarity in La Paz—and by its great, inexpensive breakfasts. *Paseo Obregón at Septiembre, no phone. No credit cards.*

★ **Samalu.** Owners Santos and Manuel Mompala operate this delightful A-frame palapa in an overgrown garden of palms and vines. Stick with anything prepared Samalu style—giant shrimp stuffed with cheese, wrapped in bacon, and deep-fried, or a thin steak fillet served with grilled onion and pepper strips, guacamole, beans, and a cheese enchilada. Be sure to check out the "Maligator" (half marlin, half alligator) mounted in the bar. *Rangel between Colima and Jalisco, tel. 682/2–2481. MC, V.*

Inexpensive

★ **El Quinto Sol Restaurante Vegetariano.** El Quinto's bright yellow exterior walls are painted with Indian snake symbols and smiling suns. The back room is a natural-foods store stocked with grains, soaps, lotions, oils, and books. The restaurant serves yogurt with bananas and wheat germ, ceviche tostadas, and *machaca,* a marinated shredded beef dish made with meat substitutes. *Belisario Domínguez and Independencia, tel. 682/ 2–1692. No credit cards. Open daily 8 AM–10 PM.*

La Fabula Pizza. With its turrets and lacy white trim, this bright yellow two-story building looks like a midwestern Victorian frame home. The pizza parlor inside, crowded and fun, could be in Ohio. It's got pizza with *chorizos* (sausages), beans, and jalapeños; with smoked oysters and tuna; and with Hawaiian ham and bananas. *Paseo Obregón at 16 de Septiembre, no phone. No credit cards.*

Lodging

La Paz has hotels clustered along the malecón, with a few of the more expensive places outside town on the road to Pichilingue and the road to the airport. If you're interested in sunbathing and relaxing on the beach, stay outside town. Highly recommended lodgings are indicated by a star ★.

Category	Cost*
Expensive	over $55
Moderate	$25–$55
Inexpensive	under $25

*All prices are for a standard double room, excluding service charge and sales tax (10%).

Expensive
★ **La Concha Beach Resort.** La Concha, which has the cleanest beach in town, is a place where you could stay put for a week and not be bored. There's tennis, scuba, snorkeling, water-skiing, wide-screen TV, movies, and a large swimming pool. *Km 5 on the Pichilingue Rd., tel. 682/2–6544; reservations in the U.S.: tel. 800/999–2252. 109 rooms. Facilities: pool, 2 tennis courts, restaurant, palapa and lobby bars, gift shop, meeting and banquet rooms. AE, MC, V.*

Los Arcos. Many say Los Arcos is the nicest hotel in La Paz, but that depends on the location of your room. Resist the waterfront view and request a room in the central courtyard, where the rush of water in the fountain drowns out the music from the street and the noise from the pool area. All rooms have balconies and TVs; some have lumpy mattresses on squeaky frames. The self-service coffee shop opens early so those headed out on fishing boats can eat and pick up a box lunch. *Paseo Obregón 498 between Rosales and Allende, tel. 682/2–2744; reservations in the U.S.: 4422 Cerritos Ave., Los Alamitos, CA 90720, tel. 213/ 583–3393 or 800/347–2252. 180 rooms. Facilities: pool, sauna, coffee shop, restaurant, bar, store, sport fishing tours. AE, MC, V.*

Moderate
★ **La Posada de Englebert.** For 25 years, divers on their way to and from trips on the sea have stayed in La Posada's casitas. The casitas have wood shutters, haphazardly tiled bathrooms, fireplaces, worn couches in the living rooms, and rocking chairs on the porches. At night miniature lights twinkle in the palm trees, guitarists stroll between the blue patio umbrellas, and guests dine on grilled fish and lobster. Saturday-night entertainment alternates between folkloric dancing and a Hawaiian luau. La Posada also operates a small 25-room inn on a little jetty across the water that opens when the main hotel is full. *Av.*

Reforma and Playa Sur, Box 152, La Paz, BCS, 23000, tel. 682/ 2–4011, fax 682/2–0663. 26 suites, 4 casitas. Facilities: pool, restaurant, palapa bar, private beach. MC, V.

Las Cabañas de Los Arcos. These small thatched-roof brick cottages on a side street beside Los Arcos are surrounded by trees and flowering hibiscus. Sidewalks lead through the small complex to a pool nearly hidden by the trees. The cabanas are a bit run-down, but private; for more modern surroundings, stay in the low-rise hotel building by the pool. *Just off Paseo Obregón at the corner of Rosales; reservations in the U.S.: 4422 Cerritos Ave., Los Alamitos, CA 90720, tel. 213/583–3393 or 800/347– 2252. 30 rooms. Facilities: pool, access to other facilities at Los Arcos hotel. AE, MC, V.*

Inexpensive **Gardenias.** By far the most pleasant of the budget hotels, Gardenias has gardens, a pool and patio, and clean, spacious rooms. The drawback is its distance from the malecón (about a half-hour walk). *Serdan Norte 520, tel. 682/2–3088, fax 682/5–0436. 56 rooms. Facilities: pool, restaurant. MC, V.*

Pension California. Backpackers and low-budget travelers find an old, run-down hacienda here, housing clean blue-and-white rooms with baths and a courtyard with picnic tables and a TV. A laid-back, friendly camaraderie prevails. *Av. Degollado 209, tel. 682/2–2896. 25 rooms. Facilities: cooking privileges. No credit cards.*

The Arts and Nightlife

El Teatro de la Ciudad (Av. Navarro 700, tel. 682/5–0004) is La Paz's cultural center. The theater seats 1,500 and is used for stage shows by visiting performers as well as local ensembles.

Nightlife in La Paz centers on the malecón and the **Okey Laser Disco** (Paseo Obregón, tel. 682/2–3133) near La Perla. The mirrored **Disco El Rollo** (tel. 682/2–4000) at the Hotel Palmira plays music videos, recorded salsa, and disco tunes.

Los Cabos

Introduction

At the southern tip of the 1,600-kilometer (1,000-mile) Baja California Peninsula the land ends in a rocky point called **El Arco** (The Arch). The waters of the **Sea of Cortés** swirl into the Pacific Ocean's rugged surf as marlin and sailfish leap above the waves. The desert ends in white-sand coves, with cactus standing at their entrances like sentries under the soaring palm trees. Although it has become a haven for sportfishers, boaters, and sun seekers, the land's end has retained its stark and mysterious beauty.

Pirates found the capes at the end of the peninsula an ideal lookout for spotting Spanish galleons traveling from the Philippines to Spain's empire in central Mexico. Missionaries soon followed, seeking to save the souls of the few thousand local Indians who lived off the sea. The good fathers established the missions of **San José del Cabo** and **Cabo San Lucas** in the mid-1700s, but their colonies did not last long. The missionaries had brought syphilis and smallpox with their preachings, and by the end of the century the indigenous population was nearly wiped out. A different sort of native brought the explorers back. They came for the underwater creatures, the massive gamefish that appeared to be trapped in the swirl of surf where the ocean meets the sea. In the 1940s and 1950s, the capes became a haven for millionaires who built lodges on rocky gray cliffs overlooking secluded coves and bays. By the 1960s, lavish resorts began rising in the barren landscape, and in the 1980s Baja's southern tip became a government-sponsored resort area. Today Los Cabos has an international airport, a marina, shopping centers, and dozens of hotels. San José del Cabo has a long stretch of waterfront that has been designated a hotel zone, a nine-hole golf course, a half-dozen luxury condo developments, and a picturesque downtown, with colored lights in the fountains along the main street and the languid pace of a Mexican village. Cabo San Lucas has changed dramatically, with a five-story condo/hotel complex under development along the bay that blocks the water view from the town's hotels, restaurants, and shops. Los Cabos is no longer a low-cost, secluded hideaway, but its natural qualities of the desert and sea are still dramatic and the towns retain their charm.

The area remains a rugged outback, a solitary place where telephones and TVs are the exception rather than the rule. Go a few kilometers down any small road off the highway, and you'll feel as if civilization is an illusion and survival a challenge.

Arriving and Departing by Plane

The **Los Cabos International Airport** (tel. 684/2–0341) is about 11 kilometers (7 miles) north of San José del Cabo and about 48 kilometers (30 miles) from Cabo San Lucas. **Aero California** (tel. 684/3–0848 or 800/253–3311) flies to Los Cabos from Los Angeles, San Diego, and Phoenix; **Mexicana** (tel. 684/3–0411 or 800/531–7921) from Denver, Los Angeles, San Francisco, and Seattle; **Alaska Airlines** (tel. 684/2–1015 or 800/426–0333) from Anchorage, Fairbanks, Portland, San Francisco, San Diego, Los Angeles, and Seattle; and **Aeroméxico** (tel. 684/2–0398 or 800/237–6639) from Los Angeles.

Vans shuttle passengers from the airport to the hotels in both towns, but not back to the airport. Many of the hotels, have sign-up sheets for guests who wish to share a cab and the $30 or so fare to the airport.

Arriving and Departing by Car, Bus, and Boat

By Car Mexico Highway 1, also known as the Transpeninsular Highway, runs the entire 1,600 kilometers (1,000 miles) from Tijuana to Cabo San Lucas. The highway is in excellent condition.

By Bus **Tres Estrellas de Oro** (tel. 684/2–0200) travels from Tijuana to Los Cabos and between San José and Cabo San Lucas daily. The peninsula-long trip takes about 22 hours.

By Boat Several cruise lines—including **Carnival** (tel. 800/327–9051), **Starlite** (tel. 800/488–7827), **Princess** (tel. 800/421–0522), and **Admiral** (tel. 800/327–0271)—use Cabo San Lucas as a port of call; there is a handicrafts market at the marina designed to accommodate cruise-ship passengers.

Getting Around

By Car The best way to see the sights is on foot. The downtown areas are small and compact. The plaza, church, shops, and restaurants are within a few blocks of one another. If you want to travel frequently between the two towns or to remote beaches and coves, you will need a car.

Most hotels and resorts have car rentals, with the cost of a Volkswagen Beetle or a Jeep averaging $60 per day, including tax and insurance, plus 18¢ per kilometer. The following car-rental agencies all have desks at the airport and in one or both towns: **Avis** (tel. 684/2–0680); **Budget** (tel. 684/3–0241); **Dollar** (tel. 684/2–0671); **Hertz** (tel. 684/3–0211); **National** (tel. 684/3–6000); and **Servitour** (tel. 684/3–0897).

By Taxi Cab fares are standardized by the government, but you should confirm the price before you get into the car. The fare between the two towns is about $15.

Important Addresses and Numbers

Tourist Information There is no tourism office in Los Cabos, but there are plenty of makeshift stands where time-share operators seek new clients under the guise of offering information. Unless you have hours to spend listening to sales spiels, you're better off using the tour desk or concierge at your hotel.

Emergencies **Police:** Cabo San Lucas (tel. 684/3–0057), San José del Cabo (tel. 684/2–0361); **Hospital:** Cabo San Lucas (tel. 684/3–0102); San José del Cabo (tel. 684/2–0316).

Guided Tours

With the water as the main attraction, most tours involve getting into a boat and diving or fishing. Nearly everyone takes a ride to El Arco, the natural rock arches at land's end, and Playa del Amor (Lover's Beach), where the Sea of Cortés blends into the Pacific. Nearly all hotels have frequent boat trips to El Arco; the fare depends on how far your hotel is from the point.

Chubasco's (Blvd. Marina 22, Cabo San Lucas, tel. 684/3–0404) offers guided tours on motorcycles and three-wheel off-road motorbikes to remote areas around Los Cabos, including the old lighthouse.

Pez Gato (tel. 684/3–0885 or 714/673–4705) has sailing and sunset cruises on a 46-foot catamaran, with live music and free drinks, and snorkeling and sailing tours. All trips depart from the marina in Cabo San Lucas; tours cost $25 per person. Call or stop by the booth at the marina for further information.

Exploring

You needn't worry about reserving lots of time for sightseeing here—each town can easily be toured in an hour or so. Only a few streets are named, but the towns are small enough for you to find what you're looking for without wandering very far.

Cabo San Lucas and **San José del Cabo** are about 32 kilometers (20 miles) apart on Mexico Highway 1. Some hotels in each offer tours to the other town, which is a good way to see the sights; or you can take a taxi between the towns. If you want to check out the lavish fishing resorts or the beaches, you're best off renting a car and stopping off for lunch or a swim along the way.

Numbers in the margin correspond to points of interest on the Los Cabos Coast, San José del Cabo, and Cabo San Lucas maps.

San José del Cabo, the larger of the two towns, has about 25,000 **①** inhabitants. The main street is **Boulevard Mijares.** The south end of the boulevard has been designated the tourist zone, with **②** the **Los Cabos Club de Golf** as its centerpiece. Fonatur owns **③** 4,000 acres along this stretch and has built a **Commercial and Cultural Center** in the middle. A few reasonably priced hotels are situated along this strip, on a beautiful long beach where the surf, unfortunately, is too dangerous for swimming. At the end of the strip, on Paseo San José by the Stouffer Presidente **④** hotel, is the **estuary,** a freshwater preserve filled with more than 200 species of birds. There is a small stand at the road's end where you can rent a boat to paddle through the thick swamp grass of the sanctuary.

Take Boulevard Mijares north into town, through a stretch of **⑤** restaurants and shops. **City Hall** is on your left near Avenida Zaragoza, where Boulevard Mijares ends. A long fountain lit at night by colored lights marks the end of the boulevard. There is a small, shaded plaza here and, in front of a public library, a mural painted by the children of San José.

⑥ One block east on Avenida Zaragoza is a large **zócalo** with a white wrought-iron gazebo and green benches set in the shade. **⑦** The town's **church** looms over the zócalo. Be sure to walk up to the front and see the tile mural of a captured priest being dragged toward a fire by Indians.

Mexicana and Aeroméxico airlines have offices by the zócalo. The bus station, hospital, market, and pharmacies are all located one block south, on Avenida Manuel Doblado. Most of the town's souvenir shops and restaurants are clustered in the surrounding streets.

As you drive south on Mexico Highway 1 toward Cabo San **⑧** Lucas you first pass **Costa Azul,** a good surfing beach, and **⑨** **Playa Palmilla,** San José's best swimming beach. Above the **⑩** beach is the **Hotel Palmilla,** a rambling, hacienda-style resort with its own small white adobe chapel. Farther south are beaches for swimming and snorkeling, and some spectacular **⑪** hotels; most worth visiting are the **Bahía Chileno** at the **Hotel** **⑫** **Cabo San Lucas** and the **Bahía Santa María** at the **Twin Dolphin** hotel. The beaches at both bays have white sand, clear blue water, and schools of fish just offshore.

Highway 1 leads into the center of **Cabo San Lucas,** ending at Kilometer 1 on the Transpeninsular Highway. The main down- **⑬** town street, Avenida Lázaro Cárdenas, passes a small **zócalo.** Most of the shops, services, and restaurants are located between Avenida Cárdenas and the waterfront.

Time Out When the sun's heat has exhausted your energy, stop at the nearest branch of **Helados Bing,** a pink- and white-striped ice cream stand serving delectable cones, shakes, and floats. One is on Blvd. Mijares in San José, and another is located on Hwy. 1 just north of Cabo San Lucas.

Los Cabos Coast

N
Los Pozos
0 — 6 miles
0 — 9 km
Los Cabos International Airport

San José del Cabo
1 — 7

Cabo San Lucas
13 — 16

Bahía Chileno
8 Costa Azul

Playa Médano
Playa de Amor
Bahía San Lucas
12 Bahía Santa María
11
10 Hotel Palmilla
9 Playa Palmilla
Bahía San José del Cabo

PACIFIC OCEAN
Golfo de California

Boulevard Mijares, **1**
Church, **7**
City Hall, **5**
Commercial and Cultural Center, **3**
Estuary, **4**
Los Cabos Club de Golf, **2**
Zócalo, **6**

San José del Cabo

0 — 500 meters
0 — 500 yards

TO LA PAZ AND AIRPORT

Ignacio Comonfort

Av. Zaragoza

7
6 **5**

Av. Manuel Doblado

N

Margarita Maza de Juárez

Cerro de la Cruz

Morelos

Miguel Hidalgo

Valerio Gonzalez Canseco

Carretera Transpeninsular

Cerro de El Vigia

1

2

Mijares Blvd.

3

4

TO CABO SAN LUCAS

Playa Hotelera

Golfo de California

Bahía de Cabo San Lucas, **15**
Handicrafts Market, **14**
Los Arcos, **16**
Zócalo, **13**

Cabo San Lucas

N

Matamoros
M. Hidalgo
Cabo San Lucas
Morelos
Lázaro Cárdenas

Golfo de California

13

14 **15**

Blvd. Marina

0 — 500 meters
0 — 500 yards

16 Los Arcos

PACIFIC OCEAN

Boulevard Marina has been transformed from a dusty main drag into a busy paved thoroughfare lined with hotels and cafés. Paved walkways now run from here to the hotels and
⓮ beaches on the east end of town and west to the **Handicrafts Market** at the Cabo San Lucas marina, where new hotels and shopping centers are under construction. The sportfishing
⓯ fleet is docked in the **Bahía de Cabo San Lucas,** and there are glass-bottom boats available at the water's edge.

⓰ The most spectacular sight in Cabo San Lucas is **El Arco.** The natural rock arch is visible from the marina and from some of the hotels but is more impressive from the water. A little farther on, and visible from the water, is **El Faro de Cabo Falso** (Lighthouse of the False Cape). You need a four-wheel-drive vehicle to reach the lighthouse by land. If you don't take at least a short boat ride out to the arches and **Playa de Amor,** the beach underneath, you haven't fully appreciated Cabo.

Shopping

Though there aren't many places to shop in Los Cabos, the selection of handicrafts and sportswear is excellent. In Cabo San Lucas, the sportswear shops—**Guess, Ferrioni, Bye-Bye, Cotton Club,** and the like—are clustered at the Plaza Cabo San Lucas on Avenida Madero. Several specialty shops are located in the modernistic Plaza Bonita at the beginning of Blvd. Marina.

Several high-class resort-wear boutiques have opened. The best are **Temptations** (Av. Lazaro Cárdenas at Vincente Guerrero, tel. 684/3–1015), **Dos Lunas** (Blvd. Marina, tel. 684/3–1280), and **La Bamba** (Guerrero, tel. 684/3–1545). Across Avenida Hidalgo from the zócalo is **La Bugambilia** (tel. 684/3–0625), a gallery with brass and copper animals by Sergio Bustamante and one-of-a-kind belts, purses, and jewelry. **La Paloma,** a few doors down, has beautiful embroidered and appliquéd clothing from Tlaquepaque, an artisan's colony outside Guadalajara.

Artes Oaxaqueños on Avenida Hidalgo is a tiny shop stuffed with gorgeous wood carvings and wool weavings from Oaxaca. **Mama Eli's** (Av. San Lucas, tel. 684/3–1616) has her three display rooms filled with high-quality pottery, jewelry, glasswork, and clothing from throughout Mexico. **Galería El Dorado** (Blvd. Marina, tel. 684/3–0817) sells fanciful bronze sculptures and beautiful watercolor paintings of the beaches of Los Cabos. Wander to the back room filled with souvenirs. High-quality folk art from throughout Mexico is also available at **Nekri** and **Galería El Dorado** (tel. 684/3–0817) on Blvd. Marina.

At the **Handicrafts Market** in the marina, you can pose with an iguana for a photo, plan a ride in a glass-bottom boat, or browse to your heart's content through stalls packed with blankets, sombreros, and pottery.

Shopping opportunities in **San José del Cabo** occur in the few streets around the zócalo and City Hall. Across Boulevard Mijares from City Hall is **Almacenes Goncanseco,** where you can get film, postcards, groceries, and liquor. **Antigua Los Cabos** on Avenida Hidalgo has handsome carved-wood furniture, woven rugs, and wrought-iron chandeliers. Along Boulevard Mijares, **La Casa Vieja Boutique** (tel. 684/2–0270) has beautiful hand-knit sweaters, designer dresses, and embroidered *guayaberas* (loose-fitting cotton shirts) for men; **Bye-Bye** has high-quality souvenir T-shirts; **La Mina** displays silver jewelry and leather bags; and **La Bamba** has colorful hand-painted T-shirts and coveralls. **Galería El Dorado** (tel. 684/2–1987), across from the City Hall on Blvd. Mijares, displays paintings and sculptures from local artists. For fresh produce, flowers, meat, fish, and a sampling of local life in San José, visit the **Mercado Municipal** off Calle Doblado, behind the bus station.

Sports and Outdoor Activities

Fishing　There are over 800 species of fish in these waters. Most of the hotels, particularly those along the stretch of highway between the two towns, will arrange fishing charters and can have your catch mounted, frozen, or smoked. Charters include a captain and mate, tackle, bait, licenses, and drinks. Prices start at $250 per day for a 25-foot cruiser. Some charters provide lunch. Most of the boats leave from the sportfishing docks in the Cabo San Lucas marina. Usually there are a fair number of pangas (small boats) for rent at about $25 per hour with a five-hour minimum. Dependable companies include **Hotel Palmilla Sportfishing** (Hotel Palmilla in San José del Cabo, tel. 684/2–0583 or 800/637–2226), the **Solmar Fleet** (tel. 684/3–0022 or 800/344–3349), and **Pisces Sportfishing Fleet** (tel. 684/3–0588).

Diving　El Arco is the prime diving and snorkeling area, as are several rocky points off the coast. Most hotels offer diving trips and equipment rental. Companies serving divers in Cabo San Lucas include **Amigos del Mar** (near the sportfishing docks at the harbor, tel. 684/3–0022); **Palmilla Divers** (Hotel Palmilla, tel. 684/2–0582); **Cabo Acuadeportes** (at the Hotel Hacienda and Playa Chileno, tel. 684/3–0117); and **Tio Watersports** (at the Melia San Lucas, tel. 684/3–1000).

Golf　The **Los Cabos Campo de Golf,** completed in April 1988, is a nine-hole course and country club that is the pride of Los Cabos. The course, on Boulevard Mijares in San José, is surrounded by villas and condos. The clubhouse has a restaurant that is open from 8 AM until 1 AM and a pro shop. The greens fee is $24 for 18 holes, $12 for 9 holes; club rentals are $10 per day.

Tennis　The **Los Cabos Campo de Golf** has lighted tennis courts open to the public; fees are $6 per hour during the day and $10 per hour at night.

Beaches

Cabo San Lucas　**Playa Médano,** just north of Cabo San Lucas, is the most popular stretch in Los Cabos (and possibly in all Baja) for sunbathing and people-watching. The 3.2-kilometer (2-mile) span of white sand is always crowded, especially on weekends.

Playa Hacienda, in the inner harbor by the Hacienda Hotel, has the calmest waters of any beach in town and good snorkeling around the rocky point. **Playa Solmar,** by the Solmar Hotel, is a beautiful wide beach at the base of the mountains leading into the Pacific, but it has dangerous surf with a swift undertow. Stick to sunbathing here.

Playa de Amor consists of a secluded cove at the very end of the peninsula, with the Sea of Cortés on one side and the Pacific

Ocean on the other. The difference between the peaceful, azure cove on the Sea of Cortés and the pounding white surf of the Pacific is dramatic.

San José del Cabo   **Playa Hotelera** is the stretch of beach that most of the finer hotels use. It's beautiful, but the current is dangerously rough, and the water is usually a long walk from the hotel. At the east end of the beach, near the Stouffer Presidente, there is a freshwater lagoon filled with tropical birds and plants; sometimes there are boats for rent at the lagoon. If you plan to spend time here, be sure to douse yourself with insect repellent. The best swimming beach in San José is **Playa Palmilla,** which is protected from the surf by a rocky point just south of San José. The northern part of the beach is cluttered with boats and shacks, but as you walk south you reach the Hotel Palmilla beach, a long stretch of white sand and calm sea.

Los Cabos   Some of the finest resorts in Los Cabos are situated off the highway between the two towns, set on some of the area's finest beaches. **Playa Bahía Santa Maria,** by the Twin Dolphins Hotel, is a picture-perfect white-sand cove protected by towering brown cliffs. The snorkeling here is superb, with hundreds of colorful fish swarming through chunks of white coral. Just north of the hotel, there is a public access trail to the beach. **Bahía Chileno,** by the Hotel Cabo San Lucas, is an underwater preserve teeming with marine life and a great place for snorkeling and diving. The beach is rocky in parts and smoothest in front of the hotel.

Dining

Fresh fish, lobster, and shrimp are the dining draws here, along with abalone and quail. Prices in Los Cabos have risen dramatically, and inexpensive restaurants are hard to find. Some restaurants add a service charge of 10%–15% to your total. Highly recommended restaurants are indicated by a star ★.

Category	Cost*
Expensive	over $25
Moderate	$10–$25
Inexpensive	under $10

per person, excluding drinks, service, and sales tax (10%)

Cabo San Lucas   **Alfonso's.** You get the feeling you're in a private dining room
Expensive   feasting on a meal prepared just for you at this small, elegant restaurant within a *petit* hotel. The fixed-price meals include six sublime courses served in a leisurely yet attentive manner. There's no more romantic room in town. *On the road to Playa Médano, tel. 684/3–0739. Reservations recommended. AE, MC, V. Dinner only.*

El Galeón. Considered the most distinguished restaurant in town, El Galeón is located across from the marina. The choice seats are on the outside terraces facing the water; the inside is decorated with lots of heavy wood furniture. Traditional Spanish, Mexican, and American dishes are prepared expertly, with an emphasis on thick, tender cuts of beef. The piano bar is a nice setting for a late-night brandy. *Across from the marina by the road to the Finesterra Hotel, tel. 684/3-0443. AE, MC, V.*

★ **Peacocks.** The ubiquitous fresh fish dinner achieves gustatory eminence when prepared by chef Bernard Roll. His dorado is coated with a crust of chopped pecans, and his shrimp masterfully tossed with spinach fettuccini. This chef is known for his incredible desserts—if you miss dinner, be sure to stop by for a cappuccino and tequila mousse. *Paseo Pescador near Playa Médano, tel. 684/3-1858. AE, MC, V.*

Moderate **El Delfin.** Other restaurants on Playa Médano seem to attract larger crowds, but El Delfin serves by far the best food. The grilled lobster receives high grades and is reasonably priced to boot; the glassed-in dining room is a cool and comfortable respite from the beach sun. *Playa Médano, tel. 684/3-0487. MC, V.*

El Rey Sol. By far one of the best and most authentically Mexican restaurants in Cabo San Lucas, El Rey Sol is a bit out of the way, on the road to Playa Médano. The abalone is succulent, and the seafood combination—lobster, oysters, crab, and fish—incredibly generous and outrageously good, though expensive. The *7-Mares* soup, with seven varieties of seafood from octopus to clams, is guaranteed to *levantar muertos* (raise the dead) or, at the very least, cure tequila hangovers. This large brick restaurant is warm and cozy, and the Mexican breakfasts are popular with both townfolk and tourists. *On the road to Playa Médano, tel. 684/3-1117. AE, MC, V.*

The Giggling Marlin. El Marlin Sonriente (as it is also known) is designed for fun, with flowers, vines, hot-air balloons, and parrots painted on the white walls of its high-ceiling room. Though the menu is extensive—burgers, sandwiches, tostadas, burritos, and steaks—the regulars advise sticking with tacos, appetizers, and drinks. This is a popular watering hole. *Av. Matamoros and Bd. Marina, tel. 684/3-0606. MC, V.*

Mi Casa. The first Los Cabos restaurant to serve authentic dishes from mainland Mexico was this small, burnt-orange café. About a dozen tables covered with bright, striped cloths fill the former living room of a small house by the plaza. Instead of serving the typical tacos and nachos so popular in this area, Mi Casa offers the adventurous eater enchiladas in mole sauce, *pozole* (corn soup), nopal cactus stuffed with *chorizo* (sausage), and fried plantains. The restaurant opened in late 1991 and was an immediate success among the locals yearning for the unadulterated flavors of Mexico. *Av. San Lucas at Serdan, no phone. AE, MC, V.*

Inexpensive **Mama's Royal Cafe.** The ideal breakfast hangout across the street from the plaza, Mama's has omelette combos to please every taste: Eggs are mixed with cheese, chorizo, jalapeños, guacamole, spinach, ham, or any other ingredient you can imagine. The burgers and sandwiches come in equally motley variations, the coffee is brewed fresh all day, and homemade orange marmalade accompanies every order of whole wheat toast. *Av. San Lucas at Cárdenas, no phone. No credit cards. Open breakfast and lunch only.*

Squid Roe. The Carlos 'n' Charlie chain hits new heights in zaniness and rowdiness with this double-layer, neon-festooned, open-air madhouse. Waiters dressed as bulls charge customers down the aisles, tequila shooters are the drink of choice, and conversation is out of the question. The food—burgers, barbeque, and fish—is always plentiful and good. *Av. Cárdenas on the east end of town, tel. 684/3–0655. MC, V.*

San José del Cabo
Expensive
★
Damiana. For a special night out, visit this small hacienda tucked beside the zócalo, past the center of town. The lounge area has overstuffed couches where you can unwind before claiming your table on the patio. Fuchsia bougainvillea wraps around the tall pines shading the wrought-iron tables, and the pink adobe walls glow in the candlelight. Start with fiery oysters diablo, then move on to the tender chateaubriand or charbroiled lobster. You'll find the setting so relaxing and charming that you will want to linger well into the night. *Bd. Mijares 8, tel. 684/2–0499. AE, MC, V. No lunch.*

Moderate
★
La Paloma. With an upstairs patio overlooking the Hotel Palmilla's pool and gardens, as well as the sea, the setting is sublime. The food is unparalleled—for a special dinner, order the mixed grill. For a light meal, have the savory tortilla soup and garlicky Caesar salad. The *pan dulce* (sweet bread) at breakfast is subtly sweet, and the flaky croissants are served with excellent raspberry preserves. Having at least one meal here is recommended. *Hotel Palmilla, Hwy. 1 just north of San José, tel. 684/2–0582. AE, MC, V.*

Inexpensive
Café Europa. Two expatriate Europeans have created a cosmopolitan coffee house/café in an old home by a small park with a few tables on the sidewalk and more inside by a long wooden bar. Cappuccino, espresso, and coffee brewed by the cup accompany French baguettes, Danish pastries, and smoked salmon with eggs. Salads washed with purified water and composed of impeccably fresh ingredients are a delightful change from the normal Cabo fare. Light jazz plays in the background of a remarkably urbane scene. *Blvd. Mijares, no phone. MC, V.*

La Fogata. The Davida family continues to offer quality Mexican dishes, steaks, and seafood in their clean, comfortable dining room, where you feel like a relative welcomed home for a good meal. *Calle Zaragoza, tel. 2–0480. MC, V.*

Lodging

The accommodations in Los Cabos are mostly expensive and exclusive. Many of the hotels offer the American Plan (AP) with three meals. Many of the resorts do not accept credit cards and often add a 10% to 20% service charge to your bill. Most properties also raise their rates for the December–April high season. Rates here are based on high-season standards. Expect to pay 25% less during the off-season. Highly recommended lodgings are indicated by a star ★.

Category	Cost*
Expensive	over $170
Moderate	$70–$170
Inexpensive	under $70

All prices are for a standard double room, excluding service charge and sales tax (10%).

Cabo San Lucas
Expensive
Hacienda. Set on the tip of a tree-filled point jutting into San Lucas Bay, the Hacienda resembles a Spanish Colonial inn with its white arches and bell towers, stone fountains, and statues of

Indian gods set amid scarlet hibiscus and bougainvillea. The white rooms have red-tile floors, tile baths, and folk art hanging on the walls; the bar is a veritable museum of Indian artifacts. *Across from the marina, tel. 684/3–0122; reservations in the U.S.: Box 48872, Los Angeles, CA 90048, tel. 800/733–2226. 112 rooms, suites, and beachfront cabañas. Facilities: beach, pool, restaurant, bar, shops, aquatic center. MC, V.*

Villa Alfonso's. Exclusive privacy is guaranteed at this five-room petit hotel, set above Médano beach. Each large guest room is furnished distinctively with custom-made bed frames and bureaus, and touches of Mexican folk art. The narrow lap pool in the backyard is a shaded hideaway, and the restaurant is one of the area's best. *On the road to the Hacienda Hotel, tel. 684/3–0739 or 800/347–1522. 5 rooms. Facilities: pool, restaurant. AE, MC, V.*

Moderate
★ **Meliá San Lucas.** From the moment you enter the Meliá and spot El Arco in the Sea of Cortés, framed by the lobby's arches, you know you're at a hotel where details are important. The blue walls and linens in the rooms enhance the views of the aquamarine sea; the outer adobe walls of the terraced hotel buildings glow orange and gold with the changing sunlight. The Meliá has a long beach with calm waters, a spacious hot tub under the palms, and all the equipment you could need for playing on and in the water. *Off Hwy. 1 at Playa Médano, tel. 684/3–4020; reservations in the U.S.: tel. 800/336–3542. 190 rooms and suites. Facilities: beach, 2 pools, hot tub, 3 restaurants, meeting facilities. AE, MC, V.*

Solmar. From afar, the Solmar looks like a space colony. The rooms are set against granite cliffs at the tip of Land's End, facing the wild Pacific. The older rooms by the cliffs are simple and comfortable; those in a two-story building on the beach are more modern; and the new condos (also available as hotel rooms) are impressively designed in a Mexico/Santa Fe style. The surf here is far too dangerous for swimming, but don't miss a stroll along the wide strip of beach. Most visitors hang out around the pool and swim-up bar, joining in with the ever-present musicians. The Solmar's sportfishing fleet is first-rate. *Bd. Marina, tel. 684/3–0022; reservations in the U.S.: Box 383, Pacific Palisades, CA 90272, tel. 213/459–9861 or 800/344–3349. 66 rooms, 4 suites, 68 condos. Facilities: pool, beach, tennis, aquatic center, restaurant, bar, shops. AE, MC, V.*

Inexpensive **Hotel Marina.** This establishment is conveniently located across from the marina (though the view is now blocked by the massive Plaza las Glorias hotel/time-share complex). The rooms are air-conditioned, with blue-and-yellow flowers painted on the walls, and bathrooms have tile baths. Some rooms face a courtyard with pools and a whirlpool and are quieter than those facing the street. *Blvd. Marina at Calle Guerrero, tel. 684/3–0030. 30 rooms. Facilities: pool, whirlpool, restaurant. MC, V.*

Between the Capes **Meliá Cabo Real.** Even if you're staying elsewhere, stop here
Expensive for a glimpse of the future. This Meliá is incredibly huge and opulent, spread over a hilltop with a meandering crystal-blue pool, fountains, waterfalls, white canopies shading rest areas, and a private beach created by a small jetty jutting from the rocky hillside. Mayan carvings and bas reliefs adorn the walls in the rooms, which all have landscaped terraces. Several other high-end hotel chains are planning construction near the Meliá,

and there will be an 18-hole golf course here someday. *Km 19.5 Los Cabos Hwy., tel. 684/3–0754; reservations in the U.S.: tel. 800/336–3542. 299 rooms. Facilities: pool, beach, fishing fleet, dive shop, water-sports, tennis courts, fitness center, 24-hour room service, 2 restaurants, 24-hour café. AE, MC, V.*

★ **Palmilla.** Just outside San José, the Palmilla is a gracious, sprawling hacienda-style resort. Tiled stairways lead up from flower-lined paths to large apartments with hand-carved furniture, French doors leading to private patios, and tile baths. Colorful serapes and *molas* (embroidered and appliquéd scenes) hang on the walls. The buildings are spread along a hillside overlooking the beach, with fountains and bougainvillea-draped statues throughout. The service is delightfully personalized, and the Palmilla is a popular honeymoon and hideaway spot. *Hwy. 1 about 8 km (5 mi) from San José, no phone; reservations in the U.S.: 4577 Viewridge Ave., San Diego, CA 92123, tel. in CA, 800/542–6082; 800/854–2608 outside CA. 62 rooms, 7 suites, 2 villas. Facilities: pool, beach, restaurant, bar, tennis, water sports, airstrip. MC, V.*

Twin Dolphin. Sleek and Japanese-modernistic with an austere air, the Twin Dolphin has been a hideaway for the rich and famous since 1977. Guest rooms are in low-lying casitas along a seaside cliff, and are furnished in minimalist style. The hotel is worth a visit if only for the reproductions of Baja's cave paintings on the lobby wall. *Km 12, Hwy. 1, tel. 684/3–0496, 213/386–3940 in CA, or 800/421–8925 outside CA. 44 rooms, 6 suites. Facilities: pool, beach, restaurant, bar, tennis, water sports. MC, V.*

San José del Cabo
Expensive

Stouffer Presidente Los Cabos. By far the nicest hotel in San José, this property sits at the end of the hotel zone, next to the estuary. It resembles a pueblo set amid beachside cactus gardens. The buildings curve around an enormous blue pool; the rooms have shaded patios, cable TVs, minibars, king-size beds, deep bathtubs, and couches facing the sliding glass doors. *At the end of the hotel zone, tel. 684/2–0038; reservations in the U.S.: tel. 800/472–2427. 250 rooms, including 6 suites. Facilities: beach, pool, tennis courts, satellite TV, 4 restaurants, bar, disco, water sports, horseback riding, fishing charters. MC, V.*

Moderate

Tropicana Inn. A welcome addition to San José, this small hotel opened in 1991, bringing a great option for those who aren't desperate to be on a beach. The new stucco buildings frame a pool and palapa bar in a quiet enclave behind San José's main boulevard. The rooms are air-conditioned, have satellite TV, and are maintained to keep looking brand new. *Blvd. Mijares 30, 684/2–0907. 20 rooms. Facilities: pool, bar, restaurant. MC, V.*

Inexpensive

Hotel Colli. This small inn in the center of town is remarkably peaceful and picturesque, with a flowering backyard and third-floor terrace. Rooms have ceiling fans and carpeting. Some have balconies over the street, which isn't very noisy. *Calle Hidalgo, no phone. 12 rooms. No credit cards.*

Hotel San José Inn. This new, small hotel is about a five-minute walk from town and offers simple rooms with concrete floors, showers, and pastel furnishings. The rates are the lowest in town, and the proprietress is very accommodating. *Calle Degollado s/n, tel. 684/2–1428. 11 rooms (more under construction). Facilities: snack bar. No credit cards.*

Posada Terranova. As with many small properties, the Terranova is undergoing changes, with construction beginning on 14 more rooms and a swimming pool. For now, you feel like you're staying in an old hacienda neatly outfitted with private tiled baths in the five colonial-style rooms. The clientele is made up mostly of regulars who return year after year. Call ahead for reservations. *Calle Degollado at Zaragoza, tel. 684/ 2-0534. 5 rooms. Facilities: restaurant, bar. MC, V.*

Nightlife

With fishing and diving boats departing by 7 AM, there's not much nightlife in Los Cabos. The nightlife in Cabo San Lucas took a definite upturn when members of the rock band Van Halen opened **Cabo Wabo** (Calle Guerrero, tel. 684/3-1188). The latest U.S. bands play over an excellent sound system, but the real highlight is the impromptu jam sessions with appearances by Van Halen's many friends in the music business. Music, dancing, and general revelry also reign at **Squid Roe** (Av. Cárdenas), **Giggling Marlin** (Blvd. Marina), **Señor Sushi** (Blvd. Marina), **Shooterz** (Calle Guerrero), and **The One That Got Away** (Calle Guerrero). Traditionally, the best disco in town has been **El Oasis** (Av. Cárdenas), but now there is competition from **Lukas** (Av. Cárdenas at Blvd. Marina).

5 Pacific Coast Resorts

Introduction

By Maribeth Mellin

Updated by Wendy Luft

Across the Gulf of California from the Baja California Peninsula lies Mazatlán, Mexico's largest Pacific port and the closest major Mexican resort to the United States, some 1,200 kilometers (750 miles) south of the Arizona border. This is the beginning of what cruise-ship operators now call the Mexican Riviera, or the Gold Coast. The coastline for the next 1,400 kilometers (900 miles) is Mexico's tropical paradise. The Gulf of California, or the Sea of Cortés, as it is also called, ends just below the Tropic of Cancer, leaving the Pacific coastline open to fresh sea breezes. The Mexican Riviera resorts—Mazatlán, Puerto Vallarta, Manzanillo, Ixtapa, Zihuatanejo, and Acapulco—are therefore less muggy than gulf towns to the north. The water, however, is colder, and waves can get very rough. Deserted palm-fringed bays and tropical jungles border high-rise hotels and luxury resorts, and the emphasis is on enjoying the tropical climate and broad sandy beaches.

The Pacific coast doesn't have the rich cultural heritage of Mexico's inland colonial villages and silver cities, and the history is sketchy at best. This is not an area for touring ruins, museums, and cathedrals, but rather a gathering spot for sun worshipers, sportfishermen, surfers, and swimmers. Sightseeing involves touring the resorts and shopping areas rather than exploring ancient Aztec ruins. Not far from the resort regions are jungle streams and ocean coves that seem remote and undiscovered. The majority of visitors never venture to these isolated sites, preferring instead to immerse themselves in the simultaneously bustling and restful resort lifestyle, where great dining, shopping, and sunbathing are the major draws.

Mazatlán is first and foremost a busy commercial center, thanks to an excellent port and the fertility of the surrounding countryside. More than 600,000 acres of farmland near Mazatlán produce tomatoes, melons, cantaloupes, wheat, and cotton, much of which is shipped to the United States. And nearly all the 150,000 tons of shrimp that are hauled in annually are processed and frozen for the American and Japanese markets.

Sportfishing accounts for Mazatlán's resort status. The port sits at the juncture of the Pacific and the Sea of Cortés, forming what has been called the world's greatest natural fish trap. Mexico's largest sportfishing fleet is based here, and fishermen routinely haul in the biggest catches in size and number on the coast. But fishing is not the only attraction. Hunters are drawn to the quail, duck, and dove that thrive in the hillsides, and surfers find great waves on nearby beaches. Another draw is the relatively low price of accommodations. El Cid, the largest resort on Mexico's Pacific Coast, is in the city's Zona Dorada (Golden Zone), as are dozens of high-rise hotels and small *posadas* (inns), all charging about half the going rate of accommodations in Cancún. Between Mazatlán and Puerto Vallarta is Tepic, capital of the state of Nayarit. Tepic is the closest station to the coast for trains from inland Mexico and the U.S. border; travelers headed for Puerto Vallarta or Mazatlán take public buses from here to the coast, some three hours west. For those driving to the coast, Mexico Highway 15 ends here, becoming Mexico Highway 200. The closest coastal town to Tepic is San Blas, some 37 kilometers (23 miles) northwest through the jun-

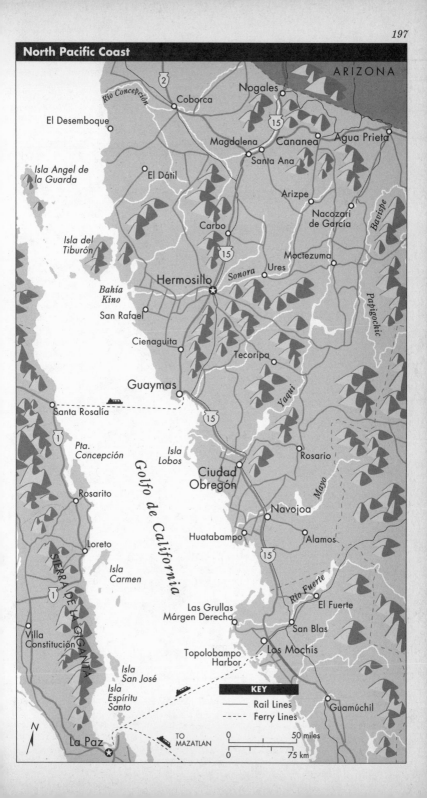

North Pacific Coast

ARIZONA

Nogales

Coborca

Río Concepción

El Desemboque

Magdalena   Cananea

Santa Ana   Agua Prieta

*Isla Angel de
la Guarda*

El Dátil

Arizpe

Nacozari
de García

Bavispe

Carbo

Moctezuma

Papigochic

Hermosillo   Ures

Sonora

*Isla del
Tiburón*

*Bahía
Kino*

San Rafael

Cienaguita

Tecoripa

Guaymas

Yaqui

Santa Rosalía

*Pta.
Concepción*

*Isla
Lobos*

Rosario

Rosarito

Ciudad
Obregón

Mayo

Loreto

Navojoa

*Isla
Carmen*

Huatabampo   Alamos

Golfo de California

SIERRA DE LA GIGANTA

Río Fuerte

Las Grullas
Márgen Derecha   El Fuerte

San Blas

Villa
Constitución

Topolobampo
Harbor   Los Mochis

*Isla
San José*

*Isla
Espíritu
Santo*

Guamúchil

KEY

——— Rail Lines

- - - - Ferry Lines

0   50 miles

0   75 km

N

La Paz

TO
MAZATLAN

South Pacific Coast

TO
LA PAZ

Navolato
Culiacán

El Dorado

*Lázaro
Cárdenas*

Santiago
Papasquiaro

15

Canatlán

La Cruz

Estación
Dimas

Presidio

El-Salto

Durango

Golfo de California

Mazatlán
Villa Unión

40

El Caimanero
Rosario

Escuinapa
de Hidalgo

Mezquital

Tecuala
*Agua
Brava*

Tuxpan

*Islas
Marías*

San Blas
Tepic

Río Grande de Santiago

Punta
Mita

*Bahía de
Banderas*

15

*Cabo
Corrientes*

200

Puerto
Vallarta

Ameca

Guadalajara

PACIFIC OCEAN

N

Tomatlán

80

Chamela
Ayotitlán

*Lake
Chapalá*

Armería

Ciudad
Guzmán

KEY
— Rail Lines
--- Ferry Lines

Barra de Navidad

54

Manzanillo

110

Colima

Tecomán

0   100 miles

0   150 km

gle. San Blas is a small seaside village, favored by budget travelers and escapists who eschew the mega-resorts.

Some 323 kilometers (200 miles) south of Mazatlán is Puerto Vallarta, by far the best-known resort on the upper Pacific coast. The late film director (and sometime resident) John Huston put the town on the map when he filmed Tennessee Williams's *The Night of the Iguana* on the outskirts of the village. One of the movie's stars, Richard Burton, brought Elizabeth Taylor with him—scandalous behavior in 1964, as Burton and Taylor were married but not to each other. Gossip columnists and the Hollywood press flocked to cover the goings-on. In between titterings, stories were filed about the Eden that Huston had discovered—this quaint Mexican fishing village with its cobblestoned lanes and whitewashed, tile-roofed houses. Before long, travel agents were deluged with queries about Puerto Vallarta, a place many had never heard of before.

More than 150,000 people live in Puerto Vallarta today, and upwards of 700,000 tourists arrive each year. The fabled cobblestoned streets are clogged with bumper-to-bumper traffic during the holiday season, and the sounds of construction often drown out the pounding surf. Despite its resort status, parts of Puerto Vallarta are still picturesque. For a sense of the Eden that once was, travel out of town to the lush green mountains where the Rio Tomatlán tumbles over boulders into the sea.

Manzanillo, at the south end of the central Pacific coast, had more of a storybook start than did Puerto Vallarta. Conquistador Hernán Cortés envisioned the area as a gateway to the Orient: From these shores, Spanish galleons would bring in the riches of Cathay to be trekked across the continent to Veracruz, where they would be off-loaded to vessels headed for Spain. But Acapulco, not Manzanillo, became the port of call for the Manila galleons that arrived each year with riches from beyond the seas. Pirates are said to have staked out Manzanillo during the colonial era, and chests of loot are rumored to be buried beneath the sands.

With the coming of the railroads, Manzanillo became a major port of entry, albeit not a pretty one. Forty or 50 years ago, a few seaside hotels opened up on the outskirts of town, which vacationers reached by train. The jet age, however, seemed to doom the port as a sunny vacation spot. Then came Antenor Patiño.

Patiño made millions mining tin in Bolivia. A healthy chunk of that fortune went into building Las Hadas (The Fairies), which, as its name implies, is a sort of fairyland. Inspired by Moorish villages along the Mediterranean, the complex took 10 years to build. The inaugural party in 1974, the "Gala in White," was the social event of the year. Patiño even provided the funds for the government to build a new airport, one that could accommodate his friends' jets. For a while Las Hadas was better known than Manzanillo itself. The film *10* made a star of the resort as well as household names of its stars, Bo Derek and Dudley Moore.

For many visitors, Manzanillo is not so much a city as an airport, the last stop before a holiday begins. Older hotels have been spruced up and condos and all-inclusive resorts built. The Jalisco state line is just a few miles up the coast from the airport. North of the line are the villages of Barra de Navidad,

Melaque, Tenacatita, and Costa de Careyes. In these towns and on the isolated beaches between them are self-contained resorts. Colima's tourist industry is working hard to turn the whole coast into a tourist zone. A four-lane toll road now cuts the driving time between Manzanillo and Guadalajara, Mexico's second largest city, to three hours. On the drawing board are plans to build a pedestrian walkway along the shore, where visitors will stroll by the sea, shop in designer boutiques, and dine in luxury.

The 967-kilometer-long (600-mile-long) coastline on the Gulf of California north of the Mexican Riviera doesn't yet sport a catchy moniker, and the resorts are few and far between. But this corner of northwest Mexico has a character and ambience similar to that of the Baja California Peninsula. The state of Sonora begins at the Arizona border with the scrubby Sonoran desert extending north into Arizona and New Mexico. Nogales is the main border town, and Americans regularly cross the border in search of bargains and treasures; from Nogales many travelers begin the drive south on Mexico Highway 15 toward the Gulf Coast.

This stretch of the northwest is reminiscent of the old Wild West in the United States. Cowboys ride the range, and ranchero ballads not unlike country-and-western songs emanate from saloons. Irrigated ranchlands feed Mexico's finest beef cattle, and rivers flowing from the Sierra Madre to the east are diverted by giant dams to the once-barren land that now produces cotton, sugarcane, and vegetables. Hermosillo, Sonora's capital, bustles with commerce in the midst of the fertile lands, which turn barren again toward the coast. Kino Bay, 104 kilometers (65 miles) west of Hermosillo, is a quiet beach resort, long favored by travelers in recreational vehicles. Visitors from Arizona seeking more luxurious accommodations have begun building condominiums and private homes along Kino Bay.

The Sierra Madre meets the Sea of Cortés 645 kilometers (400 miles) south of the border at Guaymas, the northwest coast's major resort area. An active city and seaport, Guaymas once drew only the hardy, adventuresome traveler, but hotels and restaurants now abound, along with plans for future developments. The northwest's farmland extends south into the state of Sinaloa and the city of Los Mochis. Centered in a fertile valley fed by the Rio del Fuerte, El Fuerte is a picturesque colonial town. Some 78 kilometers (48 miles) southwest is Los Mochis, the starting point for the Copper Canyon railroad trip into the Sierra Madre. From here, Mexico Highway 15 cuts inland from the coast and few roads branch off to the sea until you reach the entrance to the Mexican Riviera at Mazatlán.

Mazatlán

Mazatlán is the Aztec word for "place of the deer," and long ago its islands and shores sheltered far more deer than humans. Today it is a city of some 450,000 residents and draws more than 500,000 tourists a year. Sunning, surfing, and sailing have caught on here, and in the winter months visitors from inland Mexico, the United States, and Canada flock to Mazatlán for a break in the sun. From November through April, the temperature range is 21–27°C (70–80°F), and the summer months are not nearly as warm as in the more popular tourist areas farther south. Hotel and restaurant prices are lower than elsewhere on the coast, and the ambience is more that of a fishing town than a tourist haven.

Upscale resorts and ritzy restaurants are not part of Mazatlán's repertoire, though there is a fair dose of luxury at El Cid, Camino Real, and Pueblo Bonito resorts. Time-share condos and high-rise towers are popping up on the few remaining lots in the Zona Dorada, Mazatlán's beach/hotel/shopping/nightclub strip north of the *malecón* (wharf or waterfront embankment). The stretch north from El Cid development to Punta Cerritos (Cerritos Point) and beyond seems destined to become a retreat for the wealthy, as luxury high-rise towers are built on the beach.

Hunting and fishing were the original draw for visitors. At one time, duck, quail, pheasant, and other wildfowl fed in the lagoons; and jaguars, mountain lions, rabbits, and coyotes roamed the surrounding hills. Hunters have to search a little harder and farther for their prey these days, but there's still plenty of wildlife near Mazatlán. The city is the base for Mexico's largest sportfishing fleet; fishermen haul the biggest catches (in size and number) on the coast. The average annual haul is 10,000 sailfish and 5,000 marlin; a record 973-pound marlin and 203-pound sailfish were pulled from these waters.

The Spaniards settled in the Mazatlán region in 1531 and used the indigenous people as a labor force to create the port and village. The center of Mazatlán gradually moved north so that the original site is now 32 kilometers (20 miles) southeast of the harbor.

The port has a history of blockades. In 1847 during the Mexican War, U.S. forces marched down from the border through northeast Mexico and closed the port. In 1864, the French bombarded the city and then controlled it for several years. Mexico's own internal warring factions took over from time to time. And after the Civil War in the United States, a group of southerners tried to turn Mazatlán into a slave city.

Today Mazatlán has the largest shrimping fleet in Mexico. Sinaloa, one of Mexico's richest states, uses Mazatlán's port to ship its agricultural products.

Arriving and Departing by Plane

Airport and Airlines
Mazatlán's Rafael Buelna International Airport is serviced by several airlines. **Aeroméxico** (tel. 800/237–6639) has flights from Los Angeles and Tucson. **Alaska Airlines** (tel. 800/426–0333) flies in from San Francisco and Los Angeles; **Delta** (tel. 800/843–9378) from Los Angeles; and **Mexicana** (tel. 800/531–7921) from Denver, Los Angeles, San Francisco, and several Mexican cities.

Between the Airport and Hotels
The airport is a good 40-minute drive from town. Shuttle services using Volkswagen vans charge about $5 for the trip to the major hotels.

Arriving and Departing by Car, Train, Bus, and Ship

By Car
Mazatlán is 1,212 kilometers (751 miles) from the border city of Nogales, Arizona, via Mexico Route 15. An overnight

stop is recommended, as driving at night in Mexico is hazardous.

By Train Trains arrive daily from Mexicali, at the California border, and Nogales, at the Arizona border. Others come in from Guadalajara. The train depot is located south of town. Tickets may be purchased at the train station in the neighborhood of Col. Esperanza (tel. 69/84–67–10).

By Bus **Transportes Norte de Sonora** has service to Mazatlán from Nogales, Arizona; other companies connect the coast with inland Mexico. The bus terminal is on Av. Insurgentes (tel. 69/81–36–80).

By Ferry Ferry service between La Paz and Mazatlán has been privatized and improvements are expected. The ferry departs daily from Mazatlán's Playa Sur terminal at 5 PM and takes about 18 hours to reach La Paz. The fare is $17 for regular passage and nearly $100 for a private cabin for two with bed and bath (tel. 69/81–70–21).

By Ship Cruise ships from the **Commodore**, **Carnival**, and **Princess** lines, among others, include Mazatlán on their winter itineraries.

Getting Around

Most tourist hotels are located in the Zona Dorada, about 3 kilometers (5 miles) north of downtown, but taxis and buses cruise the strip regularly. A fun way to get around is on the *pulmonías* (open-air jitneys, literally "pneumonias") that cost about $6 for up to three passengers. Complaints have been registered, however, about one's susceptibility to fumes from other vehicles.

By Car A car is not necessary in town since public transportation is good, but you might want one for a self-guided tour of the area. Rentals usually include free mileage. A Volkswagen Beetle costs about $60 per day with insurance; a sedan with automatic transmission is about $90 per day. The following rental firms have desks at the airport: **Budget** (Av. Camarón Sábalo 402, tel. 69/83–20–00), **Hertz** (Av. del Mar 314, tel. 69/83–60–60), and **National** (Av. Camarón Sábalo in the Plaza el Camarón, tel. 69/83–40–77). **Rent Me!,** between the Quijote Inn and the Caravelle hotel, rents antique-type open cars for about $20 an hour (tel. 69/84–64–33).

Important Addresses and Numbers

Tourist Information Information on Mazatlán and city tours is available at the hotels, which do a more thorough job of promoting the area than the tourism office. The **City Tourism Bureau** is next to the Los Sábalos Hotel. *Rodolfo T. Loaiza 100, tel. 69/83–25–45. Open Mon.–Sat.; hours vary.*

Consulates U.S. (Circunvalación 120 Centro, tel. 69/85–22–05); **Canadian** (Hotel Playa Mazatlán, tel. 69/83–73–20).

Emergencies The **Public Tourism Ministry** (tel. 69/84–32–22) is an agency of the police department instituted specifically for tourists. **Red Cross** (tel. 69/81–48–08), **24-hour medical clinic** (tel. 69/84–22–44).

Guided Tours

Orientation Tour agencies have offices in most hotels and along the Zona Dorada. Mazatlán's tourist areas are filled with sidewalk stands staffed by persuasive individuals offering free tours of the area along with free drinks and meals. Their true goal is to sell time-shares and condos, and the tour/sales pitch can take up the better part of a day.

The three-hour **City Tour** is a good way to get the lay of the land, particularly downtown, which can be a bit confusing. It includes the Zona Dorada, the cathedral and *zócalo* (main square) downtown, the Mazatlán Arts and Crafts Center, and the waterfront.

Harbor Cruises Cruises feature live mariachi or marimba music and free refreshments and normally last about three hours. Cruises aboard the *Yate Fiesta* (tel. 69/85–37–26) cost about $7 and navigate the bay and the harbor, past the islands and sportfishing fleet. A five-hour tour goes to Isla de la Piedra (Stone Island), with time for lunch and a swim.

The **country tour,** also called the **mountain tour,** goes to **Concordia,** known for its furniture makers (a huge wood chair marks the entrance to the small town), then proceeds to **Copala,** a scenic colonial mining town. The **jungle tour** goes to **San Blas** and the **Rio Tovara** (in the state of Nayarit), where boats travel upriver through mangrove jungle to a small spring-fed pond. The tour companies also offer individual guided tours and sportfishing outings.

Exploring

Numbers in the margin correspond to points of interest on the Mazatlán map.

❶ The **Zona Dorada** (Golden Zone) is the tourist region, and it is from this point that most visitors begin touring the city. Unfortunately, Mazatlán's highlights are spread far and wide, and walking from one section of town to the other can take hours. The best way to travel is via pulmonías, so you can sunbathe and take pictures as you cruise along, although you won't be able to roll up any windows to protect yourself from automobile fumes. If you choose to rent a car and drive, you can tour at your own pace. There are no traffic jams in Mazatlán, except near the market in downtown, where parking can also be a major problem.

❷ The Zona Dorada begins on Avenida Camarón Sábalo at **Punta Camarón** (Shrimp Point), the rocky outcropping on which Valentino's Disco sits, resembling a Moorish palace perched above the sea. Going north, Avenida Camarón Sábalo forms the eastern border of the zone, while Avenida Loaiza runs closer to the beach. In this four-block pocket are most of the hotels, shops, and restaurants, and the majority of nonresidents intent on having a good time sunning, shopping, and partying. Head here to souvenir shop, hit the discos, and check out the hotel bars.

❸ A stroll through the **Mazatlán Arts and Crafts Center** (Av. Loaiza, tel. 69/83–50–22), at the north end of the zone, will give you a good sampling of the souvenir selection—onyx chess sets,

Mazatlán

straw sombreros, leather jackets, and Mickey Mouse piñatas. Some of the shops in the center close for siesta from 2 to 4 PM.

Time Out **No Name Café,** right in the Arts and Crafts Center, is a good spot for a beer or *agua mineral* (mineral water) and lime. Mexico's version of Baskin-Robbins, **Helados Bing,** has good hot-fudge sundaes and ice cream cones. It's at the corner of Avenida Camarón Sábalo and Avenida Gaviotas. **Panadería Panamá,** also on Camerón Sábalo across from the Las Palmas hotel, is a bakery that has tables where you can sit and enjoy fragrant cinnamon-flavored coffee.

Traveling north, Avenida Loaiza merges into Avenida Sábalo at Avenida Gaviotas, and Avenida Sábalo continues along the coast, past El Cid Resort, one of the largest tourist developments in Mexico. Along the beach side of Avenida Sábalo are some of Mazatlán's largest, most luxurious, and priciest hotels; opposite the beach are many of the better low-cost motels. Along this route there is a good view of Mazatlán's three Pacific
4 islands—**Isla de los Pájaros** (Bird Island), **Isla de los Venados** (Deer Island), and **Isla de los Chivos** (Goat Island). Just past the Camino Real resort, Avenida Camarón Sábalo becomes Avenida Sábalo Cerritos and crosses over the Estero del Sábalo, a long lagoon popular with bird-watchers. The area north of here will someday be an exclusive touring and resort area; towering condos are already being built.

South of Valentino's, this main road changes names frequently in its 15-mile length. At Punta Camarón it becomes Avenida del
5 Mar, which leads toward Old Mazatlán. The 10-mile **malecón,** Mazatlán's version of a main highway and beachfront board-walk, begins here.

6 **Acuario Mazatlán** (Mazatlán's aquarium) is a few blocks south, down Avenida de los Deportes. The aquarium, with its tanks of sharks, sea horses, eels, lobster, and multicolored saltwater and freshwater fish, is a must-see. A fanciful bronze fountain and sculpture of two boys feeding a dolphin marks the aquarium's entrance. *Av. de los Deportes 111, tel. 69/81–78–15. Small admission fee. Open daily 10–6.*

Time Out Just before you reach the road to the aquarium, you'll see **Señor Frog** (Av. del Mar, tel. 69/82–19–25), probably the most popular restaurant and bar in all of Mazatlán. There's a souvenir shop at the front that sells T-shirts and assorted paraphernalia bearing the Señor Frog logo. The restaurant is cool, dark, cluttered, and busy. Pace yourself with the margaritas and silver buckets filled with bottles of beer, or you'll never make it to the aquarium.

Avenida del Mar continues south past beaches popular with the locals and travelers staying at the budget hotels across the
7 street. The **Monumento al Pescador** (Fisherman's Monument) is Avenida del Mar's main landmark, and it is a strange sight. An enormous, voluptuous, nude woman reclines on an anchor, her hand extended toward a nude fisherman dragging his nets.

Calle Juárez and Calle Cinco de Mayo intersect with Avenida del Mar and lead to Mazatlán's real downtown, where the streets are filled with buses and locals rushing to and from work and the market. Many travelers never see this part of

Mazatlán, but it's worth a visit. Head for the blue and gold **8** spires of the **Mazatlán Catedral,** at Calles Juárez and Ocampo, and you'll be in the heart of the city. The cathedral, built in 1890 and made a basilica in 1935, has a gilded and ornate triple altar, with murals of angels overhead and many small altars along the sides. A sign at the entrance requests that visitors be appropri- **9** ately attired (no shorts or tank tops inside). The **zócalo,** called **Plaza Revolución,** just across the street, has one of the most fascinating gazebos in Mexico—what looks like a '50s diner in- side the lower level and a wrought-iron bandstand on top. The green and orange tile on the walls, ancient jukebox, and soda fountain serving shakes, burgers, and hot dogs couldn't make a more surprising sight. On the streets facing the zócalo are the City Hall, banks, post office, and telegraph office.

10 The **Teatro Angela Peralta,** built in 1860 and now beautifully re- stored, is at Sixto Osuna and Carnaval, about three blocks from the zócalo. It was declared a historic monument in late 1990.

Back along the waterfront, Avenida del Mar becomes Paseo **11** Claussen as it heads south, passing by **El Fuerte Carranza,** an old Spanish fort built to defend the city against the French, and **12** **Casa del Marino,** a shelter for sailors. Playa los Piños, a popular **13** surfing beach, stretches along this road. **High-Divers Park,** where young men climb to a white platform and plunge into the sea, is located nearby. It isn't as exciting as the performance at La Quebrada in Acapulco, but at night when the divers leap carrying flaming torches it's equally spectacular. Some of Mazatlán's best surfing beaches are along this strip.

14 The malecón continues past **Cerro de la Nevería** (Icebox Hill). Wealthy landowners in Mazatlán imported ice from San Fran- cisco in the late 1800s and stored it in underground tunnels in **15** this hill. The next landmark is the statue of **La Mazatleca,** a bronze nymph rising from a giant wave. Across the street is a small bronze deer, Mazatlán's mascot.

Paseo Claussen leads into Olas Altas, site of Old Mazatlán, the center for tourism in the 1940s. Olas Altas (which means high waves) ends at a small traffic circle. A plaque at the circle bears the state symbol of Sinaloa.

16 Above Olas Altas is **Cerro de Vigía** (Lookout Hill), with a look- out point, weather station, and rusty cannon. The view from this windy hill is fantastic, overlooking both sides of Mazatlán, its harbor, and the Pacific. It's a steep climb up and is better **17** done by taxi than on foot. The **Centenario Pérgola,** at the top of the hill, was once used by the Spaniards as a place to watch for pirates.

Time Out **El Mirador,** on top of Cerro de Vigía, is one of the best seafood restaurants in Mazatlán. If you can't make it for a meal, stop long enough to sample the ceviche (seafood marinated in lime or lemon juice) made with fresh shrimp.

At the end of the malecón, the road becomes Paseo Centenario and continues south to the tip of the peninsula. At the tip is **Cerro del Crestón** (Summit Hill) and **El Faro,** said to be the sec- ond-highest lighthouse in the world after Gibraltar, with a range of 36 nautical miles. It takes about 30 minutes to hike up to the lighthouse, but you get a great view of the harbor and sea. This side of the peninsula is devoted to boats, and the road running along the many docks and military installations is called Avenida del Puerto. The sportfishing fleet is anchored at the base of Cerro del Crestón; the next docks north are used by cruise ships and merchant vessels. Launches for **Isla de la Piedra** leave from from a small dock by the military base.

Time Out Small *palapas* (beach shacks) are sometimes set up along the sportfishing docks; many serve a tasty smoked marlin. The palapas near the launches to Isla de la Piedra sell sugarcane sticks, which look like bamboo and are good for quenching your thirst.

What to See and Do with Children

The **Acuario Mazatlán,** with its tanks of salt- and freshwater fish, sharks, and films about sea life, is a perfect child-pleaser. On Sundays in particular, it is packed with families. At the large playground next door, skateboarders practice their tricks while the little ones play on the slides and swings. A little zoo sits amid the trees in the botanical garden beside the aquarium; the most interesting animals are the crocodiles.

Shopping

In the **Zona Dorada,** particularly along Avenida Camarón Sábalo and Avenida Rodolfo T. Loaiza, you can buy everything from piñatas to designer clothing. The best place for browsing is the **Mazatlán Arts and Crafts Center,** designed as a place to view artisans at work and buy their wares. Now the center is filled with shops and boutiques, and the only craft you see is the fine art of bartering. **No Name Café** restaurant and bar in the arts center is a good spot to have a beer and compare prices with fellow shoppers. The **Mercado Viejo Mazatlán** and the **Tequila Tree,** both on Avenida Loaiza, are enormous warehouse-type stores filled with souvenirs. **Evolución** (tel. 69/86–08–39), in the Tequila Tree Center, is a new-age bookstore with a fine collection of English-language books.

For sportswear, visit **Aca Joe, Benetton, Fiorucci, Guess,** and **Bye-Bye. Sea Shell City** is a must-see; it has two floors packed with shells from around the world that have been glued, strung, and molded into every imaginable shape from lamps to necklaces. Check out the enormous fountain upstairs, covered with thousands of shells. **Designer's Bazaar,** a two-story shop near Los Sábalos Hotel, has probably the best selection of high-quality folk art, leather wallets and belts, hand-embroidered clothing, and a good sampling of fashionable swimsuits. Leather shops are clustered along the southern end of the Zona Dorada. Try on soft leather jackets dyed in the latest colors at the **Leather House** and **Rey Solomon.**

The **Mercado Central,** downtown between Calle Juárez and Serdán, is a gigantic place filled with produce, meat, fish, and handicrafts that are sold at the lowest prices in town. It takes more searching to find good-quality handicrafts, but that's part of the fun. Browse through the stalls along the street outside the market for the best crafts.

Sports and Fitness

Fishing More than a dozen sportfishing fleets operate from the docks south of the lighthouse. Hotels can arrange charters, or you can contact the companies directly. Charters include a full day of fishing, lunch, bait, and tackle. Prices range from $40 per person on a party boat to $230 to charter an entire boat. Charter companies to contact include **Bill Heimpel's Star Fleet** (tel. 69/82–26–65), **Flota Faro** (tel. 69/81–28–24), **Estrella** (tel. 69/82–38–78), **El Dorado** (tel. 69/82–62–04), and **De Oro** (tel. 69/82–31–30).

Golf The spectacular 18-hole course at **El Cid** (tel. 69/83–33–33), designed by Robert Trent Jones, is reserved for members of the resort, hotel guests, and their guests. There is a nine-hole course at the **Club Campestre de Mazatlán** (tel. 69/84–74–94), on the outskirts of town on Route 15.

Hunting Several species of duck and white-wing doves, mourning doves, and quail abound in the Mazatlán area. The season runs from October through April. **Aviles Brothers** (Box 221, tel. 69/81–37–28) is the most experienced outfitter, arranging licenses and the rental of firearms. The cost of a six-hour hunt is $110 and up, including transportation, retriever, and English-speaking guide.

Tennis Many of the hotels have courts, some of which are open to the public. There are a few public courts not connected to the hotels. Call in advance for reservations at **El Cid Resort,** 13 courts (tel. 69/83–33–33); **Racket Club,** 6 courts (tel. 69/82–46–00); and **Club de Tenis Reforma,** 8 courts (tel. 69/83–35–76).

Water Sports Jet skis, Hobie Cats, and Windsurfers are available for rent at most hotels, and parasailing is very popular along the Zona Dorada. Scuba diving and snorkeling are catching on, but there are no really great diving spots. The best is around Isla de los Venados. For rentals and trips, contact the following operators: **Caravelle Beach Club** (Av. Camarón Sábalo, tel. 69/83–02–00), **Chico's Beach Club** (Av. Camarón Sábalo 500, tel. 69/84–06–66), **El Cid Resort Aqua Sport Center** (Av. Camarón Sábalo, tel. 69/83–33–33), and **Los Sábalos** (Av. Camarón Sábalo, tel. 69/83–53–33).

Spectator Sports

Baseball The people of Mazatlán loyally support their team, Los Venados, a Pacific League, Triple A team. Games are played at the Teodoro Mariscal Stadium (Av. Deportes) from October through January.

Bullfights Spectacles are held most Sunday afternoons between December and Easter. The bullring is located on Boulevard Rafael Buelna and tickets are available at most hotels and from **Valentino's** (tel. 69/84–16–66).

Beaches

Playa Los Cerritos The northernmost beach on the outskirts of town, which runs from Camino Real Resort to Punta Cerritos, is also the cleanest and least populated. The waves can be too rough for swimming but great for surfing.

| Playa Sábalo and Playa las Gaviotas | Mazatlán's two most popular beaches are along the Zona Dorada. There are as many vendors selling blankets, pottery, lace tablecloths, and silver jewelry as there are sunbathers. Boats, Windsurfers, and parasailers line the shores. The beach is protected from heavy surf by the three islands—Venados, Pájaros, and Chivas. You can safely stroll these beaches until midnight and eavesdrop on the social action in the hotels while enjoying a few solitary, romantic moments sans vendors and crowds. |

| Playa Norte | This strand begins at Punta Camarón (Valentino's is a landmark) along Avenida del Mar and the malecón and runs to the Fisherman's Monument. The dark brown sand is dirty and rocky at some points, but clean at others, and is popular with those staying at hotels without beach access. Palapas selling cold drinks, tacos, and fresh fish line the beach; be sure to try the fresh coconut milk. |

| Playa Olas Altas | Meaning "high waves," this was the first tourist beach in Mazatlán, running south along the malecón from the Fisherman's Monument. Surfers congregate here during the summer months, when the waves are at their highest. |

| Playa Isla de los Venados | Boats make frequent departures from the Zona Dorada hotels for this beach on Deer Island. It's only a 10-minute ride, but the difference in ambience is striking; the beach is pretty, uncluttered, and clean, and you can hike around the southern point of the island to small, secluded coves covered with shells. |

| Playa Isla de la Piedra | The locals head here on weekends. Entire families, bearing toys, rafts, and picnic lunches, ride over to the island on *pangas* (small, open boats) from the dock near the train tracks. Sixteen kilometers (10 miles) of unspoiled beaches here allow enough room for all visitors to spread out and claim their own space, but this won't be the case for long: Work on another tourist mega-development is at a standstill. The project calls for the surrender of 900 acres of the island to a host of hotels, villas, two golf clubs, and tennis and riding clubs. Small shacks and palapas sell drinks and fresh fish, and on Sundays the island looks like a small village, with lots of music and fun. |

Dining

The emphasis in Mazatlán is on casual, bountiful dining, and the prices are reasonable. Shrimp and fresh fish are the highlights; be sure to have a seafood cocktail along the beach. Dress is casual in Mazatlán although shorts are frowned upon for dinner, and most restaurants require footwear at all meals. Chic resort wear is not out of place in establishments like Sr. Peppers, La Concha, and Casa Loma. When you check your bill, be aware that some restaurants, particularly in the hotels, add a service charge of 10% to 15% to your total, as well as 10% tax.

Highly recommended restaurants are indicated by a star ★.

Category	Cost*
Expensive	over $25
Moderate	$15–$25
Inexpensive	under $15

*per person, excluding drinks, service, and sales tax (10%)

Expensive **Casa Loma.** An out-of-the-way, elegant restaurant in a converted villa, Casa Loma serves international specialties such as chateaubriand and chicken *cordon bleu*. Lunch on the patio is less formal. Have a martini made by an expert, and save room for the fine pastries. *Av. Gaviotas 104, tel. 69/83–53–98. No credit cards.*

El Marinero. The best seafood house in Old Mazatlán, this restaurant offers a generous seafood platter, grilled on a hibachi at your table and piled high with frogs' legs, turtle, shrimp, oysters covered with melted cheese, and fresh fish. The decor is dark and woodsy, with lots of brick arches and seashell-covered chandeliers. Try the shrimp *machaca*, sautéed in olive oil with tomatoes, chives, and chiles. Machaca is a typical dish, often made with beef and served for breakfast. *Calle Cinco de Mayo 530, tel. 69/81–76–82. AE, D, MC, V.*

★ **La Concha.** Certainly the prettiest waterside dining spot, La Concha is a large enclosed palapa with three levels of seating at tables spread far apart, a spacious dance floor decked with twinkling lights, and outdoor tables by the sand. Adventurous types might attempt the stingray with black butter or calamari in its ink. The more conservative can try a thick filet Mignon cooked to perfection. A singer croons Las Vegas–style ballads as couples dance. The waiters are proper and refined. La Concha is also open for breakfast. *El Cid Resort, Av. Camarón Sábalo, tel. 69/83–33–33. AE, DC, MC, V.*

Sr. Peppers. Elegant yet unpretentious, with ceiling fans, lush foliage, and candlelit tables, Sr. Peppers serves choice steaks and lobsters cooked over a mesquite grill. Enjoy the dance floor and live music. *Av. Camarón Sábalo, across from the Camino Real hotel, tel. 69/84–01–20. AE, DC, MC, V.*

Moderate **El Mirador.** A real find on the top of Cerro de Vigia, this unas-
★ suming restaurant has some of the freshest, most flavorful fish around. The ceviche is made with fresh shrimp, chopped and marinated in lime juice with tomatoes, onions, cilantro, and peppers. The salsa and chips are homemade and delicious, and meals include soup, salad, and dessert. Stick with the shrimp and fish, and you'll be delighted. The strong wind atop the lookout tends to whip through the open windows, which can be quite invigorating. *Atop Cerro de Vigia, no phone. MC, V.*

Señor Frog. The Carlos Anderson chain's Mazatlán restaurant is as noisy and entertaining as the others. Bandidos carry tequila bottles and shot glasses in their bandoliers, leather belts that held ammunition in the old Westerns. Barbecued ribs and chicken, served with corn on the cob, and heaping portions of standard Mexican dishes are the specialty, and the drinking and carousing go on well into the night. The tortilla soup is excellent. *Av. del Mar, tel. 69/82–19–25. AE, MC, V.*

Shrimp Bucket. In Old Mazatlán under forest-green awnings is the original Carlos 'n Charlie's. The garden patio restaurant is much quieter than its successors—some would call it respectable. Best bets are fried shrimp served in clay buckets and barbecued ribs. Portions are plentiful. Breakfast is also served. It's the place to see where all the Carlos 'n Charlie's action began. *Olas Altas 11, tel. 69/81–63–50. AE, MC, V.*

★ **Tres Islas.** A wonderful palapa on the beach, between El Cid and the Holiday Inn, Tres Islas is a favorite with families who spend all Sunday afternoon feasting on fresh fish. Try smoked marlin, oysters *diablo*, octopus, or the seafood platter. The setting is the nicest in town, close to the water with a good view of the three islands. The waiters are friendly and eager to help. *Av. Camarón Sábalo, tel. 69/83–59–32. MC, V.*

Inexpensive   **Copa de Leche.** Though the name means "cup of milk," this indoor/outdoor café in Old Mazatlán, across from the malecón, is a good place any time of day for a cup of coffee or a beer. Locals settle in at the sidewalk tables for hours of gossip, watching the tourists, and marveling at the changes Mazatlán has undergone. The food is not spectacular, so stick with the less expensive egg dishes at breakfast and tacos and burritos at other times. *Olas Altas 33, tel. 69/82–57–53. AE, MC, V.*

★ **Doney.** This big downtown hacienda has been serving great Mexican meals since 1959. The large dining room has old photos of Mazatlán, a high brick ceiling, and embroidered tablecloths, all of which give you the feeling that you're sitting in someone's home. The Doney is named after a restaurant in Rome, though there is nothing Italian about the menu. Try the *chilaquiles* (casserole of tortillas and chile sauce), mole, or fried chicken. The meringue and fruit pies are excellent. *Mariano Escobedo at Calle Cinco de Mayo, tel. 69/81–26–51. MC, V.*

★ **Karnes en Su Jugo.** A small family-run café on the malecón, with a few outdoor tables and a large indoor restaurant, this establishment specializes in *karnes en su jugo*, literally beef in its juice, a Mexican beef stew, with chopped beef, onions, beans, and bacon—a filling, satisfying meal, especially when eaten with a basket of homemade tortillas. *Av. del Mar, tel. 69/82–13–22. AE, MC, V.*

Mucho Taco. This bright blue taco stand in the heart of the Zona Dorada is open 24 hours—a blessing for those who stay out at the discos until the wee hours. The tacos are fresh and tasty, and you can eat at the small sidewalk tables or take your feast back to your room. *Av. Camarón Sábalo, no phone. No credit cards.*

Lodging

Most of Mazatlán's hotels are in the Zona Dorada, along the beaches. Less expensive places are in Old Mazatlán, the original tourist zone along the malecón—on the south side of downtown. Most hotels raise their rates for the November–April high season; rates are lowest in the summer, during the rainy season. Price categories are based on high-season rates—expect to pay 25% less during the off-season.

Highly recommended lodgings are indicated by a star ★.

Category	Cost*
Expensive	over $80
Moderate	$50–$80
Inexpensive	under $50

All prices are for a standard double room; excluding 10% tax.

Expensive   **El Cid.** The largest resort in Mazatlán, and perhaps in Mexico,
★ El Cid has 1,000 rooms spread over 900 acres. A tower contains only suites. A private residential area away from the beach has some impressive homes and villas, most with satellite TV. Soon it will have a private marina. The spacious hotel rooms overlook the pool and beach (one of the longest and cleanest in the area),

and the hotel is popular with convention groups as well as lone travelers. The glass-enclosed arcade has nice boutiques, and La Concha is one of the most romantic spots on the beach (*see* Dining, *above*). *Av. Camarón Sábalo, tel. 69/83–33–33; reservations in the U.S., tel. 800/525–1925. 1,000 air-conditioned rooms, suites, and villas. Facilities: 18-hole golf course, 6 pools, 13 tennis courts, 14 restaurants, disco, shops, aquatic center. AE, DC, MC, V.*

Los Sábalos. A white high rise in the center of the Zona Dorada, Los Sábalos has a great location, a long clean beach, and lots of action. You feel as though you're a part of things, amid the flight attendants who lay over here, and it's only a short walk to Valentino's, the best disco in town. *Av. Loaiza 100, tel. 69/83–54–09; reservations in the U.S. 800/528–8760. 185 air-conditioned rooms. Facilities: beach, pool, restaurant, 2 bars, tennis courts, health club, shops. AE, DC, MC, V.*

★ **Pueblo Bonito.** By far the most beautiful property in Mazatlán, this all-suite hotel and time-share resort has an enormous lobby with chandeliers, beveled glass doors, and gleaming red and white tiled floors. The pink terra-cotta rooms have domed ceilings. An arched doorway leads from the tiled kitchen into the elegant seating area, which is furnished with pale pink and beige couches and glass tables. Pink flamingos stroll on the manicured lawns, golden *koi* (carp) swim in small ponds, and bronzed sunbathers repose on padded white lounge chairs by the crystal-blue pool. This is as elegant as Mazatlán gets. *Av. Camarón Sábalo 2121, tel. 69/84–37–00. 135 air-conditioned suites, each with kitchen, dining and living area, and balcony. Facilities: pool, beach, restaurant, bar. AE, DC, MC, V.*

Westin Camino Real. Location is the big plus at this property, which is far from the frenzy of the Golden Zone, past a rocky point at the northernmost edge of town. The beach is a bit of a hike from the hotel rooms, through the densely landscaped grounds and down a small hill. The hotel, one of the first in Mazatlán, has undergone drastic renovation; the rooms have shed their '70s earth-tone decor, and a blue, green, and pink color scheme now prevails. If you're more interested in relaxing in peace than in carousing, this is your best bet. *Av. Camarón Sábalo, tel. 69/83–11–11; reservations in the U.S., tel. 800/228–3000. 169 rooms. Facilities: beach, pool, 2 tennis courts, 3 restaurants, bars, disco. AE, DC, MC, V.*

Moderate **Holiday Inn.** A consistently good hotel, the Holiday Inn is a
★ long walk from the Zona Dorada, and little traffic runs by. Tour and convention groups fill the 202 rooms and keep the party mood going by the pool and on the beach, where parasailing is a big hit. Children have a small play area with swings and a wading pool, and there is live, upbeat music in the lobby. All of the rooms have been updated in whites and pastels, and there are large sliding glass doors that open to a pretty view of the islands. *Av. Camarón Sábalo 696, tel. 69/83–22–22. 202 air-conditioned rooms. Facilities: pool, beach, restaurant, 2 bars. AE, DC, MC, V.*

★ **Playa Mazatlán.** Palapas are set up on the patios by the rooms in this casual hotel, which is popular with Mexican families and laid-back singles more concerned with comfort than style. The bright, sunny rooms have tiled headboards over the beds and tiled tables by the windows. There's a volleyball net on the beach, and a small taco stand sells good, inexpensive snacks.

Av. Loaiza 202, tel. 69/83–44–44. 425 air-conditioned rooms. Facilities: beach, pool, restaurant, bar. AE, DC, MC, V.

Inexpensive **Belmar.** One of the first hotels in Old Mazatlán, built near the turn of the century, the Belmar has seen better days. It must have been charming in its heyday, with its blue-and-white tiled balconies facing a central courtyard. Now the place is a bit shabby. The dark wood arches and doorways haven't seen polish in years, and the furnishings in the rooms are quite rickety, though there are some marvelous antiques among the clutter. The newer rooms on the waterfront side have shag carpeting and paneled walls. The beach across the street is one of the best for surfing, and downtown and the market are a short walk away. *Olas Altas 166 Sur, tel. 69/85–11–11. 196 rooms. Facilities: beach, pool, parking, coffee shop, bar. MC, V.*

Bungalows Mar Sol. This older motel has clean, cluttered rooms furnished in a mishmash of colors and styles. A long garden area fronts the parking lot, and there are lounge chairs, a small fountain, and a palapa-covered ping-pong table, but no pool. The beach is across the street, and though the motel is north of town, buses do stop close by frequently. *Av. Camarón Sábalo 1001, tel. 69/84–01–08. MC, V.*

Sands. This is a beachfront hotel with many of the amenities of the larger and more expensive resort hotels, but at a fraction of the price. It is popular with retirees and wanderers who want to stay put for a while. All of the rooms are air-conditioned and have color TVs with some U.S. channels, and several have kitchenettes. *Av. del Mar 1910, tel. 69/82–06–00. Facilities: pool, restaurant, bar. AE, MC, V.*

Nightlife

Caracol Tango Palace at El Cid is Mazatlán's premier night spot. **Valentino's** still draws a glitzy crowd. Its stark white towers rise on Punta Camarón at the beginning of the Zona Dorada. Enjoy easy listening or romantic music here, or opt for rock around the clock on the dance floor.

Also at the Valentino's complex is **Bora Bora** (tel. 69/83–62–12), a casual palapa bar on the beach that stays alive with music and dancing from noon to 4 AM. **Sheik,** a new restaurant extravaganza, is also located here, but it needs a lot of improvement in the food and service departments. Still, don't miss it—stop in during early evening for a drink at least.

Fandango's, in the Las Palmas shopping center, is also popular. One of the **Mexican Fiestas,** at the Playa Mazatlan, Holiday Inn, or the Oceano Palace is also a good entertainment bet; the Fiesta at the Plaza Maya offers a buffet and a two-hour show that includes a performance of the Flying Indians of Papantla. Almost all hotel travel desks can provide you with information on days and times.

Puerto Vallarta

On the edge of the Sierra Madre range sits one of the most popular vacation spots in Mexico. When Puerto Vallarta first entered the public's consciousness, with John Huston's 1963 movie, *The Night of the Iguana*, it seemed an almost mythical, tropical paradise. Indeed, at the time it was a quiet fishing and farming community in an exquisite setting.

Puerto Vallarta's Bahía de Banderas (Bay of Flags) attracted pirates and explorers as early as the 1500s; it was used as a stopover on long sailings, as a place for the crew to relax (or maybe plunder and pillage). Sir Francis Drake apparently stopped here. In the mid-1850s, Don Guadalupe Sánchez Carrillo developed the bay as a port for the silver mines by the Río Cuale. Then it was known as Puerto de Peñas and had about 1,500 inhabitants. It remained a village until 1918, when it was made a municipality by the state of Jalisco and named after Ignacio L. Vallarta, a governor of Jalisco.

In the 1950s, Puerto Vallarta was essentially a pretty hideaway for those in the know—the wealthy and some hardy escapists. After the publicity brought on by *The Night of the Iguana*, tourism began to boom. Puerto Vallarta the fishing village is now PV (as it is called), a city with more than 150,000 residents and an additional 100,000 in the surrounding countryside. Airports, hotels, and highways have supplanted palm groves and fishing shacks. More than 700,000 tourists visit each year, and from November through April cobblestoned streets are clogged with pedestrians and cars. There are now about 10,000 hotel rooms in Puerto Vallarta.

Despite the transformation, every attempt has been made to keep the town's character and image intact. Even the parking lot at the new Gigante supermarket is cobblestoned, and by law any house built in town must be painted white. Visitors still see houses with red-tile roofs on palm-covered hills overlooking glistening blue water. Pack mules clomp down the steep cobblestoned streets. Within 16 kilometers (10 miles) of town are peaceful coves, rivers rushing to the sea, and steep mountain roads that curve and twist through jungles of pines and palms.

In the high season, from December through April, the temperature is in the 70s and 80s, the water temperature in the 60s and low 70s. The off-season brings rain: light afternoon showers in the early summer and major rainstorms in the late summer and fall. You miss out on constant sunshine in the off-season; it's humid and the temperatures are high (in the 80s and 90s), and the mosquitoes can be a nuisance; but you enjoy emptier beaches, warmer water (well into the 70s), and less-crowded streets. You also benefit from a 25% to 30% reduction in room rates and the opportunity to do a little bargaining on rental car costs.

Arriving and Departing by Plane

Airport and Airlines Puerto Vallarta's **Gustavo Díaz Ordáz International Airport** is 6.4 kilometers (4 miles) north of town, not far from the major resorts. The Mexican airlines have daily flights from Mexico City, Los Cabos, Mazatlán, and Guadalajara and connecting flights from other Mexican cities. **Mexicana** (tel. 800/531–7921) has service from Chicago, Los Angeles, San Francisco, Dallas/Fort Worth, and Denver; **Aeroméxico** (tel. 800/237–6639) from Los Angeles. Several American carriers also serve Puerto Vallarta, including **Alaska Airlines** (tel. 800/426–0333), **American** (tel. 800/433–7300), **Aero California** (tel. 800/258–3311), **Delta** (tel. 800/221–1212), and **Continental** (tel. 800/525–0280).

Between the Airport and Hotels Volkswagen vans provide economical transportation from the airport to hotels, and all the car rental agencies have desks in the airport.

Arriving and Departing by Car, Train, Bus, and Ship

By Car   Puerto Vallarta is about 1,900 kilometers (1,200 miles) from Nogales, Arizona, at the United States–Mexico border, 354 kilometers (220 miles) from Guadalajara, and 167 kilometers (104 miles) from Tepic. Driving to Puerto Vallarta is not difficult, but driving in the city can be horrid. From December to April—peak tourist season—traffic clogs the small cobblestoned streets; during the rainy season from July to October, the streets flood and the hills are muddy and slippery.

By Train   Trains run daily from Mexicali and Guadalajara to Tepic; from Tepic, it is a three-hour bus ride to Puerto Vallarta. The train is unreliable, crowded, and slow, and is best left to those with plenty of time and patience. *Tel. 322/3–4861 for the train station in Tepic.*

By Bus   There is no central bus station in Puerto Vallarta, but most of the carriers are located on Avenida Insurgentes between the Río Cuale and Calle Serdán: **Estrella Blanca** (Av. Insurgentes 180, tel. 322/2–0613), **Norte de Sonora** (Madero 343, tel. 322/2–1650), **Transportes del Pacifico** (Av. Insurgentes 282, tel. 322/2–1015), and **Tres Estrellas de Oro** (V. Carranza 322, tel. 322/2–6666). There are hourly buses to and from Tepic, Guadalajara, Mexico City, Mazatlán, and Manzanillo.

By Ship   Several cruise lines, including Carnival, Bermuda Star, Princess, and Admiral, sail to Puerto Vallarta from Los Angeles during the winter months. North Star Cruises sails in from La Paz. The ferry from La Paz and Cabo San Lucas on the Baja California Peninsula has been discontinued indefinitely. Check at the cruise ship terminal or the tourist office for information.

Getting Around Puerto Vallarta

By Bus   City buses and *combis* (Volkswagen vans) serve downtown, the northern hotel zone, and the southern beaches. Bus stops—marked by a blue and white sign with a drawing of a bus—are located every two or three blocks along the highway (Carretera Aeropuerto) and in town. To take a combi to Mismaloya or other points south, go to the Combi Terminal on Calle Piño Suárez or the bus stop at Plaza Lázaro Cárdenas just south of Los Arcos Hotel.

By Taxi   Many hotels post fares to common destinations; be sure to agree on a fare before the cab takes off. The ride from the northside hotels to downtown costs about $3, plus $1 to cross the bridge.

By Rental Car   There are several agencies in Puerto Vallarta that rent Jeeps, open-air Volkswagen Beetles, and automatic-transmission sedans. During the high season, rentals start at $70 per day, including insurance and mileage; off-season, they start at $45 per day. All the car rental agencies below have desks at the airport; some have offices along the highway, but they are spread out, so compare prices at the airport or call from your hotel. Agencies to contact include **Avis** (Carretera Aeropuerto Km 2.5, tel. 322/2–1412), **Budget** (Carretera Aeropuerto Km 5, tel. 322/2–2980), **Hertz** (Lucerna 109–A, tel. 322/2–0024), **National** (Carretera Aeropuerto Km 1.5, tel. 322/2–1107), and **Dollar** (Calle Lucerna 105, tel. 322/4–0001).

Important Addresses and Numbers

Tourist Information	The **State Tourism Office** is one of the best in Mexico. *City Hall on Av. Juárez, by the zócalo, tel. 322/2–0242 or 2–0243. Open weekdays 9–8, Sat. 9–1.*
Consulates	**U.S. Consul** (Av. Insurgentes at Libertad, tel. 322/2–0069, open weekdays 9 AM–1 PM); **Canadian Consul** (Av. Hidalgo 217, tel. 322/2–53–99; open weekdays 9 AM–1 PM).
Emergencies	**Police** (City Hall on Av. Juárez, tel. 322/2–0123); **Red Cross** (Río de la Plata and Río Balsas, tel. 322/2–1533), **Hospital** (Basilio Badillo 365, tel. 322/2–35–72).

Guided Tours

The three-hour city tour is a good way to get the lay of the land, from Gringo Gulch and the Río Cuale to Mismaloya Beach. Almost everyone goes on at least one daytime or sunset cruise around the bay, sighting pretty isolated coves and barren beaches from the deck of a sailboat or yacht. A full-day excursion to Yelapa or Las Animas, seaside communities that can be reached only by boat, gives you a feeling of what life is like in a secluded tropical paradise.

Tropical tours visit mango and banana plantations in Nayarit and include stops in Nayarit's capital, Tepic, and the small seaside town of San Blas. Other trips head south to Boca de Tomatlán, the mouth of the river that flows from the mountains into the sea. Horseback riding is available at ranches in the mountains—three hours are spent riding, and time is taken for lunch and a swim in a mountain stream or lake.

Tours may be arranged through your hotel or one of the many tour operators with offices at hotels and in town. It's worth the few extra dollars to go with a small group in a Volkswagen van rather than with a large group on a tour bus.

Exploring

Orientation	Central Puerto Vallarta has three major parts: the northern hotel and resort region, the downtown area (also called Old Town), and the Río Cuale and Playa de los Muertos. A rental car or cab is necessary to explore the hotel zone, which is basically a long stretch of shopping centers, restaurants, and hotels.

You don't want to have a car downtown and in the Río Cuale area. Most of what you want to see can be covered on foot—just be sure you wear comfortable shoes for the cobblestoned streets.

Numbers in the margin correspond to points of interest on the Puerto Vallarta map.

The Hotel Zone ❶	The big attraction in the north is the **Marina Vallarta** area, which is practically a town unto itself with a marina, hundreds of condominiums, several major hotels, shopping centers, an 18-hole golf course, and the Royal Pacific Yacht Club. A Marriott, Meliá, Velas Vallarta, Quinta Real, Plaza Iguana, Plaza las Glorias have opened. A Conrad Hilton and a Ritz-Carlton are slated to open by December 1992. Nuevo Vallarta, just over

Puerto Vallarta

TO AIRPORT, PLAYA NORTE,
NUEVO VALLARTA

the Jalisco state line in Nayarit, at the mouth of the Río Ameca, is a beautiful new community with beachfront homes and condos on canals with direct access to the bay. In addition, the area is home to an all-inclusive resort, Jack Tar Village. A Best Western hotel, Camelinas, a Paraiso Radisson, and a Sierra hotel are scheduled to open by the end of 1992.

Downtown and the Río Cuale

❷ When you start seeing cobblestoned streets, you're in the downtown area also known as Old Town. This is the heart of PV, a vestige of old Puerto Vallarta. The **malecón** begins at Díaz Ordáz. A seawall and sidewalk run along the bay, and restaurants, cafés, and shops are across the street. The malecón is downtown's main drag, a nice place to rest on a white wrought-iron bench. There are some interesting sculptures along the walkway, including the bronze seahorse that has become Puerto Vallarta's trademark.

❸ ❹ The main zócalo, **Plaza de Armas,** is just after Díaz Ordaz and merges with Morelos at the waterfront. The **City Hall** is on the north side of the plaza. This building is home to a colorful mural, painted in 1981 by Puerto Vallarta's most famous artist, Mañuel Lepe. The mural (above the stairs on the second floor) depicts Puerto Vallarta as a fanciful seaside fishing and farming village. The tourism office is on the first floor.

❺ Dominating the square from a block east is the ornate crown atop **La Iglesia de Nuestra Señora de Guadalupe** (Church of Our Lady of Guadalupe). The crown is a replica of the one worn by Carlota, the empress of Mexico in the late-1860s. There are signs posted at the entrances asking that you not visit the church wearing shorts or sleeveless T-shirts.

❻ The **Mercado Municipal** is located at Miramar and Rodríguez, at the foot of the old bridge over Río Cuale. The market is small enough to tour quickly. There are some good, clean lunch stands on the second floor that serve savory tacos and cool *licuados*, drinks made with fruit juice and water.

❼ The stretch above town along the river is called **Gringo Gulch,** named after the thousands of expatriates from the United States who settled here in the 1950s. Rumor has it that Elizabeth Taylor's home, Casa Kimberly, was sold for a lot less than the $1 million asking price.

Time Out Dining and drinking are the malecón's big attractions, from early morning till just before dawn. If you're there in the morning, have breakfast at **Las Palomas;** evening happy hours are boisterous and fun at **Carlos O'Brien's,** where a six-pack of Corona beer in a silver pail is the favored drink.

Río Cuale Island and Playa de los Muertos

❽ ❾ The Río Cuale runs into the bay just past Plaza de Armas. **Río Cuale Island** is in the middle of the river. There are steps leading under the two bridges that cross the river, then a long park and walkway from Avenida Insurgentes to the waterfront. The island has an outdoor marketplace with boutiques, souvenir stands, trendy restaurants, and inexpensive cafés. The **Museo Arqueológico** at the western tip of the island has a nice collection of pre-Columbian figures and Indian artifacts.

Time Out Close to the mouth of the Río Cuale near the beach is the **Franzi Café,** a great spot to stop for coffee and dessert. There's a library with couches and shelves filled with books, and a talented pianist plays everything from lullabies to polkas. Live jazz is performed at night. *Río Cuale, no phone. MC, V.*

⑩ Playa de los Muertos, the beach on the south side of the Río Cuale, has long been the budget traveler's domain, though it has some of the more expensive restaurants and shops. It is the most popular and most crowded beach in Puerto Vallarta. Parasailers lift off while sunbathers recline on the sand. Beach toys for rent include everything from rubber inner tubes to Windsurfers. Vendors stroll the beach, hawking lace tablecloths, wood statues, kites, and grilled fish on a stick. Plaza Lázaro Cárdenas is a pretty spot at the north end of the beach. To the south, Playa de los Muertos ends at a rocky point called El Púlpito. PV's tourism promoters have been trying to change the name of Playa de los Muertos (Beach of the Dead Ones) to Playa del Sol (Beach of the Sun), but to no avail. If you see an address for the latter, head for the former.

Time Out Eating grilled fish on a stick at Playa de los Muertos is like having a hotdog on Coney Island: it's what you *do.* Buy it from one of the stands at the south end of the beach, then stroll along and watch the show. For a sit-down break, get a beer and tacos or enchiladas at **El Dorado** on the north end.

Mismaloya and A visit to Puerto Vallarta without a side trip to **Playa**
Boca de Tomatlán **Mismaloya (Mismaloya Beach)** is nearly unthinkable, since this
⑪ is where "the movie" was made. The 13-kilometer (8-mile) drive south on Route 200 passes by spectacular homes, some of PV's oldest and quietest resorts, and a slew of condo and time-sharing developments. A pretty cove, somewhat spoiled by La Jolla de Mismaloya, a huge hotel complex built on its shores, Mismaloya is backed by rugged, rocky hills and affords a good view of Los Arcos, a rock formation in the water. Motor launches leave from here for the more secluded beaches of Los Arcos, Las Animas, Quimixto, and Yelapa for about $3.50 per person, per hour.

⑫ Boca de Tomatlán is a small village at the mouth of the Tomatlán River. It's a beautiful spot where you can wade in freshwater pools. Just before you reach the dirt road to the beach, there are several large palapa restaurants, including Chee Chee's, which is a massive restaurant, shopping, and swimming-pool complex that spreads down a steep hillside like a small village. Farther along the main road, through Boca, is Chico's Paradise, a large restaurant set amid giant boulders and surrounded by pools and small waterfalls.

Shopping

Puerto Vallarta can get into a shopper's blood. Chain stores line the main streets, selling designer-label clothing such as **Esprit, Guess?,** and **Ralph Lauren** at prices comparable to, if not higher than, those at home. Prices in the shops are fixed, and American dollars and credit cards are accepted. Bargaining is expected in the markets and by the vendors on the beach, who also freely accept American money. Most stores open at 10, close for siesta at 1 or 2, then reopen from 4 to 8 PM.

Art The late Mañuel Lepe is perhaps Puerto Vallarta's most famous artist. His works may be seen and purchased at **Galería Lepe** (Mañuel Lepe 485). Sergio Bustamante, the creator of life-size brass, copper, and papier-mâché animals, has his own gallery, **Sergio Bustamante** (Juárez 275). Other galleries of note include **Galería Uno** (Morelos 561, tel. 322/2–0908), **Galería Pacífico** (Juárez 519), **Galería Vallarta** (Juárez 263), and **Galería Fitzpatrick/de Gooyer** (Morelos 589).

Clothing Most of the brand-name sportswear shops are located along the malecón and down its side streets. Many of these stores also have branches in the shopping centers or along Carretera Aeropuerto. Some of the most popular shops are **Aca Joe** (Díaz Ordáz 588), **Guess** (Morelos and Abasolo), **Ocean Pacific** (Morelos 660), and **Calvin Klein** (Hidalgo and Libertad).

More elegant, dressier clothes, made of soft flowing fabrics in tropical prints, can be found at **Sucesos Boutique** (Libertad and Hidalgo and Villa Vallarta), which features hand-painted fabrics and fashionable gauze resortwear that is sold in exclusive boutiques throughout Mexico. **El Aguila Descalza** (Corona 179) has designer Josefa's fantastically popular and expensive handwoven cotton caftans, dresses, and skirts embroidered and appliquéd with bright primary-color ribbons. There are also designs by Opus and some beautifully embroidered ethnic clothing. **María de Guadalajara,** in the Puesta del Sol condominiums in Marina Vallarta, carries easy-to-wear clothing for women in gauzy cotton fabrics dyed in luscious colors.

Folk Art Few cities in Mexico have a collection of the country's fine folk arts that is as representative as the one in Puerto Vallarta. Masks, pottery, lacquerware, clothing, mirrors, glass dishes, windows and lamps, carved-wood animals and doors, antiques and modern art, hand-dyed woven rugs and embroidered clothing all are available in the markets, and from vendors. **Nevaj** (Morelos 223) carries high-quality folk art from Central and South America, including primitive and sublime weavings, bags, shawls, and dresses. **Olinalá** (Lázaro Cárdenas 274, tel. 322/2–4995) is a two-story gallery and shop filled with masks from all over Mexico, as well as lacquered boxes, trays, and bowls from Michoacán. **Arte Mágico Huichol** (Calle Corona 164) features beaded tapestries and weavings from the Huichol Indians of Nayarit. **Majolica** (Calle Corona 191) stocks hand-painted pottery from Puebla. **St. Valentín** (Morelos 574) carries rough-hewn pine and mahogany furniture, handwoven rugs from Oaxaca, and earthenware dishes. **Querubines** (Juárez and Galeana) displays crafts, including ceramics, glassware, and jewelry, from all over Mexico, as well as a wearable collection of intricately embroidered native clothing made from hand-loomed cloth.

Jewelry There is a good selection of Mexican silver in Puerto Vallarta, but watch out for fake silver made with alloys. Real silver carries the 925 silver stamp required by the government. It is best to visit a reputable jeweler, such as **Taxco,** on the malecón; **Joyería la Azteca** (Juárez 244 and 360) sells silver jewelry from Taxco and its own line of elaborate, heavy silver and gold necklaces and bracelets. **Arodi** (8 locations, including one on Juárez) specializes in precious and semiprecious stones in unusual settings.

Markets The **Mercado Municipal,** at Avenida Miramar and Libertad, is a typical market plopped down in the busiest part of town. Flowers, piñatas, produce, and plastics are all shoved together in indoor and outdoor stands that cover a full city block. The strip of shops along Río Cuale Island is an outdoor market of a sort, with souvenir stands and exclusive boutiques interspersed with restaurants and cafés. Bargaining at the stalls in the market and on the island is expected.

Shopping Centers The highway on the north side of town is lined with small arcades and large shopping centers that are occupied by handicrafts and sportswear shops. The best selections are at **Plaza Malecón,** at the beginning of Díaz Ordáz; **Plaza Marina,** by the airport; the **Gigante Plaza,** by the Fiesta Americana hotel; and **Villa Vallarta,** by the Plaza las Glorias hotel.

Sports

Swimming, sailing, windsurfing, and parasailing are popular sports at the beachfront hotels. The hotels have stands on the beach offering boat trips and equipment, and you need not be a guest to buy these services.

Fishing Sportfishing is good off Puerto Vallarta most of the year, particularly for billfish, roosterfish, dorado, yellowtail, and bonito. The marlin season begins in November. The Fishermen's Association has a shack on the north end of the malecón and offers a variety of options for fishing trips; most hotels can arrange your reservations. Large group boats cost about $40 per person for a day's fishing; the smaller cruisers may be chartered for $150 a day and higher, depending on the size of the boat and the length of the trip. Charters include a skipper, license, bait, and tackle; some also include lunch.

Golf **Los Flamingos Country Club** (tel. 322/8–0280) has an 18-hole golf course (called a *bucería*). Reservations should be made through your hotel a day in advance. The country club is about 12 kilometers (8 miles) north of the airport, and transportation is provided with your reservations. There is a new, Joe Finger–designed, 18-hole course at the Marina Vallarta complex (tel. 322/1–0171).

Tennis Most of the larger hotels have tennis courts. Nonmembers may also play at the **John Newcombe Tennis Club** (tel. 322/2–4850), **Los Tules** (tel. 322/4–2010), and **Los Flamingos Country Club** (tel. 322/8–0280).

Water Sports Snorkeling and diving are best at Los Arcos, a natural underwater preserve on the way to Mismaloya. Punta Mita, about 80 kilometers (50 miles) north of Puerto Vallarta, has some good diving spots, as does Quimixto Bay, about 32 kilometers (20 miles) south and accessible only by boat. Experienced divers prefer Las Tres Marietas, a group of three islands off the coast.

Some of the hotels have snorkeling and diving equipment for rent and offer short courses on diving at their pools. For dive trips and rentals, contact the following shops: **Chico's Dive Shop** (Díaz Ordáz 772, tel. 322/2–1895) and **Paradise Divers** (Olas Altas 443, tel. 322/2–4004).

Beaches

Beaches in Mexico are federal property and are not owned by the hotels; some hotels try to keep their beaches exclusive by roping off an area where the hotel's lounge chairs must be kept.

Playa Norte Also known as **Playa de Oro,** this is the northernmost beach, stretching from the marina and cruise-ship terminal to downtown. The beach changes a bit with the character of each hotel it fronts; it is particularly nice by the Fiesta Americana and the Krystal hotels.

Playa de los Muertos Dead Men's Beach is the site of a long-ago battle between pirates and Indians. The town's boosters keep trying to change the name to Playa del Sol (Beach of the Sun), but they have not been successful. The budget travelers hang out here, and vendors selling kites, blankets, and jewelry seem as abundant as the sunbathers.

Playa las Animas and Yelapa These secluded fishing villages are accessible only by boat. Both villages have small communities of hardy isolationists; of late, Yelapa has attracted more and more foreigners who settle in for good. At Yelapa, take a 20-minute hike from the beach into the jungle to see the waterfalls. Tour groups visit the beaches daily.

Dining

Puerto Vallarta has so many fine restaurants that it would be impossible to review them all here; hotel restaurants have been listed only if they are exceptional. Dining prices are comparable to those in the United States, and there are few real bargains. Dress is casual in PV, even at the most glamorous spots, though shorts are frowned upon at dinner.

Highly recommended restaurants are indicated by a star ★.

Category	Cost*
Expensive	over $25
Moderate	$10–$25
Inexpensive	under $10

per person, excluding drinks, service, and sales tax (10%)

Expensive **Chez Elena.** This restaurant is among the town's best. Located
★ up a steep street behind Vallarta's famous crown-topped church, Chez Elena is especially agreeable for an early dinner after enjoying the sunset and a delightful tropical drink on the rooftop El Nido bar. The shrimp dishes are excellent, as is the mixed *satay* (an Indonesian dish consisting of grilled, skewered chicken or meat served with a spicy peanut sauce) and the chicken mole. Top it all off with a perfect brownie and café mulatto. *Matamoros 520, tel. 322/2–0161. Reservations advised. AE, MC, V. Dinner only.*

El Set. This restaurant is located at Las Conchas Chinas Hotel, a special spot just south of town. Perched above the cliffs, El Set features rustic wood steps that lead to three dining areas. The grilled lobster is filling, but save room for the caramel crepes. Get here in time for the sunset, and stay for the splendid show of city lights. *Hwy. 200 Km 2.5, tel. 322/2–0302. Reservations advised. AE, MC, V.*

La Perla. This restaurant and its chef are frequent award winners for their sublime French nouvelle cuisine, service, and ambience. The best dish by far is the sole or salmon topped with pasta, crab, and lime sauce, though the duck with pears and the chateaubriand are also superb. The chef really shows his worth with the pastries, which are renowned throughout PV. There is a separate lounge in the restaurant for after-dinner drinks, coffee, and dessert—by all means try the flaming crepes prepared here. The restaurant has been newly redecorated in soft pastels. If you're in town on the first Thursday of the month, have dinner at La Perla and then attend the classical music performance in the Camino Real hotel. *Hotel Camino Real, Carretera a Barra de Navidad, tel. 322/3–0123. Reservations advised. AE, DC, MC, V. Dinner only.*

★ **Le Bistro.** By far the classiest restaurant along Río Cuale, Le Bistro has a black and white tiled bar, gray and white striped tablecloths, and handsome waiters. Try the brochette Brubeck, made of grilled giant shrimp and generous hunks of tenderloin. The pecan pie is a must, as is the Russian Quaalude, made with coffee, Frangelico, vodka, and cream. *Río Cuale Island, tel. 322/2–0283. No reservations. AE, MC, V. Closed Mon. evening and Sun.*

Señor Chico's. On the Alta Vista hill overlooking all of Puerto Vallarta, Señor Chico's is a magnificent spot from sunset into nighttime. The Caesar salad is good, as is any seafood choice, but it's the view that really makes the place. Enjoy live music from 8 to 11 PM. *Púlpito 377, tel. 322/2–3570. AE, DC, MC, V. Dinner only.*

Moderate **Brazz.** A big, airy place decorated with brightly colored piñatas, Brazz is a branch of the Guadalajara chain, known for its generous steaks and chops and good Mexican dishes. At lunch the excellent prime rib is only $8; at dinner it goes up to nearly $20. The salad bar is the best in town. Mariachi music plays continuously. *Morelos at Galleana, tel. 322/2–0324. AE, DC, MC, V.*

★ **El Dorado.** A must for at least one lunch, this Playa de los Muertos palapa is popular with American expatriates. The eclectic menu includes spaghetti, burgers, and crepes, but stick with specialties such as dorado-style fish, broiled with a thick layer of melted cheese. *Amapas and Púlpito, tel. 322/2–1511. AE, DC, MC, V.*

★ **Las Palomas.** Breakfast at this malecón café is a daily ritual for many and a place for the reunion of Puerto Vallarta regulars upon their return to town. Have *jugo de lima* (similar to lemonade but made with the region's tart limes). Homesick? Have hot oatmeal with cinnamon and sugar; otherwise, stick with the *huevos con chorizo* (eggs with spicy sausage) and coffee spiced with cinnamon. *Díaz Ordaz at Aldama, tel. 322/2–3675. No reservations. AE, MC, V. ID required for traveler's checks.*

★ **Le Gourmet.** The small Posada Río Cuale hotel has one of the best restaurants in town, offering a great Caesar salad, shrimp à l'orange, and a large choice of flambéed entrées and desserts. The pepper steak, sautéed at your table, is a good choice, and the piano music is a pleasant change from mariachis. *Calle Serdán 284, tel. 322/2–0450. AE, MC, V. Dinner only.*

Inexpensive **Andale.** A Playa de los Muertos hangout and a good spot for an
★ afternoon beer with the locals, this restaurant serves good fettuccine with scallops, great garlic bread, and an unusual chicken *Mestizo* with white wine, pineapple juice, and jalapeño peppers. *Paseo de Velasco 425, tel. 322/2–1054. AE, D, MC, V.*

Fresh Company. This is a good taco and burger spot in the Villa Vallarta shopping area; it only has a few small tables but serves great *chilaquiles* (similar to nachos). *Villa Vallarta, tel. 322/2–6697. No credit cards.*

★ **La Fuente del Puente.** Located just across from the market, above the riverbank, this outdoor café is popular with budget travelers. The bright pink and blue neon along the ceiling is an unusual touch for PV. The prices are low, the food good, and the crowd amiable. *Av. Miramar at the old bridge, tel. 322/2–1141. MC, V.*

Rito Baci's. This popular deli and pizza parlor delivers to homes and hotels. The crispy-crusted pizza is excellent, and the sausage spicy and flavorful. Try the sausage sandwich as well. *Calle Ortiz de Dominguez 181, tel. 322/2–6448. MC, V.*

Tutifruti. Sample great fresh-squeezed juices at a small stand in the downtown shopping area; choose your desired combination of mango, papaya, melon, and pineapple. Filling *tortas* (sandwiches) cost less than $2. *Morelos at Corona, tel. 322/2–1068. No credit cards. Closed Sun.*

Lodging

Most of PV's deluxe resorts are located to the north; south of downtown and the Río Cuale, in the Playa de los Muertos and Olas Altas areas, the rates are lower. Some of the nicest, older hotels are a few miles south of town. In the winter, budget rooms run $30 to $50, and the large resorts start at $150 per night. Rates go down from April through December by 25%–30%. Reservations are a must at Christmas, New Year's, and Easter.

Highly recommended lodgings in each price category are indicated by a star ★.

Category	Cost*
Very Expensive	over $150
Expensive	$80–$150
Moderate	$50–$80
Inexpensive	under $50

*All prices are for a standard double room; excluding 10% tax.

Very Expensive **Camino Real.** One of PV's first hotels, this Westin hotel sits on a lovely small bay south of town. A recent renovation has replaced the brown, rust, and gold color scheme with light pine handcrafted furniture and bright pink, yellow, and purple highlights against stark white walls. The hotel now has all the five-star touches—from plush robes in the rooms and the feel of an established, comfortable resort to the palapas on the beach and the fragrant white jasmine blooming along the natural waterfall. New since the renovation are an 11-story tower and a convention/banquet center. *Carretera a Barra de Navidad, tel. 322/3–0123; reservations in the U.S., tel. 800/228–3000. 337 rooms (80 in new tower). Facilities: beach, 2 pools, children's pool, 2 tennis courts, 5 restaurants and bars, shops. AE, DC, MC, V.*

★ **Fiesta Americana.** A seven-story palapa covers the lobby and a large round bar. The dramatically designed terra-cotta building rises above a deep blue pool that flows under bridges, palm oases, and palapa restaurants set on platforms over the water. The rooms have a modern blue, pink, and lavender color scheme; each has white marble floors, tiled bath with powerful shower, and balcony. The beach bustles with activity—parasailing, windsurfing, boat tours, snorkeling, and, of course, sunbathing. The restaurants are excellent, especially the breakfast buffet by the pool. Of all the full-service resorts, Fiesta Americana has the most tropical and luxurious feel. *Carretera Aeropuerto, tel. 322/4–2010 or 800/FIESTA–1. 291 rooms with bath. Facilities: pool, beach, 4 restaurants, 3 bars, 5 tennis courts, disco, shops, beauty salon, travel agency, Mexican fiestas with fireworks. AE, DC, MC, V.*

★ **Hyatt Coral Grande.** This stunning new hotel south of town is one of the prettiest on the coast, a pale pink palace surrounded by lush landscaping; rushing waterfalls mask the noise from the nearby highway. The lobby is filled with lavish floral arrangements and high-quality folk art and paintings. The rooms are all suites, with pale pink spreads and drapes, glass-top tables and wall-length sliding glass doors, white lounge chairs on the terrace, and white tile floors. The master suites have private whirlpools. *Carretera a Barra de Navidad, tel. 322/3–0707 or 800/233–1234. 120 suites with bath. Facilities: beach, pool, 2 restaurants, 2 bars, tennis court, health club, shops, beauty salon, water sports. AE, DC, MC, V.*

Marriott. Located in Marina Vallarta, Puerto Vallarta's newest resort complex, with El Salado beach to the front and the Marina's 18-hole, Joe Finger–designed golf course to the rear, the Marriott is one of Vallarta's newest, largest, and most glamorous hotels. The vast, plant-filled, marble lobbies that open onto the huge pool area are hung with chandeliers. The rooms are decorated with light woods and soft colors. All overlook the bay. And if the water sports, tennis, restaurants, night clubs, and other facilities of the hotel aren't enough, the complex houses a huge shopping center, yacht club, golf course, marina, restaurants, bar, tennis club, and spa. *Marina Vallarta, tel. 322/1–0004 or 800/228–9290. 456 rooms and suites with bath. Facilities: restaurants, pool, beach, tennis, 4 restaurants, bars, disco, tennis. AE, DC, MC, V.*

Omni. Formerly the Fiesta Americana, the Omni hotel is a spa, with a fitness center and state-of-the-art machines, a jogging trail running through the hotel grounds, beauty treatments from hydromassage to herb wraps, nutritional analysis, and computerized exercise and diet regimes. You don't have to be a fitness freak to stay here, though. The rooms in the two wings and main 14-story tower are done in peaceful mauves and blues; deluxe rooms have oceanview balconies. Additional personalized services are available to those who opt for the exclusive Omni Club. No matter where you stay, there are extra charges for spa facilities and services, although excellent packages are available. *Carretera Aeropuerto, tel. 322/2–3959. 248 rooms. Facilities: health spa, 2 pools, hot tub, beach, 2 restaurants, 2 bars, shops. AE, DC, MC, V.*

★ **Villas Quinta Real.** Reminiscent of a Palm Springs estate, this pale pink mansion with white columns is simply but elegantly decorated. Fresh flowers and plants, antiques, and original works of art grace the rooms and corridors of this spacious property. Built in 1990, the Villas Quinta Real includes 50 suites and 25 villas that command views of the golf course of the new Marina Vallarta complex. Though the hotel is not directly on the beach, its amenities are many, and its location between the first and 18th holes of the Marina Vallarta Golf Course makes it ideal for golfers. *Marina Vallarta, Pelicanos 311, 48300, tel. 322/1–0800 or 800/878–4484. 50 suites and 25 1- to*

3-bedroom villas. Facilities: golf course, outdoor pool, cable TV, 24-hour room service. AE, MC, V.

Expensive **Krystal Vallarta.** A full-service resort that sprawls over acre-
★ age equivalent to that of a small town, the Krystal has 460 rooms including 48 villas, each with a private pool. There are eight restaurants, including Tango, which serves Argentine *churrasco* (barbecue), and Kamakura, which serves Japanese food. Not all rooms are by the ocean, but the secluded beach can accommodate all sunseekers. Christine's disco has a knock-'em-dead light show. *Carretera Aeropuerto, tel. 322/4–0202. 500 rooms with bath; 48 villas with bath and pools. Facilities: 2 tennis courts, beach, pools, 7 restaurants, bars, shops, disco, travel agency. AE, DC, MC, V.*

Plaza Vallarta. A heavenly resort for tennis buffs, this Medi-terranean-style complex features the John Newcombe Tennis Club, which has 8 courts and offers daily tennis clinics. The re-sort has a shopping plaza, several restaurants and bars, a large swimming pool, and a nice beach. The Plaza Vallarta is favored by athletic types. *Carretera Aeropuerto, tel. 322/4–4448, res-ervations in the U.S.: 800/FIESTA–1. 429 rooms with bath. Fa-cilities: 8 tennis courts, pool, restaurants, bars, shopping center, beach. AE, DC, MC, V.*

Moderate **Buenaventura.** This hotel's location is ideal, on the edge of
★ downtown, within walking distance (10 blocks or so) of the Río Cuale and, in the opposite direction, of the shops, hotels, and restaurants on the airport highway. From the street it looks rather austere, but just inside the door is an enormous five-sto-ry open lobby and bar. The bright, cheerful rooms in yellows and whites have beamed ceilings and pale wood furnishings. *Av. México 1301, tel. 322/2–3737; reservations in the U.S.: 800/223–6784. 206 rooms and 4 suites with bath. Facilities: beach, pool, bar, restaurant. AE, DC, MC, V.*

★ **Conchas Chinas.** This hotel is a short distance south of town, but it's one of the most comfortable places to stay, and there is frequent bus service just out the door. The three-story build-ing is set right on the beach, and all 31 rooms and 8 suites face the water. The rooms have dark beams, orange bedspreads, heavy wood furniture, and small kitchenettes. Some rooms have whirlpool bathtubs. There's a small restaurant on the rocky beach, and **El Set**, one of PV's best restaurants, is next door. *Carretera Barra de Navidad Km 2.5, tel. 322/2–0156, reservations in the U.S.: 800/424–4441. 31 rooms and 8 suites with kitchenette and bath. Facilities: pool, beach, 2 restau-rants. MC, V.*

★ **Las Palmas.** The palapa entrance to Las Palmas is unique—four bamboo bridges suspended from the ceiling and parrots screeching under the palms. The rooms have shared balconies and green and yellow floral spreads and drapes. The accommo-dations are first-rate for this price category. *Carretera Aero-puerto Km 2.5, tel. 322/4–6784 or 800/421–0767. 153 rooms with bath. Facilities: pool, restaurant, bar, water sports. AE, DC, MC, V.*

Mar Elena. These suites on the north side of town are a good bargain for those wanting a kitchen and living-room setup. The building is rather plain, but the kitchens and bathrooms are beautifully tiled, and the bedrooms have woven rugs on the floors and flowers stenciled on the walls. The pool is on the roof; the beach is a block away. *Carretera Aeropuerto Km 2, tel. 322/4–4425. 30 suites with bath. Facilities: pool. MC, V.*

Inexpensive **Los Cuatro Vientos.** The most charming small hotel in PV, Cuatro Vientos (meaning Four Winds) is located up a steep hill behind town, tucked among the red-tile-roofed cottages. Its 16 rooms are often booked a year in advance by repeat guests. The simple rooms with arched brick ceilings have colorful flowers stenciled on the walls and folk art knickknacks. The restaurant, **Chez Elena,** is among PV's best, and there's a pleasant rooftop bar open in high season. *Matamoros 520, tel. 322/2–0161. 16 rooms with bath. Facilities: restaurant, bar. AE, MC, V.*

★ **Molino de Agua.** A real find on the Río Cuale, the hotel's bungalows are spread out along the riverbed amid lush trees and flowers. Stone pathways wind under willows, past caged parrots and monkeys, and lead to cottages with wood shutters, yellow tiled bathrooms, and redbrick walls. A bubbling whirlpool sits half-hidden under a willow by the swimming pool. *Vallarta 130, tel. 322/2–1907. 62 rooms with bath. Facilities: beach, whirlpool, restaurant. AE, MC, V.*

Playa Los Arcos. By far the most popular hotel on the beach by the Río Cuale, Los Arcos has a pretty central courtyard and pool and a friendly air. A glass elevator rises by the pool to the rooms, which have bright orange furnishings and small balconies. *Olas Altas 380, tel. 322/2–0583. 140 rooms with bath. Facilities: beach, pool, restaurant, bar. AE, DC, MC, V.*

★ **Posada de Roger.** One of the least expensive hotels, the Posada de Roger is in many ways the most enjoyable, if you like the company of Europeans and Canadians who are savvy about budget traveling. The showers are hot, the beds soft, and the pool an international meeting spot. You can have your mail held there, and the desk clerks are knowledgeable about other budget hotels and restaurants. *Basilio Badillo 237, tel. 322/2–0836. 56 rooms with bath. Facilities: rooftop pool, restaurant, bar. MC, V.*

★ **Posada Río Cuale.** This small, friendly inn on the south side of Río Cuale has one of the best gourmet restaurants in town (aptly named Le Gourmet) and a nice sense of serenity. The beds are big and cozy, flowers are placed on each nightstand; and with only 21 rooms, it rarely becomes noisy. *Calle Serdán 242, tel. 322/2–0450. 21 rooms with bath. Facilities: pool, restaurant, bar. AE, MC, V.*

Nightlife

Puerto Vallarta is a party town, where the discos open at 10 PM and stay open until 3 or 4 PM. A minimum $5 cover charge is common in the popular discos, many of which are at the hotels. The Krystal has **Christine's,** which features a spectacular light show set to music from disco to classical nightly at 11:30. **Sixties,** at the Marriott, features music for almost all ages, and **Friday López,** at the Fiesta Americana, has a video bar with live music and dancing. Tables start to disappear from the lower level of the **Hard Rock Café** at about 10:30 PM, and by 11 PM the live music starts and there is dancing everywhere. **Yesterday's** (Pulpito 127) has live music and disco tapes for dancing under the stars. **El Panorama,** at the Hotel La Siesta, is a real nightclub with a floor show and live music. Jazz can be heard at **Le Bistro** and **Franzi Café** on Río Cuale Island. **Iggy's,** at the La Jolla Mismaloya Hotel, is the perfect drinking and dancing spot for those who like to converse without shouting.

Mexican fiestas are popular at the hotels and can be lavish affairs with buffet dinners, folk dances, and fireworks. Reservations may be made with the hotels or travel agencies. Some of the more spectacular shows are at La Iguana Tourist Center, the Krystal, Plaza las Glorias, and the Sheraton. On Thursday nights a Fiesta Brava is held at the Krystal that features a mock bullfight with audience participation. Also on Thursdays, the Meliá hosts a flamenco night with Spanish buffet.

Excursion from Puerto Vallarta to Manzanillo

The coastline south of Puerto Vallarta is sprinkled with some of the Mexican Riviera's most exclusive and secluded one-of-a-kind resorts. But you'll never see them if you take 200 south—a rugged, twisting road through tropical forest of pines and palms. You've got to venture down some paved and unpaved roads to the coast. Guests usually fly to Puerto Vallarta (two hours north) or Manzanillo (one hour south) and take a taxi or hotel van to the resort. Once there, they stay put for a week or more, leaving only for the requisite shopping spree in PV. The resorts are all expensive—more than $130 a night double—but most are all-inclusive, which relieves you from carrying cash and calculating tips. Traveling south, the best resorts are in Careyes, then in Tenacatita.

Lodging **Fiesta Americana Los Angeles Loco.** Canadians come here by the charter-jet load, drawn to the amiable, surroundings, the all-inclusive drinks and meals, and the chance to relax with friends. Fiesta Americana operates the hotel, which is similar in design to their other properties, with the large, comfortable rooms clustered in a horseshoe-shaped terra-cotta building around the bay. Tours to Puerto Vallarta and Manzanillo are available, and there is a good selection of shops on the property. *Hwy. 200 in Tenacatita, tel. 333/7–0220. Reservations in the U.S. 800/223–2332. 205 rooms and suites. Facilities: beach, pool, water and land sports, horseback riding, tours, buffet and restaurant, bar, disco. AE, DC, MC, V.*

Hotel Costa Careyes. As much an architect's delight as a travelers domain, Costa Careyes looks like a watercolor still life rustling in the breeze. The sand changes from scarlet gold to pale tan with the light of the sun; the buildings carry on the sunlight theme, washed in amber, gold, and blue. Palapas and white-gauze tents and umbrellas block the sun's rays. Early morning is for horseback riding along the beach, casting a lure for sailfish, an extended tennis game, or snorkeling around rocky points. Evening is for a sumptuous meal served with casual graciousness. (Meals are not included.) At press time, a large part of the hotel was closed for renovation (only three bungalows and 12 casitas are currently available), but construction is scheduled to terminate in December 1992. Call ahead for an update. *Off Hwy. 200 at Careyes, tel. 333/7–0050, fax 333/7–0107. 90 rooms, suites, bungalows, and casitas. Facilities: beach, pool, sportfishing, diving, horseback riding, tennis courts, restaurant, bar. AE, MC, V.*

Playa Blanca. This Club Med recently underwent renovation and modernization and has all the services the pioneer all-inclusives are known for—diving, fishing, pool bars, horseback riding, and even a clown school. The food, usually served buffet style, is ample and good, and there are two restaurants where you can be served by waiters. The guests tend to be young and active, and the resort is far from having a feeling of isolation—with 300 rooms, a disco, and a tendency toward rock videos and aerobic classes, the ambience is more celebratory than somnolent. *Off Hwy. 200, next door to Costa Careyes. Reservations in the U.S. 800/CLUB–MED. 300 rooms. Facilities: beach, pool, tennis, horseback riding, water sports, buffet dining halls and 2 restaurants, bar. AE, DC, MC, V.*

Excursion to Tepic and San Blas

Tepic, the state capital of Nayarit, is the departure point for those taking the train from the border or Guadalajara to the coast. From here it is a three-hour bus trip to Puerto Vallarta on Highway 200 at the end of the shores of the Sea of Cortés. The 167-kilometer (104-mile) route traverses mountainous roads along the coast; the highway continues south to the Guatemala border.

The town was founded in 1532 by the Spanish conqueror Nuño de Guzmán, who named it Villa del Espíritu Santo de la Mayor España. Later, the name became Santiago de Galicia de Compostela, which somehow was shortened to Tepic. Tepic is best known for its sugar refineries, which cast a distinctive aroma of burning sugar into the air. Though it is the capital and has a population of more than 200,000, there is little to attract tourists. For most, it is a necessary stop-off if they're traveling toward the coast by train.

The most noted site in town is **La Iglesia de Santa Cruz,** built centuries ago when someone noticed that the grass on the site was growing in the shape of a cross. Fray Junípero Serra spent a year here, and there is a monument to him in the church. The church's two Gothic spires have been restored and tower over the flowers and trees in the Plaza Principal.

The **Museo Regional de Nayarit** is in the former palace of the Counts of Miravalle and has a collection of Mesoamerican pottery and jewelry. On weekends, the Huichol and Cora Indians come down from their villages in the mountains around Tepic to sell their crafts, including bead necklaces, God's Eyes woven of colored wool, and scarves. *Av. México 91. Open 9 AM–6 PM. Closed Mon.*

San Blas would be a tropical paradise if it weren't for the infernal gnats that swarm on the beach and riverbeds and nip at your skin—bug repellent is an absolute necessity. The drive into town from Tepic via Highway 15 is spectacular. Within 37 kilometers (23 miles), you drop 1,000 feet through the jungle to sea level. At the entrance to town, the bridge over the Estero San Cristóbal marks the mouth of the **Río La Tovara.** Small tour boats leave from here for a trip up the river, through the jungle. Huge turtles sun on the riverbank under the mangrove trees, and bright yellow birds fly out from the thick foliage. After about a half-hour ride, you reach a primitive hut by a large freshwater pool fed by mountain springs, where you can swim in the clear cool water. Jaguars are said to drink from this pool at night. The town of San Blas is a pleasant little village where the locals congregate at the small central plaza. Two churches in comparable states of disrepair fill one side of the plaza. **El Templo de San Blas,** practically a ruin, has a life-size statue of Jesus wearing the Crown of Thorns, his face dripping with blood. **La Apostólica Romana de San Blas,** the cathedral, has been under construction for more than 30 years, and its roof is not yet complete.

The beaches are about five blocks from the plaza, past the military base. The sand flies along these beaches form thick ankle-high clouds in the evening, so don't bother with sunset strolls along the sand. During the day, though, the beaches are great—nearly empty and with good surf. Shacks on the sand sell fresh grilled fish.

Cerro de San Basilio, a high hill overlooking town, has the ruins of an old Spanish fort, guarded by a rusty cannon. **Las Ruinas la Contaduría,** as the site is known, marks the place where 70 Spanish families founded San Blas in 1768. **La Iglesia de Nuestra Señora del Rosario,** a colonial church with an overgrown cemetery, sits on the side of the hill. Henry Wadsworth Longfellow wrote the poem "The Bells of San Blas" about this church.

Dining   Neither Tepic nor San Blas can boast of culinary hot spots. In fact, the best places to eat in San Blas are the palapas that serve grilled fresh fish with homemade tortillas and rice.

Category	Cost*
Expensive	over $15
Moderate	$10–$15
Inexpensive	under $10

per person, excluding drinks, service, and sales tax (10%)

San Blas   **El Delfin.** This hotel dining room is the best place in town for seafood, Mexican specialties, and a variety of international dishes. *Hotel Las Brisas, Cuauhtémoc 106, tel. 321/5–0112. No reservations. Dress: casual. MC, V. Expensive.*
La Familia. A lovely place owned by a former mayor of San Blas, whose paintings of tropical scenes hang on the walls, La Familia is known for its great seafood cocktails and shrimp. *Batellón 18, tel. 321/5–0298. No reservations. Dress: casual. No credit cards. No lunch. Moderate.*

Tepic   **Roberto's.** This family-run restaurant is known for its well-prepared international dishes and exceptionally good service. *Paseo de la Loma and Insurgentes, tel. 321/3–3005. No reservations. Dress: casual. AE, MC, V. Expensive.*
Mariscos del Farallón. An informal spot with the best seafood in town, better for fish than lobster or shrimp. *Insurgentes 282, tel. 321/3–1124. No reservations. Dress: casual. MC, V. Closed Mon. Moderate.*

Lodging   Rooms in Tepic are generally inexpensive. In San Blas they run a little higher, but the rates are nothing compared with those in the resort areas.

Category	Cost*
Expensive	over $45
Moderate	$25–$45
Inexpensive	under $25

All prices are for a standard double room; excluding 10% tax.

San Blas **Las Brisas.** The nicest hotel in town is near the beach and has air-conditioned rooms in a three-story building draped with bougainvillea. *Cuauhtémoc 106, tel. 321/5–0112. 42 rooms with bath. Facilities: pool, restaurant, parking. MC, V. Expensive.*
Los Flamingos. A pretty colonial hotel in an old hacienda, this establishment has a junglelike garden and a tiled patio. *Poniente 105, no phone. 25 rooms with bath. Facilities: restaurant, parking. MC, V. Moderate.*
Posada del Rey. A motel by the sea, Posada del Rey has only 13 rooms and is popular with families. *Calle Campeche 10, tel. 321/5–0123. 13 rooms with bath. Facilities: pool. MC, V. Moderate.*
El Bucanero. A crumbling mansion with a stuffed crocodile in the lobby and a somewhat overgrown courtyard; all rooms have ceiling fans. *Poniente 75, tel. 321/5–0101. 33 rooms with bath. Facilities: restaurant, bar, pool. MC, V. Inexpensive.*

Tepic **Corita.** Located on the main road out of town, this hotel has pretty gardens and small, clean rooms. *Insurgentes 310, tel. 321/2–0477. 35 rooms with bath. Facilities: restaurant, pool, bar, parking. MC, V. Moderate.*
Fray Junípero Serra. This hotel is centrally located on the main square and features modern, air-conditioned rooms. *Lerdo 23, tel. 321/2–2525. 85 rooms with bath. Facilities: restaurant, bar, disco. MC, V. Moderate.*
Altamirano. A small, comfortable place, Altamirano is just off the main plaza. *Minas 19 Pte., tel. 321/2–7131. 30 rooms with bath. Facilities: parking, coffee shop. No credit cards. Inexpensive.*

Manzanillo

Tourism is booming in Manzanillo, although compared with other Pacific coast resorts, the town is a sleeper. It has a sprinkling of fine hotels and restaurants, with more being built all the time. Manzanillo is also home to the most opulent resort property on the Mexican coast, Las Hadas.

Nature is undoubtedly Manzanillo's best attraction. Its twin *bahías* (bays), Manzanillo and Santiago, where crystal blue waters lap white-sand shores, have caught outsiders' eyes since Cortés conquered Mexico. In the July–September rainy season, rivers and lagoons swell, forming waterfalls and ponds. White herons and pink flamingos flock to the fertile waters, and white butterflies flutter above the flowers in the chamomile fields (*manzanillo* is Spanish for chamomile).

Santiago Peninsula, which divides Bahía Santiago and Bahía Manzanillo, is the site of Las Hadas (The Fairies) resort. From the water or points above the beach, the resort seems a mirage, a sea of white domes and peaks that radiate in the midday heat. When Bolivian tin magnate Antenor Patiño conceived of this white palace in the early 1960s, Manzanillo was easier to reach by sea than land, a rugged, primitive port that attracted the hardy who didn't mind creating their own tropical paradise. In 1974, when Señor Patiño's retreat was complete, the international social set began to visit Manzanillo, thus putting the city in magazines and on television screens around the world. Even then, Manzanillo remained essentially a port city with only a few tourist attractions.

Manzanillo is still relatively undeveloped. Investors have plenty of land to divvy up for their financially rewarding havens, and existing resorts are spread out. Many shops and hotel desks close for afternoon siesta, and on Sundays most businesses are shut (including restaurants) and everyone heads for the beach.

Arriving and Departing by Plane

Airport and Airlines Manzanillo's **Aeropuerto Internacional Playa de Oro** is 32 kilometers (20 miles) north of town, on the way to Barra de Navidad. **Aeroméxico** (tel. 800/237–6639) and **Mexicana** (tel. 800/531–7921) fly in from several U.S. and Mexican cities. **Mexicana** serves Manzanillo from Guadalajara and Mexico City.

Between the Airport and Hotels Volkswagen vans transport passengers from the airport to the major resorts; these shuttle services are less expensive than taxis.

Arriving and Departing by Car, Train, and Bus

By Car The trip south from the Arizona border to Manzanillo is about 2,419 kilometers (1,500 miles); from Guadalajara, it is 332½ kilometers (200 miles); from Puerto Vallarta, 242 kilometers (150 miles). Highway 200 runs along the coast from Tepic, Nayarit, to Manzanillo. Hazardous conditions and unexpected, drastic detours are common.

By Train Trains run to Manzanillo from Guadalajara—an adventure for some, but for most it is a tedious trip, lasting a minimum of eight hours and ending at the ship and freight yards outside town.

By Bus **Tres Estrellas de Oro** travels to Manzanillo from Nogales, Arizona, at the U.S.–Mexico border, from Mexico City and Guadalajara, and from the coastal towns. Many of the area's resorts are located 1 to 2 kilometers (2 to 3 miles) from the bus stop on the highway.

Getting Around

By Car Cars are almost essential for exploring the area on your own. The highway from Santiago to Manzanillo is commonly called Carretera Santiago–Manzanillo, Manzanillo–Aeropuerto, Salahua–Santiago, or any number of things depending on the closest landmark. It's called the Santiago–Manzanillo Road throughout this chapter to lessen confusion. Route 200 runs north along the coast past Manzanillo and Santiago bays to Barra de Navidad and Melaque; Route 110 goes east to Colima.

Avenida Morelos, the main drag in town, runs from Manzanillo Bay past the port and shipyards to the plaza. If you plan to explore the downtown, park along the waterfront across from the plaza and walk—all the shops and hotels are within a few blocks. **Avis** (tel. 333/3–0190), **Budget** (tel. 333/3–1445), and **National** (tel. 333/3–0611) have offices in the airport, and most big hotels have at least one company represented. **Hertz** has offices at Las Hadas and the Sierra hotels. Rates vary depending on where you rent your car, but rentals are generally costly ($60–$100 per day, including insurance). Most offer 200 kilometers (124 miles) free, which should give you enough roaming for one day.

Important Addresses and Numbers

Street addresses are not often used in Manzanillo; instead, locations are designated by neighborhood—the Las Brisas area, Santiago Peninsula (also known as the Las Hadas Rd.), and so on. Maps with actual street names are rare (or inaccurate).

Tourist Information Information on Manzanillo is scanty at best and rarely consistent. The **State Tourism Office** (Blvd. Costero Miguel de la Madrid Km 9.5, tel. 333/3–2277) is supposed to be open weekdays 9–3:30, but call first to be sure. More accurate information is available from tour operators and hotels.

Emergencies **Police** (tel. 333/2–0181); **Hospital** (tel. 333/2–0029).

Guided Tours

The best way to see Manzanillo is with a tour guide. Operators will arrange special-interest or private tours as well as sportfishing trips, sunset cruises, and horseback outings. Most agencies have offices along the highway that encircles Santiago and Manzanillo bays, and most hotels offer at least one agency's services. Agencies include **Bahías Gemelas Agencia de Viajes** (Las Hadas Plaza Albina, tel. 333/3–0204; Manzanillo–Santiago Rd. Km 10, tel. 333/3–1000), **Recorridos Turisticos Manzanillo** (Plaza Santiago and the Plaza Las Glorias Hotel, tel. 333/3–0434 or 333/3–0435), **Viajes Anfitriones Mexicanos** (Club Maeva Hotel, tel. 333/3–1940; and Plaza Galería, local 10, Km. 10 Costera Miguel de la Madrid tel. 333/3–1941), and **Viajes Hectur** (Santiago–Manzanillo Rd. Km 11 in Plaza la Fuente, tel. 333/3–1890).

Exploring

A vacation in Manzanillo is not spent shopping and sightseeing. You stay put, relax on the beach, and maybe take a few hours' break from the sun and sand to survey the local scene casually.

The **Santiago** area is tourist oriented, with clusters of shops and restaurants by the beach. An investment of $500,000 in private and public dollars that will create a marina for 190 boats is still in the planning stages. Also in the works are five hotels, a golf course, and shops and restaurants. The next area to the east, **Salahua**, today comprises a settlement with homes, a baseball field, and restaurants, but this area will soon become the malecón, a new waterfront park and boardwalk that will link the hotels on the east side of the road with the shore. (Highway 200 will have to be rerouted behind the hills and hotels, so it's guaranteed to be a lengthy project.) **Las Brisas** beach is farther south, past the traffic circle and Avenida Morelos, the road to town. Some of the more reasonably priced hotels are located here.

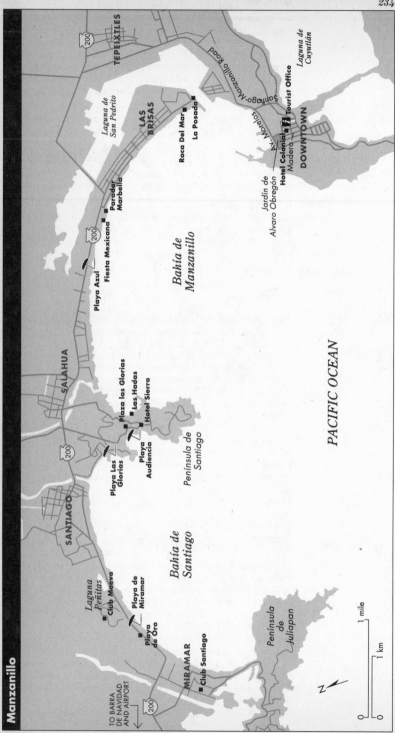

234

Manzanillo

TO BARRA
DE NAVIDAD
AND AIRPORT

MIRAMAR

SANTIAGO

SALAHUA

LAS BRISAS

TEPEIXTLES

Laguna
Peñitas

Club Santiago

Playa
de Oro

Club Maeva

Playa de Miramar

Bahía
de
Santiago

Península
de
Juliapan

Playa Las Glorias

Playa Audiencia

Plaza las Glorias

Las Hadas

Hotel Sierra

Península de Santiago

Playa Azul

Fiesta Mexicana

Parador
Marbella

Laguna de San Pedrio

Roca Del Mar

La Posada

Bahía de Manzanillo

Santiago-Manzanillo Road

Jardín de
Alvaro Obregón

Hotel Colonial

Madero

Av Morelos

Tourist Office

DOWNTOWN

Laguna
de
Cuyutlán

PACIFIC OCEAN

0   1 mile
0   1 km

N

Downtown is busy and jam-packed. At the beginning of the harbor, Route 200 jogs around downtown and intersects with Highway 110 to Colima. Avenida Morelos leads past the shipyards and into town. Just before you reach the port, stop at **Laguna de San Pedrito,** where graceful white herons and vivid pink flamingos assemble at sunset. The **zócalo** or **Jardín de Obregón** is right on the main road by the waterfront. It's a small square, quite lively in the evening.

Las Hadas resort is Manzanillo's Disneyland, a dizzying spectacle of wealth. This luxurious fantasyland is the creation of Don Antenor Patiño, who created his own "Magic Kingdom" in the 1960s on the undeveloped Santiago Peninsula in Manzanillo Bay. Dazzling white domes and spires rise amid the palms; cobblestoned paths wind past private villas veiled in blooming bougainvillea; white gauze Arabian tents billow in the breeze on the beach. Most tourists visit the hotel at least for lunch and the chance to marvel at the scenery. And yes, the movie *10* was filmed here—the most luxurious villa of all bears Bo Derek's name.

Shopping

One goes to Manzanillo to rest, not to shop. But Manzanillo has its share of sportswear boutiques, a sprinkling of fine-crafts galleries, and a substantial allotment of stores selling velvet sombreros and the like. The hotel shops have the best selections of folk art and clothing. Most of the shops are closed from 1 to 4 PM; many are also closed on Sunday.

Plaza Santiago has a good Mexican handicrafts store called **Boutique Grivel. Atico Fourzan,** at the Plaza Manzanillo mall and Marina Las Hadas, houses a variety of fine folk art. **Galería de Arte** at Plaza Albino (Puerto las Hadas) has painting and sculptures by contemporary Mexican artists including Sergio Bustamante and Pal Kepenyes. **Tane,** probably Mexico's most prestigious silver shop for tableware, art objects, and jewelry, is also at Las Hadas.

Rubén Torres, set off by itself at Kilometer 16 on the Santiago–Manzanillo Road, has the best sportswear. **Galería Jaramar,** at the Las Hadas arcade, specializes in handwoven fabrics and fine jewelry and creative designs for women. Downtown, the selection of souvenirs and clothing is more typically Mexican. Some of the best spots for crafts and clothing are **El Dorado** and **Maria de Guadalajara.**

Sports

Fishing Manzanillo claims to be the sailfishing capital of the world; the season runs from mid-October through March, with an international sailfish tournament held every November. Blue marlin and dorado are also abundant. Sportfishing charters are available at the major hotels and tour agencies.

Golf **La Mantarraya** (tel. 333/3–0000), the 18-hole golf course at Las Hadas, designed by Roy Dye, has been rated among the world's 100 best courses by *Golf Digest*. Club Santiago (tel. 333/3–0413) has a nine-hole course designed by Larry Hughes.

Tennis Most of the resort hotels have tennis courts.

Water Sports The rocky points off Manzanillo's peninsulas and coves make good spots for snorkeling and scuba diving. Small boats called *pangas* can be rented on some beaches so you can reach the better spots.

Beaches

In Manzanillo, every day is a beach day, and Sundays are downright festive, with half the town gathered to play onshore. Windsurfing has become quite popular, and jet skis roar about, but there isn't much in the way of parasailing. The sand is a mix of black, white, and brown, with the southernmost beaches the blackest. Most beaches post warning flags if the conditions are dangerous or jellyfish have been sighted.

Playa Miramar, at the north end of Santiago Bay, is populated by windsurfers and boogie-boarders. The beach in front of Club Santiago, once the favored hangout for locals, is now accessible only by walking north along the beach from the highway or by passing the guards at the club gates. The main stretch of beach is across the highway from Club Maeva. **Playa Audiencia,** in a cove along the north side of Santiago Peninsula, is a small beach between two rock outcroppings—it's a good spot for snorkeling. (The local Indians supposedly granted Cortés an audience on the beach—thus the name.) The new Intercontinental Hotel is located in the middle of the beach, making public access limited. **Playa Azul,** also called Playa Santiago, is a long strand that runs from Santiago along Manzanillo Bay to Playa Las Brisas. The surf gets rough along the north end; swimming is better toward Las Brisas. South of town is **Playa Cuyutlán,** a black-sand beach on the open sea. Legend has it the great *ola verde* (green wave) rises some 30 feet each spring during the full moon. In reality, the surf is high in spring but not quite as big as the original ola verde, which took the tiny town of Cuyutlán by surprise in 1959.

Barra de Navidad and **San Patricio Melaque,** to the north, have popular beaches, good for surfing in the fall months. Palapa restaurants along the beach serve fresh fish. In Barra there are panga trips to a small island just offshore, where unbroken seashells are abundant. When the tide is low, it is possible to walk along the beach from Barra to Melaque, a distance of about 6 kilometers (almost 4 mi).

Dining

Manzanillo has some good restaurants, several with scenic views of the jungle and water that compensate for their lack of culinary excitement. As more shops appear along the Santiago–Manzanillo Road, so do restaurants that are geared toward tourists. Dress is usually casual but not sloppy (no bathing suits or bare feet), even in the more expensive restaurants, although in L'Récif and Legazpi women and men usually wear chic resort wear. Reservations are almost never necessary, but we have indicated those places that do accept them. Be aware that some restaurants, particularly in the hotels, add a 10%–15% service charge to your tab, as well as 10% tax.

Highly recommended restaurants are indicated by a star ★.

Category	Cost*
Expensive	over $15
Moderate	$10–$15
Inexpensive	under $10

*per person, excluding drinks, service, and sales tax (10%)

Expensive **Carlos 'n Charlie's Colima Bar Café.** Yet another in the Carlos Anderson chain of fun places, where the food is well prepared and abundant, the decor is a clutter of memorabilia and graffiti, and the accent is on having a good time. *Santiago–Manzanillo Rd., near Las Brisas, tel. 333/3–1150. Reservations advised. Dress: casual. AE, MC, V. Dinner only. Closed Sun.*

El Vaquero. The setting is reminiscent of a cowboys' saloon, and the emphasis is on beef, marinated and seasoned as *carne asada* or grilled as good old American steaks. Some steaks are served and priced by weight to satisfy the healthiest appetite. *Crucero Las Brisas, tel. 333/3–1654. Reservations not required. Dress: casual. MC, V.*

★ **Legazpi.** Manzanillo's only gourmet restaurant is at Las Hadas, and it is beautiful. The service is white-gloved perfection, but friendly rather than pretentious, and the food is decidedly elegant. The emphasis is on caviar and smoked salmon, consommés and bisques, seafoods and steaks with French sauces, and wonderful pastries. *Las Hadas, tel. 333/3–0000. Reservations accepted. Jacket and tie suggested. AE, DC, MC, V. Dinner only. Closed Wed. and Fri.*

★ **L'Récif.** Situated in a fantastic cliff-top setting far from town, L'Récif has a breathtaking view and a swimming pool—you can go for lunch, spend the afternoon sunning and swimming, then stay for dinner. The restaurant's owner is French, and the menu includes pâté with Armagnac, quail with muscat, and mango mousse. The Sunday brunch (served only in winter) is a must. *Off the Santiago–Manzanillo Rd., north of Santiago, at the sign for Vida del Mar, tel. 333/3–0624. Reservations accepted. Dress: casual. AE, MC, V.*

Moderate **La Bamba.** This patio and indoor restaurant along the highway ★ is considered by locals to be the best place for Mexican food, congenial company, and soft music. *Santiago–Manzanillo Rd., tel. 333/3–1930. Reservations accepted. Dress: casual. AE, MC, V. Dinner only.*

Manolo's. The lobster and shrimp are reasonably priced, and the Mexican dishes are tasty at this longtime favorite for great seafood dinners and steaks. *Santiago–Manzanillo Rd., tel. 333/3–0475. Reservations accepted. Dress: casual. AE, MC, V. Dinner only. Closed Sun.*

★ **Osteria Bugatti.** The most popular dinner spot near downtown, Bugatti's has a loyal following of locals and tourists who crave seafood prepared in the Italian manner and oysters Rockefeller. *Santiago–Manzanillo Rd., near Las Brisas, tel. 333/3–2999. Reservations advised. Dress: casual. DC, MC, V. Dinner only. Closed Sun.*

★ **Willy's.** Some people have been known to dine at Willy's every night of their stay in Manzanillo. The food is that good, and the owner, Jean François, is that personable and gracious. The French chef prepares delicious onion soup, a sublime bordelaise sauce, and decadent desserts. A guitarist strolls through the beachfront palapa's informal setting of woven-leather tables and chairs under a bamboo roof. *Crucero Las Brisas, tel. 333/3–0023. No reservations. Dress: casual. AE, MC, V. Dinner only.*

Inexpensive
★ **Juanito's.** This American hangout is owned by an American who married a local girl and settled in Manzanillo. It specializes in great burgers and fries, American breakfasts, barbecued ribs, and fried chicken. *Santiago–Manzanillo Rd., tel. 333/3–1388. No reservations. Dress: casual. No credit cards.*

★ **La Posada.** Breakfast here is an integral part of any Manzanillo experience. Pancakes, French toast, fried eggs, and bacon are made to order and served in the large *sala* (living room) facing the sea. The mood is casual. Sandwiches and drinks are served in the afternoon, but breakfast is your best bet. *La Posada, Las Brisas, tel. 333/3–1899. No reservations. Dress: casual. MC, V.*

Marbella. *Cabrito* (roast kid) and paella are the specialties at this cozy, no-frills place, but you may also choose from a variety of international dishes. *Parador Marbella, tel. 333/3–1103. Reservations not required. Dress: casual. MC, V.*

Pancho's. A popular spot packed with fishing nets, seashells, caged parrots, and beer-drinking merrymakers, it serves fresh fish that pulls people in and keeps them coming back. *Av. Barra de Navidad, #53, tel. 333/7–0176. Reservations accepted. Dress: casual. No credit cards.*

Pirámide. This palapa restaurant at the Club Nautico Hotel is set a few steps above the sand, has a TV over the bar playing sports or soap operas, and is a good shady spot for a mid-afternoon break. Hot dogs and hamburgers are served in addition to the standards. *Madero 1, Melaque, tel. 333/7–0239. No reservations. Dress: casual. AE, MC, V.*

Lodging

Lodging in Manzanillo was at one time a bargain, but no more. The hotels you might once have booked for $10 or so a night now cost $25 or more, and budget travelers usually either stay in downtown's few remaining hotels or head to the towns of Barra de Navidad and Melaque. As with the rest of the Pacific coast, Manzanillo is undergoing a building boom. The resorts are spread out along the Santiago–Manzanillo Road.

Most hotels raise their rates for the December–April high season; the best prices are during the rainy season from July through September. Price categories are based on high-season standards—expect to pay 25% less during the off-season.

Highly recommended lodgings are indicated by a star ★.

Category	Cost*
Very Expensive	over $200
Expensive	$120–$200
Moderate	$35–$100
Inexpensive	under $35

*All prices are for a standard double room; excluding 10% tax.

Very Expensive
★ **Las Hadas.** Though Antenor is long gone, Las Hadas is still something to marvel at. A member of the Leading Hotels of the

World, Las Hadas is Manzanillo's premier resort. It is the kind of place where vacationers are content to check in and stay put. Thick, padded lounge chairs and curtained cabanas surround the waterfall and pool; on the beach, bathers rest in the shade under white Arabian-style tents. Some of Manzanillo's nicest shops are clustered in the resort's Plaza de Doña Albina and at Marina Las Hadas, next door. *Santiago Peninsula, off the Santiago–Manzanillo Rd., tel. 333/3–0000 or 800/228–3000. 220 rooms and 41 suites with bath. Facilities: pools, beach, 4 restaurants, 5 bars, golf course, 10 tennis courts, marina, shops, beauty parlor, massage, travel agency, disco, theme parties. AE, DC, MC, V.*

Expensive   **Club Maeva.** Families love the playgrounds and children's pools, small theater, tennis courts, and disco at this all-inclusive resort. The blue and white bungalows (with kitchenettes) are spread over a high hillside across the highway from the beach; a bridge crosses over the road to the water. *Santiago–Manzanillo Rd., at Playa Miramar, tel. 333/3–2223 or 800/GO–MAEVA. 514 rooms with bath. Facilities: beach access, 2 pools, waterslide (Super Maeva Splash), 12 tennis courts, several restaurants, disco. AE, MC, V.*

★ **Fiesta Mexicana.** This bright white five-story hotel stands out on the highway. It has a lovely central courtyard with a large swimming pool. The rooms have pretty wood-frame windows and comfortable bentwood lounges and are quieter on the ocean side. *Santiago–Manzanillo Rd., in Playa Azul, tel. 333/3–2180. 185 rooms with bath. Facilities: pool, beach, restaurant, bar, disco, piano bar, shops, tour desk. AE, MC, V.*

Roca Del Mar. This is a condominium complex of two rows of terraced apartments on the beach. The apartments (each is furnished differently) have full kitchens and living rooms, two bedrooms and two baths, and balconies. The apartments run about $100 per night but can easily accommodate four persons. *Las Brisas, tel. 333/3–2950. 39 units with bath. Facilities: pool, beach. MC, V.*

Sierra. Manzanillo's newest hotel is a somewhat overbearing 20-story giant with white-stucco walls and a red-tile roof. Most of the 351 rooms and suites have private balconies and a view of the bay. A large free-form pool, four tennis courts, and several bars and restaurants round out the property. Light wood and pastel colors dominate the pleasant but uninspired decor. *Avenida de la Audiencia, tel. 333/3–2000. 351 rooms and suites. Facilities: beach, pool, 4 tennis courts, restaurants, bars. AE, DC, MC, V.*

Moderate   **Club Santiago Tenisol.** This condominium complex features villas, apartments, and studios in a neighborhood setting. The view toward Santiago Peninsula and Manzanillo is lovely at night, and the beach, one of the most popular, is active all day. *Playa Santiago, tel. 333/3–0413 or 303/841–7099. 60 rooms with bath. Facilities: 2 mi of beach, restaurant, bar, 9-hole golf course. AE, MC, V.*

★ **La Posada.** This "passionate pink" hotel has been a hangout for North Americans since 1957. With only 24 rooms, most guests get to know each other well, mingling in the *sala*, a large living/dining room with a communal coffee pot. Rooms are comfortable and simple; old iron keys work the antique locks. Tipping of individual employees is discouraged; the proprietor suggests that you leave a sum equal to 10% of your final tab in the tip box by the coffee urn. *Las Brisas, tel. 333/3–1899. 24 rooms with bath. Facilities: pool, beach, bar, restaurant. MC, V.*

★ **Plaza Las Glorias.** Situated in the center of the Santiago Peninsula, Las Glorias has a lovely setting above the golf course. Rooms are spacious and comfortable, with plush white upholstered couches and chairs, firm mattresses, and glass and wood tables and dining chairs. *Av. Tesoro off the Las Hadas Rd., tel. 333/3–0440; reservations in the U.S., tel. 800/456–5000. 85 one-bedroom villas. Facilities: pool, restaurant, bar, use of Las Hadas beach, access to the Las Hadas golf course, tennis courts. AE, MC, V.*

Inexpensive **Hotel Colonial.** This was once the grandest hotel in Manzanillo. Although the Colonial has gone downhill since its heyday, it's still the best place to stay in downtown, a block away from the noise of the plaza. *Av. México 100, tel. 333/2–1080. 38 rooms with bath. Only some of the units have air-conditioning. Facilities: restaurant, bar. MC, V.*

Parador Marbella. This hotel is one of the few moderately priced places on the beach. The best rooms are on the ocean; each has a tiny balcony under the palms. The furnishings are plain and mismatched—pink sheets contrast with brown and rust bedspreads and red and yellow plastic flowers on the nightstand. *Santiago–Manzanillo Rd., Km 9.5, tel. 333/3–1103. 60 rooms with bath. Facilities: pool, restaurant, bar. MC, V.*

Nightlife

During the high season, there is nightlife at two discos on the Santiago–Manzanillo Road—**Oui** (tel. 333/32333) and **Enjoy** (tel. 333/32839)—and at **Cartouche** (tel. 333/3–000) at Las Hadas. The **Legazpi** (tel. 333/3–000) piano bar at Las Hadas is also a good spot for a nightcap. At **Bugatti's** (tel. 333/32929), music for dancing runs from 8 PM to midnight. **VOG** (tel. 333/31875) is a new disco that may be worth a visit.

Guaymas and Sonora

Sonora, Mexico's second-largest, second-richest state, is a vacationland with its own band of devoted followers, many from Arizona, just across the border, who use the coast of Sonora as their beach playground.

Most enter the state at Nogales, a riotous border town where shopping for Mexican handicrafts is the major draw. Mexico Highway 15 begins here, running inland through dry, barren desert terrain to Hermosillo, the capital of Sonora, where the first hint of the green tropics is seen. The landscape becomes brown once again as you head south to Guaymas, a resort on the Gulf of California, also called the Sea of Cortés, 418 kilometers (261 miles) south of the U.S.–Mexico border.

In 1540, Francisco Vázquez de Coronado, governor of the provinces to the south, was the first Spaniard to walk the plains of Sonora. More than a century later, Fray Eusebio Francisco Kino led a missionary expedition to Sonora and founded several towns in the state. For the next three centuries, no one paid much attention to Sonora, and it was not part of the Mexican territory that ended up under the American flag after the War of 1847. International squabbles over Sonora bloomed and faded away as the border became a haven for Arizona outlaws.

During the last quarter of the 19th century, Porfirio Díaz, dictator of Mexico for 30-odd years, moved to secure the state by settling it. For Don Porfirio, however, developing the region was a mistake—the men who overthrew him in the revolution came from Sonora. In fact, Mexico was ruled for almost a quarter of a century by the Sonora dynasty. The Mexican Revolution brought prosperity to Sonora.

Sonora continues to thrive. Its inhabitants have adopted the most modern farming techniques, growing enough wheat for Mexico and sending excess grain abroad. Route 2 leads into Sonora from Baja California. As you cross the Colorado River, you move from Pacific time to Mountain time. The highway hugs the border, and there are a number of crossing points.

The largest border town in Sonora is Nogales (adjacent to the U.S. town of Nogales, Arizona). For many years, liquor was the favored attraction. Folks from Phoenix and Tucson would load up the family and head down to the border, where Mom, Dad, and the kiddies each picked up a gallon. The law has since changed; and now only a quart per adult may be brought home duty-free. For a time Nogales suffered economically from this restriction, but the town has rebounded and does a lot of business as a point of entry. Winter fruit and vegetables exported to the United States cross the border at Nogales.

Below Nogales is Magdalena, where the grave of Father Kino was discovered in 1966. His remains are in a mausoleum outside Mission San Francisco Xavier, one of the 22 missions he founded. A million-dollar monument to the memory of this pioneer priest also stands here. To the northeast of Magdalena is Cananea, a mining center made famous by a Mexican song for its jail. Today, Sonora leads the nation in copper mining, its huge, open pits spewing out about 80% of Mexico's production.

Hermosillo (population about 600,000) is the capital of the state, a status it has held on and off since 1831. It is the seat of the state university and benefits from the cultural activities of that institution. Although the city's name, to those who know a bit of Spanish, sounds as if it means "little beauty," it actually honors José María González Hermosillo, one of the leaders in Mexico's War of Independence. Settled in 1742 by Captain Agustín de Vildosola and a contingent of 50 soldiers, Hermosillo was originally called Pitic, the Pima name for "the place where two rivers meet." A business center for the state of Sonora, Hermosillo is largely modern, but some lovely plazas and parks hark back to a more graceful post-colonial past.

Some 104 kilometers (65 miles) west of Hermosillo lies Kino Bay on the shore of the Sea of Cortés. The coast highway is excellent and the beaches are magnificent. For many years, Kino Bay was undiscovered except by the RV owners and others who sought the unspoiled and beautiful; but a great change has recently taken place. The area is a convenient distance south of Phoenix and Tucson and thus a good location for a series of fine condos that have been constructed for American owners.

Guaymas (population 225,000), about 135 kilometers (83 miles) south of Hermosillo (and Kino Bay), is an active port where visitors come to do some serious fishing. The port was founded in 1771 and christened San Fernando de Guaymas. A nearby Jesuit mission was named San José de Guaymas. The city's off-the-beaten-path tranquillity may soon come under the heading of "what used to be." Government and private concerns have selected this area for intense economic development. Guaymas is slated to become an international "megaport," designed to compete with the Port of Los Angeles for Pacific Rim shipping traffic. In addition, currently inadequate tourist facilities are being expanded with a view toward turning Guaymas into a major resort with several deluxe hotels. Already there is a Club Med, a new Howard Johnson's resort, and the San Carlos Country Club, which has an 18-hole golf course, a dozen tennis courts, and two swimming pools. (Hotels can arrange for temporary memberships so guests can use country-club facilities.) It is hoped that plans will also include the provision of some means of adequate public transportation.

South of Guaymas, Route 15 continues toward Mazatlán by way of Ciudad Obregón and Navojoa. Obregón is an ultramodern agricultural center. Alamos is less than an hour from Obregón and is the most authentic colonial-style town in Sonora, such a gem that it has been declared a national monument. A Jesuit mission was founded here in 1630, but the boom really started with the discovery of silver in the 1780s. The church dates to this era; the mint was built in the 19th century. Take a look at the paintings on the ceiling of the kiosk in the plaza in front of the church. Alamos's second claim to fame is as the original home of the Mexican jumping bean (caused by a hyperactive larva).

Important Addresses and Numbers

Hermosillo There is a **tourist information office** at the Palacio Administrative (Calles Tehauntapec and Comonfort, tel. 62/14–73–99 or 800/4–SONORA from the U.S.).

Emergencies **Police** (tel. 62/16–15–64), **Red Cross** (tel. 62/14–07–69), **Hospital** (tel. 62/12–18–70).

U.S. Consulate The consulate is on Calle Monterrey, in back of the Hotel Calinda (tel. 62/17–26–13 and 17–23–75 [emergencies]).

Guaymas **Tourist Information** is on Avenida 22, behind the Palacio Municipal (tel. 622/4–2932).

Emergencies **Police** (tel. 622/2–0030), **Red Cross** (tel. 622/2–0879), **Hospital** (tel. 622/2–0122).

Arriving and Departing By Plane

Airport and **Aeroméxico** (tel. 800/257–6639) has daily flights from Tucson,
Airlines Arizona, to Hermosillo ($59 one way) and to Guaymas ($80 one way), and flights on Sunday, Monday, and Wednesday from Los Angeles to Hermosillo ($180 one way). There are direct flights from Guaymas to Guadalajara, La Paz, and Tijuana; from Hermosillo to Chihuahua, Ciudad Obregón, Los Mochis, Guadalajara, and Tijuana. Connections to other destinations may be made from these points. All of these flights are either on **Mexicana** (tel. 800/531–7921) or **Aeroméxico.**

Arriving and Departing by Car, Train, and Bus

By Car Many visitors to Sonora and Guaymas travel by car from Tucson via I–19 and Mexico 15. The highways are paved and quite good but are best driven during the day. Highway 15 is now a divided four-lane highway, making the ride much quicker and easier than it used to be.

By Train The train arrives in Hermosillo daily from Nogales and Mexicali.

By Bus Frequent buses travel to Hermosillo and Guaymas from Nogales, Tijuana, and Mexicali, via **Tres Estrellas de Oro** and **Transportes de Sonora. Autobus Plus** (tel. 62/13–24–26 in Hermosillo) runs a deluxe air-conditioned coach daily from Nogales to Hermosillo (price around $10).

Getting Around

By far the easiest way is by automobile, either yours or a rented one. Guaymas and its beaches are particularly spread out, and the only convenient means of getting around is by automobile. Most hotels have car-rental agencies. Buses are frequent and inexpensive between towns; the train runs daily but is unreliable and scheduled at inconvenient hours. There is ferry service from Guaymas to Santa Rosalia on the Baja coast, leaving at 10 AM. The crossing takes about seven hours and returns on the same day at 11 PM. At this time, management of the ferry is changing, and schedules are erratic. Check with the tourism office (tel. 622/4–2932) for the latest information and schedule. Cars can be shipped on the ferry; reserve at least 3 days in advance.

By Rental Car *Hermosillo* Car-rental agencies include **Hertz** (Bds. Rodriguez and Tamaulipas, tel. 62/14–85–00 and 62/12–07–35) and, across the street, **Budget** (tel. 62/14–30–33).

Guaymas Here the agencies to contact are **Budget** (tel. 622/2–1450) and **Hertz** (tel. 622/2–1000), both on the main highway.

Exploring Sonora

Hermosillo Although Hermosillo is usually just considered a jumping-off point for Kino Bay or Guaymas, it has a number of attractions in its own right, as well as the best accommodations and restaurants in the area. The city's main boulevard is lined with monuments to Sonora's famous sons: Adolfo de la Huerta, Alvaro Obregón, Plutarco Elías Calles, and Abelardo Rodríguez (after whom the boulevard is named), all presidents of the state after the revolution. At the center of town, the **Plaza Zaragoza** boasts the impressive Catedrál de San Agustín (1878), recently regilded at great expense. Across from the cathedral is the Palacío de Gobierno del L'Estado, its graceful courtyard surrounded by somewhat disjunctive modern murals depicting Sonoran history, and between the two buildings sits an ornate Victorian gazebo. On the south edge of town, the **Plaza de los Tres Pueblos** marks the original settlement.

Two museums are worth a visit: overlooking the city, on the Cerro la Campana (Hill of Bells), the **Museo de Sonora,** a former penetentiary, now hosting a variety of regional history displays; and the **Museo de la Universidad de Sonora** (on Bds. Luis Encinas and Rosales), with interesting exhibits of pre-Columbian artifacts. *Both museums are open Wed.–Sun., 9–3.*

Kino Bay An interesting trip from Kino Bay is a run across the narrow channel to Isla del Tiburón (Shark Island). The island is being developed into one of the finest wildlife and game refuges in

North America. Special permits are needed to visit the island, but they are not hard to get; boatmen usually handle this chore for their passengers. Only the Seri Indians—for whom Isla del Tiburón is a traditional turtle-fishing ground—need no special permit. You might see some of these Indians at Kino Bay selling their fine ironwood carvings of animals. Though they have lost many of their traditions, some still conduct rituals for events such as a girl's arrival at puberty, the capture of a turtle, or the finishing of a fine basket. (Note: The Seris will request money if you take their picture. The polite way to handle this is to request permission and offer them a dollar or so before taking the photo.)

Guaymas One of the great attractions in Guaymas is its beauty. In many of Mexico's ports, it can be said that the mountains come down to meet the sea, but at Guaymas, both the mountains and the desert abut the water. The clear air and the sun striking the mountains provide panoramas of striking, ever-changing beauty.

Guaymas has not one bay but two: Bacochibampo and San Carlos. San Carlos has beaches, many white adobe homes owned by retired Americans, a marina with a good number of yachts, a country club, and a Club Med. From Bacochibampo boats set out to catch marlin, yellowtail, red snapper, sea bass, and sailfish. In the backcountry, hunters go after deer, duck, and dove. Higher up in the hills, they track coyotes and mountain lions.

Guaymas Marina, a port in the Sea of Cortés with security dock facilities and electricity, is upgrading and expanding its facilities. Fishing boats may be rented for $100–$200 a day. Smaller outboards for waterskiing, fishing, or pleasure jaunts are also available.

Shopping

Nogales is Sonora's best shopping area, with a wide selection of handicrafts, furnishings, and jewelry. **El Zarape Curios** (Av. Obregón 161) specializes in sterling silver jewelry and designer clothing. For upscale imports, particularly French perfumes, try **Mickey's** (Av. Obregón 128), **Via Veneto** (Avds. Obregón and Aguirre), and **Versailles** (Av. Obregón 111). **Continental Curios** (Av. Obregón 98) is a large department store with a wide selection of *rebozos* (shawls), appliquéd and embroidered clothing, hand-blown glassware, and leather huaraches. **El Changarro** (Calle Elías 93) specializes in high-quality furniture, antiques, pottery, and handwoven rugs. The selection of handicrafts is less abundant as you travel farther south in Sonora. Aside from *charro* (Mexican cowboy) items in Hermosillo, the best crafts may be bought from tourist-oriented shops in San Carlos: **Lourdes Gift Shop,** at the entrance to Hotel Posada San Carlos; **Sagitario's Gift Shop,** in front of the entrance to the San Carlos Country Club; **El Pescador Curios,** at the Plaza Comercial La Mar; and **La Casita,** at the Plaza San Carlos.

Sports

Diving **San Carlos Diving Center** (Apdo. 655, San Carlos, tel. 622/6–0049), on the main street of San Carlos, has diving excursions in the Sea of Cortés.

Fishing **Navagentes de Cortez** (Plaza Bahia 5 and 6, tel. 622/6–0608 or 602/885–9848 in Tucson) offers deep-sea fishing and diving charters in San Carlos Bay. Other smaller outfitters have boats for rent in the bay.

Hunting Hunting for birds (duck, dove, and pigeon) and for deer draws an increasing number of Americans to Sonora every winter. The bird season is from October through March, and deer season is during November and December. Hunting is not permitted without a Mexican guide; a reliable one in Hermosillo is Alberto Noriega at **Sonora Outfitters** (Aguascalientes 132, tel. 62/14–10–11 or 62/14–03–30). In Guaymas, contact **Solimar Hunting Adventures** (c/o Hotel Armida, Carraterra Internacional Salida Norte, tel. 622/4–3035).

Beaches

All the main beaches of the state have paved access roads. There are hotels and restaurants at San Carlos and in Guaymas, in Puerto Peñasco, and at Kino Bay. Miles and miles of secluded beaches run along the Sea of Cortés, but access is difficult and there are no facilities.

Dining

Category	Cost*
Expensive	over $10
Moderate	$8–$10
Inexpensive	under $8

*per person excluding drinks, service, and sales tax (10%)

Guaymas/ San Carlos **Del Mar.** On the main street of town, this place does surf and turf Guaymas style. A series of small dining rooms with beamed ceilings and tiled floors are separated by bricked arches, from which hang fishing nets and assorted flotsam and jetsam. The fish Santo Domingo (broiled local bass with mushrooms, green peppers, and melted cheese) is popular, as is the mixed seafood grill. *Avenida Serdan 17, tel. 622/2–4650. Reservations accepted. Dress: casual. AE, MC, V. Expensive.*

El Paradise. This small restaurant in town features seafood. Fresh fish is prepared in several ways but is best simply grilled with oil and garlic. *Abelardo Rodríguez 20, Guaymas, tel. 622/ 2–1181. No reservations. Dress: casual. No credit cards. Moderate.*

Rosa's Cantina. Picnic tables fill two large dining rooms where diners feast on ample breakfasts of eggs with *chorizo* (sausage) or *huevos rancheros* (Mexican-style eggs). The tortilla soup is great for lunch or dinner. *Carreterra San Carlos, no phone. No reservations. Dress: casual. No credit cards. Inexpensive.*

Hermosillo **La Siesta.** A family-run inn, La Siesta is known for its fine cuts of Sonoran beef. *Bd. Kino Norte, no phone. No reservations. Dress: casual. MC, V. Expensive.*

Xochimilco. A friendly place popular with locals and regulars visiting from across the border, serving typical Sonoran dishes. *Av. Obregón 5, tel. 62/13–34–84. No reservations. Dress: casual. AE, MC, V. Expensive.*

Chalet de Guitarra. A small, intimate restaurant specializing in pasta and Italian dishes. *Bd. Kino at Villareal, tel. 62/14–91–41. Reservations accepted. Dress: casual. AE, MC, V. Moderate.*

Hotel Bugambilia Restaurant. A small dining room with beamed ceilings and red-checked tablecloths, this cheerful place serves excellent tortilla soup and Mexican-style veal cutlets. *Blvd. Kino 712, tel. 62/14–50–50. Dress: casual. No reservations. AE, MC, V. Moderate.*

Kino Bay   **El Pargo Rojo.** As befits a restaurant near the sea, this plain but friendly dining room has a nautical motif. Entrées include an excellent *sopa de marisco* (seafood soup) and fresh flounder stuffed with clams, scallops, and shrimp. There's live music weekend nights. *Av. Mar de Cortez 1426, tel. 624/2–1232. Dress: casual. Reservations accepted. AE, MC, V. Expensive.*

Lodging

Category	Cost*
Very Expensive	over $100
Expensive	$50–$100
Moderate	$25–$50
Inexpensive	under $25

All costs are for a standard double room; excluding 10% tax.

Alamos   **Casa de los Tesoros.** This hotel, the House of Treasures, is a pic-
Expensive   turesque and romantic converted 18th-century convent. The rooms are former nuns' cells and have fireplaces, tiled baths, antique furnishings, and high-quality handicrafts on the walls. *Av. Obregón 10, tel. 622/8–0011. 14 rooms. Facilities: pool, shops, gardens, restaurant, bar, parking. MC, V.*

Guaymas/San   **Club Med Sonora Bay.** Although San Carlos is expanding rapid-
Carlos Bay   ly in its direction, this Club Med is still secluded from the main
Very Expensive   tourist area, its verdant 42-acre complex spread behind a large gate fronted by saguaro cactus. Accommodations are characteristically charming but plain, and the range of available activities is as great as one would expect from the chain. All meals, drinks, tips—and many sports, such as sailing and scuba diving—are included. It's worth paying extra for the dawn horseback ride to the foothills of the nearby Sierra Madres. *Playa de los Algodones, tel. 622/6–0176, 800/CLUB–MED for U.S. reservations. 375 rooms. Facilities: beach, pool, 2 saunas, 31 tennis courts, sailboats, Windsurfers, golf course, horseback riding, restaurant, bar. AE, MC, V.*

Howard Johnson's. Forget the familiar orange roofs: This huge structure, rising from San Carlos Bay en route to Club Med, is thoroughly, strikingly pink. Opened in February 1992. *Pasco Mar Bermejo, 4, Los Algodones, tel. 622/60777. 148 rooms, 17 suites. Facilities: 3 restaurants, 2 bars, night club, disco, 2 swimming pools, Jacuzzi, exercise room, video game room, tennis and volleyball courts, shops. AE, MC, V.*

Expensive   **La Posada de San Carlos.** You're paying for the view (in the case of the tower rooms) and proximity to the beach (for the bungalows), but don't expect luxury at this relatively pricey hotel—or even a phone in your room. All accommodations are large and cheerful, if somewhat oddly laid out. *San Carlos Bay, tel. 622/*

6–0015. 150 rooms. Facilities: beach, restaurant with live ma-
riachi music, bar, ramada bar, pool, parking, gardens, tennis,
golf, disco, shops, paddle boats. MC, V.

Playas de Cortés. This fine, older hotel, built in the colonial
style, is set amid lush gardens that lead down to the sea. The
rooms are furnished with hand-carved antiques and many have
fireplaces; unfortunately, accommodations are not kept up as
well as they might be. *2 mi off Bacochibampo Bay, tel. 622/4–*
0131 or 622/4–0191. 142 rooms. Facilities: restaurant, bar,
pool, shops, nightclub, parking, car rental, gardens, tennis,
water sports. MC, V.

Moderate **Fiesta San Carlos.** This small, well-maintained hotel on the bay
has mismatched furnishings but a comfortable feeling. *San*
Carlos Bay, tel. 622/6–0229. 33 rooms. Facilities: restaurant,
bar, pool, parking. MC, V.

Inexpensive **Las Playitas.** The best deal in town, this combination trailer
★ park/motel on Guaymas Bay has plain but characterful
rooms—with tinwork mirrors and beamed ceilings, opening
out onto a cobbled, bougainvillea-lined path—for $22 a night
($15 if you stay a week). Even if you don't sleep here, come out
for the lively, eclectically decorated restaurant and bar. The
food is good and inexpensive, but if you'd rather eat what you
caught that day, you can get it cooked up with trimmings added
for a small price. *Carraterra al Varadero Nacional, tel. 622/2–*
2727 and 622/2–2753. 29 bungalows with shower, 93 RV spaces.
Facilities: pool, pier, restaurant, bar, live weekend entertain-
ment. MC, V.

Shangri-La Beach Cottages. These modest cabanas by the
beach go for under $40 a night and can fit four (if you're a friend-
ly group). The cottages are near an RV park, which can be
noisy, but are air-conditioned and have comfortable beds. *San*
Carlos Bay, tel. 622/6–0235. 36 cottages. Facilities: beach,
pool, bar, restaurant, minimarket. MC, V.

Hermosillo **Calinda Comfort Inn.** Although there's nothing special about
Expensive this hotel chain, it is well managed and comfortable. *Rosales*
and Calle Morelia, tel. 62/17–23–96; reservations in the U.S.,
tel. 800/228–5151. 111 rooms. Facilities: restaurant, cafeteria,
bar, pool, garden, travel agency. AE, MC, V.

Holiday Inn. This full-service property is the largest in town
and popular among business travelers. The decor is predictable, but some rooms have excellent views and the beds are
large and firm. *369 Bd. Kino, tel. 62/15–11–12 or 62/15–18–20,*
800/HOLIDAY for U.S. reservations. 222 rooms. Facilities:
restaurant, cafeteria, lobby bar, pool, Jacuzzi, disco, shops,
video bar, tennis, travel agency, beauty parlor. AE, MC, V.

Valle Grande Pitic. Two-thirds of the attractive rooms in this
contemporary Spanish-style hotel look out on extensive, well-
kept gardens and a good-size pool. The staff, geared toward accommodating the many Mexican business travelers who stay
here, don't all speak English. *Blvd. Kino and Ramon Corral,*
tel. 62/14–45–70. 144 rooms with shower. Facilities: nightclub,
bar, restaurant, pool, direct-dial long distance, beauty parlor,
travel agent, gift shop. AE, MC, V.

Moderate **Kino.** One of the few places in town featuring a hot tub and sauna, the Kino has dark, somber furnishings in the rooms, but
bright, colorful gardens. *Piño Suárez 151, tel. 62/13–31–32.*
114 rooms. Facilities: restaurant, pool, hot tub, sauna. MC, V.

Monte Carlo. Set on a somewhat seedy downtown plaza, the

Monte Carlo has a good restaurant and bar. *Juárez and Sonora, tel. 62/12–08–53. 24 rooms. Facilities: restaurant, bar. AE, MC, V.*

San Andrés. Near the plaza and fairly well maintained, this hotel has somewhat unpredictable accommodations. Check a few rooms before choosing one, and test the mattresses—some are very thin and lumpy. *Oaxaca 14, downtown, tel. 62/17–40–99. 48 rooms. Facilities: restaurant. AE, MC, V.*

Inexpensive **Pima.** A small, fairly comfortable hotel with clean white rooms and hot showers, the Pima is among the best bargains in town. *Bd. Kino Norte, tel. 62/14–62–70. 32 rooms. No credit cards.*

Kino Bay **Posada del Mar.** The most pleasant property in Kino Bay, the
Moderate Posada is decorated mission-style, with folk art on the brick walls in the rooms and pretty gardens by the pool. *Mar de Cortéz and Creta, Box 132, tel. 62/42–01–55; in Hermosillo, tel. 62/ 18–12–05. 48 rooms. Facilities: beach, restaurant, bar, pool, gardens, parking. MC, V.*

Posada Santa Gemma. A good place for families, this hotel consists of two-story bungalows with fireplaces, full kitchens, and upstairs balconies overlooking the sea. *Bd. Mar de Cortez, tel. 624/4–5576. 14 bungalows, each with 2 bedrooms and kitchen. Facilities: beach, grocery store. MC, V.*

Nightlife

Guaymas/ Nightlife in Guaymas can be found at the following locales:
San Carlos **Xanadu,** a disco located at Malecón Malpica; **Bar El Yate,** a sports bar at the Marina San Carlos; **Casanova Discoteque,** at the Armida Hotel (Carraterra Internacional Salida Norte); **Charles Baby,** for the younger set, at Avenidas Serdan and Malecón; the **Playitas** bar (*see* Lodging, *above*) on weekends; and **Pappas Tappas,** on the main highway of San Carlos, a fun place with neon cacti.

Hermosillo Hermosillo is home to several lively night spots: **Bar Ali Baba** at the Plaza Pitic, Boulevards Kino and Roman Yocupicio, open daily 9–11 PM; **Disco Sonovision** at the Hotel San Alberto, open Thursday–Sunday 9 PM–2 AM; and **Blocky'O Disco,** Rodríguez at Aguascalientes, open nightly except Sunday.

6 The Copper Canyon: From Los Mochis to Chihuahua City

Introduction

By Edie Jarolim

Edie Jarolim is a free-lance writer currently living in Tucson, Arizona.

The magnificent series of gorges known collectively as the Copper Canyon (in Spanish, *Barranca del Cobre*) is the real hidden treasure of the Sierra Madre. Inaccessible to the casual visitor until 30 years ago and still largely uncharted, the canyons may now be explored by taking one of the most breathtaking rides in North America: The *Chihuahua al Pacífico* railroad whistles down 661 kilometers (410 miles) of track, crossing 86 tunnels and 35 bridges through rugged country as rich in history and culture as in physical beauty.

The five barrancas of the Sierra Tarahumara, as this portion of the Sierra Madre Occidental is known, are on the western edge of the Pacific "Ring of Fire." Formed by seismic and volcanic activity, which at the same time hurled a good quantity of the earth's buried mineral wealth to the surface, the canyons were carved over the millenia by the Urique, Septentrion, Batopilas, and Chinapas rivers and further defined by wind erosion. Totaling more than 1,452 kilometers (900 miles) in length and capable of enveloping four of the Arizona Grand Canyons, the gorges are nearly a mile deep and wide in places; the average height of the peaks is 8,000 feet, and some rise to more than 12,000 feet. Each of the five barrancas—Urique, Sinforosa, Batopilas, Guaynopas, and Copper—descends deeper than the Grand Canyon, Urique by nearly 1,500 feet.

The idea of building a rail line to cross this region was first conceived in 1872 by Albert C. Owen, an idealistic American socialist. Owen met with some success initially. More than 1,500 people came from the states to join him in Topolobampo, his utopian colony on the Mexican west coast, and in 1881 he obtained a concession from Mexican president General Manuel Gonzáles to build the railroad. Construction on the flat stretches near Los Mochis and Chihuahua presented no difficulties, but eventually the huge Sierra Madre mountains got in the way of Owen's dream, along with the scourge of typhoid and disillusionment within the community.

After Owen abandoned the project in 1893, it was taken up in 1900 by American railroad magnate and spiritualist Edward Arthur Stilwell. One of Stilwell's contractors in western Chihuahua was Pancho Villa, who ended up tearing up his own work during the Mexican revolution in order to impede government troop movements. By 1910, when the Mexican Revolution started, the Mexican government had taken charge of building the railroad line, but progress was very slow until 1940, when surveying of the difficult Sierra Madre stretch finally began in earnest. Some 90 years and more than $100 million after it started, the Ferrocarril Chihuahua al Pacífico was dedicated on November 23, 1961.

The rail line no longer starts at Topolobambo but at nearby Los Mochis. Chihuahua City, at the other end of the line, was established in 1709. Today Chihuahua, the capital of the state of that name and a prosperous economic center, derives its wealth from mining—the Spanish discovered silver in the region as early as 1649—as well as from ranching, agriculture, and lumber.

The Tarahumara Indians, who once occupied the entire state of Chihuahua, were not unaffected by the foreign activity in the area: They were forced to serve in the mines by the Spanish and on the railroad by the Mexicans and the Americans. The threat of slavery and the series of wars that began in the 1600s and continued to the 20th century forced them to retreat deeper and deeper into the canyons. Seminomadic, many roam the high plateaus of the Sierra Madre in summer and move down to the canyon floor in winter to live in stone cliff dwellings or hidden wooden houses. Numbering about 50,000 some 20 years ago, the Tarahumara population, ravaged by disease and poverty, is now estimated at approximately 20,000.

Essential Information

Important Addresses and Numbers

Tourist Information
Los Mochis

The **Oficina de Turismo** (tel. 681/2–76–10), located on Degollado and Cuauhtemoc, provides a variety of information to travelers.

Chihuahua

The **Government Tourist Office** (Av. Libertad and Calle 13, 2nd floor, tel. 14/16–24–36 or 14/15–91–24, ext. 106) has many informative brochures and a helpful, English-speaking staff. *Open weekdays 9–3.*

Emergencies
Los Mochis

Police (tel. 681/2–00–33); **Cruz Roja** (Red Cross) (Guillermo Prieto and Rosendo G. Castro, tel. 681/2–02–92).

Chihuahua

Two facilities for handling the injured or sick are **Clínica del Parque** (Calle de la Llave and Calle 12, tel. 14/15–74–11) and **Hospital del Centro** (Ojinaga 816, tel. 14/16–00–22).

Late-night Pharmacies
Los Mochis

Farmacia Tecolote (Av. Leyva, 326-sur, tel. 681/2–76–28 and Blv. Rosales, 379-1 sur, tel. 681/5–45–43) is open 24 hours per day.

Chihuahua

Chihuahua has an abundance of pharmacies with late-night service in the center of the city. **Farmacia Mendoza** (Calle Aldama 1901, tel. 14/16–44–14) is open 24 hours.

Money Exchange

Make sure to change money before you get into real barranca country: There are no banks in Cerocahui and Divisadero/Posada Barrancas, and no guarantee that the hotels in those places will have enough cash to accommodate you. A bank in the main plaza at Creel only transacts foreign exchanges from 10:30 AM to noon. Even in Los Mochis, banking hours are limited, for the most part, to weekdays between 9 AM and 1 PM; some banks reopen at 3 PM and a few are open Saturday morning. In Chihuahua, banks are open weekdays from 9 AM to 1:30 PM and from 3:30 to 7:30 PM, and Saturday from 9 to 1:30; the **Casa de Cambio Rachasa** (Calle Victoria 401) and **Rubarza** (Aldama 202A) both offer good exchange rates and quick service. In general, you're best off getting your pesos at the hotels in Los Mochis and Chihuahua; the exchange rate is slightly lower, but no commission is charged, and you won't have to spend a confusing half hour or more switching lines at the bank.

Guided Tours

Almost all of the larger hotels in Los Mochis and Chihuahua have in-house travel agencies that can arrange both city tours and tours of the Copper Canyon area, as well as hiking, hunting, and fishing expeditions. In Los Mochis, the Santa Anita and La Colinas hotels (*see* Lodging, *below*) offer city tours for about $17 per person; these take approximately 3½ to 4 hours and include a boat trip around Topolobampo Bay. In Chihuahua, independent travel agents include **Turismo Espectacular de México** (Victoria 1410, tel. 14/15–59–33); the American Express agent **Rojo y Casavantes** (Calle Vincent Guerrero 1207, tel. 14/12–60–30); and, particularly recommended, **Turismo Al Mar** (Av. Reforma 400, tel. 14/16–59–50 or 14/16–92–32). Half-day city tours for a minimum of two people average $10 per person; full-day van trips into Mennonite country run about $25 per person, with a minimum of six needed.

From the United States, the oldest and most reliable operator in the area is **Pan American Tours** (Box 9401, El Paso, TX 79984, tel. 915/778–5395 or 800/876–3942). Prices for tours between Los Mochis to Chihuahua, based on double occupancy and including train but not airfare, range from about $170 to $420 per person, depending on length of stay and number of stops made; some meals and all transfers are covered.

Arriving and Departing by Plane

Los Mochis **AeroCalifornia** (tel. 800/237–6225) has daily flights from Los Angeles to Los Mochis, and also flies every day from Tijuana, Mexico City, and Guadalajara. On **Aeroméxico** (tel. 800/237–6639) you can get to Los Mochis from Tucson and from Mexico City every day. **Leo López** (tel. 915/778–1022) departs from El Paso to Los Mochis via Chihuahua on Monday, Wednesday, and Friday.

Chihuahua **Leo López** flies to Chihuahua from El Paso daily. **Mexicana** (tel. 800/531–7921) has a daily direct flight from Dallas/Fort Worth, as well as a connecting flight from Guadalajara and Mexico City. **Aeroméxico** departs every day to Chihuahua from Tucson, with a plane change at Hermosillo; within Mexico, the airline has three daily flights to Chihuahua from Mexico City, two from Monterrey, one from Guadalajara, and one from Tijuana.

Arriving and Departing by Car, Train, Bus, and Boat

By Car Drive down to Los Mochis from Nogales on the Arizona border.
Los Mochis Mexico Highway 15, four lanes much of the way, will take you all the way there, a distance of 763 kilometers (474 miles).

Chihuahua Most U.S. visitors drive to Chihuahua via Mexico Highway 45 from the El Paso/Ciudad Juárez border, a distance of 375 kilometers (233 miles), or up from Mexico City, 1,440 kilometers (895 miles).

Copper Canyon Paved roads now connect Chihuahua to Creel: Take Mexico Highway 16 west to San Pedro, then State Highway 127 south to Creel. The 300-kilometer (186-mile) trip takes 3½ to 4 hours if the weather is good. This drive, through the pine forests of the Sierra Madre foothills, is more scenic than the railroad route via the plains area. Driving is a good option if you have an all-terrain vehicle, because there are many worthwhile, if difficult, excursions into the canyons from Creel. A new road from Chihuahua to Bahuichivo via Divisadero has recently been finished but an all-terrain vehicle is still advised. A route to Urique Canyon is also planned.

By Train The Ferrocarril Pacífico, which travels from Nogales to Guada-
Los Mochis lajara, stops at the San Blas (Sufragio) station between Los

Mochis and El Fuerte. Arriving at about 2 AM, it is not a viable option for most. But if you don't mind spending the night at a no-frills train station, you can pick up the *Chihuahua al Pacífico* train here the next morning at about 6:45.

Chihuahua The daily train that runs between Ciudad Juárez and Mexico City stops in Chihuahua at 10 PM and takes about 4½ hours. Fares vary; the best seats, *primera especial* or *servicio estrella*, cost about the same as the bus (*see* By Bus, *below*).

Copper Canyon A new luxury touring train makes a round-trip run from Nogales through the Copper Canyon area. From September through May, **Sierra Madre Express of Tucson** (Box 26381, Tucson, AZ 85726, tel. 602/747–0346 or 800/666–0346) offers eight-day, seven-night trips once or twice a month. Traveling on the same track as the *Chihuahua al Pacífico*, the train stops in Cerocahui, Posada Barrancas, and Creel. Prices are $2,190 per person, based on double occupancy.

By Bus The **Tres Estrellas de Oro, Transportes del Pacífico,** and **Norte**
Los Mochis **de Sonora** bus lines all leave every hour from Nogales to Los Mochis; with luck, the trip should take about 12 hours. The cost is approximately [TK]

Chihuahua The **Transportes de Norte, Chihuahuenses,** and **Omnibus de México** lines run clean, air-conditioned buses from Ciudad Juárez to Chihuahua; these leave approximately every 15 minutes from 7 AM to 8 PM. The cost for the trip, which takes about five hours, is approximately $10. Buses shuttle between El Paso and Ciudad Juárez every two hours; the price is $3.

By Boat The **Baja Express** (tel. 682/563–11 or 682/563–13 in La Paz) has catamaran service every day except Wednesday from La Paz to Topolobampo; it takes about four hours, and costs vary from $37 to $47. A slower ferry runs every day except Saturday; the trip takes about eight hours and costs about $11.

Getting Around

By Car Car companies in town include **Budget** (Leyva and Angel Flo-
Los Mochis res, behind the Santa Anita Hotel, tel. 681/5–83–00 or 681/5–84–00); **Hertz** (Leyva 167 Nte., at Callejón Narciso Mendoza, tel. 681/2–12–00), and **Aga** (Leyva and Callejón Municipal, tel. 681/2–53–02).

Chihuahua **Avis** (Av. Universidad 1703, tel. 14/14–19–99), **Hertz** (Av. Revolución 514, tel. 14/16–64–73), and **Budget** (Av. Independencia 1205, tel. 14/16–09–09) all have offices at the airport also.

By Taxi Taxis are easy to find, but not very cheap for long distances.
Los Mochis You're better off renting a car to Topolobampo. It costs about $13 to get to the airport from downtown Los Mochis.

Chihuahua Easy to find, taxis can be engaged at your hotel or hailed on the street. Since fares are negotiable, always agree on a price before entering the cab. You'll usually pay less if you speak Spanish.

By Train The Ferrocarril Chihuahua al Pacífico line runs two trains daily
Copper Canyon in each direction from Chihuahua and Los Mochis. The one designed for tourists, with plush seats and a bar and dining car, is called *El Tren Estrella*. Eastbound, this train departs from Los Mochis at 6 AM and arrives in Chihuahua 12 hours later; west-

bound, it departs from Chihuahua at 7 AM and arrives in Los Mochis around 7 PM (most of the time, but problems with the weather may cause long or short delays). Tickets can be purchased through almost any hotel in Los Mochis or Chihuahua or directly at the train station. The price is about $29 each way, but there's a 15% charge for any stopovers en route. These should be arranged at the time of ticket purchase. Reservations (tel. 14/12–22–84 or 14/15–77–56 in Chihuahua, tel. 681/57775 in Los Mochis) should be made at least a week in advance, especially in July and August and around Christmas and Easter.

The second-class train leaves an hour later from each terminus, but makes many stops and is scheduled to arrive 3½ hours later in both directions than the first-class train. While less comfortable, this train is a good way to meet the locals. Don't rely on served snacks—bring your own food. No reservations are needed; prices are approximately $8.50 each way.

It's possible to ship your car on the train, but it's not worth the expense and the bother. If you're driving down to Los Mochis, you're better off leaving your car there and taking the train round-trip. If you're coming via Chihuahua, however, you should consider driving to Creel and doing a round-trip from there (*see* Arriving and Departing by Car, *above*).

Exploring the Copper Canyon

Imagine visiting the Grand Canyon in the days before it was tamed by tourist facilities, and you'll have some sense of what a trip through the Copper Canyon will be like—for better and for worse. That is, with the opportunity to encounter a relatively untouched natural site come some of the attendant discomforts of the rustic experience. But if you are careful in your choice of time to visit and are properly prepared, the trip's myriad rewards should far outstrip any temporary inconveniences.

You'll see some beautiful scenery if you just ride the railroad, including a panoramic look at Copper Canyon during a 15-minute stop at Divisadero, but you'll only experience a fraction of what the canyons have to offer if you don't get off the train. If possible, plan on a night in Cerocahui (Bahuichivo stop), one at Posado/Barrancas or Divisadero (the train stations are 10 minutes apart from each other), and one or two at Creel.

About 60% of the people who visit the Copper Canyon come via Los Mochis, which is the easiest route if you're traveling from California or Arizona. It's also by far the most desirable route if you come in winter, because some of the best scenery is to be seen at the western end of the ride and you're likely to miss it if you approach Los Mochis in the evening. Your choice of route matters less in the extended daylight hours of summer.

In general, winter—December through February—is not the best time to come; many of the hotels in the region are inadequately prepared for the cold, and the minor rainy season in January renders some of the roads for side excursions impassable. The warm months are May through September; the rainy season, June through September, brings precipitation for a short period every day, but this shouldn't interfere with your enjoyment in any way. It's temperate in the highlands during the summer; if you're planning to hike down into the canyons, however, remember that the deeper you go, the hotter it'll get. The best months to visit are October and November, when the weather is still warm and rains have brought out all the colors in the Sierra Tarahumara.

Many people visit during Christmas and Easter, specifically to see the Tarahumara celebrations of those holidays. Closely related to the Pima Indians of southern Arizona, the Tarahumara are renowned for their running ability. (*Tarahumara* is a Spanish corruption of *Raramuri,* which means "running people" in their language; it is said that in earlier times they survived as hunters by chasing deer to the point of collapse.) Around Christmas, Easter, and other religious feast days, the Tarahumara compete in races, which can last up to three days. The men run in small groups, kicking a wooden ball for a distance of 161 kilometers (100 miles) or more. On these and other feast days, tribal elders consume peyote or *tesguino,* a sacred fermented corn liquor.

Numbers in the margin correspond to points of interest on the Copper Canyon map.

❶ The first stop on the western end of the rail line, **Los Mochis** (population about 300,000) is an agricultural boomtown; its location near the harbor at Topolobampo and the railroad makes it the export center of the state of Sinaloa, which produces many of Mexico's basic crops. Visitors can tour Benjamin Johnston's sugar refinery, the Ingenio Azucarero, around which the town grew. Near Johnston's estate you can still see the American colony, the group of brick bungalows that housed his associates, as well as a worker's hostel and the country club. Not far away, on Calles Obregón and Mina, the Museo Regional de Los Mochis has rotating exhibits of paintings and crafts by local artists, and the public library next door displays pictures of the early days of the city.

Cottonwood trees and bougainvillea line the highway from Los Mochis to **Topolobampo;** on both sides of the road are fields planted with crops ranging from sugar cane to marigolds and mangos (36 varieties are produced here). Once the site of Albert Owen's utopian colony and the center of the railroad building activity in the area, Topolobampo is now considered a suburb of Los Mochis, 15 minutes away. A huge tuna-packing factory sits at the entrance to the bay, and local fisherman—90% of the population—ply the harbor in small shrimp boats; they compete for their catch with the many dolphins that cavort in the bay. Isla El Farallón, just off the coast, is a breeding ground for the sea lions that gave the town its name: In the language of the Mayo Indians who once dominated the area, Topolobampo means "watering place of the sea lions."

❷ Eighty kilometers (50 miles) east of Los Mochis, **El Fuerte** is a small colonial town, named after the 17th-century fort built by the Spaniards to protect against attacks by the local Mayo, Sinaloa, Zuaque, and Tehueco Indians. Originally called San Juan de Carapoa, it was founded in 1564 by Spanish conquistador Don Francisco de Ibarra and a small group of soldiers. Located on the central El Camino Real route, El Fuerte was at one time the frontier outpost from which the Spanish set out to explore and settle New Mexico and California. For three centuries, it was also a major trading post for gold and silver miners from the nearby Sierras and the most important commercial and farming center of the area; it was chosen as Sinaloa's capital in 1824 and remained so for several years. Some intact colonial mansions remain in what is now a rather sleepy town of 25,000; one of the best is the Hotel Posada del Hidalgo (*see* Lodging, *below*). Most of El Fuerte's historic houses are set off the cobblestone streets leading from the central plaza; a number of them have been converted into government offices.

If you want to catch an extra hour and a half of sleep, spend the night at El Fuerte and board the train at 7:30 AM. As the train ascends almost 1,800 meters (5,906 feet) into the mountains from here to Bahuichivo, it passes through 54 tunnels and over 24 bridges, including the longest and highest ones of the rail system. The scenery shifts from Sinaloan thornforest, with cactus and scrublike vegetation, to the pools, cascades, and tropical trees of the Rio Septentrion canyon, to the oak and pine forest that begins to take over past Temoris, where a plaque marks the dedication of the railroad by President López Mateos in 1961.

A free bus operated by the Hotel Misión meets the train at the Bahuichivo stop to take visitors for a 45-minute ride up a bumpy, unpaved road to the quiet mountain village of **Cerocahui**. This is a good place to get a sense of how people live in the canyon area. Next door to the hotel is a Jesuit mission, established around 1690 by Juan María de Salvatierra, who proselytized widely in the region; it is said that because the Tarahumara were the most difficult Indians to convert, he considered this mission his favorite among the many he founded. Nearby, the church operates a boarding school for Tarahumara children. Visitors can hike or ride horses to two nearby waterfalls and to a silver mine (closed for the last three years), but the prime reason to come to Cerocahui is for the views the area affords of Urique Canyon. A kidney-crunching bus ride offered by the hotel (about four hours round-trip) will take you up to the Cerro del Gallego lookout point where, amid mountains spread against the horizon, you can make out the Urique River and the town of Urique, a slim thread and a dot on the distant canyon bottom. On the way up you'll stop at a Tarahumara cave, where Indian women sell baskets, and at a nearby shrine to the Virgin.

For the most comfort in the most spectacular setting on the route, get off at the Posada Barrancas or the Divisadero stop. **④** There's little to do in **Divisadero,** a postage stamp of a place on the Continental Divide, but it's impossible to remain unastounded by the vistas of the Copper Canyon, said to have derived its name from the facts that copper used to be mined in the area and that the canyon turns copper-colored at sunset. You can also glimpse a bit of the distant Urique and Tararechua canyons from here. A popular excursion, which takes about four hours whether you're traveling on two feet or on horseback, is a visit to Bacajipare, a Tarahumara village.

⑤ Nestled in pine-covered mountains, **Creel** is a rather charmless mining and logging town that grew up around the railroad station. It's easy to imagine American frontier towns at the turn of the century looking like Creel—without, of course, the backpacking contingent that makes this town its base. A cluster of small hotels here offers tours to the many points of interest in the area. It's a short drive from Creel to Cusarare, where an impressive waterfall can be reached via an easy hike through a lovely piñon forest, and to the Valley of the Mushrooms, with its strange volcanic rock formations; along the way you'll pass Lake Arareco and a 300-year-old mission built by the Jesuits for the Tarahumara. If the unpaved roads are passable, consider taking the longer trips to the Recohuata Hot Springs, a fairly strenuous hike down from the rim of the Tararecua Canyon, and to El Tejaban, a spectacular overlook into the Copper Canyon. It's a five-hour drive along rough roads to Basaseachic Falls, and you'll have to stay overnight if you want to visit Batopilas (*see* Off the Beaten Track, *below*), but several worthwhile day trips en route to the latter include Basihuare, where huge vertical outcroppings of rock are crossed with wide horizontal bands of color; the Urique Canyon overlook, affording another perspective of that barranca than the one from Cerocahui; and La Bufa, site of a former Spanish silver mine.

⑥ After the peaceful Copper Canyon, the sprawling city of **Chihuahua,** with nearly 1 million inhabitants, may come as a bit of a jolt. Two of the most famous figures in Mexico's revolutionary wars are closely tied to the city. Father Miguel Hidalgo, the father of Mexican independence, and his coconspirators were executed by the Spanish here in 1811. And Chihuahua was home to General Pancho Villa, whose revolutionary army, the División del Norte (Army of the North), was decisive in overthrowing dictator Porfirio Díaz in 1910 and securing victory in the ensuing civil war. In addition, Benito Juárez, known as the Abraham Lincoln of Mexico, made Chihuahua his base in 1865 during the French invasion of the country.

Whatever you do, don't miss a visit to the Museo Histórico de la Revolución en el Estado de Chihuahua, better known as **Pancho Villa's House.** Villa lived in this home, completed in 1909, with his second wife, Luz Corral (he had three wives, none of whom he divorced). She stayed here until her death on June 6, 1981, willing the residence to the government, which restored it as a national museum. The 50 small rooms that used to board Villa's bodyguards have been converted into exhibition rooms displaying artifacts of Chihuahua's cultural and revolutionary history. Parked outside the museum's courtyard is the bullet-ridden 1919 Dodge in which Villa was assassinated in 1923 at the age of 45. *Calle Décima 3014, tel. 14/16–29–58. Admission: 2,000 pesos. Open daily 10–1 and 3–7.*

Another must see is the **Catedral** on the central Plaza de la Constitución. Construction on this beautiful baroque structure was started by the Jesuits in 1726, but not completed until 1825 because of Indian uprisings in the area. The exterior is made out of the pinkish limestone quarried in this region; inside, the opulent church has altars made of Carrera marble, a 24-karat solid gold ceiling, a beautiful cedar-and-brass carved depiction of St. Peter and St. Paul, and a huge German-made organ. In the back of the cathedral, the Museum of Sacred Art displays the work of seven local artists of the 18th-century Mexican Baroque tradition, as well as commemorations of the 1990 visit of Pope John Paul II. *Admission: 1,500 pesos. Open weekdays 10–2 and 4–6.*

At the nearby Plaza Hidalgo, the **Palacio del Gobierno** (State Capitol) was built by the Jesuits as a convent in 1882. Converted into government offices in 1891, it was destroyed by a fire in the early 1940s and rebuilt in 1947. Murals around the patio by artist Pino Mora depict famous episodes from the history of the state of Chihuahua; a plaque commemorates the spot where Father Hidalgo was shot on the morning of July 30, 1811. *Open daily 8–6.*

Around the corner from the entrance to the Palacio del Gobierno, on Calle Libertad, the **Palacio Federal** (Federal Building) houses the city's main post office and telegraph office, as well as the dungeon where Hidalgo was imprisoned before he was executed by the Spanish; his pistols, traveler's trunk, crucifix, and reproductions of his letters are on display here. *Open daily 9–7.*

Also connected to the history of Father Hidalgo is the **Iglesia de San Francisco** (San Francisco Church), the oldest (1721) church built in Chihuahua that is still standing. Hidalgo's decapitated body was interred in the chapel of this simple church from 1811 to 1827, when it was sent to Mexico City (his head was publicly displayed for 10 years by Spanish Royalists in Guanajuato on the Alhóndiga de Granaditas (*see* Chapter 7).

Slightly outside the center of town but well worth a visit is the Cultural Museum of the University of Chihuahua, known as **Quinta Gameros.** This Art Nouveau mansion, with beautiful stained-glass windows, ornate carved wooden staircases, and Italian blown-glass chandeliers, was built in 1910 by Julio Corredor, a Columbian architect, for Manuel Gameros, a wealthy mining engineer. An eclectic collection includes European art from the 18th and 19th centuries, pottery of the local Paquime Indians, and artifacts of the nearby Mennonite community. Concerts, lectures, and exhibitions of local artists are also held here. *Calle Bolívar 401, tel. 14/12–38–34. Admission: 2,000 pesos. Open Tues.–Sun. 9–1 and 3:30–7.*

A restoration project has made the site of the town's original settlement, **Santa Eulalia,** particularly appealing. The 20-minute drive southeast of town is compensated by the colonial architecture and cobblestoned streets of this small town; the religious artwork in the 18th-century cathedral is noteworthy, and the Mesón de Santa Eulalia Restaurant owns a lovely spot.

Off the Beaten Track

Seventy-three kilometers (45 miles) northeast of Creel, but reached via an unpaved, winding road, the 806-foot **Basaseachic Falls** are the highest cascades in Mexico and the fourth-highest in North America.

A remote village of about 5,000 people, **Batopilas** was once the richest town in Mexico. On the bottom of Batopilas Canyon, 80 kilometers (50 miles) south of Creel, the city used to be part of the silver trade route that extended from Batopilas, where the silver was mined, to Alamos, where coins were minted, via the trade center of El Fuerte. At one point, it is said, Batopilas was the only city besides Mexico City to have electricity. Most of the buildings in town date from 1880 to 1910, the silver mine's last period of prosperity. Reached via a scenic 4-mile hike from Batopilas, the triple-domed "lost" cathedral, at least three centuries old, stands mysteriously isolated in the Satevo Valley. There are three modest posadas in Batopilas at which to spend the night (the María is the best of them), and at this writing a new hotel is being built by the company that owns the Copper Canyon Lodge (*see* Lodging, *below*). A local bus leaves from Creel to Batopilas once a week.

A rather anomalous experience in Mexico is a visit to the large **Mennonite community** (Campos Menonitas) in the town of Cuauhtemoc, about 105 kilometers (65 miles) west of Chihuahua. Approximately 20,000 Mennonites came to the San Antonio Valley in 1922 at the invitation of President Alvaro Obregón, who gave them the right to live freely and autonomously in return for farming the 100,000 hectares (247,000 acres) of land they purchased. Tours can be arranged either in Chihuahua or at the Tarahumara Inn in Cuauhtemoc.

Shopping

Tarahumara crafts, which provide the Indians with their only cash income, include lovely hand-woven baskets, made from palm leaves and pine bark; carved wooden dolls; crude pottery; brightly colored belts and sashes woven using backstrap looms; and wooden fiddles, sometimes with mask faces, from which the men produce haunting music. The Tarahumara, who are generally shy about talking with tourists, sell their wares throughout the Copper Canyon area; their prices are fair, so bargaining is unnecessary (as well as inappropriate). Baskets run from $1 for the smallest to about $15 for the largest. Tarahumara wares are sold at the market outside the train station at Divisadero and at a number of shops in Creel, the best one of which is **Artesanías Misión,** right off the central plaza.

In Chihuahua, **Mercado de Artesanías,** on Calle Victoria 506 across from the cathedral, sells everything from jewelry, candy, and T-shirts to crafts from all over the region. The small **gift shop at the Museo de Arte Popular** (Calle Reforma 5) has a good selection of items from all over Mexico, including many made by the Tarahumara.

Sports and Outdoor Activities

Hiking   Even the most experienced trekkers should enlist the help of local guides, who can be contacted through all the hotels in the area or through travel agents in Los Mochis and Chihuahua. Few adequate maps are available for even the so-called marked trails, and many of the better-worn routes into the canyon are made by the Tarahumara, whose prime concern is to get from one habitable area to the next rather than to get to the bottom.

The Copper Canyon is most accessible from Divisadero; trails range from easy rim walks to a 27-kilometer (17-mile) descent to the bottom, which takes seven or eight hours. If you're in Creel, a gentle and rewarding hike is the 5-kilometer (3-mile) walk from the Copper Canyon Lodge to the Cusarare Falls. More difficult but equally scenic are the treks down to Recohauta Hot Springs and to the base of Basaseachic Falls; both are about three hours round-trip.

Horseback Riding   All hotels in the canyon area can arrange for local guides with gentle horses. Most trips are not for couch potatoes, however. The trails into the canyon are badly defined and can be rocky as well as slippery if the weather is icy or wet; at rough spots, you might be asked to dismount and walk part of the way. A fairly easy and inexpensive ride is to the falls at Cerocahui, about two hours round-trip, including a half-hour hike at the end, where the trail is too narrow for the horses. From Divisadero, the trip to Bacajipare, a Tarahumara village in the Copper Canyon, affords stunning vistas; it's an exciting four-hour ride round-trip, not for the faint of heart.

Hunting and fishing   More than a million and a half game birds—quail, white-winged dove, duck, and geese—migrate to Sinaloa in the winter, making Los Mochis a magnet for hunters. Most of them either hire a guide—through their hotels—or stay at one of the hunting lodges outside Los Mochis, where guns, ammunition, and licenses are provided. Nearby Topolobampo attracts sportsmen who come to catch corbina, yellowtail, red snapper, and cabrilla, while El Fuerte serves as a base camp for those interested in fishing for black bass or hunting for trophy deer and javelina as well as birds.

Dining and Lodging

Dining

Along the Copper Canyon trail, you'll encounter rustic areas where there's no place besides the lodges to eat, and sophisticated culinary centers, like Chihuahua.

In Los Mochis and Topolobampo, your best bet is seafood. Restaurants tend to be inexpensive. At the hotels in Cerocahui and Divisadero/Posada Barrancas, food is included in the price of the room. Don't even think about dieting here: You'll get three freshly cooked, hearty meals a day, served family-style, often with meat courses and dessert at both lunch and dinner. There are a few more dining options in Creel, where, in addition to the hotel dining rooms, there are a number of inns along the town's main street, Avenida López Mateos; **La Cabana** and **Lupita** both offer good, inexpensive Mexican fare.

You'll have the most choice in Chihuahua. The state is a large producer of beef, so upscale steakhouses and places serving *carne asada* (charbroiled strips of marinated beef) abound, but a variety of Mexican specialties and seafood flown in from the coast is also available. Many of Chihuahua's well-appointed international restaurants are located in the Zona Dorada, on Calle Juárez starting from its intersection with Calle Colón.

Highly recommended restaurants are indicated by a star ★.

Category	Cost*
Expensive	over $20
Moderate	$10–20
Inexpensive	under $10

*per person, excluding drinks, service, and sales tax (10%)

Lodging

Accommodations in this area tend to fall into two categories: comfortable but characterless in the larger cities and charming but to varying degrees rustic in the smaller ones. In Cerocahui, Divisadero/Posada Barrancas, and Creel, all the hotels send buses or cars to meet the train; if you don't have a reservation, you'll have to make a quick decision and then hop on a vehicle sent out by the hotel of your choice. During the summer and around Christmas and Easter, it's important to book in advance. Rates for hotels in Cerocahui and Divisadero/Posada Barrancas all include meals.

Highly recommended lodgings are indicated by a star ★.

Category	Cost*
Very Expensive	over $100
Expensive	$65–$100
Moderate	$30–$65
Inexpensive	under $30

*All prices are for a standard double room, excluding 10% tax.

Cerocahui
Dining and Lodging

Hotel Misión. Part of the Balderrama chain—the Copper Canyon's equivalent of the Grand Canyon's Fred Harvey hotel empire—this is the only tourist accommodation in town. The main house, which looks like a combination ski lodge and hacienda, contains the hotel's office, small shops, dining room, bar, and lounge. In winter, guests huddle for warmth around two large fireplaces, the prime sources of heat and light: Cerocahui isn't wired for electricity, and the hotel uses its generator for only a few hours at night, generally from 7 to 9:30 PM. The plain but characterful rooms, with beamed ceilings and Spanish Colonial-style furnishings, are a pyromaniac's dream: They're equipped with fuel and matches for guests to light the wood-burning stove and a kerosene lamp for light. *Cerocahui (train stop: Bahuichivo; mailing address: Santa Anita Hotel, Box 159, Los Mochis, Sinaloa), tel. 681/5-7046, ext. 432, fax 681/2-0046. 30 rooms with bath. Facilities: gift shop, restaurant, bar, vineyard (which produces red and white wine sold at the hotel). AE, MC, V. Very Expensive.*

Chihuahua   **El Galeón.** Nautical almost to the point of inducing seasickness,
Dining   this upscale seafood restaurant serves steak and chicken as well as fish. Yachty details include a bell tower, rigging, and a pirates' deck; in the downstairs bar, which has live music on Tuesday through Saturday nights, fish swim behind simulated portholes. You can get everything here from seabass, conch, and eel (a specialty) to lobster; the *camarones a la plancha*, grilled jumbo shrimp served with rice pilaf and steamed vegetables, is a good choice. *Av. Juárez 3312 B, tel. 14/15-20-50. Reservations accepted. Jacket advised. AE, DC, MC, V. Expensive.*

★   **Club de Los Parados.** Thirty-seven years of Chihuahua's history have passed through the doors of this landmark restaurant, set in an adobe-style house that would seem more at home in New Mexico. It was started by Tony Vega, a wealthy cattle rancher who died two years ago, as a place for him to come with his fellow ranchers. The story goes that when they went out drinking, the one who sat (or fell) down first had to pick up the tab; Los Parados means "the standing ones." Excellently grilled steaks and chicken as well as tasty Mexican specialties are served in a large room, decorated in muted southwestern colors, with a wood-burning kiva fireplace; the *carne asada* (charbroiled strips of marinated beef) with guacamole is particularly good. A private dining room is lined with photographs of Tony Vega and all the important people in town, including native Chihuahuan Anthony Quinn. *Av. Juárez 3616, tel. 14/15-95-85. Reservations accepted. Dress: casual but neat. AE, V. Moderate.*

La Calesa. A large, dimly lit room with wood paneling and red tablecloths and curtains, this looks like the classic steakhouse it is. The onion soup and chile with *aserdo* (a local cheese) make good appetizers. The filet Mignon and ribeye steaks from the area are particularly recommended as entrées; try the former cooked in garlic with shrimp and mushrooms. The clubby bar has a good selection of wines and liquors. *Av. Juárez 3300, tel. 14/12-85-55 and 14/16-12-22. Reservations recommended for large groups. Dress: casual. AE, MC, V. Moderate.*

El Taquito. Three blocks south of the Palacio del Gobierno, this modest restaurant specializes in tacos and other typical Mexican dishes, although the dining room, with vines and black-and-white etchings of local scenes on the wall, looks somewhat Mediterranean. The chiles rellenos, enchiladas suizas, and chicken burritos with mole sauce are all good choices; you can get a bottle of sangria to accompany your meal for about $6. *Venustiano Carranza 1818, tel. 14/12-71-81. No reservations. Dress: informal. No credit cards. Inexpensive.*

La Parilla. A good place to take a break from downtown sightseeing, this fast-food place across the street from the Hotel San Francisco will delight dedicated carnivores. After the waiter hands you an order form/menu on which you mark your choice, he'll come over with a tray bearing the cuts of meat being offered that day. A strolling guitarist makes the rounds of this plain, white-walled room with plastic tables and chairs and an open grill in the back. The *menu turístico* includes steak with mashed potatoes, soup, and salad for about $6.50; you'll get your own grill if you order the house special, *parillados*, a sirloin platter served with guacamole and chile sauces as well as potatoes. *Victoria 420, tel. 14/50–58–56. No reservations. Dress: informal. No credit cards. Inexpensive.*

Lodging
★
Villa Suites. This new (1988) property combines comfort, style, and convenience: Ten minutes from the downtown sights, but set off in a quiet area, this is the first all-suite hotel in Chihuahua. Each of the rooms, tastefully decorated in contemporary style with a green or blue and beige color scheme, has a kitchenette with stove, dishwasher, and coffeemaker, as well as a VCR and an exercycle. A complimentary Continental breakfast buffet is served at the Clubhouse, which also houses the hotel's indoor pool, Jacuzzi, and exercise equipment. Eager to accommodate the many American business travelers who stay here, the English-speaking staff is friendly and helpful. *Escudero 702, tel. 14/14–33–50. 72 suites with private bath. Facilities: restaurant, indoor and outdoor pool, spa, health club, ping-pong, basketball, free videos, cable TV, room service, laundry. AE, DC, MC, V. Very Expensive.*

Posada Tierra Blanca. Across the street from the Palacio del Sol but considerably less expensive, this modern motel-style property is convenient to the downtown sights. Rooms, decorated in red and black with pseudo-antique furnishings, are large and well heated in winter; all have TVs. The striking "Stages of Man" mural in the lobby was painted by Pina Mora, the same artist who decorated the courtyard of the Palacio del Gobierno (*see* Exploring, *above*). *Niños Heroes 100, tel. 14/15–00–00. 103 rooms with bath. Facilities: restaurant, pool, piano bar. AE, MC, V. Moderate.*

Victoria. This lovely hotel, built in 1940, used to be *the* place to stay in town. It's seen better days—rooms, decorated in pinks and blues, are a bit small and carpets are somewhat worn—but the public areas, with blue and white tiles, carved wood archways, and wrought-iron electric candelabras, have lost none of their charm. The best rooms look out over the pretty garden surrounding a large swimming pool. *Av. Juárez and Colón, tel. 14/10–05–47. 131 rooms with bath. Facilities: TVs in room, restaurant, bar, pool, car rental company, travel agency. AE, D, DC, MC, V. Moderate.*

Creel
Dining and Lodging
★
Copper Canyon Lodge. About 15 miles from the train station, near Cusarare Falls and overlooking a piñon forest, this rustic hotel couldn't have a nicer setting. The pine-walled rooms, with their light-wood, Spanish-style furnishings and tiled modern baths, are very attractive, and the lodge where hearty meals are served family-style is cozy and appealing. The only catch is that there's no electricity. The kerosene lamps are fine for light year-round. You'll just have to get used to bounding out of bed on cold winter mornings to light the wood-burning stove. *Apdo. Postal #3, Creel 33200, Chih., tel. 145/60179 or 800/77–MEXICO in the U.S., fax 145/60036. 23 rooms. Facilities: restaurant, bar, gift shop. Moderate (without meals)—Very Expensive (meals included).*

Dining
The Steak House. The restaurant of the Hotel Cabanas, this is a fun place to have dinner. If you don't see the sign—down the

gated alleyway just past the Parador de la Montaña Motel—in the dark, you may be drawn in by the strains of music: The restaurant will provide a mike and guitar to anybody who wants to come up and entertain. Two rows of tables covered with serapes line the sides of a small room blessed by a potbelly stove. Add a brick bar twinkling with Christmas lights for a year-round festive spirit. As the name suggests, steak is the focus of the menu, but there are tasty seafood dishes, all reasonably priced, as well. *López Mateos 49, tel. 145/6–01–51 or 145/9–11–45. No reservations. Dress: casual. MC, V. Moderate.*

Lodging **Parador de la Montaña Motel/The Little Resort.** Built 19 years ago, the Parador is considered the fanciest hotel in town, but it's showing its age. The furniture is dark—as is the lighting—and unappealing, and the rooms smell like Lysol. A better bet is to stay in the back of the hotel at the affiliated Little Resort, owned by the Parador's manager, Eduardo Melidi. Guests have access to all the Parador's facilities and pay $15 per person to stay in more cheerful, pine-walled rooms; suites have kitchenettes and fireplaces. *Creel, tel. 145/6–00–75 or 145/6–00–67 (Little Resort); reservations: Allende No. 114, Chihuahua, Ch., tel. 14/12–20–62 or 14/15–54–08. 48 rooms with shower; 7 rooms in the Little Resort. Facilities: restaurant, bar, gift shop, TV and phone in room. AE, MC, V. Moderate.*

★ **Margarita's.** If a small boy at the train station offers to take you to Margarita's, go with him. Otherwise you might miss one of the best deals in town: There's no sign on the door, and, even if you follow directions (right off the main town plaza, between the two churches perpendicular to each other), you're likely to think you're walking into a private kitchen when you open the door. At this gathering spot for backpackers, you can get anything from a bunk bed in the dorm ($5) to a double room with two beds (around $8 per person); all prices include a tasty homecooked breakfast and dinner. The rooms, with wrought-iron lamps, light-wood furnishings, and clean, modern baths, are as pleasant as anything you'll find for twice or three times the price. *Av. López Mateos y Parroquia 11, tel. 145/6–00–45. 21 rooms, most with private bath. Facilities: restaurant. No credit cards. Inexpensive.*

Divisadero/Posada Barrancas **Hotel Cabanas Divisadero-Barrancas.** The two other hotels in the area have nearby lodges for viewing the Copper Canyon, but this is the only property that overlooks it directly; the dining room and rooms one through 10 in the old section and 35 through 52 in the new section all enjoy panoramic views. The old rooms, with dark furnishings, have decks, while the new ones, somewhat farther from the dining room but lighter in decor, have balconies. Food and service get mixed reviews from the international visitors who sign the guest log, but you're not likely to notice what you're eating when you look out the dining-room window. *Reservations: Calle 71, No. 1216, Box 661, Chihuahua, Chih., tel. 14/10–33–30 and 14/15–11–99, fax 14/15–65–75. 52 rooms with shower. Facilities: gift shop, restaurant, bar. AE, MC, V. Very Expensive.*

Dining and Lodging

Hotel Mansion Tarahumara. It's a bit disconcerting to come across a red-turreted, medieval-style castle out here in barranca country, but somehow this whimsical property works. The newest (1988) hotel in the area and the least expensive, this is also the nicest. All the rooms (15 of them in individual cabins) have light pine furniture beautifully designed in Spanish contemporary style. The newest units have pine log walls; the older rooms feature gray cobblestone walls, which match the castle's exterior. The large dining room with its high-vaulted ceiling is hard to keep warm in winter but has wonderful views of the Sierra Madres. *Apdo. Postal No. 1666–C, Chihuahua, Ch., tel. 14/15–47–21 and 14/10–24–93, fax 14/16–54–44. 46 rooms with bath and fireplace. Facilities: restaurant, stables, bar, disco, gift shop. AE, MC, V. Very Expensive.*

Hotel Posada Barrancas. Perhaps the least distinctive member of the Balderrama chain, this hotel nevertheless provides a good base from which to explore the Barranca del Cobre. Guest rooms, with undistinguished, dark, contemporary furniture, pseudo-stucco walls, and linoleum-tiled floors, have comfortable beds and effective overhead reading lights. From the vertical beams in the main lodge/dining room hang strings of butterfly cocoons used in Tarahumara ceremonial dances, sometimes performed at the hotel in the evening. Rates include four meals (two lunches), rather than the usual three. *Posada Barrancas; reservations: Hotel Santa Anita, Box 159, Los Mochis, Sin., tel. 681/2–00–46. 39 rooms with fireplace and bath. Facilities: restaurant, bar, gift shop. AE, MC, V. Very Expensive.*

El Fuerte
Dining and Lodging
★

Hotel Posada Hidalgo. You'll be transported back to a more gracious era at this lovely restored hacienda, with its lush tropical gardens and cobblestone paths. Designated an Historic Landmark in 1913, it was built in 1895 by Rafael Almada, a rancher and the richest man in nearby Alamos; he had furniture shipped from as far as San Francisco for his lavish home, where he entertained the local elite. It's difficult to choose between the larger rooms with balconies, set off of a lobby filled with period artifacts, and the ones that open out onto the gardens; all are decorated with rough-hewn handcrafted furniture in Spanish Colonial style. *Langostino* (crayfish) is a specialty of the hotel dining room. *Hidalgo 101, tel. 681/3–0242; reservations: Hotel Santa Anita, Box 159, Los Mochis, Sin., tel. 681/57046, fax 681/2–00–46. 30 rooms with bath. Facilities: dining room/bar, gardens, pool, disco. AE, MC, V. Moderate.*

Los Mochis
Dining

El Farallón. With its nautical decor and murals, the dining room of this simple restaurant sets the tone for the excellent fish served here. *Obregón and Angel Flores, tel. 681/2–14–28. No reservations. Dress: informal. MC, V. Inexpensive.*

Lodging

Hotel Colinas. A Best Western high-rise on a hill overlooking Los Mochis, this hotel offers a resortlike atmosphere in a quiet location. Rooms are generic contemporary-style but have all the amenities. *Carretera Internacional 15, Apdo. 600, tel. 681/2–01–17, 681/2–02–42 or 681/2–01–01. 120 rooms with bath. Facilities: restaurant, bar, 2 pools with water slide, hot tub, basket and volleyball courts. AE, MC, V. Expensive.*

Hotel Santa Anita. The central reservations link of the Balderrama chain, this downtown hotel is also an informal information center for what's happening along the Chihuahua al Pacífico route, as well as the place to book tours. Built in 1959, the property has been continuously renovated; rooms are large and tastefully furnished in muted pastels, with comfortable modern furniture. All have cable TV, and many have hairdryers, unusual for this part of the country. *Leyva and Hidalgo, Apdo. 159, Los Mochis, Sin., tel. 681/5–70–46, fax 681/2–00–46. 130 rooms with bath. Facilities: restaurant, bar, travel agency, gift shop. AE, MC, V. Expensive.*

El Dorado. On the main street of town and, as a result, noisy as well as convenient to restaurants and shops, this modest hotel is a clean place to stay and a good value. *525 N. Valdez, tel. 681/ 5–11–11. 96 rooms with bath. Facilities: restaurant, bar, travel agency. AE, MC, V. Moderate.*

Posada Barrancas (*See* **Divisadero,** *above.*)

Topolobampo **Yacht Hotel.** Open to cool breezes from Topolobampo Bay, this
Dining hotel restaurant is a pleasant place to enjoy well-prepared Mexican dishes as well as the fresh seafood caught in the small fishing boats that sail by. *Yacht Hotel, on the waterfront, tel. 681/ 2–38–62. No reservations. Dress: informal. MC, V. Inexpensive.*

Nightlife

Sitting around and chatting with fellow guests in your lodge is about the extent of nighttime activity in the heart of Sierra Madre country, though occasionally one of the hotels in Divisadero/Posada Barrancas will have performances in the evening by Tarahumara dancers. In Creel, head to the **Steak House** (*see* Dining, *above*) for an after-dinner drink. Things are a bit more lively in Los Mochis, where locals kick up their heels at **Mr. Owens** and **Boccacio,** two downtown discos, but Chihuahua has the most nightlife options in the area. **La Reggae** (Blvd. Ortiz Mena and Bosque de la Reina, tel. 14/15–47–55) draws a crowd with dancing feet for its rock-and-roll bands. At **Chihuahua Charlie** (Av. Juárez 3329, tel. 14/17–70–65), DJs spin discs nightly; come early for dinner—the food is as good as the music. The popular **La Puerta de Alcalá** (Revolución 1608, tel. 14/ 15–83–93) disco sometimes has live music.

7 The Heartland of Mexico

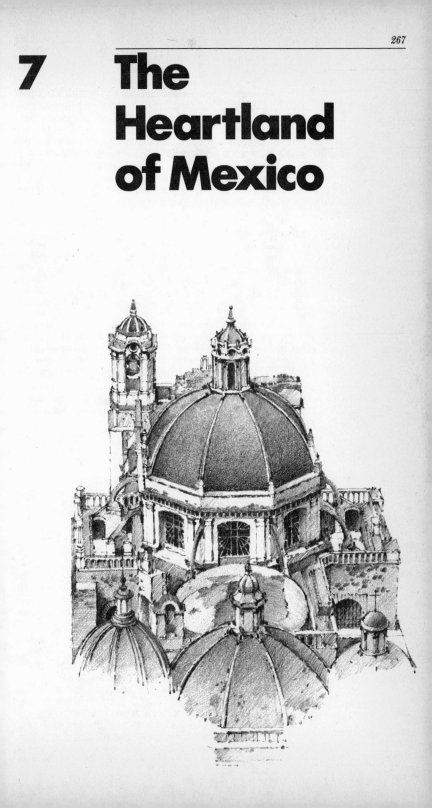

Introduction

By Laura Anne
Broadwell

A New York–based
free-lance writer,
Laura Anne
Broadwell lived in
Michoacán for six
months, where she
apprenticed with a
Tarascan Indian
weaver and taught
English to
Mexican students.
She currently
writes for a
variety of business
and travel
magazines.

Updated by
Eleanor S. Morris

Mexico's heartland, so named for its central location, has neither the beaches of the west coast nor the ruins of Yucatán. Rather, this fertile farmland and the surrounding mountains is known for its leading role in Mexican history, particularly during the War of Independence, and for its especially well-preserved examples of colonial architecture. The Bajío (ba-**hee**-o), as it is also called, corresponds roughly to the states of Guanajuato and parts of Querétaro and Michoacán. In the hills surrounding the cities of Guanajuato, Zacatecas, Querétaro, and San Miguel de Allende, the Spaniards found silver in the 1500s, leading them to heavily colonize the area.

Three centuries later, wealthy Creoles (Mexicans of Spanish descent) in Querétaro and San Miguel took the first audacious steps toward independence from Spain. When their clandestine efforts were discovered, two of the early insurgents, Ignacio Allende and Father Miguel Hidalgo, began in earnest the 12-year War of Independence. One of the bloodiest skirmishes was fought in the Alhóndiga de Granaditas, a mammoth grainstorage facility in Guanajuato that is now a state museum.

When Allende and Hidalgo were executed in 1811, another native son, José María Morelos, picked up the independence banner. This mestizo priest-turned-soldier, with his army of 9,000, came close to gaining control of the land before he was killed in 1815. Thirteen years later, the city of Valladolid was renamed Morelia in his honor.

Many travelers barrel past the Bajío to points north or west of Mexico City. But there are many reasons others make it their destination. Some stop for a few days to browse in the shops of San Miguel or Guanajuato for bargains in silver and other local crafts. Others venture to the state of Michoacán, renowned for its folklore and folk crafts, especially ceramics and lacquerware.

For those who stay longer, the rewards are ample, as each of these colonial cities has a wealth of architectural styles. La Parroquia, the Gothic-style parish church of San Miguel de Allende, designed by an Indian mason, puts a Gallic touch on an otherwise very Mexican skyline; Guanajuato boasts a 17th-century Baroque centerpiece, the Basílica Colegiata de Nuestra Señora; Zacatecas, a national monument city, has the best example in Mexico of a Mexican baroque cathedral; in Morelia, the 200-foot baroque towers of the central cathedral are among the tallest in Mexico; and in Pátzcuaro and Querétaro, ornate 16th-century colonial mansions surrounding the city squares today are hotels and government offices.

Driving through the Bajío, especially scenic Michoacán, is recommended. Within hours the landscape can change from lakeside pine forests to lush subtropical terrain. Day-trippers from Pátzcuaro can explore the crater of an extinct volcano in San Juan Parangaricútiro or the ruins of an ancient Tarascan Indian capital, Tzintzuntzán. Harried city dwellers often head to the state of Querétaro for the weekend, where they unwind in the thermal springs of San Juan del Río and Tequisquiapan. Though the restorative powers of these springs have never been scientifically proven, the waters are said to ease arthritis pain, cure insomnia, and improve digestion.

Heartland

ZACATECAS

N

JALISCO

Ojuelos de Jalisco

Ocampo

Villa de Reyes

Santa María del Rio

KEY

Rail Lines

0   20 miles

0   30 km

80

51

57

Lagos de Moreno

San Luis de la Paz

León

SIERRA DE GUANAJUATO

Dolores Hidalgo

110

45

Guanajuato

San Miguel de Allende

Silao

111

Manuel Doblado

GUANAJUATO

51

57

Irapuato

45 D

Querétaro

45 D

Salamanca

Celaya

La Piedad de Cabadas

Lago Yuriria

Lerma

Moroleón

51

Acámbaro

15

43

Lago de Cuitzeo

Quiroga

Morelia

Ciudad Hidalgo

Angahuán

Lake Pátzcuaro

15

51

14

Pátzcuaro

Zitacuaro

Uruapan

Parque Nacional Eduardo Ruíz

120

MICHOACAN

Tuzantla

Nueva Italia

La Huacana

Nocupétaro

134

Bejucos

Infiernillo

Balsas

Huetamo

Long after the War of Independence ended in 1821, the cities of the Bajío continued their prominent role in Mexico's history. Three major events took place in Querétaro alone: In 1848, the Mexican-American War ended with the signing of the Treaty of Guadalupe Hidalgo; in 1867, Austrian Maximilian of Hapsburg, crowned Emperor of Mexico by Napoleon III of France, was executed in the hills north of town; 50 years later, the Mexican Constitution was signed here.

The heartland today honors the events and people that helped to shape modern Mexico. In ornate cathedrals or bucolic plazas, down narrow alleyways or high atop hillsides, the traveler will discover monuments—and remnants—of a heroic past. During numerous fiestas, the visitor can savor the region's historic spirit. On a night filled with fireworks, off-key music, and tireless celebrants, it's hard not to be caught up in the vital expression of national pride.

Tourism is welcomed in the heartland, especially in these hard economic times, and tourists are treated naturally by residents, who go about their lives in an ordinary fashion. Families visit parks for Sunday picnics, youngsters tussle in school courtyards, old men chat in shaded plazas, and Tarascan women in traditional garb sell their wares in crowded *mercados* (markets). Though a tour operator or vendor may attempt to persuade foreign passersby to part with their money, rarely is the overture less than good-natured. Unlike areas where attractions have been specifically designed for tourism, the Bajío relies on its historic ties and the architectural integrity of its cities to appeal to the traveler.

San Miguel de Allende

San Miguel de Allende first began luring foreigners in the late 1930s when Stirling Dickinson, an American, and prominent locals founded an art school in this mountainous settlement. The school, now called the Instituto Allende, has grown in stature over the years—as has the city's reputation as a writers' and artists' colony. Walk down any cobblestoned street and you're likely to see residents of various national origins. Some come to study at the Instituto Allende or the Academia Hispano-Americana, some to escape the harsh northern winters, and still others to retire.

Cultural offerings in this town of about 110,000 reflect its large American community. There are literary readings, art shows, a lending library, and aerobics classes. Nevertheless, San Miguel retains its Mexican characteristics and warrants further exploration. The town was declared a national monument in 1926. Wandering down streets lined with 18th-century mansions, you'll also discover fountains, monuments, and churches, all reminders of the city's illustrious—and sometimes notorious—past. The onetime headquarters of the Spanish Inquisition in New Spain, for example, is located at the corner of Calles Hernández Macías and Pila Seca; the former Inquisition jail stands across the way.

Arriving and Departing

By Car Driving time from Mexico City to San Miguel is roughly four hours via Route 57 (to Querétaro) and Route 111 (Querétaro to San Miguel). Cars can be rented at various outlets in Mexico City; in San Miguel, **Renta de Autos Gama** (Calle de Hidalgo 3, tel. 465/2–08–15), has a limited selection of standard-shift compacts available.

By Train First-class train service between Mexico City and San Miguel is available daily via the **Mexican National Railways** (tel. 547–5819; in Mexico City, 5/547–3190). The *Constitucionalista* departs Mexico City at 7 AM and arrives in San Miguel at 11:10 AM; the reverse trip leaves San Miguel at 4 PM and arrives in Mexico City at 9:15 PM. Tickets cost approximately $6.50 and are best purchased one day in advance. The price includes either a full breakfast or dinner. The San Miguel train station (tel. 465/2–00–07) is located on La Calzada de Estación (Station Highway).

By Bus Direct bus service is available daily between the Central del Norte (North Bus Station) in Mexico City and the new Central de Autobuses in San Miguel. Several major lines—including **Flecha Amarilla, Herradura de Plata,** and **Tres Estrellas de Oro**—offer frequent service; travel time is about four hours. Inexpensive, second-class bus service is also available from San Miguel to other area cities.

Getting Around

San Miguel de Allende is best negotiated on foot, keeping in mind two pieces of advice. The city is 1,870 meters (more than a mile) above sea level, so visitors not accustomed to high altitudes may tire quickly during their first few days there. Streets are paved with rugged cobblestone, and some of them do not have sidewalks. Sturdy footwear, such as athletic or other rubber-soled shoes, is therefore highly recommended.

By Taxi Taxis can easily be hailed on the street or found at taxi stands such as **Sitio Allende** in the main plaza (tel. 465/2–05–50), **Sitio San Francisco** on Calle Juárez (tel. 465/2–02–90 or 2–01–92), or **Sitio San Felipe** on Calle Mesones (tel. 465/2–04–40). Flat rates to the bus terminal, train station, and other parts of the city apply.

Important Addresses and Numbers

Tourist Information The **Delegación de Turismo** is located in the center of town. Most of the brochures here are in Spanish, but an English-speaking staff member can help with basic information. You can also pick up a good map of the city that locates major hotels, restaurants, and historic attractions. *Plaza Principal s/n, tel. 465/2–17–47. Open weekdays 10–2:45 and 5–7, Sat. 10–1, Sun. 10–noon.*

Information in English is available at a new service, **Pack 'N' Mail** (Calle Jesus 2A, tel. 465/2–31–91) with reliable U.S. mail and Express Mail, 24-hour message and answering service, gift wrap, copy and fax service.

U.S. Consulate The U.S. Consular agent is Colonel Phil Maher. *Calle Hernández Macías 72, tel. 465/2–23–57 during office hours; tel. 465/2–*

00–68 or 2–09–80 for emergencies. *Open Mon. and Wed. 9–1 and 4–7; Tues. and Thurs. 4–7.*

Emergencies **Police** (tel. 465/2–00–22). **Ambulance–Red Cross** (tel. 465/2–16–16).

Hospital The staff at **Union Médica** (Calle de San Francisco 50, tel. 465/2–22–33) can refer you to an English-speaking doctor.

Pharmacies San Miguel has many pharmacies, but American residents recommend **Botica Agundis,** where English speakers are often on hand. *Calle de Canal 26, tel. 465/2–11–98. Open daily 10 AM–midnight.*

Money Exchange Banks will change dollars or traveler's checks at certain hours of the day, usually in the morning. Lines, however, are often long and move slowly. A better bet is the **Casa de Cambio.** *Calle del Correo 15, tel. 465/2–17–06. Open weekdays 9–2 and 4–6, Sat. 9–12.*

English-language Bookstores **El Colibrí,** *Sollana 30, tel. 2–07–51. Open Mon.–Sat. 10–2 and 4–7.*
Lagundi, *Calle de Canal 21, tel. 2–08–30. Open Mon.–Sat. 10–2 and 4–7, Sun. 11–3.*

Travel Agencies Major agencies are **Viajes Vértiz** (American Express representative at Calle de Hidalgo 1A, tel. 465/2–19–09 or 2–04–99); **Viajes San Miguel** (Hotel Real de Minas, tel. 465/2–25–37); and the **Travel Institute of San Miguel** (Calle Cuna de Allende 11, tel. 465/2–00–78).

Guided Tours

The **Travel Institute of San Miguel** (tel. 465/2–00–78) offers two walking tours of the city, conducted in English. At press time, each cost $10 per person. Its orientation tour takes in the central plaza, churches, mansions, museums, and public buildings, and also provides practical advice on the town's pharmacies, newsstands, library, and post office. The tour of historic San Miguel takes travelers by minibus to El Mirador (the lookout). Visitors then walk down a winding cobblestoned street to El Chorro natural springs, through Juárez Park, past the bullring, to La Parroquia (parish church), and finally to the Allende Museum. They also offer guided tours of other sections of the Bajio.

Exploring

Numbers in the margin correspond to points of interest on the San Miguel de Allende map.

Most of San Miguel's historic sights are clustered in the downtown area and can be seen in a couple of hours. Begin at the main plaza, commonly called **El Jardín** (the garden). Seated on one of its gray wrought-iron benches, you'll quickly get a feel for the town: Old men with canes exchange tales, youngsters in school uniform bustle by, fruit vendors hawk their wares, and bells from the nearby Parroquia (parish church) pierce the thin mountain air at each quarter hour.

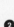 Leaving the Jardín, cross Calle del Correo to reach **La Parroquia** on the south side of the plaza. This imposing pink Gothic-style parish church, made of local *cantera* sandstone, was designed in the late-19th century by self-trained Indian

mason Ceferino Gutiérrez, who sketched his designs in the sand with a stick. Gutiérrez was purportedly inspired by postcards of European Gothic cathedrals. Since the postcards gave no hint of what the back of those cathedrals looked like, the posterior of La Parroquia was done in quintessential Mexican style.

La Parroquia still functions as a house of worship, though its interior has been changed over the years. Gilded wood altars, for example, were replaced with neoclassical stone altars. The original bell, cast in 1732, still calls parishioners to mass several times daily.

❸ Three blocks from La Parroquia, the **Iglesia de San Francisco,** on Calle Juárez, has one of the finest Churrigueresque facades in the state of Guanajuato. (José Churriguera, a 17th-century Spanish architect, was noted for his extravagantly decorative Baroque style.) Built in the late-18th century, the church was financed by donations from wealthy patrons and by revenue from bullfights. Topping the elaborately carved exterior is the image of Saint Francis of Assisi; below are sculptures of Saint John and Our Lady of Sorrows, as well as a crucifix.

Continue a few steps north on Calle Juárez until you reach Calle Mesones and the colorful **Mercado Ignacio Ramírez.** During the week, the market occupies the small plaza directly in front of the Oratorio de San Felipe Neri and spills over onto the surrounding streets (for about six blocks). This market is particularly active on Sundays, when country folk come to town with pigs, chicken, and other livestock and succulent produce. During the week, rows of fresh fruits and vegetables are supplemented by racks of cheaply made clothing, inexpensive American toys, and blaring Mexican-made tapes and records. The ❹ dome of the **Oratorio de San Felipe Neri** is visible just beyond the market. This church, located across the market plaza on Calle de los Insurgentes, was built by local Indians in 1712. The pink stone of the eastern facade (with its figure of Our Lady of Solitude) is a remnant of the original chapel; its newer southern front was built in an ornate Baroque style. In 1734, the wealthy Count of Canal paid for an addition to the Oratorio. His **Templo de Santa Casa de Loreto** (dedicated to the Virgin of Loreto) is just behind the Oratorio; its main entrance, now blocked by a grille, is in the left rear of the Oratorio. Peer through the grille to see the heavily gilded altars and effigies of the count and his wife, under which they are buried.

❺ Continue down Calle de los Insurgentes for another block to **La Biblioteca Pública** (tel. 465/2–04–35). Posted on the bulletin board in the entranceway to the library are many notices (mostly in English) about events such as literary readings or yoga and aerobics classes. Inside are the offices of the English-language newspaper, *Atención San Miguel*, as well as a reading room with back issues of popular publications. On Sundays, the library offers a two-hour house-and-garden tour of San Miguel, departing at noon. Tickets cost about $6, with all proceeds going to the library.

Time Out The **reading room** is a great place to take a breather, grab a magazine, or one of the many English books in stock, and find a quiet spot to read in the shaded courtyard. *Calle de los Insurgentes 25 tel. 465/2–02–93. Open Mon.–Sat. 10–2 and 4–7.*

From the library, walk two blocks west to Calle Hernández Macías. At No. 75, across the street from the building that ❻ houses the U.S. Consulate, is the **Bellas Artes** cultural center. This impressive cloister, once the Royal Convent of the Conception, is now an institute for the study of music, dance, and the visual arts. Several murals, including one by the famed Mexican painter David Siqueiros, are on exhibit.

Directly behind Bellas Artes, the **Iglesia de la Concepción** touts one of the largest domes in Mexico. The two-story roof, completed in 1891, boasts both elegant Corinthian columns and ornamental pilasters and is said to have been inspired by the dome of Les Invalides in Paris. Ceferino Gutiérrez (of La Parroquia fame) is credited with its design.

❼ Heading back to the main plaza, stop at the **Casa de Ignacio Allende,** at Calle Cuna de Allende 1. Now housing a museum and gallery, this is the birthplace of Ignacio Allende, one of Mexico's great independence heroes. Allende was a Creole aristocrat who, along with Father Miguel Hidalgo, plotted in the early 1800s to overthrow the Spanish regime. At clandestine meetings held in San Miguel and nearby Querétaro, the two discussed strategies, organized an army, gathered weapons, and enlisted the support of clerics for the struggle ahead.

Spanish Royalists learned of their plot and began arresting conspirators in Querétaro on September 13, 1810. Allende and Hidalgo received word of these actions and precipitated their plans. At dawn on September 16, they rang out the cry for independence, and the fighting began. Allende was the military leader of the insurrection and was captured and executed by the Royalists the following year. As a tribute to his brave efforts, San Miguel El Grande became San Miguel de Allende in the 20th century. *Calle Cuna de Allende 1, tel. 465/2-24-99. Open Tues.-Sun. 10-3:30.*

Time Out Across the street from El Jardín is **La Terraza,** a refreshing
8 stop for weary walkers. Though food prices are high, it's possible to order a coffee, beer, juice, or soda and enjoy the open-air ambience of the restaurant's long, stone-columned terrace. *Plaza Principal and Calle del Correo. No phone. Open daily 9-9. DC, MC, V.*

After exploring downtown, take a leisurely stroll to sights in San Miguel's outlying neighborhoods. From the south side of the plaza (the side with La Parroquia), head west four blocks on Calle de Umarán until you reach Calle Zacateros. Turn south on this narrow cobblestoned street to reach some of the town's most interesting crafts shops—stocked with everything from silver jewelry to Mexican ceremonial masks. Keep in mind that many stores close for siesta from 2 to 4 PM.

Past the shops, Calle Zacateros becomes Ancha de San Antonio.
9 On your left at No. 20 is the entrance to the celebrated **Instituto Allende** (tel. 465/2-01-90). The school is set in the former hacienda of the Count of Canal. Since its founding in 1951, thousands of students from around the world have come to learn Spanish and to take classes in social studies and the arts. Courses last a couple of weeks to a month or longer. Lush with bougainvillea, rose bushes, and ivy vines, the grounds provide a quiet refuge for students and visitors alike.

From the institute, continue south on Ancha de San Antonio until you reach Callejón del Cardo on your left. This road, unlike so many in town, is wide and paved, looking as though it might lead to a private estate. Continue past St. Paul's Episcopal Church, where many Americans worship, until you arrive at the cobblestoned Calle Aldama on your left.

Heading downhill, walk briefly through a neighborhood of
10 whitewashed houses before reaching the north entrance to **Parque Benito Juárez,** a favorite of joggers, sweethearts, and children. The five-acre park—the largest in San Miguel—is a shaded labyrinth of evergreens, palm trees, and gardens. Take a few minutes to stroll around or find a bench and observe the activity around you.

Return to the north rim of the park, where Calle Aldama turns into Calle Diezmo Viejo. Continue until the imposing terracotta colored La Huerta Santa Elena is in front of you. From
11 here, turn left and walk one block uphill to reach the **Lavandería,** one of San Miguel's most endearing places. At this outdoor public laundry—a collection of cement tubs set above Juárez Park—local women gather daily to wash clothes and gossip as their predecessors have done for centuries. Though some women claim to have more efficient washing facilities at home, the lure of the spring-fed troughs—not to mention the chance to gossip—brings them daily to this shaded courtyard.

Calle de Recreo, the road above the Lavandería, heads north back toward the plaza. At times narrow and dusty, it leads uphill past quiet pastel-colored residences and lovely views of the surrounding mountains. To return to town, follow Recreo north for several blocks until you reach Calle del Correo. Make a left, and in three blocks you'll be back at the main plaza.

⓬ For energetic exploration, consider a climb to **El Mirador** (the lookout). One block before town, turn right off Recreo onto Calle Hospicio. Follow Hospicio for three blocks until you reach Calle Pedro Vargas, a narrow, busy two-way street. Make a right and head uphill. Soon you'll notice a statue of Ignacio Allende on your left; a panorama of the city, mountains, and reservoir will be below on your right. The vista is most commanding at sunset, and chances are you won't be alone, as El Mirador is popular both with locals and tourists.

The walk back to town is an approximately 15-minute downhill trek. (Calle Pedro Vargas hits Calle del Correo, which takes you back to the plaza.) Taxis are usually available and the trip back should cost no more than $1.

Off the Beaten Track

Roughly 50 kilometers (30 miles) north of San Miguel via Route 51 is the town of **Dolores Hidalgo,** which played an important role in the fight for independence. It was here, before dawn on September 16, 1810, that Father Miguel Hidalgo—the local priest—gave an impassioned sermon to his clergy that ended with the cry, "Mexicanos, Viva México!" At 11 PM on September 15, politicians throughout the land repeat the "grito," signaling the start of Independence Day celebrations. On September 16 (and only on this day), the bell in Hidalgo's parish church is rung.

Casa Hidalgo, the house where the patriot lived, is now a museum. It contains copies of important letters Hidalgo sent or received and other independence memorabilia. *Calle Morelos 1, tel. 468/20–1–71. Open Tues.–Sat. 10–6, Sun. 10–5. Admission: about $3.*

The town is also known for its output of hand-painted ceramics, most prominently tiles and tableware. Dolores Hidalgo can be reached easily by bus from San Miguel de Allende. Buses depart frequently from the Central de Autobuses; travel time is about one hour.

Shopping

For centuries San Miguel's artisans have been creating a wide variety of crafts, ranging from straw products to metalwork. Though some boutiques in town (including a branch of Benetton) may be a bit pricey, there are good buys on silver, brass, tin, woven cotton goods, and folk art.

Jewelry Established in 1963, **Joyería David** has an extensive selection of gold, silver, copper, and brass jewelry, all made on the premises. A number of pieces contain Mexican opals, amethysts, topaz, malachite, and turquoise. *Calle Zacateros 53, tel. 465/2–00–56. Open Mon.–Sat. 9–8. AE, V.*

Other recommended jewelers include:

Beckmann Joyería, *Calle Hernández Macías 115, tel. 465/2–16–13. Open Mon.–Sat. 9–2 and 4–7. AE, V.*

Plateria Cerro Blanco, *Calle de Canal 17, tel. 465/2–05–02. Open Mon.–Sat. 11–2 and 5–8. AE, MC, V.*
Platería y Joyería Julio, *Calle del Correo 8, tel. 465/2–02–48. Open Mon.–Sat. 9–2 and 4–8, Sun. 9–2. AE, MC, V.*

Clothing **El Pegaso** sells hand-embroidered blouses and dresses from Mexico and Guatemala as well as leather goods, hand-painted masks, jewelry and men's and children's clothing. The second floor contains rare folk art. A small café is located in the middle of the store. *Corregidora 6, tel. 465/2–13–51. Open Mon.–Sat. 10–2 and 4–7:30. AE, MC, V.*

For chic designer clothing, try **Casa Canal,** *Calle de Canal 3, tel. 465/2–04–79. Open weekdays 9–2, 4–7; Sat. 10–2, 4–8. AE, V.* **De Selva,** *Calle de Selva, Umaràn 1. Open daily 10–7. No credit cards.* **Sidell,** *Jesus, 21, tel. 465/2–04–86. Open Mon.–Sat. 10–1:30 and 4:30–6:30. MC, V.* A **Benetton** outlet is located in the Plaza Colonial, a minimall with an upscale restaurant, a coffee shop, an English-Spanish bookstore, and designer shops. *Calle de Canal 21, tel. 465/2–08–30. Open Mon. and Tues. 10:30–8, Wed. and Thurs. 10:30–2 and 4–8. Fri. 10:30–8, Sat. 10:30–5:30. AE, MC, V.*

Brass and Tinware Several stores in town sell locally crafted metal objects, such as plates and trays, chests, mirrors, and decorative animals and birds. The best selections can be found at: **La Carreta de Arte,** *Calle Zacateros 26-A, tel. 465/2–17–32, open Mon.–Sat. 9–2 and 4–8, Sun. 9–2, MC, V;* and **Casa Cohen,** *Reloj 12, tel. 465/ 2–14–34, open Mon.–Sat. 9–2 and 4–6. MC, V.*

Folk Art For hand-painted masks, ceremonial art objects, and other regional handcrafts, try **Cactus,** *Calle Zacateros 39. Open Mon.–Sat. 10–3 and 5–8, Sun. 11–4. AE, MC, V.* **La Calaca,** *Mesones 93. Open Mon.–Wed., Fri. and Sat. 11–2 and 4–7, Sun. 11–2. No credit cards.* **Artes de México,** *Aurora 47 at the Dolores Hidalgo exit, tel. 465/2–07–64, open Mon.–Sat. 9–7:30, AE, DC, MC, V;* **Arte Reve Tonatiu/Meztli,** *Calle de Umarán 24, tel. 465/ 2–08–69, open Mon.–Sat. 10–2 and 5–8, Sun. 10–4, MC, V;* and **Casa Maxwell,** *Calle de Canal 14, tel. 465/2–02–47, open weekdays 9–2 and 4–7, Sat. 10–2 and 4–8, AE, MC, V.*

Sports

Participant Sports Travelers who enjoy the sporting life will find good facilities for swimming, tennis, horseback riding, and golf at deluxe and first-class hotels situated near the Instituto Allende or on the outskirts of town. (The San Miguel tourist office can provide a list of these properties.) The **Hotel Hacienda Taboada** (Km 8 on the Dolores Hidalgo Hwy., tel. 465/2–08–50) has simmering thermal pools that are open to the public for a nominal fee. The **Club de Golf Malanquin** (Km 3 on the Celaya Hwy., tel. 465/2–05–16) features a heated pool, steam baths, tennis courts, and nine holes of golf, all of which are open to the public.

Spectator Sports Visitors who want to witness the pageantry of a traditional Mexican bullfight can do so at the **Plaza de Toros Oriente** (situated off Calle de Recreo) several times a year. The most important contest takes place during the last week of September when St. Michael the Archangel, the town's patron saint, is commemorated. Posters announcing fights are set up in El Jardín in the center of town and at the Fonda La Mesa del Matador restaurant at Calle Hernández Macías 76.

Dining

For its size, San Miguel has a surprising number of international restaurants (about 124 at last count). The recent influx of Americans has given rise to new Tex-Mex and health-food establishments; a European influence has contributed to nearly authentic French, Italian, and Spanish cuisine. Regional Mexican food is available in a variety of price ranges. Much of this fare is made from pork, chicken, or ground beef and often broiled, fried, or covered with a bread-crumb batter. Dishes are prepared with onions or garlic and served with a red or green chile sauce.

Highly recommended restaurants are indicated by a star ★.

Category	Cost*
Expensive	over $15
Moderate	$10–$15
Inexpensive	under $10

per person, excluding drinks, service, and sales tax (10%)

Expensive　**La Antigua Restaurant y Tapa Bar.** The name of this restaurant is something of a joke, as it only opened in 1990. A cheerful room with less than a dozen tables (each with a baby-blue tablecloth and a vase of orange carnations) and a polished wood bar that can seat up to 15 people, La Antigua puts its clientele in the mood for a large variety of tapas with its European café furniture and Spanish bolero music. Among its specialties are *queso antiguo*, baked cheese with chiles; *chisterra*, a sliced and fried Spanish-style sausage; *camarones con tocineta*, jumbo shrimp fried with bacon; and *pulpo antiguo*, squid sautéed in garlic and herbs. All dishes are served with bread or tortillas. *Calle Canal 9, tel. 465/2–25–86. Reservations accepted. Dress: casual. AE, MC, V. Closed Tues.*

La Princesa. More upscale restaurants have opened in San Miguel recently, but La Princesa is still *the* place to go for intimate dining. The romantic ambience is enhanced by cloth-covered tables, dark wood paneling, lazily turning ceiling fans, a large wine selection, and musicians who entertain from 8 PM to 3 AM. The Executive Menu, served daily 1–8 PM, includes soup, one of eight entrées (ranging from fillet of red snapper to Mexican-style stuffed peppers), dessert, coffee or tea, and a complimentary margarita, all for about $4 a person. After 8 PM the menu features steak dishes, including chateaubriand for two, and the prices climb. *Calle de Recreo 5, tel. 465/2–14–03. Reservations not accepted. Dress: informal. AE, MC, V.*

La Vendimia. Fast becoming one of San Miguel's most excellent restaurants, La Vendimia offers cuisine described by chef Jack Jesse as continental with a touch of southern California. In a setting designed and furnished by a local Mexican artist, the British Cordon Bleu Jesse serves such dishes as oysters pancetta, warm scallop salad, fillet of beef Toreado as well as English high tea and fish-and-chips. *Hidalgo 12, tel. 465/2–26–45. Reservations suggested. Dress: casual. AE, MC, V.*

Moderate　**Fonda Meson de San José.** On a tree-shaded cobblestone patio
★　inside a complex of small shops, this relatively new restaurant is a first for San Miguel, offering German as well as Mexican

cuisine. Owner-chef Angela Merkel is enthusiastic about her rouladen, potato pancakes, and German chocolate cake. The German Buffet, originally offered for Oktoberfest, is in great demand. *Mesones 38, no phone. No credit cards. Open daily 1– 10 PM.*

Mamá Mía. It might seem odd to order Italian food in Mexico, but Mamá Mía has a satisfying assortment of pastas and pizzas, as well as a decent *fettuccine bolognese* and *spaghetti parmesana.* House specials include *fettuccine Alex* (flat egg noodles with white wine, ham, cream, and mushrooms) and *fettuccine à la Mexicana* (with ground sausage, peppers, onion, and tomato). Folk musicians entertain on the lush outdoor patio come dusk. *Calle de Umarán 8, tel. 465/2–20–63. Reservations not accepted. Dress: informal. MC, V.*

Inexpensive   **Virginia's Restaurante.** Walk through a turquoise-painted hallway to enter a scene that resembles a crafts gallery more than a dining room, with splashy, colorful rugs displayed on the walls and exotic jewelry in showcases. Ceilings, archways, walls, and tables are painted from a magenta-lilac-turquoise palette. Most of the crafts (also including crocheted halter tops and earrings) are for sale, but the draw for many expatriate Americans is the nut brownies, homemade ice creams, cappuccinos, baked bread, and mixed salads that Virginia (an American) serves. *Calle Mesones 58, tel. 465/2–07–13. Reservations not accepted. Dress: informal. MC, V.*

Lodging

San Miguel has a wide selection of hotels ranging from cozy bed-and-breakfasts to elegant all-suite properties. Rooms fill up quickly during summer and winter seasons, when northern tourists migrate here in droves. Make reservations several months in advance if you plan to visit at these times.

Highly recommended accommodations are indicated by a star ★.

Category	Cost*
Very Expensive	over $100
Expensive	$75–$100
Moderate	$30–$75
Inexpensive	under $30

*All prices are for a standard double room; excluding 10% tax.

Expensive–   **Casa de Sierra Nevada.** Once the home of the Archbishop of
Very Expensive Guanajuato and the Marquise of Sierra Nevada, this elegant
★ country-style inn (built in 1850) hosted George Bush in 1981 and continues to attract ambassadors, diplomats, heads of state, film stars, and bullfighters. Its complex of four colonial buildings, on either side of a cobblestoned street a few blocks from La Parroquia, contains 18 individually decorated suites and five standard rooms. Lace curtains, handwoven rugs, chandeliers, and prints by artist Diego Rivera adorn some rooms; fireplaces, cozy private terraces, and skylights enhance others. From the terrace of room No. 1, there's an excellent view of La Parroquia. *Calle Hospicio 35, 37700, tel. 465/2–04–15 or 800/223–9868; 800/372–1323 or 212/696–1323 from N.Y. 18*

rooms with bath. Facilities: formal restaurant; multilingual receptionist; facials, massage, and acu-puncture (by appointment only); medical evacuation; pool under construction. No credit cards.

Expensive **Villa Jacaranda.** An all-suite hotel located near the Parque Benito Juárez, the Villa Jacaranda boasts a full range of amenities. Rooms, though unimaginatively decorated, have space heaters and cable TVs (with feeds from the United States). The hotel's Cine/Bar shows American movies Tuesday–Saturday at 7:30 PM and live sports events on a giant screen. The price of admission—roughly $3—includes a drink. *Calle Aldama 53, 37700, tel. 465/2–10–15 or 465/2–08–11. 15 suites with bath. Facilities: restaurant, pool, Jacuzzi, cable TV. AE, MC, V.*

Moderate **Casa de LuJo.** A local art dealer, Josh Kligerman, opened this hotel and has decorated each of its seven rooms with original prints, oil paintings, pastels and small sculptures. All have either a private or shared terrace; the ones facing Calle Pila Seca have beautiful vistas of the surrounding hills. Located on a quiet and secluded street no more than a ten-minute walk from the principal plaza, Casa de LuJo includes in its price a rich breakfast, such as *chilaquiles* (baked tortillas with cheese and chicken) or Mexican-style scrambled eggs with chiles, tomatoes, and onions, as well as coffee and pastries in the afternoon. A private house until 1983, most of Casa de LuJo's rooms are flooded with sunlight during the day. Its cozy and intimate atmosphere provides visitors a welcome distinction from the larger, less personal hotels in the area. It also offers its guests use of the Club de Golf, free of charge. Given its size, reservations are recommended. *Pila Seca 35, 37700, tel. 465/2–15–64. 7 rooms with bath. Facilities: cable T.V. MC, V.*

★ **La Mansión del Bosque.** Located on a quiet side street across from the Parque Benito Juárez, this renovated hacienda opened as a guest house and restaurant in 1968. Its American owners, George and Ruth Hyba, cater to long-term guests in the winter and more transient visitors in the off-season. The hotel, which operates on a Modified American Plan that includes breakfast and dinner, has guest rooms with such homey touches as handwoven cotton spreads, locally made throw rugs and artifacts, and bookshelves. Many rooms feature working fireplaces as well as private, plant-filled terraces. The lounge off the foyer has books and magazines, a telephone for long-distance calls, and a house cat that watches over the premises. *Calle Aldama 65, 37700, tel. 465/2–02–77. 23 rooms with bath. Facilities: restaurant, bar. No credit cards.*

Inexpensive **Posada de las Monjas.** This 19th-century structure has been operating as a hotel for the past 50 years. It caters to long-term students (from the Instituto Allende or Academia Hispano-Americana) but welcomes guests of shorter duration. Rooms are furnished in a colonial style, with some furniture in the old wing looking worn enough to be authentically colonial. The rooftop public terrace has tables and lounge chairs and offers commanding views of mountains and city. Some rooms have fireplaces, and there's a communal television in the lobby. *Calle de Canal 37, 37700, tel. 465/2–01–71. 65 rooms with bath; 37 are located in a new wing. Facilities: restaurant, bar, solarium, laundry service. AE, DC, MC, V.*

★ **Posada de San Francisco.** This colonial-style property, located on the main plaza downtown, resembles an old Spanish monastery—a crucifix hangs in the lobby beneath a stone archway, and some rooms have crosses over the beds. Rooms on the plaza will appeal to people-watchers, but on weekends and during the busy season, these quarters can be rather noisy. For a quieter setting, request a room on the second or third floor (some overlook nearby mountains and churches) or one inside, facing the bougainvillea-draped courtyard. *Plaza Principal 2, 37700, tel. 465/2–14–66 or 465/2–00–72. 46 rooms with bath. Facilities: patio restaurant, bar, lounge. AE, MC, V.*

The Arts and Nightlife

San Miguel, long known as an artists' colony, continues to nurture that tradition today. Galleries, museums, and art shops line the streets near El Jardín, and two government-run salons—at **Bellas Artes** (Calle Hernández Macías 75) and the **Instituto Allende** (Ancha de San Antonio 20)—showcase the work of a variety of Mexican artists. For a sampling of regional talent, visit the **Galería San Miguel** (Plaza Principal 14, tel. 465/2–04–54), **Galería Atenea** (Calle Cuna de Allende 15, tel. 465/2–07–85), and the **Kligerman Gallery** (Calle de Umarán 6, tel. 465/2–09–51). If a rather large painting or photograph strikes your fancy, don't despair: Some gallery owners will ship your newfound treasure back to the States for you.

Nightlife in San Miguel is also plentiful. On most evenings you can readily satisfy a whim for a literary reading, an American movie, a theatrical production, or a turn on a disco dance floor. The most up-to-date listings of events can be found in the English paper *Atención San Miguel*, published every Friday. The bulletin board at the public library (Calle de los Insurgentes 25) is also a good source of current events.

La Taberna de los Reyes (Hidalgo 3, no phone) features dance music from 9 until 2 Thursday through Sunday, with dinner/theater on Wednesday at 9:30. Other places that feature live music include: **Pancho and Lefty's** (Calle Mesones 99, tel. 465/2–19–58), rock, jazz, and blues bands, depending on the night. **La Fragua** (Calle Cuna de Allende 3, tel. 465/2–11–44), traditional Mexican bands; **Mamá Mía** (Calle de Umarán 8, tel. 465/2–20–63), Peruvian folk music and classical guitar; **El Jardín** (San Francisco 4, tel. 465/2–17–06), piano bar; **Laberintos Disco** (Calle Ancha de San Antonio 7, tel. 465/ 2–03–62), and **El Ring Disco Club** (Calle de Hidalgo 25, tel. 465/2–19–98).

Guanajuato

Once Mexico's most prominent silver-mining city, Guanajuato is a colonial gem, tucked into the mountains at 6,700 feet. This provincial state capital is distinguished by twisting cobble-stoned alleyways, pastel-walled houses, 15 shaded plazas, and a vast subterranean roadway (where a rushing river once flowed). In the center of town is Alhóndiga de Granaditas—an 18th-century grain-storage facility that was the site of the first battle in Mexico's War for Independence from Spain.

The city comes alive in mid-October with the International Cervantes Festival, a two-week-long celebration of the arts. Day-to-day affairs, however, continue as usual. Students still rush to class with books tucked under their arms, women eye fresh produce at the Mercado Hidalgo, and old men utter greetings from behind whitewashed doorways. On weekend nights, *estudiantinas* (student minstrels dressed as medieval troubadours) serenade the public in the city squares.

At first Guanajuato's underground roadways and poorly marked streets may seem daunting. Armed with a good map and a sense of adventure, however, you can enjoy exploring the city's hidden passages. If you do get lost, just remember that the top of the Alhóndiga (which can be seen from many spots in town) points north, and the spires of the Basílica Colegiata Nuestra Señora de Guanajuato, at the Plaza de la Paz, point south.

Arriving and Departing

By Car Guanajuato is 432 kilometers (268 miles) northwest of Mexico City via Route 57 (to Querétaro) and Route 45 (through Celaya and Irapuato), approximately a five-hour drive.

By Train The first-class *Constitucionalista* leaves Mexico City daily at 7 AM and arrives in Guanajuato at 1:25 PM; the return trip leaves Guanajuato at 2:30 PM and arrives in Mexico City at 8:57 PM. Tickets are approximately $12 and should be purchased one day in advance; a full breakfast or dinner is included in the price.

By Bus Direct bus service is available between the Central del Norte (North Bus Station) in Mexico City and Guanajuato's Central Camionera. Several lines—including **Flecha Amarilla** and **Estrella Blanca**—offer hourly service; travel time is about five hours. Frequent inexpensive bus service is available from Guanajuato to other Bajío cities.

Getting Around

Don't bother with a car in Guanajuato. Many of the attractions are within strolling distance of one another and located between Avenida Juárez and Calle Positos, the city's two major north–south arteries. The twisting subterranean roadway— El Subterráneo—also has a primarily north–south orientation.

By Taxi Nonmetered taxis can be hailed on the street or found at *sitios* (taxi stands) near the Jardín la Unión, Plaza de la Paz, and Mercado Hidalgo. Traffic moves north on Avenida Juárez and Calle Positos and south along the underground road system.

Important Addresses and Numbers

Tourist Information The **Guanajuato tourist office** is on Calle Cinco de Mayo, on the north side of the street at the intersection of Ave. Juárez (tel. 473/2–00–86 or 2–15–74; open weekdays 8:30–7:30, weekends 10–2). There is also a tourist information kiosk at the Central Camionera bus station. Maps and brochures (mostly in Spanish) are available at both locations.

Emergencies **Police** (tel. 473/2–02–66). **Ambulance-Red Cross** (tel. 473/2–04–87). Since few people in Guanajuato have a good command of English, in an emergency it's best to contact your hotel manager or the tourist office.

Hospital **Hospital General** (tel. 473/2–08–59 or 2–00–08).

Travel Agencies **Viajes Georama,** the American Express representative, is at Plaza de la Paz 34 (tel. 473/2–59–09 or 2–51–01). **Wagon-Lits Viajes** has an office in the lobby of Hotel Real de Minas (Calle Nejayote 17, tel. 473/2–18–36 or 2–23–11).

Guided Tours

Transporte Exclusivo de Turismo (Av. Juárez and Calle 5 de Mayo, tel. 473/2–59–68) offers several tours of Guanajuato and its environs. A 3½-hour tour, with an English-speaking guide, of the Museum of Mummies, the church and mines of Valenciana, the monument to Pípila, the Panoramic Highway, subterranean streets, and residential neighborhoods is $4 per person. A five-hour evening tour to the Pípila monument and one or two nightclubs, including one drink, is about $12 per person. Estudiantinas perform during the weekend tours.

Exploring

Numbers in the margin correspond to points of interest on the Guanajuato map.

Many of Guanajuato's major attractions are located within an oblong downtown loop. After picking up a detailed city map at the tourist office (corner of Av. Juárez and Calle 5 de Mayo), find the market by walking south on Avenida Juárez 1½ blocks ❶ until you reach **Mercado Hidalgo** on your right. The 1910 cast-iron and glass structure is reminiscent of English Victorian stations and markets. Though the balcony stalls try to lure tourists with tacky T-shirts and cheap plastic toys, the lower level is replete with authentic local wares, including fresh produce, peanuts, honey-drenched nut candies, and colorful basketry. Vendors line the sidewalks in front of the market, hawking flowers and local crafts.

As you leave the market, continue south on Avenida Juárez until the road splits near the Jardín Reforma. (Av. Juárez, crowded and heavy with exhaust fumes, veers to the right; keep to the left and cut down Calle Reforma, a short alleyway lined with shops.) Bear right at the end of Calle Reforma and you'll come to two pleasant courtyards: Plaza San Roque, which hosts outdoor performances during the fall Cervantes Festival, and, just beneath it, Plaza San Fernando, a shady square where many book fairs are held.

This short detour will return you to Avenida Juárez, where the ❷ road climbs slightly toward **Plaza de la Paz.** Built from 1895 to 1898, this square is surrounded by some of the city's finest colonial buildings. Chief among them is the 18th-century residence of the Count of Rul and Valenciana, owner of the country's richest silver mine of the time. The two-story structure, located at the corner of Avenida Juárez and Callejón del Estudiante, was designed by famed Mexican architect Eduardo Tresguerras.

❸ Toward the back of the plaza is the imposing **Basílica Colegiata de Nuestra Señora de Guanajuato,** a 17th-century Baroque church, painted a striking yellow. Inside is the oldest Christian statue in Mexico: the highly venerated jewel-laden 8th-century wood statue of the Virgin, which, as one story goes, was a gift in 1557 from Philip II of Spain. On the Friday preceding Good

284

Guanajuato

Alhóndiga de
Granaditas, **8**
Basílica Colegiata de
Nuestra Señora de
Guanajuato, **3**
El Museo Casa Diego
Rivera, **7**
El Pípila Monument, **6**
Jardín la Unión, **4**
Mercado Hidalgo, **1**
Plaza de la Paz, **2**
Teatro Juárez, **5**

Friday, miners—accompanied by floats and mariachi bands—parade to the basilica to pay homage to the Lady of Guanajuato.

 As you pass the plaza, bear to the right and continue south along Avenida Juárez. Within a few blocks on your left is **Jardín la Unión,** a tree-lined plaza that is Guanajuato's central square. On Thursdays and Sundays musical performances take place in the bandshell. At other times, impromptu groups of musicians break into song along the plaza's shaded tile walkways.

Time Out   For alfresco dining, try the terrace at the **Hotel Museo Posada Santa Fe.** The menu includes pricey specialties, such as broiled trout and chicken with mole sauce, but a cappuccino and slice of cake will cost about $2. *Plaza Principal at Jardín Unión 12, tel. 473/2-00-84. Open 7 AM-11 PM. AE, DC, MC, V.*

Another outdoor café, **El Agora,** located down an alley off the plaza's southeast corner, has cheaper offerings. A four-course lunch, including soup, rice, an entrée, and dessert, costs under $3. *El Agora del Baratillo, tel. 473/2-33-00. Open 8 AM-10 PM. No credit cards.*

❺ The ornate **Teatro Juárez** is just past the Jardín on Calle de Sopeña. Adorned with bronze lion sculptures and figures of Greek muses, the theater was inaugurated by Mexican dictator Porfirio Díaz in 1903 with a performance of *Aida*. It now serves as the principal venue of the annual Cervantes Festival, when the city resounds with symphony recitals, plays, dance performances, movies, and *callejoneadas* (student street serenades). A brief tour of the plush interior is available for a nominal fee. *Open Tues.–Sun. 9:15–1:45 and 5–7:45.*

❻ From Teatro Juárez you can walk or take a taxi or bus to **El Pípila Monument**. If you choose to walk (it's a steep climb that takes nearly an hour), bear right on Calle de Sopeña just past the theater. A sign marked *Al Pípila* will direct you onto Callejón de Calvario, which eventually leads to the hillside memorial. If you prefer to save energy, you can hire a taxi or catch a bus marked Pípila from the Jardín.

From the monument, you'll see a splendid panorama of the city. You can also pay tribute to the young miner, nicknamed El Pípila, who was one of the martyrs of the independence movement. El Pípila crept into the Alhóndiga de Granaditas (where Spanish Royalists were hiding) and, with a stone shield strapped to his back, set the front door ablaze. El Pípila died, but the Spanish troops were captured by Father Miguel Hidalgo's army in this early battle, giving the independence forces their first major military victory.

Heading back to town, pick up Calle Cantarranas, a main street behind the Jardín la Unión. You'll pass the **University of Guanajuato** (tel. 473/2-41-50) on your right. This institution was begun as a Jesuit seminary in 1732 (the original Baroque church, La Compañia, still stands next door) and became a state university in 1945. Among the school's most famous alumni is Diego Rivera, one of Mexico's great muralists. The current university building, constructed in the 1950s, was designed to blend in with the town's architecture, but its modern interior betrays the colonial facade. If you do wander inside, check out the bulletin boards for notices of cultural events in town.

Head briefly uphill past middle-class residences. This road, Calle Positos, leads to **El Museo Casa Diego Rivera**—the birthplace of Guanajuato's illustrious son. On view are family portraits, the bed in which Rivera slept as a child, other family furniture, and 97 works by Rivera, among them his studies for the controversial mural that was commissioned for Rockefeller Center in New York City. The painting, completed in 1933, contained a portrait of Russian revolutionary Vladimir Lenin and was removed immediately after it was first displayed. *Calle Positos 47. Open Tues.–Sat. 10–1:30 and 4–6:30, Sun. 10–2:30.*

Calle Positos weaves past more residences and eventually becomes Calle 28 de Septiembre. The massive stone structure on the left with horizontal slit windows is the **Alhóndiga de Granaditas**, one of the city's most prominent attractions. This 18th-century grain-storage facility was a fortress during the war for independence and the site of El Pípila's courageous act. It is now a state museum with exhibits on local history, crafts, and archaeology. The hooks on which Spanish Royalists displayed the decapitated heads of Father Hidalgo, Ignacio Allende, and two other independence leaders still hang on the exterior. *Calle 28 de Septiembre #6, tel. 473/2–11–12. Admission: about $3, Sun. free. Open Tues.–Sat. 10–2 and 4–6, Sun. 10–4. Group tours for up to 30 people are available during museum hours.*

A little over a mile north from the Alhóndiga is the **Iglesia de San Cayetano,** known all over Guanajuato as **La Valenciana.** Constructed over 20 years in the latter part of the 18th century, it is one of the most well-known colonial churches in all of Mexico. The pink stone facade is brilliantly, baroquely ornate. Inside are three altars, each hand-carved in wood and covered in gilt, in separate styles: Plateresque, Chiaroscuro, and Baroque. There are also fine examples of religious painting from the viceregal period. La Valenciana is included in the guided tour of the city; there are also frequent buses from the center.

Return to Calle 5 de Mayo, one block north of the Alhóndiga. If you make a left, you'll be back at Avenida Juárez, where you began your journey. From here, you can take a taxi to the **Museo de la Momias,** at the north end of town. At the museum, mummified human corpses—once buried in the nearby municipal cemetery—are on display. Until the law was amended in 1958, if a gravesite had not yet been paid for, the corpse was removed after five years to make room for new arrivals. Because of the mineral properties of the local soil, these cadavers (the oldest is about 100 years old) were in frighteningly good condition upon exhumation. The most gruesome are exhibited in glass cases. *Panteon Municipal. tel. 473/2–06–39. Admission: about 75 cents. Open Tues.–Sun. 9–6.*

Dining

Guanajuato's better restaurants are located in hotels near the Jardín la Unión and on the highway to Dolores Hidalgo. For simpler fare, private establishments around town offer a good variety of Mexican and international dishes.

Highly recommended restaurants are indicated by a star ★.

Category	Cost*
Expensive	over $15
Moderate	$5–$15
Inexpensive	under $5

*per person, excluding drinks, service, and sales tax (10%)

Expensive **El Comedor Real.** Continental cuisine served in a medieval environment defines El Comedor Real. The bright, whitewashed, and brick-domed restaurant in the Hotel Castillo Santa Cecilia serves such specialties as *filete pimiente* (steak au poivre); breaded trout with tartar sauce, and fish soup with vegetables. Troubadours perform every Friday and Saturday at 10:30 PM at La Cava, the bar next door. *Carretera a la Valenciana s/n, tel. 473/2–04–85. Reservations advised on weekends. Jacket suggested. AE, DC, MC, V.*

Moderate **El Retiro.** This traditional Mexican restaurant up the street from the Teatro Juárez lives up to its name, the Retreat. Though it is often crowded for the main midday meal, at other times you can relax with a steaming cappuccino and listen to classical music. For more substantial fare, try the mole poblano with chicken, broiled steak with mushroom sauce, or a Spanish omelet. *Calle de Sopeña 12, tel. 473/2–06–22. Reservations not accepted. Dress: informal. MC, V.*

Restaurant Valadez. Dark wood-paneled walls give way to large windows overlooking the Teatro Juárez at this downtown restaurant. House dishes include *filete à la Tampiqueña* (beefsteak served with guacamole, cheese enchiladas, and beans), hamburger Valadez (topped with cheese and bacon), and crepes with tequila and blackberries. The bar serves Campari, Dubonnet, and tequila drinks for under $2. *Jardín la Unión 3, tel. 473/2–11–57. Reservations not accepted. Dress: informal. AE, DC, MC, V.*

★ **Tasca de Los Santos.** This cozy restaurant, located across the street from the Basílica, specializes in Spanish and international cuisines. Waiters recommend the *sopa de mariscos* (shellfish soup with shrimp, clams, and crabs), *pollo al vino blanco* (chicken in white wine sauce with tomatoes, onions, olives, raisins, almonds, and parsley), and *filete parrilla* (grilled beef with baked potatoes and spinach). A variety of music, ranging from French to Russian, enhances the cosmopolitan mood. *Plaza de la Paz 28, tel. 473/2–23–20. Reservations not accepted. Dress: informal. MC, V.*

Inexpensive **Cafeteria Nueva.** Cheap and plentiful food attracts the university crowd to this spartan eatery. A midday meal, consisting of soup, Mexican rice, a chicken or beef dish, dessert and coffee, costs about $2. The service can be slow, but vibrant music and a lively crowd will keep you entertained. While you wait, note the posters of Mexican art on the walls. *Jardín la Unión at Allende 3, tel. 473/2–14–14. Reservations not accepted. Dress: informal. No credit cards.*

Lodging

Guanajuato's less expensive hotels are located near the bus station, along Avenida Juárez and Calle de la Alhóndiga. Moderately priced and upscale properties are near the Jardín la Unión and on the outskirts of town. It's best to secure reservations at least six months in advance if you plan to attend the Cervantes Festival, which usually runs from mid- to late October.

Highly recommended lodgings are indicated by a star ★.

Category	Cost*
Expensive	$40–$100
Moderate	$20–$40
Inexpensive	under $20

All prices are for a standard double room; excluding 10% tax.

Expensive **Hotel Museo Posada Santa Fe.** This colonial-style property, located at the Jardín la Unión, has been in operation since 1862. Large historic paintings by local artist Don Manuel Leal hang in the wood-paneled lobby; a sweeping carpeted stairway leads to second-floor quarters. Each room, decorated in warm, autumnal colors, has a wood minibar, black-and-white TV, and telephone. Rooms facing the plaza can be noisy; quieter rooms face narrow alleyways. *Plaza Principal at Jardín la Unión 12, 36000, tel. 473/2–00–84 or 2–02–07. 46 rooms with bath. Facilities: restaurant, bar, rooftop terrace with Jacuzzi, satellite TV. AE, DC, MC, V.*

★ **Parador San Javier.** This immaculately restored hacienda was converted into a hotel in 1971. In fact, a safe from the Hacienda San Javier and old wood trunks still decorate the large, plant-laden lobby. The rooms are clean and have modern appointments: lace curtains, crisp coverlets, and blue-and-white-tiled baths. The 16 rooms reached via a stone archway have some rugged colonial details. A word of caution: Large convention groups sometimes use the facility. *Plaza Aldama 92, 36020, tel. 473/2–06–26. 115 rooms with bath. Facilities: 2 restaurants, bar, café, disco, outdoor swimming pool, gardens, bullring. AE, DC, MC, V.*

Inexpensive **Hotel Socavón.** One of Guanajuato's newest hotels, this modest five-story property was built in 1981. Open-air walkways, with views of surrounding mountains, lead to guest quarters. Each room has a wood-beamed ceiling, is simply furnished with a bed and a desk, and has a modern bath. Fourth-floor corner rooms offer some good views; second-floor rooms are near the hotel restaurant. *Calle de la Alhóndiga 41A, 36060, tel. 473/2–48–85 or 2–66–66. 37 rooms with bath. Facilities: restaurant. AE, MC, V.*

The Arts and Nightlife

Guanajuato, on most nights a somnolent provincial capital, awakens each fall for the **International Cervantes Festival.** During two weeks in October world-renowned actors, musicians, and dance troupes (which have included the Bolshoi Ballet) perform nightly at the Teatro Juárez and at other venues in town. The **Plaza San Roque,** a small square near the Jardín Reforma, hosts a series of *Entremeses Cervantinos*—swashbuckling one-act farces by classical Spanish writers. Grandstand seats require advance tickets, but crowds often gather by the edge of the plaza for free. If you plan to be in Guanajuato for the festival, contact the Cervantes ticket office in Mexico City (Emerson 304, Colonia Polanco, tel. 905/250–0095) at least six months in advance for top-billed events.

At other times of the year, nightlife in Guanajuato is mostly relegated to dramatic, dance, and musical performances at the **Teatro Juárez** (Calle de Sopeña, tel. 473/2–01–83) and the **Teatro Principal** (Calle Hidalgo, tel. 473/2–15–23), which has begun showing American movies several times a week. Some hotels, including the Parador San Javier and the Castillo Santa Cecilia, provide evening musical entertainment. There are also several nightclubs located in or near the downtown area, including **Discoteque El Pequeño Juan** (Panorámica Al Pípila at Callejon de Guadalupe, tel. 473/2–23–08), whose panoramic view of the city at night is stunning, and **Discoteque La Fragua** (Calle Tepetapa 45, tel. 473/2–27–15).

Excursion to León

León, 56 kilometers (35 miles) northwest of Guanajuato, is best known as the shoemaking capital of Mexico. It is also an important center for industry, and commerce. With more than 1 million people, it is the state's most populous urban area.

If you know footwear and have the time (and patience) to browse through the downtown shops, you may find some good buys in León. First try the Plaza de Zapatos, a mall with 70 stores located on Boulevard Adolfo López Mateos roughly one block from the bus station. From here, take a taxi west (about a 10-minute ride) to the Zona Peatonal, a pedestrian zone with several shoe stores. On Calle Praxedis Guerrero there are various artisans' stands selling leather goods.

Flecha Amarilla buses leave Guanajuato's Central Camionera every 15 minutes for León; the ride takes about 45 minutes and costs under $1. Pick up a map of León at the tourist office in Guanajuato.

Excursion to Zacatecas

Back in colonial days, Zacatecas was the largest silver-producing city in the world. Still a large silver-mining center, with factories producing silver jewelry and trade schools training apprentices in the fine art of handmade silver craft, Zacatecas is a relatively undiscovered jewel for tourists. Although a state capital with a population of 300,000, it has the feel of a much smaller place and is spotlessly clean, kept so by Zacatecan pride. Allow yourself an excursion from Guanajuato despite the distance (311 kilometers/193 miles; 4–5-hour drive), if only to experience the following gems, a mere introduction to this light-splashed town of arches and cobblestones.

The elaborately carved 18th-century Mexican Baroque **Cathedral** on Avenida Hidalgo is considered one of the best examples of this style in the country. Each of the three facades tells a different legend, while a fourth tale has it that an anticlerical governor of the state took the cathedral's silver cross and baptismal font to mint Zacatecas' first silver coins.

Adjoining the cathedral is the **Plaza de Armas** and the **Governor's Palace,** an 18th-century mansion containing flower-filled courtyards, and on the main staircase, a powerful mural depicting the history of Zacatecas.

A treasure, the **Rafael Coronel Museum,** is located in the Exconvento de San Francisco, out of town center toward Lomas del Calvario. The 17th-century facade of mellowed pink tones conceals a rambling structure of open-arched corridors, all leading through garden patios to rooms containing an amazing collection of some 3,700 masks. Saints and devils, wise men and fools, animals and humans, make up this startling assortment of handmade mascaras used in regional festivals all over Mexico. There is also an outstanding display of puppets. *Tel. 492/28116. Open Tues.–Sun. 10–5; closed Mon.*

Not to be confused with the Rafael Coronel Museum is the **Pedro Coronel Museum** (the men were brothers), also in a historical building, originally a Jesuit monastery, then used as a jail in the 18th century. In the Plaza Santo Domingo, north of the cathedral, the museum is one of a kind in Mexico and Latin America, housing the work of Zacatecan artist and sculptor Pedro Coronel and his extensive collection of the works of Picasso, Dali, Miro, Braque, and Chagall among others, as well as an abundance of art from Africa, China, Japan, India, Greece, and Egypt. *Open Fri.–Wed. 10–2 and 4–7, Sun. 10–2 and 4–5; closed Thurs.*

At Cerro del Grillo (Cricket Hill) on the northeast side of the city you catch the **Teleferico,** the only cablecar in the world that crosses an entire city. True, it crosses at the narrowest point, but it presents a magnificent panoramic view of the city and its many baroque church domes and spires. For a cost of a little more than a dollar, the ride takes you up to Cerro de la Bufa. The price is the same whether you ride both ways or walk one, and it's quite a climb going up.

Cerro de la Bufa, the trademark of the city, is the site of Pancho Villa's definitive battle against dictator Victoriano Huerta in June of 1914. The spacious **Plaza de la Revolución,** paved with the three shades of pink Zacatecan stone, is crowned with three huge equestrian statues of Villa and two other heroes, Felipe Angeles and Panfilo Natera.

The **Eden Mine** (El Mina Eden), functioning from 1586 until the 20th century, is now a tourist attraction. From the entrance on Antonio Dovali off Ave. Torreon beyond the Alameda Garcia de la Cadena, an open mine train runs down into the underground tunnels; there is a small gift shop at the entrance. The tour, for a nominal fee, is in Spanish, but you won't have any trouble imagining for yourself what the life of the miners was like. Be sure to wear sturdy shoes, and remember that mines are pretty dark. This one is no exception; through much of the tour your only light may be the guide's flashlight. *Open daily noon–7:30 PM.*

Finally, since this is a silver town, you won't want to miss a visit to the **Centro Platero Zacatecas** (tel. 492/2–10–27), a school and factory for fine handmade silver jewelry and other items. In the 18th century mansion of one Don Ignacio de Bernardez you can watch student silversmiths master this fine tradition. Jewelry and other silver products are for sale on the premises (Ex-Hacienda de Bernardez, Colonia Bernardez, tel. 492/3–10–07) or in the factory's shop located downtown in **Centro Commercial "El Mercado,"** a group of boutiques in what was once a covered market. *Calle Hidalgo next to the Cathedral.*

Querétaro

A state capital and industrial center of nearly 800,000 people, Querétaro, like other Bajío cities, has played a significant role in Mexican history. In 1810, in the home of Josefa Ortiz de Dominguez, a heroine of the independence movement, known as La Corregidora, the first plans for independence were hatched. In 1848, the Mexican-American War was concluded in this city with the signing of the Treaty of Guadalupe Hidalgo. Emperor Maximilian made his last stand here in 1867 and was executed by firing squad in the Cerro de las Campañas (Hill of the Church Bells) north of town. A small memorial chapel, built by the Austrian government, marks the spot. A gigantic statue of Benito Juárez crowns a park on the crest of the hill just above it. In 1917, the Mexican Constitution, which still governs the land, was signed in this city.

Throughout Querétaro there are markers, museums, churches, and monuments that commemorate its heroes and historic moments. A prevailing sense of civic pride is evident in the impeccably renovated mansions, the flower-draped cobblestoned pedestrian walkways, and the hospitable plazas, which are softly lit at night. The people are among the most congenial in central Mexico and are quick to share their favorite sites and tales with travelers.

Though Querétaro's boundaries extend for some distance, the historic district is in the heart of town. A day or two can easily be spent here, visiting museums, admiring the architecture, and learning the local history.

Arriving and Departing

By Car   Querétaro is 220 kilometers (136 miles) northwest of Mexico City, a three-hour drive via Route 57. Cars can be rented at various outlets in Mexico City; in Querétaro try **Budget** (Av. Constituyentes Oriente 73, tel. 463/2–43–45), **Auto Rent** (Av. Constituyentes Oriente 24, tel. 463/4–20–39), or **National** (Calle 13 de Septiembre #34, tel. 463/6–35–44).

By Train   First-class train service between Mexico City and Querétaro is available daily on **Mexican National Railways** (tel. 905/547–5819 or 547–3190 in Mexico City; 463/2–17–03 in Querétaro). The *Constitucionalista* departs from Mexico City at 7 AM and arrives in Querétaro at 10 AM; the return trip leaves Querétaro at 6 PM and arrives in Mexico City at 8:57 PM. Tickets should be purchased one day in advance; the price (about $7) includes a full breakfast or dinner.

By Bus   Direct bus service is available daily between the Central del Norte (North Bus Station) in Mexico City and Querétaro's Central de Autobuses. Major lines—including **Flecha Amarilla, Omnibus de México, Tres Estrellas de Oro,** and **Transportes del Norte**—offer frequent service; travel time is about three hours. Frequent inexpensive bus service is available from Querétaro to other heartland cities.

Getting Around

Many of Querétaro's historic sites are within walking distance of one another in the downtown district, and can be reached by a series of walkways that are closed to automobile traffic most of the day. If you want to venture farther afield, you will find that buses and taxis run frequently along the main streets and are inexpensive.

Important Addresses and Numbers

Tourist Information
The **Dirección de Turismo del Estado** is located near the Plaza de la Independencia. City maps and brochures of the state of Querétaro are available, and the bilingual staff is extremely helpful. *Calle 5 de Mayo #61, tel. 463/4–01–79 or 4–04–28. Open weekdays 9–3 and 6–8, weekends 10–1.*

Emergencies
Police (tel. 463/6–19–37). **Ambulance-Red Cross** (tel. 463/2–17–06 or 463/2–83–01). **Protectur** (tel. 463/4–04–28) offers legal assistance with robberies, fraud, and detention/arrest.

Hospital
Sanatorio Alcocer Pozo (Calle Reforma 23, tel. 463/2–01–49 or 2–17–87).

Money Exchange
Casa de Cambio de Querétaro (Av. Madero 6, tel. 463/4–42–55) is open Monday–Thursday 9–3, Fri., 9–1:30.

Travel Agencies
Wagons-Lits Viajes (Centro Comercial Plaza Niza at Zaragoza y Tolsa 2, tel. 463/4–30–20 or 4–33–44).

Guided Tours

On request, the tourist office conducts a free 90-minute English-language walking tour of the city's historic landmarks. To arrange a city tour, call the office (*see* Important Addresses and Numbers, *above*) one day in advance.

Exploring

Numbers in the margin correspond to points of interest on the Querétaro map.

The city's most noteworthy sites are near the tourist office. Pick up a map, make a right, and walk directly to the **Plaza Independencia** or **Plaza de Armas**. Bordered by carefully restored colonial mansions, this immaculate square is especially lovely at night, when the central fountain is lit. Built in 1824, the fountain is dedicated to the Marquis de la Villa del Villar, who constructed Querétaro's elegant aqueduct and provided the city with drinking water. The old stone aqueduct with its 74 towering arches still stands at the east end of town, though it no longer brings water into the city.

The **Palacio Municipal**, also known as the Palacio de la Corregidora, is on the plaza's northwest corner. Today it houses municipal government offices, but in 1810 it was the home of Querétaro's mayor-magistrate (El Corregidor) and his wife, Josefa Ortiz de Domínguez (La Corregidora). On many evenings, conspirators—including Ignacio Allende and Father Miguel Hidalgo—came here under the guise of participating in La Corregidora's literary salon. When the mayor-magistrate learned that they were actually plotting the course for independence, he imprisoned his wife in her room. La Corregidora managed to whisper a warning to a coconspirator, who notified Allende and Hidalgo. A few days later, on September 16, Father Hidalgo tolled the bell of his church to signal the beginning

of the fight for freedom. A replica of the bell can be seen atop
the Palacio Municipal.

Continue counterclockwise around the square. At Plaza
Independencia 4 is the **Palacio de Justicia,** and beside it, **Casa
de la Cultura** (the sign out front reads "*Bazar Ideas y Artesanias*"). The baroque palace, also known as **Casa de Ecala,** is
tains its original facade. As the story goes, its 18th-century
owner adorned his home so ornately to better his neighbor.
When the neighbor complained, City Hall stepped in and halted
construction.

Just past the Casa de la Cultura is Avenida Libertad Oriente,
one of the city's bougainvillea-draped pedestrian walkways.
Turn west here and walk two blocks to reach Calle Corregidora, named after the heroine. Bear right again, and in the
middle of a long block, you'll find the entrance to the **Museo
Regional de Querétaro.** This bright yellow 17th-century Franciscan monastery displays the works of colonial and European
artists in addition to historic memorabilia, including early copies of the Mexican Constitution and the table on which the
Treaty of Guadalupe Hidalgo was signed. *Calle Corregidora 3,
tel. 463/2–20–36 or 2–20–31. Admission, about $3. Open Mon.,
Wed.–Sat. 10–6; Tues. 10–3:30.*

Cross the street to Avenida Madero, another "pedway," this
one lined with shops. (Cars have use of the street between 2 and
4 PM daily.) The **Jardín Obregón,** the city's main square, will be
on your right. You'll also pass a number of lapidary shops selling opals (not blue like Australian opals but beautiful nonethe-

less) and other locally mined gems. If you're in the market for loose stones or opal jewelry, do some comparison shopping, as you're apt to find better prices here than in the United States.

4 One block past Avenida Juárez on the corner of Allende Sur, you'll see the former **Casa de la Marquesa** on your left at No. 41. The structure currently houses Querétaro's Center of Cultural Services, but it was once the ostentatious home of the Marquesa de la Villa del Villar, who apparently had a penchant for things Arabic. Notice the studios on the second floor, one of which is covered with Middle Eastern tiles.

5 Cross Allende to reach the neoclassical **Fountain of Neptune** next to the Church of Santa Clara at the corner of Calle Allende. It was built in 1797 by Eduardo Tresguerras, the renowned Mexican architect and a native of the Bajío. The fountain originally stood in the orchard of the Monastery of San Antonio, but when the monks faced serious economic problems, they sold part of their land and along with it the fountain.

6 From the fountain, make a left on Calle Allende and walk nearly one block to a fine example of Baroque architecture, the **State Museum of Art,** housed in an 18th-century Augustinian monastery that contains a collection of European and Mexican paintings from the 17th through the 20th centuries. *Calle Allende 14, no phone. Admission: about 35 cents. Open Tues.–Sun. 11–7.*

7 Retrace your steps back to Calle Corregidora. Make a left and walk one block to Calle 16 de Septiembre. Across the street is the **Jardín de la Corregidora,** prominently marked by a statue of the heroine. Behind this monument stands the **Arbol de la Amistad** (Tree of Friendship). Planted in 1977 in a mixture of soils from around the world, the tree symbolizes Querétaro's hospitality to all travelers.

Time Out At Jardín de la Corregidora, you may want to find a bench and sit for a while. This is the calmest square in town, with many choices for outdoor eating (*see* Dining, *below*).

Dining

Many of Querétaro's dining spots are located near the main plaza (Jardín Obregón), along Calle Corregidora, near the Teatro de la República, and particularly in the Jardín de la Corregidora. There are more upscale restaurants in hotels on the Plaza Independencia or off Route 57, north of the city. In early evenings women set up stoves in a square near the Plaza Independencia and tempt passersby with cheap and hearty fare, but for health reasons, food cooked on the street should be avoided throughout Mexico.

Highly recommended restaurants are indicated by a star ★.

Category	Cost*
Expensive	over $15
Moderate	$5–$15
Inexpensive	under $5

*per person, excluding drinks, service, and sales tax (10%)

Expensive **Fonda del Refugio.** Situated in the Jardín de la Corregidora, this restaurant offers intimate indoor and outdoor dining. Inside, fresh flowers adorn white-clothed tables; outside, comfortable leather chairs face the surrounding gardens. Seafood and beef fillets are a specialty; order the fillet of beef cooked in red wine, lemon, mustard, and peppers, or the scallops prepared in marsala. Cocktails are served on the terrace at night. *Jardín de la Corregidora 26, tel. 463/2-07-55. Dress: informal. AE, DC, MC, V.*

★ **Restaurante Josecho.** Bullfight aficionados and other sports fans frequent this highway road stop as much for the lively atmosphere as for the food. Wood-paneled walls are hung with hunting trophies, including geese, elk, bears, and leopards; waiters celebrate patrons' birthdays by banging on pewter plates and blasting a red siren. Though the place can be raucous, it does quiet down at night, when a classical guitarist performs. House specialties include *filete Josecho* (steak with cheese and mushrooms), *filete Chemita* (steak sautéed in butter and onions), and shrimp crepes, smothered in a cheese and tomato sauce. *Dalia 1, next to the Plaza de Toros Santa María, tel. 463/4-02-01 or 6-02-29. Reservations not accepted. Dress: informal. AE, DC, MC, V.*

Moderate **El Cortijo de Don Juan.** At lunchtime, businessmen and families favor this garden location, making it the busiest spot in the shaded Jardín. Vendors, too, stroll by with a variety of wares, from homemade cheeses to large, inflatable crayons, and children sing songs for a small donation. Free snacks are served with drinks in the afternoon, or you can order from a menu that includes *pollo adobado* (chicken in a rich chile sauce), *jamón serrano* (a proscuitto-type ham), and *paella Valenciana* (rice casserole with chicken, sausage, and seafood), served on Saturdays only. The inside rooms are filled with photos of famous matadors; a bull's head is mounted prominently on the wall. *Jardín de la Corregidora 14, tel. 463/2-97-08. Reservations not accepted. Dress: informal. AE, DC, MC, V.*

Inexpensive **Comedor Vegetariano Natura.** This natural-food kitchen, one of a chain of four in Querétaro, will be of interest to the vegetarian traveler. (A second one, not far away, is located at Juárez 47, off Plaza Obregón.) Traditional vegetarian fare, such as soy burgers with cheese, is on the menu, as are Mexican-influenced dishes, such as guayaba- or papaya-flavored yogurt, enchiladas stuffed with soy and cheese, or a vegetarian alternative to *huevos rancheros* (Mexican-style eggs). Vitamins, protein powders, and natural soaps are also in stock. *Vergara Sur 7, tel. 463/4-10-88. Reservations not accepted. Dress: informal. No credit cards. Closed Sundays.*

La Mariposa. Celebrating more than 50 years in business, La Mariposa is easily recognized by a wrought-iron butterfly (mariposa) over the entrance. This is the place for light Mexican lunches—enchiladas, tacos, tamales, and *tortas* (sandwiches). *Angela Peralta 7, tel. 463/2-11-66 or 463/2-48-49. Dress: casual. No credit cards.*

Lodging

Several new properties in various price ranges have opened in Querétaro in the past 10 years. Lower-priced hotels are located near the main plaza and thus tend to be noisy; newer high rises are near the bus station but are quiet inside; and deluxe properties, including a Holiday Inn, are on the outskirts of town.

Highly recommended lodgings are indicated by a star ★.

Category	Cost*
Very Expensive	over $50
Expensive	$25–$50
Moderate	$15–$25
Inexpensive	under $15

All prices are for a standard double room; excluding 10% tax.

Very Expensive
★ **Mesón de Santa Rosa.** Located on the quiet Plaza Independencia, this elegant all-suite property occupies a restored hacienda. Rooms are clustered around a quiet courtyard. Each has a lace-hung glass door and a decor that includes warm autumn colors and wood-beamed ceilings. *Pasteur Sur 17, 76000, tel. 463/4–56–23. 21 suites with bath. Facilities: restaurant, bar, swimming pool, satellite TV. AE, DC, MC, V.*

Expensive
Hotel Amberes. A modern high rise built in 1981, Hotel Amberes faces the Alameda Hidalgo park on a rather busy street, but rooms are well insulated and fairly quiet. Standard features include beds with floral spreads, small black-and-white TVs, free-standing fans, and modern baths with purified tap water. *Corregidora Sur 188, 76000, tel. 463/2–86–04. 140 rooms with bath. Facilities: restaurant, bar. AE, DC, MC, V.*
Hotel Mirabel. A favorite among business travelers and conventioneers, this modern high rise hums with activity. Its carpeted rooms, however, are insulated and quiet and feature color TVs, telephones, wood desks, and air-conditioning. Some double rooms have views of the Alameda Hidalgo park; some single rooms overlook a soccer stadium. *Av. Constituyentes Oriente 2, 76000, tel. 463/4–35–85 or 4–30–99. 171 rooms with bath. Facilities: restaurant, bar, convention salon. AE, MC, V.*

Moderate
Hotel Señorial. Built in 1981, this sprawling four-story property has clean, modern rooms with telephones and TVs. Beds are covered with printed spreads that clash with the floral drapes; baths are tiled and almost sterile in appearance. Rooms in front face a narrow, busy street, but traffic slows in the evening. There are purified-water dispensers in the hallways. *Guerrero Norte 10-A, 76000, tel. 463/4–37–00 or 4–19–45. 45 rooms with bath. Facilities: restaurant. MC, V.*

Inexpensive
Hotel Plaza. This modest property, located on the main plaza, offers clean accommodations and lots of hot water. Rooms facing the principal square are extremely noisy—even at night. Inside rooms, particularly those on the second floor, are much quieter, but dark. All rooms have telephones and most have TVs, but for those that do not, there is a small color TV above the soda machine in the tiled lobby. *Av. Juárez Norte 23, 76000, tel. 463/2–65–62. 29 rooms with bath. MC, V.*

Excursion to San Juan del Río and Tequisquiapan

San Juan del Río and Tequisquiapan, both within an hour's drive of Querétaro, have long been frequented by harried Mexican urbanites who come to soak in the area's thermal waters and to shop for semiprecious gems. If you have time for a day's excursion, grab a bathing suit and your credit card and go exploring. The tourist office in Querétaro can supply you with brochures.

The simplest way to reach these towns is by car. Route 57, the quick, well-traveled road to Mexico City, passes by San Juan del Río 51 kilometers (32 miles) from Querétaro. Tequisquiapan is 19 kilometers (12 miles) east of San Juan, off Route 120. Buses service both towns from Querétaro, but the trip is longer.

To break up the day, you'll probably want to do your shopping in San Juan del Río (a center of commerce), then head to Tequisquiapan to relax at its lush resort spas. Most of San Juan's gem shops are located near the main plaza downtown. Two places have particularly good selections.

Mercado de Artesanías Minerales specializes in opal, amethyst, turquoise, and topaz jewelry. *Av. Juárez Poniente 4, tel. 463/ 2–14–81. Open daily 9–8. No credit cards.*

La Guadalupana—a cluster of shops in a large courtyard— sells opal, amethyst, topaz, and onyx jewelry, hand-embroidered blouses, brassware, and wood carvings. *Calle 16 de Septiembre #5, tel. 463/2–01–03. Open daily 9–6:30. AE, MC, V.*

Your first stop in Tequisquiapan should be the tourist office. The staff has a list of all 22 spas in town and can tell you which hotels rent out facilities for the afternoon. There is no phone but during the week the office of municipal government may be able to answer questions at 467/3–07–57. *Andador Niños Héroes at the corner of Morelos. Open weekdays 9–2 and 5–8, weekends 10–1.*

A few hours soaking in the local spas' waters of volcanic origin is said to ease the pain of arthritis, cure insomnia, and improve digestion. Avoid Tequisquiapan on weekends, when area urbanites book up hotels. During the week, however, some spas clean their pools, so call before going.

After visiting the spas, stop in the verdant main plaza for a beverage or snack and then head to the shops or to the Mercado de Artesanías where woven goods, jewelry, and locally made furniture are sold. Each summer, the city hosts a week-long wine and cheese festival, which is quite a lively affair. Aside from sampling locally grown products, visitors can attend bullfights, purchase handicrafts, and dance to the tunes of mariachi bands.

Morelia

Morelia, with its long, wide boulevards and earth-tone colonial mansions, is the gracious capital of the state of Michoacán. Founded in 1541 as Valladolid (after the Spanish city), it changed its name in 1828 to honor José María Morelos, the town's most famous son. The legendary mule skinner-turned-priest took up the battle for independence after its early leaders were executed in 1811.

Morelos began with an ill-equipped army of 25 but soon organized a contingent of 9,000 that nearly gained control of the country. Though he was defeated and executed in 1815, he left behind a long-standing reformist legacy that called for universal suffrage, racial equality, and the demise of the hacienda system.

The city today still pays tribute to Morelos: His former home has been turned into a museum, and his birthplace is now a library. Morelia's colonial heritage is preserved by its status as a national monument. The city is also forward-thinking. It's the site of a politically liberal university that often holds rallies supporting social and political causes. Look closely along Avenida Madero and you'll see political fliers posted on buildings.

Morelia has the dubious distinction of being the candy capital of Mexico. So strong, in fact, is the sweet-eating tradition that the city houses a *Mercado de Dulcería*, or sweets market. If you want to sample some local confections (made from candied fruit or evaporated milk), walk over to Calle Gómez Farías, three blocks west and a half block north of the main plaza.

Morelia is also the home of writers, artists, philosophers, and poets, as well as American retirees. To explore Morelia and its surrounding hillside neighborhoods thoroughly would take some time. However, if you stroll through the historic plazas and frequent the cafés (as many locals do), you will begin to feel the city's vitality.

Arriving and Departing

By Plane There are daily flights between Francisco Mujica International Airport, 24 kilometers (15 miles) north of Morelia, and Mexico City's International Airport on **Aeromar Airlines** (tel. 451/3-05-55 in Morelia; 5/2-85-45 or 207-6666 in Mexico City). Flights are subject to cancellation and flight times change often and must be confirmed one day in advance.

By Car Recent construction on Federal Highway 126 has cut travel time from Mexico City to Morelia from 6 to 4½ hours. Take the highway through Toluca, Atlacamulco, Contepec and Maravatio. Cars can be rented at various locations in Mexico City. In Morelia, **Budget** has an office at the Misión Hotel (tel. 451/5-00-23) but will pick up clients at the airport.

By Train There is daily train service between Mexico City and Morelia on the Mexican National Railway. The *Purepecha* leaves Mexico City at 10:20 PM and arrives in Morelia at 6:15 AM; the return trip departs Morelia at 10:05 PM and arrives in Mexico City at 7:20 AM. Sleeping cars are available, but tickets, which begin at $17, should be purchased one day in advance.

By Bus Direct bus service is available daily between the Terminal Poniente (West Terminal) in Mexico City and Morelia's Central de Autobuses. Several bus lines offer frequent service; the most direct trip, which takes five hours, is on Herradura de Plata (via Corta). Frequent inexpensive bus service is also available from Morelia to other points in Michoacán and throughout the heartland.

Getting Around

As in many of the heartland cities, Morelia's principal sights are near the center of town and you can reach them on foot. Street names in Morelia change frequently, especially on either side of Avenida Madero, the city's main east–west artery. Taxis in Morelia can be hailed on the street or found near the main plaza. Buses run the length of Avenida Madero.

Important Addresses and Numbers

Tourist Information The **Secretaría Estatal de Turismo** in the Palacio Clavijero provides city maps and brochures of the state of Michoacán. Only a few of the brochures are in English. *Calle Nigromante 79, tel. 451/3–26–54 or 451/3–26–54. Open daily 9–2 and 4–8.*

Federal tourism offices are at Acueductor 303–Bis, Altos Central (tel. 451/2–01–23 or 451/2–05–22).

Emergencies **Police** (tel. 451/2–22–22). **Ambulance-Red Cross** (tel. 451/4–51–51). **Consumer Protection Office** (tel. 451/2–40–49).

Hospital **Municipal Hospital** (tel. 451/2–22–16).

Money Exchange **Casa de Cambio** (Calle Melchor Ocampo, at the corner of Calle Ignacio Zaragoza) is open Monday–Saturday, 9–2 and 4–6.

Travel Agencies **Viajes Lopsa** is the American Express representative. (Service Las Américas, Local 27, Artilleros del 47, tel. 451/4–19–50). **Wagons-Lits Viajes** is located at Ignacio Zarazoga 95 (tel. 451/2–42–95 or 2–42–99).

Guided Tours

The following operators conduct tours of Morelia: **Autoturismo Morelia** (Calle Colima 486, tel. 451/4–08–26), **Michoacán Tour Guides and Conductors Association** (Calle Nigromante 79, tel. 451/3–26–54), **Tours Lindo Michoacán** (Calle Colima 486, tel. 451/4–99–43), **Transportación Turística Valladolid** (Av. Lázaro Cárdenas 1966, 2nd floor, tel. 451/4–73–84).

Exploring

Numbers in the margin correspond to points of interest on the Morelia map.

❶ Many of Morelia's points of interest are located within a few blocks of the main square, the **Plaza de Armas** or **Plaza de los Mártires**. Several rebel priests were brutally murdered on this site during the War of Independence, and the plaza is named after them. Today, however, the square belies its violent past: Sweethearts stroll along the tree-lined walks, vendors sell mounds of peanuts, placards boast of cultural events, and lively, recorded music blasts from a silver-domed bandshell.

❷ Slightly east of the plaza lies Morelia's famed **Catedral**, a majestic structure built between 1640 and 1744. It is known throughout Mexico for its 200-foot Baroque towers, among the tallest in the land, and for its 4,600-pipe organ, one of the finest in the world. The organ is on the balcony at the back of the cathedral. An international organ festival is held here each May.

As you leave the cathedral, cross Avenida Madero and walk to
❸ the **Palacio de Gobierno**. This former Tridentine Seminary,

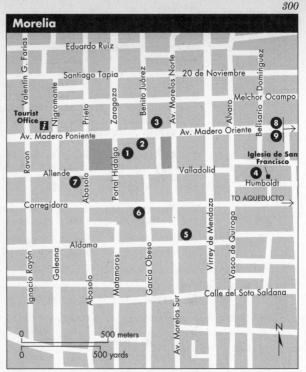

built in 1770, has had such notable graduates as independence hero José María Morelos, social reformer Melchor Ocampo, and the first Emperor of Mexico, Agustín de Iturbide. Striking murals decorate the stairway and second floor. Painted by local artist Alfredo Zalce in the early 1960s, they depict dramatic, often bloody, scenes from Mexico's history. From the second floor, you can catch a glimpse of the cathedral's spires across the way. *Av. Madero 63, tel. 451/2-78-72. Open daily 7 AM–11 PM.*

From the palace, walk four blocks east along Avenida Madero (past a number of banks) until you reach Calle de Belisario Domínguez. Make a right and walk one block to the Church of San Francisco. To the rear of the church, in the former convent ❹ of San Francisco, is the entrance to the **Casa de las Artesanías del Estado de Michoacán.** This two-story marketplace is a virtual cornucopia of crafts from around the state. In the 16th century, Vasco de Quiroga, the Bishop of Michoacán, helped the Tarascan Indians develop artistic specialties so they could be self-supporting. The rooms display the work the Tarascans still produce: copper goods from Santa Clara del Cobre, lacquerware from Uruapan, straw items and pottery from Pátzcuaro, guitars from Paracho, macabre ceramic figures from Ocumicho. Upstairs in the **Museo Michoacana de las Artesanías,** which is open daily 9–8, some of these items are showcased behind glass while artists demonstrate how they are made. Though the market offers an excellent selection of goods, prices are often better in the indigenous villages. If you plan to explore these outlying towns, you may want to do your shopping there.

⑤ Next visit the **Casa Museo de Morelos**, a home acquired in 1801 by the independence leader Morelos. Generations of the Morelos family lived there until 1934. Walk two blocks south on Calle Vasco de Quiroga, a street lined with vendors, until you reach Calle del Soto Saldana. Walk west another two blocks to Avenida Morelos Sur. The museum, now owned by the Mexican government, is the corner building on your right. The two floors contain family portraits (including one of Morelos's mother who, he said, "gave him constant spirit and strength"), a copy of Morelos's birth certificate, various artifacts from the independence movement (such as a camp bed used by Ignacio Allende), and the blindfold Morelos wore for his execution. A guide conducts an excellent free tour (in Spanish only). *Av. Morelos Sur 323. Small admission fee. Open daily 9–6:30.*

From the museum, walk one block north to Calle Corregidora, then one block west to Calle García Obeso. On this corner **⑥** stands **Casa Natal**, Morelos's birthplace, now a library and national monument housing mostly history and literature books (as well as two murals by Alfredo Zalce). Be sure to visit the courtyard in back. It's a tranquil square, adjacent to the Church of San Agustín, with rose bushes, evergreens, and wild poinsettias; a marker and eternal flame honor the fallen hero. *Calle Corregidora 113. Admission free. Open weekdays 9:30–2 and 4–8, Sat. 9:30–3:30 and 4:30–7, Sun. 9:30–3.*

Walk west on Calle Corregidora until you reach Calle Abasolo; head north one block to Calle Allende, where you'll find the **⑦** **Museo Michoacana**. An 18th-century former palace, the museum traces the history of Mexico from its pre-Hispanic days through the Cardenista period, which ended in 1940. President Lázaro Cárdenas, a native of Michoacán, was one of Mexico's most popular leaders because of his nationalization of the oil industry and his support of other populist reforms. The ground floor contains an art gallery, plus archaeological exhibits from Michoacán and other parts of Mexico. Upstairs is an assortment of colonial objects, including furniture, weapons, and religious paintings. *Calle Allende 305, tel. 451/2–04–07. Admission: about $3. Open Tues.–Sat. 9–7, Sun. 9–2.*

From the museum, take Calle Abasolo one block north to return to Avenida Madero. The plaza will be one block to the east.

Time Out When you've finished your tour, walk across the street to the *portales*. A number of popular sidewalk cafés are set among these colonial stone arcades. For a sandwich or a fruit cocktail, or a good selection of juices, coffees, and teas, try **Café Catedral**. No one will mind if you linger over a book or newspaper for the better part of an hour. *Portal Hidalgo 213, tel. 451/2–32–89. Open 8 AM–10 PM. No credit cards.*

After refueling at the portales, continue east on Avenida Madero to the **Bosque Cuauhtémoc**, Morelia's largest park. This **⑧** walk should take about 15 minutes, providing you aren't sidetracked en route by temptations such as Helados Bing (Av. Madero 422), an ice cream shop offering more than 20 flavors.

Avenida Madero forks as you near the park. Keep to the right, passing the **Fountain of the Tarascans** on a square to your left. Just past the square, Morelia's mile-long **aqueduct** begins. This structure, which consists of 250 arches, was built in 1785 and was once the city's main source of drinking water. It's particularly beautiful at night when its arches—some rising to 30 feet—are lit.

Two blocks farther (Madero is now called Avenida Acueducto) is the entrance to Bosque Cuauhtémoc. If you happen by during the week, you may encounter university students studying (or lounging) beneath the palms and evergreens; on weekends, especially Sundays, the park is filled with families on outings.

❾ Continue past the park entrance for two blocks to the **Museo de Arte Contemporáneo** on your right, where the works of contemporary Mexican and international artists are on view. *Av. Acueducto 18. Small admission fee. Open Tues.–Sun. 10–2 and 4–8.*

Dining

Some of Michoacán's tastiest dishes—Lake Pátzcuaro white fish, tomato-based Tarascan soup, corn products like *huchepos* and *corundas*, and game (rabbit, quail, and kid)—are featured at Morelia restaurants. Traditional chicken and beef fare are also available as well as international dishes. As a rule, more upscale restaurants are located in hotels near the plaza and on the outskirts of town.

Highly recommended restaurants are indicated by a star ★.

Category	Cost*
Moderate	$10–$15
Inexpensive	under $10

*per person, excluding drinks, service, and sales tax (10%)

Moderate **Boca del Rio.** Large picture windows opening onto a busy inter-
★ section provide lots of light for this cheerful restaurant, which claims to have fresh fish and seafood trucked in daily from Sinaloa and Veracruz. Located between the bus station and the Mercado de Dulceria, it provides light snacks, such as *cocktel de camarones* (shrimp cocktail) or *sopa de mariscos* (a rich broth filled with clams, mussels, shrimp and crab) or heartier fare like *pescadillos* (tostadas stuffed with lightly cooked, marinated fish and served with a salad), or *jaiba rellena* (crabs stuffed with mushrooms and cheese and liberally seasoned with garlic). *Valentin Gomez Farías 185, tel. 451/2–99–74. Reservations accepted. Dress: informal. AE, DC, MC, V.*

★ **El Rey Tacamba.** Friendly, attentive service and brightly colored decorations mark this three-year-old restaurant, located on the north side of the Plaza de Armas. Among its specialties are *mixiote de carnero*, a piquant (although not spicy), mutton dish, first stewed and then steamed in banana leaves; *pollo moreliano*, chicken roasted in a rich, red chile sauce and served with enchiladas covered in vegetables; and *carne tampiqueña*, a grilled flank steak accompanied by guacamole, refried beans, and tostadas. *Portal Galeana 157, tel. 451/2–20–44. Reservations accepted. Dress: informal. MC, V.*

Inexpensive **Café del Bosque.** During the week, university students frequent this 1960s-style restaurant. It's tacky—floral carpet and bright green booths—but the food is good and fairly cheap. Most students can afford sandwiches or burgers; if you feel like spending a bit more, order *pollo moreliano* (chicken with enchiladas, vegetables, and french fries) or *carne à la Mexicana* (grilled beef cooked with onions, tomatoes, lemon juice, and salsa). There's a small but pleasant terrace for outdoor dining. *Plaza Rebullones, Local C-7, tel. 451/3–28–13. Reservations not accepted. Dress: informal. AE, MC, V.*

El Paraíso. To jump-start your day, have a cup of the strong, rich cappuccino at El Paraíso. Breakfasts—the recommended meal at this downtown eatery—run the gamut from eggs and pancakes to fresh fruit, granola, and exotic juices (watermelon, mango, pineapple, and guayaba). The specialty is *jamón Paraíso*, fried eggs, ham, and grated cheese. The plain surroundings—Formica tables and yellow-tiled walls—don't deter locals. *Portal Galeana 103, tel. 451/2–03–74. Reservations not accepted. Dress: informal. MC, V.*

★ **Los Comensales.** This garden restaurant, a downtown favorite among the bullfight crowd, is set in an old colonial house north of the main plaza. Tables are spaced casually around a plant-filled courtyard where caged birds sing briskly. Regional dishes include *pollo de plaza* (chicken with enchiladas, carrots, potatoes, and cheese) and *huchepos* (tamales and sour cream). For breakfast, try *calabaza con leche* (baked squash with brown sugar and milk). *Calle Zaragoza 148, tel. 451/2–93–71. Reservations not accepted. Dress: informal. No credit cards.*

Lodging

Morelia offers a number of pleasant colonial-style properties both in the downtown and outlying areas. Generally, the cheapest hotels are located near the bus station, moderately priced selections are clustered around the plaza (or on nearby side streets), and deluxe resort properties are in or near the Santa María hills.

Highly recommended lodgings are indicated by a star ★.

Category	Cost*
Very Expensive	over $75
Expensive	$35–$75
Moderate	$15–$35
Inexpensive	under $15

All prices are for a standard double room; excluding 10% tax.

Very Expensive ★ **Villa Montana.** This deluxe property, owned by French Count Philippe de Reiset, has all the markings of a wealthy Mexican estate. Set high above Morelia in the Santa María hills, its five impeccably groomed acres are dotted with a pool, tennis court, and fanciful stone sculptures. Each individually decorated unit has at least one piece of antique furniture and often a fireplace and private patio. A renowned restaurant offers North American, French, and Mexican food. *Calle Patzimba s/n, 58090, tel. 451/4–02–31 or 4–01–79. 55 rooms with bath. Facilities: restaurant, piano bar, outdoor terrace with bar, game room, pool, tennis court, laundry service, convention hall. MC, V.*

Expensive **Hotel Catedral.** Located in a restored colonial mansion, this three-story property began operating as a hotel some 30 years ago. Its modern rooms are clustered around a skylit courtyard; some overlook the main plaza and cathedral on Avenida Madero. Interior quarters have less dramatic views but are less noisy. All rooms have dark, wood furnishings, telephones, and color TVs. *Calle Zaragoza 37, 58000, tel. 451/3–07–83 or 3–04–67. 44 rooms with bath. Facilities: restaurant, bar, pharmacy, tobacco shop, laundry, dry cleaning, medical referrals. AE, DC, MC, V.*

★ **Hotel Posada de la Soledad.** Set in a restored private mansion built in the late-17th century, the Posada de la Soledad is conveniently located one block from the Plaza de Armas. The rooms in the front of the hotel, the oldest section, are surrounded by an elegant patio with a large fountain and bougainvillea trees, as well as vintage carriages from the colonial era. Rooms located here also have sturdy wooden furnishings, elegantly hand-carved by Michoacán craftsmen. The rooms facing north on Calle Melchor Ocampo, however, should be avoided due to heavy traffic on that street. Rooms in the back of the hotel were added in the 1960s; the newer section's accommodations are smaller and less elaborately furnished but stay quiet and are comfortably appointed with earthtone carpeting and bedspreads. In the off-season, they can be had for a discount. The Posada also has an elegant restaurant and a darkly lit bar where a guitar trio plays plaintive, romantic music. *Ignacio Zaragoza 90, 58000, tel. 451/2–18–88. 58 rooms with bath. Facilities: restaurant, bar. AE, DC, MC, V.*

Moderate **Hotel Mansion Acueducto.** An elaborate wood and wrought-iron staircase leads from the elegant lobby to more modest quarters upstairs. Rooms have dark, colonial-style furniture, telephones, and black-and-white TVs. Older rooms overlook the aqueduct and nearby park; rooms in the motel-like wing have views of the garden, pool, and surrounding mountains. Student groups at times book the entire property. *Av. Acueducto 25, 58000, tel. 451/2–33–01 or 2–20–20. 36 rooms with bath. Facilities: restaurant, bar, pool. AE, MC, V.*

Inexpensive **Hotel Concordia.** New owners have spruced up this property in the past few years, giving it a coat of paint and a large skylight. Rooms are simply furnished (some spreads are slightly worn), but sheets are clean and showers have hot water throughout the day. On weekends, Mexican families with young children frequent this spot and tend to rise (and wake others) early. *Valentín Gómez Farias 328, 58000, tel. 451/2–30–52. 51 rooms with bath. Facilities: restaurant. DC, MC.*

Pátzcuaro

Pátzcuaro, the 16th-century capital of Michoacán, exists in a time warp. A bit more than an hour by car from Morelia, this beautiful lakeside community set at 7,250 feet in the Sierra Madre is home to the Tarascan Indians, who fish, farm, and ply their crafts as they have for centuries. Women, wrapped tightly in their striped wool *rebozos* (shawls), hurry to market in the chill, smoky morning air. Men, in traditional straw hats, wheel overburdened carts down crooked, dusty back streets.

The architecture, too, has remained largely unchanged over the years. In the 16th century, under kindly Bishop Vasco de Quiroga, Pátzcuaro underwent a building boom of sorts. After he died in 1565, the state capital was moved to Morelia, and the town became a cultural (and architectural) backwater for hundreds of years. Modern visitors will see 16th-century mansions surrounding the downtown plazas; one-story whitewashed houses with sloping tile roofs line the side streets and hills.

Despite the altitude, the weather in Pátzcuaro is temperate year-round. (Autumn and winter nights, however, are cold; sweaters and jackets are a must.) On November 1—the night preceding the Mexican Day of the Dead—the town is inundated with tourists en route to Janitzio, an island in Lake Pátzcuaro, where one of the most elaborate graveyard ceremonies in all of Mexico takes place. Unless you have hotel reservations six months in advance, avoid going anywhere near Pátzcuaro on November 1.

Arriving and Departing

By Car Driving time from Mexico City to Pátzcuaro is about seven hours. From Morelia, two roads lead to Pátzcuaro: the newer passes through Tiripetio; the older passes through Quiroga and Tzintzuntzán. Cars can be rented at locations in Mexico City or Morelia; there are no rental outlets in Pátzcuaro.

By Train Train service with sleeping cars between Mexico City and Pátzcuaro is available daily on the Mexican National Railways. The *Purepecha* departs Mexico City at 10 PM and arrives in Pátzcuaro at 7:37 AM; the return trip leaves Pátzcuaro at 9:41 PM and arrives in Mexico City at 7:17 AM. Sleeping-car accommodations run about $20 per person.

By Bus Direct bus service is available daily between the Terminal Poniente (West Terminal) in Mexico City and Pátzcuaro's Central Camionera. Several bus lines offer frequent service; the most direct trip, which takes six hours, is on **Herradura de Plata** (via Corta). Frequent inexpensive bus service is available from Pátzcuaro to other points in Michoacán and throughout the heartland.

Getting Around

Many of Pátzcuaro's principal sites are located near the Plaza Vasco de Quiroga and Plaza Bocanegra in the center of town. Taxis and buses to the lake can also be found at these main squares. If you want to visit surrounding villages, taxi drivers will drive you for a reasonable rate. Be sure to agree on a fee before setting out.

Important Addresses and Numbers

Tourist Information The **Delegación de Turismo** distributes city maps and brochures (in Spanish). *Portal Hidalgo 9, off the Plaza Vasco de Quiroga, tel. 454/2-09-67. Open weekdays 9-2 and 4-7, Sat. 9-7, Sun. 9-4.*

Emergencies **Police** (tel. 454/2-05-65). **Ambulance** (tel. 454/2-18-89).

Clinic **Centro Médico Quirúrgico** (Portal Hidalgo 76, tel. 454/2-19-98).

Pharmacy **Farmacia La Paz** (at the corner of La Paz and Bocanegra in the Plaza Bocanegra tel. 454/2-08-10).

Money Exchange **Banca Promex** (tel. 454/2-03-97), **Banca Serfin** (tel. 454/2-22-10), **Banamex** (tel. 454/2-05-88), **Bancomer** (tel. 454/2-03-34).

Many Pátzcuaro restaurants and hotels do not accept traveler's checks, though some will take major credit cards.

Exploring

Numbers in the margin correspond to points of interest on the Pátzcuaro map.

Most of Pátzcuaro's sites can be visited in a few hours, but the town deserves to be explored at a leisurely pace. Begin at the ❶ **Plaza Vasco de Quiroga,** the larger of two downtown squares. A tranquil courtyard surrounded by ash trees and 16th-century mansions (since converted into hotels and shops), the plaza commemorates the bishop who restored dignity to the Tarascan people. During the Spanish conquest, Nuño de Guzmán, a lieutenant in Hernán Cortés's army, committed atrocities on the local population in his efforts to conquer western Mexico. He was eventually arrested by the Spanish authorities, and in 1537 Quiroga was appointed Bishop of Michoacán. a number of model villages in the area and promoted the development of commerce among the Tarascans. Quiroga died in 1565, and his remains were consecrated in the basilica.

❷ From the plaza, cross over to the **tourist office** at Portal Hidalgo 9, where you can collect maps and brochures on the region. (As you face the front of the Quiroga's statue, Portal Hidalgo is the street to your right.) As you leave the office, turn right again and continue around the plaza until you reach Calle Dr. José María Coss on the east side.

Turn right on this street, and in less than a block you'll see a ❸ long cobblestoned walkway leading to **La Casa de los 11 Patios,** an 18th-century convent with a number of high-quality shops featuring Tarascan handiwork. As you meander through the gardens and courtyards, you'll encounter weavers producing large bolts of cloth, artists trimming black lacquerware with gold, and seamstresses embroidering blouses. Children may approach you and ask if you'd like to hear the history of the Casa. In return, they expect a small donation. If you plan to shop in Pátzcuaro, this is a good place to start. You can view the selection of regional goods and begin to compare prices.

As you leave the shops, continue up a stone walkway to Calle Lerín. Though only one block east of the plaza, its aging stone walls and whitewashed houses with sloping tile roofs have an ancient feel about them. Another block down (past Calle ❹ Portugal) is the **Templo de la Compañia,** Michoacán's first cathedral. It was begun in 1540 by order of Vasco de Quiroga and completed in 1546. When the state capital was moved to Morelia some 20 years later, the church was taken over by the Jesuits. Today it remains much as it was in the 16th century. Moss has grown over the crumbling stone steps outside; the dank interior is planked with thick wood floors and lined with bare wood benches. Though not architecturally striking, a visit inside the cathedral will transport you back four centuries.

❺ Continue down Calle Lerín another half block to the **Museo de Artes Populares** on your right. The Colegio de San Nicolás Obispo in the 16th century, this museum today displays colonial and contemporary crafts, such as ceramics, masks, lacquerware, colonial paintings, and ex-votos in its many rooms. Behind this building is a *troje* (traditional Tarascan wood house) braced

Pátzcuaro

N

TO RAILROAD
STATION

atop a stone platform. *Admission: about $3. Open Tues.–Sat.
9–7, Sun. 9–3.*

6 Directly down Calle Lerín and across a cobblestoned courtyard
is **La Basílica de Nuestra Señora de la Salud.** Out front,
Tarascan women sell hot tortillas, herb mixtures for teas, and
religious objects. From this point you can glimpse Lake
Pátzcuaro in the distance. The church was begun in 1554 by
Vasco de Quiroga but was never completed. Over the centuries,
others—undaunted by earthquakes and fires—took up the
cause and constructed a church in honor of the Virgin of
Health. Near the main altar is a statue made of cornstalk paste
and orchid "juice." Several masses are still held here daily; the
earliest begins shortly after dawn.

7 Continue downhill from the basilica for about two blocks to
reach the **Biblioteca Pública Gertrudis Bocanegra.** In the back
of this library is a vast mural depicting in great detail the history of the region and of the Tarascan people. It was completed
by Juan O'Gorman in 1942. If you look closely at the bottom,
you may be able to make out images of Vasco de Quiroga, portrayed as friend and protector of the Indians, and Gertrudis
Bocanegra, a local heroine who was shot in 1814 for refusing to
divulge the revolutionaries' secrets to the Spaniards. *Open
weekdays 9–7, Sat. 9–1.*

From the library, continue again to your right for a half a block
to the large outdoor **mercado** sprawled along Calle Libertad
and its side streets. At times, the road is so crowded with people and their wares—fruits, vegetables, beans, rice, herbs,

and sponges—that it is difficult to walk. On Friday, market day, the street is particularly packed. If you press on for about a block, you'll see an indoor market to your left, filled with more produce, large hanging slabs of meat, vendors selling hot food, and a variety of cheap trinkets.

When you've completed your market stroll, retrace your steps down Calle Libertad. Across the street from the library, stop
❽ in at the **Plaza Bocanegra**. This square, marked by a statue of the local heroine, is just one block north of Plaza Vasco de Quiroga, your starting point. While Bocanegra is the smaller of the two squares, it is the center of Pátzcuaro's commercial life. Bootblacks, pushcart vendors and bus and taxi stands to Lake Pátzcuaro are all found in this plaza.

Time Out   Before heading to the lake, sit in the shady square for a moment and enjoy a rich Michoacán ice cream or fruit bar. Then grab a taxi or the San Bartolo/Lago bus to the *embarcadero* (wharf).

A 10-minute ride will bring you to the tranquil shore of Lake Pátzcuaro. There are a few lakeside restaurants here that serve fresh white fish and other local catches. Amble along the dock or peek into the waterfront crafts shops. If you have time, a boat trip to **Janitzio** (the largest of Lake Pátzcuaro's five islands) is highly recommended.

Wooden launches, with room for 25 people, depart for Janitzio daily from 8 AM to 5 PM. Purchase round-trip tickets at a dockside office (where prices are controlled by the tourist department). The ride to Janitzio takes about 30 minutes and is particularly beautiful in late afternoon, when the sun is low in the sky. Once you're out on the lake, fishermen with butterfly nets may approach your boat. The nets are no longer used for fishing, but for a small donation, these locals will let you take their picture.

On most days (November 2 being the exception), Janitzio is a quiet island inhabited by Tarascan Indians. It is crowned by a huge statue of independence hero José María Morelos, which is accessible by cobblestoned stairway. Though the road twists past many souvenir stands as it ascends, don't be discouraged. The view from the summit—of the lake, the town, and the surrounding hills—is well worth the climb. Inside the statue are some remarkable murals that spiral up from the base to the tip of the monument.

Off the Beaten Track

The remains of **Tzintzuntzán,** the ancient capital of the Tarascan Indian kingdom, lie 17 kilometers (10.5 miles) northeast of Pátzcuaro. When the Spanish came to colonize the region in the 16th century, some 40,000 Tarascans lived and worshiped in this lakeshore village, which they called "place of the hummingbirds." The ruins of their pyramid-shape temples, or *yacatas*, still stand today and are open to the public for a small admission charge. Visitors can also find vestiges of a 16th-century Franciscan monastery where Spanish friars attempted to convert the Indians to Christianity. Though Tzintzuntzán lost some prominence when Bishop Vasco de Quiroga moved the seat of his diocese to Pátzcuaro in 1540, the village is still well known for its handicrafts. The Tarascan Indians turn out a variety of products in straw and ceramics, which are sold in numerous shops along the main street of town. To reach Tzintzuntzán, take the bus marked Quiroga from Pátzcuaro's Central Camionera; travel time is about 30 minutes.

Dining

Most restaurants in Pátzcuaro specialize in seafood. In addition to white fish (which is featured on most menus), look for *trucha* (trout) and *charales* and *boquerones* (two small, locally caught fish served as appetizers). Tarascan specialties, such as a tomato-based soup, are also common. As a rule, restaurants are located around the two plazas and in hotels. Since the large meal is served at midday, many dining establishments are shuttered by 9 PM.

Highly recommended restaurants are indicated by a star ★.

Category	Cost*
Moderate	over $10
Inexpensive	$5–$10

*per person, excluding drinks, service, and sales tax (10%)

Moderate
★ **El Patio.** Though this newly renovated restaurant features mouth-watering white-fish platters, it's possible to duck in at midday for just a strong cappuccino or glass of local wine. (There are several varieties of wine; waiters can help you choose among them.) For a late-afternoon snack, a plate of quesadillas with a side order of guacamole is highly recommended. For full-blown meals, try the white fish served with salsa, vegetables, and french fries. *Plaza Vasco de Quiroga 19, tel. 454/2–04–84. Dress: informal. DC, MC, V.*

Restaurante Gran Hotel. Though this one-room restaurant is connected to the Gran Hotel, it is independently owned and attracts a mix of locals and tourists to its midday meal. The furnishings are simple: tables covered with amber-colored cloths and set beneath wood chandeliers. The food is good and wholesome. Specialties include lightly breaded white fish and chicken with mole sauce. Tarascan soup (with a tomato base, cheese, cream, and tortillas) is also worth trying. *Portal Regules 6, tel. 454/2–04–98. Reservations not accepted. Dress: informal. No credit cards.*

Restaurante Los Escudos. This colonial-style restaurant, located on the Plaza Vasco de Quiroga, is frequented by foreigners who stay in the adjoining hotel. The varied menu ranges from club sandwiches to several-course midday meals. Two particularly tempting treats are the Tarascan soup and *pollo especial Los Escudos* (chicken sautéed in tomato sauce and vegetables). Checked tablecloths and yellow chimney lamps lend a cozy atmosphere. *Portal Hidalgo 74, tel. 454/2–01–38 or 2–12–90. Reservations not accepted. Dress: informal. MC, V.*

Inexpensive
★ **Restaurante Hotel Posada La Basílica.** From a corner table in this glass-enclosed restaurant, patrons have views of the mountains, the lake, and tile-roofed homes. Open for breakfast and lunch, this dining spot offers such regional specialties as broiled trout with garlic, fried *charales*, and *sopa de corunda* (tamales with cheese and cream). Mexican-style eggs and a fresh fruit platter are recommended morning fare. *Calle*

Arciga 6, tel. 454/2–11–08. Reservations not accepted. Dress: informal. No credit cards.

Lodging

Though Pátzcuaro has no deluxe properties, there is an ample number of clean, moderately priced hotels. Most are located on or within a few blocks of the Plaza Vasco de Quiroga. Several more expensive properties are situated on Avenida Lázaro Cárdenas, the road to Lake Pátzcuaro. If you're planning to be in town on or near November 2, the Mexican Day of the Dead, make hotel reservations at least six months in advance.

Highly recommended lodgings are indicated by a star ★.

Category	Cost*
Expensive	over $40
Moderate	$15–$40
Inexpensive	under $15

All prices are for a standard double room, excluding 10% tax.

Expensive
★ **Hotel Posada de Don Vasco.** Located several minutes out of town on the road to Lake Pátzcuaro, this sprawling resort hotel offers a wide range of indoor and outdoor amenities. Its 30 new rooms are thickly carpeted and have either balconies or patios; the older quarters, decorated in a colonial style, are smaller and open onto a courtyard. The manicured grounds are relatively quiet despite the occasional rumbling of a passing bus or truck. *Av. Lázaro Cárdenas 450, 61500 tel. 454/2–02–27. 103 rooms with bath, including 4 suites. Facilities: restaurant, pool, tennis and badminton courts, bowling alley, billiard tables. AE, DC, MC, V.*

Moderate
Los Escudos. The 16th-century home of the Count de la Lama and the Marquis de Villahermosa de Alfaro on the Plaza Vasco de Quiroga is today a cozy hotel. Its courtyards brim with potted plants, and some guest rooms contain small murals of Tarascan Indian scenes. Ten rooms situated in back and shielded from street noise, open onto an outdoor patio. Twenty-five rooms have color TVs; five rooms offer fireplaces. *Portal Hidalgo 73, 61600, tel. 454/2–01–38 or 2–12–90. 30 rooms with bath. Facilities: restaurant. MC, V.*

★ **Mansión Iturbe.** This hotel, housed in a 17th-century mansion, still retains much of its colonial charm. Plant-filled courtyards are ringed by stone archways. Rooms have large wood and glass doors; their interiors are partially carpeted and decorated with red-and-black checked spreads and drapes. The tranquil second-floor courtyard has a good view of the neighborhood. *Portal Morelos 59, 61600, tel. 454/2–03–68. 12 rooms with bath. Facilities: restaurant, tobacco/souvenir shop. MC, V.*

Inexpensive–Moderate
Mesón del Gallo. Located on a fairly quiet side street near the Casa de los 11 Patios, this two-story property offers modern rooms in a garden setting. In the rooms, beds have wood-and-tile headboards and magenta spreads and drapes. Suites, complete with minibars, are furnished in more subdued hues. The pool is encircled by bougainvillea, fruit trees, and a rock garden. When the second-floor banquet room is rented out for af-

ternoon parties, the decibel level rises. *Calle Dr. José María Coss 20, 61600, tel. 454/2–14–74. 25 rooms with bath, including 5 suites. Facilities: restaurant, bar, pool. AE, MC, V.*

Inexpensive **Hotel Posada La Basílica.** This colonial-style inn, housed in a 17th-century building, faces the Basilica of the Virgin of Health. On some mornings, strains from a postdawn mass filter softly into the hotel; in the evenings, when there's a fair across the way, louder, more resonant music is audible. Though noisy, the property deserves a positive mention for its comfortable, individually decorated rooms. Thick wood shutters cover floor-to-ceiling windows, walls are trimmed in hand-painted colonial designs, and the rugs are handwoven. Some rooms have fireplaces, but check with management before attempting to use them, as not all of them are working. *Calle Arciga 6, 61600, tel. 454/2–11–08. 11 rooms with bath. Facilities: restaurant, fireplaces (in lobby and in 7 rooms). No credit cards.*

Excursion to Uruapan

The subtropical town of **Uruapan,** located about 64 kilometers (40 miles) west of Pátzcuaro, is distinctly different from its lakeside neighbor. At an elevation of 5,300 feet, it is a populous, commercial center with a warm climate and lush vegetation. The town's name is derived from the Tarascan word *urupan,* meaning "where the flowers bloom."

Uruapan can be reached from Pátzcuaro by either car or bus. Route 14 is the most direct route between the two cities. There is also frequent bus service on the Flecha Amarilla and other major lines; travel time is about 70 minutes.

You can see several points of interest within a few hours. The first, **La Huatapera,** is located off Uruapan's Plaza Principal. This 16th-century hospital, which abuts two 17th-century churches, has been converted into the **Museo Regional de Arte Popular.** It houses a collection of crafts from the state of Michoacán, including an excellent display of lacquerware made in Uruapan. *Tel. 452/2–21–38. Open Tues.–Sun. 9:30–1:30 and 3:30–6.*

The **Mercado de Antojitos,** an immense sprawling market, begins directly in back of the museum and extends for quite a distance north along Calle Constitución. Along the road are Tarascan Indians selling large mounds of produce, fresh fish, beans, homemade cheese, and a variety of cheap manufactured goods. If you travel south along Calle Constitución, you'll come to a courtyard where vendors set up cooking stoves and sell hot food to passersby. Frequented by locals, it is a choice place for a quick lunch of *carnitas* (a traditional Michoacán specialty of sliced pork fried in seasonings), or even just a soda.

Another recommended eatery is the **Parrilla Tarasca.** This two-level restaurant, specializing in grilled meats, cooks all dishes to order. For a delicious treat, try the *carne asada;* it's served with grilled scallions, avocado, and *frijoles charros,* a popular Mexican side order of beans in broth. The varieties of salsa are also outstanding. *Calle Alvaro Obregón 4, no phone. Open daily 8–11. MC, V.*

Head over to the **Parque Nacional Eduardo Ruiz,** located about a half mile from the Plaza Principal off Calle Independencia.

Stroll through the verdant acreage to the source of the River Cupatitzio and abundant fountains, waterfalls, and springs.

Eleven kilometers (7 miles) south along the river is the magnificent waterfall at **Tzaráracua.** At this point, the Cupatitzio plunges 150 feet off a sheer rock cliff into a riverbed below; a rainbow seems to hang perpetually over the site. Buses marked Tzaráracua leave sporadically from the Plaza Principal in Uruapan. You can also take a taxi or drive there via Avenida Lázaro Cárdenas.

Farther afield, about 32 kilometers (20 miles) north of Uruapan, lies the extinct **Paricutín volcano.** Its initial burst of lava and ashes wiped out the nearby village of San Juan Parangaricutiro in 1943. Today travelers can visit this buried site by hiring gentle mountain ponies and a Tarascan guide in the town of Angahuan. To reach Angahuan, take the Los Reyes bus from Uruapan's Central Camionera or go by car via the Uruapan–Carapan highway.

8 Guadalajara

Introduction

*Updated by David
Lida*

Traditions are preserved and customs perpetuated in Guadalajara; it's a place where the siesta is an institution and the fiesta an art form. The city is the birthplace of *el jarabe tapatío* (the Mexican hat dance), *charreadas* (rodeos), *mariachis*, and tequila.

Mexico's second-largest city is engaged in a struggle to retain its provincial ambience and colonial charm as its population approaches 6 million. Emigrés from Mexico City after the devastating 1985 earthquake and staggering numbers of the rural poor seeking employment have created a population explosion that strains the capacity of public services and the city's often outdated infrastructure. Visitors to the city can enjoy the tree-lined boulevards, parks, plazas, and stately Churrigueresque architecture, but recent years have indeed brought traffic jams and occasional heavy pollution, coming from the industrial zone outside of the city, to the downtown area.

Guadalajara has always been one of the most socially traditional and politically conservative cities in Mexico. It has also been the seat of Christian fundamentalism, and indeed, was one of the strategic areas of the *Cristeros*, a movement of Catholic fanatics in western Mexico, in the 1920s. *Tapatíos*, as the city's residents are called, even seem to take a certain amount of pride in their straight and narrow outlook. The International Gay and Lesbian Association (ILGA) wanted to hold its 1991 annual conference here, but such a public outcry ensued—protests ranging from mass marches to death-threatening graffiti to indignant newspaper editorials—that the municipal and state government refused permission. At the last minute, the convention found a friend in Acapulco.

Still, *Tapatíos* are historically accustomed to challenge and change. (The name comes from *tlapatíotl*, or three units or purses of cacao or tortillas used as currency by the Indians of Jalisco.) Within 10 years of its founding in 1532, the location of the city changed three times. In 1542, the City Council again deliberated on a new site for the fledgling municipality. After days of discussion and indecision, an intrepid woman, Doña Beatriz de Hernández, rose to address the assembly: "If you cannot make up your minds, I will. The only place suitable to build the capital is in the center of the Atemajac Valley, where the city can expand."

The governor immediately accepted the proposal, which placed Guadalajara on a mile-high plain of the Sierra Madre, bounded on three sides by rugged cliffs and on the fourth by the spectacular Barranca de Oblatos (Oblatos Canyon). A near-perfect semitropical climate and proximity to the Pacific Ocean (240 kilometers, or 150 miles) ensure warm, sunny days with just a hint of humidity and cool, clear nights.

Geographically isolated from the rest of the republic during the nearly 300 years of Spanish rule, the city cultivated and maintained a political and cultural autonomy. By the end of the 16th century, tons of silver were flowing into Guadalajara from area mines, creating the first millionaires of what was then known as New Galicia. Under orders from Spain, much of the wealth was lavished on magnificent churches, residences, and monuments. Many of these reminders of the golden era still stand in a series of contiguous plazas in downtown Guadalajara. The imposing 16th-century cathedral is the symbol of the city and an ideal starting point for a leisurely day or two of exploration.

The city also has numerous modern attractions and activities, including a new zoo, a planetarium, and the immense Parque Agua Azul (park), with carnival rides, a minitrain, swimming pool, and Sunday concerts. There are exhibitions of contemporary art at the Instituto Cultural Cabañas and in private galleries throughout the city, and tours of Museo Orozco, the former home and studio of Guadalajara's most famous muralist, José Clemente Orozco.

Guadalajara is also a great place to shop. The Mercado Libertad, Latin America's largest enclosed market, and El Baratillo, the world's largest flea market, offer a seemingly endless variety of merchandise and the opportunity to bargain with vendors. The Plaza del Sol, Latin America's biggest shopping mall, and Calle Esteban Alatorre, encompassing eight city blocks with more than 60 shoe stores, sell products you could buy at home, but usually with much lower price tags.

The suburbs of (San Pedro) Tlaquepaque and Tonalá produce some of Mexico's finest and most popular traditional crafts and folk art, including intricate blown-glass miniatures, jewelry, silver and copperware, leather and hand-carved wood furniture, and handwoven clothing. In Tlaquepaque (Tla-kay-**pah**-kay), located on the southeastern fringe of Guadalajara, over 300 shops line pedestrian malls and plazas. This charming town, which gained international acclaim for its production of ceramics, is also the birthplace of mariachi music.

Tonalá (Toe-na-**la**) is 8 kilometers (5 miles) east of and centuries removed from its commercial neighbor. One of Mexico's oldest pueblos, Tonalá is a quiet village with dusty, cobblestoned streets and adobe houses. Only in the past few years have craftsmen—primarily ceramicists—welcomed tourists into their homes and workshops.

Perhaps it is the Mexican arts and culture, perhaps the favorable exchange rate, perhaps the springlike climate; whatever the reason, more than 25,000 U.S. and Canadian citizens have retired in the Guadalajara area. The majority reside along the shores of Lake Chapala, Mexico's largest inland body of water. In the towns of Chapala (45 kilometers or 28 miles south of Guadalajara) and nearby Ajijic (Ah-he-**heek**), residents enjoy most of the amenities and services they were accustomed to north of the border.

Finally, it is worth noting the tragedy that befell Guadalajara in April, 1992. Over 200 citizens died in a succession of sewer explosions that went off mid-morning on the 23rd. As a tourist, you will not directly encounter the effects—they were restricted to a working-class neighborhood of the city where virtually no visitor attractions exist—but residents of the city suffered greatly. An investigation of the cause was still underway at press time.

Essential Information

Arriving and Departing by Plane

Airport and Airlines Libertador Miguel Hidalgo International Airport (tel. 36/89–02–49) is 16.6 kilometers (11 miles) south of Guadalajara. Unfortunately, Guadalajara's only commercial airport is frequently unable to meet the demands of the increased air service to the city. A new international terminal is planned in the next decade.

Aeroméxico (tel. 800/237–6639) and **Mexicana** (tel. 800/531–7921) have nonstop service from many major U.S. cities. Through Dallas, **American Airlines** (tel. 800/433–7300) provides service to Guadalajara from all cities in its system. **Continental Airlines** (tel. 800/525–0280) provides the same service through Houston. Nonstop flight times are: from Chicago, 4 hours; Dallas, 2 hours; Los Angeles, 2 hours and 40 minutes; and New York, 4 hours and 50 minutes.

Between the Airport and Downtown

By Van **Autotransportes Aeropuerto** (tel. 36/89–00–32) is a *combi* (VW minibus) service to city hotels and other destinations in the Guadalajara area. Fares, based on distance from the airport, are between $7 and $10 per person.

By Taxi Taxis charge between $12 and $18 to city hotels. You can bargain with drivers, but make sure you both agree on the fare before entering the cab.

By Limousine **Royal Limousines** (Miguel de Cervantes 382, Sector Juárez, tel. 36/42–56–05) has chauffeur-driven stretch limousines to downtown Guadalajara for $55.

By Car The Chapala Highway 23, a well-paved, four-lane thoroughfare, stretches north from the airport to the city. The 30-minute trip can be delayed by slow-moving caravans of trucks and weekend recreational traffic. To reach downtown hotels, just past El Tapatío Resort, turn left from the highway onto Calzada Gonzales Gallo and then right onto Av. 16 de Septiembre at Parque Agua Azul; to hotels on Avenida López Mateos Sur, just past El Tapatío Resort, turn left from the highway onto Calzada de las Torres, which turns into Calzada Lázaro Cárdenas.

Most international and domestic car rental agencies have booths at the airport in both the domestic and the new international terminals.

Arriving and Departing by Train and Bus

By Train To celebrate the 100th anniversary of railroad passenger service in 1988, the Mexican government spent millions to improve service and facilities. The upgrading of Mexico's rail system makes it a comfortable and economic option for traveling to Guadalajara. The scenic trip from the border cities—including Ciudad Juárez, Nogales, and Tijuana—takes 34 hours and features new cars and hot meal service. Information about the Mexican National Railways, including schedules and fares, can be obtained from any Mexican Government Tourism Office. The Estación de Ferrocarril (train station) is located on the south end of Avenida 16 de Septiembre, near Parque Agua Azul.

By Bus First-class, air-conditioned buses with rest rooms provide daily service to Guadalajara from most major cities on the border. **Greyhound** (tel. 800/237–8211) has lists of the telephone numbers of bus terminals in border cities served by Mexican bus lines. English-speaking representatives of the Mexican carriers will give you schedule and fare information. The **Nueva Central Camionera** (New Central Bus Station) is located 9.6 kilometers (6 miles) southeast of downtown Guadalajara on the highway to Zapotlanejo.

Important Addresses and Numbers

Tourist Information There is an **Information Booth** in the new international terminal at the airport staffed by bilingual tourism representatives.

State Tourist Offices The main office is well stocked with timely information on area hotels, restaurants, and attractions, and has a helpful, bilingual staff. *Calle Morelos 102, in the Plaza Tapatía, tel. 36/58–00–49. Open weekdays 9–9, Sat. and Sun. 9–1.*

Branch offices are located in **Tlaquepaque** (Guillermo Prieto 80, near the main entrance to El Templo Parroquial de San Pedro, the parish church, tel. 36/35–15–03), and **Zapopan** (20 de Noviembre No. 103, in the Municipal Palace, tel. 36/33–05–71). *All offices are open weekdays 9–8:30, Sat. 9–1.*

Municipal Tourism Office The **Guadalajara Tourist Office** has a very limited amount of printed information. *Av. Vallarta and Los Arcos (the Arches), tel. 36/16–33–33. Open weekdays 9–9 and Sat. 9–1.*

The **Guadalajara Visitors and Convention Bureau** sometimes has a selection of maps and brochures. *Chamber of Commerce building, Av. Vallarta Poniente 4095, tel. 36/47–93–31. Open weekdays 9–5.*

Associations and Organizations The U.S. and Canadian communities are eager to provide information and recommendations and answer any questions about the Guadalajara area.

American Society of Jalisco. The Personal Services Committee chairman is Judy Furton (tel. 36/21–23–48). *San Francisco 3332, in Chapalita, tel. 36/21–23–95. Open weekdays 9:30–4:30.*

Fellowship for Unos. This group meets at members' homes every Saturday at 5 AM. Visitors traveling alone are welcome. Contact Gail Benedict (tel. 36/15–20–91).

New Yorkers. This group, which meets the first Sunday of each month at 5 PM at members' homes, is made up of people who have lived, worked, or gone to school in New York. Contact Gail Benedict (36/15–20–91).

Senior Citizens Club. The club meets every Wednesday at 5 PM in the Hotel Calinda Roma (Av. Juárez 110, tel. 36/14–86–50).

Unitarian Fellowship. This club meets every Sunday at noon at the American Society of Jalisco (*see* address, *above*); contact chairperson Gail Benedict (tel. 36/15–20–91).

Publications *Retiring in Guadalajara* (Retiring in Guadalajara Publications, Apdo. 5-409, Guadalajara, Jalisco, Mexico, tel. 36/21–23–48 or 36/47–99–24), by Fran and Judy Furton, is a detailed, up-to-date newsletter for prospective American and Canadian retirees. It discloses tons of information on living costs, housing and work opportunities, medical services, English-speaking organizations, and the sundry advantages of retirement in Guadalajara. Mr. and Mrs. Furton offer one free issue in response to written requests.

Consulates **United States** (Progreso 175, near the intersection of Av. Chapultepec and Av. La Paz, tel. 36/25–27–00; after-hours emergency tel. 36/30–31–31).

Canada: Offices are in the Fiesta Americana Guadalajara (Aurelio Aceves 225, tel. 36/25–34–34).

Emergencies **City police** (tel. 36/17–60–60); **state police** (tel. 36/17–58–38); **highway patrol** (tel. 36/21–71–94); **fire department** (tel. 36/19–52–41 and 36/23–08–33); **Cruz Roja** (Red Cross) (tel. 36/13–15–50), and **Cruz Verde** (Green Cross) (tel. 36/43–71–90).

Hospitals **Hospital del Carmen** (Tarascos 3435, near the Plaza México, tel. 36/47–48–82), **Hospital México-Americano** (Colomos 2110, tel. 36/41–31–41), and **Hospital Santa María Chapalita** (Niño Obrero 1666, in the Chapalita neighborhood, tel. 36/21–40–50).

Doctors The U.S. Consulate (*see* Consulates, *above*) maintains a list of English-speaking doctors. All major hotels have names of doctors on 24-hour call.

English-language **Sandi Bookstore** features a variety of newspapers, magazines,
Bookstores and books. *Tepeyac 718 in the Chapalita neighborhood, tel. 36/ 21–08–63. Open weekdays 9:30–2:30 and 3:30–7, Sat. 9–2.*

Late-night **Farmacias Guadalajara** has several branches that are open 24
Pharmacies hours. *Avenida Las Americas 2, tel. 36/15–85–16; Av. Javier Mina 221, tel. 36/17–85–55.*

Travel Agencies Many of the city's 150 travel agencies are in the two hotel zones, El Centro (downtown) and on Avenida López Mateos Sur (on the southwest side of the city). There is an American Express office at Avenida Vallarta 2440, near Los Arcos (tel. 36/30–02–00).

Telephones The pay phones found on street corners, many of them around
Local Calls the Plaza Tapatía, accept 100-peso coins. All major hotels have telephones in the lobbies from which guests can make local calls at no charge.

Opening and Closing Times

Banks are open weekdays 9–1:30. A few branch offices located in shopping centers are now open on Saturday 9–1.

Museums are open Tuesday–Sunday 9–4.

Stores in downtown Guadalajara and in shopping malls are open weekdays 10–8, Saturday 10–6; Sunday hours vary.

Getting Around

Guadalajara's major attractions are best seen on foot. For points of interest outside the city center, Guadalajara has an inexpensive, well-organized public transportation system.

By Bus This is, without a doubt, the most economical and efficient but least comfortable means of traversing the city. Buses run from the center of the city to all local attractions, including Tlaquepaque and Zapopan. The 20¢ fare makes buses the preferred mode of transportation for Guadalajara natives, so expect to stand during daylight hours.

By Tram The *tren ligero* (light train), which began operating in mid–1989, should ease the city's overburdened public transportation system. It runs along Avenida Federalismo from the Periférico (city beltway) Sur to Periférico Norte, near the Benito Juárez Auditorium. The system has 16 trains running at five-minute intervals between 19 stations and costs about 25¢.

By Taxi Taxis are readily available and reasonably economical. Tell the driver where you are going and agree on a fare *before* you enter the cab. Fare schedules, listing prices to downtown and all major attractions, are posted in the lobby of all hotels. *Sitios* (cab stands) are located near all hotels and attractions.

Guided Tours

City Tours **Copenhagen Tours** (tel. 36/21–10–08 or 21–18–90) has several city tours, with admission to attractions included in the price. Transport can be by van or car. The branch office is located at Boulevard de las Cordilleras 152; phone for hotel pickup.

Panoramex (Calzada Federalismo Sur 948, tel. 36/10–51–09 and 10–50–05), Guadalajara's largest tour company, provides many tours of city and area attractions. Air-conditioned buses with bilingual guides depart each morning from Los Arcos and Parque San Francisco.

Royal Limousines (Miguel de Cervantes 382, Sector Juárez, tel. 36/42–56–05) offers a variety of city and area tour packages in a stretch limousine with bilingual guide; domestic liquor is included in all tours. Limousines can also be rented for $40 per hour for self-guided tours. Phone for reservations between 9 and 2 and between 4 and 7 daily.

Personal Guides The federal government maintains a list of licensed bilingual guides. They charge an hourly rate of about $10 for orientation or special-interest tours in their own automobiles. Included in the list are Cristina Alvarez González (tel. 36/35–26–86 and 36/16–11–55), Roberto Arellano Deyra (tel. 36/23–18–56), Luis Govea García (tel. 36/31–10–08), and Susana Rodríguez Anguiano (tel. 36/23–29–95).

Calandrias You can hire a horse-drawn carriage in front of the Museo Regional, the Mercado Libertad, or Parque San Francisco. The charge is about $10 for a half-hour tour, and about $17 for a full hour, for up to four passengers. Few drivers speak English, so stop by the Federal Tourist Office (*see* Important Addresses and Numbers, *above*) first and ask for brochures that describe the attractions in downtown Guadalajara.

Exploring the Guadalajara Area

Beginning around 1960, 20th-century architecture started to threaten the historical integrity of this provincial state capital. In the early 1980s, city fathers declared a 30-square-block area in the heart of the city a cultural sanctuary. The 16th-century buildings here are connected by a series of large Spanish-style plazas where today's inhabitants enjoy life: young children chase gaily colored balloons, young lovers cuddle on tree-shaded park benches, and grandparents stroll hand-in-hand past vendors and marble fountains. At nearby Mariachi Plaza can be heard the nostalgic songs and music of costumed troubadors. The downtown walking tour (Tour 1) visits the churches, monuments, and museums of colonial Guadalajara.

The second tour focuses on the traditional arts and crafts of Tlaquepaque and Tonalá, two towns that are a 20-minute drive from downtown Guadalajara. The third tour (Chapala) covers the lakeside towns of Chapala and Ajijíc, 45 kilometers (28 miles) south of Guadalajara. This scenic area is a weekend retreat for wealthy Tapatíos and a retirement haven for *norteamericanos*.

Highlights for First-time Visitors

Catedral
Instituto Cultural Cabañas
Isla de Mezcala
Posada Ajijíc
Museo Regional de la Cerámica.
Regional Museum of Guadalajara
Restaurant with No Name
Teatro Degollado

Colonial Guadalajara

Numbers in the margin correspond to points of interest on the Guadalajara map.

❶ The focal point of downtown is the **catedral,** consecrated in 1618. It is an intriguing mélange of architectural styles, the result of design and structural modifications during the 60 years of construction. Its emblematic twin towers replaced the original much shorter ones, which were toppled in the devastating earthquake of 1818. The interior contains fine examples of 16th-through 18th-century Spanish art and decor. Ten of the silver and gilt altars were gifts of King Fernando VII (in appreciation of Guadalajara's financial support of Spain during the Napoleonic Wars); the 11th, of sculpted white marble, was carved in Italy in 1863. The altar and statue dedicated to Our Lady of the Rose are exquisite. The statue, carved from a single piece of balsa wood, was a gift from King Charles V in the 16th century. The image and remains of Saint Innocence, brought here from the catacombs of Rome, are on the left side of the main altar. On the walls of the cathedral hang some of the world's most beautiful *retablos* (altarpieces); over the sacristy is the priceless 17th-century painting of Bartolomé Esteban Murillo, *The Assumption of the Virgin.* The sign near the front door requests that visitors be appropriately attired. *Av. Alcalde between Av. Hidalgo and Calle Morelos. Open daily 7 AM–9 PM.*

The main entrance to the cathedral overlooks the **Plaza de los Laureles,** a spacious square that is ideal for serious people-watching, since Tapatíos use it as a short cut. Walk across Avenida Hidalgo from the north side of the plaza (to your left as ❷ you face the cathedral) to the **Municipal Palace** (City Hall). Though this building has a colonial facade, it was not built until 1952. You may wish to stop in to see the mural by Gabriel Flores—a prominent and prolific Tapatío—on the center stairwell; you may *have* to visit the palace to pay a 50¢ fine to

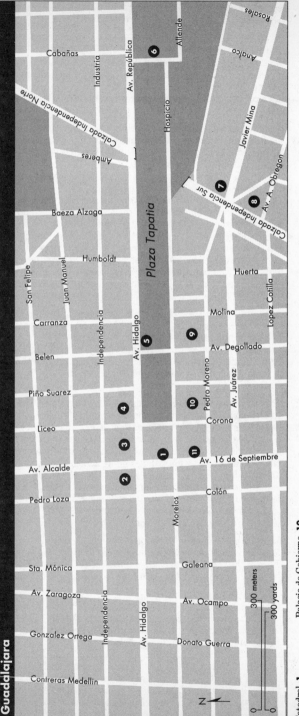

Guadalajara

Catedral, **1**
Degollado Theater, **5**
Iglesia de San
  Augustín, **9**
Instituto Cultural
  Cabañas, **6**
Mercado Libertad, **7**
Municipal Palace, **2**

Palacio de Gobierno, **10**
Plaza de Armas, **11**
Plaza de los
  Mariachis, **8**
Regional Museum of
  Guadalajara, **4**
Rotonda de los
  Hombres Ilustres de
  Jalisco, **3**

retrieve your front license plate—traffic police remove them from illegally parked cars.

❸ Directly across Avenida Alcalde, on the north side of the cathedral, is the **Rotonda de los Hombres Illustres de Jalisco** (Monument to the Illustrious Men of Jalisco). A tree-shaded rotunda encircled by 17 Doric columns, it is actually a mausoleum containing the remains of 11 of Jalisco's favorite sons. Surrounding the monument are brass sculptures representing those buried inside.

❹ From the east side of the monument, walk across Calle Liceo to the **Regional Museum of Guadalajara** (also known as the State Museum). Constructed at the end of the 17th century, this stately Baroque and colonial building served as a seminary until 1918. Since then, it has housed the art, archaeology, and history museum. The first-floor galleries, which surround a courtyard of Roman arches and tropical gardens, contain artifacts and memorabilia that trace the history of western Mexico from prehistoric times through the Spanish Conquest. In the main gallery are the royal carriages of Emperor Maximilian and President Juárez. On the second floor is an impressive collection of works by European and Mexican artists, including Bartolomé Esteban Murillo and Diego Rivera. *Av. Hidalgo between Calle Liceo and Pino Suárez, tel. 36/14–99–57. Admission: about $3; Sun. free. Open Tues.–Sun. 9–3:45.*

Occupying the next block to the left on Avenida Hidalgo is the **Palacio de Legisladores** (Legislative Palace). Over the past 300 years this building has been a customs house, tobacco warehouse, and *posada* (inn). On the next block, across Calle Belén, is the **Palacio de Justicia** (Hall of Justice), the state courthouse. This colonial building was originally part of the city's first convent.

❺ Directly across Avenida Hidalgo is the **Degollado Theater,** Guadalajara's famous opera house. Inaugurated in 1866, the magnificent structure was modeled after Milan's La Scala. Above the Corinthian columns gracing the entranceway is a relief depicting Apollo and the seven Muses. Inside, red and gold balconies ascend to a multitiered dome adorned with Gerardo Suárez's depiction of Dante's *Divine Comedy*. Reopened in September 1988 after a year-long renovation, the theater is the permanent home for the Guadalajara Philharmonic and the Ballet Folklórico. Open during performances (*see* The Arts and Nightlife, *below*, for information).

Walk around to the rear to **Founders Square.** According to tradition, this is the spot on which the city was founded; the sculpted frieze of the theater's rear wall depicts the ceremony with 60 of the founding fathers. *Av. Degollado between Av. Hidalgo and Calle Morelos.*

You are now at the head of the **Plaza Tapatía,** a five-block-long pedestrian mall that ends at the **Instituto Cultural Cabañas.** The plaza is lined with stores and galleries and filled with trees, fountains, and whimsical sculptures.

Time Out   An outlet of the city's most popular ice cream franchise, **Helados Bing** is located two blocks east of the Degollado Theater on the north side of the plaza, just east of the Children's Fountain. For natives, a stop at Helados Bing is a custom (if not an obsession); for tourists, it is a welcome respite from an afternoon of sightseeing. Choose from 30 flavors of pasteurized ice cream and find a shaded bench from which to take in the activity.

⑥ On the east end of the plaza is the **Instituto Cultural Cabañas,** the city's cultural center. Bishop Juan Cruz Ruíz Cabañas founded an orphanage in this building in 1801, and it was home for 400 orphans and indigent children until the 1970s. The rooms, which surround 23 flower-filled patios, contain permanent and revolving art exhibits. The central dome of the main chapel displays a series of murals painted by José Clemente Orozco in 1938–39. *The Man of Fire,* which depicts a man enveloped in flames who is ascending toward infinity and yet not consumed by the fire, represents the spirit of mankind. It is generally considered to be his finest work. There is a permanent exhibit of Orozco's paintings, cartoons, and drawings in Room 189. Ask the attendant at the front desk for an English-speaking guide. *Calle Cabañas 8 at the Plaza Tapatía, tel. 36/ 17–43–22. Admission: about $3. Open Tues.–Sun. 9–7.*

As you leave the Instituto, walk back west through the Plaza Tapatía to the **Quetzalcóatl Fountain** at the center of the plaza; turn **⑦** left and walk down the stairs to the **Mercado Libertad** (Liberty Market). Inside a modern three-story building is Latin America's largest enclosed market. Within a three-square-block area you can browse over 1,000 privately owned stalls selling everything that is grown, manufactured, or handmade in Mexico.

Turn left as you leave the market and cross Avenida Javier Mina (we recommend that you use the pedestrian overpass to avoid the constant flow of traffic) to **Iglesia de San Juan de Díos** (San Juan de Díos Church). In front of the church, you will see a line of colorful calandrias, each behind a patient, motionless **⑧** horse. Next to the church is the **Plaza de los Mariachis,** a picturesque little plaza where mariachi groups perform. While the action and ambience are best during the evening, you might enjoy a break from sightseeing in one of the cafés. A mariachi serenade is $5 a song.

From the intersection in front of the church, turn right on Calzada Independencia; walk two blocks and then go back up the stairs to Plaza Tapatía. Turn left as you enter the mall and continue west for four blocks (giving you the opportunity to see the stores on this side of the plaza) to the oldest church in the **⑨** city. **Iglesia de San Agustín** (St. Augustine Church) at Avenida Degollado and Calle Morelos. Though this venerable building has been remodeled many times since its consecration in 1574, the sacristy has been preserved in its original form. The building to the left of the church, originally a cloister of the Augustinian monks, is now the School of Music of the University of Guadalajara.

As you leave the church, turn left and continue down Calle Morelos to Avenida Corona, then left a half block to the main entrance of the **Palacio de Gobierno** (Governor's Palace). A **⑩** Churrigueresque and neoclassical structure built in 1643, it is the residence of the governor of the state of Jalisco and the site of Orozco's most imaginative and passionate murals. As you enter the palace, on the stairwell to your right is a dramatic mural depicting Father Hidalgo and the Mexican people's struggle for freedom. Its inspiration was Father Hidalgo's 1810 proclamation abolishing slavery in Mexico. *Open weekdays 9–6.*

⓫ As you leave the palace, cross Avenida Corona to the **Plaza de Armas.** Trees and benches in this lovely square surround an ornately sculpted kiosk, a gift from France in 1910.

Exploring Tlaquepaque and Tonalá

Tlaquepaque is known throughout the country as an arts and crafts center. The distinctive hand-painted pottery, sold in stores throughout the town, was first fashioned here by Tonaltecan Indians in the mid-16th century. The small village remained virtually isolated until June 13, 1821, when the Mexican Treaty of Independence was signed here. Soon after, the wealthy residents of Guadalajara, who had used the village as a weekend retreat, began to build palatial mansions in which to spend the summers. Many of these magnificent buildings have been restored and today house shops and restaurants.

During this period, according to one legend, a growing French colony living in the area was (inadvertently) responsible for naming one of Mexico's most renowned musical institutions. French aristocrats hired groups of street singers and musicians to entertain at weddings. The French word *mariage* was soon deformed into *mariachi.*

In 1870, the art of glass-blowing was introduced from Europe. As people started coming to purchase the pottery and intricate glass creations, more artisans—weavers, jewelers, and wood carvers—arrived and built workshops. A new tradition was born.

In 1973, downtown Tlaquepaque underwent a major renovation, the highlight of which was the creation of a wide pedestrian mall. Twentieth-century commercialism had arrived.

You can spend the day browsing in the shops and boutiques and stop at lunch to listen to the lively songs of the mariachis.

The village of Tonalá is one of the oldest pueblos in Mexico. It was both the pre-Hispanic capital of the Indians of the Atemajac Valley and the capital of New Spain. Captain Juan de Onate moved the city of Guadalajara here in 1532. Within three years, however, unfriendly Indians and a lack of water forced the Spaniards to abandon the location.

Over the past 400 years, the village has existed in contented seclusion. The simple adobe houses and dusty streets belie the artistic refinement of Tonalá's residents. It is in this small pueblo that most of the ceramics and pottery sold in Tlaquepaque (and in many other parts of the world) are made. Behind the tall gray walls, families create the lovely dinnerware, vases, and playful animals with the same material and techniques their ancestors used centuries ago. If you are traveling without a guide, stop by the plaza and ask one of the young men to take you to the artisans' homes and workshops. Your guide will charge about $5 an hour.

Tlaquepaque is a 20-minute ride, which will cost about $7 in a cab, from downtown Guadalajara. Take Avenida Revolución southeast from the city; at the Plaza de la Bandera (at the intersection of Calzada del Ejército), jog to your right onto Boulevard Tlaquepaque and into the town.

Tlaquepaque

Numbers in the margin correspond to points of interest on the Tlaquepaque map.

Continue on Boulevard Tlaquepaque to the *glorieta* (traffic circle), and follow the circle around to Avenida Niños Héroes. At the first intersection, Calzada Independencia (the pedestrian **①** mall), turn left; walk one block to the **Museo Regional de la Cerámica** (Regional Museum of Ceramics). Exhibits in the museum, housed in a colonial mansion, trace the evolution of ceramics in the Atemajac Valley during the last century. There is also an exhibit of Indian folk art from the area and prize-winning entries from the national ceramics competition. *Calle Independencia 237, tel. 36/35–54–04. Admission free. Open Tues.–Sat. 10–4, Sun. 10–1.*

② Walk across the street to the **Sergio Bustamante Gallery,** whose work is found in galleries throughout the world. You can purchase one of Bustamante's whimsical sculptures for considerably less here. Silver- and gold-plated jewelry and bronze sculptures are on display in this modern gallery; the flamingos under the waterfall in the rear are real. *Calle Independencia 236, tel. 36/39–55–19. Open Mon.–Sat. 10–7.*

③ Next door is Tlaquepaque's oldest blown-glass factory, **Artmex la Rosa de Cristal.** The store contains a large variety of hand-blown glass objects and figures; the intricate miniatures are surprisingly inexpensive. Plan to arrive before lunch so you can go back into the factory (open weekdays 9–2:30, Sat. 10–2) and watch the craftsmen shove long tubes into a white-hot fire, retrieve a bubbling glob, and in a few minutes create one of the pieces you saw in front. *Calle Independencia 232, tel. 36/39–71–80. Open Mon.–Sat. 10–6:30, Sun. 10–2.*

④ On the next block east (left) is **Bazar Hecht,** a 12-room hacienda filled with hand-carved furniture, antiques, and designer fashions. The Hecht family is known throughout Mexico for its high-quality, ornately sculpted tables and chairs. Part of the fun is wandering through this beautiful building, wondering what it would have been like to grow up in the colonial ambience of 19th-century Tlaquepaque. *Calle Independencia 158, tel. 36/35–22–41. Open Mon.–Sat. 10–2:30 and 3:30–6:30.*

Turn left as you leave the bazaar, and left again at the next corner (Prisciliano Sánchez); walk one block along Calle Morelos, which, with Calle Guillermo Prieto, forms an L-shape arcade. **⑤** In the center of the arcade is the **Templo Parroquial de San Pedro** (Parish Church of St. Peter). Franciscan friars founded the church during the Conquest, naming it in honor of San Pedro de Analco. According to custom, the town was named after the principal church, and in 1915 the name was officially changed to San Pedro Tlaquepaque. The altars of Our Lady of Guadalupe and Saint Joseph are intricately carved in silver and gilt; the chapel of the Daughters of Mary has a most effectual oil painting of *La Purísima. Open daily 7 AM–9 PM.*

Time Out Turn right as you leave the church and walk through the arcade to Constitution; make another right at the next intersection

Tlaquepaque

(Madero) and walk a half block to the **Restaurant with No Name** considered by food critics and patrons to be one of Mexico's best. There are tables both indoors and on the patio of this 17th-century colonial mansion. High adobe walls surround the hacienda and extensive gardens, which are filled with orchids and exotic birds. The restaurant serves Spanish nouvelle cuisine, a combination of pre-Hispanic and modern recipes. Daily entertainment includes mariachis, a vocal trio, and singing waiters. After 15 years, the No Name's owner hung a sign above the restaurant's front door (the restaurant opened as a speakeasy, and the proprietor says he never got around to installing a sign). *Francisco Madero 80, tel. 36/35–45–20. Reservations for large parties. Dress: casual. AE, DC, MC, V.*

⑥ The next door to the left is the **Ken Edwards Gallery.** In 1959 Mr. Edwards developed a technique to transform the fragile Tonalá pottery into a lustrous, hardened, glazed stoneware. The store is filled with brightly colored, hand-painted plates, cups, and vases. Prices are much less than you would pay outside Mexico; ask to see the seconds, some real bargains. *Madero 70, tel. 36/35–54–56. Open Mon.–Sat. 10–6:30, in summer and winter high seasons, Sun. 12–5.*

⑦ One block south (left) of the gallery is **El Parián,** a square block of outdoor cafés frequented by mariachis anxious to perform. El Parián (named after the Chinese section of Manila, with which the conquistadors traded) is the heart of Tlaquepaque. The atmosphere is festive, if not boisterous, on weekends. The shops in the arcades around El Parián should be used only to compare prices; do your shopping in the galleries and boutiques on Calzada Independencia or another main street.

Tonalá The village of **Tonalá** is a 10-minute ride (about $5 for a cab)
8 from Tlaquepaque. Take Avenida Revolución south to Carretera Tonalá and make a left on the Carretera into Tonalá. Follow Avenida Tonalá (the same street you were on) to the main square in the center of the village. Follow Avenida Juárez one block away from the plaza to reach **La Iglesia Parroquial** (the parish church) built in 1533. Inside is a sculpture of Pope Pius IX.

From the northwest corner of the plaza, at Calles Hidalgo and Zapata, walk west (left) one block on Calle Zapata to Avenida Morelos, then right a half block to the **workshop of Jorge Wilmot** (Av. Morelos 76, no phone). This factory produces intricately designed, hand-painted stoneware ceramic plates, cups, and figurines that are sold throughout the world. Unfortunately, the opening hours of this shop, like many others in the village, vary greatly, although the artist lists his hours as weekdays from 10–6 and Saturday from 10–5.

Turn right as you leave the workshop, and right again at the next intersection, to the **Museo Nacional de la Cerámica** (National Ceramics Museum). On exhibit are the ceramics and pottery dating from pre-Columbian times to the present of several Mexican states. There are also a workshop and small store. *Constitución 110, tel. 36/83–04–94. Admission free. Open Tues.–Fri. 10–5, weekends 10–3.*

Turn left and continue a half block on Avenida Morelos to the **workshop of Ken Edwards.** Meet the man who revolutionized the centuries-old technique of firing ceramics. Either Edwards or his wife is usually on hand to show visitors their facilities. *Av. Morelos 184, tel. 36/83–03–13. Open weekdays 10–6.*

On Thursday and Sunday mornings, there is a *tianguis* (market) on the street in front of the church. Most of the ceramics here are seconds, either chipped or with slight flaws in design or glaze; if you are planning on buying, stop by one of the stores here or in Tlaquepaque.

Lake Chapala and Ajijic

This tour visits the lakeside communities of Chapala and Ajijic. Unfortunately, Lake Chapala—Mexico's largest inland body of water—is polluted, and water levels have been so low in the past few years that some Mexican ecologists predict there will be no lake at all in a few years' time. It does, however, provide a setting for spectacular sunsets, afford enough humidity to keep the abundant bougainvillea blooming, and ensure that there are no drastic temperature fluctuations.

The town of Chapala is 45 kilometers (28 miles) south of Guadalajara, on the northwest shore of the lake. With its proximity to the large city and its comfortable climate, it is surprising that tourists did not frequent the area until the late-19th century. Then-President Porfirio Díaz heard that aristocrats had discovered the ideal place for weekend getaways. The president began spending holidays here in 1904. Soon summer homes were built, and in 1910 the Chapala Yacht Club opened. Word of the town, with its lavish lawn parties and magnificent estates, spread quickly to the United States and Europe.

Nowadays this town of 35,000 attracts a less influential but equally fun-loving assortment of visitors. On weekends, the streets are full of Mexican families. During the week, American and Canadian retirees stroll along the lakeside promenade, play golf, and relax on the verandas of downtown restaurants.

Keep in mind, however, that despite the art galleries, upscale boutiques, and restaurants, Ajijic is still a traditional Mexican village with narrow cobblestoned streets and whitewashed buildings.

Lake Chapala Area *Numbers in the margins correspond to points of interest on the Lake Chapala Area map.*

From downtown Guadalajara take Calzada del Federalismo south to Calzada Lázaro Cárdenas (the Sports Stadium is on the corner); turn left on Calzada Cárdenas and continue south. Follow the signs as Calzada Cárdenas converges with Highway 23 to Mexico City; the trip takes 50 minutes. There is also frequent bus service to Chapala from Guadalajara's old bus station on the corner of Calles Analco and Cinco de Febrero. From the Chapala bus station there are buses every hour to Ajijic.

After passing the turnoff to Ajijic, the highway becomes Avenida Madero as you enter Chapala. Follow Avenida Madero
❶ down to the **San Francisco Church** (two blocks north of the lake) and park your car. The church was built in 1528 and reconstructed in 1580. In 1538, Franciscan Friar Miguel de Bolonio founded the town and began to convert the Taltica Indians to Christianity. Their chief was named Chapalah, from which the name Chapala originated.

❷ Walk across the street to the **Hotel Nido** (Av. Madero 202, tel. 376/5–2116), the oldest hotel on the lake. It was built in the beginning of the century to accommodate President Porfirio Díaz and his entourage during their frequent visits. In the 1940s, Mexican film star Maria Felix spent the first of her numerous honeymoons at the Nido. There are pictures of turn-of-the-century Chapala on the walls of the hotel and a picturesque patio and garden in the rear.

Turn right as you leave the hotel and walk two blocks to the lake. On the corner (Av. Madero and Paseo Ramón Corona) is the **Cazadores Restaurant,** once the summer home of the Braniff (Airlines) family, an ideal place to enjoy a cool liquid refreshment and watch the action along the *malecón* (lakeside promenade). Walking left down the Paseo Ramón Corona as you leave the restaurant, you will pass a number of open-air cafés featuring *pescado blanco* (white fish). Because of the pollution of the lake, we do not recommend that you partake of this regional delicacy. There is a small **handicrafts market** at the end of the Paseo Ramón Corona (two blocks from Avenida Madero).

Walk back to Avenida Madero and then to the end of the pier, where *marineros* (sailors) rent boats that will take you for a
❸ tour of the lake or its islands. The most popular trip is to **Isla de los Alacránes** (Scorpion Island) to enjoy a meal in one of the tiny restaurants there. The price for a round-trip cruise is between $20 and $35 (for the launch, with a capacity of six adults). An-
❹ other interesting trip is to **Isla del Presidio** (Prison Island), offi-

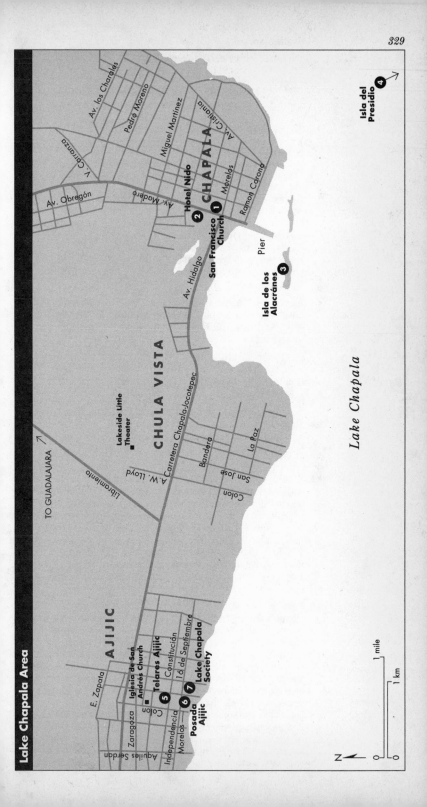

Lake Chapala Area

CHAPALA

Av. los Charales
Pedro Moreno
Miguel Martínez
Av. Cristianía
V. Carranza
Av. Obregón
Av. Madero
Hotel Nido
San Francisco Church
Morelos
Ramon Corona
Av. Hidalgo
Pier
Isla de los Alacránes
Isla del Presidio

CHULA VISTA

Lakeside Little Theater
Carretera Chapala-Jocotepec
A.W. Lloyd
Libromiento
TO GUADALAJARA
Bandera
Colon
San José
La Paz

AJIJIC

E. Zapata
Zaragoza
Independencia
Morelos
Aquiles Serdán
Colon
Iglesia de San Andrés Church
Telares Ajijic
Constitución
16 de Septiembre
Posada Ajijic
Lake Chapala Society

Lake Chapala

① ② ③ ④ ⑤ ⑥ ⑦

N

0 1 km
0 1 mile

cially **Isla Mezcala.** On this primitive, undeveloped island, designated a national historic site, stand the remains of an early 19th-century fortress. Climb to the top of the thick-walled fortress and look over the large courtyard and surrounding brick buildings for a spectacular view of the lake and nearby mountains. The cost for the four-hour trip is $90 (for up to 10 passengers).

Return to your car, and take a right at the traffic light (the only one in town) onto Avenida Hidalgo. You will be heading west to the village of Ajijic. Three kilometers (2 miles) from Chapala is the community of **Chula Vista,** the most American colony in Mexico. Just west of the Chapala suburb, above the PAL Trailer Park (and next to the Oak High School) is the new, 120-seat **Lakeside Little Theater** (tel. 376/5–2368). The theater stages English-language musicals and plays throughout the year. There is a small cafeteria in the trailer park. The **Lake Chapala Department of Tourism** is 1.6 kilometers (1 mile) west of the trailer park. *Auditorio Ribera de Chapala, tel. 376/5–31–36. Open weekdays 9–3, Sat. 9–1.*

As you enter Ajijic, turn left onto Avenida Colón for two blocks until you reach the plaza and the **Iglesia de San Andrés** (Church of St. Andrew). Weekly events and festivities take place on this lovely plaza.

Park your car at the plaza and walk down Morelos toward the lake; along the way you can stop in at the many stores and boutiques selling everything from designer fashions to traditional arts and crafts.

⑤ Walk in and watch weavers work on traditional hand looms at **Telares Ajijic.** Indian women weave cotton, wool, and acrylic into fabrics used for both native costumes and designer fashions. *16 de Septiembre No. 1, tel. 376/5–24–02. Open 9–2 and 4–7.*

⑥ Where Calle Morelos meets the lake, you'll find the **Posada Ajijic,** a hacienda-style building that is the social, commercial, and political convocation center for Ajijic residents. Many people come to the restaurant and bar, under sculpted wood archways, for the daily happy hour and stay to watch the spectacular sunsets. For the past few years, members of the Huichole Indian tribe have set up shop in a corner of the lush gardens, where they weave their colorful serapes. *Frente al Lago, esquina Morelos, Ajijic, Jalisco, 45920, tel. 376/5–44–22 and 376/5–33–95.*

⑦ Back across 16 de Septiembre is the headquarters of **Lake Chapala Society,** a nonprofit organization that can answer your questions about the area. *16 de Septiembre No. 16A, no phone. Open weekdays 10–1.*

Time Out Stop in for some authentic Mexican atmosphere and cooking at the popular **El Mesón de Ajijic.** Enter through a flower-filled courtyard to dine either inside or on the patio. The white stucco walls, red-tile ceiling, and an antique fireplace will put you in the mood for some serious Mexican food. The *pollo al vino blanco* (chicken sautéed in a rich white-wine sauce) is a favorite of the locals. For American tastes, try the barbecued pork chops and spareribs in a tangy sauce. Don't miss the desserts: crepes suzette, bananas Foster, and strawberries Romanoff.

Av. Hidalgo 17, tel. 376/5–36–11. Reservations recommended on weekends. Dress: casual. AE, MC, V.

Guadalajara for Free

The **Municipal Band of Guadalajara** performs every Tuesday at 6:30 PM in the bandstand of the Plaza de Armas (Moreno and Av. 16 de Septiembre); the **State Band of Jalisco** performs here every Sunday and Thursday at the same time. In the **Concha Acústica** (outdoor theater) in Agua Azul Park there are music or dance shows every Sunday at 5 PM (Av. 16 de Septiembre and Calzada Gonzales Gallo).

Museums

Many of Guadalajara's museums are free, and the rest charge a nominal fee.

Callejón Del Carmen. Along the wide passage between the Agora Café and the Ex-Convento del Carmen, there are alfresco displays of sculpture and paintings. Information and schedules are available in the café.

Fiesta Americana Hotel. Galleries on the second and third floors of the hotel display works by Mexican artists.

Las Calas Cultural Center (Tepeyac 1156, in Chapalita, tel. 36/47–03–83 or 42–07–79) holds monthly exhibitions of contemporary and postcolonial art. It also has a vegetarian café in an enclosed patio, and evening concerts on Wednesday, Friday, Saturday, and Sunday nights. *Gallery open Tues.–Sun. 8 AM–11 PM.*

What to See and Do with Children

Parque Agua Azul is Guadalajara's largest and most popular park. Amid acres of trees and flowers are carnival rides, a miniature train, and a swimming pool. *Calzada Independencia Sur and Calzada Gonzales Gallo. Admission: 35¢. Open 9 AM–10 PM.*

If you're looking for a place to relax on a warm day, head to **Parque Alcalde.** Amble along the shores of the lake or rent a boat; next to the picnic grounds are children's games. *Jesús García and Mariano Barcena. Open 9–9.*

Planetario Severo Díaz Galindo (The Planetarium). A modern facility with astronomy shows and aeronautical displays, the planetarium also features exhibits that allow children to test the forces and laws of nature. *Av. Ricardo Flores Magón 599, tel. 36/37–21–19. Admission: about 75¢. Open Tues.–Sun., 10–7.*

Zoológico Guadalajara (Guadalajara Zoo). Built in 1988, the zoo and entertainment center are located in the Barranca Huentitán (Huentitán Canyon). There are 1,800 animals representing 250 species. For 50¢ a train provides guided tours. There are picnic areas, a children's zoo, and shows in the auditorium on weekends. The adjacent *Selva Mágica* (Magic Jungle) amusement park has carnival rides and attractions. *Paseo del Zoológico 600 next to the Planetarium, tel. 36/38–44–05. Admission: about $1. Open Tues.–Sun. 10–6.*

Off the Beaten Track

Many of the activities at the **Rancho Río Caliente** health resort and vegetarian, alcohol-free spa are literally in hot water—therapeutic hot mineral water. You can steam away your mental tensions and body toxins in front of the 20-foot-high wall of volcanic rock and then dip into one of the mineral-water-filled swimming pools. The restorative waters of the Río Caliente (Hot River) have soothed the mental and physical maladies of the Indians of this region for thousands of years. The resort offers sparse but comfortable accommodations, facials and massages, T'ai Chi instruction, hiking, horseback riding, and classes in yoga and body awareness. Meals, served buffet style, feature locally grown fruits and vegetables and whole-wheat bread. *Apdo. 1187, Guadalajara, Jalisco, tel. 36/15–78–00. The spa is 30 km (19 mi) from Minerva Fountain on Hwy. 15.*

Barranca de Oblatos (Oblatos Canyon). Ten kilometers (6 miles) northeast of downtown Guadalajara via Calzada Independencia is a spectacular 2,000-foot-deep gorge. The view from the top of the canyon (similar to, but smaller than the Grand Canyon) is impressive.

Basilica of the Virgin of Zapopan (Calzada Avila and Av. Las Américas, 6 mi northeast of downtown). The church, with an ornate *Plateresque* facade and Mudejar tiled dome, was consecrated in 1730. It is known throughout Mexico as the home of La Zapopanita, Our Lady of Zapopan. The 10-inch-high statue is venerated as the source of many miracles in and around Guadalajara. Every year on October 12, over 1 million people crowd the streets leading to Zapopan as the Virgin is returned to the basilica after a five-month absence during which she visits every church in the city.

Huichol Museum. The Monastery of the Basilica of Zapopan has a small museum that displays and sells costumes and handicrafts produced by the Huichol and Cora Indians of northern Jalisco. It is not uncommon to see colorfully dressed Huicholes in and around the church. *Tel. 36/33–66–14 and 36/33–01–41. Open 9–2 and 4–7.*

Centuries ago, the Tiquilas, a small Nahuatl-speaking tribe, established a settlement 56 kilometers (35 miles) northwest of Guadalajara in **Tequila** in the picturesque Jaliscan countryside. The Tiquilas discovered that the heart of the maguey cactus exuded *mezcal* (a kind of honey). When fermented, it produced a highly appreciated drink, which they called tequila. Today you can tour the famous Sauza Distillery or one of the other modern distilleries in town. Follow the signs, and plan to arrive between 10 AM and 1 PM.

The modern administration building of the **Universidad de Guadalajara** houses the first murals painted by Orozco after he returned to Guadalajara at age 53. In addition to these two powerful works—located behind the stage and in the dome of the auditorium—there are beautiful murals by Amado de la Cueva and David Alfaro Siqueiros. *Av. Juárez at Tolsa, 2 mi west of downtown, tel. 36/25–88–88. Open 8–9.*

Behind the university building is the **Templo Expiatorio** (Tolsa and Av. Francisco Madero). Though this church is nearly a century old, construction is still under way, albeit at a leisurely pace. The church is modeled after the Cathedral of Orvieto in

Italy, and it is an outstanding example of unadulterated Gothic architecture.

Sightseeing Checklist

This list includes attractions covered in the preceding tours and others described here for the first time.

Museo de Arqueología de Occidente de México (Archaeological Museum of Western Mexico). Artifacts from the states of Colima, Jalisco, and Nayarit. *Calzada Independencia and Calzada del Campesino, in front of Parque Agua Azul. Admission free. Open weekdays 10–6, Sat. 10–4.*

Catedral (*see* Colonial Guadalajara, in Exploring the Guadalajara Area, *above*)

Nuestra Señora de Aranzazu. The Churrigueresque altar at the Church of Our Lady of Aranzazu is considered to be one of the finest in the world. *Av. 16 de Septiembre and P. Sanchez. Open 7 AM–8 PM.*

El Museo Orozco (Orozco Museum). The artist's workshop was converted into a museum after his death in 1949. It contains a large collection of his paintings and frescoes. *Aurelio Aceves 27, just west of Los Arcos, tel. 36/25–33–65. Admission: 35¢. Open Tues.–Sat. 10–4, Sun. 10–2.*

Instituto Cultural Cabañas (*see* Colonial Guadalajara in Exploring the Guadalajara Area, *above*)

Isla Mezcala (*see* Lake Chapala Area, *above*)

Posada Ajijic (*see* Lake Chapala Area, *above*)

Iglesia de San Francisco. The statue-laden facade gives this colonial church the most impressive exterior of any church in the city. *Av. 16 de Septiembre and Av. Corona, facing the Jardin de San Francisco 6 blocks south of the city center. Open 7 AM–8 PM.*

Iglesia de Santa Monica. Residents of Guadalajara think this church, built in 1720, is the loveliest in the city. It has an elaborately carved Churrigueresque facade. *Santa Monica and San Felipe, 8 blocks west of Parque Morelos. Open 8–8.*

Sergio Bustamante Gallery (*see* Tlaquepaque, in Exploring Tlaquepaque and Tonalá, *above*)

Participant Sports and Fitness

Golf

Golf clubs that admit foreign travelers include **Atlas Golf Club** (Carretera Guadalajara-Chapala, in front of Montenegro Park, tel. 36/89–00–85) and the **San Isidro Golf Club** (highway to Zacatecas, Km 14.5, tel. 36/33–28–14 or 36/33–27–08). If you have credentials from a U.S. golf club, you can play at the **Guadalajara Country Club** on weekdays (tel. 36/41–40–45 or 36/41–40–02).

Tennis

Try **Tennis Del Sol** (Av. Tizoc 17, tel. 36/22–38–31), **Tennis Patria** (Plaza Patria, tel. 36/33–38–11), or the **Holiday Inn** (tel. 36/34–10–34), which allows nonguests to use its courts for a fee.

Fitness Clubs

The **Carlton, Fiesta Americana,** and **Holiday Inn** fitness clubs are open to nonmembers. At **Gold's Gym** (Chimalhuacán 3574, off Av. López Mateos Sur, tel. 36/47–85–94) guest passes are available for about $7 per day.

Spectator Sports

Bullfights

Corridas begin at 4:30 PM every Sunday in October and every other Sunday from November through April at **Plaza Nuevo Progreso.** You can buy tickets for either the *sol* (sunny) or *sombra* (shady) side of the bullring. Since the action does not begin until just before sunset, opt for the cheaper seats on the sunny side. *Calzada Independencia across from the Estadio Jalisco, tel. 36/25–19–74. Admission: $6–$22.*

Charreadas

The Mexican rodeo takes place at **Lienzo Charros de Jalisco** every Sunday at noon. The *charros* (cowboys) compete in 10 events; mariachis perform during breaks in the action. *Campo Charro Jalisco, Dr. R. Michel, 577, next to Agua Azul Park, tel. 36/19–32–32. Admission: about $3.*

Soccer

Estadio Jalisco. Professional soccer matches are on Saturday at 8:45 PM and sometimes on Sunday at 2 PM. *The north end of Calzada Independencia, near the bullring, tel. 36/37–05–63. Admission: 75¢–$7.*

Shopping

Shoppers in Guadalajara can choose from a broad variety of high-quality merchandise at low prices. Of course, you will also find low-quality products at high prices; *caveat emptor.* Store hours are traditionally 10–2 and 4–7 on weekdays, Saturdays 9–2. Many large stores, however, are open daily and don't close for siesta.

Malls

In Guadalajara, as in all major cities, shopping malls are springing up everywhere; the city now has 24 of them.

Plaza del Sol. The city's largest mall has 500,000 square feet of commercial space, enough room for 300 businesses and services and parking for 500 cars. *Av. López Mateos and Mariano Otero* *(across from the Hyatt Hotel), tel. 36/21–59–50. Open weekdays 10–8, weekends 10–6.*

Plaza México. There are 100 commercial establishments in the city's second most popular shopping mall. *Av. México 3300, at the corner of Calle Yaquis, on the city's west side, tel. 36/47–00–98. Open weekdays 10–8, weekends 10–6.*

Plaza Galería del Calzado. The 60 stores in this new mall all sell shoes. Guadalajara is one of Mexico's leading shoe centers, and high-quality footwear and accessories sell here for a fraction of what you would pay back home. *Av. México and Calle Yaquis, next to the Plaza México, tel. 36/47–64–22. Open weekdays 10–7, weekends 10–4.*

Traditional Arts and Crafts

Tlaquepaque and Tonalá
Artisans in these two towns produce some of the finest handiwork in Mexico. Tlaquepaque's 300 stores and galleries, and Tonalá's workshops and factories are replete with ceramics, pottery, jewelry, leather, blown glass, brass, and copper creations. *Located on the southeastern fringe of the city. Most stores are open weekdays 10–2 and 4–7, Sat. 10–6.*

Markets

In **Mercado Libertad,** Latin America's largest enclosed market, more than 1,000 vendors sell everything from clothing to crafts, and live animals to gold watches. *Calzada Independencia and Av. Javier Mina. Open weekdays 9–2 and 4–8, weekends 9–6.*

El Baratillo is the world's largest flea market. Thirty city blocks are lined with stalls, tents, and blankets piled high with new, used, and antique merchandise. *On Calle Juan Zavala, east of Mercado Libertad. Open Sun. 6–2.*

Dining

The quality and variety of Guadalajara's restaurants have improved to accommodate the tastes and budgets of the international business community. While native restaurateurs and chefs continue to present traditional and classic Mexican dishes, a new breed of immigrant *cuisinier* has introduced such ethnic delicacies as French Creole *chicken sauté Louisiane*, classic Japanese *shabu shabu*, and Spanish *paella*. Many restaurants close early, so if you are accustomed to dining after 9 PM, it's advisable to call first to check if the establishment remains open.

Highly recommended restaurants are indicated by a star ★.

Category	Cost*
Very Expensive	over $35
Expensive	$25–$35
Moderate	$15–$25
Inexpensive	under $15

per person excluding drinks, service, and sales tax (10%)

Very Expensive **Place de la Concorde.** Booths throughout the elegant multilevel
★ restaurant overlook Minerva Fountain and surround the baby-
grand piano, where a pianist provides a musical backdrop for
outstanding French cuisine. Specialties include appetizers
such as vol-au-vent (escargot and mushrooms sautéed in oil and
garlic) and tureen of rabbit in rich port sauce; entrées such as
tenderloin steak encircled by giant shrimp and medallions of
beef in an imaginative sweet grape sauce; and desserts flambéed tableside. *Hotel Fiesta Americana, tel. 36/25–34–34, ext.
3077. Reservations advised on weekends. Dress: formal. AE,
DC, MC, V. Closed Sun.*

Expensive **Cazuelas Grill.** Pedro Olivares personally oversees the operation of this family-operated restaurant and entertainment
lounge. Cazuelas Grill serves traditional cuisine both inside
and on an open-air patio with red-tile floor and bamboo ceiling.
Three shows are presented daily (3:30, 6:30, and 10:30 PM), featuring the songs and music of one of Guadalajara's best mariachi
groups; live music for dancing follows. *Pollo parrilla* (mesquite-
grilled chicken) and *borrego al pastor* (barbecued goat) are two
specialties. The tangy barbecued ribs are popular with visitors
from north of the border. *Av. López Mateos Sur 3755, 2 blocks
south of the Holiday Inn, tel. 36/31–57–80. Reservations advised for dinner. Dress: casual. AE, MC, V. Closed Christmas
Eve.*

★ **La Vianda.** Classical Mexican elegance pervades this intimate
bilevel room overlooking a neat, lush garden; cobalt-blue water
glasses provide a charming accent to the white-on-white decor.
Chef Salvador Rodriguez masterfully combines traditional native recipes with New Orleans Creole. Begin with the *ceviche*
(fresh white fish marinated in a blend of onions, tomatoes, olive
oil and lemon juice) and the dry lima bean and shrimp soup (per-
fumed with fresh coriander). Entrées from the extensive dinner menu include crabmeat crepes in a rich Hollandaise sauce, a
spicy shrimp Creole in a tangy tomato sauce, and mignonettes
of veal Normandy. *Av. Chapalita 120, tel. 36/21–78–23. Reservations advised. Dress: formal. AE, DC, MC, V.*

Moderate **Copenhagen.** This multilevel, mirrored restaurant bills itself as
★ the "Paella Place." Since 1952, the Copenhagen has featured
the famous dish of Valencia, Spain. The secret of a great paella
lies in the texture of the rice. The grain in both presentations,
Copenhagen (in white wine) and *à la marinera* (with seafood),
is loose and dry, but still tender. The menu also features beef
and seafood entrées. Copenhagen is also the unofficial headquarters for Guadalajara's jazz aficionados; it showcases some
of the city's best jazz musicians, who entertain each evening at
8 PM. *López Cotilla and Marcos Castellanos, tel. 36/25–28–03.
Reservations advised on weekends. Dress: casual. AE, DC,
MC, V. Closed Sun. and national holidays.*

Guadalajara Grill. Fun and revelry share top billing with the
food at this Carlos 'n Charlie's affiliate. The large, trilevel room
is decorated with Mexican knickknacks and antique street
lamps; turn-of-the-century photographs of Guadalajara are
displayed in the foyer and on the back wall. The tender barbecued baby-ribs are by far the favorite of both natives and tourists. Shrimp lovers will be happy to find the crustaceans
grilled, baked, boiled, or served in a casserole. Enthusiastic
waiters promote the convivial atmosphere and urge patrons to
join in the fun. There is live entertainment every evening. *Av.*

López Mateos 3771, tel. 36/31–56–22. Reservations recommended. Dress: casual. AE, MC, V. Closed on national holidays.

La Copa de Leche. This downtown, family-owned and operated restaurant is an institution in Guadalajara. You can choose between three distinct dining areas: El Portal, a sidewalk café, El Balcon, an open-air terrace overlooking Avenida Juárez; and the main dining room with traditional Mexican decor, a 40-foot ceiling, and an antique fireplace. Specialties include *pescado California* (California white fish sautéed in a sauce of avocados and oranges and then bathed in butter), *camarones copa de leche* (giant shrimp smothered with bacon and cheese), and *pierna de cerdo* (pork shank baked in a tangy port wine sauce); for dessert try one of the flambés. *Av. Júarez 414–B, tel. 36/ 14–18–45. Reservations advised on weekends. Dress: informal. AE, MC, V. Closed on national holidays.*

La Rinconada. This enclosed patio of a restored colonial mansion houses hanging plants, stone pillars, hand-carved doors with frosted glass windows, and a piano and bass duo plucking out American standards. La Rinconada exudes an old-plantation graciousness in a centrally located position on Calle Morelos between the Teatro Degollado and the Instituto Cultural Cabañas. Specialties of the house include shrimp scampi (jumbo shrimp cooked in white wine and garlic sauce), prime rib, and the *Plato Mexicano Arrachera*, a flank steak served with guacamole, enchiladas, and beans and rice. Schedule your private parties in the rooms in the back. *Calle Morelos 86, tel. 36/ 13–99–14. Reservations accepted. Dress: casual but neat. AE, DC, MC, V.*

Moravia. Both Tapatios and tourists come to enjoy the elegant ambience and superb Continental cuisine. A full-length stained-glass window in the rear of the main room overlooks manicured gardens. Appetizers include select oysters Rockefeller (eight choice oysters on the half-shell lightly breaded and covered with a rich mornay sauce) and piñon creme with spinach soup, a Moravia specialty. Entrées include fish fillet Florentina (tender white-fish fillets in a tangy white-wine sauce served on a bed of spinach) and *filete pimienta*, steak in a green peppercorn and cream sauce. *López Mateos Nte. 1143 on the corner of Colomos, tel. 36/41–84–87. Reservations recommended on weekends. Dress: casual. AE, MC, V. Closed on Sun. and national holidays.*

Inexpensive **Cafe Madrid.** If you want good solid portions of home cooking at a steal, try the center of the city, two blocks north of Calzada Independencia and the Plaza de los Mariachis. A classic diner where locals hang out, Cafe Madrid services an eight-stool counter and six tables in the front plus a larger room toward the back with a mural that, admittedly, kind of kills the appetite. Here's a sampler: hot cakes, waffles, *filete tampiqueña* (a steak served with guacamole, refried beans, and enchiladas), *huevos a la Mexicana* (scrambled eggs with tomatoes, onions, and chile peppers), club sandwiches, and *molletes* (a huge toasted roll with butter, refried beans, grated cheese and bacon). *Avenida Juárez 264, tel. 36/14–95–04. No reservations. Dress: casual. No credit cards.*

Dainzu. Pablo Garcia Ojeda introduced the cuisine of Mexico's southern state of Oaxaca to the city in 1986. The restaurant takes its name from the centuries-old Mixtec ruin just outside of Oaxaca City. The eight-table room (additional seating is planned for the rear garden) has white plaster walls and a red-tiled ceiling, with regional posters and ornamentation on the walls. The owner greets each patron with a smile and a large basket of warm homemade corn chips. Featured among the Oaxacan specialties are tender beef, pork, and chicken dishes prepared in a tangy green or black mole sauce (the thick dark sauce of chocolate, chiles, onions, and more than a dozen other spices and herbs), and *pollo almendro* (chicken smothered in onions). Traditional Mexican specialties include a combination plate of tacos, enchiladas, and tamales. Dainzu doesn't appear in any city guidebooks. The faithful, and growing, clientele would keep it that way. Tell your cabdriver to take Calle Mariano Otero to the Chocolate Ibarra (chocolate factory), and then turn east to Avenida Diamante (between the Plaza del Sol and the Plaza Arboledas). *Av. Diamante 2598, no phone. No reservations. Dress: casual. MC, V. Closed Mon.*

La Trattoria. Michelli Prumcci's Italian eatery has swiftly become the favorite of the city's American and Canadian communities. Under the vigilant eye of Michelli's brother-in-law Alberto, this unpretentious, squeaky-clean restaurant churns out superb Italian dishes, which are reasonably priced. The *combination la trattoria* is lasagna, fettuccine, and spaghetti in a zingy house sauce. In addition to pasta plates, the restaurant offers a limited selection of beef and seafood entrées. All meals come with a trip to the salad bar. The popularity of La Trattoria is increasing to include a large contingent of young natives—especially for Saturday-night dates. *Av. Niños Héroes 3051, tel. 36/22–18–17. No reservations. Dress: casual. AE, MC, V. Closed Christmas.*

Saint Michael. A unique addition to Guadalajara's growing register of restaurants. With its stone walls and arches, you would expect to find the front dining room in a French castle; the room to the rear has a contemporary Mexican flair, with its beige walls, beamed ceilings, and a pleasant view of the patio and gardens. Saint Michael serves more than 50 varieties of crepes. Crepe specialties include *Azteca* (with chicken and cheese), beef Stroganoff (with thin slices of beef and mushrooms in a red-wine sauce), *Hawaiana* (with ham and pineapple), and *Gran Amirante* (with shrimp in a thick white-wine sauce). Meals include a trip to the salad bar. *Av. Vallarta 1700, tel. 36/30–18–20. Reservations advised. Dress: casual. AE, DC, MC, V. Closed national holidays.*

Lodging

Until 20 years ago, most of Guadalajara's hotels were in the downtown area. As commercial interest in the city grew and businesses began springing up throughout the metropolitan area, hotels were constructed on Avenida López Mateos, a 10-mile strip extending from Minerva Fountain to the Plaza del Sol shopping center. Expo-Guadalajara (Latin America's largest convention center) opened in 1987, and the city's hotels immediately began major remodeling projects to accommodate the convention business.

Guadalajara today offers a fine variety of hotels in all price ranges. Hotels in this city follow the tradition initiated by the hotels in resort areas of raising prices every year on December 15. An excellent time to visit Guadalajara is from the beginning of October (during the *Fiestas de Octubre)* until mid-December.

Call ahead if you're apprehensive about noise levels outside your hotel room. Many hotels are located on busy intersections, and you'd be well advised to consult the reservation clerk on the matter of a room away from the hubbub.

The rates given are based on the year-round or peak-season price; off-peak (summer) rates may be slightly lower. Highly recommended lodgings are indicated by a star ★.

Category	Cost*
Very Expensive	over $120
Expensive	$90–$120
Moderate	$55–$90
Inexpensive	under $55

*All prices are for a standard double room; excluding 10% tax.

Very Expensive
★

Quinta Real. Stone and brick walls, colonial arches, and objets d'art highlight the classical Mexican architecture in all public areas of this luxury hotel, located in a quiet residential neighborhood on the city's west side. Suites are plush and intimate, with select neocolonial furnishings, including glass-top writing tables with carved-stone pedestals, fireplaces with marble mantelpieces, and original art. Bathrooms are carpeted, with marble sinks and bronze fixtures (some suites have sunken tubs with Jacuzzis). Suites on the first floor facing the lobby tend to be a bit musty (the result of drapes being drawn to ensure privacy). *Av. México 2727, 44680, tel. 36/15–00–00. 43 suites and 8 deluxe rooms. Facilities: restaurant, piano bar/lounge, small pool with Jacuzzi, boutique, limousine transfer to airport, English-language TV channels (with remote control), purified water system. AE, DC, MC, V.*

Expensive

Camino Real. A 15-minute cab ride from downtown will bring you to this sprawling resort located 3.2 kilometers (2 miles) west of Minerva Fountain. Public areas were remodeled in 1988. The rooms, in two-story wings surrounding manicured lawns and tropical gardens, were redecorated in 1989. By day, you can indulge in any of a long list of activities and sports; by night, you can enjoy the turn-of-the-century Aquellos Tiempos restaurant or live entertainment in La Diligencia lounge. The large rooms have placid pastel color schemes, matching bedspreads and curtains, and modern furniture. The rooms in the rear wing face busy, noisy Avenida Vallarta. *Av. Vallarta 5005, 45050, tel. 36/47–80–00 or 800/228–3000. 208 rooms with bath, including 6 suites. Facilities: 2 restaurants, bar with live music, coffee shop, 5 pools, tennis court, putting green, children's playground, English-language TV channels, purified water system, baby-sitting service. AE, DC, MC, V.*

Carlton. The only first-class property in downtown Guadalajara, this modern 20-story tower hotel was totally remodeled in 1988 (it had been a Sheraton until mid-1987). The oversize rooms with light beige walls and ceilings have matching dark-blue curtains and bedspreads. Public areas are decorated in a colonial style; the rear gardens and fountain are surrounded by ivy-draped walls. Though the hotel is convenient for tourists, it caters to the business traveler. The view of the city from the rooftop meeting rooms is spectacular. The best rooms are on the upper floors, above the terribly loud street noises. *Av. Niños Héroes 105, at the corner of Av. 16 de Septiembre, 44100, tel. 36/14–72–72. 200 rooms with bath, including 7 suites. Facilities: restaurant, 2 bars, discotheque, outdoor heated pool, health club, video disco club. AE, MC, V.*

★ **Fiesta Americana.** The dramatic glass facade of this luxury high rise faces the Minerva Circle. The location, warm contemporary Mexican ambience, and excellent service make this hotel a popular choice for both business travelers and tourists. Four glass-enclosed elevators ascend over the 11-story atrium lobby and adjoining Lobby Bar (one of Guadalajara's most popular night spots). The ample rooms, remodeled in 1988, have a pastel color scheme, modern furnishings (including molded seating and desk areas), and panoramic city views. The hotel presents a German Cafe Night (Thursday), an Italian Fiesta (Tuesday), and an International Buffet (Sunday afternoon). The best rooms are on the upper floors, well away from the revelers down in the Lobby Bar. *Aurelio Aceves 225, 45050, tel. 36/25–34–34 or 800/223–2332. 396 rooms with bath, including 46 suites. Facilities: restaurants, including the gourmet Place de la Concorde; cafeteria; 2 bars; shopping center; outdoor heated pool; 2 lighted tennis courts, complete health club (with health food bar); English-language TV channels; purified water system. AE, DC, MC, V.*

Hyatt Regency. A striking ziggurat (tiered) glass facade defines this 13-story hotel located in the middle of the hotel strip. Opened in 1983, the Hyatt is popular with vacation charter groups and business travelers seeking the comfortable uniformity that the hotel chain affords; unfortunately, this large property lacks any semblance of intimacy or charm. Street-level escalators lift you past cascading waterfalls to the plush 12-story atrium lobby; two glass-enclosed elevators whisk you up to your floor. Spacious rooms, redecorated in 1990, feature hypoallergenic carpets and twin or queen-size orthopedic mattresses. The hotel's indoor Polaris Ice Skating Rink (the only such facility in the city) is open to nonguests. For the best city view, request a room on an upper floor facing the bustling Plaza del Sol shopping center. *Av. López Mateos Sur and Moctezuma, 45050, tel. 36/22–77–78 or 800/228–9000. 346 rooms with bath, including 29 suites. Facilities: 2 restaurants; 2 bars; pool; VIP club and business center with a bilingual staff; large, upscale shopping arcade; complete health club for men only; English-language TV channels; purified water system. AE, DC, MC, V.*

Moderate **Aranzazú.** This downtown hotel is popular with business travelers and conventioneers. The Aranzazú's two towers are on either side of Avenida Revolución; they are connected by an underground passageway. Each modern tower has a full complement of amenities and services. The public areas are ample and airy, with pleasant traditional decor and appointments. The standard-size rooms, remodeled in 1985, have pastel color schemes, with chatoyant walls and ceilings, and simple but comfortable furnishings. The Factory (in Tower 1) is one of the city's most popular night spots, with live entertainment each evening. *Av. Revolución 110, 44100, tel. 36/13–32–32 or 800/421–0000. 500 rooms with bath, including 14 suites. Facilities:*

1 restaurant, 2 coffee shops, 2 pools, nightclub, shops/boutiques, sauna, bottled water. AE, MC, V.

Calinda Roma. Located on a busy downtown street, this hotel caters to business travelers and senior citizens, with discounts offered to the latter. As the national headquarters for Señor Citizens, the chain's retirement club, the hotel hosts meetings here each Wednesday night and throws in free margaritas to boot. Public areas and rooms, all remodeled in 1984, combine modern Mexican decor and traditional appointments with a simple, hospitable ambience. The spacious lobby, with cushioned chairs and fireplace, doubles as a cocktail lounge, with nightly entertainment. From the Roma's rooftop, you have a panorama of the colonial center of the city and can swim in the pool. Rooms in the old wing are smaller and have black-and-white TVs; those in the new wing have color TVs and many have a great view of the Teatro Degollado. *Av. Juárez 170, 44100, tel. 36/14-86-50. 172 rooms with bath, including 3 suites. Facilities: restaurants, bar, lounge, bottled water. AE, DC, MC, V.*

De Mendoza. Mature travelers from the United States and Canada often choose this downtown hotel because of its convenient location (on a quiet side street just one block from the Degollado Theater) and charming postcolonial architecture and ambience. Beamed ceilings, hand-sculpted wood furniture and doors, and wrought-iron railings decorate public areas and rooms. Recent correspondence indicates that the quality of service and hotel facilities has been erratic, however. *Venustiano Carranza 16, 44100, tel. 36/13-46-46. 104 rooms with bath, including 17 suites. Facilities: restaurant, bar, pool, bottled water. AE, DC, MC, V.*

Fénix. This mid-rise downtown hotel caters to business travelers and national tourists. The lobby is active and busy and the staff efficient. The location, just off a principal downtown intersection, makes this hotel an ideal choice for the short-term visitor. The comfortable standard-size rooms, remodeled in 1988, have simple appointments and furnishings. *Av. Corona 160, 44100, tel. 36/14-57-14. 255 rooms with bath, including 25 suites. Facilities: 24-hour restaurant, bar, disco, nightclub, shops, English-language TV channels, bottled water. AE, DC, MC, V.*

Plaza Del Sol. Location and price make families and young adults head for this hotel's two towers rising over the south end of the Plaza del Sol shopping center. The intimate Solaris Restaurant and the Bar Sol provide enjoyable and romantic evenings. Public areas and rooms incorporate mauve and aquamarine-on-white color schemes. The accommodations, redecorated in 1987, have modern furniture and wall-to-wall carpeting. Rooms in the newer tower are a bit larger, and have a view of the shopping center below. *Av. López Mateos and Calle Mariano Otero, 45050, tel. 36/47-82-40. 355 rooms with bath, including 14 suites. Facilities: restaurant, cafeteria, bar, nightclub, outdoor swimming pool, solarium, English-language TV channels, bottled water, AE, DC, MC, V.*

Posada Guadalajara. Rooms in this colonial-style hotel's four contiguous six-story towers open onto airy, wrought-iron railed hallways overlooking the small patio and circular pool. The unassuming accommodations are clean and comfortable, with traditional appointments. In addition to a loyal cadre of international patrons, the Posada welcomes visiting sports teams. Depending on your disposition (and the age and inclinations of your fellow guests), you will find the evenings here to be either festive or raucous. The hotel is just south of Calzada Lázaro Cárdenas (arterial access to downtown). *Av. López Mateos Sur 1280, 45050, tel. 36/21–20–22. 180 rooms with bath, including 18 kitchenette suites. Facilities: restaurant, bar, outdoor heated pool, English-language TV channels, bottled water. AE, DC, MC, V.*

Inexpensive   **Diana.** Mexican and European tourists favor this six-story hotel, located two blocks from Minerva Fountain. The beige stucco lobby adjoins a small lounge and busy restaurant. Standard-size rooms have white-on-white walls and ceilings with brightly patterned curtains and bedspreads; all have desks and window air conditioners. The best rooms are on the upper floors in the rear, away from the activity and traffic on Yáñez. *Circunvalacíon Agustín Yáñez 2760, 44100, tel. 36/15–55–10. 200 rooms with bath, including 4 suites. Facilities: restaurant, cafeteria, bar, outdoor heated pool, English-language TV channels, bottled water. AE, DC, MC, V.*

★   **Frances.** The brothers Oliveros carefully renovated Guadalajara's oldest hotel (1610), preserving and restoring its original architecture and charm. During reopening ceremonies in 1981, the eight-story downtown hotel was designated a national monument. The venerable Frances has a three-story enclosed atrium lobby with stone columns and colonial arches surrounding a polished marble fountain and cut crystal-and-gilt chandelier. Even if you're not a guest, you may enjoy a ride in the antique cage elevator that holds three adults. Though room sizes vary, all share a colonial ambience, with white stucco walls, polished wood floors, and high-beamed ceilings. For the best city views, ask for a room facing Calle Maestranza. The Frances is ideal for travelers willing to exchange the amenities of a modern hotel for the hospitality of Guadalajara's grande dame. *Calle Maestranza 35, 45050, tel. 36/13–11–90. 60 rooms with bath. Facilities: 2 restaurants, cantina with live music, TV with English-language channels, bottled water. AE, DC, MC, V.*

Malibu. Behind Malibu's characterless two-story motel facade on the western fringe of the city are sprawling tropical gardens with wrought-iron chairs and tables scattered beneath imposing trees. During a 1982 renovation of this popular neocolonial-style resort, an eight-story hotel tower was built to accommodate guests without cars. Public areas in all of the buildings feature traditional Mexican accents: beamed ceilings, arches, and tiled floors. The ample rooms are decorated in beiges and browns with plain but functional furnishings (tower rooms have balconies). Unfortunately, early morning and late-night arrivals and departures of driving guests tend to mar an otherwise serene environment. The best rooms are on the upper floors of the tower. *Av. Vallarta 3993, 45050, tel. 36/21–76–76. 174 rooms with bath, including 5 suites. Facilities: restaurant, cocktail lounge (with nightly entertainment), outdoor heated pool, tennis court, English-language TV channels, purified water system. AE, DC, MC, V.*

The Arts and Nightlife

Guadalajara has a reputation as a cultural and performing arts center. Over the past 20 years, the active U.S. and Canadian communities have developed a schedule of English-language cultural events. You can attend a performance, an exhibition, or a recital almost any day of the year. The most extensive cultural events calendar appears in *The Colony Reporter*, an English-language weekly, which can be purchased in many downtown newsstands and most of the major hotels. The "Around the Town" column on the front page of the *Guadalajara Weekly* lists major events taking place in the city. This tabloid is available in hotel lobbies throughout the city.

The Arts

Symphony **Filarmónico Jalisco** (tel. 36/14–47–73 or 13–11–15). This famous symphony orchestra, conducted by Maestro Guadalupe Flores, performs Sundays and Fridays at the Degollado Theater.

Theater Degollado (Degollado and Belén, tel. 36/14–47–73 or 14–16–14). This magnificent theater was built in 1886 and totally remodeled in 1988. The theater presents nationally and internationally famous artists for performances throughout the year. The new velvet seats are comfortable, the acoustics are excellent, and the central air-conditioning is a treat.

Callejón Del Carmen In the passageway between the ex-Convento del Carmen and the Agora Café, there are performances by singers, dancers, and musical groups on weekday evenings. Fliers distributed to hotels list the schedule of events.

Concha Acústica. The outdoor theater in Parque Agua Azul presents festivals of music and dance every Sunday at 5 PM.

Instituto Cultural Cabañas (Calle Cabañas and Hospicio, tel. 36/17–30–97 or 18–60–03). Built in 1810, this former orphanage has 23 flowered patios and permanent and revolving art exhibits. Theater, dance, and music performances take place on an open-air stage within the institute. The Instituto also has a movie theater.

Music **Plaza De Armas.** Every Sunday and Thursday evening, the **State Band of Jalisco** performs at 6:30 PM. On Tuesday evening, the **Municipal Band of Guadalajara** performs at 6:30 PM.

Ballet **Ballet Folklórico of the University of Guadalajara.** This world-renowned dance troupe performs traditional Mexican folkloric dances and music in the Degollado Theater every Sunday at 10 AM.

Nightlife

Guadalajara is not known for its nightlife. The nightclubs in major hotels provide good local entertainment and, occasionally, internationally known recording artists. The best hotel clubs are the **Lobby Bar,** in the Hotel Fiesta Americana; **Memories,** in the El Tapatío; **La Diligencia,** in the Camino Real; and **La Fiesta,** in the Holiday Inn.

Discos You can dance all night at **Elipsis** (Av. Mariano Otero and Av. López Mateos) and **Osiris** at (Calzada Lázaro Cárdenas 3898).

Hotel discos include **Da Vinci,** in the Holiday Inn, and **The Factory,** in the Hotel Aranzazú.

Peñas As in the coffeehouses of the 1960s, patrons sit around a small stage at **Peña Cuicacalli** (Av. Niños Héroes 1988, tel. 36/25–46–90) and listen to jazz, blues, and folk, or Latin American music Wednesday through Saturday nights.

9 Acapulco

Introduction

By Anya Schiffrin

Now based in Turkey, Anya Schiffrin is a well-traveled free-lance writer whose credits include the Village Voice *and such British publications as* City Limits, Time Out, *and* New Society.

For sun lovers, beach bums, and other hedonists, Acapulco is the ideal holiday resort. Don't expect high culture, historic monuments, or haute cuisine. Anyone who ventures to this Pacific resort 260 miles south of Mexico City does so to relax. Translate that as swimming, shopping, and nightlife. Everything takes place against a staggeringly beautiful natural backdrop. Acapulco Bay is one of the world's best natural harbors, and it is the city's centerpiece. By day the water looks clean and temptingly deep blue; at night it flashes and sparkles with the city lights.

The weather is Acapulco's major draw—warm waters, almost constant sunshine, and year-round temperatures in the 80s. It comes as no surprise, then, that most people plan their day around laying their towel on some part of Acapulco's many miles of beach. Both tame and wild water sports are available—everything from waterskiing to snorkeling, diving, and the thrill of parasailing. Less-strenuous possibilities are motorboat rides and fishing trips. Championship golf courses, tennis courts, and the food/crafts markets also occasionally lure some visitors away from the beach, but not out of the sun.

Apart from these options, most people rouse themselves from their hammocks, deck chairs, or towels only when it is feeding time. Eating is one of Acapulco's great pleasures. You will find that in most dishes the ingredients are very fresh. Seafood is caught locally, and restaurateurs go to the *mercado* (market) daily to select the produce, meats, and fish for that night's meals. There are many good no-frills, down-home Mexican restaurants. Prices are reasonable and the food in these family-run places is prepared with care—spiced soups filled with red snapper (and red snapper heads), baskets filled with hot corn tortillas instead of bread. Eating at one of these spots gives you a glimpse into the real Mexico: office workers breaking for lunch, groups of men socializing over a cup of coffee.

At night, Acapulco is transformed as the city rouses itself from the day's torpor and prepares for the long hours ahead. Even though Acapulco's heyday is past, its nightlife is legendary. This is true despite the fact that many of the city's discos look like they were designed in the early '70s by an architect who bought mirrors and strobe lights wholesale. Perpetually crowded, the discos are grouped in twos and threes, so most people go to several places in one night. Last year's disco hits and huge fruity cocktails are trademarks of the Acapulco disco experience.

A relaxed, holiday atmosphere pervades Acapulco; shorts and T-shirts are the standard dress. The Mexicans you meet are friendly, and many travelers return to Acapulco every year to catch up on friendships begun on a previous vacation. The only drawback to this laid-back air is that everything takes much longer than you might expect. But there is no point in getting annoyed—just sit back and relax while you wait.

Acapulco was originally an important port for the Spanish, who used it to trade with countries in the Far East. The Spanish built Fuerte de San Diego (Fort San Diego) to protect the city from pirates, and today the fort houses a historical museum with exhibits about Acapulco's past. The name of the late

Teddy Stauffer, an entrepreneurial Swiss, is practically synonymous with that of modern Acapulco. He hired the first cliff divers at La Quebrada in Old Acapulco, and founded the Boom Boom Room, the town's first dance hall, and Tequila A Go-Go, its first discotheque. The Hotel Mirador at La Quebrada and the area stretching from Caleta to Hornos beaches, near today's Old Acapulco, were the center of activity in the 1950s, when Acapulco was a town of 20,000 with an economy based largely on fishing.

Former President Miguel Alemán Valdés bought up miles of the coast just before the road and the airport were built. The Avenida Costera Miguel Alemán bears his name today. Since the late 1940s, Acapulco has expanded eastward so that today it is one of Mexico's largest cities, with a population of approximately 2 million. Currently under development are a 3,000-acre expanse known as Acapulco Diamante and the areas known as Punta Diamante and Playa Diamante.

Essential Information

Arriving and Departing by Plane

Airport and Airlines From the United States: **American** (tel. 800/433–7300) has nonstops from Dallas; connections from Chicago and New York through Dallas. **Continental** (tel. 800/525–0280) has nonstop service from Houston. **Delta's** (tel. 800/843–9378) nonstop service is from Dallas and Los Angeles. **Mexicana** (tel. 800/531–7921) has nonstop service from Chicago and connecting service from New York, Miami, Denver, Dallas, Los Angeles, San Francisco, and San Jose, California, all via Mexico City. **Aeromexico's** (tel. 800/237–6639) flight from New York to Acapulco stops in Mexico City. Other major carriers fly into Mexico City, where you can make a connection to Acapulco.

From Canada: At press time **Sunquest** (tel. 800/776–3000) had charter service from Toronto on a biweekly basis using La Tur airlines; **Delta** has flights from most major Canadian cities via Los Angeles to Acapulco; **Canadian Holidays** (tel. 800/387–7663) has nonstop charter flights from Toronto to Acapulco.

From the United Kingdom: There are no direct flights to Acapulco, though the following airlines have service via Mexico City or major U.S. or European cities: **Air France** (tel. 081/759–2311); **Iberia** (tel. 071/437–5622); and **KLM** (tel. 081/568–9144).

From New York via Dallas, flying time is 4½ hours; from Chicago, 4¼ hours; from Los Angeles, 3½ hours.

Between the Airport and City Center Private taxis are not permitted to carry passengers from the airport to town, so most people rely on **Transportes Terrestres,** a special airport taxi service. The bus system looks confusing, but there are dozens of helpful English-speaking staff to help you figure out which bus to take.

Look for the name of your hotel and the number of its zone on the overhead sign on the walkway in front of the terminal. Go to the desk for your zone and buy a ticket for an airport taxi that goes to your zone. The ride from the airport to the hotel zone on the trip costs about $8. The drivers are usually helpful and will often take you to hotels not on their list. Tips are optional. The journey into town takes 20 to 30 minutes.

Arriving and Departing by Car, Ship, Train, and Bus

By Car A car can be handy in these parts, but we don't recommend you drive from either the United States or Canada. Except for major highways, the roads are not well maintained and distances from the border are great. If you prefer to see the sights by car, we suggest renting a car once you're there. Whether you drive from the United States or Canada or rent a car in Acapulco, bear in mind that Mexico is a developing country and things are much different than in North America or Western Europe. Unleaded gasoline is now available at the green-and-white Pemex stations along major tourist routes, but sometimes you'll find the supply has been depleted. It's a good idea to fill up your tank whenever possible, especially before starting out on long stretches of road. Spare parts are another worry. Parts for a Ford or Chevy are plentiful, but getting a new transmission for a Toyota or Mercedes is not easy.

The best highway, although two lanes most of the way, is Route 85 from Laredo to Monterrey and Route 57 on to Mexico City. Driving time is about 16 hours. The trip to Acapulco from Mexico City takes about six hours, but many people opt for going via Taxco.

By Ship Many cruises include Acapulco as part of their itinerary. Most originate from Los Angeles. Cruise operators include **Carnival Cruise Lines** (tel. 800/327–9501); **Clipper Cruise Line** (tel. 800/325–0010); **Cunard Line** (tel. 800/221–4770); **EuropAmerica Cruises** (tel. 800/221–1666); **Holland America Lines** (tel. 800/426–0327); **Krystal Cruises** (tel. 213/785–9300); **Norwegian Cruise Line** (tel. 800/327–3070); **Paquet French Cruises** (tel. 800/556–8850); **Princess Cruises** (tel. 800/421–0522); **Royal Caribbean Cruise Line** (tel. 365/539–6000); **Royal Cruise Line** (tel. 800/227–4534); **Royal Viking Line** (tel. 800/422–8000); and **Seaborn Cruise Line** (tel. 415/391–7444). Bookings are generally handled through a travel agent.

For details on freighter travel to or from Mexico, consult **Pearl's Travel Tips** (9903 Oaks La., Seminole, FL 34642, tel. 813/393–2919, fax 813/392–2580).

By Train and Bus There is no train service to Acapulco from anywhere in the United States or Canada. Buses to Acapulco can be boarded on the U.S. side of the border, but the trip is not recommended; even the most experienced travelers find the trip exhausting and uncomfortable. Bus service from Mexico City to Acapulco, however, is worth trying, especially if you want to see some of the Mexican countryside. Buses are comfortable and in good condition, and the trip takes six hours. They leave three times a day from Tasqueña station. A first-class ticket costs about $15. You check your baggage and collect it from the baggage window at the Estrella de Oro bus station in Acapulco when you arrive.

Getting Around Acapulco

Getting around in Acapulco is quite simple. You can walk to many places and the bus costs only 20¢. Taxis cost less than in the United States, so most tourists quickly become avid taxi takers.

By Bus The buses tourists use the most are those that go from Puerto Marqués to Caleta and stop at the fairly conspicuous metal bus stops along the way. If you want to go from the Zócalo to The Strip, catch the bus that says *"La Base"* (the naval base near the Exelaris Hyatt Regency). This bus detours through Old Acapulco and returns to the Costera just east of the Ritz Hotel. If you want to follow the Costera for the entire route, take the bus marked "Hornos." Buses to Pie de la Cuesta or Puerto Marqués say so on the front. The Puerto Marqués bus runs about every half hour and is always crowded.

By Taxi How much you pay depends on what type of taxi you get. The most expensive are hotel taxis. A price list that all drivers adhere to is posted in hotel lobbies. Fares in town are usually about $1.50 to $5; to go from downtown to the Princess Hotel or Caleta beach is about $10 to $15. Hotel taxis are by far the plushest and are kept in the best condition.

Cabs that cruise with their roof light off occasionally carry a price list. But don't expect to find a running meter because they are all mysteriously "broken." You need to reach an agreement with these drivers, but the fare should be less than at a hotel. There is a minimum charge of $1. Some taxis that cruise have hotel or restaurant names stenciled on the side, but are not affiliated with any establishment. Before you go anywhere by cab, find out what the price should be and agree with the driver on a price. You can usually persuade one to overcharge you by only 50¢ to $1. Alternatively, you can hand him the correct fare when you arrive, but that can lead to a nasty scene where the driver is disappointed to receive the correct fare and argues with you for more.

The cheapest taxis are the little Volkswagens. Officially there is a $1 minimum charge, but many cab drivers don't stick to it. A normal, i.e., Mexican-priced, fare is $1 to go from the Zócalo to American Express, but lots of luck getting a taxi driver to accept that from a tourist. Rates are about 50% higher at night and though tipping is not expected, Mexicans usually leave small change.

You can also hire a taxi by the hour or the day. Prices vary from about $12 an hour for a hotel taxi to $8 an hour for a street taxi. Never let a taxi driver decide where you should eat or shop, since many get kickbacks from some of the smaller stores and restaurants.

By Motorscooter Little Honda motorscooters can be rented from a stand outside CiCi, the children's water park on the Costera. They are also available at the Plaza Hotel. Cost: $15 to $20 for up to four hours, depending on the size, or $30 to $40 per day.

By Horse and Carriage Buggy rides up and down The Strip are available on weekends. Bargain before you get in—they cost about $20 a half hour.

Important Addresses and Numbers

Tourist Information The **State of Guerrero Department of Tourism (SEFOTUR)** will help you find your way around and answer questions. The office is in the Centro Internacional, tel. 74/84–70–50. It is open Monday through Saturday from 9 to 3 and 6 to 9. Much more helpful is the **Secretaía de Turismo,** across from the Super-Super, Costera Miguel Alemán 187, which is open weekdays 8–8, Saturday and Sunday 10–6. The staff speaks English, has brochures and maps on other parts of Mexico, and can help you find a hotel room. Tel. 74/85–12–49 or 74/85–13–04.

Consulates The consular representative for the United States is Bonny Urbaneck. Her office is in the Club del Sol Hotel on the Costera, tel. 74/85–72–07. The Canadian representative is Diane McLean de Huerta, and her office is on the mezzanine level of the Club del Sol Hotel, tel. 74/85–66–21.

Emergencies **Police,** tel. 74/85–08–62.

The **Red Cross** can be reached at tel. 74/85–41–00 or 74/85–41–01. Two reliable hospitals are **Hospital Privado Magallanes,** Wilfrido Massiue 2, tel. 74/85–65–44, and **Hospital Centro Médico,** J. Arevalo 99, tel. 74/82–46–92.

Doctors and Your hotel and the Secretaría de Turismo can locate an En-
Dentists glish-speaking doctor. But English-speaking doctors don't come cheap—house calls are about $50. The Secretaría de Turismo has a list of dentists and suggests Dr. Guadalupe Carmona, Costera Miguel Alemán 220–101, tel. 74/85–71–76, or Dr. Arturo Carmona, Costera Miguel Alemán 220, Suite 110, tel. 74/85–72–86.

English-language English-language books and periodicals can be found at
Bookstores Sanborns, a reputable American-style department store chain, and at the newsstands in some of the larger hotels. Most reading material costs more than at home. Many small newsstands and the Super-Super carry the *Mexico City News,* an English-language daily newspaper with a large Sunday edition carrying reports from many cities, including Acapulco. Social events and evening activities in the area are often covered. Every day several pages are devoted to foreign news drawn from the wire services with reprints of articles from the *Washington Post, New York Times,* and *Los Angeles Times. The Sun,* an English-language weekly sold at newsstands on Sundays, usually includes a report from Acapulco. *Time* and *Newsweek* magazines are also available.

Travel Agencies **American Express,** at Costera Miguel Alemán 709, tel. 74/84–60–60, and **Viajes Wagon-Lits,** at Scenic Highway 5255 (Las Brisas Hotel), tel. 74/82–28–64.

Guided Tours

Orientation Tours There are organized tours everywhere in Acapulco, from the red-light district to the lagoon. Tours to Mexican fiestas in the evenings or the markets in the daytime are easy to arrange. Tour operators have offices around town and desks in many of the large hotels. If your hotel can't arrange a tour, contact **Consejeros de Viajes** at the Torre de Acapulco, Costera Miguel Alemán 1252, tel. 74/84–74–00, or **Acuario,** Costera Miguel Alemán, opposite the Plaza Hotel, tel. 74/85–61–00.

Special-interest The Acapulco Princess runs a Mexican cooking school featur-
Tours ing the techniques of executive chef George Olah, who teaches dishes from the Aztec time to nouvelle Mexican. The school is limited to 20 participants per session, and there are two 5-day/4-night sessions a year. Contact the Acapulco Princess hotel, tel. 800/223–1818.

Exploring Acapulco

Acapulco is a city that is easily understood, easily explored. During the day the focus for most visitors is the beach and the myriad activities that happen on and off it—sunbathing, swimming, waterskiing, parasailing, snorkeling, deep-sea fishing, and so on. At night, the attention shifts to the restaurants and discos. The Costera Miguel Alemán, the wide boulevard that hugs Acapulco Bay from the Scenic Highway to Caleta Beach (a little less than five miles), is central to both day and night diversions. All the major beaches, big hotels—minus the more exclusive East Bay properties, such as Las Brisas, Pierre Marqués, and the Princess—and shopping malls are off the Costera. Hence most of the shopping, dining, and clubbing takes place within a few blocks of the Costera, and many an address is listed only as "Costera Miguel Alemán." Because street addresses are not often used and streets have no logical pattern, directions are usually given from a major landmark, such as CiCi or the Zócalo.

Old Acapulco, the colonial part of town, is where the Mexicans go to run their errands: mail letters at the post office, buy supplies at the Mercado Municipal, and have clothes made/repaired at the tailor. Here is where you'll find the Zócalo, the church, and Fort San Diego. Just up the hill from Old Acapulco is La Quebrada, where, four times a day, the cliff divers plunge into the surf 130 feet below.

The peninsula just south of Old Acapulco contains remnants of the first version of Acapulco. This primarily residential area has been prey to dilapidation and abandonment of late, and the efforts made to revitalize it—such as reopening the Caleta Hotel and opening the aquarium on Caleta Beach and the zoo on Roqueta Island—haven't met with much success. The Plaza de Toros, where bullfights are held sporadically, is in the center of the peninsula.

If you've arrived by plane, you've had a royal introduction to Acapulco Bay. Driving from the airport, via the Scenic Highway, the first thing you see on your left is the golf course for the Acapulco Princess. Just over the hill is your first glimpse of the entire bay, and it is truly gorgeous, day or night.

Numbers in the margin correspond to points of interest on the Acapulco map.

❶ La Base, the Mexican naval base next to Plaza Icacos, anchors the eastern terminus of the Costera. There are no tours.

❷ The **Centro Cultural Guerrerense** is on the beach side of the Costera, just past the Hyatt Regency. It has a small archaeological museum and the Zochipala art gallery with changing exhibits. *Admission free. Open weekdays, 9–1 and 5–8.*

❸ CiCi (short for Centro Internacional para Convivencia Infantil), on the Costera, is a water-oriented theme park for children. There are dolphin and seal shows, a freshwater pool with wave-making apparatus, water slide, mini-aquarium, and other attractions. *Admission: $7 adults; $5 children. Open daily 10–6.*

About a half mile past CiCi, on the right side of the Costera, is **❹ Centro Internacional** (the Convention Center), not really of in-

PACIFIC OCEAN

Av. Rancho Acapulco

Paseo del Farallon

Cuauhtemoc

Av. Almirante

Magallanes

Anfiente Cristobal Colon

Horacio Nelson

Golf Course

Lobo Solitario

4

Diana Glorieta

Costera Miguel Alemán

Costera Miguel

Playa Icacos

3

2

Alemán

Playa Condesa

Playa Hornos

1

Punta Guitarrón

Escénica

Bahía de Acapulco

Carretera

E A S T

B A Y

TO AIRPORT →

el Rey

ical

ya
eta

Bahía de
Puerto
Marqués

Punta Bruja

Playa Roqueta

TO PUNTA DIAMANTE →
AND BARRA VIEJA

N

0 — 880 yards
0 — 800 meters

terest unless you are attending a conference there. There is a **Mexican Fiesta** Tuesday, Thursday, and Saturday nights from 7 to 10:30 ($45 pays for the show, dinner, and open bar; entrance to the show alone is $10).

Continue along the Costera, through the heart of The Strip, until you reach **Papagayo Park,** one of the top municipal parks in the country for location, beauty, and variety. Named for the hotel that formerly occupied the grounds, Papagayo sits on 52 acres of prime real estate on the Costera, just after the underpass at the end of The Strip. Though aimed at children, there is plenty for all ages to enjoy. Youngsters enjoy the life-size model of a Spanish galleon like the ones that once sailed into Acapulco when it was Mexico's capital of trade with the Orient. There is an aviary, a roller-skating rink, a racetrack with mite-size Can Am cars, a replica of the space shuttle *Columbia*, bumper boats in a lagoon, and other rides. The aviary is Papagayo's best feature: Hundreds of species of birds flitter overhead as you amble down shaded paths. *Admission free, though rides cost $1–$3.50. Open daily 10–6.*

The sprawling **Mercado Municipal,** a few blocks from the Costera, is Acapulco at its most authentic. It is also the city's answer to the suburban shopping mall. Locals come to purchase their everyday needs, from fresh vegetables and candles to plastic buckets and love potions. Go between 10 AM and 1 PM and ask to be dropped off near the *flores* (flower stand) closest to the souvenir and craft section. If you've driven to the mercado, locals may volunteer to watch your car; be sure to lock your trunk and tip about 35¢.

The stalls within the mercado are densely packed together but luckily are awning covered, so things stay quite cool despite the lack of air-conditioning. From the flower stall, as you face the ceramic stand, turn right and head into the market. There are hundreds of souvenirs to choose from: woven blankets, puppets, colorful wooden toys and plates, leather goods, baskets, hammocks, and handmade wooden furniture including child-size chairs. You can also find some kitschy gems: Acapulco ashtrays and boxes covered with tiny shells or enormous framed pictures of the Virgin of Guadalupe. Bargaining hard is the rule: Start at half the asking price. The exception is silver. Under no circumstance pay more than one-fourth the asking price for hallmarked jewelry. A bracelet will be offered for $50 but the price should drop to less than $20 within five minutes. The silver vendors speak English.

The mercado is patronized primarily by Mexicans and, like many markets, is divided into departments. One area sells locally made brushes and wooden spoons. In another, artisans put finishing touches on baskets and wooden furniture. There are dozens of exotic blossoms—many arranged into FTD-like centerpieces—in the flower market. Prices are a fraction of what you'd pay at home. The beans, spices, and vegetable section has a number of unfamiliar tropical products. There is even a stand offering medicinal herbs from China along with good luck charms. Allow at least an hour and a half to take it all in.

Built in the 18th century to protect the city from pirates, **El Fuerte de San Diego** is on the hill overlooking the harbor next to the army barracks in Old Acapulco. (The original fort, destroyed in an earthquake, was built in 1616.) The fort now houses the **Museo Historico de Acapulco,** under the auspices of Mexico City's prestigious Museum of Anthropology. The exhibits portray the city from prehistoric times through Mexico's independence from Spain in 1821. Especially noteworthy are the displays touching on the Christian missionaries sent from Mexico to the Far East and the cultural interchange that resulted. Exhibits are mounted in separate air-conditioned rooms of the old fort. *Tel. 74/82–38–28. Admission: $3.50. Open Tues.–Sun. 10:30–4:30.*

8 Acapulco is still a lively commercial port and fishing center. If you stroll along the **waterfront,** you'll see all these activities at the commercial docks. The cruise ships dock here, and at night Mexican parents bring their children to play on the small tree-lined promenade. Farther west, by the Zócalo, are the docks for the sightseeing yachts and smaller fishing boats. It's a good spot to join the Mexicans in people-watching.

9 The **Zócalo** is the center of Old Acapulco, a shaded plaza in front of **Nuestra Señora de la Soledad,** the town's modern but unusual—stark white exterior with bulb-shaped blue and yellow spires—church. If there is any place in Acapulco that can be called picturesque or authentic, the Zócalo is it. Overgrown with dense trees, it is the hub of downtown, a spot for socializing. All day it's filled with vendors, shoeshine men, and people lining up to use the pay phones. After siesta, they drift here to meet and greet. On Sunday evenings there's music in the bandstand. There are several cafés and news agents selling the English-language *Mexico City News,* so tourists lodging in the area linger here, too. The Flor de Acapulco is a lovely old-fashioned café with a 1950s ambience. Groups of Mexicans stop in for breakfast before work, and in the evening it is popular for drinks and meals. European hippie types and retired Canadians hang out at Flor de Acapulco for hours. Around the Zócalo are several souvenir shops, and on the side streets you can get hefty, fruity milk shakes for about 50¢. The "flea market," inexpensive tailor shops, and Woolworth's (*see* Shopping, *below*) are nearby.

Time Out The café across from the Flor de Acapulco, below the German restaurant, at 455 de Mayo, serves *churros* every afternoon beginning at 4. This Spanish treat of fried dough dusted with sugar and dipped in hot chocolate is popular at *merienda,* which means snack.

10 A 10-minute walk up the hill from the Zócalo brings you to **La Quebrada.** This is home to the famous Mirador Hotel and a large silver shop, Taxco El Viejo (*see* Shopping, *below*). In the 1940s this was the center of action for tourists, and it retains an atmosphere reminiscent of its glory days. Most visitors eventually make the trip here because this is where the famous cliff divers jump from a height of 130 feet every evening at 7:30, 8:30, 9:30, and 10:30. The dives are thrilling, so be sure to arrive early. Before they dive, the brave divers say a prayer at a small shrine near the jumping-off point. Sometimes they dive in pairs; often they carry torches.

What to See and Do with Children

CiCi and **Papagayo Park** (*see above*). Kids might also like to see the aquarium on Caleta beach, where there are also swimming pools, a toboggan, scuba diving, and (for rent) jet skis, inner tubes, bananas (inflatable rubber tubes pulled along the beach by motorboats), and kayaks—not to mention clean rest rooms. From here you can take the launch to Roqueta Island for a visit to the small zoo, or a glass-bottom boat to La Quebrada and Puerto Marqués. *Aquarium admission: $5. Ferry service to Roqueta Island, including zoo admission: $3.50. Glass-bottom boat: $6.50.*

Palao's. This restaurant on Roqueta Island has a sandy cove for swimming, a pony, and a cage of monkeys that entertain the youngsters. Children enjoy the motorboat ride out to the island. Other good restaurants for children are **Beto's Mimi's Chili Saloon,** and **Carlos 'n Charlies** (*see* Dining, *below*).

Shopping

There is quite a lot of shopping to do in Acapulco, and the abundance of air-conditioned shopping malls and boutiques makes picking up gifts and souvenirs all the more pleasurable. Except for the markets, most places shut for siesta. The typical hours of business are 10–1 and then 4–7, though these hours vary slightly. Most shops close on Sunday.

Though the fall of the peso has given most travelers to Acapulco a shopping edge, those who master the art of bargaining and understand how the Mexican sales tax (IVA) works will have their purchasing power increased even more (*see* Shopping in Staying in Mexico, Chapter 1).

Gift Ideas

Mexicans produce quantities of inexpensive collectibles and souvenirs such as colorful serapes, ceramics, glassware, silver, straw hats, leather, shell sculptures, wooden toys, carved walking canes, and, in season, Christmas ornaments. Most of these trinkets can be found everywhere. In fact, you may tire of the hawkers who traverse the beaches and approach passersby on the street. Crafts sold on the street include stone wind chimes, painted wooden birds (each about $3.50–$5), shell earrings for 50¢, shell sculptures, sets of wooden dishes, and rugs. Bargaining is essential in these situations. Prices are often lower in the markets and on the street, so it makes sense to buy outside the shops or to visit the shops first, note the prices, and then venture to the markets to try and beat the store prices. Don't buy any article described as "silver" on the street. Street vendors sell a silver facsimile called alpaca. In the morning they buy bracelets from a wholesale supplier for 50¢ that they sell to unsuspecting tourists in the afternoon for $5. Buy silver in shops and look for the .925 hallmark, which means you are getting sterling. The large AFA (Artesanías Finas de Acapulco) crafts shop, though, has fixed prices and will ship, so this is the place to purchase onyx lamp stands and other larger items (*see* Food and Flea Markets, *below*). Clothes are another reasonably priced gift item. There are a couple of fashionable boutiques with designer clothes, but the majority of shops stock cotton sportswear and casual resort clothes. Made-to-order clothes are well made and especially reasonable. Otherwise, be careful, since quality is not high and many goods self-destruct a few months after you get back home.

Shopping Districts

The biggest shopping strip surrounds the Fiesta Americana Condesa Hotel and is where you can find Gucci, Acapulco Joe, Ocho Rios, Rubén Torres, Fiorucci, and others. Downtown (Old) Acapulco doesn't have many name shops, but this is where you'll find the inexpensive tailors patronized by the Mexicans, lots of little souvenir shops, and the flea market with crafts made for tourists. The tailors are all on Calle Benito Juárez, just west of the Zócalo. Also downtown are Woolworth's and Sanborns.

Food and Flea Markets

The **Mercado Municipal** is described in Exploring, *above*.

El Mercado de Artesanías is a 20-minute walk from the Zócalo. Turn left as you leave Woolworth's and head straight until you reach the Multibanco Comermex. Turn right for one block and then turn left. When you reach the Banamex, the market is on your right. There are also "fleamarket" signs posted. The market itself is shamelessly inauthentic; everything here is made strictly for foreign consumption, so go just for the amusement. It is a conglomeration of every souvenir in town: fake tribal masks, the ever-present onyx chessboards, the $20 hand-embroidered dresses, imitation silver, hammocks, ceramics, even skin cream made from turtles. (Don't buy it because turtles are endangered and you won't get it through U.S. Customs.) *Open daily 9–9*. If you don't want to make the trip downtown, try **Noa Noa** on the Costera at Calle Hurtado de Mendoza. It's a cleaner, more commercial version of the Mercado Municipal and has T-shirts and jewelry, as well as the dozens of souvenirs available in the other markets.

Artesanías Finas de Acapulco (AFA) is one block north of the Costera behind the Baby O disco. All the souvenirs you have seen in town and lots more are available in 13,000 square feet of air-conditioned shopping space. AFA also carries household items, complete sets of dishes, suitcases, leather goods, and conservative clothing, as well as fashionable shorts and T-shirts. The staff is helpful. AFA ships to the United States and accepts major credit cards.

The **Crafts Shop,** in the same building as Taxco El Viejo in La Quebrada before you reach the Mirador Hotel, has not only all the usual crafts but also the best selection of glassware in Acapulco.

Two blocks west of the Zócalo is **Calle José M. Iglesia,** home to a row of little souvenir shops that have a smaller selection than the big markets, but many more T-shirts and more shell sculptures, shell ashtrays, and shell key chains than you ever imagined possible.

Art

Galerías Artesanales, at the Princess, carries the work of contemporary Mexican artists, including Felgueres, as well as handcrafts that almost border on art. *Open Mon.–Sat. 10–8*.

Galería Rudic, across from the Hyatt Continental, is one of the best galleries in town, with a good collection of top contemporary Mexican artists, including Armando Amaya, Leonardo Nierman, Norma Goldberg, Trinidad Osorio, José Clemente Orozco, and José David Alfaro Siqueiros. *Open weekdays 10–2 and 5–8.*

Galería Victor is the most noteworthy shop in the El Patio shopping center across from the Hyatt Continental. On display is the work of the late Victor Salmones. *Open 10–2 and 4–8. Closed Sun.*

The sculptor **Pal Kepenyes** continues to receive good press. His jewelry is available in the Hyatt Regency arcade. It's also on display in his house at Guitarrón 140. Good luck with his perennially busy phone number, tel. 74/84–47–38.

Sergio Bustamante's whimsical painted papier-mâché and giant ceramic sculptures can be seen at the Princess Hotel shopping arcade and at his own gallery (Costera Miguel Alemán 711-B, next to American Express). **El Dorado Gallery,** next door, carries works by his former partner, Mario Gonzáles.

Boutiques

The mall section (*see below*) lists clothing shops, but there are a few places, mainly near the Fiesta Americana Condesa Hotel, that are noteworthy. **Mad Max** has tasteful cotton separates in bold colors for children, and shirts sporting the shop's logo (all under $20). **Ocho Ríos** has a line of smashing women's bathing suits for equally smashing bodies. **Acapulco Joe, Rubén Torres, Polo Ralph Lauren, Benetton, Fiorucci,** and **OP** are scattered around the Costera, too. At No. 143 are three interconnected shops: Explora, Poco Loco, and Maria de Guadalajara. **Explora** and **Poco Loco** stock shirts imprinted with beer and alcohol logos, with casual separates and bathing suits, as well. The **Maria de Guadalajara** line of comfortable casual clothes for women is made from crinkly cotton in subdued and pastel colors. There are also a few high-fashion boutiques that will make clothes to order, and many can alter clothes to suit you, so it is always worth asking.

Sassafrass, in the Galería Plaza, is a boutique stocked with stylish bathing suits, shorts, and handpainted T-shirts for men and women.

In Plaza Bahía, **Lassere** has a selection of very stylish casuals, designed in France and made in Mexico for men and women.

Marietta is located at the Acapulco Princess Hotel arcade and on the Costera at the Torre de Acapulco. It has a large collection that ranges from simple daywear to extravagantly sexy party dresses. This is a standby for expats in Acapulco. Though the clothes may seem expensive (cotton dresses from $70 to $150), they are quite a bit cheaper than they would be in the United States. It also has a good selection of men's shirts.

Pit, located in the Princess arcade, is another bonanza. It is one of the few places that carries sweaters and coats as well as bathing suits and light dresses.

Custom-made Clothes The most famous of the made-to-order boutiques is **Samy's** at Calle Hidalgo 7, two blocks west of the Zócalo, a little crammed shop next to a florist. It boasts a clientele of international celebrities and many of the important local families. Samy, the charming owner, takes all customers to heart and treats them like old, much-loved friends. He makes clothes for men and women, all in light cottons. The patterns are unusual and heavily influenced by Mexican designs, with embroidery and gauze playing a supporting role in the Samy look. The outfits are appropriate for trendy over-30s. Anything that doesn't fit can be altered, and Samy will even work with fabric that you bring in. Prices start at about $30. There is also a ready-to-wear line.

Esteban's, the most glamorous shop in Acapulco, is on the Costera near the Club de Golf. Like Samy, Esteban will make clothes to order and adapt anything you see in the shop. The similarity ends there. Esteban's clothes are far more formal and fashionable. His opulent evening dresses range from $200 to $1,000, though daytime dresses average $120. If you scour the racks, you can find something for $85. Esteban has a back room full of designer clothes.

Jewelry

Aha, on the Costera next to the Crazy Lobster, has the most unusual costume jewelry in Acapulco. Designed by owner Cecilia Rodriguez, this is really campy, colorful stuff that is bound to attract attention. Prices range from $12 to $300.

Emi Fors (Galería Plaza and the Continental Plaza) are tony jewelry shops owned by Mrs. Fors, a former Los Angelino. The stores stock gold, silver, and some semiprecious stones.

Arles, at the Galería Acapulco Plaza, carries the beautiful Oro de Monte Alban collection of gold replicas of Oaxacan artifacts, as well as watches, handicrafts, and handpainted tin soldiers.

Silver

Many people come to Mexico to buy silver. Taxco, three hours away, is one of the silver capitals of the world. Prices in Acapulco are lower than in the United States but not dirt-cheap by any means. Bangles start at $8 and go up to $20; bracelets range from $20 to $60. Just look for the .925 sterling silver hallmark, or buy the more inexpensive silver plate that is dipped in several coats *(baños)* of silver. **Antonio Pineda** and **Los Castillo** are two of the more famous design names. Designs range from traditional bulky necklaces (often made with turquoise) to streamlined bangles and chunky earrings. Not much flatware can be found, although Emi Fors and Taxco El Viejo do carry some.

Taxco El Viejo (La Quebrada 830), in a large colonial building in Old Acapulco, has the largest silver selection in Acapulco. Pieces seen all over town crop up here as do more unusual designs. Also for sale are flatware and a large range of ornamental belt buckles. If you buy several pieces, you can request a discount. Beware of heavy-handed sales techniques such as offering to send a taxi to pick you up at your hotel, a tactic meant to make you feel obligated to buy something.

La Joya (Acapulco Plaza) stocks a good collection of inexpensive silver jewelry in modern designs and an extensive array of low-priced bangles (in the $6 range). Joya sells wholesale and will give a 30% discount on every item. *Open weekdays 9–6, Sat. 9–5.*

Dudu (Acapulco Princess shopping center) has the finest selection of silver jewelry and decorative pieces in town. There are signed pieces by Los Castillo (including brightly colored high-temperature ceramic dinnerware inlaid with silver), and enameled pieces by Miguel Pineda.

Malls

Malls are all the rage in Acapulco, and new ones are constantly being built. These range from the lavish air-conditioned shopping arcade at the Princess to rather gloomy collections of shops that sell cheap jewelry and embroidered dresses. Malls are listed below from east to west.

The **Princess's** cool arcade is one of Acapulco's classiest, most comfortable malls. Serious shopping takes place here. Best bets are quality jewelry, clothes, leather, accessories, and artwork. Even if you are staying on The Strip, it is worth the cab ride out here just to see the shops.

La Casita, which carries Mexican-inspired clothes for women, is the only shop left in **Plaza Icacos,** at the bottom of the hill, across from the Hyatt Regency. Across from the Fiesta Americana Condesa Hotel is the **Plaza Condesa,** which offers a cold-drink stand, an Italian restaurant, a weight-training center, and a greater concentration of silver shops than anywhere else in Acapulco. Next door to Plaza Condesa is a high-tech, two-story building with a gym, OP for trendy sportswear, Rubén Torres, Acapulco Joe, and two branches of Mad Max. The multilevel **Marbella Mall,** at the Diana Glorieta, has Peletier Paris jewelers and Bing's Ice Cream, as well as several restaurants and a Century 21 office. **Aca Mall,** which is on the other side of the Diana Glorieta, is all white and marble. Here you'll find Polo Ralph Lauren, Esprit, Perry Ellis, Amarras, Ellesse, and Marti (which carries a huge variety of sports equipment). **El Patio,** across from the Hyatt Continental, has two recommendable art galleries, Gucci, and a fairly generic collection of clothing and silver shops.

Plaza Bahía, next to the Acapulco Plaza, is a huge, completely enclosed and air-conditioned mall, where you can easily spend an entire day. Here you'll find Calvin Klein; Benetton; Aspasia, which carries a line of locally designed glitzy evening dresses and chunky diamanté jewelry; Bally; Armando's Girasol, with its distinctive line of women's clothing; restaurants and snack bars; Marti; a video-games arcade; and silver and handicraft shops. The list goes on and on.

Galería Plaza is a new two-story structure of lusciously air-conditioned shops built around a courtyard. Except for the silver, you could find many similar items at home. But this is a good place to pick up some cotton sportswear or a pretty dress to wear to a disco. For fancier duds, try Arles, upstairs. Guess! is one block west as you leave the plaza. Across from the Galería Plaza is the **Flamboyant Mall,** similar in style to El Patio.

Department Stores

Sanborns is the most un-Mexican of the big shops. It sells English-language newspapers, magazines, and books, as well as a line of high-priced souvenirs, but its Mexican glassware and ceramics cannot be found anywhere else in town. This is a useful place to come for postcards, cosmetics, and medicines. Sanborns's restaurants are recommended for glorified coffee-shop food. *The branch adjacent to the Condesa, Costera Miguel Alemán 209, is open until 1 AM; the downtown branch, Costera Miguel Alemán 1206, closes at 10:30 PM.*

Two branches of **Super Super** and **Gigante,** all on the Costera, and one Super Super downtown sell everything from light bulbs and newspapers to bottles of tequila and postcards. If you are missing anything at all, you should be able to pick it up at either of these stores or at the **Commercial Mexicana,** a store a little closer to The Strip. *Open until 9 PM; Super Super on La Costera until 11 PM, downtown until 8 PM.*

Woolworth's, at the corner of Escudero and Matamoros streets in Old Acapulco, is much like the five-and-dime stores found all over the United States, but with a Mexican feel. You can purchase American brands of shampoo for less than they cost at home, as well as paper goods, cheap clothes, handmade children's toys, and the ubiquitous Acapulco shell ashtrays. There are also several mini-Woolworths along the Costera. *Open until 9 PM.*

Sports and Fitness

Participant Sports and Fitness

Acapulco has lots for sports lovers to enjoy. Most hotels have pools, and there are several tennis courts on The Strip. The weight-training craze is beginning to catch on and gyms are opening. You'll find one at Plaza Condesa across from the Fiesta Americana Condesa Hotel.

Fishing Sailfish, marlin, shark, and mahimahi are the usual catches. Head down to the docks near the Zócalo and see just how many people offer to take you out for $35 a day. It is safer to stick with one of the reliable companies whose boats and equipment are in good condition.

Fishing trips can be arranged through your hotel, downtown at the Pesca Deportiva near the *muelle* (dock) across from the Zócalo, or through travel agents. Boats accommodating four to ten people cost $200–$500 a day, $60 by the chair. Excursions usually leave about 7 AM and return at 2 PM. You are required to get a license ($7) from the Secretaría de Pesca above the central post office downtown, but most fishing outfits take care of it. Don't show up during siesta, between 2 and 4 in the afternoon. For deep-sea fishing, **Arnold Brothers** (Costera Miguel Alemán 205, tel. 74/82–18–77) has well-maintained boats for five passengers (two lines). Small boats for freshwater fishing can be rented at **Cadena's** and **Tres Marías** at Coyuca lagoon. **Divers de México** (*see* Scuba Diving, *below*) rents chairs on fishing boats for about $30 per person.

Fitness and Swimming Acapulco weather is like August in the warmest parts of the United States. This means that you should cut back on your workouts and maintain proper hydration by drinking plenty of water.

Acapulco Princess Hotel (Carretera Escénica, Km 17, tel. 74/8 4–31–00) offers the best fitness facilities, with five pools, 11 tennis courts, and a gym with stationary bikes, Universal machines, and free weights. Because the Princess is about nine miles from the city center, you can even swim in the ocean here, avoiding the pollution of Acapulco Bay. Beware: The waves are rough and the undertow is strong.

Villa Vera Spa and Fitness Center (Lomas del Mar 35, tel. 74/84–03–33) has a new spa and fitness center, is equipped with exercise machines (including step machines), free weights, and benches. Masseuses and cosmetologists give facials and massages inside or by the pool, as you wish. Both the beauty center and gym are open to non-guests.

Westin Las Brisas (Carretera Escénica 5255, tel. 74/84–15–80) is the place to stay if you like to swim but don't like company or competition. Individual *casitas* come with private, or semiprivate, pools; the beach club has two saltwater pools, a Home Fitness System, and workout machines.

Most of the major hotels in town along the Costera Miguel Alemán also have pools.

Golf There are two 18-hole championship golf courses shared by the Princess and Pierre Marqués hotels. Reservations should be made in advance (tel. 74/84–31–00). Greens fees are $50 for guests and $60 for nonguests. There is also a public golf course at the Club de Golf (tel. 74/84–07–81) on The Strip across from the Acapulco Malibú hotel. Greens fees are $30 for nine holes.

Jogging The only real venue for running in the downtown area is along the sidewalk next to the seafront Costera Miguel Alemán. Early morning is the best time, since traffic is heavy along this thoroughfare during most of the day and the exhaust fumes can make running unpleasant. The sidewalk measures close to five miles. The beach is another option but, like beaches everywhere, the going is tough with soft sand and sloping contours. Away from the city center, the best area for running is out at the Acapulco Princess Hotel, on the airport road. A 2-kilometer (1.2 mi) loop is laid out along a lightly traveled road and, in the early morning, you can also run along the asphalt trails on the golf course.

Scuba Diving **Divers de México,** (tel. 74/82–13–98 or 74/83–60–20). owned by a helpful and efficient American woman, provides English-speaking captains and comfortable American-built yachts. A four- to five-hour scuba-diving excursion, including equipment, lessons in a pool for beginners, and drinks, costs about $55 per person. If you are a certified diver, the excursion is $45; if you bring your own equipment, it is $30.

Arnold Brothers (*see* Fishing, *above*) also runs daily scuba excursions and snorkeling trips. The scuba trips cost $30 and last for 2½ hours.

Tennis Court fees range from about $7 to $20 an hour during the day, and are $2–$3 more in the evening. Non-hotel guests pay about $5 more per hour. Lessons, with English-speaking instructors, are about $25 an hour; ball boys get a $2 tip.

Acapulco Plaza, 4 clay courts, 3 lighted for evening play (tel. 74/84–80–50). **Acapulco Princess,** 2 indoor courts, 9 outdoor (tel. 74/84–31–00). **Club de Tennis and Golf,** across from Hotel Malibu, Costera Miguel Alemán (tel. 74/84–48–24). **Hyatt Regency,** 5 lighted courts (tel. 74/84–12–25). **Pierre Marqués,** 5 courts (tel. 74/84–20–00). **Tiffany's Racquet Club,** Avenue Villa Vera 120, 5 courts (tel. 74/84–79–49). **Villa Vera Hotel,** 3 outdoor lighted clay courts (tel. 74/84–02–24).

Water Sports Waterskiing, broncos (one-person motorboats), and parasailing can all be arranged for on the beach. Parasailing is an Acapulco highlight and looks terrifying until you actually try it. Most people who do it love the view and go back again and again. An eight-minute trip costs $10–$15 (tel. 74/82–20–56). Waterskiing is about $20 an hour; broncos cost $15 an hour. Windsurfing can be arranged at Caleta and most of the beaches along the Costera, but is especially good at Puerto Marqués. At Coyuca Lagoon, you can try your hand (or feet) at barefoot waterskiing. The main surfing beach is Revolcadero.

Spectator Sports

Bullfights The season runs from Christmas to Easter, and *corridas* are held—sporadically—on Sundays at 5:30. Tickets are available through your hotel or at the Plaza de Toros ticket window (open Mon.–Sat. 10–2 and Sun. 10:30–3; tel. 74/82–11–81). Tickets cost from $20 to $25, and a $25 seat in the first four rows—in the shade (*sombra*)—is worth the extra cost. Also check the local paper and signs around town to find out if any noteworthy matadors can be seen in action.

Beaches

The lure of sun and sand in Acapulco is legendary. Every sport is available and you can shop from roving souvenir vendors, eat in a beach restaurant, dance, and sleep in a *hamaca* (hammock) without leaving the water's edge. If you want to avoid the crowds, there are also plenty of quiet and even isolated beaches within reach. However, at some of these, such as Revolcadero and Pie de la Cuesta, there are a very strong undertow and strong surf, so swimming is not advised. Despite an enticing appearance and claims that officials are cleaning up the bay, it remains polluted. If this bothers you, we suggest you follow the lead of the Mexican cognoscenti and take the waters at your hotel pool.

Beaches in Mexico are public, even those that seem to belong to a big hotel. The list below moves from east to west.

Barra Vieja About 16 miles east of Acapulco, between Laguna de Tres Palos and the Pacific, this magnificent beach is even more inviting than Pie de la Cuesta because you're not bothered by itinerant peddlers and beggars.

Revolcadero A wide, sprawling beach next to the Pierre Marqués and Princess hotels, its water is shallow and waves fairly rough. People come here to surf and ride horses.

Puerto Marqués Tucked below the airport highway, this strand is popular with Mexican tourists, so it tends to get crowded on weekends.

Icacos Stretching from the naval base to El Presidente, this beach is less populated than others on The Strip. The morning waves are especially calm.

Condesa Facing the middle of Acapulco Bay, this stretch of sand has more than its share of tourists, especially singles. The beachside restaurants are convenient for bites between parasailing flights.

Hornos and Hornitos Running from the Paraiso Radisson to Las Hamacas hotels, these beaches are packed shoulder to shoulder with Mexican tourists. These tourists know a good thing: Graceful palms shade the sand and there are scads of casual eateries within walking distance.

Caleta and Caletilla On the peninsula in Old Acapulco, these two once rivaled La Quebrada as the main tourist area in Acapulco's heyday. Now they attract families. Motorboats to Roqueta leave from here.

Roqueta Island A ferry costs about $3.50 round-trip, including entrance to the zoo; the trip takes 10 minutes each way. Acapulqueños consider Roqueta Island their day-trip spot.

Pie de la Cuesta You'll need a car or cab to reach this relatively unpopulated spot, about 15 minutes west of town. A few rustic restaurants border the wide beach and straw *palapas* provide *sombra* (shade).

Dining

Dining in Acapulco is more than just eating out—it is the most popular leisure activity in town. Every night the restaurants fill up, and every night the adventurous diner can sample a different cuisine: Italian, German, Japanese, American, Tex-Mex, and, of course, plain old Mex. The variety of styles matches the range of cuisines: from greasy spoons that serve regional specialties to rooftop gourmet restaurants with gorgeous views of Acapulco Bay. Most restaurants fall somewhere in the middle, and on The Strip there are dozens of palapa (palm frond)–roofed beachside restaurants, as well as wildly decorated rib and hamburger joints popular with visitors under 30.

One plus for Acapulco dining is that the food is garden fresh. Each morning the Mercado Municipal is abuzz with restaurant managers and locals buying up the vegetables that will appear on plates that evening. Although some top-quality beef is now being produced in the states of Sonora and Chihuahua, many of the more expensive restaurants claim that they import their beef from the States. Whether or not they're telling the truth, the beef is excellent in most places. Establishments that cater to tourists purify their drinking water and use it to cook vegetables. In smaller restaurants, ask for bottled water with or without bubbles (*con* or *sin gas*).

The top restaurants in Acapulco can be fun for a splurge and provide very good value. Even at the best places in town, dinner rarely exceeds $35 per person, and the atmosphere and views are fantastic. Ties and jackets are out of place, but so are shorts or jeans. Unless stated, all are open daily from 6:30 or 7 PM until the last diner leaves.

Highly recommended restaurants are indicated by a star ★.

Category	Cost*
Very Expensive	over $45
Expensive	$25–$45
Moderate	$15–$25
Inexpensive	under $15

*per person excluding drinks, service, and sales tax (10%)

Very Expensive

French Le Gourmet. Although its food is wildly inconsistent, this restaurant is thought by many to be one of Acapulco's premier establishments. Many people staying down on the Costera brave the 15-minute taxi ride to partake of a tranquil meal in a plush setting. The French menu has all the classics: vichyssoise, steak au poivre sautéed in cognac, and such Acapulco favorites as lobster and red snapper fillets. The atmosphere is luxurious and genteel, with roomy, comfortable chairs, silent waiters, and air-conditioning. *Acapulco Princess Hotel, tel. 74/84–31–00. Reservations advised. AE, DC, MC, V.*

Gourmet Coyuca 22. This is possibly the most expensive restaurant in
★ Acapulco; it is certainly one of the most beautiful. Diners eat on terraces that overlook the bay from the west, on a hilltop in Old Acapulco. The understated decor consists of Doric pillars, sculptures, and large onyx flower stands near the entrance. Diners gaze down on an enormous illuminated obelisk and a small pool. The effect is like eating in a partially restored Greek ruin sans dust. The tiny menu centers on seafood, with lobster the house specialty. Prime ribs are also available. *Avenida Coyuca 22 (a 10-minute taxi ride from the Zócalo), tel. 74/82–34–68 or 74/83–50–30. Reservations required. AE, DC, MC, V. Closed Apr. 30–Nov. 1.*

Expensive

Continental Maximilian's. An exception to the rule that says hotels don't serve top-quality food, Maximilian's is a haven for American expatriates who like to dress up and come for a treat. It is one of few beachside restaurants with air-conditioning. Lobster bisque, duck, and seafood cooked with classic ingredients are the specialties, and steak is available, too. *Acapulco Plaza, tel. 74/85–80–50. Reservations advised. AE, DC, MC, V.*

Italian Casa Nova. This restaurant in the exclusive Las Brisas area has
★ fantastic sunset views of all Acapulco. It specializes in southern Italian cuisine, and the pastas are homemade. You might try the fettuccine scampi, prepared with shrimp, mushrooms, and scallops; the grilled veal chops; or the grilled fresh Norwegian salmon. The piano bar is open until midnight. *Scenic Hwy. 5256, tel. 74/84–68–19 or 74/84–68–16. Reservations a must on weekends. AE, DC, MC, V.*

Seafood Blackbeard's. A dark, glorified coffee shop with a pirate ship
★ motif, Blackbeard's—owned by the proprietors of Mimi's Chili Saloon—has maps covering the tables in the cozy booths, and the walls are adorned with wooden figureheads. Every movie star, from Bing Crosby to Liz Taylor, who ever set foot here has his or her photo posted in the lounge. A luscious salad bar and jumbo portions of shrimp, steak, and lobster keep customers satisfied. A new disco on the premises starts throbbing at 10:30 PM. *Costera Miguel Alemán, tel. 74/84–25–49. Reservations advised. AE, DC, MC, V.*

Moderate

American Carlos 'n Charlies. This is without a doubt the most popular res-
★ taurant in town; a line forms well before the 6:30 PM opening. Part of the Anderson group (with restaurants in the United

Acapulco Dining and Lodging

N

| 0 | 880 yards |
| 0 | 800 meters |

Paseo del Farallón

Diana
Glorieta

16 17
15
18 19 20 21 22

24
23
25
26

27
28
29

Golf
Course

Centro
International

Lobo Solitario

Costera Miguel

Av. Almirante Horacio Nelson

Almirante
Cristóbal Colón

Magallanes

30
31
**Playa
Icacos**

32 Alemán

*Bahía de
Acapulco*

33
34

La Base

35

36

*Punta
Guitarrón*

37

38 39
40

Escénica

Carretera

42
43
41

TO AIRPORT →

States and Spain as well as Mexico), Carlos 'n Charlies cultivates an atmosphere of controlled craziness. Prankster waiters, a jokester menu, and eclectic decor—everything from antique bullfight photos to a tool chest of painted gadgets hanging from the ceiling—add to the chaos. The crowd is mostly young and relaxed, which is what you need to be to put up with the rush-hour traffic noise that filters up to the covered balcony where people dine. The menu straddles the border, with ribs, stuffed shrimp, and oysters among the best offerings. *Costera Miguel Alemán 999, tel. 74/ 84–12–85 or 84–00–39. No reservations. AE, DC, MC, V.*

D'Joint. Locals as well as tourists love D'Joint—a claustrophobic restaurant with a funky, publike atmosphere and a popular sports bar—so, in season, prepare for a wait. In addition to the usual steaks, salads, and nachos, prime ribs are the house specialty. The four types of roast beef sandwiches are another hit. After your meal, try "sexy coffee"—cappuccino with liqueur. *Costera Miguel Alemán 79, next door to the Hotel Acapulco Malibú, tel. 74/84–19–13. No reservations. AE, DC, MC, V. Closed one week in summer.*

Embarcadero. A nautical motif pervades Embarcadero, which is well-loved by both Acapulco regulars and resident Americans. It is designed to look like a wharf with the bar as the loading office. Wooden bridges lead past a fountain to the thatched eating area, piled high with wooden packing crates and maps. The food is American with a Polynesian touch. You can have deep-fried shrimps with garlic sauce, tempura, chicken, or steak. The "salad barge" is enormous. *Costera Miguel Alemán, west of CiCi Park, tel. 74/84–87–87. Open 6 PM–midnight. No reservations. AE, DC, MC, V. Closed Mon. out of season.*

★ **Hard Rock Café.** A bar, restaurant, and dance hall filled with rock memorabilia, this is one of the most popular spots in Acapulco, and with good reason. The southern-style food—fried chicken, ribs, chili con carne—is very well prepared and the portions are more than ample. The taped rock music begins at noon, and a live group starts playing at 11 PM. There's always a line at the small boutique on the premises where you can buy sports clothes and accessories bearing the Hard Rock label. *Costera Miguel Alemán 37, tel. 74/84–66–80. AE, MC, V.*

Continental **Madeiras.** It vies with its neighbor Miramar for most chichi
★ place in Acapulco, and there are fierce arguments as to which has the best food. Madeiras is very difficult to get into; many people make reservations by letter before their arrival. At the very least, call the minute you get to Acapulco. Children under 8 are not welcome, however. All the tables at Madeiras have a view of glittering Acapulco by night. The furniture is certainly unusual: the bar/reception area has art nouveau-style carved chairs, plump sofas, and startling coffee tables made of glass resting on large wooden animals. All the dishes and silverware were created by silversmiths in the nearby town of Taxco. Dinner is served from a four-course, prix fixe menu and costs about $25 without wine. Entrées include the delicious Spanish dish of red snapper in sea salt, tasty chilled soups, stuffed red snapper, and a choice of steaks and other seafood, as well as the *crepas de huitlacoche* (huitlacoche, or cuitlacoche, is a corn fungus that was a delicacy to the Aztecs). Desserts are competently prepared but have no special flair. There are two seatings, at 6:30 and 9. Unfortunately, diners coming at the later time may find selections limited. *Scenic Highway just past La Vista*

shopping center, tel. 74/84–73–16. Reservations required. AE, DC, MC, V.

French **El Fuerte del Virrey.** El Real at El Fuerte del Virrey has already set up house as one of Acapulco's best. The setting is unlike any in Acapulco: an antiques-filled dining room and bar and a military museum—all in a building designed to look like an 18th-century fort. High wooden booths ensure intimate meals. Several private rooms are also available for small groups, as is the lusciously cool wine cellar. Chef Leonardo Anzures produces some of the best food in Acapulco by melding the cuisines of Mexico and France. Octopus stew in cognac, and oysters and red snapper baked in pastry are some of the specialties, but beef lovers also will find a healthy selection. *El Fuerte del Virrey, Roca Sola 17, Club Deportivo (behind Carlos 'n Charlies), tel. 74/84–33–21. Reservations not required. AE, DC, MC, V.*

★ **Miramar.** Light wood furniture and a fountain provide the decoration for this understated place, but the real glamour comes from the view of the bay and the flickering lights of Acapulco. Traditional dishes, like pâté and lobster thermidor, are served alongside classics with a new twist: ceviche with a hint of coconut and red snapper papillote. Shrimp mousse and duck are both specialties. Miramar is not as intimate as its neighbor, Madeiras, and many large groups from the Princess book long tables, so the noise level is rather high. *Scenic Highway at La Vista shopping center, tel. 74/84–78–74. Reservations advised. AE, D, MC, V. Closed Sept.–Oct.*

Normandie. Recognized as the only authentic French restaurant in town, this small place is run by the charming Nicole Lepine. The Normandie has pastel blue walls and a little fountain reminiscent of a Parisian tearoom, and the platters of cakes near the door add to this impression. The menu touches all bases, including beef bourguignon and seafood gratinée. *On the Costera near the Super-Super, tel. 74/85–19–16. AE, MC, V. Closed Apr. 1–Dec. 1.*

Mexican **Los Rancheros.** With a view of the water in the posh East Bay, here's Mexican food at about half what you'd pay at Madeiras or Miramar. The decor is colorful, folksy Mexican with paper streamers, checked tablecloths, and lopsided mannequins in local dress. Specials include *carne tampiqueña* (fillet of beef broiled with lemon juice), chicken enchiladas, and *queso fundido* (melted cheese served as a side dish to chips). Live music noon to midnight, daily. *Scenic Highway just before Extasis disco (on the left as you head toward the airport), tel. 74/84–19–08. MC, V.*

Pancho's. The only source for Mexican food right on the beach. During the day you get a free drink with your meal. Though the food is good, the selection is rather generic. *Costera Miguel Alemán, behind the El Pescador restaurant in the Continental Plaza, tel. 74/84–30–08. No reservations. AE, MC, V.*

Mixed Menu **Hard Times.** With an unusually large menu for Acapulco, Hard
★ Times features the usual Tex-Mex dishes as well as plenty of barbecue, fresh fish, and the largest salad bar in town. The dining area is an attractive open terrace, with a partial view of the bay. Although right in the center of The Strip, Hard Times is a tranquil haven—decorated with palms and incandescent lights—in which to enjoy generous portions of American food and, sometimes, jazz. Arrive early; there is often a wait in high

season. *Costera Miguel Alemán, across from the Calinda Quality Hotel (look for the red neon lights), tel. 74/84–00–64. Reservations advised during high season. AE, DC, MC, V. Closed Sun. during summer.*

Seafood **Paradise.** This is the leading beach-party restaurant. T-shirted waiters drop leis over your head as you arrive and hand roses to the ladies. The menu (primarily seafood) has the same number of dishes as drinks, a pretty good indicator of what this place is like. Paradise has one of the biggest dance floors in Acapulco and live music day and night. Chaos reigns at lunchtime (from 2 to 5), and the mood picks up again from 8:30 to 10:30. Expect a young crowd. *Costera Miguel Alemán 107, next to Mimi's Chili Saloon, tel. 74/84–59–88. No reservations. AE, DC, MC, V.*

Sirocco. This beachside eatery is numero uno for those who crave Spanish food in Acapulco. The tile floors and heavy wooden furniture give it a Mediterranean feel. Specialties include *pulpo en su tinta* (octopus in its own ink) and 10 varieties of fresh fish. Order paella when you arrive at the beach—it takes a half hour to prepare. *Costera Miguel Alemán, across from Super-Super, tel. 74/85–23–86 and 74/85–94–90. Reservations not required. AE, MC, V. Open 2–10 PM.*

Inexpensive

Health Food **100% Natural.** Six family-operated restaurants specialize in
★ light, healthful food—yogurt shakes, fruit salads, and sandwiches made with whole-wheat bread. The service is quick and the food is a refreshing alternative to tacos, particularly on a hot day. Look for the green signs with white lettering. *Costera Miguel Alemán 204, near the Acapulco Plaza, no phone. Another branch is near the Acapulco Princess Hotel, tel. 74/85–39–82. No credit cards.*

★ **Zorrito's.** The old Zorrito's, a rather dingy but popular café, is no longer, but a new, very clean restaurant of the same name is now attracting tourists. The menu features a host of steak and beef dishes, and the special, *filete tampiqueña,* comes with tacos, enchiladas, guacamole, and frijoles. *Costera Miguel Alemán and Anton de Alaminos, next to Banamex, tel. 74/85–37–35. No reservations. AE, MC, V.*

Mexican **El Cabrito.** This is another local favorite for true Mexican cuisine and ambience. The name of the restaurant—"the goat"—is also its specialty. In addition you can choose among mole; forged cheese; jerky with egg, fish, and seafood; and other Mexican dishes. *Costera Miguel Alemán, between Mariscos Pipo and Ninas, tel. 74/84–77–11. No reservations. MC, V.*

★ **Mimi's Chili Saloon.** Right next door to Paradise is this two-level wooden restaurant decorated with everything from Marilyn Monroe posters to cages of tropical birds and a collection of ridiculous signs. It's frequented by those under (and frequently over) 30 who gorge on Tex-Mex, onion rings, and excellent burgers and wash them down with peach and mango daiquiris. Or the waiters will bring you anything on the menu next door at Blackbeard's. Be prepared for a wait in the evenings. *Costera Miguel Alemán, tel. 74/84–25–49, at Blackbeard's. No reservations. AE, MC, V. Closed Mon. and Labor Day (May 1).*

★ **Tlaquepaque.** As hard to find as it is to pronounce, this is one of the best restaurants in Acapulco. It's well worth the 15-minute cab ride into the northwestern residential section of Acapulco (tell your driver it is around the corner from where the Oficina de Tránsito used to be). Owner/chef José Arreola was a chef at the Pierre Marqués for 15 years and he takes his job very seriously. Don't insult him by asking if the water is purified or if the vegetables are safe. The menu is 100% Mexican, excellent and authentic. If your party numbers four or more, Señor Arreola likes nothing better than to select a family-style meal, which can include quail liver tostadas, deep fried tortillas, and *chiles rellenos.* The alfresco dining area sits on a stone terrace bordered by pink flowering bushes and an abandoned well. The outside tables have a perfect view of the kitchen filled with locally made pots. Thursday is *pozole* day, when a thick soup of hominy and pork is served. *Calle Uno, Lote 7, Colonia Vista Alegre, tel. 74/85–70–55. Reservations advised Thurs. only (pozole day). Closed Mon. Cash only.*

Mixed Menu **Acapulco Fat Farm.** High-school and college students at the Acapulco Children's Home run this cozy place in the center of town. The specialties include ice cream made with all natural ingredients, U.S.-style cakes and pies, sandwiches, hamburgers, and good Mexican food as well. The background music is classical, which is unusual for Acapulco, and there's an exhibition of paintings and masks, as well as a book exchange. *Juárez 10, tel. 74/83–53–39. No reservations. No credit cards.*

Seafood **Beto's.** By day, you can eat right on the beach and enjoy live
★ music; by night, this palapa-roofed restaurant is transformed into a dim and romantic dining area lighted by candles and paper lanterns. Whole red snapper, lobster, and ceviche are recommended. There is a second branch next door and a third—where the specialty is *pescado a la talla* (fish spread with chili and other spices and then grilled over hot coals)—at Barra Vieja beach. *Beto's, Costera Miguel Alemán, tel. 74/84–04–73. Beto's Safari, Costera Miguel Alemán, next to Beto's, tel. 74/84–47–62. Beto's Barra Vieja, Barra Vieja beach, no phone. Reservations unnecessary. AE, MC, V.*

Lodging

Accommodations in Acapulco run the gamut from sprawling, big-name complexes with nonstop amenities to small, family-run inns where hot water is a luxury. Wherever you stay, prices are reasonable compared with those in the United States, and service is generally good, since Acapulqueños have been catering to tourists for 40 years. Accommodations above $80 (double) are air-conditioned (but you can find air-conditioned hotels for less) and include a mini-bar, TV, and a view of the bay. There is usually a range of in-house restaurants and bars, as well as a pool. Exceptions exist, such as Las Brisas, which, in the name of peace and quiet, has banned TVs from all rooms. So if such extras are important to you, be sure to ask ahead. If you can't afford air-conditioning, don't panic. Even the cheapest hotels have cooling ceiling fans.

Because Acapulco is a relatively new resort, it lacks the converted monasteries and old mansions found in Mexico City. But the Costera is chockablock with new luxury high rises and local franchises of such major U.S. hotel chains as Hyatt and Sheraton. Since these hotels tend to be characterless, your choice will depend on location and what facilities are available. Villa Vera, Acapulco Plaza, Las Brisas, and both Hyatts have tennis courts as well as swimming pools. The Princess and Pierre

Marqués share two 18-hole golf courses, and the Malibú is across from the Club de Tennis and Golf. All major hotels can make water-sports arrangements.

In Acapulco geography is price, so where you stay determines what you pay. The most exclusive area is the Acapulco Diamante, home to some of the most expensive hotels in Mexico. Travelers come here for a relaxing, self-contained holiday; the Acapulco Diamante hotels are so lush and well equipped that most guests don't budge from the minute they arrive. The minuses: Revolcadero Beach is too rough for swimming (though great for surfing), and the East Bay is a 15-minute (expensive) taxi ride from the heart of Acapulco. There is also very little to do in this area except dine at three of Acapulco's better restaurants (Madeiras, Casa Nova, and Miramar), and dance at the glamorous Extravaganzza and Fantasy discos.

Highly recommended hotels are indicated by a star ★.

Category	Cost*
Very Expensive	$185–$285
Expensive	$100–$185
Moderate	$55–$100
Inexpensive	under $55

All prices are for a standard double room, excluding 10% sales (called IVA) tax.

Acapulco Diamante

Very Expensive
★

Acapulco Princess. This is the first hotel you come to from the airport. Three pyramid-shaped buildings, the Princess has the largest capacity of any hotel in Acapulco. The hotel's fact sheet makes fascinating reading: 50 chocolate cakes are consumed daily and 2,500 staff meals are served. The Princess is one of those mega-hotels always holding at least three conventions with an ever-present horde in the lobby checking in and greeting their fellow dentists or club members. But more rooms equals more facilities. The Princess has eight restaurants, five bars, a disco, tennis, golf, and great shopping in a cool arcade. The pool near the reception desk is sensational—fantastic tropical ponds with little waterfalls and a slatted bridge leading into a swimming/sunning area. It forms a jungle backdrop to the lobby, which is always fresh and cool from the ocean breezes. Rooms are light and airy, with cane furniture and crisp yellow and green rugs and curtains. Guests can also use the facilities of the hotel's smaller sibling, the Pierre Marqués; a free shuttle bus provides transport. Accommodations include breakfast and dinner (mandatory in high season). *Box 1351 Playa Revolcadero, tel. 74/84–31–00 or 800/223–1818. 1,019 balconied rooms, with bath. Facilities: two 18-hole golf courses, 11 tennis courts (2 indoor), 4 freshwater pools, 1 salt-water pool, 8 restaurants, 5 bars, disco, banquet rooms. AE, DC, MC, V.*

Camino Real Acapulco Diamante. Acapulco's newest hotel was still under construction as we went to press but should be open by the time you read this. It's set on a secluded beach surrounded by tropical gardens and will have "modern Mexican" decor. *Playa Pichilingue, tel. (Westin in U.S.) 800/228–3000. 160 rooms with ocean view, 2 terraced pools, tennis courts, fitness center, shopping arcade, restaurants, bars. AE, MC, V.*

★ **Las Brisas.** This Westin hotel claims the dubious distinction of "most expensive hotel in Mexico"; some say it's overpriced, but at least you get a lot for your money. Privacy is a major advantage (especially in rooms with a private pool) in this spread-out yet self-contained luxury complex; most of the facilities are open only to guests, though outsiders with a reservation may dine at the El Mexicano restaurant any day but Wednesday or Saturday, and La Concha Beach Club is open to nonguests on Wednesday for shrimp and fillet night. There are almost three employees per guest during the winter season. Transportation is by white and pink jeep. You can rent one for $60 to $70 a day, including tax, gas, and insurance; or, if you don't mind a wait, the staff will do the driving. And transport is necessary—it is a good 15-minute walk to the beach restaurant, and all the facilities are far from the rooms. Everything at Las Brisas is splashed with pink, from the bedspreads and staff uniforms to the stripes in the middle of the road. Attention to detail is Las Brisas's claim to fame: Rooms are stocked with cigarettes, liquor, and snacks. A complimentary bowl of fresh fruit arrives each afternoon. Hotel registration takes place in a comfortable lounge to avoid lines. There is an art gallery and a few other stores. On Thursday is a jungle picnic, and Friday night is Mexican Fiesta. Tipping is not allowed, but a service charge of $20 a day is added to the bill. The rate includes Continental breakfast. *Box 281, Carretera Escénica 5255, tel. 74/84–15–80 or 800/228–3000, fax 74/84–22–69. 309 rooms with bath. Facilities: beach club, fitness machines, 2 saltwater pools, 1 freshwater pool, Jacuzzi and sauna, 4 lighted tennis courts, water sports, 4 restaurants, 1 bar, 2 conference rooms. AE, DC, MC, V.*

★ **Pierre Marqués.** This hotel is doubly blessed: It is closer to the beach than any of the other East Bay hotels, and guests have access to all the Princess's facilities without the crowds. In addition, it has three pools and five tennis courts illuminated for nighttime play. Rooms are furnished identically to those at the Princess, but duplex villas and bungalows with private patios are available. Many people stay here to relax, then hit the Princess's restaurants and discos at night—the shuttle bus runs about every ten minutes. Accommodations include mandatory breakfast and dinner in high season. *Box 474, Playa Revolcadero, tel. 74/84–20–00 or 800/223–1818. 344 rooms with bath. Facilities: two 18-hole golf courses, 5 tennis courts, 3 pools, valet service, bar, 3 restaurants, shops. Open only during the winter season. AE, DC, MC, V.*

Expensive **Sheraton Acapulco.** Perfect for those who want to enjoy the sun and the sand but don't have to be in the center of everything, this Sheraton is isolated from all the hubbub of the Costera and is rather small in comparison with the chain's other properties in Mexico. The rooms and suites are distributed among 17 villas that are set on a hillside on secluded Guitarrón beach 6 miles (10 km) east of Acapulco proper. Rooms for the handicapped and nonsmokers are available, and all units have private balconies and a sweeping view of the entire bay. *Costera Guitarrón 110, tel. 74/84–37–37 or 800/325–3535. 226 rooms and 8 suites with bath. Facilities: 2 pools, 2 restaurants, 2 bars, water sports. AE, DC, MC, V.*

The Strip

"Costera" is what locals call the Costera Miguel Alemán, the wide shoreline highway that leads from the bottom of the Scenic Highway, around the bay, then past Old Acapulco. The Paraíso Radisson Acapulco Hotel anchors the end of The Strip. This area is where you'll find discos, American-style restaurants, airline offices, and the majority of the large hotels. It is also home base for Americans—lounging on the beaches, shopping in the boutiques, and generally getting into the vacation spirit. Acapulco's best beaches are here, too. The waves are gentle and water sports are plentiful. Hotels on the Costera take full advantage of their location. All have freshwater pools and sun decks, and most have restaurants/bars overlooking the beach, if not on the sand itself. Hotels across the street are almost always cheaper than those on the beach. And because there are no private beaches in Acapulco, all you have to do to reach the water is cross the road.

Very Expensive
★

Villa Vera. A five-minute drive north of the Costera leads to one of Acapulco's most exclusive hotels. Guests are primarily affluent American business travelers, actors, and politicians. This luxury estate, officially the Villa Vera Hotel and Racquet Club, is unequaled in the variety of its accommodations. Some of the villas, which were once private homes, have their own pools. Casa Lisa, the swankiest, costs $1,300 a day. Standard rooms, in fashionable pastels and white, are not especially large. No matter. No one spends much time in the rooms. The main pool, with its swim-up bar, is the hotel's hub. During the day, guests lounge, lunch, snack, and swim here (a diet menu is available for calorie-conscious guests). By night, they dine at the terraced restaurant, with its stunning view of the bay. There's a new exercise facility, and three championship tennis courts host the annual competition for the Miguel Alemán and Teddy Stauffer cups. For those guests who don't have their own cars, transportation is by hotel jeep. Book well in advance; guests have been known to make reservations for the following year as they leave. *Box 560, Lomas del Mar 35, tel. 74/84–03–33 or 800/223–6510. 80 rooms with bath. Facilities: pool with swim-up bar, 3 lighted tennis courts, sauna and massage, water sports, beauty salon, restaurant, banquet room. AE, DC, MC, V.*

Expensive

Acapulco Plaza. This Holiday Inn resort is the largest and one of the newest hotels on the Costera. Like the Princess, the Plaza has more facilities than many Mexican towns: 12 bars and restaurants, four tennis courts, Jacuzzis, steam baths, and two pools. The Plaza Bahía next to the hotel is the largest shopping mall in town. The lobby bar is most extraordinary—a wooden hut, suspended by a cable from the roof, reached by a gangplank from the second floor of the lobby. About 35 people can fit inside the bar, which overlooks a garden full of flamingos and other exotic birds. Guest rooms tell the same old story: pastels and blond wood replacing passé dark greens and browns. People rave about the rooms and facilities, but we have heard several reports of inferior service and unfriendly treatment at the front desk. *Costera Miguel Alemán 123, tel. 74/85–80–50 or 800/HOLIDAY. 1,008 rooms with bath. Booked solid Dec. 20–Jan. 3. Facilities: health club, sauna, freshwater pools, 4 lighted tennis courts, water sports, 5 restaurants, 7 bars, conference rooms. AE, DC, MC, V.*

★ **Fiesta Americana Condesa Acapulco.** Right in the thick of the main shopping/restaurant district, the Condesa, as everyone calls it, is ever popular with tour operators. The rooms are furnished with wall-to-wall pastel plushness. This is the best hotel on the Costera. *Costera Miguel Alemán 1220, tel. 74/84–26–03 or 800/FIESTA–1. 500 rooms with bath. Facilities: 2 pools, water sports, 4 restaurants, bar, conference rooms. AE, DC, MC, V.*

Hyatt Regency Acapulco. Another mega-hotel that you never have to leave, this property is popular with business travelers and conventioneers. (Ex-President López Portillo used to stay in—what else?—the Presidential Suite.) All the rooms were recently redecorated in soft pastels. Four tennis courts, five restaurants (including a beachside seafood place and a Mexican dining room), four bars, and a lavish shopping area provide the action. The Hyatt is a little out of the way, a plus for those who seek quiet. Rooms on the west side of the hotel are preferable for those who want to avoid the noise of the maneuvers at the neighboring naval base. *Costera Miguel Alemán 1, tel. 74/84–28–88 or 800/223–1234. 690 rooms with bath. Facilities: 4 tennis courts, pool, sauna and massage, shops, 5 restaurants, 4 bars, 6 conference rooms, parking. AE, DC, MC, V.*

★ **Paraíso Radisson.** The last of the big Strip hotels is a favorite of tour groups, so the lobby is forever busy. The rooms look brighter and roomier since the management replaced the heavy Spanish-style furniture with light woods and pastels. Guests lounge by the pool or at the beachside restaurant by day. The rooftop Gaviotas restaurant provides a sensational view of the bay at night. The pool area is rather small and the beach can get crowded, but the restaurants are exceptionally good and the staff couldn't be nicer. Book early—the hotel is often full in high season with tour groups. *Costera Miguel Alemán 163, tel. 74/85–55–96 or 800/228–9822. 422 rooms with bath. Facilities: pool, sauna, 2 restaurants, coffee shop, bar, water sports, shops, 5 conference rooms. AE, DC, MC, V.*

★ **Ritz.** From its brightly painted exterior, it's clear that the Ritz is serious about vacations. The lobby also is seriously colorful. Parties are a hotel specialty; outdoor fiestas are held weekly, and every night is Italian night in the lobby restaurant. The pink and rattan rooms add to the 1950s beach-party flavor. *Box 259, Costera Miguel Alemán and Magallanes, tel. 74/85–75–44 or 800/527–5919. 252 rooms with bath. Facilities: pool, wading pool, sauna, water sports, beach clubs, 3 restaurants, 3 bars (including a beach bar), disco, conference rooms. AE, DC, V.*

Moderate **Copacabana.** Here's a good buy if you yearn for a modern hotel in the center of things. The staff is efficient and helpful, the ambience relaxed and festive. The lobby and pool (with a swim-up bar) are always crowded with people enjoying themselves. The psychedelic pseudo-Mexican lemon-and-lime hues pervade the halls and bedrooms. *Tabichines 2, tel. 74/84–32–60 or 800/221–6509. 422 rooms, showers only. Facilities: pool, 2 restaurants, 2 bars, shops, conference rooms. AE, DC, MC, V.*

Gran Motel Acapulco. This is a find for its reasonable price and central location. Bare walls and floors and blond-wood furniture give the newly decorated rooms a monastic appeal. The small pool has a bar, but there is no restaurant. Ask to stay in the old section, where the rooms are larger and quieter and have a beach view. *Costera Miguel Alemán 127, tel. 74/85–59–*

92. 88 rooms with bath. Facilities: pool, 3 lighted tennis courts, bar, parking. MC, V.

Hotel Acapulco Tortuga. A helpful staff and prime location make the "Turtle Hotel" an appealing choice. It is also one of the few non-beach hotels to have a garden (handkerchief-size) and a pool where most of the guests hang out. At night, the activity shifts to the lobby bar, with the crowd often spilling out onto the street. The downside of this merriment is the noise factor. The best bet is a room facing west on an upper floor. All rooms have blue-green pile rugs and small tables. Breakfast is served in the lobby café; lunch and dinner can be taken in the more formal restaurant. *Costera Miguel Alemán 132, tel. 74/ 84–88–89 or 800/832–7491. 252 rooms with bath. Facilities: pool, swim-up bar, lobby bar, 2 restaurants, snack bar, conference rooms. AE, DC, MC, V.*

★ **Maralisa Hotel and Beach Club.** The Villa Vera's sister hotel sits on the beach side of the Costera. The sun deck surrounding two small pools—palm trees and ceramic tiles—is unusual and picturesque. The rooms are light, decorated in whites and pastels. This is a small, friendly place; all rooms have TVs and balconies, and the price is right, especially since guests have access to all Villa Vera's facilities. *Box 721, Enrique el Esclavo, tel. 74/85–66–77 or 800/448–8355. 90 rooms with bath. Facilities: 2 pools, private beach club, water sports, restaurant, bar. AE, DC, MC, V.*

Inexpensive   **Autotel Ritz.** A good buy for its faily central location, this hotel attracts bargain-hunters and seniors. The uncarpeted rooms are simply decorated, but the furniture is chipped and smudged with paint. Facilities include a restaurant, a decent-size pool with a bar, and room service until 9 PM. Rooms not on the Costera are quite quiet. A useful note for nonguests: The long-distance surcharge is half what it is at many other hotels. *Avenue Wilfrido Massieu, Box 257, tel. 74/85–82–84 or 800/ 448–8355. 102 rooms with bath. Facilities: pool, restaurant, bar. AE, DC, MC, V.*

Old Acapulco

Moving off The Strip and west along the Costera leads you to downtown Acapulco, where the fishing and tour boats depart, and the locals go about their business. The central post office, Woolworth's, and the Mercado Municipal are here, along with countless restaurants where a complete meal can cost as little as $5. The beaches here are popular with Mexican vacationers, and the dozens of little hotels attract Canadian and European bargain-hunters.

Moderate   **Boca Chica.** This small hotel is in a secluded area on a small pen-
★ insula, and its terraced rooms overlook the bay and Roqueta Island. It's a low-key place that's a favorite of Mexico City residents in the know. There's a private beach club with a natural saltwater pool for guests, and a seafood, sushi, and oyster bar. Accommodations include mandatory breakfast and dinner in high season. *Caletilla Beach, tel. 74/83–66–01 or 800/346–3942. 40 rooms. Facilities: 2 pools. AE, DC, MC, V.*

Hotel Misión. Two minutes from the Zócalo, this attractive budget hotel is the only colonial hotel in Acapulco. The English-speaking family that runs the Misión lives in a traditional house built in the 19th century. A newer structure housing the guest rooms was added in the 1950s. It surrounds a greenery-rich courtyard with an outdoor dining area. The rooms are small and by no means fancy, with bare cement floors and painted brick walls. But every room has a shower, and sometimes there is even hot water. The Misión appears in several European guidebooks, so expect a Continental clientele. The best rooms are on the second and third floors; the top-floor room is large but hot in the daytime. *Calle Felipe Valle 12, tel. 74/82–36–43. 27 rooms, showers only. No credit cards.*

★ **Playa Hermosa.** Right behind the El Cid Hotel and steps away from Playa Hornos and the Normandie restaurant is this tiny hotel. Owner Edward Mackissack's guests return every year, so in high season rooms are hard to come by. Staying here is a good way to make friends. The mostly above-40 guests meet on the patio/dining room for drinks every night, although every spring brings a contingent of students from the University of Texas. Built in 1936, Playa Hermosa was originally Ed Mackissack's private home, and it still feels like it. Each room is unique, with a Japanese print in one, a low coffee table in the next. There are shelves of English books, a garden, and a pool. With its Old Acapulco ambience, this is one of the more charming hotels around. All rooms have hot water, breakfast is included, and lunch can be provided if ordered the day before. *Vasco Núñez de Balboa, tel. 74/85–14–91. 20 rooms, showers only. Facilities: pool, restaurant, bar. No credit cards.*

Plaza las Glorias El Mirador. The old El Mirador has been taken over by the Plaza las Glorias chain, which is part of the Sidek conglomerate responsible for marina and golf developments all over Mexico. Very Mexican in style—white with red tiles—the Plaza las Glorias is set high on a hill with a spectacular view of Acapulco and of the cliff divers performing at La Quebrada. *Quebrada 74, tel. 74/83–11–55. 143 rooms with bath. Facilities: 3 pools, 2 restaurants (including La Perla restaurant-nightclub). AE, DC, MC, V.*

Inexpensive **Belmar.** With its white exterior and green awnings, this stately resort hotel—typical of the 1950s—looks like a ship landlocked in the middle of a huge garden. It's situated on a hill a few blocks from Caleta beach and is a favorite with budget travelers. The rooms are spacious, simple, clean, and comfortable, with large terraces. The walls are white, but almost everything else is some shade of green. This is one of the few Acapulco hotels with a rooftop restaurant; it has a great view of the bay. *Av. de los Cumbres and Gran Vía Tropical, tel. 74/82–15–26. 70 rooms with bath (50 with air-conditioning, 20 with fans). Facilities: pool, wading pool, miniature golf, restaurant, bar. AE, MC, V.*

The Arts and Nightlife

Acapulco has always been famous for its nightlife, and justifiably so. For many visitors the discos and restaurants are just as important as the sun and sand. The minute the sun slips over the horizon, The Strip comes alive with people milling around window-shopping, deciding where to dine, and generally biding their time till the disco hour. Obviously, you aren't going to find great culture here; theater efforts are few and far between and there is no classical music. But disco-hopping is high art in Acapulco. And for those who care to watch, there are live shows and folk dance performances. The tour companies listed in the

Exploring section can organize evening jaunts to most of the dance and music places listed below.

Entertainment

Lienzo Charro, near the Princess, has shows that feature Mexican horseback riders and folkloric dances on given Tuesday, Wednesday, and Saturday, 7–10 PM. The cost, including dinner, open bar, contests, gifts, and free transportation, is about $32. Acuario Tours opposite the Plaza also organizes visits here.

The **Acapulco International Center** (also known as the convention center) has two shows nightly featuring mariachi bands, singers, and the "Flying Indians" from Papantla. The show with dinner and drinks costs about $42; entrance to the show alone is $10. Performances begin at 7:30 and 10. For $30, there's a Mexican fiesta at the **Marbella Shopping Center** on Monday, Wednesday, and Friday nights during the winter season, and on Wednesday and Friday, off-season, at 8 PM. Javier de Leon's folkloric ballet performs at the **Calinda Hotel.** On Friday, at El Mexicano restaurant in **Las Brisas** hotel, the fiesta starts off with a *tianguis* (marketplace) of handicrafts and ends with a spectacular display of fireworks.

The famous **cliff divers** at La Quebrada (*see* Exploring Acapulco, *above*) perform every night. **Divers de México** organizes sunset champagne cruises that provide a fantastic view of the spectacle from the water. For reservations, call 74/82–13–98, or stop by the office downtown near the *Fiesta* and *Bonanza* yachts. The *Fiesta, Bonanaza* (tel. 74/83–18–03 or 83–25–31 for both), and *Aca Tiki* (tel. 74/84–61–40) all run nightly cruises of the bay that include dinner, drinks, and a show. All boats leave from downtown near the Zócalo. Many hotels and shops sell tickets, as do the ticketsellers on the waterfront. At the Colonial, on the Costera next door to Extasis, there's a professional **ski show** Tuesday through Sunday at 9 PM (tel. 74/83–91–07).

Don't forget the nightly entertainment at most hotels. The big resorts have live music to accompany the early-evening happy hour, and some feature big-name bands from the United States for less than you would pay at home. Many hotels sponsor theme parties—Italian Night, Beach Party Night, and similar festivities.

Dance

Nina's is a dance hall specializing in salsa music. *On The Strip near CiCi, tel. 74/84–24–00.*

Flamenco performances take place at **La Flor de Acapulco Condesa.** A $30 tab includes dinner with wine and the show; $13 includes the show, two drinks, and tips. *Costera Miguel Alemán 112, near Carlos 'n Charlies, tel. 74/84–40–00. Nightly at 10:15.*

Discos

The legendary Acapulco discos are open 365 days a year from about 10:30 PM until they empty out, often not until 4 or 5 AM. Reservations are advisable for a big group, and late-afternoon or after 9 PM are the best times to call. New Year's Eve requires advance planning.

Except for Tiffany, Fantasy, and Extravaganzza, all the discos are on The Strip and, except for Le Dome, are in three different clusters. They are listed here roughly from east to west:

Tiffany, the posh disco at the Princess Hotel, is a bit more sedate than other places in town. It's great for people who enjoy conversation as well as dancing because the sound system directs the music toward the dance floor. *Princess Hotel, tel. 74/ 84-33-95.*

Extravaganzza. Acapulco's most splendiferous disco was inaugurated in late 1989. Word has it that it cost over $3 million to build—absolutely everything was imported—and it has the ultimate in light and sound. It accommodates 700 at a central bar and in comfortable booths, and a glass wall provides an unbelievably breathtaking view of Acapulco Bay. No food is served, but Los Rancheros is just a few steps away. The music (which is for all ages) starts at 10:30. *On the Scenic Highway to Las Brisas, tel. 74/84-71-64.*

Fantasy is without a doubt one of the most exclusive of all the discos in Acapulco. If there are any celebrities in town, they'll be here, rubbing elbows with or bumping into local fashion designers and artists—since Fantasy is quite, shall we say, snug. As we've said already, this is one of the only discos where people really dress up, the men in well-cut pants and shirts, and the women in racy outfits and cocktail dresses. The crowd is 25–50 and mainly in couples. Singles gravitate to the two bars in the back. A line sometimes forms, so people come here earlier than to other places. By midnight the dance floor is so packed that people dance on the wide windowsills that look out over the bay. At 2 AM there is a fireworks display. Capacity is 300, so although seating is cramped, all seats have a view of the floor. "Siberia" consists of an upstairs balcony. Around the floor are long plastic tubes filled with illuminated bubbles, and there is a good light show. In spite of everyone's proximity to the sound system, it is just possible to have a conversation—although not about anything complicated. A glassed-in elevator provides an interesting overview of the scene and leads upstairs to a little shop that stocks T-shirts and lingerie. *On the Scenic Highway, next to Las Brisas, tel. 74/84-67-27.*

Magic is all black inside and has a fabulous light show each night after midnight. This is a good-size place with tables on tiers looking down at the floor. This is one of the few discos where on weekdays you can find a fair number of Mexicans. Any day of the week, this is a good bet to catch up on the Top 10 from Mexico City, as well as the American dance hits. The atmosphere is friendly and laid-back. *Across the Costera from Baby O, tel. 74/84-88-15.*

Baby O and Le Dome (*see below*) are both old favorites. Even mid-week, Baby O is packed. The dance floor is a New York City subway at rush hour, the bar is Grand Central Terminal. Coming here is not a comfortable experience, nor is it quiet or peaceful; it is total chaos. Baby O bucks the trend of most discos in Acapulco. Instead of the usual mirrors and glitz, Baby O resembles a cave in a tropical jungle, with simple plants and walls made of a strange stonelike substance. The crowd is 18–30 and mostly tourists, although many Mexicans come here, too. In fact, this is one of Acapulco's legendary pick-up spots, so feel free to ask someone to dance. When the pandemonium gets to you, retreat to the little hamburger restaurant. Watch your step at all times, however, to avoid falling on the tables and waiters. The architect clearly thought he was designing for acrobats. *Costera Miguel Alemán 22, tel. 74/84-74-74.*

Hard Rock Café, filled with rock memorabilia, is part bar, part restaurant, part dance hall, and part boutique (*see* Dining, *above*). *Costera Miguel Alemán 37, next to CiCi, tel. 74/84-66-80.*

Le Dome, an Acapulco standby, is still one of the hot spots. Even before the music starts at 11:30, there is already a small crowd at the door, and in spite of the capacity of 800, this club is always full. Le Dome doesn't look very different from other clubs on The Strip—it has the usual black wall and mirror mix, although it does have a larger video screen than most. Le Dome is the only club in Acapulco, if not in the world, where you can play basketball, yes, basketball, every Wednesday. Winners get a bottle of tequila. *Costera Miguel Alemán 402, next door to Fiorucci, tel. 74/84-11-90.*

Discobeach is Acapulco's only alfresco disco and its most informal one. The under-30 crowd sometimes even turns up in shorts. The waiters are young and friendly, and every night they dress to a different theme. One night they're all in togas carrying bunches of grapes, the next they're in pajamas. Other nights feature a Hawaiian luau or a mock bullfight. Every Wednesday, ladies' night, all the women receive flowers. The coco loco is the house special. *On The Strip, one minute east of Eve's, tel. 74/84-70-64.*

News is billed as a "disco and concert hall." Disco it is—and it's enormous, with seating for 1,200 people in love seats and booths, but "concert hall" is just a figure of speech. There are different theme parties and competitions nightly—bikini contests on Tuesday, and Carnival Night (with lambada and limbo contests and a Brazilian-style show) on Thursday. Winners walk off with a bottle of champagne or dinner for two; occasionally the prize has been a trip to Hawaii. From 10:30 (opening time) to 11:30, the music is slow and romantic; then the disco music and the light show begin, and they go on till dawn. *Costera Miguel Alemán, across from the Hyatt Regency, tel. 74/84-59-02.*

Delirio used to operate under the name Jackie O, but now one can only sigh nostalgically for the days when the bathrooms were preciously dubbed "Jackie O" and "Aristotle." Comfortable is the operative word here; big booths and wrap-around sofas all have a view of the dance floor. Lasers and lights penetrate the seating area without irritating, and there are numerous relatively quiet spaces. *Opposite the Hyatt Continental, tel. 74/84-08-43.*

Planet is very sophisticated. The seats are comfortable armchairs and sofas with a good view for people-watching. The managers wear suits, and the disco is an art gallery—the walls are covered with tasteful renditions of the beach and other typical Mexican scenes. In addition to the usual videos and disco music, there is a show every night during the winter season (Friday and Saturday night during the rest of the year), complete with mariachis. This club is less crowded than most. There is always room to dance. The crowd is mostly Mexican.

Calle Vicente Yañez Pinzón 12, just behind Delirio, tel. 74/84–82–95.

Antillanos has replaced the old Cats, which is, sadly, no more. Now it's all palm "trees" and lanterns, the crowd is mostly local, and the music is strictly salsa and tropical. The live groups start playing at 10:30, and at midnight there's a drag show. The $15 cover charge includes local-brand drinks. *Juan de la Cosa 32, tel. 74/82–72–35. Open Tues.–Sun.*

Excursions from Acapulco

Taxco, the Silver City

It's a picture-postcard look—Mexico in its Sunday best: white stucco buildings nuzzling cobblestoned streets, red-tile roofs and geranium-filled window boxes bright in the sun. Taxco (pronounced **tahss**-co), a colonial treasure that the Mexican government declared a national monument in 1928, tumbles onto the hills of the Sierra Madre in the state of Guerrero. Its silver mines have drawn people here for centuries. Now its charm, mild temperatures, sunshine, and flowers make Taxco a popular tourist destination.

Hernán Cortés discovered Taxco's mines in 1522. The silver rush lasted until the next century, when excitement tapered off. Then, in the 1700s a Frenchman, who Mexicanized his name to José de la Borda, discovered a rich lode that revitalized the town's silver industry and made him exceedingly wealthy. After Borda, however, Taxco's importance faded, until the 1930s and the arrival of William G. Spratling, a writer/architect from New Orleans. Enchanted by Taxco and convinced of its potential as a silver center, Spratling set up an apprentice shop, where his artistic talent and his fascination with pre-Columbian design combined to produce silver jewelry and other artifacts that soon earned Taxco its worldwide reputation as the Silver City. Spratling's inspiration lives on in his students and their descendants, many of whom are the city's current silversmiths.

Getting There There are several ways to travel to Taxco from Acapulco, and all involve ground transport.

By Car It takes about 2½ hours to make the drive from Acapulco to Taxco, now that the new road connecting the town to Highway 95 eliminates most of the tortuous hairpin turns of the previous route. A new superhighway connecting Acapulco to Cuernavaca, which should be finished by winter 1993 (much of it is already open), promises to cut down on driving time even more. It is also common practice to hire a chauffeured car or a taxi. Check with your hotel for references and prices.

By Bus First-class **Estrella de Oro** buses leave Acapulco several times a day from the Terminal Central de Autobuses de Primera Clase (Av. Cuauhtemoc 1490, tel. 74/85–87–05). The cost for the approximately four-hour ride is about $7 one way. The Taxco terminal is at Avenida John F. Kennedy 126 (tel. 762/2–06–48). First-class **Flecha Roja** buses depart Acapulco several times a day from the Terminal de Autobuses (Av. Cuauhtemoc 97, tel. 74/82–03–51). The one-way ticket is about $6.50. The Taxco terminal for this line is at Avenida John F. Kennedy 104 (tel. 762/2–01–31).

Getting Around Unless you're used to byways, alleys, and tiny streets, maneuvering anything bigger than your two feet through Taxco will be difficult. Fortunately, almost everything of interest is within walking distance of the Zócalo. Minibuses travel along preset routes and charge only a few cents, and Volkswagen bugs provide inexpensive (average $2) taxi transportation. Remember that Taxco's altitude is 5,800 feet. If you have come from sea level, wear sensible shoes for negotiating the hilly streets, and take it easy on your first day.

Exploring *Numbers in the margin correspond to points of interest on the Taxco Exploring map.*

❶ Begin at the **Zócalo,** properly called **Plaza Borda,** heading first into the **Church of San Sebastián and Santa Prisca,** which domi-
❷ nates the main square. Usually just called **Santa Prisca,** it was built by French silver magnate José de la Borda in thanks to the Almighty for his having literally stumbled upon a rich silver vein. The style of the church—sort of Spanish baroque meets rococo—is known as churrigueresque, and its pink exterior is a stunning surprise.

Just a block from the Zócalo, behind Santa Prisca, is the
❸ **Spratling Museum,** formerly the home of William G. Spratling (*see* Introduction, *above*). This wonderful little museum explains the working of colonial mines and displays Spratling's collection of pre-Columbian artifacts. *Porfirio Delgado and El Arco. Small entrance fee. Open daily 10–5.*

❹ **Casa Humboldt,** a few blocks away, was named for the German adventurer Alexander von Humboldt, who stayed here in 1803. The Moorish-style 18th-century house has a finely detailed facade. At press time it was being remodeled to house a museum of colonial art. *Calle Juan Ruiz Alarcón 6.*

❺ Down the hill from Santa Prisca is the **Municipal Market,** which is worth a visit, especially early on Saturday or Sunday morning.

Time Out Around the plaza are several *neverías* where you can treat yourself to an ice cream in a delicious fruit flavor, such as coconut.

Off the Beaten About 15 minutes northeast of Taxco are the Caves of
Track Cacahuamilpa (Grutas de Cacahuamilpa). The largest caverns in Mexico, these 15 large chambers comprise 12 kilometers (8 miles) of geological formation. Only some caves are illuminated. A guide can be hired at the entrance to the caves.

Shopping Most of the people who visit Taxco come with silver in mind.
Silver Three types are available: sterling, which is always stamped .925 (925 parts in 1,000) and is the most expensive; plated silver; and the inexpensive *alpaca,* which is also known as German silver or nickel silver. Sterling pieces are usually priced by weight according to world silver prices, and of course fine workmanship will add to the cost. Work is also done with semiprecious stones; you'll find garnets, topazes, amethysts, and opals. If you plan to buy, check prices before leaving home. When comparison shopping in the more than 200 silver shops in Taxco, you will see that many carry almost identical merchan-

dise, although a few are noted for their creativity. Among them:

Galería de Arte Andrés (Av. John F. Kennedy 28) has unique designs created by the personable Andrés Mejía.

Pineda's Taxco (Plaza Borda) has fine designs and fine workmanship.

Los Castillo (Plazuela Bernal 10) is the most famous and decidedly one of the most exciting silver shops; it's known for innovative design and for combining silver with ceramics and such other metals as copper and brass. The artisans are disciples of Spratling.

The Spratling Workshop (south of town on Highway 95) turns out designs using the original Spratling molds.

Joyería Elena Ballesteros (Celso Muñoz 4) is a very elegant shop with work of outstanding design.

Local Wares   Lacquered gourds and boxes from the town of Olinala, masks, bowls, straw baskets, bark paintings, and many other handcrafted items native to the state of Guerrero are available from strolling vendors and spread on the cobblestones at "sidewalk boutiques." **Acácia** (Convention Center, Calle Florida) has an interesting selection of Guerrero handicrafts. **Gracias a Dios** (Bernal 3) has women's clothing, with brightly colored ribbons and appliqués, designed by Tachi Castillo, as well as a less original selection of crafts. **La Calleja** (Calle Arco 5, 2nd floor) has a wide and well-chosen selection of native arts and handcrafts.

Sunday is market day, which means that artisans from surrounding villages descend on the town, as do visitors from Mexico City. It can get crowded, but if you find a seat on a bench in Plaza Borda, you're set to watch the show and peruse the merchandise that will inevitably be brought to you.

Sports and Fitness You can play golf or tennis, swim and ride horses at various hotels around Taxco. Call to see if the facilities are open to nonguests. Bullfights are occasionally held in the small town of Acmixtla, 6 km (3.75 mi) from Taxco. Ask at your hotel about the schedule.

Dining Gastronomes can find everything from tagliatelle to iguana in Taxco restaurants, and meals are much less expensive than in Acapulco.

Category	Cost*
Moderate	$20–$30
Inexpensive	under $15

per person excluding drinks, service, and sales tax (10%)

Cielito Lindo. This charming restaurant features a Mexican-international menu. Give the Mexican specialties a try, for example, *pollo en pipian verde*, a chicken simmered in a mild, pumpkinseed-based sauce. *Plaza Borda, tel. 762/2–06–03. Open daily, breakfast–dinner. No reservations. Dress: casual. MC, V. Moderate.*

★ **La Taberna.** This is the latest venture of the proprietors of Bora Bora, Taxco's popular pizza place. The menu is varied, with the likes of pastas, beef Stroganoff, and crepes to choose from. *Benito Juárez 8, tel. 762/2–52–26. Reservations suggested. Dress: casual. MC, V. Moderate.*

★ **La Ventana de Taxco.** Mario Cavagna traveled from Como, Italy, to Taxco with many of his favorite recipes intact. That food, coupled with Mexican specialties and a fantastic view, makes this the town's finest. *Hacienda del Solar Hotel, Hwy. 95, south of town, tel. 762/2–05–87. Reservations required on weekends. Dress: casual. AE, MC, V. Moderate.*

Pagaduría del Rey. In the Posada Don Carlos, south of town via Avenida John F. Kennedy, this restaurant has a long-standing reputation for Continental fare served in comfortable surroundings. *Calle H. Colegio Militar (formerly Cerro de la Bermeja), tel. 762/2–34–67. Reservations not necessary. Dress: casual. Open daily breakfast–dinner. MC, V. Moderate.*

Toni's. Prime rib and lobster are the specialties. There's also a great view and a romantic setting. *Monte Taxco Hotel, tel. 762/2–13–00. Reservations required. Dress: casual. AE, DC, MC, V. Moderate.*

★ **Bora Bora.** Exceptionally good pizza is what's on the menu here. *Callejón de las Delícias, behind Paco's Bar, tel. 762/2–17–21. No reservations. Dress: casual. MC, V. Inexpensive.*

La Hacienda. In the Hotel Agua Escondida, this charming restaurant serves Mexican and international specialties. The best buy: the daily fixed-price meal called a *comida corrida*. *Guillermo Spratling 4, tel. 762/2–06–63. Open daily, breakfast–dinner. No reservations. Dress: casual. MC, V. Inexpensive.*

Los Arcos. This local favorite serves international cuisine in a delightful patio setting. *At the Hotel los Arcos, tel. 762/2–18–*

36. Reservations advised. Dress: casual. AE, MC, V. Inexpensive.

Piccolo Mondo. More casual than its neighbor Toni's, this place serves pizza baked in a wood-burning brick oven and meats and chicken charcoal broiled at your table. *Monte Taxco Hotel, tel. 762/2–13–00. Reservations advised. Dress: casual. AE, DC, MC, V. Closed Mon.–Thurs. Inexpensive.*

Señor Costilla. That's right. This translates as Mr. Ribs, and the whimsical name says it all. The Taxco outpost of the zany Anderson chain serves ribs and chops in a restaurant with great balcony seating. *Plaza Borda, tel. 762/2–32–15. Reservations advised. Dress: casual. MC, V. Inexpensive.*

Lodging Whether your stay in Taxco is a one-night stopover or a few days' respite from the madness of Acapulco, there are several categories of hotel to choose from within Taxco's two types: the small inns nestled on the hills skirting the Zócalo and the larger, more modern hotels on the outskirts of town.

Category	Cost*
Moderate	$65–$100
Inexpensive	$40–$65
Very Inexpensive	under $40

All prices are for standard double room, exluding 10% sales (called IVA) tax.

★ **Hacienda del Solar.** This intimate and elegant small resort (off Hwy. 95 south of town) has well-appointed rooms. Its restaurant is the top-notch La Ventana de Taxco (*see above*). *Box 96, 40200, tel. 762/2–03–23. 22 rooms with bath. Facilities: 1 tennis court, pool, restaurant. MC, V. Moderate.*

Monte Taxco. A colonial style predominates at this hotel, which has a knockout view and two restaurants, a disco, and nightly entertainment. *Box 84, Lomas de Taxco, 40200, tel. 762/2–13–00. 160 rooms with bath. Facilities: 3 tennis courts, 9-hole golf course, horseback riding, two restaurants, disco. AE, DC, MC, V. Moderate.*

De la Borda. Long a Taxco favorite, but getting very run-down now, the hotel's rooms overlook town from its hillside perch. There's a restaurant with occasional entertainment, and many bus tours en route from Mexico City to Acapulco stay overnight here. *Box 6, Cerro del Pedregal 2, 40200, tel. 762/2–00–25. 95 rooms with bath. Facilities: pool, restaurant. MC, V. Inexpensive.*

★ **Posada de la Misión.** Laid out like a village, this hotel is close to town and has dining room murals by the noted Mexican artist Juan O'Gorman. *Box 88, Cerro de la Misíon 84, 40230, tel. 762/2–00–63. 150 rooms with bath. Facilities: pool, tennis court. AE, DC, MC, V. Inexpensive.*

Rancho Taxco-Victoria. This in-town hotel, in two buildings connected by a bridge over the road, is under the same management as the De la Borda, and suffers from the same neglect. It has its rooms done in classic Mexican decor. There's also the requisite splendid view. *Box 83, Carlos J. Nibbi 5, 40200, tel. 762/2–00–10. 100 rooms with bath. Facilities: 2 pools, restaurant, bar. AE, MC, V. Inexpensive.*

Santa Prisca. The patio with fountains is a plus at this colonial-style hotel. *Cena Obscuras 1, 40200, tel. 762/2–00–80. 40 rooms. Facilities: restaurant, bar. AE, MC, V. Inexpensive.*

Agua Escondida. A favorite with some regular visitors to Taxco, this small hotel has simple rooms decorated with Mexican-style furnishings. *Guillermo Spratling 4, 40200, tel. 762/2–07–26. 50 rooms with bath. Facilities: pool, La Hacienda restaurant. MC, V. Very Inexpensive.*

Loma Linda. This is a basic motel on the highway just east of town. *Av. John F. Kennedy 52, 40200, tel. 762/2–02–06. 90 units. Facilities: pool, restaurant, bar. AE, MC, V. Very Inexpensive.*

Los Arcos. An in-town inn, Los Arcos has a fine restaurant (*see* Dining, *above*). *Calle Juan Ruiz de Alarcón, 40200, tel. 762/2–18–36. 30 rooms with bath. Facilities: heated pool, restaurant. MC, V. Very Inexpensive.*

Posada de los Castillo. This inn in town is straightforward, clean, and good for the price. *Juan Ruiz de Alarcón 7, 40200, tel. 762/2–13–96. 15 rooms. Facilities: restaurant, bar. DC, MC, V. Very Inexpensive.*

The Arts and Nightlife Taxco has no abundance of cultural events, but it's noted for its festivals, which are an integral part of the town's character.

The Arts These fiestas provide an opportunity to honor almost every saint in heaven with music, dancing, marvelous fireworks, and lots of fun. The people of Taxco demonstrate their pyrotechnical skills with set pieces—wondrous "castles" made of bamboo. (Note: Expect high occupancy at local hotels and inns during fiestas.)

January 18, the feast of Santa Prisca and San Sebastián, the town's patron saints, is celebrated with music and fireworks.

Holy Week, from Palm Sunday to Easter Sunday, brings processions and events that blend Christian and Indian traditions, the dramas involving hundreds of participants, images of Christ, and, for one particular procession, black-hooded penitents. Most events are centered on Plaza Borda and the Santa Prisca Church.

September 29, Saint Michael's Day (Dia de San Miguel), is celebrated with regional dances and pilgrimages to the Chapel of Saint Michael the Archangel.

In **early November,** on the Monday following the Day of the Dead celebrations on November 1 and 2, is the day the whole town takes off to a nearby hill for the Fiesta de los Jumiles. The *jumil* is a crawling insect that is said to taste strongly of iodine and is considered a great delicacy. Purists eat them alive, but others prefer them stewed, fried or combined with chili in a hot sauce.

In **late November or early December,** the National Silver Fair (Feria Nacional de la Plata) draws hundreds of artisans from around the world for a variety of displays, concerts, exhibitions, and contests held around the city.

Nightlife Travelers should satisfy their appetite for fun after dark in Acapulco. Although Taxco has a disco or two, a couple of piano bars, and some entertainment, the range is limited.

Still, you might enjoy spending an evening perched on a chair on a balcony or in one of the cafés surrounding the Plaza Borda. Two traditional favorites are the **Bar Paco** and **Bertha's,** where a tequila, lime, and club-soda concoction called a "Bertha" is the house specialty.

Or immerse yourself in the thick of things, especially on Sunday evening, by settling in on a wrought-iron bench on the Zócalo to watch children, lovers, and fellow people-watchers.

Most of Taxco's nighttime activity is at the Monte Taxco hotel, either at the **Windows** discotheque or at **Tony Reyes's,** where the price of the show includes a performance of the Papantla fliers, dancing, drinks, and transportation. On Saturday nights, there's a buffet, a terrific fireworks display (Taxco is Mexico's fireworks capital), and a show put on by the hotel's employees.

Some of the best restaurants, like La Ventana de Taxco, have music.

Ixtapa and Zihuatanejo

In Ixtapa/Zihuatanejo, 3½ hours by car (250 kilometers/150 miles) up the coast from Acapulco, you can enjoy two distinct lifestyles for the price of one—double value for your money.

Ixtapa/Zihuatanejo is a complete change of pace from hectic Acapulco. The water is comfortably warm for swimming, and the waves are gentle. The temperature averages 78° year-round. During the mid-December–Easter high season, the weather is sunny and dry, and in the June–October rainy season, the short, heavy showers usually fall at night.

Ixtapa (pronounced ees-**tah**-pah), where most Americans stay—probably because they can't pronounce Zihuatanejo (see-wha-tah-**nay**-ho)—is big, modern, and scarcely 17 years old. Exclusively a vacation resort, it was invented and planned, as was Cancún, by Fonatur, Mexico's National Fund for Tourism Development. Large world-class hotels cluster in the Hotel Zone around Palmar Bay, where conditions are ideal for swimming and water sports, and just across the street are a couple of football fields' worth of shopping malls. The hotels are well spaced; there's always plenty of room on the beach, which is lighted for strolling at night; and the pace is leisurely.

Zihuatanejo, which means "land of women" in Purepecha, the language of the Tarascan Indians, lies 5 kilometers (3 miles) to the southeast. According to legend, Caltzontzin, a Tarascan king, chose this bay as his royal retreat and enclosed it with a long protective breakwater, which is known today as Las Gatas. Zihuatanejo is an old fishing village that has managed to retain its charm; but it's also the area's commercial center, with banks and airline offices, and its *malecón* (waterfront) and cobblestoned streets are lined with hotels, restaurants, and boutiques.

Getting There You can fly direct to Ixtapa on **Mexicana Airlines** from San
By Plane Francisco and Los Angeles via Guadalajara, and from Chicago via Mexico City. **Delta** flies to Ixtapa nonstop from Los Angeles. Both **Mexicana** and **Aeromexico** have daily nonstop service from Mexico City and most other major cities in Mexico, but there is no direct air service from Acapulco.

By Car The trip from Acapulco is a 3½-hour drive over a good road that passes through small towns and coconut groves and has some quite spectacular ocean views for the last third of the way. At three inspection stops, soldiers checking for drugs and arms generally only look into the car and wave you on.

By Bus **Estrella de Oro** and **Flecha Roja** offer deluxe service (which means that the air-conditioning and toilets are likely to be functioning) between Acapulco and Zihuatanejo. The trip takes about five hours and costs $6. You must reserve and pick up your ticket one day in advance and get to the terminal at least a half hour before departure. Estrella de Oro buses leave from the Terminal Central de Autobuses de Primera Clase (Av. Cuauhtémoc 1490, tel. 74/85–87–05). The Flecha Roja buses leave from the Terminal de Autobuses (Av. Cuauhtémoc 97, tel. 74/82–03–51).

Escorted Tours Most Acapulco-based travel agencies can set up one-day tours to Ixtapa/Zihuatanejo for about $50–$150, including guide, transportation (car, minibus, or bus), and lunch. If your hotel travel desk can't arrange it for you, contact **Turismo Caleta** (Calle Andrea Dória 2, tel. 74/84–61–72), **Fantasy Tours** (Costera Miguel Alemán 50, tel. 74/84–25–28), or **Excursiones Acapulco** (Costera Miguel Alemán 40, Suite 204, tel. 74/84–65–54).

Getting Around Unless you plan to travel great distances or to visit remote beaches, taxis and buses are by far the best way to get around. Rental cars cost about $100 per day; jeeps about half that.

By Taxi Taxis are plentiful, and fares are reasonable. The average fare from the Ixtapa Hotel Zone to Zihuatanejo or to Playa La Ropa or Playa Quieta is about $4. There's no problem getting cabs, and there are taxi stands in front of most hotels.

By Bus The buses that operate between the hotels and from the Hotel Zone to downtown Zihuatanejo run approximately every 20 minutes and charge about 20¢.

By Motor Scooter Scooters can be rented at **Hola Renta Motos** (next door to the Villa Sakura restaurant in the El Portal shopping center; no phone) for $10–$15 an hour.

By Pedicab Pedicabs (*carcachas*) decorated with balloons can be rented in the shopping mall across the street from the Dorado Pacifico hotel for $10 per hour. Bikes cost $1 per hour. The rental tent is open daily 9–8.

By Car Rental-car offices in Zihuatanejo: **Dollar** at the Dorado Pacífico hotel (tel. 753/3–20–25) and at the Hotel Krystal (tel. 753/3–03–33, ext. 1110), and **Hertz** (Calle Nicolás Bravo 9, tel. 753/4–30–50 or 753/4–22–55). In Ixtapa: **Avis's** only office is in the airport (tel. 753/4–22–48), and the other companies have branches there. Jeeps can be rented at the airport from **Dollar** (tel. 753/4–23–14).

Exploring No matter where you go in Ixtapa/Zihuatanejo, you get the fresh-air, great-outdoors feeling of a place in the making, with plenty of room to spare.

Zihuatanejo is a tropical charmer. The seaside promenade overlooks the town dock and cruise-ship pier; tiny bars and restaurants invite you to linger longer. From town, the road soars up a hill that has a handful of restaurants and hotels perched on breezy spots overlooking the bay. Another sprinkling of hotels surrounds pancake-flat **Madera Beach. La Ropa,** farther along, is Zihuatanejo's most popular beach and the location of one of Mexico's best small hotels, Villa del Sol. **Las Gatas** beach, beyond, lined with dive shops and tiny restaurants, is also popular, but is accessible only by water.

On the opposite end of the area, about five minutes beyond the Ixtapa Hotel Zone, is pretty **Playa Quieta,** a small beach used by Club Med. From here, you can take a boat ride to **Isla Ixtapa** for pennies and spend a wonderful day in the sun far from other people. Once the boat lands, take the path to the other side of the island for better sunning and swimming.

For another perspective, take a three-hour cruise for $25 on the 12-passenger catamaran *Tequila* (tel. 753/3–00–07). It cruises the bay with a stop for snorkeling at Isla Ixtapa. **Sailboats of the Sun** (tel. 753/3–07–82) sets sail weekdays at 10 AM from the Puerto Mío marina in Zihuatanejo for a seven-hour cruise that includes a stop for snorkeling and a fresh-fish lunch at Ixtapa Island. Both the *Tequila* and Sailboats of the Sun also have two-hour sunset cruises of Zihuatanejo Bay.

Shopping At last count, there were seven shopping malls in Ixtapa. La Puerta, the first one built, is now flanked by terra-cotta-colored Ixpamar, colonial-style Los Patios, and bright white Las Fuentes. The ubiquitous **Aca Joe** and **Polo Ralph Lauren** are in Las Fuentes, as is **Africán,** which carries 100%-cotton safari-style clothing for men and women. **Ferrioni** is in La Puerta; **Chiquita Banana,** a good source of decorative items for your house, and **La Fuente,** which sells clothes with native-inspired designs, are in Los Patios. **El Amanecer,** selling some of the best folk art in the state, is in Ixpamar. Don't let the modern facades and sparkling decor fool you: Most prices are within everyone's range. There is sometimes free live entertainment on the patio at Ixpamar.

Downtown Zihuatanejo has a municipal minimarket and a host of tiny stores. You must go inside to discover bargains in souvenirs and decorations, T-shirts, and embroidered dresses. On Calle Vicente Guerrero is one of the best handicrafts shops in all of Mexico—**Coco Cabaña,** which is owned by the same people who run Coconuts restaurant. **Los Almendros,** at Calles Guerrero and Alvarez, has an especially good selection of handpainted ceramics from Oaxaca, and at **La Zapoteca,** on the waterfront, you'll find hand-loomed woolen rugs, wall hangings, and hammocks. On Calle Juan N. Alvarez, Indians sell baskets and other handmade wares that they bring from the surrounding areas.

Sports and Fitness Although several hotels have tennis courts, and there are two beautiful championship golf courses in Ixtapa, most of the outdoor activities in Ixtapa/Zihuatanejo center on the water. At the **water-sports center** in front of Villa del Sol on La Ropa you can arrange for waterskiing, snorkeling, diving, and windsurfing.

Deep-sea Fishing Boats with captain and crew can be hired at the **Cooperativa de Lanchas de Recreo and Pesca Deportiva** (Av. Ruíz Cortines 40 at the Zihuatanejo pier; tel. 753/4–20–56), or through **Turismo Caleta** (La Puerta shopping center in Ixtapa, tel. 753/3–04–44). The cost is $80 to $100 for a boat with two lines, and up to $250 for a boat with four to six lines.

Golf and Tennis The **Ixtapa Golf Club** (tel. 753/3–11–63) is open to the public. The greens fee is $35; tennis costs $8 an hour in the daytime, $9 at night. Caddies cost $10 an hour and carts go for $26. A second 18-hole golf course is located at Marina Ixtapa.

Horseback Riding You can rent horses at La Manzanilla Ranch, near Playa La Ropa, and at Playa Linda. **Turismo Caleta** (La Puerta shopping center, tel. 753/3–04–44) picks tourists up at their hotel and transports them to either one.

Parasailing You can try this scary-looking sport on the beach in the Ixtapa Hotel Zone. A 10-minute ride will cost about $12.

Sailing Hobie Cats and larger sailboats are available for rent at La Ropa Beach for $20–$60 per hour.

Scuba Diving **Carlos** operates day and night diving excursions on Las Gatas, and **Oliverio,** who is now over 70, runs diving excursion on Ixtapa Island. Both have kiosks on the beach. A one-tank dive with either costs about $25 to $30. The **Zihuatanejo Scuba Center,** at the foot of the Zihuatanejo pier (tel. 753/4–21–47), is operated by marine biologist Juan Barnard.

Windsurfing This popular activity can be arranged at Las Gatas and La Ropa beaches for about $20 per hour—$30 per hour with lessons.

Dining Meals are generally less expensive in downtown Zihuatanejo than in Ixtapa or in the restaurants up in the hills, and even the most expensive ones will cost considerably less than in Acapulco. The restaurants will fall at the lower end of our price categories, verging on the category below, and casual dress is acceptable everywhere. A delicious, inexpensive snack is a *licuado*, a milkshake made with fresh fruit. It's filling and nutritious, and usually costs less than $1.

Category	Cost*
Expensive	$30–$45
Moderate	$20–$30
Inexpensive	under $20

*per person excluding drinks, service, and sales tax (10%)

Ixtapa **Bogart's.** Romantic and elegant, with moorish/arabic decor and an international menu. The *Crepas Persas* filled with cheese are topped with sour cream and caviar. Or try *Suprema Casablanca*: chicken breasts stuffed with lobster, then breaded and fried. *Hotel Krystal, Playa Palmar, tel. 753/3–03–33. Reservations required. No shorts or T-shirts. AE, DC, MC, V. Expensive.*

El Faro. El Faro sits atop a hill next to the funicular that goes up to the Club Pacifica complex. It has an extensive menu that includes *camarones en salsa de albahaca* (shrimp in a basil sauce), piano music, and a spectacular view. *Playa Vista Hermosa, tel. 753/3–10–27. Reservations advised. Dress: casual. AE, MC, V. Expensive.*

El Sombrero. This popular place serves Mexican food, seafood, and international dishes. The potpouri Mexicana, with chicken in mole sauce, an enchilada, and a spicy sausage, is a good introduction to real Mexican cookery. *Los Patios Shopping Center, tel. 753/3–04–39. Reservations advised. Dress: casual. MC, V. Closed Sun. Expensive.*

★ **Las Esferas.** This place in the Westin Ixtapa is a complex of two restaurants and a bar. **Portofino** specializes in Italian cuisine

Ixtapa Dining and Lodging

and is decorated with multicolored pastas and scenes of Italy. In **El Mexicano** the specialties are obviously Mexican, as is the decor—bright pink tablecloths, Puebla jugs, a huge tree of life, antique wood carvings, and blown glass. *Playa Vista Hermosa, tel. 753/3-21-21, ext. 3444. Reservations necessary at Portofino, advised at El Mexicano. No shorts or T-shirts. AE, DC, MC, V. Expensive.*

Villa de la Selva. Just past the Hotel Camino Real, this restaurant has tables set up on multilevel terraces under the stars. Excellent international dishes and grilled steaks and seafood are served in a romantic setting, and special lighting after dark illuminates the sea and the rocks below. *Paseo de la Roca, tel. 753/3-03-62. Open daily 6–midnight. Reservations advised. Dress: casual. AE, MC, V. Expensive.*

Carlos 'n Charlies. Hidden away at the end of the beach, this outpost of the famous Anderson's chain serves pork, seafood, and chicken in a Polynesian setting almost on the sand. It has a minizoo, too. *Next to Posada Real Hotel, tel. 753/3-00-35. No reservations. Dress: casual. AE, DC, MC, V. Moderate.*

Da Baffone. The atmosphere is easy and informal at this well-run Italian restaurant with two dining areas; you can choose the air-conditioned dining room or the open-air porch. Try the spaghetti siubeco, prepared with cream, peppers, shrimp, and wine. *La Puerta Shopping Mall, tel. 753/3-11-22. Reservations advised. Dress: casual. AE, MC, V. Moderate.*

Café Onyx. Mexican and international dishes are served under an awning at this alfresco eatery. *Across from the Holiday Inn, in the Galerías shopping mall. No phone. No reservations. Dress: casual. MC, V. Inexpensive.*

★ **Nueva Zelanda.** This is a fast-moving cafeteria with good food that you order by numbers. Chicken enchiladas with green sauce, *sincronizadas* (flour tortillas filled with ham and cheese), and the licuados (*see above*) are all tasty. Families with young children gather here, and there is usually a line on weekends. Dinner for two can cost less than $8. *Behind the bandstand, no phone. No reservations. No credit cards. Inexpensive.*

Zihuatanejo Restaurants in Zihuatanejo are usually small and friendly. Talking to people can be part of the fun. If you want to find out what the town is about, go to the bar before dinner.

Coconuts. Excellent seafood and salads are served in elegant surroundings. *Calle Agustin Ramírez 1, tel. 753/4-25-18. Reservations required. Dress: casual. AE, DC, MC, V. Closed Sept.–Oct. Expensive.*

★ **Villa del Sol.** This restaurant, in the hotel that bears the same name, has earned a worldwide reputation for excellent quality and service. The international menu is prepared by Swiss, German, and Mexican chefs. *Hotel Villa del Sol, Playa La Ropa, tel. 753/4-22-39. Dinner reservations advised. Dress: casual. No credit cards. Expensive.*

Casa Elvira. Joaquin Vasquez, the owner, claims that this is the oldest restaurant in town—it's been around since 1956. It's quaint and clean, decorated with talavera tiles from Puebla and handicrafts from Pátzcuaro, and the prices are reasonable. There's a fairly large selection of fish and seafood, including an excellent *parrillada de mariscos* (seafood grill), as well as such traditional Mexican dishes as poblano peppers stuffed with cheese and *puntas de filete albañil* (a kind of goulash). *Paseo del Pescador 16, tel. 753/4-20-61. MC, V. Open Wed.–Mon. 8 AM–10 PM. Moderate.*

Chez Juan. In spite of the name, this restaurant is neither French nor Mexican but Chinese. Hot and spicy Szechuan dishes are the specialty of the house. There's also a sports bar with backgammon and checkers. *Calle Hermenegildo Galeana 4, tel. 753/4-51-55. Dress: casual. Open Sun.–Fri. 5–11. MC, V. Moderate.*

Garrabos. A delightful restaurant that specializes in seafood and Mexican cuisine. Try the seafood brochettes. *Calle Juan N. Alvarez 52, near the church and museum, tel. 753/4-29-77. Reservations advised. Dress: casual. MC, V. Moderate.*

La Gaviota. A mini-beach club where you can spend an afternoon swimming and sunning after having a seafood lunch. Lots of locals like this one, and the bar is pleasant. Ask the taxi driver to come back for you around 4 PM. *On Playa La Ropa, no phone. No reservations. Dress: casual. MC, V. Moderate.*

★ **La Mesa del Capitán.** Now a tradition in Zihuatanejo, this restaurant has been around since 1975. The steaks, ribs, and seafood dishes are prepared under the watchful eye of the proprietor, Luz Maria. Indoor and terrace seating are available. *Calle Nicolás Bravo 18, tel. 753/4-20-27. Reservations for groups only. Dress: casual. AE, MC, V. Moderate.*

La Bocana. A favorite with locals as well as visitors. The service is good and the seafood is a treat. You can eat three meals a day here. Musicians sometimes stroll through. *Calle Juan N. Alvarez 13, tel. 753/4-35-45. Dress: casual. MC, V. Inexpensive.*

La Perla. At Doña Raquel's popular seaside restaurant and vid-

Zihuatanejo Dining and Lodging

eo sports bar, the hands-down favorite is *Filete La Perla*, a fish fillet baked in aluminum foil with cheese, garlic, onion, and tomato. *Playa La Ropa, tel. 753/4–27–00. Dress: casual. Open daily 9 AM–10 PM. MC, V. Inexpensive.*

★ **La Sirena Gorda.** The specialty here is seafood tacos (try the shrimp-and-bacon combo); meals are served in rustic, yet pleasant, surroundings. *Paseo del Pescador 20-A, tel. 753/4–26–87. Dress: casual. MC, V. Open Thurs.–Tues. 7 AM–10 PM. Inexpensive.*

★ **Nueva Zelanda.** From breakfast through dinner everybody drops in to this little coffee-shop–style place, which serves *tortas* (Mexican sandwiches on crusty rolls), tacos, and enchiladas. *Calle Cuauhtémoc 23, no phone. No reservations. Dress: casual. No credit cards. Inexpensive.*

★ **Pepper's Garden.** This Mexican restaurant has beautifully carved doors that lead onto the patio dining area and many picturesque colonial touches. *Calle Ignacio Altamirano 46, tel. 753/4–37–67. Reservations suggested. Dress: casual. MC, V. Inexpensive.*

Puntarenas. This plain place serves Mexican food and great breakfasts. It's a favorite with those in the know and there's often a line, but it's worth the wait. *Across the bridge at the end of Calle Juan N. Alvarez, no phone. No reservations. Dress: casual. No credit cards. Open only in high season. Inexpensive.*

Lodging Ixtapa/Zihuatanejo hotel rates vary widely, and after Easter they drop 30%–40% and sometimes more. Most of the budget accommodations are in Zihuatanejo. Rooms everywhere are clean and have private baths with showers.

Category	Cost*
Very Expensive	$185–$285
Expensive	$100–$185
Moderate	$55–$100
Inexpensive	under $55

All prices are for a standard double room, excluding 10% sales (called IVA) tax.

Ixtapa   **Costa Club Ixtapa.** Located at the very end of the hotel zone, on a beach protected by Ixtapa Island (which makes it good for swimming), this is the former Hotel Playa Linda, with enlarged rooms and a new restaurant, lobby, and shopping area. The rooms—each with a private terrace—are strung through one- and two-story buildings. *Carretera Escenica s/n, Municipio Teniente Azueta 40880, tel. 753/3–19–85 in Ixtapa or 5/520–6457 in Mexico City. 150 rooms with bath. Facilities: 2 tennis courts, 2 pools, 2 restaurants, outdoor disco. AE, DC, MC, V.*

★ **Krystal Ixtapa.** This attractive beachfront property is part of an excellent Mexican chain. Home to Christine's, Ixtapa's most popular disco, and Bogart's restaurant, the Krystal is one of the liveliest spots in town. *Playa Palmar, 40880, tel. 753/3–03–33. 260 rooms and suites with bath. Facilities: 2 restaurants, coffee shop, disco, 2 tennis courts, pool. AE, DC, MC, V. Expensive.*

Stouffer Presidente. A beautifully landscaped resort that was among Ixtapa's first beachfront properties. The rooms are divided between colonial-style villas that line winding paths through the grounds and a tower with a glass elevator that provides a sensational view of Ixtapa. *Playa Palmar, 40880, tel. 753/3–00–18. 401 rooms with bath. Facilities: 3 restaurants, bar, 2 tennis courts, 2 pools, wading pool. AE, DC, MC, V. Expensive.*

★ **Westin Ixtapa.** Formerly known as the Camino Real, this is a pyramid-shaped hotel whose rooms (all with private balconies) seem to cascade down the hill to secluded Vista Hermosa beach. It is one of Ixtapa's largest hotels, and is noted for excellent service. *Playa Vista Hermosa, Box 91, 40880, tel. 753/3–21–21. 428 rooms with bath. Facilities: 3 restaurants, 2 bars, 4 tennis courts, 3 pools, wading pool. AE, DC, MC, V. Expensive.*

Posada Real. Smaller and more intimate than most of the Ixtapa hotels, the colonial-style Posada Real sits on Palmar Beach, has lots of charm, and offers good value. A Best Western hotel. *Playa Palmar, 40880, tel. 753/3–16–85 and 753/3–17–45. 108 rooms with bath. Facilities: 3 restaurants, 2 bars, disco, 2 pools, wading pool, tennis court. AE, DC, MC, V. Moderate.*

Zihuatanejo   The best hotels are on La Madera or La Ropa beaches or overlooking them; the least expensive ones are downtown.

★ **Villa del Sol.** A small hotel with a reputation as one of the best in Mexico, the Villa del Sol is set on the best beach in Zihuatanejo. Although the hotel has all the amenities of a large resort, guests are welcome to do nothing if they so desire.

Playa La Ropa, Box 84, 40880, tel. 753/4–22–39. 21 air-condi-tioned suites (1 and 2 bedrooms). Facilities: restaurant, pool, beach club, tennis court. Rate includes breakfast and dinner. Children under 14 not accepted in high season. AE, MC, V. Very Expensive.

Puerto Mío. This small hotel overlooking Zihuatanejo Bay is part of a marina and residential development. The suites, dis-tributed among several Mediterranean-style villas, are taste-fully furnished, and the decor makes wonderful use of the bright colors always associated with Mexico. *Playa del Almacen, Bahía de Zihuatanejo, 40880, tel. 753/4–37–45, fax 753/4–20–48. 35 suites. Facilities: pool, 2 tennis courts, restau-rant, bar. AE, DC, MC, V. Expensive.*

Villas las Urracas. Each of the units has a porch in a shaded gar-den, a kitchen, and a stove. Bungalows las Urracas is a great bargain—and lots of people know it, which places it greatly in demand. *Playa la Ropa, Box 141, 40880, tel. 753/4–20–49. 16 bungalows. No credit cards. Moderate.*

Catalina-Sotovento. Really two hotels in one, this oldie-but-goodie sits on a cliff overlooking the beach, to which you de-scend on stairs. The rooms are large and decorated in Mexican colonial style, with ceiling fans. *Playa La Ropa, Box 2, 40880, tel. 753/4–20–32 or 753/4–21–37. 124 rooms with bath. Facili-ties: 2 restaurants, 2 bars. Rate includes breakfast and lunch or dinner. AE, DC, MC, V. Moderate.*

★ **Villas Miramar.** Overlooking La Madera beach, the pretty stuc-co rooms are nicely decorated and have tile showers, air condi-tioning, and ceiling fans. This all-suite hotel is an excellent value, but you need to book three months in advance and some-times as much as two years ahead for Christmas and Easter. *Playa La Madera, Box 211, 40880, tel. 753/4–21–06. 18 suites. Facilities: restaurant, bar. AE, MC, V. Moderate.*

Avila. Downtown and close to all the pier activity, the Avila has large clean rooms (some are air-conditioned), TVs, and ceiling fans. *Calle Juan N. Alvarez 8, 40880, tel. 753/4–20–10. 27 rooms with bath. AE, MC, V. Inexpensive.*

Bungalows Pacíficos. Each of these bungalows features two spacious, well-ventilated rooms (sleeping four between them), a kitchen, and a large terrace. *Playa la Madera, 40880, tel. 4–21–12. 6 bungalows. No credit cards. Inexpensive.*

Fiesta Mexicana. The pretty Mediterranean-style rooms are surrounded by inviting palm-shaded gardens. Make reserva-tions well in advance, especially for the winter season. *Playa la Ropa, Box 4, 40880, tel. 753/4–37–76. 63 rooms with bath. Fa-cilities: restaurant, bar, pool. AE, DC, MC, V. Inexpensive.*

Irma. Simple and clean, this hotel on a bluff overlooking Playa La Madera (and accessible by a stairway) gets lots of repeat visitors. Guests may use the beach club at the Fiesta Mexicana. *Playa la Madera, Box 4, 40880, tel. 753/4–20–25. 75 rooms with bath. Facilities: restaurant/bar, 2 pools, tennis. AE, DC, MC, V. Inexpensive.*

The Arts and Nightlife A good way to spend an evening is at a happy hour in one of Ixtapa's hotels. Drinks are two for the price of one, and there is no cover charge to enjoy the live music. And don't miss the sun-set. **The Bay Club,** on the road to Playa La Ropa, has a marvel-ous ocean view. **Mariano's** bar in Zihuatanejo is where the locals hang out. The decor is nothing special, but everyone goes, especially singles. **Benji-Pio Bar,** in the El Portal shop-ping center, and **Le Club,** at the Westin Ixtapa, are also popular. **Christine's** at the Krystal in Ixtapa is the town's liveliest disco. **Tropicana Ixtapa,** behind Bancomer in the La Puerta Shopping Mall, is a combination restaurant, bar, and nightclub featuring live music and entertainment.

Euphoria is a spectacular new disco across from the Posada Real hotel. Every night, **Carlos 'n Charlies** has a dance party on a raised platform on the beach. On Friday night, the **Sheraton Ixtapa** and the **Villa del Sol** hotel in Zihuatanejo stage lively Mexican Fiestas that are lots of fun.

There is a movie house with several screens, the **Multicinema Vicente Guerrero,** next to the Somex bank on Calle Vicente Guerrero. Tickets cost about $1. Movies in English generally have Spanish subtitles.

10 Oaxaca

Introduction

Updated by Jim Budd

A former editor of The News, *Mexico City's English-language newspaper, and later a correspondent for* Copley News Service, the *New York Times and* Time-Life, *Jim Budd has lived in Mexico City for nearly 35 years. He is now a contributing editor to* Travel Weekly.

The city of Oaxaca (wah-**hah**-kah), one of Mexico's colonial treasures, sits on the vast, fertile, mile-high plateau of the Oaxaca Valley, encircled by the majestic Sierra Madre del Sur mountain range. It is located in the geographic center of the State of Oaxaca, of which it is the capital.

The state, Mexico's fifth largest, is situated in the country's southernmost section, bordered by the states of Chiapas to the east, Veracruz and Puebla to the north, and Guerrero (whose touristic claims to fame are Acapulco and Ixtapa) to the west. The south of Oaxaca State spans 509 kilometers (316 miles) of lush tropical Pacific coastline with magnificent beaches. Until recently, *las playas de Oaxaca* (the beaches of Oaxaca) have been relatively unknown and unexploited, except for the long-established small fishing town and seaside hideaway of Puerto Escondido and the even smaller town of Puerto Angel. But now newly created Huatulco, 125 kilometers (75 miles) west of Puerto Escondido, is beginning to appear on maps and is scheduled to become a world-class resort that someday may rival Acapulco and Cancún (*see* The Oaxacan Coast, *below*).

Oaxaca is endowed with a vast geographic and ethnic diversity. Together with neighboring Chiapas, Oaxaca is the most Indian state in Mexico, which explains its richness and variety in handicraft, folklore, culture, and gastronomy. Most are descendants of the Mixtec or Zapotec Indians, whose villages dot the valleys, mountainsides, and coastal lowlands. Today, two out of every three Oaxaqueños are Indians and come from one of 16 distinct groups within the Mixtecs and Zapotecs. They speak 52 dialects of eight distinct languages, and for the most part can barely understand each other. If they speak Spanish, it is a second language to them.

The Zapotecs and Mixtecs flourished in the area thousands of years ago. The archeological ruins of Monte Albán, Mitla, and Yagul are among the vivid reminders of their splendid legacies. Within a 40-kilometer (25-mile) radius of the city of Oaxaca, they all bear witness to highly religious, creative, advanced civilizations that were knowledgeable in astronomy and had a system of writing that may be the oldest in North America.

Their civilizations were conquered by the Aztecs who, in the 15th century, gave Oaxaca its name: *Huaxyaca*. In the Náhuatl language it probably means "by the acacia grove," referring to the location of the Aztec military base. Then came the Spanish Conquest in 1528. Cortés fell in love with the area and claimed much of it for himself, planning to build an estate for himself befitting his title, Marqués del Valle de Oaxaca. The estate was never built, although Cortés's descendants kept the property until Mexico's bloody 1910 Revolution.

Oaxaca's gift to Mexican politics were Presidents Benito Juárez and Porfirio Díaz, two of the country's most important leaders. Juárez, a Zapotec, was a sheepherder from San Pablo Gelatao, a settlement about 64 kilometers (40 miles) north of Oaxaca. As a child, he spoke only his native Zapotec tongue. Often referred to as Mexico's Abraham Lincoln, Juárez was trained for the clergy, but later studied law and entered politics. He was elected governor of the state (1847), chief justice of the Supreme Court of Mexico (1857), and then president (1859–1872),

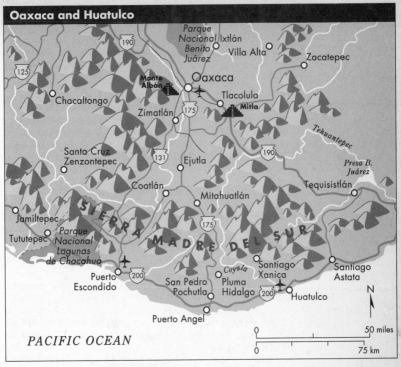

Oaxaca and Huatulco

Parque Nacional Benito Juárez
Villa Alta
Zacatepec
Ixtlán
Oaxaca
Monte Albán
Tlacolula
Mitla
Tehuantepec
Chacaltongo
Zimatlán
Santa Cruz Zenzontepec
Ejutla
Presa B. Juárez
Coatlán
Mitahuatlán
Tequisistlán
Jamiltepec
Parque Nacional Lagunas de Chacahua
Tututepec
SIERRA MADRE DEL SUR
Coyula
Santiago Xanica
Santiago Astata
Puerto Escondido
San Pedro Pochutla
Pluma Hidalgo
Huatulco
Puerto Angel
N
0   50 miles
0   75 km
PACIFIC OCEAN

defeating efforts to convert the country into a monarchy under
Maximilian. Porfirio Díaz, a Juárez general, seized the presi-
dency by coup in 1877 and held office until overthrown by the
Mexican Revolution in 1911.

Today, the capital is still the state's major attraction, with 2
million visitors a year. The city is traditionally Indian, but cosmopolitan touches are everywhere. Children sell woven bracelets and shoeshines around the city's many parks and squares,
while painters and weavers display their wares on grassy
lawns. Stark white galleries exhibit the pottery, textiles, and
fanciful wooden animals, called *animalitos*, that have drawn international attention to Oaxaca's artisans. Mariachis blare in
the streets; salsa and jazz bands percolate in intimate clubs.

The large, lively, and very European-looking zócalo draws both
visitors and locals to its shaded walks, commodious white park
benches, and, in its center, an ornate bandstand. Closed to mo-
tor-vehicle traffic, the zócalo still bustles at all hours of the
day—Indians on their way to the market early in the morning,
schoolchildren hurrying to their lessons in midday, and tourists strolling to the sidewalk cafés surrounding the square for
lunch or dinner.

Oaxaca celebrates Mexican holidays and its own state's fiestas
with an intensity of color, tradition, and talent that attracts
visitors in hordes. Hotels usually are booked solid around
Christmas, but the Tourist Office (*see* Important Addresses
and Numbers, *below*) often can help. On December 23, the
Noche de Rabanos (Night of the Radishes), the zócalo is packed

with growers and artists displaying their hybrid radishes carved and arranged in tableaux that depict everything from Nativity scenes to space travel. Prizes are awarded for the biggest and the best, and the competition is fierce. Other arrangements are made with *flores immortales* (small dried flowers) or *totomoxtl* (corn husks). Bring plenty of film.

Oaxaca's other major celebration is the *Guelaguetza* (Zapotec for offering or gift) held on the last two Mondays in July. Dancers from all the various mountain and coastal communities converge on the city bearing pineapples, baskets, weavings, and pottery. They perform elaborate dances in authentic costumes—everything from feathered headdresses to fluted white halos—from early morning until late at night at the Guelaguetza Auditorium, often shown on maps as *Lunes del Cerro* (Monday of the Hill). Contact the tourist office for information. Various hotels in town offer mini-Guelaguetzas at night; the best is at the Stouffer Presidente on Fridays.

Essential Information

Important Addresses and Numbers

Tourist Information
The English-speaking staff at the local tourist office can help plan your stay in the city as well as any excursions you might want to make to nearby ruins, such as Monte Albán, Mitla, and Yagul. *Cinco de Mayo 200 (corner of Morelos), tel. 951/6–48–28. Open daily 9–8.*

U.S. Consulate
The U.S. consular representative has offices at Macedonio Alcalá 201, int. 204 (tel. 951/4–30–54). *Open weekdays 9–2.*

Emergencies
Dial 06 locally for all emergencies, including police and hospital. The **police** direct line is 6–11–55 or 6–32–18; **hospital** (Red Cross) is 6–20–56.

Arriving and Departing by Plane

Airports and Airlines
There are no international flights to the city of Oaxaca, so travelers must fly into Mexico City and connect to either Aeroméxico or Mexicana, both of which fly nonstop to Oaxaca's **Zozocatlán Airport,** about 8 kilometers (5 miles) south of town. Their phone numbers in Oaxaca are: **Aeroméxico** (951/6–7101), **Mexicana** (951/6–7352). There is also service for triangle flight itineraries including the Oaxacan coastal resorts of Huatulco or Puerto Escondido. Local domestic airlines serving Oaxaca are: **Aerocaribe** (tel. 951/6–2247) from Mérida, Cancún, and Villahermosa; **Aerovias Oaxaqueñas** (tel. 951/6–1600) from Puerto Escondido, and **Aviacsa** (tel. 951/3–1809) from Tuxtla Gutiérrez, Villahermosa, and Palenque; **AeroVega** (tel. 951/6–27–77) from Puerto Escondido and Huatulco; and **Aeromorelos** (tel. 951/6–30–10) from Puerto Escondido and Huatulco. Taxis are plentiful, and microbuses are available from the airport to hotels in town.

Arriving and Departing by Car, Train, and Bus

By Car
From Mexico City take Mexico 190 (Pan American Highway) south and east through Puebla and Izúcar de Matamoros to Oaxaca—a distance of 546 kilometers (338 miles).

By Train The *Oaxaqueño* leaves Mexico City daily at 7 PM, arriving in Oaxaca the next morning at 9:30. The trains are clean, pleasant, and have sleeping and dining cars. Contact the **Mexican National Railways** (tel. 5/872–8245) or the train station at Calzada Madero, tel. 951/6–2564.

By Bus There are direct bus trips from Mexico City to Oaxaca, with innumerable stops in between. The first-class bus terminal is at Calzada Niños Héroes de Chapultepec, tel. 951/6–2270; the second-class bus station is on the Periferico at Las Casas, tel. 951/6–5776. Several bus lines serve the surrounding states and have desks at one or both terminals. Most routes are tortuous and grueling, going through on narrow mountain roads.

Guided Tours

Unless you're on a strict budget, take advantage of the many tour companies that offer guided trips to the archaeological sites, colonial churches and monasteries, the dozen or more outlying towns (some of which have weekly market days), and the folk-art centers. Several routes take in a sampling of each of the above, and each is different in character and color. The city tour runs $15 or so, and those to outlying areas cost $20 and up. There are licensed individual guides as well, available through the tourism office and the various agencies at $10–$20 per hour. **Turismo El Convento** (Calle Cinco de Mayo 300, in the main lobby of the Stouffer Presidente Hotel, tel. 951/6–0611), **Jade Tour Operators** (Porfirio Díaz 311, tel. 951/6–68–47), and **Agencia Marqués del Valle** (Portal de Clavería s/n, tel. 951/6–32–95) are among the most established agencies.

Exploring Oaxaca City

Numbers in the margin correspond to points of interest on the Oaxaca City map.

❶ The colonial heart of Oaxaca is laid out in a simple grid, with all major attractions within walking distance of one another. Most explorations of the town begin at the shady **zócalo,** the heart of the city and its pedestrian-only main square.

❷ On the zócalo's northwest corner is the **Catedral.** Begun in 1544, it was partially destroyed by earthquakes and not finished until 1733. The facade is Baroque, with a wood-cogged clock presented to the city by the King of Spain. *Av. Independencia 50, tel. 951/6–55–80. Open daily 8–8.*

Standing opposite the cathedral is the splendid 19th-century neoclassical **Palacio de Gobierno,** which serves as Oaxaca State House.

Walk north from the zócalo along the pedestrian mall whose full name is *Andador Turístico Macedonio Alcalá*. Pastel, restored colonial mansions and some of Oaxaca's best galleries, shops, and restaurants line this street. It is also lively and well-lit at night, and there are frequent outdoor art and crafts exhibits.
❸ After five short blocks you will come to the **Iglesia y ex-Convento de Santo Domingo,** the church and exmonastery of Santo Domingo. It is one of the most brilliantly decorated churches in Oaxaca, a city renowned for its many churches. The 16th-century monastery has an ornate carved facade between two high bell towers. The interior is a profusion of white and

Oaxaca City

gold, typical of the energy with which Mexico seized on the Baroque style and made of it something unique. *Calle Macedonio
Alcalá and Calle A. Gurrión, tel. 951/6–3720. Open Mon.–Sat.
7–1 and 4–8, Sun. 7–2.*

4 The old convent alongside the church houses the **Museo
Regional de Oaxaca,** or state museum, which is laid out in a series of galleries around the cloister. This ethnological collection
focuses on the various Indian groups (there were at least 52 dialects spoken in the state at last count) within Oaxaca. The centerpiece of the collection is the gold and jade treasures taken
from the tombs at Monte Albán, the Mixtec and Zapotec ruin
just outside Oaxaca. There is also a large collection of ceremonial masks and costumes from the different tribes of the valley;
some of the Indian women who come into town for the market
still wear traditional costumes and, with a bit of study here at
the museum, you will be able to identify their home villages.
*Tel. 951/6–2991. Small admission fee; free Sun. and national
holidays. Open Tues.–Fri. 10–6, Sat.–Sun. 10–5.*

As you leave the church and enter the wide Santo Domingo Plaza, you are likely to be accosted by Indian boys selling rough
sketches on bark (they make an easy-to-carry gift) and a variety of other crafts, or by smiling Indian girls with trays of fresh
gardenias that they will want to put in your hair or pin to your
clothes. From the front of the plaza, walk south, back down
Macedonio Alcalá until one block before the zócalo, you reach
Avenida Independencia. Turn right and walk six blocks until
5 you reach the Baroque **Basílica de la Soledad,** the Basilica of
Our Lady of Solitude. This 1682 structure houses the statue of

the Virgin, Oaxaca's patron saint. She stands in a gilded shrine and wears a magnificent robe of jewel-studded black velvet. She was found in the pack of a stray mule that had died. This event was construed by the faithful as a miracle and the church was built to commemorate it. To the faithful the statue had supernatural healing powers and has since been the object of fervent piety for the devout populace. *Av. Independencia 107 at Galeana, tel. 951/6–7566. Open daily 5:30 AM–9 PM.*

6 Backtracking toward the zócalo, take the first street north to Morelos and head east on Morelos to the **Museo de Arte Prehispánico "Rufino Tamayo"** (Tamayo Museum of Pre-Hispanic Art). This old, carefully restored colonial mansion with interior courtyard has a small but excellent collection of pre-Hispanic pottery and sculpture.

It was originally the private collection of the late painter-muralist Rufino Tamayo, who presented it to his hometown in 1979. There are exhibits from all over the country, arranged geographically and chronologically. Perhaps the most delightful item is the model of a ball court for sacred Indian games with figurines representing the participants and spectators. *Av. Morelos 25, tel. 951/6–4750. Small admission fee. Open Mon. and Wed.–Sat. 10–2 and 4–7, Sun. 10–3.*

7 Oaxaca has almost as many small museums as it has churches. Of particular note is the **Museo de Oaxaca** (City Museum), housed in the Casa de Cortés (Cortés's House), a former colonial residence. Inside are exhibits featuring the crafts and artworks of local artists in a variety of media. *Calle Macedonio Alcalá 202–204, tel. 951/6–8499. Admission free. Open Tues.–Fri. 10–2 and 5–8, weekends 10–2.*

8 Another colonial home is the **Museo Casa de Benito Juárez** (the Juárez House Museum). Memorabilia of the Mexican hero is displayed in this 19th-century house where he was a servant during his youth. *Calle García Vigil 609, tel. 951/6–1860. Small admission fee; free Sun. and holidays. Open Tues.–Sun. 9–7.*

9 An impressive tribute to the natives of the region is the **Fuente de las Siete Regiones** (the Fountain of the Seven Regions). It includes six statues of Indian women in regional garb and is topped by the figure of a male dancer from the Teotitlán del Valle wearing a plumed headdress.

Time Out | **Choco-Chips,** at Macedonio Alcalá 200 in the middle of the pedestrian walkway, is a *fuente de sodas* (soda fountain) selling ice-cream cones, sundaes, sodas, and hot dogs and popcorn to nibble on as you stroll.

Excursions from Oaxaca

10 The one-time holy city of more than 40,000 Zapotecs, **Monte Albán** is among the most interesting and well-preserved archaeological ruins in the country. Monte Albán overlooks the Oaxaca Valley from a flattened mountaintop 8.8 kilometers (5.5 miles) southwest of Oaxaca. The Zapotecs leveled the area in about 600 BC. They arranged the buildings along a perfect north-south axis, with the exception of one structure thought to have been an observatory that is more closely aligned with the stars

Monte Albán

than with the earth's poles. The oldest of the four temples is the **Temple of the Dancers,** so named because of the remains of elaborate carved stone figures that once covered the building. The figures are nude and, because of their distorted positions, have since come to be thought of not as dancers but as patients in what might have been a hospital or school of medicine. Another major point of interest is the ball court, site of a complicated game—part basketball, part soccer. The players' objective was to navigate the ball into a lowered area in the opponents' court with only their hips and elbows. There is some speculation that the captain of the losing team was sacrificed, but this has never been confirmed. About 1,000 years ago, the Zapotecs were conquered by the Mixtecs. The Mixtecs never lived in Monte Albán, but used it as a city of the dead, a massive cemetery of lavish tombs. More than 160 have been discovered, and in 1932, **Tomb 7** yielded a treasure unequaled in North America. Inside there were more than 500 priceless Mixtec objects, including gold breastplates; jade, pearl, ivory, and gold jewelry; and fans, masks, and belt buckles of precious stones and metals. All are now on view at the Regional Museum of Oaxaca.

There are special tourist buses to Monte Albán from the Mesón del Angel hotel running every hour on the half hour from 8:30 to 1:30, and one at 3:30; the last bus back is at 5:30. The fare is about $2 round-trip, or you can hire a taxi from your hotel or the zócalo. Most of the drive is straight up and tortuously slow but extremely scenic. *Follow Veinte de Noviembre out of the city across the Atoyac River (Río Atoyac); at the end of the bridge, take the right fork to the site. Small admission fee; Sun. and holidays free. The ruins are open daily 8–6.*

⓫ Thirty-four kilometers (24 miles) southeast of Oaxaca is **Mitla,** another complex of ceremonial structures started by the Zapotecs but taken over and heavily influenced by the Mixtecs. The name, from the Aztec word *mictlan,* means "place of the dead." The architecture here is totally different from that of any of the other ruins in the area. The walls of stone and mud are inlaid with small stones cut into geometric patterns, forming a mosaic that is Grecian in appearance. Unlike other ancient buildings in North America, there are no human figures or mythological events represented—only abstract designs. Another unique feature of Mitla is the fact that it was still in use after the Spanish conquest of Mexico. A trip here can be nicely combined with a stop at the Tule Tree (*see* Off the Beaten Track, *below*), the colonial church of Mitla, built against the walls of other Mixtec ruins, and the large open-air crafts market by the ruins. *Small admission fee; Sun. and holidays free. Archeological zone open daily 8:30–6.*

⓬ About 30 kilometers (19 miles) southeast of Oaxaca on the road to Mitla is **Yagul,** another group of ruins. Not as elaborate as Monte Albán, but set in a lovely spot on top of a hill, Yagul is certainly beautiful and interesting enough to make it worth the trip. This city is predominantly a fortress that is set slightly above a group of palaces and temples; it includes a ball court and more than 30 uncovered underground tombs. *Small admission fee; Sun. and holidays free. Archaeological zone open daily 8–6.*

Off the Beaten Track

No trip to Oaxaca would be complete without visiting at least some of the dozen or more villages surrounding the city. Many are known for the skills of their artisans, who use both ancient and modern techniques to create indigenous folk-art pieces that sell for hundreds of dollars around the world. Few who purchase the treasures have the opportunity to see the tiny towns and humble homes where the artists live, often among generations of families who have their own special designs for pottery, woven rugs, and wood carvings. A trip to a few of these towns can be combined with a visit to at least one archaeological site, a colonial church or two, and a regional market.

A west-to-south counterclockwise route from the city takes in **Atzompa,** where the descendants of Teodora Blanca create fanciful *muñecas* (dolls) from clay and other potters make the regions traditional green-glazed plates, bowls, and cups, all in array on Tuesday market day. In **Arrazola,** artists carve *animalitos,* grand dragons, and snakes from copal wood, then paint them with surrealistic designs in vivid colors. On Thursdays, **Zaachila** has the most authentic livestock and food market in the area, while **Etla's** Wednesday market is famous for its cheeses, mole, and chocolate. The southern route goes to **San Bartolo Coyotepec,** the center for glossy black pottery sold in people's yards and from a multistalled building on the side of the road. In **Santo Tomás Jalietza,** women work on small looms in the center of town, weaving elaborate belts and table runners from pastel cotton. Friday's market in **Ocotlan** is known for its handicrafts, especially woven baskets and cutlery.

An eastward route includes **Teotitlán del Valle,** where giant rug looms sit in front of many houses, and **Tlacolula,** where the Sunday market spreads for blocks around a Baroque 16th-century chapel. On Sundays it seems that all of Oaxaca take this route, starting at the Tule Tree (*see below*), then the ruins of Mitla and on to the crafts centers and market. The markets on other routes are held on special days throughout the week, and you can easily fill a week with tours and never see the same sight twice. If you have to budget your time, use tour guides for these trips so you don't miss out on the fascinating details.

(Prospective folk-art buyers should heed one major caveat, or risk being saddled with more than they expected. It is not too difficult to ship your purchases home from many of the city's shops and shipping services, provided you have a receipt showing that you paid the 10% sales tax on all items purchased. Since many of the artisans do not charge tax or pay tax to the government, you may have a hard time finding someone to ship your wares for you, and when you do, it will be very expensive. Ask for receipts, and for referrals to shipping agents. Also, check out the displays at the shops in town and learn about quality and design before you start spending millions of pesos. The people of Oaxaca are deservedly proud of their arts and will help you make wise selections.)

Standing 6.5 kilometers (4 miles) east of Oaxaca in Santa María del Tule is the **Tule Tree** (located on Tehuantepec Highway en route to Mitla), a huge ahuehuete cypress that is estimated to be more than 2,000 years old. One of the biggest in the world, it is some 140 feet high with roots buried more than 60 feet in the earth; it takes 35 adults with their arms outstretched to embrace it. The tree is the traditional center of the town of Santa María and is larger than the church behind it.

Shopping

Oaxaca City was and remains the focus of Indian life, mostly that of Zapotecs and Mixtecs who live in the valley and nearby mountains. They come to town to buy and sell, especially on Saturdays. While the market is no longer as colorful as in D. H. Lawrence's day (see his *Mornings in Mexico*), it remains an authentic exotic spectacle. This is the largest Indian market in all of Mexico, and only Michoacán can rival Oaxaca in the variety and quality of crafts. Expect hectic activity and bright colors. (It might come as a surprise not to hear much Spanish spoken at the markets, but rather the singsong Zapotec and Mixtec languages in which changes in the pitch of the voice change the meaning of the word.)

The Saturday market is held at the **Mercado Central de Abastos** (Central Supply Market) on the southern edge of town. Late Friday and Saturday, Indians stream to this site, spreading their wares over blocks and blocks of empty lots and through an enormous central warehouse. By noon on Saturday, the market is swarming with thousands of sellers and shoppers, and the experience can be quite overwhelming. Don't burden yourself with a lot of camera equipment or purses and bags; you'll have a hard enough time keeping track of companions in the jostling, bumping crowd. If you see something you really want, purchase it on the spot—you'll never find your way back. Check out the mounds of multicolored chiles and herbs, the piles of tropical fruits, the aisles of baskets, rugs, and jewelry. Some sections are filled with plastic household products, others with automotive and electronic gadgets. In the midst of it all are some great handicrafts: *huipiles* (embroidered blouses) that vary with the village of origin; *rebozos* (shawls) of cotton and silk; pottery shaped without a wheel; colorful woven baskets; wooden and tin toys; machetes with leather sheaths. A long row of flower stands line the outside of the warehouse; buy some gladiolas or tuberoses for your room. Bargaining is expected in the market. Exercise sensible caution with what you eat, however; pineapple peeled and sprinkled with chile powder will quench your thirst just as well as drinks made with questionable water.

The several market areas in Oaxaca are active daily, though Saturday is the busiest day. **Mercado Juárez** (Juárez Market) and **Mercado 20 de Noviembre** are two blocks south of the zócalo between Calle las Cases and Calle Mine. This two-block area has some crafts, but most tempting are the food stalls, which serve simple meals for locals and budget travelers alike. Two blocks farther south is **Mercado de Artesanías** (Crafts Market) at the corner of Calles José P. García and Ignacio Zaragoza, which features mostly textiles. While they tend their stands, Trique Indian women and children weave wall hangings with simple backstrap looms.

Besides having a mother lode of markets, Oaxaca also has some spectacular shops and galleries, most near the zócalo. To get a good overview of the arts and crafts from throughout the region, start your serious shopping at **Aripo** (about nine blocks north of the zócalo on Av. García Vigil 809, tel. 951/6–9211), a large showcase for all the regions of Oaxaca. The **Fonart** store (García Vigil at Nicolás Bravo) also has a representative selection of arts and crafts. Several gallery-style shops have opened, featuring the works of the true masters of the folk arts. The prices can be astounding, but as your eye becomes adjusted to the differences in quality and technique, you can appreciate the talent involved. **Chimalli** (García Vigil 513–A) has shelves and shelves of bright pink, orange, and purple carved copal cats, dogs, tigers, rabbits, and snakes with comical expressions. **La Mano Mágica** (Macedonio Alcalá 203, tel. 951/6–42–75) is an enormous gallery inside a hacienda, with rotating shows from Oaxaca's premier artists, working in pottery, textiles, wood, and paint. **Yalalag** (Macedonio Alcalá 104, tel. 951/6–2108) has delicately woven huipiles and a courtyard filled with pottery. Leading local artists exhibit and sell their paintings and sculptures at **Galería de Arte de Oaxaca** (Trujano 102, tel. 951/6–97–17).

Several shops specialize in gold and silver jewelry designed in the style of the jewels found at Monte Albán. Try **Palacio de las Gemas** (Morelos at Macedonio Alcalá, tel. 951/6–9596), **Artesanía Del Convento** (Macedonio Alcalá 503, tel. 951/6–4224), and **Oro de Monte Albán** (Adolfo C. Gurrión, tel. 951/6–4528). Most shops close from 2 to 4 in the afternoon; many are closed on Sunday.

Dining

Though you can dine on overpriced Continental food, one of the highlights of visiting Oaxaca is the opportunity to enjoy its traditional cuisine, one of the finest and most elaborate in all Mexico. Oaxaca is known as "the land of seven moles" because of its seven distinct kinds of multispiced mole sauces. Only one of them is made with chocolate, rivaling that of Puebla (mole poblano) in thickness and flavor because of the outstanding quality of the local chocolate. Cheeses and tamales are another treat. The tamales are steamed corn dough stuffed with chicken or pork. The home- and factory-produced mezcal differs in flavor with its maker, and can be as high as 80 proof, so be careful when you imbibe. One variety, slightly sweet, is flavored with oranges; others are sold in festive ceramic containers. The open-air cafés surrounding the zócalo are good for drinks, snacks, and people-watching, with the scene changing from peaceful serenity over early-morning coffee to pulsating frenzy in late evening. If you want to join the crowds at these restaurants, the *comida corrida* (set menu served at midday) makes an economical choice.

Highly recommended restaurants are indicated by a star ★.

Category	Cost*
Expensive	over $25
Moderate	$10–$25
Inexpensive	under $10

*per person, excluding drinks, service, and sales tax (10%)

Expensive

★ **La Morsa.** The name means "walrus," the setting is tastefully tropical amid gardens and fountains, and super-fresh seafood is the specialty. Try the *platón de mariscos* (shellfish platter) with oysters, shrimp, squid and octopus; or fish fillet *a la veracruzana* (with tomato sauce), *a la mexicana* (with green chile sauce), or *amarillo*, (with yellow *chile ancho* sauce). *Calzada Porfirio Díaz 240, Col. Reforma, tel. 951/5–2213. Reservations recommended. Dress: casual but neat. AE, DC, MC, V. Weekdays 1–5. Closed Sun.*

Stouffer Presidente. The El Refectorio dining room at this historic landmark hotel does not disappoint. The best meal is the weekend brunch, served from 8 to noon. Fragrant strawberry soup simmers in huge green *ollas* (ceramic pots), and colonial wooden tables are laden with fresh papaya and pineapple, *pan dulce* (sweet rolls), egg dishes, and *chilaquiles* (corn tortillas simmering in chicken sauce). Choose a table overlooking the garden courtyard, and linger over breakfast in this 16th-century convent. *Cinco de Mayo 300, tel. 951/6–0611. AE, DC, MC, V.*

★ **Victoria.** On a hill to the west of town, the Victoria Hotel's prime location is enhanced by the offering of the veranda dining room—Oaxacan specialties—and the view of hotel gardens and the countryside below. *Km 545 of Rte. 190, tel. 951/5–2633. AE, DC, MC, V. Closed Sun.*

Moderate

El Asador Vasco. Basque (*vasco*) cuisine is featured here along with an outstanding Oaxacan version of mole sauce—steamy, black, and marvelous on chicken and *cazuelas* (small casseroles of baked cheese, mushrooms, and garlic.) The tables overlooking the zócalo are in great demand; dine before 8 and you have a chance at one, if the dour waitresses approve of you. There's live music every night at 9 PM. Live serenading by the *tuna* student minstrels comes medieval Spanish style. *On the west side of the zócalo, upstairs, Portal de Flores 11, tel. 951/6–9719. AE, DC, MC, V.*

★ **Los Guajiros.** The inner courtyard of an old hacienda has been transformed into a tasteful restaurant/club where live salsa bands draw crowds after 10 PM. The waiters are pleasantly attentive, and the decor fascinating, with its pottery fountain, eclectic display of art and artifacts, and posters of jazz greats. *Macedonio Alcalá 303, tel. 951/6–5038. AE, MC, V. Open 6 PM–1 AM. Closed Sun.*

Mi Casita. Many in the know consider this the best place to enjoy the cuisine of Oaxaca. The actual dishes are displayed in the case by the door, so you can see what your food will look like before you order. This eatery is especially famous for *chapulines* (grasshoppers), but there are also more conventional dishes, such as enchiladas with chicken and spicy mole sauce. Try to get a table by the window (it's on the second floor), so you can watch the activity in the zócalo while you dine. *South side of the zócalo at Av. Hidalgo 616 altos, tel. 951/6–9256. AE, MC, V. Lunch only. Closed Thurs.*

★ **Ñuu-Luu.** The name in Mixtec, "picturesque place," couldn't be more appropriate. Located in a quaint colonial suburb in the northern part of town (just 8 minutes from the zócalo), this delightful veranda restaurant overlooks a large country garden lush with exotic fruit trees. Renowned chef-owner Guadalupe Salinas prepares gourmet Oaxacan specialties, including all seven kinds of moles, as well as pre-Hispanic delicacies. Also enticing is her filet of grouper in green sauce wrapped in banana leaves. Delicate desserts follow. *Iturbide 100, San Felipe del Agua, tel. 5–3187. Reservations recommended, especially on weekends. (Private transportation is provided from and to your hotel.) Dress: casual. AE, MC, V. Open daily; breakfast from 8 AM, lunch until 6 PM.*

Inexpensive **Catedral.** This local favorite is nicknamed the House of Filets. It offers no fewer than 11 tenderloin cuts, as well as regional dishes, hamburgers, sandwiches, and a variety of soups. Paintings by Guadalajara artist Miguel Angel Expanas fill the two pleasant dining rooms. *1 block from the zócalo, at the corner of Calle García Vigil and Av. Morelos, tel. 951/6–3285. MC, V.*

El Mesón. The spanking clean dining room and open-air kitchen in this restaurant right off the zócalo make it a favorite for locals and visitors, who stop by for a snack or full meal from the long paper menu, where you check off your items of choice. Try the *cebollitas* (grilled whole green onions) as a side dish with your *enchiladas cecina* (grilled strips of pork covered with chile powder) and fresh corn tortillas made at the torilleria at the entrance. For an intense sugar fix, have a cup of rich Oaxacan chocolate and a slice of nut pie. *Av. Hidalgo 805, at Cinco de Mayo, tel. 951/6–2729. MC, V.*

Lodging

Oaxaca has no high-rise hotels or luxury resorts, but it does have some magnificently restored properties and dozens of smaller, moderately priced accommodations, most in downtown locations.

Highly recommended lodgings are indicated by a star ★.

Category	Cost*
Expensive	over $100
Moderate	$50–$100
Inexpensive	under $50

*All prices are for a standard double room; excluding 10% tax.

Expensive

★ **Stouffer Presidente.** A monastic air lingers in the breezy patios and small enclosed gardens of this beautifully restored former convent (1576), which brings to mind its former name, El Convento. However, all rooms have deluxe conveniences. Stop in for a drink and look around even if you don't stay here. On Friday nights, the restaurant offers a variety of traditional Oaxacan dishes, and there is an excellent performance of regional dances. *Cinco de Mayo 300, tel. 951/6–0611 or 800/468–3571. 91 rooms. Facilities: restaurant, bar, pool. AE, DC, MC, V.*

★ **Victoria.** Surrounded by terraced grounds and well-kept gardens, this sprawling salmon-colored complex is perched on a hill overlooking the city. Draw back your curtains at dawn and catch your breath at the view: Oaxaca awakening under the Sierra Madre. The two-story hotel has a very good restaurant, tennis courts, heated pool, and disco, and the property is strewn with picture-perfect bougainvillea vines. Rooms, bungalows, and suites are available; be sure to request one with a view. *Km 545 of Mexico 190, tel. 951/5–2633. 151 rooms. Facilities: restaurant, disco, heated pool, tennis courts. AE, DC, MC, V.*

Moderate

Misión de los Angeles. Though this resort-style hotel is 10 blocks from the zócalo (a long, dark walk at night), its peaceful gardens, relaxed ambience, and colonial-style rooms make it a good choice. The hotel is near Plaza Juárez, a central park and plaza frequented more by locals than tourists, and the commodious dining room is popular with tour groups. *Calzada Porfirio Diaz 102; tel. 951/5–1500. 155 rooms. Facilities: bar, disco, game room, heated pool, gardens, tennis court, and jogging path. AE, DC, MC, V.*

Inexpensive

Marqués del Valle. Right on the plaza and in the middle of things, the property's restaurant serves a good breakfast, from bananas and cream to hotcakes. The cavernous marble hallways act like echo chambers for the cathedral bells from next door, which ring with appalling frequency. *Portal de Clavería 1, tel. 951/6–3295. 95 rooms. Facilities: TV, restaurant. AE, DC, MC, V.*

Mesón de Angel. This huge, plain hotel near the markets is a favorite with Mexican families and traveling salesmen. There is a big pool with a playground nearby, but few decorative touches. Still, the rooms are clean, the mattresses firm, the water hot, and the rates low. Tourist buses to Monte Albán and Puerto Escondido leave from here, and the travel agency is one of the best in town. *Francisco J. Mina 518, tel. 951/6–6666. 50 rooms. Facilities: restaurant, pool, private parking. MC, V.*

Principal. This popular budget hotel fills up quickly, but the owners can refer you to other hotels in the area as well as provide insider touring tips. Rooms in this colonial hacienda face a central courtyard abloom with red geraniums. Each room has small folk art touches, and the whole place has a friendly, homey feeling. *Cinco de Mayo 208, tel. 951/6–2535. 23 rooms. Facilities: small courtyard restaurant. No credit cards.*

Señorial. Beside El Jardín café on the zócalo, the Señorial caters quite comfortably to those who like being in the center of the action. Choose a room overlooking the zócalo if you like watching people rushing to work down freshly hosed-down streets, and enjoy the nightly reverie of mariachis and mingling. The rooms are large and casually comfortable, with little in the way of distinguishable touches. *Portal de Flores 6, off the zócalo, tel. 951/6–3933. 91 rooms. Facilities: bar, roof garden, pool. No credit cards.*

The Oaxacan Coast

Introduction

Oaxaca's 520-kilometer (322-mile) coastline is mainland Mexico's last Pacific frontier. Huatulco, 291 kilometers (180 miles) from the capital, is the newest project of Fonatur, the Mexican government's tourism developers. Already the tiny settlement has the state's only international airport, composed of a cluster of humble buildings with palm-frond roofs. Thus far fewer than a dozen hotels are in operation. The Bahías de Huatulco, as the area is being called, covers 51,900 acres of mountain lowlands and coastal stretches, the vast majority of which have never been developed.

Today Huatulco's beauty can best be seen from a boat (*see* Guided Tours, in Essential Information, *below*), since most of the bays are inaccessible by road. Tangolunda Bay is the site of the first three major hotels, and more hotels, condos, and time-share projects are under way. The towns of Santa Cruz and Crucecita are being developed as well. Santa Cruz has the waterfront pier and sightseeing boats, a sprawling artisan's market, and the major banks; Crucecita has a lavishly landscaped town square and the best restaurants outside the hotels. The town of Santa María Huatulco, for which the tourism destination is named, is 18 kilometers (11 miles) from the bays and is largely ignored by developers.

Puerto Escondido, 111 kilometers (69 miles) northwest of Huatulco, has long been prime territory for international surfers seeking the thrills of the Mexican Pipeline. For much of the year the waves here are rated right up there with the surf in Hawaii and Australia by those who can handle the murderous undertow. International surfing champions congregate here for tournaments in August and November. And when the crowds of surfers are gone in June and July, the town turns into a peaceful village where those seeking solitude stay at shaded, bougainvillea-covered haciendas and cabanas and alternate between their hammocks and crystalline blue pools. Puerto

Escondido has the coast's first airport (not international) and is in many ways better developed for travelers than Huatulco. Puerto Angel, midway between the two airports, is the budget traveler's destination, with a ragtag selection of hotels and bungalows spread into the hills overlooking the bay with, incongruously, a military installation smack in its center.

Essential Information

Arriving and Departing by Plane
Airports and Airlines

Puerto Escondido has a national airport with daily service from Oaxaca on **Aerovías Oaxaqueñas** (Av. Gasga, tel. 958/2–0132), and on tiny Cessnas run by **AeroVega** (tel. 958/2–0151). **Mexicana** (at the airport, tel. 958/2–0300) flies to Puerto Escondido daily from Mexico City and U.S. gateway cities.

Aeropuerto Bahías de Huatulco, the state's only international airport, is about 68 kilometers (42 miles) north of the Bahías de Huatulco. **Mexicana** (at the airport, tel. 958/4–0077) flies to Huatulco from Mexico City, Guadalajara, and several U.S. gateways. Regional carriers and private charters connect Huatulco with Oaxaca City, Mérida, and Cancún. Make reservations at the airport or through travel agencies, and be sure to confirm them 24 hours before your flight.

Arriving and Departing by Bus and Car
By Bus

Don't attempt to take the bus from Oaxaca to Puerto Escondido or Huatulco unless you have an iron-clad stomach and lots of time. The twisting, jarring ride through the mountains takes about 10 hours. The 370-kilometer (230-mile) trip from Acapulco is less strenuous, and buses run hourly. The bus station in Puerto Escondido is on the main highway and Avenida Oaxaca (tel. 958/2–0427). Huatulco's bus station is in La Crucecita, on Avenue Gardenias (no phone).

By Car

The drive from Oaxaca to the coast on Highways 175 and 190 is rough, and although the scenery through the mountains is superb, all your attention will be focused on the twisting, roughly paved road. Do not attempt this drive at night. Plan on taking 10 hours or so, and leave early enough to be at your destination before dark. Rental cars are available at major hotels along the coast, but the cost is prohibitive—over $100 a day for a Volkswagen Beetle, including insurance.

Getting Around
By Bus

As yet there are no direct buses stringing together Puerto Escondido, Puerto Angel, and Huatulco. Instead you must change buses at Pochutla, just off the highway near Puerto Angel, where buses converge in a large dirt lot. Drivers yell out their destinations and refuse to leave unless the bus has a sufficient number of passengers. If you are going to Huatulco do not take the bus marked "Huatulco," since it will leave you in the town of Santa María Huatulco, some 18 kilometers (11 miles) from the bays. Instead take a bus marked "Santa Cruz" or "Salina Cruz," both of which stop in Crucecita.

By Car

The drive on Highway 200 from Puerto Escondido to Huatulco is relatively hassle-free, and having a car allows you to turn off the main road onto unmarked dirt roads leading to secluded beaches. But rental cars are extremely expensive (about $100 per day, including insurance and unlimited mileage), and there is an additional drop-off fee if you don't return the car where you picked it up. **Budget** has franchises in Huatulco (tel. 958/4–0078) and Puerto Escondido (tel. 958/2–0312), and **Hertz** is present in Puerto Escondido (tel. 958/2–0035); nonaffiliated local firms often quote lower rates, but their vehicles may be in questionable condition.

Important Addresses and Numbers
Tourist Information

Information is scanty at best in this area. The **Puerto Escondido tourism office** (tel. 958/2–0358) is in the old part of town by the market, at the corner of Av. Hidalgo and Av. Oaxaca, on top of the Super Estrella grocery store. The office is open Monday–Friday 9–2 and 5–8, and Saturday 10–1. In Huatulco the **Fonatur** office (tel. 958/1–0094) is across from the Sheraton Hotel in Tangolunda Bay. Hours are erratic, information scarce, and there is no state tourism office yet. You're better off using the travel agents in the hotels.

Guided Tours

In **Puerto Escondido** the most exciting tours are run by ornithologist Michael Malone, who offers dawn and sunset tours into the Manialtepec Lagoon, a prime bird-watching area. Tours are $30 per person and can be arranged through your hotel, through **Turismo Rodimar** (Av. Gasga, tel. 958/2–0734), or through the **Agencía García Rendon** (Av. Gasga, tel. 958/2–0114). This last agency is the most comprehensive in town for all sorts of information and is open daily 7 AM–9 PM.

The safest swimming and snorkeling beaches in Puerto Escondido are **Puerto Angelito** and **Carrizalillo,** a 10-minute boat ride from the town beach. Transportation is available from the Agencía García Rendon (*see above*) or from the many fishermen who park their *pangas* (small boats) on the sand near town. The ride should cost $5–$10.

In **Huatulco** you can't possibly grasp the beauty of the bays without touring them by boat. The venture takes four to six hours, with stops at Bahía San Augustín or El Maguey (where fishermen grill their catch over open fires) and at one of several secluded beaches for swimming and snorkeling. Bay cruises cost about $35 per person and are available at the boat dock in Santa Cruz.

Turismo Tangolunda, with offices in the Royal Maeva hotel (tel. 958/1–0000) and in Santa Cruz (Av. Oaxaca and Calle Zoquiapan, tel. 958/1–0024; in the U.S., 800/468–5639) is the most comprehensive travel agency in Huatulco and has bay and bus tours to Puerto Angel and Puerto Escondido (about $60 per person) and plane tours to Oaxaca ($220 per person). The **Sheraton** (Blvd. Benito Juárez, tel. 958/1–0055) and **Club Med** (Tangolunda Bay, tel. 958/1–0161) also have travel agencies.

Exploring the Oaxacan Coast

Puerto Escondido is the first coastal town in Oaxaca south of Acapulco on Highway 200. The airport is on the northern edge of town, as are the hotels favored by charter groups. **Playa Bacocho,** just south of the airport, is being developed as a new housing-and-hotel development, and some inviting bars and restaurants have opened in this area. Be sure to catch the sunset at least once from the gardens of the **Posada Real hotel,** and walk down the cliff to Coco's Beach Club, a lavish restaurant (with erratic quality and service) and a pool right on the beach.

The main intersection in Puerto Escondido is at Highway 200 and Avenida Alfonso Perez Gasga, which travels south into the tourist zone. On the north side of the highway this street is called Avenida Oaxaca, which leads to the dirt streets and markets of the town. The bus station is on this corner. Traveling down a steep hill, Avenue Gasga passes many of the tourist hotels; at the bottom, traffic is prohibited and the street becomes a four-block-long pedestrian mall lined with shops, restaurants, and lodgings that spread to the sands of the main beach. The panga fleet is at the north end of this beach, where the water is calm albeit polluted. **Laguna Agua Dulce** is at the south end of the tourist strip, followed by **Marinero Beach,** then a sharp outcropping of rocks, and, finally, the most famous beach of all, **Zicatela.**

One of the top 10 surfing beaches in the world, Zicatela is a long stretch of cream-color sand battered by the **Mexican Pipeline,** as this stretch of mighty surf is called. In August and November international surfing championships are held here, and the town fills with sun-bleached blonds of both sexes intent on serious surfing and hard partying. Do not swim in these waters unless you can withstand deadly undertows and rip currents. Instead watch the surfers at sunset from the palapa restaurant at the **Hotel Santa Fe,** surely the prettiest hotel in town.

Puerto Angel, about 81 kilometers (50 miles) south of Puerto Escondido, is a small village on a beautiful bay which, sadly, shows signs of pollution these days. The central town beach has been taken over by the Navy, and the most popular swimming-and-sunning territory is at **Playa Panteón,** just past the oceanfront cemetery. The biggest attraction in Puerto Angel is **Playa Zipolite,** a bay 6 kilometers (3.7 miles) west of town. Known for its nude sunbathing, Zipolite is a favorite with surfers and travelers who are content with a hammock on the beach and little else in the way of creature comforts. The undertow is dangerous here, and the local officials occasionally ban nudity.

Bahías de Huatulco, the Fonatur development, is suffering growing pangs, with some bizarre results. Modern streets and lightposts are in place, but telephones are scarce except in the first-class hotels. There are branches of Mexico's main banks, but pesos are sometimes hard to come by. Although rental cars are available, maps are nonexistent, and the vast majority of Huatulco's tourists rarely leave their hotels. The Huatulco of the future is most evident at **Tangolunda Bay,** where three major hotels are in full swing, and parasailers glide over fleets of sightseeing boats. A small shopping/restaurant center is located by the entrance to the Sheraton, but most of the shopping and dining takes place in the towns of Santa Cruz and Crucecita, each about 10 minutes from the hotels by taxi. **Santa Cruz** is located on the bay of the same name, where glass-bottom boats and sightseeing tours are available. The waterfront is lined with bright-blue, pink, and orange shacks offering a disappointing selection of crafts and souvenirs for sale. A central zócalo with a wrought-iron gazebo has been built nearby, and tourists and locals alike mingle in the grassy plaza. At press time several hotels and restaurants were under construction in Santa Cruz.

Crucecita, just off Highway 200, is more developed, with a few condominium complexes and a central park. Modern buildings with arches and balconies are going up along the streets by the park, and this is becoming the place to hang out at sidewalk cafés and to shop in trendy boutiques. The bus station and long-distance telephone office are here, along with a smattering of budget rooms.

Dining

.Seafood is the coast's best dining bet; everything else is mediocre. Unfortunately, Oaxacan cuisine—the cheeses, moles, and meats that make dining in the capital memorable—is in short supply here. Still, it's hard to spend more than $15 on a meal in any establishment. The best choices for restaurants continue to be in the hotels or on the beach. Puerto Escondido now has three vegetarian restaurants; Puerto Angel has meager offerings; and Huatulco's restaurants are gradually struggling to their feet. Dress is casual at all restaurants except where noted, and reservations are not necessary.

Highly recommended restaurants are indicated with a ★.

Category	Cost*
Expensive	over $15
Moderate	$10–$15
Inexpensive	under $10

*per person, excluding drinks, service, and 10% sales tax

Huatulco   **Cardinale.** Your only choice for glamorous dining thus far is in the Sheraton Hotel. The menu emphasizes Northern Italian dishes—any of the pastas are a good choice—and the ambience is decidedly upscale, with heavy polished tables and chairs, and stained-glass doors, and elaborate floral arrangements. Try the hotel's Mexican restaurant as well. *Sheraton Hotel, Blvd. Benito Juárez, Tangolunda Bay, tel. 958/1–0055. AE, MC, V. Closed lunch. Expensive.*

Restaurante María Sabina. This is a great place to sit at a sidewalk table and watch the locals and tourists mingle in Crucecita's pretty plaza. No mystery exists here about how your food is prepared, since the grill is on the sidewalk, and the cook will chat with you as he chars your steak or fish. *West side of plaza, Crucecita, no phone. No credit cards. Moderate.*

1/2 Carlos 'n Charlie's. The odd name refers to the size of this closetlike addition to the Carlos 'n Charlie's chain, with all the trappings of the famous franchise packed in meager space. 1/2 has dependable food—barbequed ribs, tortilla soup, burgers, and fries—and fun for those who like downing shots of tequila and beer. *Ave. Flamboyan, Crucecita, tel. 958/7–0005. Closed lunch. MC, V. Inexpensive.*

Puerto Angel   **Posada Cañon Devata.** The communal health-food dinner at this small hotel is a local institution, and most travelers stop by at least once to compare notes with others. The menu changes daily, so you're never sure what the meal will be, but it's always healthy, filling, and unusual. *Posada Cañon Devata Hotel, past Playa Panteón, no phone. No credit cards. Closed lunch. Moderate.*

El Capi. There's nothing to distinguish this small hotel and restaurant from all the rest, except the gargantuan portions of fresh fish and Mexican dishes served by the friendly, talkative owners. In fact, this is one of the best spots in town to get the lowdown on what's happening. *Blvd. Virgilio Uribe, near cemetery, no phone. No credit cards. Inexpensive.*

Restaurant Ley vis Y Vincente. This standard palapa on the beach is a good place to stop for a cold drink and a filling meal of

Huevos Mexicana (scrambled eggs with green pepper, tomatoes, and onions) for breakfast or for tacos any other time of day. *Playa Panteón, no phone. No credit cards. Inexpensive.*

Puerto Escondido
★

Art 'n Harry's. Formerly La Fonda de los Tres Osos, this favorite gathering place is now run by a pair of Canadians. Burgers and steak are popular, but the shrimp and snapper are far more flavorful. One flight up, this seafront bistro overlooks the beach, and occasionally offers live guitar music in the evenings. *South end of Zicatela Beach, no phone. No credit cards. Expensive.*

Santa Fe. By all means treat yourself to at least one meal here. Half the menu is vegetarian and the other half filled with healthy portions of grilled fish, meats, and poultry. The fruit salad is a pyramid of papaya, pineapple, and melon; the coconut ice cream tastes like it just came off the tree; and the substantial shrimp salad with avocado is delicious. The tables overlooking the surf are great at dawn and sunset, and it's nice to relax in the shade under a whirring fan in the noonday heat. *Hotel Santa Fe, Calle del Moro, tel. 958/2–0170. MC, V. Expensive.*

La Perla Flameante. The fresh dorado, shark, tuna, and red snapper come with teriyaki, cajun, or garlic seasonings at this second-story bamboo restaurant overlooking the beach. Make sure to order the deep-fried onion rings and zucchini. *Av. Gasga, near end of tourist strip, no phone. MC, V. Closed lunch. Moderate.*

La Posada. The open grill at the front of the restaurant draws crowds—patrons spot the lobster or steak they want and personally hand it to the chef. An eclectic selection of background music includes fifties rock 'n' roll, jazz, and show tunes and keeps the atmosphere lively. Sit in the big open-air dining room or at one of the tables on the beach, then order the house cocktail (a cooling blend of fruits and tequila) and settle back for a relaxing dinner. *Av. Gasga, no phone. MC, V. Closed lunch. Moderate.*

Pizzaland. Mario the proprietor is a courtly, generous Italian who makes his customers feel very much at home. Pizzas with all sorts of exotic toppings are the menu's main attraction; even better are the gigantic green salads made with vegetables washed in purified water (a precaution one cannot rely on at other restaurants). *Av. Gasga just past the chain ending tourist zone, no phone. No credit cards. Moderate.*

Cafe Il Capucccino. Coconut-shell masks adorn the rustic bamboo walls in this small coffeehouse, where locals play backgammon for hours in the shade at tiny wrought-iron tables. Try the lime mousse or *crepas con cajeta* (crepes with caramel sauce) for dessert, and sample yogurt and fruit for breakfast. *Av. Gasga, tel. 958/2–0334. No credit cards. Inexpensive.*

Restaurante Cabañas Marinero. Located just south of the lagoon, this palapa restaurant offers several varieties of pizza (baked in an open-air, wood-burning oven on the beach) and fresh-fish dinners for $6 or so. The most expensive item on the menu is the *Vuelve a la Vida*, or "Come Back to Life" seafood cocktail, made with four kinds of fish and shellfish, for $7—definitely worth trying. An added attraction is the parade of extremely large brown pigs that wanders through the lagoon and down the beach, oblivious to the diners nearby. A wonderful unnamed bakery is just up the dirt street from here; it sells great breads and croissants. *Playa Marinero, no phone. No credit cards. Inexpensive.*

Restaurante Vegeteriano. This small café and health-food store on the upper end of the Gasga hill has all sorts of salads, as well as *licuados* (milkshakes), made with yogurt, papaya, and mango; or the fresh carrot juice, all for under $5. Try the vegetable soups. *Av. Gasga, no phone. No credit cards. Inexpensive.*

Lodging

Hotel rates vary considerably in this area. Even the fanciest hotels in Puerto Escondido charge less than $100 per day for a double, yet those in Huatulco can cost considerably more. The Club Med and Royal Maeva have the highest rates but are all-inclusive, which works well in Huatulco because restaurants and other tourist services are scarce. The high season along the coast runs from December 21 to April 15; rates increase by 20% during this time. Budget accommodations are scarce in Huatulco, although more moderately priced rooms are becoming available.

Category	Cost*
Very Expensive	over $100
Expensive	$50–$100
Moderate	$30–$50
Inexpensive	under $30

*All prices are for a standard double room, excluding 10% tax.

Huatulco **Club Med.** The club's biggest compound in Mexico sprawls over a sloping hillside overlooking Tangolunda Bay. The 500 rooms are spread out in lavender-and-blue clusters with giant color-coded towers on top to help guests find their way home. There are three beaches, and the list of amenities is endless. The emphasis is to keep the guests so absorbed in Club Med's goings on that they never leave the grounds. Week-long fitness programs are particularly popular. Packages with air-fare included are usually available. Advance booking is mandatory. *Tangolunda Bay, tel. 958/1–0161. Reservations: 40 W. 57th St., New York, NY 10019, tel. 800/CLUB–MED. 500 rooms. Facilities: 5 restaurants, 3 pools, 3 beaches, tennis courts, arts-and-crafts center, fitness center, water sports. AE, MC, V. Very Expensive.*

Royal Maeva. This all-inclusive resort caters to charter groups and Mexican families as well as lone travelers. The emphasis is on fun, fun, fun, and if you're not a fan of loud music, stay in a room that's away from the pool area. The ever-present, ever-upbeat recreation leaders here are fanatically in love with Huatulco and will do all they can to make sure you feel the same. The beach is colorfully littered with sunbathers sipping piña coladas while watching the tow boats depart for the more secluded bays; and the rooms are spacious, colorful, and adorned with heavy blue-and-peach fabric and light-wood furniture. The meals, included in your tab, are uninspired but generous; breakfast is by far the best. There are plenty of activities, from talent shows to sports demonstrations. *Tangolunda Bay, Blvd. Benito Juárez, 227, Bahías de Huatulco, tel. 958/1–0000. Reservations in U.S., tel. 800/431–2822. 300 rooms. Facilities: restaurant, pool, beach, tennis, water sports, fitness center. AE, MC, V. Very Expensive.*

Sheraton. The only hotel on Tangolunda that's not all-inclusive, the Sheraton is also the most user-friendly, with boutiques, a travel agency, a selection of restaurants, and a triangular pool. The rooms are done in soft peaches and pinks, with blessedly powerful air-conditioning, heavy drapes to block the sun, and bathtubs—a real luxury in these parts. *Tangolunda Bay, Blvd. Benito Juárez, tel. 958/1–0055. Reservations in U.S., tel. 800/325–3535. 346 rooms. Facilities: 4 restaurants, 3 bars, pool, tennis courts, beach, fitness center, water sports. AE, MC, V. Very Expensive.*

Hotel Castillo Huatulco. The closest accommodations to the plaza and Santa Cruz Bay are the brand-new rooms at the Castillo, which looks like a motel from the front and a quasi-resort inside. New in 1991, the Castillo is a good choice if you want to be near the marina and rental boats, close to the luxury hotels, and away from the business bustle of Crucecita. *Blvd. Bahía Santa Cruz, tel. 958/7–0051. 56 rooms. Facilities: restaurant, bar, pool, tennis court. MC, V. Expensive.*

Posada Binniguenda. The first hotel in Santa Cruz, the Binniguenda is not on the beach but stands close to the marina. As development continues the hotel will be in the center of the town's hotel/restaurant/shopping scene. The dusty-pink adobe, red-tile-roof building forms a "U" around the courtyard and pool. The rooms have heavy colonial furnishings, commodious showers, and wood-and-glass French doors leading to small wrought-iron balconies. The pool bar is an ideal retreat from the midday sun—try the fresh lemonade for a quick reviver. *Blvd. Benito Juárez 5, Box 44, Santa Cruz, tel. 958/4–0077. Reservations in U.S., tel. 800/262–2656. 75 rooms. Facilities: restaurant, pool. MC, V. Expensive.*

Hotel Griffer. Crucecita's only hotel is the least expensive place to stay in Huatulco and thus fills up quickly. Located on a busy in-town corner, the hotel feels like a business traveler's quarters, with a no-nonsense desk clerk, simple serviceable rooms, and no frills. The restaurant is operated separately from the hotel, and is a good spot for down-home breakfasts and lunch with the locals. *Av. Guamuchil at Carrizal, Crucecita, tel. 958/7–0048. 18 rooms. Facilities: restaurant. MC, V. Inexpensive.*

Puerto Angel   **Angel del Mar.** The road to Puerto Angel's most expensive hotel is a steep, twisting affair you wouldn't want to attempt on foot except in the coolest hours of the morning. The view from the top takes in the panorama of town and coast, and sunsets are spectacular. The rooms, however, are only adequate, and the restaurant is expensive. Because all supplies have to be carted up the hill, the hotel sometimes runs out of water, among other essentials. The telephone number is now simply 2; the hotel can be reached only through operator assistance since dial phones have yet to arrive in Puerto Angel. *Dirt road past Playa Panteón, in Puerto Angel, no phone. 45 rooms. Facilities: restaurant, pool. MC, V. Moderate.*

Posada Cañon Devata. The buildings look like colonial-style tree houses nestled in a shady, forested canyon. Rocking chairs carved from logs sit outside the rooms, which are small, clean, and cool. The beach is a three-minute walk away and is visible from the rooftop restaurant shaded by a giant palapa. The bungalows here have kitchenettes. *Off Blvd. Virgilio Uribe at end of road, Box 74, Pochutla, no phone. 10 rooms, 3 bungalows.*

Facilities: restaurant. No credit cards. Closed May–June. Moderate.

La Cabaña de Puerto Ángel. Just across from Playa Panteón, this is the best located hotel in town. The accommodating proprietors keep a big pot of coffee at the front desk for early risers, along with a library of paperback novels and maps of Mexico. The rooms have small balconies, louvered windows with screens, ceiling fans, and cheery yellow-stripe spreads on the thin mattresses. Some rooms don't have curtains. *Across from Playa Panteón. 23 rooms. MC, V. Inexpensive.*

Puerto Escondido
★

Hotel Santa Fe. Your room here will have colonial furnishings, a tile bath, drapes and spreads of heavy woven Mexican cloth in soothing lavenders and blues, a telephone, air-conditioning and a ceiling fan, a television if you request one, and maybe a balcony overlooking the pool. All the fine details come from Mexico's crafts centers—the multicolor tiles lining the steps are from Puebla, the cowhide chairs from Guadalajara. No wonder more than half the hotel's guests come back year after year, and stay put for weeks at a time. The owners of the Santa Fe also operate a small country inn about two hours from Puerto Escondido, in the pine forests of the Oaxaca mountains, amid coffee plantations and crystal-clear rivers. *Calle del Morro by Zicatela beach, Box 95, tel. 958/2–0170. 39 rooms. Facilities: restaurant, pool, tours. AE, MC, V. Expensive.*

Paraíso Escondido. Puerto Escondido's only funky, colonial-style hotel climbs the hillside overlooking Avenue Gasga and has a down-home, friendly aura that encourages mingling around the pool. No two rooms are alike, and they are furnished with a mishmash of wood dressers, tin mirrors, and bright-blue drapes and spreads. Take time to examine the stone statues spread about the property. *Av. Gasga, tel. 958/2–0444. Reservations: Box 20–187, Mexico 20, Mexico City D.F. 20 rooms. Facilities: restaurant, bar, pool. MC, V. Expensive.*

Posada Real. Here's a resort that almost satisfies the term "luxurious." It sits atop a hill overlooking the sea with air-conditioned rooms in a complex of four-story buildings surrounding lovely gardens. One drawback is the chore involved in clambering down to the beach, where you'll find the surf is too rough for safe swimming. Nearby, however, a pool and Coco's Beach Club, one of the best restaurants in the area, offer refreshment. Two more pools, a coffee shop, a lively bar, and well-trained staff round out the amenities. *Blvd. Benito Juárez, Playa Bacocho, about 3 miles above the village, tel. 958/ 2–0133. 100 rooms. Facilities: restaurant, 3 pools, bar, coffee shop. AE, MC, V. Expensive.*

Villas Los Delfines. An enterprising couple from the capital have created this solitary paradise atop a hill overlooking the coast, with eight first-class cabañas spread along the hillside. The cabañas have full kitchens, separate bedrooms, and hammocks hanging outside. The husband is an architect with a fine eye for classical Mexican design, and blooming bougainvillea climbs all over the grounds. The cool blue pool sits in the middle of the compound, beside a palapa restaurant. Staying here is like visiting gracious friends who happen to have a few extra homes for guests. There's a long path down the hill to Zicatela Beach, and there is a market nearby. *Cerro de la Iguana, Carretera Costera del Pacífico Km. 71 Box 150, tel. 958/2– 0467. 8 cabañas. Facilities: restaurant, bar, pool, satellite TV. MC, V. Expensive.*

Casas de Playa Acali. You can choose from four sizes and styles of accommodations at this cluster of cabañas by the main beach. The least expensive rooms are in small bungalows without air conditioning or patios; prices rise with the size of the cabañas, number of beds, and the extent of kitchen facilities. This is a good choice for groups of four or six surfers who want to share expenses and prepare their own meals. *Calle del Morro, tel. 958/2–0754. 10 cabañas. Facilities: kitchens. MC, V. Moderate.*

★ **Jardín Escondido.** Of the dozens of bungalow/cabaña hotels near the beach, this place stands out for its cleanliness and its long lap pool. The cabanas have hammocks hanging out front, mosquito nets over the beds, tile baths and showers, and freshly painted white brick walls. There's a small restaurant by the pool, and bottles of purified water to take to the beach are available at the front desk. Weekly and monthly rates are available. *Calle del Morro 300, Box 97, tel. 958/2–0348. 8 bungalows. Facilities: restaurant, pool. MC, V. Moderate.*

Casa de Huespedes Pakololo. Surfers congregate in the patios of this small guest house, keeping an eye on the waves while listening to the latest rock tunes on their boom boxes. The two bungalows have full kitchens; the eight simple rooms have refrigerators, ceiling fans, louvered windows, and mosquito netting over the beds. The rates are just about the lowest on the beach, and the clientele is young and ready to party. *Calle Morro, Zicatela Beach, tel. 958/2–0759. 2 bungalows, 8 rooms. No credit cards. Inexpensive.*

Castillo del Reyes. Proprietor Don Fernando runs an amiable show in his small, immaculately clean establishment. With no pool or restaurant, the clients tend to congregate around the front desk, drinking their own sodas and beer. The simple rooms have clean white walls and powerful showers with plenty of hot water and may be getting air-conditioning soon. *Av. Gasga, tel. 958/2–0442. 17 rooms. No credit cards. Inexpensive.*

Hotel Arco Iris. This three-story colonial style hotel is on Zicatela Beach, south of the Santa Fe, and is a good choice for those who want privacy and security but cannot afford the Santa Fe. Most rooms overlook the beach and have ceiling fans, fairly firm double beds, and private balconies with hammocks. Eight of the rooms have kitchenettes. The third-floor restaurant is a great spot for sunset watching. *Calle del Morro, Zicatela Beach, Box 105, tel. 958/2–0432. 18 rooms. Facilities: restaurant, pool, surfboard rental. MC, V. Inexpensive.*

11 Chiapas and Tabasco

Introduction

By Erica Meltzer

Updated by
Barbara Franco

Newcomers to Mexico might want to save Chiapas and Tabasco for a later visit. Although uniquely interesting, they are not an easy region to see and to appreciate. For those truly looking for an outstanding travel experience, however, a well-planned trip to this area can be very satisfying. Though the two states have several American-style deluxe hotels, it is the smaller, locally run properties, with their foibles as well as their charms, that are more representative of the area's accommodations. Unlike beach resorts such as Cancún and Acapulco, this area is not one that visitors can jet to in a few hours from major U.S. gateways. Substantial ground transportation, either by bus or by car, is absolutely necessary. People working in the tourist industry often don't speak English and are not as practiced in dealing with tourists as they are elsewhere in Mexico. Tourist information can be more difficult to obtain, and locals may be a bit more reserved.

On the other hand, the less touristic nature of these states has its own appeal. In Chiapas, at least, the locals are less self-conscious, less sophisticated, and they seem less out to make a quick buck. And though gringos are hardly a novelty, it can be refreshing to be noticed as an outsider rather than ignored as one more anonymous face in an ongoing "invasion."

The Indians' wariness of strangers has a historic basis. A bloody past of exploitation by and fierce confrontation with outsiders remains vividly present, as already impoverished indigenous communities in Chiapas are continually forced to compete for their lands with wave after wave of new settlers. Most of eastern Chiapas borders on Guatemala, and during the past 20 years it has been overrun, first by the landless poor relocated from other parts of Mexico, and then by tens of thousands of Guatemalan refugees. Because of its isolation, Chiapas has been at the margin of the nation's development. It is one of the poorest states in Mexico, with appallingly high rates of alcoholism, violence, illiteracy, and death due to unhygienic conditions. Land distribution, too, is skewed: 1% of the landowners hold 45% of the territory, keeping the colonial system nearly intact, and repression is rampant. Not surprisingly, tensions are high among the various Indian groups themselves; between the Indians and the mestizos (those of both Spanish and Indian descent); and between the Indians and PEMEX, the state oil monopoly, which has built a highway along the Guatemalan border, destroying lands and wildlife in the process.

Although it was nominally made rich half a century ago with the discovery of oil in the gulf, Tabasco maintains a rebellious tradition. During the 1920s and 1930s, Tomás Garrido Canabal, a vehemently anticlerical dictator, outlawed priests and had all the churches either torn down or converted to other uses. Riots, deportations, and property confiscations were common. When British writer Graham Greene visited Tabasco in 1938, he called it "the Godless state." No wonder he found people voicing "the rather wild dream . . . of a rising which will separate Chiapas, Tabasco, Yucatán, and Quintana Roo from the rest of Mexico and of an alliance with Catholic Guatemala"! These somber facts are not likely to intrude on the visitor's consciousness, although they should be borne in mind. The rest of

Mexico, too, has a turbulent past. But if Tabasco's past is barely evident today, a wholly different spirit prevails in Chiapas.

Chiapas will not be off the tourist track for long. In the planning stage is an American-sponsored "Mayan Route," which
will carve highways of tourism into the hinterland in the name
of preservation and development. And the Lacondon jungle is
already disappearing, its Indian inhabitants being driven to
adopt poor imitations of Western lifestyle. Massive erosion and
deforestation are taking their toll as the new settlers burn the
forest and exhaust the soil by planting corn and raising cattle.

For the present, however, travelers threading their way along
tortuous mountain roads—full of dramatic hairpin turns along
the edges of desolate ravines—will come upon remote clusters
of huts and cornfields planted on near-vertical hillsides. They
will pass Indian women wrapped in deep blue shawls and
coarsely woven wool skirts, and Indian children selling fruit by
the roadside. Chiapas has 14 separate Indian groups, primarily
the highland-dwelling Maya Tzeltals and Tzotzils, many of
whom do not speak Spanish. As they have for centuries, the Indians travel seasonally between their homes in the highlands
and the plantations in the lowlands, which still need subsist-
ence-wage workers, and between Mexico and Guatemala.

Tabasco is of interest primarily to hardy adventure-seekers,
lured by its minor ruins and the wild rivers surging through the
jungle. Less adventurous travelers will find Villahermosa's
CICOM museum of pre-Columbian archaeology and the collection of Olmec heads at Parque La Venta a good introduction to
the Indian heritage so evident in Chiapas. (And no, Tabasco
sauce does not come from here or from anywhere else in Mexico; it originated in Louisiana.)

The highlight of Chiapas and Tabasco is the town of San Cristóbal de las Casas. It can be reached by car or bus from either
Villahermosa, a convenient point of departure because of its
airport and museum, or Tuxtla (**Tus**-tla) Gutiérrez, which has
the only other major airport in the region. A sample itinerary
might begin in Villahermosa, then head southeast to take in the
ruins of Palenque, stay for a few nights in San Cristóbal, then
on to Tuxtla. From Palenque you can arrange an excursion to
the Mayan ruins of Bonampak and Yaxchilán (Yas-chee-**lan).** A
popular day trip from San Cristóbal is to the Lagunas de Montebello (Lakes of Montebello).

San Cristóbal de las Casas

San Cristóbal, the chief city of the Chiapas highlands, is a pretty town of about 125,000 situated in a valley of pine forests and
orchards. Common sights are Indian women, who stand comb-
ing and braiding their hair, and hippies, because the place is
inexpensive and relatively unfettered by tourism. More
Europeans than Americans visit San Cristóbal, and it is the
preferred stopping point before venturing on to Palenque and
Guatemala.

San Cristóbal is also among the finest colonial towns in Mexico:
It has churches, red-tile roofs, elegant Spanish mansions, and
cobblestone streets. The cold, haunting atmosphere of the
place is intensified by the remarkable quality of the early morning and late-afternoon light. Small enough to be seen on foot in

the course of a day, San Cristóbal is also captivating enough to invite a stay of three days, a week, or even a month.

In addition to viewing the monuments from the colonial era, visitors usually plan an early morning visit to see the Indians gather at the *mercado* (market), browse for local handicrafts, or explore one of the indigenous villages in the vicinity. Just soaking up the ambience in one of San Cristóbal's little cafés or unpretentious restaurants is a pleasure. But more than anything else, San Cristóbal is safe and comfortable, and can serve as an unintimidating prelude to Guatemala.

In 1524, the Spaniards under Diego de Mazariegos decisively defeated the Chiapan Indians at a battle outside town. Mazariegos founded the city, which was called Villareal de Chiapa de los Españoles, in 1528. For most of the viceroyalty, or colonial era, Chiapas, with its capital at San Cristóbal, was a province of Guatemala. It was of greater strategic than economic importance to the Spaniards, lacking the gold and silver of the north. Instead, the state's agricultural resources became entrenched in the *encomienda* system, tantamount to slavery. "In this life all men suffer," lamented a Spanish friar in 1691, "but the Indians suffer most of all."

The situation improved only slightly through the efforts of Bartolomé de las Casas, the eponymous bishop of San Cristóbal who in the mid-1500s protested the colonialists' torture and massacre of the Indians. The Indians protested in another way, murdering priests and other *ladinos* (whites), in infamous uprisings. (Chiapans still refer to whites as either ladinos or *Españoles*—Spaniards—whether they are "pure-blooded" or mestizo.)

Mexico, Guatemala, and the rest of New Spain declared independence in 1821. For a brief two years, Chiapas was independent of both Spain and Mexico, electing by plebescite to join the latter on September 14, 1824, the *día de la mexicanidad* of Chiapas (the day is still celebrated in San Cristóbal). In 1892, because of San Cristóbal's allegiance to the Royalists during the War of Independence, the capital was moved to Tuxtla Gutiérrez; with it went all hope that the town would keep pace with the rest of Mexico. It was not until the 1950s that the roads into town were paved and the first automobiles arrived. Modern times came late to San Cristóbal, for which most visitors are thankful.

Arriving and Departing

By Plane
Airports and
Airlines

The closest major airport is in Tuxtla Gutiérrez, 85 kilometers (52.8 miles) west. There are daily flights from Mexico City on **Mexicana** (airport, tel. 961/3–49–21; in Tuxtla, 961/2–00–20 or 961/2–54–02, fax 961/2–70–86). **Aviación de Chiapas** (Aviacsa, tel. 961/2–80–81 or 961/2–68–80; Mexico City, tel. 563–44–00 or 590–24–26, fax 590–25–64) also has daily flights between Tuxtla and Mexico City. For charter flights to the ruins of Bonampak and Yaxchilán, contact a travel agency or Na-Bolom. The San Cristóbal airport south of the city is currently closed.

Between the Airport
and Center City

The easiest way to get from Tuxtla to San Cristóbal is by taxi. The two-hour ride is about $50. Many travel agencies in both cities provide private taxi service. By car, follow Route 190.

First-class bus service on **Cristóbal Colon** costs under $10; from the Tuxtla airport, you must first catch the *colectivo* (shared taxi service in a van or minibus) into town (about $5).

By Car From Tuxtla, Route 190 goes east through Chiapa de Corzo to San Cristóbal. Route 190 continues southeast to Comitán and the Guatemalan border. Route 199 is the preferred route from San Cristóbal to Villahermosa via Palenque and Agua Azul. Route 195 is a more circuitous route between San Cristóbal and Villahermosa. Though expensive, car rentals are available at the Tuxtla and Villahermosa airports as well as in San Cristóbal.

By Bus The **Cristóbal Colon** terminal is at Avenida Insurgentes and Pan American Highway, Route 190. Second-class service to Tuxtla and Guatemala departs from the terminal at Allende and Pan American Highway. **Transportes Tuxtla** (Panamerican Highway at Allende) runs second-class buses northeast along the road to Ocosingo.

Getting Around

The most enjoyable and thorough way to explore San Cristóbal, as with many other colonial Mexican towns, is on foot. Trying to maneuver a car on its narrow, cobblestone streets filled with pedestrians is a needless test of patience. If you do come to town with a car, leave it in the hotel garage except for excursions outside San Cristóbal. **Budget Rent-a-Car** has offices at Calle Diego de Mazariegos 36 in San Cristóbal (tel. 967/8-18-71). Taxis can be found at the *sitio* (taxi stand) next to the cathedral (tel. 967/8-03-96), and there is colectivo service to outlying villages, departing from and returning to the market. For maps and information, inquire at the tourist office.

Important Addresses and Numbers

Tourist Information The **San Cristóbal tourist office** (tel. 967/8-07-15 and 967/8-05-53) is on the ground floor of the Palacio Municipal, right on the *zócalo* (main square). Check the bulletin board here upon arrival for information on tours and side trips. *Open Mon.–Sat. 8–8, Sun. 9–2.*

Emergencies **Municipal police** (tel. 967/8-05-54). The **Hospital del Campo** is located at Diagonal Centenario and the Pan American Highway (tel. 967/8-17-18). The **Social Security Clinic** is outside of town on Calle Tabasco and Diagonal Centenario (tel. 967/8-03-50).

English-language Bookstores Good selections of English-language books can be found at **Cafetería El Mural** (Av. Crescencio Rosas 4), the **Casa de las Imagenes** (Av. B. Domínguez 9, tel. 967/8-03-70), and **Soluna** (Calle Real de Guadalupe 24-D).

Travel Agencies The best travel agencies are **A.T.C.** (Av. 5 de Febrero 15, tel. 967/8-25-50 and 8-11-53, fax 967/8-31-45) **Jovel** (Av. B. Domínguez 11A, tel. 967/8-27-27), and **Lacantún** (Calle Madero 19-2, tel. 967/8-25-87 or 8-25-88).

Guided Tours

Most tour operators transport passengers in minibuses and can arrange hotel pickup.

Orientation Tours A pleasurable way to explore this entire region is with a VTP (*Viajes Todo Pagado*) on **Mexicana** (tel. 800/531–7921) airlines. These all-inclusive packages are available in several combinations to fit your personal needs and budget. The A.T.C. travel agency (Av. 5 de Febrero 15, tel. 967/8–25–50 and 967/8–11–53, fax 967/8–31–45) runs full-day city tours that also cover Na-Bolom, San Juan Chamula, and the San Cristóbal Caves. Five-hour horseback tours to outlying villages can also be arranged.

Regional Tours **A.T.C., Lacantún,** and **Jovel** travel agencies all organize tours to Bonampak, Yaxchilán, Palenque, Agua Azul, Lagunas de Montebello, Amatenango, Belize, Chincultik, Comitán, Guatemala, Sumidero Canyon, Tuxtla Gutiérrez, and Yucatán. Special-interest tours and treks—Lacandon Indians, bird-watching, flora and fauna, river trips, rain-forest excursions—are also available.

Personal Guides The tourist office can put you in touch with Mercedes Hernández Gómez, a licensed English-speaking guide, who leads tours to San Juan Chamula, Zinacantán, and the area ruins.

Exploring

Numbers in the margin correspond to points of interest on the San Cristóbal de las Casas map.

San Cristóbal is laid out in a grid pattern and centered around the zócalo, with street names changing on either side of the square. For example, Francisco Madero to the east of the square becomes Calle Diego de Mazariegos to the west (rather like New York City's East and West 50th streets, divided by 5th Avenue).

The heart of San Cristóbal is small and can be seen on foot in ❶ two hours or less. Begin at the **zócalo,** around which the Spaniards built all their colonial cities. In its center stands the gazebo, which is used by musicians on festive occasions. Surrounding the square are a number of 16th-century buildings, many former mansions of the conquistadores. Tile roofs and wood-beamed ceilings adorn corridors flanking central patios, which are surrounded by arched columns and filled with huge potted plants. (Don't be afraid to go into buildings whose doors are open.) Perhaps the most famous mansion is the so- ❷ called **Casa de Diego de Mazariegos,** opposite the square on the southeast corner of Calle Diego de Mazariegos. One of the most exquisite specimens of colonial architecture in Mexico, the Casa is now the Hotel Santa Clara. The stone mermaid and lions outside it are typical of the period's Plateresque style, as ornate and busy as the work of a silversmith.

Continue in a northwesterly direction around the zócalo to the ❸ **Palacio Municipal,** which was the state capitol building until 1892, when San Cristóbal lost that honor to Tuxtla Gutiérrez. Stop at San Cristóbal's tourist office, on the ground floor, for maps and information.

Perpendicular to the Palacio Municipal, on the north side of the ❹ zócalo, is **La Catedral,** built in 1528, then demolished and rebuilt in 1693, with subsequent additions during the 18th and 19th centuries. Noteworthy attractions in the cathedral include the painting of Our Lady of Sorrows, to the left of the altar; the gold-plated *retablo de los Reyes* (altarpiece); the

Casa de Diego de Mazariegos, **2**

Centro de Estudios Científicos Na-Bolom, **7**

La Catedral, **4**

Mercado, **6**

Palacio Municipal, **3**

Templo de Santo Domingo, **5**

Zócalo, **1**

San Cristóbal de las Casas

Chapel of Guadalupe; and the gold-encrusted pulpit. *Open daily 7–2 and 4–8.*

Time Out   **Cafetería El Mural** (Crescencio Rosas 4 at the corner of Calle Diego de Mazariegos) is a pleasant café serving standard Mexican snacks. The café also has an excellent bookshop.

Head north about four blocks on Avenida General Utrilla toward the **Templo de Santo Domingo,** a three-block-long complex housing the church, former convent, regional history museum, and Templo de la Caridad. The church dates to 1547–1569, and the two-headed eagle—emblem of the Hapsburg dynasty that once ruled Spain and its American dominions—broods over its pediment. The pink stone facade, carved in an intensely ornamental style known as Baroque Solomonic, was clearly influenced by the church of Antigua, Guatemala: Saints' figures, angels, and grooved columns overlaid with vegetation motifs abound. The interior is dominated by lavish altarpieces; an exquisitely fashioned pulpit; a sculpture of the Holy Trinity; and wall panels of carved cedar, one of the precious woods of Chiapas that centuries later lured the woodsmen of Tabasco to the obscure highlands surrounding San Cristóbal. At the southeast corner of the church park lies the tiny **Templo de la Caridad,** built in 1711 to venerate the Immaculate Conception. Its highlight is the finely carved altarpiece. The **Ex-convento de Santo Domingo,** immediately adjacent to the church, now houses Sna Jolobil, an Indian cooperative selling rather expensive local weavings and a good selection of colorful postcards (open daily 9–2 and 4–6). The small regional history museum, also part of the Templo de Santo Domingo complex, is open Tuesday–Sunday 9–6.

6 The municipal **mercado** occupies an eight-block area to the northeast of Santo Domingo. Best visited early in the morning—especially on the busiest day, Saturday—the market is the social and commercial center for the Indians from surrounding villages. Stalls overflow with local produce such as turkeys, medicinal herbs, flowers, firewood, and wool, as well as huaraches, grinding stones, and candied fruit. The market is open daily, but it is busiest and most colorful on Saturdays. Be very discreet about taking photographs.

Visitors interested in the culture and history of the Indians, particularly the Lacandones, should set aside an afternoon to
7 tour the **Centro de Estudios Científicos Na-Bolom**, a handsome former colonial building built in 1891 on the outskirts of town. Na-Bolom began as the residence of Franz and Gertrude Blom, the modern heroes of San Cristóbal and the Chiapan highlands. Franz Blom, a Danish-born archaeologist and explorer who died in 1963, first came to southern Mexico in 1919, as a worker for a Veracruz oil company. By 1923, he was directing excavations at Palenque for the Mexican government. In 1943, on an expedition into the jungle, he met Gertrude (Trudy) Duby, a Swiss socialist, antifascist, and journalist.

The Bloms were married in 1950; that same year they purchased the 22-room house they called Na-Bolom (house of the jaguar). Together they founded an institute dedicated to ethnological and ecological research on the region. The property is blissfully isolated from the rest of San Cristóbal, notably because of its extensive garden of firs, fruit trees, vegetables, and flowers. The Bloms documented and helped to preserve the traditions of the Lacandones, a primitive tribe descended from the ancient Maya. The Lacandones' existence and lifestyle were threatened by the encroachment of modern civilization on their natural habitat, the selva lacandona. Thanks to the Bloms' friendship and assistance, the Lacandones (there were about 160 in 1959) now number almost 450. Though they are now considerably Westernized—many speak Spanish, dress in Western clothing, and are adept at bargaining—their survival is no longer in question. They are also frequent visitors to the center.

Na-Bolom features the Bloms' collection of religious treasures that had been hoarded in attics during the anticlerical 1920s and 1930s. A museum houses Franz Blom's findings from the classic Mayan site of Moxviquil (Mosh-vee-**keel**), found in the outskirts of San Cristóbal, which he excavated in 1952–53, and there is a room full of objects from the daily life of the Lacandones. The library, a storehouse of more than 15,000 volumes on Chiapas and the Maya, is a warm, cozy room with wood card catalogues, overstuffed armchairs draped with blankets, wood-beamed ceilings, a fireplace, Chamula hats, and Mayan relics. Na-Bolom is also a guest house, and revenues from guests, tours, and the bookshop go to support the work of the institute (*see* Lodging, *below*). Arrange for a meal at Na-Bolom at the very least, even if you are not staying there.

Na-Bolom runs a program for visiting scientists and artists-in-residence and is dedicated to reforestation of the surrounding area, planting 35,000 trees each year in a never-ending battle against land-poor settlers and avaricious traders. Trudy Blom, who was born in 1901, still resides here; at her death, the non-profit, private institute will be run by a carefully selected board of directors. In 1991, Mrs. Blom went to Sweden where she received the 500 Global Roll of Honor award granted to her by the United Nations for her lifelong work on the preservation of the environment. *Av. Vicente Guerrero 31 between Comitán and Chiapa de Corzo, tel. 967/8–14–18 with fax. Small admission charge; library free. Tours Tues.–Sun. 4:30 PM in English and Spanish. Library open Tues.–Sat. 9–1.*

Off the Beaten Track

One of the few statues of the conquistadores to be found anywhere in Mexico stands modestly in the overgrown grass fronting the **Templo de Santo Domingo.** The statue, a tiny, unmarked likeness of Diego de Mazariegos, looks westward into the hills, toward Cortés's capital of Mexico City. The vista is particularly dramatic after one of the city's frequent downpours, when dark blue and gray clouds billow above the surrounding hills.

After an early-morning venture to San Cristóbal's market, head four blocks south to the little **plaza at Calle Dr. Navarro and Avenida B. Domínguez.** When the sun edges in over the red-tile roofs, the square is bathed in golden light and is wonderfully cozy and private.

San Cristóbal is divided into several **barrios** (neighborhoods) that might appeal to amateur anthropologists who also like to walk. The barrios originated in colonial times, when the Indian allies of the triumphant Spaniards were moved onto lands on the outskirts of the nascent city. Today, as four centuries ago, each barrio is dedicated to a different occupation and populated by descendants of the original tribes. There are Mexica weavers, Tlaxcala fireworks manufacturers, Chiapa machete makers, and Quiché pig butchers. The San Cristóbal tourist office (tel. 967/8–07–15 or 967/8–05–53) can provide more details and arrange trips to the barrios.

Surrounding San Cristóbal are many small and seldom-visited Indian villages that are celebrated for the exquisite colors and embroidery work of their inhabitants' costumes. Huixtán (Hwees-**tan**) and Oxchuc (Os-**chuc**) are about 38 and 54 kilometers (24 and 34 miles) respectively, on the road to Ocosingo; Chenalhó and Pantelhó lie 56 and 72 kilometers (35 and 45 miles) respectively, along the partially unpaved road beyond Chamula. Buses are available, but because of scheduling, visitors must often stay overnight; renting a car is more convenient. The Sunday market, weavers' cooperative, and ethnographic museum in Tenejapa (19 kilometers, or 11.8 miles, northeast of San Cristóbal) are worth seeing. Tenejapa has a small pensión.

Major festival dates in the area (check with the tourist office for a broader sampling) are: January 20–22, San Sebastian festival in Zinacantán; Carnival and Easter Week in San Juan Chamula, Zinacantán, and other villages; every Friday during Lent in Zinacantán; June 22–24, San Juan festival in Chamula; July 24–25, festival of the patron saint of San Cristóbal; August 9–10, celebration of San Lorenzo in Zinacantán; and at year's end in several villages, celebrations to install the new civil officials, December 30–January 1.

Shopping

The artisans of San Cristóbal and Chiapas—with some help from Guatemalan importers—produce some of the most striking indigenous folk art of Mexico. Best are the *huipiles* (white cotton women's smocks) finely embroidered with native designs; brightly colored *fajas* (sashes); and leather goods, such as belts and purses. Lacandon bows and arrows, and the beribboned hats worn by local men, also make good souvenirs.

Always ask if an item comes from Guatemala. If the answer is yes—you'll be lucky to encounter such honesty—bargain fiercely: Guatemalan goods are priced several times higher in San Cristóbal than they would be if purchased in Guatemala. Guatemalan cloth is easily recognizable: Most of it is rough, dark blue cotton with multicolor cotton needlepoint or trim.

Good selections are available at **Sna Jolobil,** the regional crafts cooperative in the Ex-convento de Santo Domingo on 20 de Noviembre; **La Galería,** at Hidalgo 3; and the many shops clustered along **Real de Guadalupe;** and the government-run **Casa de las Artesanías** at Calle Niños Heroes and Av. Hidalgo. Indian women and children often accost visitors on the streets with their wares, mostly textiles, but their selections are not as varied as those in the shops, and prices will not necessarily be any better. You can be assured, though, that the proceeds go directly to the craftspersons themselves. San Cristóbal is also known for its quality wrought-iron work, especially its crosses. There are no department stores in San Cristóbal. The market, while picturesque, sells more produce than handicrafts.

Sports

Hiking There are many sights on the outskirts of town that make agreeable sojourns on foot (*see* Off the Beaten Track, *above*).

Horseback Riding A ride into the neighboring indigenous villages can exercise the mind as well as the body. Most hotels can arrange for rentals of horses. Guides working through the tourist office and travel agencies can also hire horses and accompany tourists. Allow a minimum of six hours for the trip.

Dining

San Cristóbal's restaurants offer an ample choice of Mexican and international cuisines, but the fare is seldom outstanding when compared with other areas of Mexico. Chiapas has regional specialties but borrows heavily from Yucatán and Oaxaca. Adventurous palates should try *atole* (cornmeal gruel), tamales, candied fruit, and *aguardiente*, literally "firewater," which is made from fermented sugarcane (the Tzotzils call it *posh*). Although the region raises cattle, the best beef is exported. Prices, however, are quite reasonable: a filling dinner (helped out by tortillas in one of their myriad forms) with beer rarely costs more than $10 per person. The town closes down early, so unlike other parts of Mexico, it is a fairly common practice to eat dinner before 8 PM. There is no dress code to speak of in this part of Mexico, and no reservations are necessary.

Highly recommended restaurants are indicated by a star ★.

Category	Cost*
Expensive	$25–$35
Moderate	$15–$25
Inexpensive	under $15

*per person, excluding drinks, service, and sales tax (10%)

Inexpensive　**Fogón de Jovel.** This new restaurant is owned by A.T.C., one of the largest travel agencies in town, which has installed a crafts shop and brought in a marimba band and costumed waiters. A cover charge is in effect when folkloric dances are performed. The menu leans toward southeast Mexican cooking and the variety is impressive. Warning: Fogón de Jovel caters mainly to tourists. *Av. 16 de Septiembre 11, tel. 967/8–11–53 or 8–25–57. MC, V.*

★　**Misión del Fraile.** The decor features wood-beamed ceilings, red-checked tablecloths, hand-carved chairs, and local baskets and birdhouses everywhere. The menu includes delicious, if greasy, *antojitos* (appetizers), and *huaraches* (elongated, stuffed tortillas), broiled scallions, and *anafres* (mixed grill). *Prolongación Insurgentes 10 at Calle José Flores, tel. 967/8–12–98. MC, V.*

★　**Normita.** A popular place and a good deal in an unpretentious setting. They have big breakfasts, Mexican dishes like *pozole* (a kind of pork stew), and specialties of the region. Fruits juices and *antojitos* (appetizers) are a favorite. *Juàrez 6, corner of Dr. Felipe Flores, no phone. MC, V.*

Restaurante del Teatro. Decorated with both Continental and local artwork, this popular French/Italian restaurant specializes in steaks, crepes, and fresh pasta dishes. The atmosphere is romantic and relaxing, with candlelight and live guitar music on the weekends. It is across from the Hotel España. *Av. 1 de Marzo 8, tel. 967/8–31–49. AE, MC, V.*

Lodging

San Cristóbal is small enough that almost any hotel is within walking distance of the major attractions. Most of the hotels listed are colonial, either architecturally or decoratively, in keeping with the rest of town. All rooms in hotels listed have baths; air-conditioning is not necessary at this high altitude and, in fact, fireplaces are welcome. Hotels are open year-round.

Highly recommended lodgings are indicated by a star ★.

Category	Cost*
Very Expensive	over $55
Expensive	$40–$55
Moderate	$25–$40
Inexpensive	under $25

*All prices are for a standard double room; excluding 10% tax.

Very Expensive　**Flamboyant.** Newly inaugurated in spring 1992, the hotel is a sister to the Flamboyant in Tuxtla Gutierrez. The colonial charm of the former Hotel Español, with its fireplaces and bougainvillea-filled courtyard, blue-tiled seats, and fountain, has been retained. The older section, a restored colonial house, has rooms with fireplaces. *1 de Marzo 15, 29200, tel. 967/8–00–45 or 967/8–06–23, fax 967/8–05–14. 54 rooms, 30 with fireplace. Facilities: TV, bar, restaurant, travel agent, car rental, meeting room, shop. AE, MC, V.*

Expensive **Bonampak.** Built in 1987 in the colonial style, this hotel is easily reached on the Panamerican Highway. The modern amenities coupled with the colonial feeling evoke the particular charm of San Cristóbal. There are bungalows for families, and a courtesy shuttle bus transports guests downtown. Request a room away from the highway. *Calzada Mexico 5, tel. 967/8–16–21, fax 967/8–16–22. 52 rooms. Facilities: restaurant, bar, satellite TV, minigolf, trailer park, tennis, pool. AE, D, MC, V.*

Moderate **Mansión del Valle.** A few blocks from the zócalo, this property is very clean and more modern San Cristóbal's moderately priced hotels. *Calle Diego de Mazariegos 39, 29240, tel. 967/8–25–82 or 967/8–25–83, fax 967/8–25–81. 42 rooms, all with phone and TV. Facilities: restaurant/bar, cafeteria, garage. AE, MC, V.*

★ **Na-Bolom.** A dozen guest rooms are available at this center for the study and preservation of the Lacandon Indians and the rain forest. Each of the rustic, but cozy, rooms is decorated with the accoutrements of a specific indigenous community—crafts, photographs, and books—and contains what might be the only bathtubs in San Cristóbal hostelries. Guests staying at Na Bolom receive a free tour of the house, free entrance to a documentary presentation, access to the Library, and information about the area. Book well in advance; ask for a garden view. Guests share the dining room with staff and volunteers at a separate charge. *Av. Vicente Guerrero 33, tel. 967/8–14–18 with fax. 12 rooms, all with fireplace. V.*

Posada Diego de Mazariegos. This hotel is in two sections that face each other across the street. Rooms on the second floor of the older and quieter half, a 200-year-old mansion that also houses the restaurant, have been recently renovated with wrought-iron window frames, oak balustrades, red-tile floors, and wood-beamed ceilings; some rooms have fireplaces. The new section is covered with a giant fiberglass dome that keeps out rain but seals in noise. Many consider the Posada to be San Cristóbal's most elegant property, but others feel it has become tacky and pretentious. *5 de Febrero 1, 29200, tel. 967/ 8–06–21 or 8–05–13, fax 967/8–27–44. 77 rooms. Facilities: restaurant/bar, cafeteria, rental car and travel agency, garage, solarium. AE, DC, V.*

Rincón del Arco. On the way out of town, near Na-Bolom, this hotel has charming touches, especially the quilts and the clay stoves in each room, shaped like bulls and jaguars. Rincón del Arco was recently renovated; the best room is No. 11. The dining room has two fireplaces, wrought-iron wagon-wheel chandeliers, and other regional touches. *Calle Ejército Nacional 66, tel. 967/8–13–13, fax 967/8–15–68. 37 rooms. AE, MC, V.*

Inexpensive **Molino de la Alborada.** This is a ranchlike cottage property with horses for rent. It's 3 kilometers (1.9 miles) outside of town—the management runs buses to and from the center—in a relaxing forest location. *Periférico Sur s/n, next to the airport, tel. 967/8–09–35. 10 rooms, all with fireplace. Facilities: restaurant, trailer park. MC, V.*

Villa Real. This is a plain but functional property, with a small restaurant. *Av. Benito Juárez 8, tel. 967/8–29–30. 24 rooms. V.*

Guest Houses and Camping

Casa de Huéspedes Margarita. This is one of five guest houses recommended by the tourist office. It serves home-cooked meals. *Calle Real de Guadalupe 34, tel. 967/8–09–57. 24 rooms.*

Hotel Bonampak. The campsite here has drainage, electricity, drinking water, and hot water for showers 24 hours a day. *Calzada México 5, tel. 967/8–16–21, fax 967/8–16–22.*

Rancho San Nicolás Camping and Trailer Park. East of town, this property has electricity, drainage, cabins, hot water for showers, and kitchen facilities. *Calle Francisco León s/n, tel. 967/8–00–57.*

The Arts and Nightlife

San Cristóbal has just a modest offering of cultural events. Inquire at the tourist office and bookshops about upcoming lectures on regional ethnography and the selva. **Na-Bolom** occasionally sponsors talks and audiovisual presentations. Although San Cristóbal has several Spanish-language movie theaters and two discos—frequented mostly by young locals—nightlife is not one of the city's main draws. Dinner is eaten early by Mexican standards—about 8 PM. While a few of the restaurants and hotels that cater to gringos provide some form of musical entertainment (and the usual spectacle available at bars), the best diversion can be found in front of a fireplace. Bring along one of B. Traven's jungle novels.

Excursions from San Cristóbal

Caves of San Cristóbal

The spectacular limestone stalactites and stalagmites are illuminated for one entire kilometer (less than a mile) inside these labyrinthine caves, which were discovered in 1960 and have never been fully explored. The park surrounding the caves has a picnic area with barbecue grills. A Spanish-speaking guide is usually available for a small fee. Horses can be rented on weekends. The caves are located in the San Cristóbal Recreational Park, in the midst of a pine forest. *11 km (6.8 mi) southeast of town off Rte. 190. Nominal admission charge. Open daily 9–5.*

San Juan Chamula

The spiritual and administrative center of the Chamula Indians is justly celebrated, as much for its rich past as for its turbulent present. The Chamula are a Tzotzil-speaking Mayan group of about 16,000 individuals who live in hamlets scattered throughout the highlands; there are some 300 of them in San Juan Chamula. Virtually the only thing to see is the church and the rituals performed inside, which are central to the Chamula culture.

The village has been minutely studied for its economic and reli gious/political systems. The Chamulas grow subsistence crop on the region's badly eroded lands and trade actively with th outside world, despite their traditional distrust of stranger: They raise sheep for wool and manure, but their religion—a cu rious mélange of pagan and Christian rites and beliefs— forbids them to eat its flesh. As the land is depleted, Chamul men hire themselves out as laborers on the Soconusco coffe plantations in the south of Chiapas. Soil erosion is so sever that many Chamula have emigrated permanently, particularl to the selva lacandona.

The horrendous working conditions of the coffee-pickers an woodcutters in the early part of this century have bee tellingly described by B. Traven in such novels as *The Rebellio of the Hanged*. More recently, Ricardo Pozas drew a portrai that is nearly as abysmal in his classic monograph, *Juan th Chamula*.

Chamula society is organized around revolving *cargos*, or pub lic posts. The chosen men must leave their homes and serve th community for a year in San Juan Chamula, frequently as po licemen or religious leaders. The position carries with it muc prestige, and although a burden for their families, it is willing ly undertaken.

The Chamula are fiercely religious, a trait that has played a important role in their history. The Chamula uprising of 186 started when some tribesmen were imprisoned for crucifying boy in the belief that they should have their own Christ. Som 13,000 Chamula then rose up to demand their leaders' releas and massacred scores of ladino villagers in the process.

As recently as 1968, the Chamula responded to an attempt t build a Catholic chapel in a neighboring hamlet with armed re sistance and a warning to the priest. The priest later tried t stop indigenous ceremonies from being performed in th church and was evicted; he now returns only for mass and bap tisms. Incursions by American evangelical groups have als met with resistance. Very recently, 10,000 Chamula were ex pelled from the region for rejecting ancient beliefs.

Getting Around   San Juan Chamula is 12 kilometers (7.5 miles) northwest of Sa
        By Car   Cristóbal. Head west on Guadalupe Victoria, which forks to th right onto Ramón Larrainzar. Continue for 4 kilometers (2. miles) until you reach the entrance to the village. Most of thes roads are unpaved, but they are far more interesting than th alternate route, which is to take the main road to Tuxtla for kilometers (4.9 miles) and then turn right when you see signs You can catch one of the colectivos that run regularly from th market in San Cristóbal, or you can hire a taxi or ride horse back (*see* Sports, in San Cristóbal de las Casas, *above*). To ge permission to enter the church and to pay a small fee, go first t the office of the Presidente Municipal (Municipal President) i the main square.

Exploring   Physically and spiritually, life in San Juan Chamula revolve around the church, a white stucco building with red, blue, an yellow trim. Extreme care must be exercised in entering th church. A policeman will either accompany you in or meet yo inside, and he is likely to tell you that taking photographs is ab solutely prohibited.

There are no pews in the church, the floor of which is strewn with fragrant pine needles. Indian families sit chanting on low stone platforms, facing colorfully attired saints' statues that are so highly polished they resemble porcelain dolls. For the most part, worshipers appear oblivious to intruders, continuing with their sacraments: They burn candles of various colors, drink Coca-Cola, kill chickens, and break eggs over themselves to plead for help with crops, illness, and disaster.

Outside the church, there is no taboo against photography. Visitors may be accosted by barefoot children speaking broken Spanish at best who want payment for being photographed. The children are eager for any handouts, but coins, *chicle* (chewing gum), and pens are favorites. If you are lucky, they will take you to their homes—mud-thatched huts—where a female relative will try to sell you locally woven goods. Village elders may question you as you leave the vicinity of the church. The best time to visit San Juan Chamula is on Sundays, when the market is in full swing and more formal religious rites are performed.

Zinacantán

The village of Zinacantán (place of the bats) is even smaller than San Juan Chamula and is reached by taking a paved road west just before San Juan Chamula. Here photography is totally forbidden, even outside the churches. It is the scenery en route to Zinacantán—terraced hillsides with cornfields and orchards—that draws visitors. There isn't much to see in the village itself except on Sundays, when people gather from the surrounding parishes, or during religious festivals. The men wear bright pink *serapes* (ponchos); the women cover themselves with deep blue *rebozos* (shawls). Watch for the plethora of crosses around the springs and mountains on the way to Zinacantán: They are not Christian symbols, but instead mark the abodes of Mayan gods, honored and propitiated through gifts of food, drink, and candles. Zinacantán is 4 kilometers (2.5 miles) west of Chamula. From Chamula, follow signs along a paved road. From San Cristóbal, take the Tuxtla road about 8 kilometers (4.9 miles) and look for the turnoff on your right. Colectivos depart for the village from the San Cristóbal market.

Villahermosa and Tabasco

Numbers in the margin correspond to points of interest on the Chiapas and Tabasco map.

Graham Greene's succinct summation of Tabasco as a "tropical state of river and swamp and banana grove" captures its essence. Though the state played an important role in the early history of Mexico, its past is rarely on view; instead, it is Tabasco's modern-day status as a supplier of oil that overwhelms the visitor. Set on a humid coastal plain and crisscrossed by abundant rivers, low hills, and unexplored jungles, the landscape is marred by shantytowns and refineries reeking ❶ of sulfur. The capital city of **Villahermosa** epitomizes the mercurial development of Tabasco (the airplane was here before the automobile). Though ugly and modern, Villahermosa is the home of a fine archaeology museum. It is also the place to see

Chiapas and Tabasco

the giant stone heads carved by Tabasco's ancient inhabitants, the Olmecs.

This is not to say that the rest of Tabasco has nothing to offer the visitor. There are beaches, but the tourist infrastructure is minimal, and in some places strollers might come away with tar on their feet due to the oil industry. The fired-brick Mayan ruins of Comalcalco attest to the influence of Palenque. Probably the most interesting region is the rivers and canyons to the south and east of Villahermosa, which are home to jaguars, deer, and alligators; this was where the English pirate Sir Francis Drake hid from the Spaniards.

Tabasco—specifically the mouth of the River Grijalva—lay along the route of the Spanish explorations of Mexico in 1518–19. At that time, the state's rivers and waterways, along which the Olmecs and their descendants lived, served as a trade route between the peoples of the north and those of the south. When the Spaniards came to Tabasco, they had to bridge 50 rivers and contend with swarms of mosquitoes, beetles, ants, and almost unbearable heat, but the region was so lush that one early chronicler termed it a Garden of Eden.

The Spanish Conquest was facilitated by the state of almost constant tribal warfare between the Tabascans and their Mayan and Aztec overlords, and by the fact that the Indians, who had never seen horses, perceived both horse and rider to be one supernatural being. Among the 20 slave women turned over to the victors was a Chiapan named Malintzín, who was singled out by the Spaniards for her beauty and her ability to speak both the Maya and the Nahuatl languages. Called Marina by the Spaniards, she became not only Cortés's mistress and the mother of his illegitimate son but also the willing interpreter of Indian customs. Marina's cooperation helped the conquistador trounce both Moctezuma and Cuauhtémoc, the last Aztec emperors.

Until the early 20th century Tabasco slumbered; it did not become a state until 1824. After the American Civil War, traders from the southern United States began operating in the region and on its rivers, hauling the precious mahogany trees upstream from Chiapas and shipping them north from the small Tabascan port of Frontera. This was Tabasco's most prosperous era until the discovery of oil 50 years ago.

Arriving and Departing

By Plane **Aeroméxico** has daily nonstop service from Mexico City. The Aeroméxico ticket office is at Periférico Carlos Pellicer, Camara No. 511. (airport, tel. 931/4–16–75 or 2–09–04; in town, tel. 931/2–69–91, 2–15–28 or 2–95–54). **Mexicana** has two daily nonstop flights from Mexico City, and both airlines offer connecting flights to other Mexican cities. Mexicana has a ticket office in the Tabasco 2000 complex, Av. 4 and Calle 13, (tel. 931/3–50–44; airport, tel. 931/2–11–64). Travel agencies book charter flights to Palenque and Bonampak.

By Car Take Route 186 from Palenque and points east (Campeche, Chetumal, Mérida), Route 195 from Tuxtla, or Route 180 from Coatzacoalcos and Veracruz.

By Bus There is frequent first- and second-class service to Campeche, Chetumal, Mérida, Mexico City, Palenque, San Cristóbal, Tapachula, Tuxtla Gutiérrez, Veracruz, and elsewhere.

Getting Around

Villahermosa—population 500,000—is surrounded by three rivers but oriented toward the River Grijalva to the east, which is bordered by the *malecón* (boardwalk). The city is huge, and driving can be tricky. The main road through town is almost a highway; exit ramps are about 1 kilometer (.62 mile) apart, and tourist destinations are not clearly marked. Nevertheless, driving is the best way to get around. Several major rental car companies, including Avis, Dollar, Hertz, and National, have offices in Villahermosa. Most taxi service is collective and runs along fixed routes; information about buses, on the other hand, can be difficult to find.

Important Addresses and Numbers

The main tourist office is located in the huge Tabasco 2000 complex, opposite the municipal palace. *Paseo Tabasco 1504, Tabasco 2000 complex, tel. 931/5–06–93 or 5–06–98, ext. 115, 116, 117. Open daily 9–3 and 6–8.*

Exploring

Downtown Villahermosa contains a pedestrian shopping mall, a museum of popular culture, and a folk-art shop, but the **CICOM Museum of Anthropology** should be seen first. Located on the right bank of the Grijalva, the museum is part of a huge cultural complex dedicated to research on the Olmec and Maya (which is what the Spanish acronym CICOM stands for), and provides one of the last tranquil vistas of Villahermosa as it might have looked 50 years ago. Although most of the explanations are in Spanish, that should not detract from the visual pleasure of the displays. The entire ground floor is devoted to Tabasco and the Olmec, or "inhabitants of the land of rubber," who flourished in Tabasco as early as 1800 BC and disappeared about 1,600 years later. The Olmecs have long been honored as the "mother culture" of Mesoamerica and as inventors of the numerical and calendrical systems that spread throughout the region, though recent research suggests that the Olmecs might actually have been influenced by the Maya, rather than the other way around.

Some of the most interesting artifacts of the Olmec, other than the giant stone heads on view at Parque La Venta (*see below*), are the remnants of their jaguar cult, which are displayed in the museum. The jaguar symbolized the earth fertilized by rain, and many Olmec sculptures portray werejaguars (half-human, half-jaguar, similar to a werewolf) or jaguar babies. Other sculptures portray jaguars swallowing human heads, bat gods, bird-headed humans, female fertility figurines, and the mysterious smiling faces of Veracruz. All of Mexico's ancient cultures are represented on the upper two floors, from the red-clay dogs of Colima and nose rings of Nayarit to the huge burial urns of the Chontal Maya, who built Comalcalco. Don't miss the vivid reproductions of the Mayan murals from Bonampak. CICOM also houses a handicrafts shop, restaurant, library, and theater. *Carlos Pellicer 511, an extension of the malecón. Admission: about $3.50. Open daily 9–7.*

Time Out | Stop off for a beer and a plate of fresh shrimp at the **Capitán Beulo,** a small riverboat restaurant that also runs 90-minute cruises along the Grijalva. *Paseo Malecón Madrazo and Zaragoza, no phone and no reservations necessary. No admission charge for the cruise, but passengers must order food ($10 maximum). Departures at 1:30, 3:30, and 9 PM. Closed Mon.*

The giant stone heads carved by the Olmec and salvaged from the oil fields of La Venta, on the western edge of Tabasco near the state of Veracruz, are on display in **Parque La Venta,** situated west of CICOM in a tropical garden on the Lago de las Ilusiones (Lake of Illusions). These six-foot-tall, baby-faced Negroid heads, weighing upward of 20 tons, have sparked endless scholarly debate. It has been theorized that they depict ancient Phoenician slaves who wound up on the coasts of Mexico, that they were meant to represent space invaders, and that because of the obesity and short limbs of the figures, they are proof of endocrine deficiencies among the ancient Olmec. More likely, they simply celebrate the earth's fecundity. La Venta contains 30 sculptures, not all of them heads. There are also werejaguars, priests, monsters, stelae, and stone altars oddly reminiscent of ancient Mesopotamian art. *Blvd. Ruiz Cortines near Paseo Tabasco, tel. 931/5–22–28. Admission: about $3.50. Open daily 9–4:30.*

Off the Beaten Track

Some 210 kilometers (130.5 miles) southeast of Villahermosa on Route 203, deep in the jungle in the least explored region of Tabasco, are the ruins of **Pomoná.** This classic Mayan city, which contains 60 buildings, was discovered in 1960 but is only now being restored. Pomoná is situated just outside Tenosique, the closest town in Tabasco to the Guatemalan border, right on the banks of the Usumacinta.

Dining

For price categories, *see* Dining for San Cristóbal, *above.* Highly recommended restaurants are indicated by a star ★.

Moderate | **El Mesón de Castilla.** This newly renovated Spanish-owned restaurant specializes in such Iberian fare as *cabrito* (goat), *lechón* (roast pork), paella, steaks, and *fabada* (white beans with sausage, bacon, and spices), as well as fresh local seafood (lobster, shrimp, squid, and *huachinango,* or red snapper). Rustic stucco walls, wood chairs and 24 tables surround an inner garden; an organist plays nightly. *Pagés Llergo 125, tel. 931/2–56–21. AE, DC, V.*

El Mesón del Duende. This restaurant, which translates as the House of the Elf, serves Spanish cuisine similar to the food at El Mesón de Castilla, including a savory Galician broth, veal, goat, fabada, paella, and seafood. The modest decor is in keeping with the family-style atmosphere. *Gregorio Méndez 1703, tel. 931/5–13–24. MC, V.*

★ **Los Tulipanes.** Next door to the CICOM Museum, the spacious Los Tulipanes specializes in steaks and seafood and has a tranquil view of the river. Try the stuffed crab or shrimp. *Carlos Pellicer 511, tel. 931/2–92–09 or 2–92–17. AE, MC, V.*

Inexpensive **Leotabasco.** This is a very popular spot for tasty beef and pork tacos, which has recently expanded its menu and enlarged its dining area. *Paseo Tabasco 429, tel. 931/2–44–63. MC, V. Open daily till 1AM.*

Lodging

Villahermosa hotels are relatively expensive, especially when compared with those in San Cristóbal. Generally speaking, the newer, American-style hotels are outside of town, near Tabasco 2000 and Parque La Venta, and the older and more modest hotels are downtown. For price categories, *see* Lodging for San Cristóbal, *above*.

Highly recommended lodgings are indicated by a star ★.

Very Expensive **Exelaris Hyatt.** Built in 1983, this nine-story Hyatt has 211 air-★ conditioned rooms, all with color TVs, phones, and minibars. *Juárez 106, 86050, tel. 931/3–44–44, 931/5–12–34, or 800/228-9000, fax 931/5–12–35, 5–58–08. Facilities: 2 restaurants, 3 bars, heated pool, 2 tennis courts. AE, DC, MC, V.*
Holiday Inn. Situated across from La Choca Park in Tabasco 2000, this nine-story resort property has 144 climate-controlled rooms, all with color TVs, minibars, and room service. There's live entertainment in the Jaguar Lounge. *Paseo Tabasco 1407, 86030, tel. 931/6–44–00 or 800/HOLIDAY, fax 931/6–45–69. Facilities: lounge, restaurant, pool. AE, DC, MC, V.*

Expensive **Calinda Viva Villahermosa.** This business traveler's hotel has 241 rooms, all with air-conditioning, FM stereos, color TVs, and phones; many have balconies. *Paseo Tabasco 1201, 86050, tel. 931/5–00–00, fax 931/5–30–73. Facilities: restaurant, 2 bars, coffee shop, disco, pool, gift shop. AE, DC, MC, V.*
Cencali. This colonial-style hotel in the new hotel zone is situated in parklike grounds and surrounded by lakes and lush greenery. All 116 rooms and 3 suites are air-conditioned. *Juárez and Paseo Tabasco, 86040, tel. 931/5–19–94 through 5–19-99. Facilities: restaurant, lobby bar, pool. AE, DC, MC, V.*
Maya Tabasco. The recently renovated Maya Tabasco has 156 rooms, all with air-conditioning, TVs, and phones. *Ruiz Cortines 907, 86000, tel. 931/2–11–11, fax 2–10–97. AE, DC, MC, V.*

Excursions from Villahermosa

The most important Mayan site in Tabasco is **Comalcalco,** about 60 kilometers (37.3 miles) northwest of Villahermosa off Route 187. The abundant cocoa plants in the region provided food and livelihood for a booming population during the late classic period (AD 600–900), when Comalcalco was built; the site marks the westernmost reach of the Maya. Descendants of the Chontal Maya, who constructed Comalcalco, still live in the vicinity. This site is unique among Mayan cities for its use of fired brick, as the Tabasco swamplands lacked the stone for building that was found elsewhere in the Mayan empire. The bricks were apparently inscribed and painted with enigmatic "anonymous messages" before being covered with stucco. The major pyramid, on the Great Eastern Acropolis, is decorated with large stucco masks and carvings, and the museum houses many of the artifacts uncovered there. *Admission: about $3.50. Open daily 9–4:30.*

If you will feel deprived without seeing the Gulf of Mexico, continue on for 19 kilometers (11.8 miles) to **Paraíso.** Bear in mind, however, that Tabasco is not known for its beaches: For the most part, they are dirty and almost totally lacking in tourist infrastructure. There is one hotel on the beach and others in the town of Paraíso, a few kilometers inland.

Palenque

2 The ruins of **Palenque** are to many people the most beautiful in all Mexico. Chichén Itzá may be more expansive, and Teotihuacán more monumental, but Palenque possesses a mesmerizing quality, perhaps because of its intimacy. It is, after all, just a cluster of ocher buildings intermingled with grassy mounds and tall palm groves, set in a rain forest. But in the early morning or late afternoon, sunlight illuminates the structures in a hazy, iridescent glow; there are the eerie shrill calls of birds, and the local Indians, descendants of the Maya, wander about collecting banana leaves, oranges, and avocados. Whether or not visitors are archaeology fans, they cannot fail to be moved by the sanctity of Palenque.

A Spanish priest first stumbled on the site in the 16th century; it was rediscovered in 1750 and a royal Spanish expedition undertaken in 1785. In about 1833, an eccentric Austrian count set up house with his mistress for three years in a building known as the **Templo del Conde** (Temple of the Count). American explorers John Lloyd Stephens and Frederick Catherwood lived briefly in the palace during their 1840 expedition. In 1923, serious excavations began under the direction of Franz Blom, cofounder of Na-Bolom in San Cristóbal. Work continued intermittently until 1952, when Alberto Ruz Lhuillier, a Mexican archaeologist, uncovered the tomb of the 7th-century King Pacal beneath the Temple of the Inscriptions. Seeing Palenque, one can understand why archaeologist Sylvanus Morley honored the Maya as the "Greeks of the New World." The site dates to the mid- to late-classic period (6th–9th centuries), although it was inhabited as early as 1500 BC. Palenque marks the architectural apogee of the western Mayan empire, and it has been called "second only to the Acropolis in terms of unadulterated beauty." (Even Graham Greene, grumpier than usual because of illness, was impressed by the "gnarled relics.")

Ground-breaking work has been done on the Maya in the past 12 years by archaeologists, linguists, and astronomers. The deciphering of 98% of Palenque's hieroglyphics in 1988 has revolutionized scholars' understanding of both the Maya and of the bloody history of Palenque. For example, the glyphs have revealed the complex history of the Palenque dynasties and shown how prevalent self-mutilation was. It is now hypothesized that Palenque reached its peak during a period of transition for Mayan civilization, when the rulers—Pacal in particular—were bent on expanding the city-state's power over rival polities. The site was abandoned around AD 800 for reasons still hotly disputed, making it one of the earliest Mayan sites to be deserted in a west-to-east extinction pattern. In its heyday, Palenque encompassed nearly 25 square miles; the excavated portions of the ruins cover only half a mile.

Arriving and Departing

By Plane Chartered flights are available through travel agencies in San Cristóbal and Villahermosa; many of them continue on to the ruins of Bonampak and Yaxchilán.

By Car The 90-minute, 143-kilometer (89-mile) trip from Villahermosa on Route 186 to Catazajá, then on Route 199 to Palenque, is easy, as for most of the way the roads are straight and paved (if full of potholes). It takes about seven hours to drive from Palenque to San Cristóbal on scenic Routes 199 and 190. For the first 30 kilometers (18.6 miles) out of Palenque, the roads are flat and newly paved. The worst stretches of unpaved roadway are on the curvy 116 kilometers (72 miles) between Palenque and Ocosingo, with numerous hillocks, lush green riverbeds, and savannas. After Ocosingo, the road is more mountainous and paved. It is also extremely beautiful, with dense vegetation, hillsides planted with maize, and occasional thatched huts of the indigenous villages. You may see *campesinos* (peasants), machete in hand. Exercise caution during the rainy season (June through October) when the roads are slick.

By Train Daily trains from Mexico City take at least 24 hours. First-class service from Mérida takes 11 hours; second-class service makes more stops and takes 16 hours. The train station is 10 kilometers (6.2 miles) from town.

By Bus First- and second-class service is available from Villahermosa (2.5 hours), San Cristóbal (6 hours), and Mexico City (14 hours); there is second-class only from Mérida (8 hours), Campeche (6 hours), and Tuxtla Gutiérrez (9 hours).

Getting Around

The town of Palenque, some 8 kilometers (5 miles) east of the ruins, is dusty, unsightly, and commercial, providing only the most basic dining and lodging. Shops on the main street have an adequate selection of regional crafts, though there are much better offerings in San Cristóbal. The tourist office, on the second floor of the Palacio Municipal, on the zócalo, is open Monday through Saturday 8:30–8 and 9–noon Sunday, tel. 934/5–01–14 or 5–01–53.

Visitors with a car will have the easiest time reaching both Palenque and its surrounding attractions, but colectivo service is available from the town center to the ruins and neighboring waterfalls.

Exploring

The ruins are open daily 8–5, and there is an admission charge of about $3.50. Since no formal guides are available, we suggest that you buy a guidebook in town.

Temple of the Inscriptions On your right as you enter the site is a 75-foot pyramid. To reach the tomb inside involves a relatively easy, if slow, climb. The pyramid is dedicated to Pacal, the "Mesoamerican Charlemagne," who took Palenque to its most glorious heights during his 70-year reign, which ended circa AD 692.

Once at the summit, take a good long look around you, particularly at the imposing palace to your right, which fills the field of vision. This is the best view of Palenque, and it provides an

Palenque

North Group

Museum of Ruins

Temple of the Count

Ball Court

Pyramid

East Court of Palace

Palace

Entrance

Tower

Temple of the Inscriptions

Temple of the Cross

Temple of the Bas Relief

Temple of the Foliated Cross

Temple of the Sun

Río Otolum Aqueduct

N

0   100 yards

0   100 meters

excellent orientation to the other buildings. Atop this temple and the smaller surrounding ones are vestiges of roof combs, one of the most distinctive architectural features of the southern Mayans. (Roof combs are delicate vertical extensions that resemble ornamental combs worn by Spanish women on the crowns of their heads.) Then descend 80 feet down a steep, damp flight of stairs into the tomb, one of the only crypts ever found inside a Mexican pyramid. Pacal's diadem and majestic jade, shell, and obsidian mask were stolen from Mexico City's Museum of Anthropology in the early 1980s and recovered in 1989. The intricately carved sarcophagus lid, weighing some 5 tons and measuring 10 by 7 feet, however, remains. A "psychoduct," or hollow stone tube through which his soul was thought to have passed to the netherworld, leads up to the temple.

It can be difficult to make out the carvings on the slab, but they depict Pacal, prostrate beneath a sacred ceiba tree. The lords of the nine underworlds are carved into stucco reliefs on the walls around him; his more earthly companions were several youths, whose remains were uncovered alongside the sepulcher. *The tomb is open daily 10:30–4.*

Palace Built at different times, the palace is a complex of patios, galleries, and other buildings set on a 30-foot-high platform. Stucco work adorns the pillars of the galleries and the inner courtyards. There are numerous friezes and masks inside, most of them depicting Pacal and his dynasty. Remarkably well preserved, their style is sinuous and linear, stylized but restrained. Steam baths in the Southwestern Patio suggest that priests once dwelled in the adjoining cellars and that the galleries were probably used for religious ceremonies.

Group of the Cross To the right of the palace, you cross the tiny Otulum River, which in ancient times was roofed over to form a nine-foot-high vaulted causeway or aqueduct. Tombs were discovered beneath the largest, the Temple of the Cross, and the most exquisite roof combs are found on these buildings.

Northern Group To reach this cluster, walk north along the river (little more than a creek), passing the palace and then the unexcavated ball court on your left. This group includes five buildings in varying states of disrepair, of which the largest and best preserved is the Temple of the Count.

Museum The small but worthwhile museum includes fine stelae, hieroglyphs, and, especially noteworthy, the stucco fragments of handsome Mayan faces. There are also maps of the Mayan zone and of Palenque itself. The museum northeast of the ball court is open daily from late morning to late afternoon.

Off the Beaten Track

Just 18 kilometers (11.2 miles) from Palenque is the waterfall of **Misol-Ha,** 2 kilometers (1.2 miles) to the right off Route 199; swimming is permitted in the pool formed by the 100-foot cascade. The falls of **Agua Azul** are another 22 kilometers (13.7 miles) toward Ocosingo (4 more kilometers—2.5 miles—off the highway). The falls are much larger and faster than Misol-Ha, and swimming is permitted. These cataracts are surrounded by giant palm fronds and tropical flowers; monkeys and toucans frolic in the vicinity. There are restaurants, camping facilities, and rest rooms.

Dining

Generally speaking, the food served in Palenque town is modest in both quality and price. On the other hand, most of the restaurants are open-air, which is where you want to be in this part of Mexico (except when it rains, and then the thatched roofs are welcome). Try **El Paraíso,** 2 kilometers (1.2 miles) from the ruins; **La Selva,** next door to the Hotel La Cañada, Merle Green 14; or the **Nututún Viva,** at the hotel of the same name. Don't expect to use credit cards.

Lodging

For prices, *see* Lodging for San Cristóbal, *above.* Highly recommended lodgings are indicated by a star ★.

Very Expensive **Misión Palenque.** This new motel-style resort is the town's only luxury hotel. Located on the north side of town off Route 199, it has a free shuttle bus to the ruins. All rooms are air-conditioned and have a terrace, minibar, and phone. *Rancho San Martín de Porres, tel. 934/5-02-41, fax 934/5-03-00. 144 rooms. Facilities: restaurant/bar, pool, tennis court. AE, DC, MC, V.*

Expensive **Chan Kah.** Four kilometers (2.5 miles) from the ruins in a para-
★ disiacal jungle setting, this property has a stone-lined pool, a resident spider monkey, aromatic jasmine bushes, and a stream flowing around the back. The restaurant is overpriced,

and meals are accompanied by Muzak and movie soundtracks, but the 14 bungalows feature mahogany furnishings and have ceiling fans (surprisingly adequate, despite the humidity); bungalows 6 through 10 offer views of both the pool and the stream. *Km. 3 Carr. Ruinas 29960, tel. 934/5–03–18, fax 934/ 5–04–89. 38 units. Facilities: restaurant/bar, lagoon-style pool. MC, V.*

Moderate **Nututún Viva Palenque.** This property has 60 air-conditioned rooms, restaurant/bar, disco, natural pool, and trailer park. *Apdo. 74, Carretera Ocosingo Km. 3.5, 29960, tel. 934/5–01– 00, 5–01–61. AE, DC, MC, V.*

Excursions from Palenque

Because access is difficult, only the most devoted Mayan fans will attempt the trip to the ruins of **Bonampak** and **Yaxchilán** (Yas-che-**lan**), 183 and 133 kilometers (113.7 and 82.6 miles), respectively, southeast of Palenque. Bonampak is renowned for its vivid murals of ancient Mayan life, though they are sadly deteriorated. (The reproductions at the archaeological museums in Mexico City and Villahermosa are better.) Recent excavations at Yaxchilán, on the other hand, have uncovered captivating temples and carvings in a superb jungle setting.

Bonampak, a satellite of Yaxchilán, was built on the banks of the Lacanjá River during the 7th and 8th centuries and remained undiscovered until 1946. Explorer Jacques Soustelle called it "a pictorial encyclopedia of a Mayan city." Indeed, the scenes portrayed in the three rooms of the Templo de las Pinturas graphically recall subjects such as life at court and the prelude and aftermath of battle with unusual realism.

Yaxchilán, which means "place of green stones," is a contemporary of Bonampak. It is dominated by two acropolises containing a palace, temples with finely carved lintels, and great staircases leading to the banks of the Usumacinta (Guatemala is on the other side). Until very recently, the Lacandon, who live in the vicinity, made pilgrimages to this site in the heart of the jungle, leaving behind "god pots" (incense-filled ceramic bowls) in honor of ancient deities. They were particularly awed by the headless sculpture of Xachtun (Wa-sha-**tun**) at the entrance to the temple (called structure 33), and believe that the world will end when its head is replaced on its torso.

Yaxchilán was situated on the trade route between Palenque and Tikal; the site was recently threatened with destruction by plans for a huge dam to be built by Mexico and Guatemala. The plans have been put on hold for lack of funds, though they may yet come to fruition. Meanwhile, ambitious highways under construction in the region are already changing the ecosystem and lifestyle. Yaxchilán in its present state is probably doomed, so you should see it now.

Arriving and Both sites can be reached by making arrangements for a small
Departing chartered plane in Palenque or San Cristóbal. In San Cristóbal, contact **A.T.C.** (5 de Febrero 15, tel. 967/82–5–50 or 8–11–53). The six-hour, round-trip tour costs about $300 (possibly less, with a minimum of four people) and includes lunch. The same agency has a branch in Palenque (Allende, Esq. Av. Juárez, Local 6, tel. 934/5–02–10 or 5–03–56). The trip takes five hours and costs the same as the trip from San Cristóbal. Some trips

add the Lacandon village of Lacanjá. (For other tours to the ruins, *see* San Cristóbal, *above*). A road is being built that will connect Yaxchilán with Bonampak. In any case, wear sturdy shoes, carry insect repellent, and cover yourself against mosquitoes, ticks, sandflies, and undergrowth.

Lagunas de Montebello

East of San Cristóbal lies one of the least explored and most exotic regions of Chiapas: the selva lacandona or Lacandon jungle. In this largely uninhabited area, a major drama is being played out that rarely makes the news in North America. Incursions of developers, land-hungry settlers, and refugees from neighboring Guatemala are transforming Mexico's last frontier, which for centuries has been the homeland of the Lacandones, a small tribe descended from the ancient Maya. This trip can be done in a day, as the lakes themselves are 155 kilometers (96.3 miles) or about 2½ hours by car from San Cristóbal. If you are driving during the rainy season, however, the trip may take longer. For extended exploring of the lakes, we suggest an overnight stay in Comitán. The itinerary can be covered by car, bus, or tour, but a car is highly preferable because of the freedom it allows for exploration on one's own.

Head south 35 kilometers (21.7 miles) on Route 190 to **Amatenango del Valle,** a small village known for its handsome, primitive pottery. By the side of the road, women sell ocher, black, and brown clay flowerpots and animal figurines that have been fired on open kilns. The rugged foothills and pine groves surrounding San Cristóbal subside into a low plain along the next stretch of the road; the mountains appear to have been sliced in two, revealing their rust-red innards, sad artifacts of the devastating erosion caused by the clearing of the forests. **Comitán** is at the halfway point to the lakes, and though the city has few attractions, it is one of the few places on the way to Guatemala that offer lodgings and restaurants. From the zócalo there are fine views of the hills. Comitan's tourist office, located on the ground floor of the Municipal Palace, facing the zócalo, is open Monday–Saturday 9–8:30, Sunday 9–2, tel. 963/2–23–03 through 2–23–07, ext. 138 or 139.

Many of the Mexicans who work at the few remaining Guatemalan refugee camps in Chiapas live in Comitán. Beginning in 1981, some 46,000 Guatemalan peasants fled a wave of political repression by crossing the border into ramshackle camps, only to be hunted down by the Guatemalan army. Mexico eventually moved more than half of the refugees to safer, more distant camps, but many Guatemalans preferred to remain in Chiapas, and there are still camps near Comitán at Las Margaritas and La Trinitaria. Comitán, whose original Mayan name was Balún-Canán, or "Nine Stars," flourished early on as a major center linking the lowland temperate plains to the edge of the Mayan empire on the Pacific. Even today, it serves as the principal trading point for the Tzeltal Indians and Guatemalan goods, such as sugarcane liquor and orchids. The present city was built by the Spaniards, but few traces of the colonial era remain. Notable exceptions are two churches, Santo Domingo de Guzmán and San Sebastián, in which part of Chiapas's struggle for independence from Spain took place.

The **Casa-Museo Dr. Belisario Domínguez,** former home of a martyr of the revolution, opened as a museum in 1985 and re-creates that turbulent era with an array of documents and photographs. *Av. Dr. Belisario Domínguez Sur 17. Admission: about 35¢. Open Tues.–Sat. 10–6:45, Sun. 9–12:45.*

The small, late-classic Mayan site of **Chincultik** will only interest hard-core archaeology buffs, although it has a lovely forest location, a view of the Montebello lakes, and a large *cenote* (sacred well). From Comitán, continue south for 15 kilometers (9.3 miles) on Route 190 until you see a very small turnoff for the lakes (marked only by a green-and-white sign depicting a tree) outside of La Trinitaria. After 39 kilometers (24.2 miles), there is a dirt road on the left to the ruins, which are another 5 kilometers (3.1 miles) off the highway; a 10-minute hike is then required. The ruins, which are only partially restored, include a ball court, pyramid, *cenote*, and stelae. *Admission: about $2.75. Open daily 8–4.*

Time Out At Km. 22 is the **Parador Museo** (no phone), a modest lodging with seven rooms and a restaurant. These are adequate, inexpensive accommodations.

❹ Ample signs and guardposts mark the entrance to the **Lagunas de Montebello** (Montebello Lakes), 9 kilometers (5.6 miles) away. Together, the 60-odd lakes and surrounding selva compose a 2,437-acre national park. A different color permeates each lake, whose waters glow with vivid emerald, turquoise, amethyst, azure, and steel-gray tints, caused by various oxides. Practically the only denizens of the more accessible part of the forest are the clamorous goldfinch, mockingbirds, and the rare quetzal bird. To the east, wild animals roam: pumas and jaguars, deer and bears. The serenity and majesty of the place, with its clusters of oak, pine, and sweet gum, recall the Alps or the lakes of Minnesota.

At the park entrance, the road forks. The left leads to the Lagunas Coloradas (Colored Lakes). At **Laguna Bosque Azul,** the last lake along that road, there are picnic tables, rest rooms, and, at the end of the road, a shabby but serviceable café. At Laguna Bosque Azul, you may encounter José Alvarez, who runs 10-day walking tours into the jungle, including a visit to the Lacandon village of Lacanjá (near the ruins of Bonampak). José is a bit of a charlatan, but he knows the region well; if he is not there, other quasi-"native" guides are sure to have taken his place. The right fork at the park entrance continues along dirt roads for 14 kilometers (8.7 miles) before dwindling into a footpath. If you walk down the right fork, you will see some of the more beautiful lakes. The largest, **Tziscao,** is on the Guatemalan border and it is the site of the Tziscao Lodge and the Hospedaje La Orquidia hostelries, both of which are dirt-cheap and very basic (no hot water), but there are food service, horses, and boats, and the fishing is excellent. Buses leave infrequently from Comitán (2 Av. Poniente Sur #4, tel 963/2–10–44) to Laguna Bosque Azul and Tziscao. There is also colectivo service.

Head back toward San Cristóbal on Route 190, and continue to Tuxtla Gutiérrez. The 85-kilometer (52.8-mile) drive from San Cristóbal to Tuxtla winds through densely wooded peaks and valleys. Indians by the roadside sell food, crafts, flowers, and fruits. You descend gradually onto vast plains punctuated by hills. At the bottom—Tuxtla is only 1,739 feet above sea level—the change to a temperate climate is striking. Just a few kilometers before Tuxtla is Chiapa de Corzo.

"All pink wash and palms and tropical fruit and old wounded churches and dusty desolation," Graham Greene remarked, in **⑤** a rather romantic vein. **Chiapa de Corzo** was founded in 1528 by Diego de Mazariegos, who one month later fled the mosquitoes and transported all the settlers to San Cristóbal (then called Chiapa de los Españoles, to distinguish it from Chiapa de los Indios, as Chiapa de Corzo was originally known).

Chiapa is still pink, still dusty, and perhaps because of its climate, the people smile more than they do in the colder highlands. Life in this small town on the banks of the Grijalva revolves, inevitably, around the zócalo, lorded over by a bizarre 16th-century Mozarabic fountain modeled after Isabella's crown. The interior is decorated with stories of the Indians.

Chiapa's lacquerware museum, facing the plaza, contains a modest collection of delicately carved and painted *jícaras* (gourds). ("The sky is no more than an immense blue jícara, the beloved firmament in the form of a cosmic jícara," explains the *Popul Vuh*, a 16th-century chronicle of the Quiché Maya.) The lacquerware on display is both local and imported, coming from Michoacán, Guerrero, Chiapas, and Asia. The museum is open Tuesday–Saturday 9–2 and 4–6, Sunday 9–1. A workshop behind the museum is open during the week, generally keeping the same hours as the museum.

Time Out Stop for lunch or refreshments at the **Jardines de Chiapa** (Portal Oriente s/n) on the opposite side of the square from the museum. Occupying a lovely patio setting, this restaurant serves an excellent and inexpensive variety of regional cuisine, including *chipilín con bolita* (a soup made with balls of ground corn paste cooked in a creamy herbal sauce and topped with Chiapas's famous cheese), *tasajo* (sun-dried beef served with squash-seed sauce), and *butifarra* (minced pork and beef sausage).

Several handicraft shops line the square, selling huaraches, ceramics, lacquerware, masks, and regional costumes. Just outside of town, behind the Nestlé plant, are some nearly unnoticeable Maya-Olmec ruins dating from 1450 BC.

Next stop—18 kilometers (11.2 miles) north of Tuxtla—is the **⑥** **Sumidero Canyon**, whose gaping, almost vertical walls descend 4,000 feet for some 15 kilometers (9.3 miles). North Americans may compare it to the Grand Canyon; it was formed about 12 million years ago, and the Grijalva River slices through it, erupting in waterfalls and coursing through caves. Ducks, pelicans, herons, raccoons, iguanas, and butterflies live at the base, which can be viewed either from five lookout points off the highway or by boat (a two- to three-hour trip). As you visit the canyon, think about the fate of the Chiapa Indians, who jumped into it rather than face slavery at the hands of the Spaniards. Boat trips (about $5 for collective service) depart daily between 7 AM and 4 PM from the tiny island of Cahuaré and the dock at Chiapa de Corzo, also stopping at the hydroelectric dam in Chicoasen. You can rent your own boat for about $50.

Tuxtla Gutiérrez

Tuxtla Gutierrez is the thriving capital city of the state of Chiapas. In 1939, Graham Greene characterized it as "not a place for foreigners—the new ugly capital of Chiapas, without attractions . . . It is like an unnecessary postscript to Chiapas, which should be all wild mountain and old churches and swallowed ruins and the Indians plodding by." That bleak description is even more true today. Nonetheless, Tuxtla Gutiérrez is a city through which most visitors to Chiapas will pass, and it is of vital economic and political importance. It is the state's transportation hub, and it does have what is probably the most exciting zoo in Latin America, along with a comprehensive archaeology museum. It is also convenient for its proximity to Chiapa de Corzo and the Sumidero Canyon, which have little in the way of accommodations.

The state capital since 1892, Tuxtla's first name derives from the Nahuatl word *tochtlan* meaning "abundance of rabbits." Its second name, Gutiérrez, honors Joaquín Miguel Gutiérrez, who fought for the state's independence and incorporation into Mexico.

Arriving and Departing

By Plane **Mexicana** flies nonstop to Mexico City from the Tuxtla airport, which is in the town of Ocozocoautla, 22 kilometers (13.7 miles) west. Mexicana's ticket office is located at Av. Central Ote 1520, tel. 961/2–53–75. **Aviacsa** also operates daily flights to Mexico City (Tuxtla, tel. 961/2–80–81 or 2–68–80; Mexico City, tel. 563–44–00).

By Car Route 190 goes from San Cristóbal to Tuxtla and west into Oaxaca. If you are skipping Palenque, an alternative road to or from Villahermosa is via Pichucalco, on Route 195. It's in excellent condition and the scenery en route is gorgeous.

By Bus Regular first- and second-class bus service runs between Tuxtla and Oaxaca, Villahermosa, Tapachula, and Mérida. For Palenque, you must transfer in Villahermosa or San Cristóbal.

Exploring

❼ The highway into town is endless and honky-tonk. **Tuxtla** (population 525,000) does not have many conveniences for tourists, and it can be difficult to get your bearings. If you stay on the main drag you will run smack into the zócalo, known locally as the *parque central*, which is fronted by huge government buildings. Marimba music is played here. The Tuxtla tourist office is on the mezzanine of Edificio Plaza de las Instituciones (Blvd. Dr. Belisario Domínguez 950, tel. 961/2–55–09 or 2–45–35). It is open weekdays 8 AM–9 PM.

Only the most obstinate animal-hater would fail to be captivated by the free-roaming inmates of the **Tuxtla Zoomat,** all native Chiapans. The 100-plus species on display include black widows, jaguars, marsupials, iguanas, quetzal birds, boa constrictors, tapirs, eagles, and monkeys. *Southeast of town off Libramiento Sur. Admission free but a donation is appreciated. Open Tues.–Sun. 8:30–5:30.*

Amateur archaeologists and botanists should head for **Parque Madero,** which includes the Regional Museum of Chiapas, (open Tues.–Sun. 9–4), Botanical Garden (open Tues.–Sun. 8–6), and orchid house (open Tues.–Sun. 10–1). One of the largest collections of Maya artifacts worldwide is on the ground floor of the museum, an innovative structure of glass, brick, and marble. On the upper floor are displays of colonial pieces and regional handicrafts and costumes. *Northeast of downtown, between 5a Av. Norte and 11a Calle Oriente. Admission: approx. $3.50.*

A good selection of regional handicrafts is on sale in the **Casa de las Artesenias,** a government-run shop on the ground floor of the state tourism office (Blvd. Dr. Belisario Domínguez 950). Amber from Chiapas and gold filigree jewelry, lacquerware, and leather are among the local specialties.

Dining

For price categories, *see* Dining for San Cristóbal. Highly recommended restaurants are indicated by a star ★.

Moderate **La Selva.** Specialties from Chiapas top a menu that satisfies multiple tastes with a broad sampling of international dishes. A tropical atmosphere sizzles with marimba music. *Belisario Dominguez 1360, tel. 961/2–62–51.*

Inexpensive **Cafeteria San Marcos.** For the youthful crowd, this is a popular place on weekends for light meals and mingling. *Plaza Crystal 2-D, tel. 961/1–29–41.*

★ **Las Pichanchas.** This restaurant features an outstanding variety of regional dishes, as well as live marimba music and weekly folkloric dances. *Central Oriente 837, tel. 961/2–53–51. AE, MC, V.*

Lodging

Lodgings are plentiful in Tuxtla. For prices, *see* Lodging for San Cristóbal, *above.* Highly recommended lodgings are indicated by a star ★.

Very Expensive **Hotel Flamboyant.** If you want something splashy and Ameri-
★ can style, try one of the 118 guest rooms in this luxury hotel. All rooms are air-conditioned and have TVs. Capacious is the byword: the pool is huge, and so are the public areas. The only disadvantage is the location—a 10-minute drive west of town. *Blvd. Dr. Belisario Domínguez Km. 1081, 29000; tel. 961/2–93–11 or 2–92–59. Facilities: restaurant, bar, disco, gardens, travel agency, car rental, parking. AE, MC, V.*

Expensive **Bonampak.** A fine hotel that has just been completely and tastefully redone, Bonampak has spacious rooms and an enormous pool set in lush gardens. The cafeteria and restaurant have a well-deserved reputation for good regional cooking, steaks, and soups. *Blvd. Dr. Belisario Dominguez 180, 29030, tel. 961/3–20–50, fax 961/2–77–37. Facilities: restaurant, cafeteria, bar, gardens, tennis, pool, cable TV, travel agency, car rental, beauty shop. AE, MC, V.*

Moderate **Gran Hotel Humberto.** Much closer to the main square is the Gran Hotel Humberto, which has 112 air-conditioned rooms, all with TVs. *Central Poniente 180; tel. 961/2–20–80 or 2–20–44. Facilities: restaurant, cabaret, parking. AE, MC, V.*

12 Huasteca Country

Introduction

By Jim Budd

Mexico City bureau chief for the Reed Travel Group, Jim Budd is the former editor of The News of Mexico City and the Spanish-language business magazine Expansion. He has concentrated on travel writing for nearly 20 years.

Updated by Eleanor S. Morris

Huasteca Country is not Mexico at its best. The Gulf Coast from the Rio Grande down to Veracruz and inland to the eastern Sierra Madre is not the Mexico touted in glossy color brochures and full-page magazine ads. Each of the three border towns— Nuevo Laredo, Reynosa, and Matamoros—seems more industrial and commercial than the next. However, with the new four-lane tollroad from Nuevo Laredo and Reynosa to Monterrey completed, as well as stretches of other highways (Mexico 2, Reynosa-Matamoros; Mexico 80, Manuel, 47 kilometers [29 miles] north of Tampico, to Tampico), the country is on its way to bringing major highways up to U.S. standards. The number of Customs and Immigration inspections has lessened, and most roadblocks have been discontinued.

The flip side of the Huasteca story is appreciated by day-trippers from Texas, who pop across the border to pick up excellent handicrafts in Nuevo Laredo and Matamoros, sample authentic Mexican dishes, and perhaps take in a bullfight—all at a bargain. Those seeking an urban respite make the three-hour drive from the border to Monterrey, an attractive cosmopolitan city founded on steel and beer. Sportsmen are lured by magnificent hunting and fishing at Lake Vicente Guerrero, not far from Ciudad Victoria. And the archaeologically curious visit the spectacular pyramid and stone carvings of El Tajín, one of Mexico's most fascinating and least-visited ruins.

The Huastecs, linguistically related to the Maya, have inhabited the region for the last 3,000 years. They developed a fairly advanced pre-Hispanic civilization, though they were scorned by the Aztecs for their immoral ways. It seems the Huastecs were more interested in worshiping the goddess of fertility and carnal pleasures than in building monuments. The lack of Huastecan ruins is more than compensated for by El Tajín, in the state of Veracruz, one of the premier archaeological zones in Mexico. It was built by the Totonacs, vassals of the Aztecs, and contains the 60-foot Pyramid of the Niches, several ball courts, and carvings of human sacrifice. El Tajín was apparently abandoned around the year AD 1100, but the Totonacs remained a tribe to be reckoned with: They were the people who greeted Cortés when he landed in Veracruz.

Many Texans weekend in Monterrey, Mexico's third-largest city and the area's cultural highlight. They come for the Alfa Cultural Center, museums of history and art, the Mexican Baseball Hall of Fame, the five-star hotels, restaurants, and shopping required of a major commercial center. Huasteca Country has its share of natural attractions, such as the dramatic Barranca de Huasteca (Huasteca Canyon) and Grutas García, caves with an underground lake and a stalactite and stalagmite forest both of which lie west of Monterrey. Cola de Caballo (Horsetail Falls), south of the city, sits amid wooded parkland right off Mexico 85.

A growing number of vacationers head to Huasteca Country, especially on coach tours down the coast, to visit only Tampico, but they occasionally travel as far as Veracruz. With unleaded gasoline becoming easier to find in Mexico, more motorists are venturing into Huasteca Country, the appeal being that they're able to go where and when they want and stay for as long as they choose.

Essential Information

Important Addresses and Numbers

Tourist Information Ironically, the best information about Mexico is found in Texas border towns, especially at places that sell Mexican automobile insurance, which is mandatory in Mexico. This list will give you a head start in searching out such sources: **Sanborns,** 2007 S. 10th St., McAllen, tel. 512/682–1353; **Bravo Insurance,** 2212 Santa Ursula, Laredo, tel. 512/722–0931; **Sanborns,** 2235 Boca Chica Blvd., Brownsville, tel. 512/542–7222. Keep in mind that good road maps are especially hard to come by in Mexico. PEMEX, the national petroleum company, however, has a fairly detailed *Atlas de Carreteras y Ciudades Turísticas* (Road Atlas and Tourist Cities) available at bookstores, hotel newsstands and some PEMEX stations.

Border Towns The Tamaulipas State Tourist Authority maintains information offices at Mexican customs and immigration posts in **Nuevo Laredo** (tel. 871/2–0104); in **Reynosa** (tel. 892/2–1189); and in **Matamoros** (tel. 891/2–3630). All are open weekdays, usually 9–3.

Monterrey The main information center (Infotur) of the Nuevo Leon State Tourism Office is at Zaragoza and Matamoros on the Gran Plaza (tel. 83/45–08–70, 83/45–09–02, or 800/235–2438). It is open weekdays 9–1 and 3–7, weekends 10–5. Recorded information in English and Spanish can be heard by dialing 83/42–21–66. For toll-free information, call 800/235–2430.

Tampico The local tourism office is well hidden one flight up at Olmos Altos and Carranza (tel. 12/12–26–68), but it has so little information that the walk up is rarely worth the effort.

Veracruz There is a tourism information office on the ground floor of the City Hall (Ayuntamiento) on Montesinos 220 (tel. 29/32–70–26 or 32–16–13).

The federal government also maintains tourism offices in the states of Tamaulipas, Veracruz, and Nuevo Leon. **Tamaulipas** (for Nuevo Laredo, Reynosa, Matamoros, and Tampico): Oaxaca 360 Altos, Col. Rodriguez, Reynosa, tel. 892/2–46–60 or 892/2–24–49; **Nuevo Leon:** Av. Loma Grande and San Francisco, Monterrey, tel. 83/44–43–43, 40–10–80 or 44–11–69; **Veracruz:** Esq. (corner) Zaragoza and Prima Verdad, tel. 29/7–3030 or 7–3796.

U.S. Consulates **Matamoros** (Primera at Azalias, tel. 891/6–7270); **Nuevo Laredo** (Allende 3330, tel. 871/4–0512); **Monterrey** (Constitución 411 Poniente, tel. 83/43–06–50 and 83/45–21–20); and **Veracruz** (Juárez 110, tel. 29/31–01–42).

Emergencies **Matamoros: Police:** González and Calle Venteuno, tel. 891/2–
Border Towns 0732; **Cruz Roja (Red Cross) Hospital:** Canales and Durango, tel. 891/2–0044. **Nuevo Laredo: Police:** Maclovio Herréa and Ocampo, tel. 871/2–2146; **San José Hospital:** Comonfort and Independencia, tel. 871/4–9506. **Reynosa: Police:** Morales between Veracruz and Nayarit, tel. 891/2–0008; **Cruz Roja (Red Cross) Hospital:** Morelos and Veracruz, tel. 891/2–1314.

Monterrey **Police:** Gonzalitos and Lincoln, tel. 83/43–25–76; **Cruz Roja (Red Cross) Hospital:** Universidad and Camelo, tel. 83/75–12–12.

Tampico **Police:** Mendez and Sor Juana Inés de la Cruz, tel. 12/12–11–57; **Cruz Roja (Red Cross) Hospital:** Tamaulipas and Gochicoa, tel. 12/12–13–33.

Veracruz **Police:** Playa Linda 222, tel. 29/32–28–33 or 32–37–61. **Hospital:** Córdoba and Lafragua, tel. 29/37–54–11, and **Cruz Roja** (Red Cross), tel. 29/37–55–00.

Arriving and Departing by Plane

Airports and Airlines All major cities in Huasteca Country are served either by **Aeroméxico** (tel. 800/AEROMEX), **Mexicana,** (tel. 800/531–7921), and **aeromonterrey** (reservations handled in U.S. by Mexicana, tel. 800/531–7921; in Monterrey, tel. 83/40–55–11). Limited intraregional service is provided by **Litoral** (tel. in Veracruz, 29/335–008 or 29/355–287; in Monterrey, 83/407–979; or, elsewhere in Mexico, 800/2–9020). Monterrey and Tampico are the only cities in the region with direct airline flights from the United States.

Border Towns Nuevo Laredo: **Mexicana** flies in daily from Mexico City. **Aeroméxico** flies into Matamoros and Reynosa via Mexico City. **Continental** (tel. 800/525–0280) flies into Laredo, Texas, and McAllen, Texas (border city for Reynosa) from Houston.

Monterrey **Mexicana** has seven to eight flights daily from Mexico City. **Aeroméxico** has service from Houston and Los Angeles. **Continental** has several flights daily from Houston. **aeromonterrey** has 11 weekly flights from San Antonio and four weekly flights from Harlingen, Texas. **Litoral** links Monterrey, Tampico, and Veracruz.

Tampico **Mexicana** has two to three flights daily from Mexico City. **Litoral** has flights from Monterrey and Veracruz, and from Brownsville, Texas.

Veracruz **Mexicana** operates two to three flights daily from Mexico City; **aeromonterrey** links Matamoros, Monterrey, Tampico, and Veracruz; **Litoral** links Veracruz with Monterrey and Tampico.

Arriving and Departing by Car, Train, and Bus

By Car With unleaded gasoline now more widely available, an increasing number of American motorists are exploring Mexican highways. Cars should be in good mechanical condition, and Mexican insurance is mandatory. Car-rental agencies rarely permit their vehicles to be taken into Mexico. Although Mexico is busy building improved highways, driving at night should be avoided as many of the two-lane roads do not have shoulders; Mexico is also still an open range country where animals meander back and forth across the roads. The old Pan-American Highway, Mexico 85 (now under construction as a four-lane tollroad), leads from Laredo to Monterrey and on to Mexico City via Ciudad Victoria and Pachuca. From Monterrey, Mexico 57 is the preferred way to reach Mexico City, but it does not pass through what is called the Huasteca Country. From Matamoros (across from Brownsville), Mexico 180 runs down the Gulf Coast to Tampico, Veracruz, and beyond. A turnoff on Mexico 101 leads to the hunting and fishing camps at Lake Vicente Guerrero. Mexico 97 leads from Reynosa (McAllen) into Mexico 101.

Distances are deceiving in this part of Mexico because of the Sierra Madre Oriente. It generally takes 3 hours to drive from the border to Monterrey; from Monterrey to Cuidad Victoria is another 4 hours; from Cuidad Victoria to Pachuca (a mountainous route with hairpin turns) takes approximately 6 hours; and from Pachuca to Mexico City is about 2 hours.

Border Towns Downtown Nuevo Laredo is reached by International Bridge 1, the point of entry required for vehicles heading to the interior. The New Bridge is the best route from downtown Brownsville to downtown Matamoros. U.S. 281 leads down to Hidalgo, Texas, and the bridge crossing into Reynosa.

Monterrey Mexico's third-largest city is about 242 kilometers (150 miles) south of Nuevo Laredo on Mexico 85; it can also be reached from Matamoros and Reynosa on Mexico 40.

Tampico The port is roughly a seven-hour drive from Matamoros on Mexico 180, or eight hours from Monterrey via Mexico 84.

Veracruz The city can be reached within about eight hours by traveling south from Tampico via Mexico 180, or within six hours from Mexico City via Mexico 150.

By Train

There is no longer train service to Huasteca Country; *El Regiomontano* between Nuevo Laredo and Monterrey has been discontinued, and *El Tamaulipeco* (800/228–3225) now runs between Monterrey and Mexico City (for bus connections, *see* By Bus, *below*).

By Bus

Huasteca Country is well connected by buses, and fares are low. Information on Mexican bus service is available from terminals in Laredo (tel. 512/723–4324), McAllen (tel. 512/682–5513), and Brownsville (tel. 512/546–7171). There is first-class bus service between Nuevo Laredo and Monterrey, to connect with *El Tamaulipeco* to Mexico City (tel. 800/228–3225 in Texas; tel. 905/546–7171 in Mexico City). **Sanborn's Viva Tours** (2015 S. 10th St., McAllen, Texas, tel. 800/395–VIVA or 512/682–9872) runs daily tours to Monterrey and one weekly tour through Tampico to Veracruz.

Guided Tours

Several U.S. tour operators, including **Gray Line** (tel. 512/943–2144) and **Viva Tours** (tel. 512/682–9872), run shopping and sightseeing tours to the border towns and coach excursions into the interior of Huasteca Country. **Viva** has also inaugurated a four-day tour to El Tajín. **Viajes Pozo** (tel. 12/13–58–71 or 12/12–01–50) in Tampico, **Veracruzana de Turismo** (tel. 29/31–00–11) in Veracruz, and **Servicios Turisticos** (tel. 83/43–79–48) in Monterrey provide sightseeing excursions in their respective areas.

Exploring

Numbers in the margin correspond to points of interest on the Huasteca Country map.

❶ Two bridges connect **Nuevo Laredo** with Laredo, Texas. However, tourists must use International Bridge 1, the only one
with facilities for clearing people and vehicles for travel to the
interior of Mexico. The newer Juárez Lincoln Bridge leading
into I–35 is obligatory for the trip back across the border. For
brief excursions across the border, consider leaving your car in
Laredo and walking over. This eliminates the hassle of purchasing Mexico auto insurance as well as the long wait—often a
half hour or more—to bring a car back into the United States.

Nuevo Laredo is the major port of entry for trucks and trains
heading into Mexico and also a manufacturing center for U.S.
firms that take advantage of cheap Mexican labor. It in no way
resembles a beautiful city and has no historical sights. Some of
the shops, however, are quite attractive, and there are a few
good restaurants in town. It's the shopping and dining that
bring Americans to Nuevo Laredo. Avenida Guerrero, which
runs from the border and eventually becomes Reforma, is the
main shopping street. The Nuevo Laredo racetrack closed in
1988, and while there are promises of a reopening soon, don't
bet on it. Occasionally there are bullfights on Sundays.

❷ **Reynosa,** some 242 kilometers (150 miles) southeast of Laredo,
is an oil-refining and gas-processing center of little charm.
There are a few curio shops and a couple of bars and restaurants
clustered around the **Zona Rosa** (Pink Zone) tourist district.
Beyond lies a very typical Mexican town complete with cathedral and central square, the **Plaza Principal.**

The cathedral on the square is of some interest, too: The original colonial church has been joined like a Siamese twin to an ultramodern arched and stained-glass windowed, newer
addition. There are also an inordinate number of dentists in
this area (Texans save money by having their teeth fixed south
of the Rio Grande). The main part of the city, around Plaza
Principal, is nearly 20 blocks from the International Bridge.
Hidalgo Street itself, leading from the plaza, is a colorful pedestrian mall of shops and street vendors.

❸ While **Matamoros**—across from Brownsville, Texas (the southernmost point in the continental United States)—has much
more to offer than Reynosa, it scarcely glitters. Some 20 years
ago, Avenida Alvaro Obregón, which leads from the main
bridge, was spruced up to "dignify" the Mexican side of the
border, but the area has not been maintained and is decidedly
shabby. Nonetheless, this is where you'll find some of the best
shops, restaurants, accommodations, and the local museum. In
fact, the **Casa Mata Museum** in the remains of old Fort Mata,
whose stone walls, turrets, and cannon are a legacy from the
city's turbulent past, will hold special interest to local history
buffs. *Calle Cuba and Lauro Villar. No phone. Admission
free. Open Wed.–Mon. 9:30–5:30.*

Matamoros, the most historic of the border towns, dates to the
18th century. It is named H. Matamoros, or Heroic Matamoros,
for one of the many rebellious priests who were executed by the
Spaniards during the War of Independence (1810–1821). The
first major battle of the Mexican-American War was fought
here when guns in Matamoros began shelling Fort Brown on
the north side of the river. Shortly afterward, troops of Zachary Taylor occupied Matamoros and began their march south.
During the U.S. Civil War, nearby Bagdad became a major

Huasteca Country

Sabinas

Nuevo Laredo **1**   Laredo

TEXAS

Padre Island

85

Sabinas Hidalgo

Rio Grande   McAllen

Laguna Madre

Grutas García

Monterrey **4 — 10**

54

Reynosa **2**   Brownsville

3 Matamoros

Barranca de Huasteca **11**

40

Saltillo   Cola de Caballo

85

97

180

Laguna Madre

Linares

57

Boca Jesús Maria

101   180

Lake **12** Vicente Guerrero

Golfo de Mexico

Matehuala

Ciudad Victoria

101   85

Ciudad Mante

80

Ebano   Ciudad Madero

13 Tampico

San Luis Potosí   Cárdenas   Ciudad Valles

70

180   *Laguna de Tamiahua*

120   105

Tuxpan

Querétaro   85

El Tajín   Poza Rica

Celaya   130   **14** **15** Papantla

Tula   Pachúca   131

120   Cuautitlán   Teotihuacán   180

Morelia   Mexico City   Jalapa

Zitácuaro   Cholula   Zempoala

Toluca   140   Veracruz **16**

Puebla

Córdoba

0   50 miles

0   75 km

N

port for Confederate blockade runners. A wild and wicked place, Bagdad was destroyed by a hurricane a century ago; treasure hunters often discover bits and pieces of it among the dunes on the beach. Today Matamoros is the commercial center of a rich agricultural area and a manufacturing center for Mexico's in-bond industry.

Numbers in the margin correspond to points of interest on the Monterrey map.

❹ Mexico's third-largest city, **Monterrey** is home to some 3 million people who claim to be the hardest-working in Mexico. The capital of Nuevo León state, this is an industrial center, a brewer of beer and forger of steel, with nothing in the way of a laid-back lifestyle. Still, it is a favorite with weekenders and "winter Texans" from the Rio Grande Valley who find Monterrey so near—a three-hour drive from the border or a short flight from Dallas, Houston, or San Antonio—and yet so foreign. The top hotels are clustered close together downtown, and several streets, including Avenida Morelos—the main drag—are now pedestrian malls.

❺ The impressive **Gran Plaza,** which covers 100 acres and was completed in 1985 as part of an urban renewal scheme, is within walking distance of downtown hotels. The plaza extends from
❻ the new and modernistic **Palacio Municipal** (City Hall) for several blocks past the cathedral, the old City Hall, and the Legis-
❼ lative Palace to the neoclassical **Palacio de Gobierno** (State Palace). Towering above it is a concrete slab topped by the Light of Commerce, a laser beam that flashes from 8 to 11 PM Tuesday–Sunday. Handsome Saddle Mountain and the craggy Sierra Madre provide a majestic backdrop.

Gran Plaza now has the brand-new **Museum of Contemporary Art** to brag about as well. Its purpose is to promote the visual arts of Mexico and Latin America. *Gran Plaza, corner of Zuazua and Ocampo, tel. 83/42–4820 or 83/42–4830. Admission: about $3.35. Open Tues., Thurs., Sat. 11–7; Wed., Sun. 11–9; closed Mon.*

Monterrey dates to 1596, although for the first couple of centuries it was little more than an outpost. Construction of the cathedral—on the Gran Plaza a block or so from Palacio Municipal—began in 1600 but took some 250 years to finish. The
❽ **Obispado** (Bishop's House) is the only landmark to be completed in the colonial era (1788). About a mile from the city center, along Avenida Padre Mier and built on a hilltop as a home for retired prelates, the Obispado was used as a fort during the Mexican-American War (1847), the French Intervention (1862), and again during the Mexican Revolution (1915). Today it is the **Regional Museum of Nuevo León,** its exhibits focusing on the history of the area, but the major appeal is the splendid view it provides of Monterrey. *Small admission fee. Open Tues.–Sun. 10–6.*

In recent years, Mexican beer has taken the world by storm. Monterrey is where all this started when the Cuauhtémoc Brewery opened a century ago. Today the brewery complex in-
❾ cludes the **Mexican Baseball Hall of Fame,** a sports museum, an art gallery, and a beer garden with free beer. *Av. Universidad 2202, tel. 83/72–48–94. Admission free. Open daily.*

Monterrey

KEY
— Rail Lines

Alfa Cultural
Center, **10**
Gran Plaza, **5**
Mexican Baseball Hall
of Fame, **9**
Obispado, **8**
Palacio de Gobierno, **7**
Palacio Municipal, **6**

The brewery spawned a glass factory for bottles, a steel mill for caps, a carton factory, and eventually several industrial con-

⓾ glomerates, one of which, Alfa, gave Monterrey the **Alfa Cultural Center,** probably the best museum of science and technology in the country. The museum has many hands-on exhibits and an IMAX theater. *Av. Gómez Morín at Roberto Garza Sada, tel. 83/78–35–10. Admission fee. Open Tues.– Sun. 3–9.*

Numbers in the margin correspond to points of interest on the Huasteca Country map.

⓫ Mexico 40 leads to scenic **Barranca de Huasteca** (Huasteca Canyon) in the western suburb of Santa Caterina. The canyon is about two miles down a paved road to the south of the village. Although the road is rocky and unpaved, the drive through the 1000-feet-deep canyon is spectacular. **The Grutas García** (García Caves) are farther west on 40, about 40 kilometers (25 miles) from downtown Monterrey. A swaying funicular leads to the caves, where guides lead the way through a mile of underground grottoes. This site is far less commercialized than are similar attractions north of the border. *Funicular cost is approximately $1.*

From Monterrey the Pan-American Highway, Mexico 85, runs south through Huasteca Country to Ciudad Victoria, capital of

⓬ Tamaulipas state. This is the route to man-made **Lake Vicente Guerrero,** a favorite with American bass fishermen year-round and, during the winter months, an excellent place to hunt duck and white-wing dove. Several camps in the area, such as White Wing and Lago Vista, cater to American sportsmen. For information, contact White Wing (tel. 516/682–3113) and Lago Vista (tel. 516/546–9101).

About 35 kilometers (20 miles) south of Monterrey on Mexico 85 is **Cola de Caballo** (Horsetail Falls), a magnificent waterfall park 4 miles off the highway at the small town of El Cercado. At the park entrance is Hacienda Cola de Caballo, a relaxing retreat surrounded by forests and mountains (tel. 828/5–0260 or 5–0660).

⓭ Highway 40 continues toward the coast and to **Tampico,** a picturesque if raffish port adjoining Ciudad Madero, an oil-refining center. Because of its relative proximity to the border, Tampico gets a smattering of tourists and is a fascinating place to wander around for a spell. Plaza Libertad, near the harbor, is shaggy and unkempt—very much the tropical waterfront. A block away is the regal Plaza de Armas, with its majestic City Hall guarded by towering palms. The cathedral here, started in 1823, was completed with funds donated by Edward L. Doheny, an oil magnate implicated in the Teapot Dome scandal of the 1920s. Oil made Tampico what it is today. Shortly after the conquest, the Franciscans established a mission in the area near a Huastec fishing village, but the settlement was constantly battered by hurricanes and pirate attacks. In 1828, the Spaniards attempted to reconquer then-independent Mexico by landing troops at Tampico, but they were soundly defeated. With later invasions by the Americans and then the French, the port languished until oil was discovered in the region at the turn of the 20th century. The British and Americans developed the industry until a strike in 1938 led to its nationalization. Petroleum helped Tampico prosper but ruined the area for tourism. Río Pánuco is so polluted that it no longer attracts tarpon fishermen, and Miramar beach has become grubby. Except for one international flight from Brownsville, Texas, Tampico airport now handles only regional flights, and the hotel chains have returned their properties to local owners.

⑭ The pyramids and temples at **El Tajín** compose the only major archaeological site in Huasteca Country. The center was built by the Totonacs, the people who met Cortés when he landed at Veracruz. El Tajín, being remote, is perhaps the least-visited of the major archaeological sites in Mexico, but it is very much worth seeing even if you have to be your own guide. Much of the site remains unexcavated; the largest and most famous structure at El Tajín is the pyramid of the Niches. Consisting of six levels into which 365 altars are carved, the pyramid towers some 60 feet. It is generally believed that the niches contained small altars, but this has not been confirmed. For the past year, 300 workers have been busy excavating the site after a long hiatus.

By some accounts, El Tajín was the most influential center in Mexico 1,000 years ago. It was a source of cacao beans, which were used as money in pre-Hispanic times. And the sacred ball game, similar to soccer, that was played throughout Mesoamerica is said to have originated here. In this game, players used a hard rubber ball that could not be touched with the hands. Two ball courts at El Tajín that have been fairly well restored show carvings of players suited up in knee pads and body protectors. They also indicate that games ended with human sacrifice. *El Tajín is 13 km (8 mi) west of Papantla. Small admission and parking fees. Open Tues.–Sun. 9–6.*

⑮ The city that is closest to the ruins at El Tajín is **Papantla,** the center of a vanilla-producing region and home of the Flying Indians, who perform their ancient ritual all over Mexico. The ceremony, which in pre-Conquest times had religious significance, consists of five men, called *voladores* (flyers), who climb to a tiny platform atop a 100-foot pole. There four of the five tie to their ankles ropes that have been wound maypole-style around the pole. While the untied performer plays a flute and beats a drum, the others hurl themselves from their perches and whirl gradually toward the ground as the ropes unwind. At the last moment they flip neatly to their feet on the ground. The gods surely are impressed.

⑯ **Veracruz** is about an eight-hour drive south from Tampico. This was the first European city to be established on the American mainland, although the spot where Cortés supposedly landed is about 50 kilometers (30 miles) north. What is professed to be his home, a rustic compound now in a state of decay, is located on the north edge of the city and is worth seeing if only for its crumbling, roofless masonry, taken over by clinging vines and massive tree roots. During the viceregal era, Veracruz was the only east-coast port permitted to operate in New Spain. As a result, it was frequently attacked by pirates. The great fort of San Juan de Ulúa, built shortly after the conquest, is a monument to that swashbuckling era. The fort was the last territory in Mexico to be held by the Spanish Royalists. After independence, it was used in unsuccessful attempts to fight off first the invading French, the Americans, then the French again and, in 1914, the Americans. It also served as a prison but today is a museum. *Reached via causeway from downtown Veracruz. Small admission fee. Open Tues.–Sun. 10–6.*

Also of interest is **Baluarte de Santiago,** a fortress and museum. It's all that's left of old city walls and was also built (in 1636) as a defense against pirates. *Rayon and Gomez Farias. Open Wed.–Mon. 10 AM–7 PM.*

Until a few decades ago, Veracruz was Mexico's premier seaside resort and the port of entry for most foreign visitors; travelers arrived by ship, then boarded a train to Mexico City, often looking wistfully back. Today relatively few foreigners find their way to Veracruz's beaches, and domestic vacationers are lured into the area by prices that are far lower than those found in Acapulco, Puerto Vallarta, or Cancún. The beaches begin on the southern edge of town and extend to Mocambo, about 7 kilometers (4 miles) farther. Beyond Mocambo is the fishing village of Boca del Río, where a little Atoyac river meets the sea and every other house seems to be a restaurant. The seafood is some of the best in Mexico. Most of these cafés feature live musical entertainment, but customers are expected to pay for the songs they order.

Veracruz itself is famed as a musical city, hometown of La Bamba and its own special brand of song played by lively trios outfitted all in white and slapping away at tiny guitars and portable harps. In the evening, mariachis entertain outside the sidewalk cafés around the main plaza. The port is a fun-loving but not particularly sophisticated town, enjoyed by those who care little about spending hours baking on the beach. The best time of all, for many, is *Carnaval*, Mexico's version of Mardi Gras. It takes place during the week before Ash Wednesday and is wild, merry, and far less self-conscious than the better-known celebrations in Rio or New Orleans. The biggest problem at such times is finding a room, but the local tourist office can usually come up with acceptable accommodations. The same is true during Christmas and Easter week, when all of Mexico goes on vacation and heads for the beach.

Shopping

Matamoros The most appealing shops are on Calle Obregón, the street that leads from the border bridge to the center of town. **Barbara** (tel. 891/2–3627) has an attractive assortment of quality handicrafts, carved wood, home furnishings, and even good costume jewelry and imported cosmetics. **Garcia's** (tel. 891/3–1566), across from the Hotel del Prado, and **The Drive Inn** (tel. 891/2–0022), also near the hotel, are both restaurants with gift shops as big as their dining room and a nice selection of craft items.

Matamoros Market, downtown, is the place to haggle for bargains; you get what you pay for.

Nuevo Laredo International Bridge 1 leads into Avenida Guerrero and the more prestigious stores. Few have street numbers, but their signs are big. **Marti's** (tel. 871/8–3759) has perhaps the best selection of quality crafts, with prices to match. **Galva's** (tel. 871/2–8348), a few blocks farther, has a wider variety when it comes to prices, and **Rafael de Mexico** (tel. 871/8–5329), where Guerrero widens into Avenida Reforma, is the biggest and finest shop in town. In between there are countless garish outlets selling plaster matadors, giant sombreros, sunsets painted on black velvet, and the like. Most shops remain open until 8 PM.

Monterrey Top-quality shops center on Plaza Hidalgo, near the major hotels, with leather and cowboy boots the local specialties. **Sanborns,** just off Plaza Hidalgo, has an excellent selection of silver, onyx, and other Mexican craft items. The **Mercado Indio,** at Bolívar Norte 1150, is another favorite with souvenir hunters. Superb lead crystal is made in Monterrey by **Krystaluxus** at José María Vigil 400 (take a taxi from your hotel) although there are showrooms (and higher prices) in town. There are guided tours of the factory Monday–Friday, 9 AM–1 PM and 2:30 PM–6:30 PM; Saturday 9 AM to 1 PM.

Veracruz There are many seashells and dried and varnished frogs, iguanas, and armadillos heaped in stacks at the stands lining the waterfront. Independencia, the main shopping street, has little to interest tourists.

Sports

Reynosa **Bullfights** are staged most Sundays in winter, with tickets and transportation available from McAllen, Texas, across the border. Contact Viva Tours (2011 S. 10th St., tel. 512/682–9872).

Monterrey From March through June there are Sunday **bullfights** at the Plaza Monumental starting at 4. Hotel travel desks can provide tickets and transportation, as well as arrange visits to **charreadas** (Mexican rodeos), held most Sunday mornings. Hotels can arrange temporary memberships in one of the areas three **golf courses** but only on weekdays.

Tampico **Golf** can be played at the local country club on weekdays; local hotels can arrange temporary memberships. **Tarpon and snapper fishing** is popular at Chairel Lagoon, with boats and equipment available for rent. Lake Vicente Guerrero, near Ciudad Victoria, has some of the best **bass fishing** and **duck hunting** in the country.

Beaches

Matamoros About 30 kilometers (18 miles) from downtown Matamoros is **Playa Lauro Villar,** sometimes referred to by its old name, Playa Washington. Facilities are limited, though there are some good seafood shanties.

Tampico **Playa Miramar,** about 5 kilometers (3 miles) from town, is a favorite with locals. Facilities are limited, but many people enjoy its unspoiled, if grubby, charm.

Veracruz The beach begins on the southern edge of the city at **Villa del Mar** but is at its best down toward **Mocambo,** about 7 kilometers (4 miles) from downtown Veracruz. Buses run out this way. Umbrellas and chairs are available for rent, and wandering vendors peddle beer and seafood snacks.

Dining

One of the most attractive features of Huasteca Country is the extensive variety and the low cost, compared with other regions of Mexico. *Cabrito* (roast kid) are found on many menus and *huachinango* (red snapper). Restaurants are generally casual, with the exception of Monterrey's Residence restaurant, where a jacket and tie are necessary. Highly recommended restaurants are indicated by a star ★.

Category	Cost*
Expensive	over $25
Moderate	$15–$25
Inexpensive	under $15

per person, excluding drinks, service, and tax

Border Towns
Expensive

The Drive Inn. In spite of the name, it's a formal restaurant with crystal chandeliers, linen tablecloths, orchestra, and dance floor. Expect a romantic evening, and stick with steak and seafood specialties. *Avenida Hidalgo at Calle 6a, Matamoros, tel. 891/2-00-22. Jacket advised. No reservations. MC, V.*

★ **Garcia's.** Recently relocated across from the Hotel Del Prado, this is a romantic place for dancing and dining on lobster or steak. *Calle Alvaro Obregón, Matamoros, tel. 891/3-1566. Reservations advised. AE, DC, MC, V.*

★ **Winery.** This Mexican version of a Continental wine bar serves regional specialties such as *tampiqueña* steak and *queso fundido* (melted cheese) often served in a bowl with *chorizo* (spicy sausage) to be spread on tortillas. It has the best selection of Mexican wines in town. *Calle Matamoros 308, Nuevo Laredo, tel. 871/2-0895. No reservations. Dress: casual. AE, DC, MC, V.*

Moderate

Cadillac. Dating to the Prohibition era, this spot is a favorite with the Texas crowd—a hangout better known for its atmosphere than for its cuisine. *Ocampo at Belden, Nuevo Laredo, tel. 871/2-0015. No reservations. Dress: informal. AE, DC, MC, V.*

Mexico Tipico. This establishment offers both indoor and outdoor patio dining, with *mariachis* (strolling musicians) coming in off the street to entertain diners. The patio has both open and covered dining, and a waterfall. Specialties are *carne asada* (grilled meat) and *cabrito* (baby goat). True to its name, Mexico Tipico serves the typical Mexican plate of beef, chicken, or cheese enchiladas with rice and refried beans. *Guerrero 934, tel. 871/2-1525. No reservations. Dress: casual. MC, V.*

Sam's. Wild game and seafood are the specialties here, but prices are reasonable. Sam's is frequented by Americans from the Rio Grande Valley in the winter and snowbirds from Minnesota. *Allende 990, Reynosa, tel. 892/2-0034. No reservations. Dress: informal. MC, V.*

Monterrey
Expensive

★ **Luisiana.** Perhaps the most elegant dining room downtown, this is a taste of how New Orleans is imagined in Mexico. There are no Cajun specialties on the menu, but rattlesnake is occasionally served. The usual menu consists of steak and seafood dishes. *Plaza Hidalgo, tel. 83/43–15–61. Reservations advised. Jackets appreciated but not required. AE, DC, MC, V.*

★ **Residence.** A clubby meeting place for the industrialists and executives who make Monterrey what it is, the menu here features both Mexican specialties and Continental dishes. *Degollado and Matamoros, tel. 83/42–83–39 and 83/42–73–0. Lunch reservations advised. Jacket and tie appreciated. AE, DC, MC, V.*

Moderate **El Pastor.** Roast kid is the regional specialty in northeastern Mexico, and this is where Monterrey folk go to enjoy it. *Madero Poniente 1067, tel. 83/74–04–80. No reservations. Dress: informal. MC, V.*

Sanborns. Part of a national chain that is a Mexican institution, this is the place to go for hamburgers and malts as well as tacos and enchiladas. *Just off Plaza Hidalgo, tel. 83/42–14–41. No reservations. Dress: informal. AE, MC, V.*

Tampico **Deligencias.** Stuffed crabs are the specialty at this plain water-
Moderate front café that ranks as one of the most famous seafood restaurants in Mexico. *Ayuntamiento 2702, tel. 12/13–76–42. No reservations. Dress: casual. MC, V.*

Inexpensive **Cafe y Neveriá Elite** is a popular gathering spot for breakfast, coffee, and ice cream treats as well as other short-order meals. Shiny and bright with Formica tables, it's decidedly informal. *Av. Diaz Miron 211 Ote. tel. 83/12–03–64. No credit cards.*

Veracruz **La Bamba.** On the waterfront with a lovely view, the menu at
Expensive this eatery includes steak and chicken as well as seafood. *Malecon at Avila Camacho, tel. 29/32–53–55. No reservations. Dress: casual. AE, DC, MC, V.*

Moderate **Pardiños,** in Boca del Rio about 10 kilometers (6.2 miles) south
★ of downtown, is a star in a village of seafood restaurants. Plain tables in a storefront setting belie the elegant preparation of such dishes as crabs Salpicon, grilled sea bass, and *huachinango* (red snapper) a la Veracruzana, served with *plantanos fritos* (fried plantains). *Boca del Rio (take a bus or taxi). Dress casual. MC, V.*

Inexpensive **La Paroquia.** Possibly the most famous sidewalk café in Mexico, this is the place to breakfast on sweet rolls and *café con leche* (bang your glass for a refill) and sip a beer while munching shrimp as marimbas play around sunset. *Independencia 106 (across from the cathedral), no phone. No credit cards.*

Lodging

There are good hotels in a few Mexican border towns, and staying overnight in a foreign country can be fun. The interior Huasteca Country cities offer a wide choice of accommodations. Highly recommended lodgings are indicated by a star ★.

Category	Cost*
Very Expensive	over $100
Expensive	$85–$100

Moderate	$50–$85
Inexpensive	under $50

All prices are for a standard double room; excluding taxes.

Border Towns
Expensive

Del Prado. A pleasant low rise built along Spanish colonial lines with a large pool in the patio, this is the center of activity for much of Matamoros. Rooms are plain but comfortable. *Alvaro Obregón at Amapolas (6 blocks from border bridge), Matamoros, tel. 891/3–9440. 122 rooms. Facilities: restaurant, bar, pool, satellite TV. AE, MC, V.*

Moderate

Astromundo. Downtown and handy to the bullring, the market, and the few good local restaurants, this popular hotel gets a lot of traffic from weekending winter Texans. *Juárez at Guerrero, Reynosa, tel. 892/2–5625. 106 rooms. Facilities: restaurant, bar, pool. MC, V.*

El Rio. A modern white structure spread out on large landscaped grounds, this motel has a spacious lobby and large guest rooms decorated in white and burgundy with dark Spanish Colonial furniture. All units include shower and telephone. *5 km (3 mi) south on Hwy 85, tel. 871/4–3666. 152 rooms. Facilities: dining room, bar, 2 swimming pools, parking on grounds.*

Hotel Reforma. An older hotel just a few blocks south of Plaza Hidalgo, Reforma has a restaurant opening both off the lobby and the street, and secure parking a block away. Rooms in the older section, although somewhat small and rather nondescript, are comfortable; junior suites in the new section are spacious and modern. All units come with shower, TV, and telephone. *Guerrero 822, tel. 871/2–6250. 38 rooms. Facilities: restaurant, bar, parking.*

Monterrey
Very Expensive
★

Ambassador. A downtown landmark recently restored as a Westin/Camino Real with spacious, comfortable rooms, a piano bar in the lobby, and a health club; this is the best hotel in Huasteca Country. *Hidalgo at Emilio Carranza, tel. 83/44–93–00 or 800/228–3000. 241 rooms and suites. Facilities: satellite TV, shops, travel desk. AE, DC, MC, V.*

Gran Ancira. A grand old lady, built in 1912 but kept like new, the property is reminiscent of the grand hotels of Europe. It features good dining, a popular bar, and large, comfortable rooms. *Hidalgo at Escobedo, tel. 83/45–10–60 or 800/626–0591. 240 rooms and suites. Facilities: satellite TV, shops. AE, MC, DC, V.*

Expensive
★

Chipinque. This hilltop resort property overlooking the city is wonderful if you have a car. The view from the restaurant is extraordinary, especially at night. *Meseta de Chipinque, tel. 83/78–11–00. 43 rooms. Facilities: restaurant/bar, pool, tennis court. AE, MC, V.*

Moderate

Río. A large commercial establishment, the Río is centrally located but somewhat noisy. *Padre Mier and Garibaldi, tel. 83/44–90–40. 408 rooms. Facilities: restaurant, lobby bar, pool. MC, V.*

Royalty. Good location and low prices are the main attractions here. *Hidalgo Oriente 402, tel. 83/40–98–00 or 83/40–98–06. 66 rooms. Facilities: restaurant, bar. MC, V.*

Tampico
Expensive

Camino Real. Attractively decorated, this low-rise property near the city center comes close to being a resort. *Madero 210 Oriente, tel. 12/13–88–11 or 800/228–3000. 132 rooms. Facili-*

ties: pool, bar, restaurant, tour desk, evening entertainment. AE, MC, V.

Moderate **Inglaterra.** The convenient location of this property may be a plus to business travelers, while others may find it too commercial and noisy. *Díaz Mirón 116 Oriente, tel. 12/12–56–78. Facilities: restaurant, bar, evening entertainment. AE, MC, V.*

Veracruz **Emporio.** This big, commercial hotel, recently renovated, is
Expensive fun and well situated—right on the malecón. Ask for a room with a sea view. *Paseo de Malecon s/n, tel. 29/32–00–20 or 29/31–22–06. 201 rooms. Facilities: indoor and outdoor pools, satellite TV, restaurant, lobby bar, disco. AE, MC, V.*

Mocambo. One of the first beach resorts in Mexico, this landmark is showing its age, and, thankfully, an ambitious renovation is underway. But in the meantime, it's still a must-see with its sprawling grounds and fine dark-wood fixtures. *Playa Mocambo, tel. 29/37–15–00 or 29/37–17–10. Facilities: beach, indoor and outdoor pools, restaurant, bar, evening entertainment. AE, MC, V.*

Moderate **Colonial.** A comfortable, but unimpressuve place to stay, the Colonial is 2 blocks from the harbor. *Miguel Lerdo 117, tel. 29/32–52–93, 29/32–04–41, or 29/32–01–93. 180 rooms. Facilities: indoor pool, sidewalk café and bar. MC, V.*

Inexpensive **Gran Hotel Diligencias.** Centrally located, on the Zócalo, this hotel is quite clean and the rooms have an imaginative decor, such as frescos around the door frames. *Independencia 1115, tel. 29/31–21–16, 29/31–31–57, or 29/32–29–67. 134 rooms. Facilities: restaurant/bar. MC, V.*

Nightlife

Border Towns In Nuevo Laredo, **O'Henry's** is a noisy favorite, with **The Winery** and **Cadillac** somewhat more sedate; **The Lion's Den** is the local disco. **Garcia's, Blanca White's** and the **Hotel del Prado** are where the action is in Matamoros. The **Hosteria del Bohemio,** in downtown Reynosa, has traditional mariachi music.

Monterrey Fashionable folk, residents and visitors alike, flock to the downtown hotels for after-dark action. The **Crowne Plaza Lobby Bar** is loud enough to dismay guests who turn in early, but it delights the young-at-heart crowd. At the **Ambassador** the pianist is more reserved. **El Cid,** at the Hotel Monterrey, features cheek-to-cheek dance music, and **Bar 1900** (Gran Anciera Hotel) is a classic Mexican cantina. **Aja** (Prolongación Madero Poniente 201) and **Sgt. Pepper's** (Río Orinoco Oriente 105), the two top discos, are best reached by taxi.

Tampico The **Camino Real, Inglaterra** and **Posada de Tampico** hotels usually have lively entertainment; **Plaza Casino** (Universidad 36) is Tampico's top disco, but don't expect the staff to understand English.

Veracruz Head to the hotels for the best nightlife, especially **Tilingo Charlie's,** at the Emporio, and the bars at the **Torremar** and **Mocambo,** with the **Puerto Bello** offering a cozy piano bar. Leading dance clubs are the downtown **Plaza 44** and **Perro Saldo,** out toward Mocambo beach.

13 The Yucatán Peninsula

Introduction

When asked what attracts them to Mexico, most visitors will mention beaches and ruins—and some of the best of each are found on the Yucatán Peninsula.

Yucatán comprises Mexico's most popular tourist destination—Cancún—and some of the country's most celebrated ruins, the pre-Columbian cities of the Maya. While much of the peninsula is vast, scrubby desert—"one living rock," as an early Spanish priest put it—with a smattering of jungles and hills, its eastern coastline on the clear, turquoise waters of the Caribbean has superb natural endowments. In addition to a semitropical climate, the Caribbean coast has unbroken stretches of beach and the world's fifth-longest barrier reef, which lies just off the island of Cozumel. Also part of Yucatán is the diminutive Isla Mujeres (Isle of Women), and on the west side of the peninsula, Mérida, a city that deserves more tourism than it gets. Mérida was one of the first cities built by the Spaniards, and it retains its colonial ambience and charm.

The peninsula's spectrum of attractions is matched by an equal range of accommodations, from the never-leave-the-site resorts of Cancún to more modest properties near the ruins and humble but adequate beach shacks. Yucatán therefore appeals to travelers of all budgets and inclinations, from package-tour-takers to backpackers and travelers who prefer to rent a car. It offers bird-watching, water sports, archaeology, handicrafts, and the savory Yucatecan cuisine. Above all, however, there are the *Yucatecos* themselves: Veteran travelers to Mexico often remark on the openness and friendliness of these people, who, like their Mayan ancestors, are short and swarthy, with prominent cheekbones and aquiline noses.

The peninsula encompasses the states of Yucatán, Campeche, Quintana Roo (until 1974 a Mexican territory), Belize, and a part of Guatemala, and covers 113,000 square kilometers (43,630 square miles). International airports at Cancún and Cozumel provide nonstop service from several North American cities; the Mérida airport handles primarily domestic flights. Cruise ships call at Cozumel and Playa del Carmen, and other harbor facilities are being developed at Progreso on the north coast off the Gulf of Mexico.

There are hundreds of Mayan sites in Yucatán, only a handful of which have been excavated. Chichén Itzá, the best-known, was once a huge city, including imperious pyramids, the shaved dome of an astronomical observatory, a ball court, and the sacred well into which the remains of sacrificial victims were flung. Uxmal is smaller and has simpler and more elegant buildings. The soft curves of the Temple of the Magicians contrast wonderfully with the geometrically whimsical mosaics adorning the Nunnery. The only Mayan site many beach lovers see is Tulum, which is unfortunate. Although dramatically situated right on the Caribbean (the only Mayan city with that distinction), Tulum is one of the least interesting from an archaeological standpoint. It boasts none of the sophisticated structures of other Mayan cities to the north, and can be seen in less than an hour.

Some of the more obscure Mayan ruins warrant a visit, if for no other reason than because they are not overrun with tourists.

The dusty, neglected remains of Kabah, Sayil, Dzibilchaltún, and Cobá are in some ways more haunting than their better-preserved neighbors. Farther south, in the state of Campeche, the ruins of Edzná have been partially restored by Guatemalan refugees, descendants of ancient Maya builders. (Because of both the excessive midday heat and the busloads of tourists, visitors are advised to get to the ruins as early as possible in the morning.)

Choosing between Cancún and Cozumel will depend on your proclivities. Cancún is more glamorous as well as more expensive, and its lodgings more sybaritic; other than the beaches, the accent is on the usual resort diversions: shopping, dining, and disco-hopping. Cozumel, the diver's island, is more casual and its hotels less flashy.

Cancún is the world's first "created" resort. Its developers selected the site by computer and built it according to a well-honed formula of what most tourists want: sun, sand, beauty, and tranquillity. Cancún represents "enclave tourism" at its most refined: a physically flawless foreign spot where modern hotels offer endless amenities to wealthy western tourists, nightlife, restaurants, shopping that caters to youthful American tastes, and just enough of an "authentic Mexican flavor" piped in to remind tourists that they are in Mexico, while keeping them well away from the less attractive realities of the country.

Put another way, Cancún has all the virtues of the Caribbean—translucent aquamarine waters, a balmy clime, palm trees—all the modern conveniences of chain hotels, and few of the inconveniences found in such older Mexican destinations as Acapulco, Mexico City, or the colonial towns. The hotel strip is even more glittering than Miami or the French Riviera, and nearly as international: Almost all the Mexicans one is likely to meet are employed by the predominant tourism industry. And construction—particularly of time-share condominiums—is rampant.

Cozumel, on the other hand, is older. Its tourism infrastructure is a bit on the faded side; there are fewer entertainment and dining options. It is larger than Cancún, and to get around, visitors must either make extensive use of taxis or rent a jeep or moped. This is precisely what makes it preferable to those seeking a more "laid-back" experience. Because of the excellence of the diving, however—the large barrier reef off the island offers giant brain coral, sponges, and butterfly fish—Cozumel is often packed with chartered planeloads of young divers from Denver and Houston.

There is much more to Yucatán, however, than the beaches and ruins. The poverty of the region is mirrored in its scrubby terrain, rocks protruding harshly through thin, parched topsoil, and bottle-brush trees adding a dab of red to the dull green, amber, and gray countryside. At white thatched-roof huts along the roadside, naked children play; iguanas, deer, and turkeys dart aimlessly about. There are scorpions, black widows, red ants; less visible, in the hinterland, live armadillos and puma.

Yucatán has its riches, too. Conch, *ceviche* (marinated seafood), venison, and duck are common fare, with papaya and mamey (a tropical fruit with juicy, yellow flesh) used to sweet-en the palate. Such writers as Somerset Maugham, John Dos Passos, Lawrence Ferlinghetti, and Allan Ginsberg have come to this area. Nearly 2 million Mayan Indians constitute a majority of the population, which historically has been among the most rebellious—and mistreated—in Mexico. Oil now outpaces tourism, fish-processing plants, and the traditional henequen industry in the local economy, but tourism is catching up fast, as more and more of Yucatán is transformed by development.

Yucatán is a land apart. It is maddeningly hot, with as much sorrow as beauty in its landscape, but it is one of the most fascinating and evocative provinces of Mexico.

Our itinerary for Yucatán begins in Cancún, the port of entry for most international arrivals by air. From there, we suggest a day trip to the beaches at Akumal, the Xel-Há Lagoon, and the Mayan ruins of Tulum. An overnight excursion to Isla Mujeres, 10 kilometers (6 miles) southeast of Cancún and a real change of pace, follows. Travelers who are particularly interested in archaeology may find the longer excursion to Cobá—a far less accessible but more fascinating ruined Mayan city—more rewarding.

The next major destination is the island of Cozumel, which represents a compromise between the luxury (and cost) of Cancún and the hippie atmosphere of Isla Mujeres. After a few days set aside for relaxing on the beaches, the itinerary continues to Mérida, capital of the state of Yucatán and its only major city. While Mérida warrants a couple of days in its own right, it also makes a good base for visiting the most famous Mayan ruins of the peninsula—Chichén Itzá and Uxmal. Other ruins are also described here for Maya buffs.

Finally, the itinerary covers the eastern and southern parts of the region—the states of Quintana Roo and Campeche—which are best visited by travelers using rental cars. This area includes a long stretch of more secluded beaches and some of the lesser-known Mayan ruins inland.

Cancún

Numbers in the margin correspond to points of interest on the Yucatán Peninsula map.

Mexico's leading tourist destination did not exist before 1974. ❶ **Cancún** was virtually created from nothing—a skinny little barrier island inhabited by 170 squatters—at the behest of a computer. The Mexican government, realizing the importance of tourism to the national economy, and equally aware of how overgrown and shabby Acapulco had become, decided to find a new site that would both make money and help provide employment for Yucatán, still one of the most impoverished regions in the country.

Variables such as "beaches," "sun," and "distance from the United States" were punched into a computer, and out came a spot given the name Cancún. It now has more than 20,000 hotel rooms and draws upwards of 1 million visitors a year, accounting for some 12% of Mexico's foreign-exchange earnings from tourism. Even Hurricane Gilbert, which devastated much of Yucatán and Quintana Roo in September 1988, barely made a

The Yucatán Peninsula

Golfo de México

Dzilam de Bravo

Santa Clara

Progreso 🟡**17**

Yucalpetén

Telchac Puerto

Dzibilchaltún
🟡**18** Motul

Temax

Sisal

Punta Baz

🛣️261

Mérida
🟡**8**–🟡**16**

Celestún

Umán

🛣️180 Hoctún

Holca

Punta Nimun

🛣️281

🛣️180

Maxcanú

Y U C A

Santa Cruz

Uxmal
🟡**19**

Ticul

Kabah

🛣️184

Sayil

Loltún

Labná

Xlapak

Tzucac

🛣️261

Tenabó

Campeche
🟡**25**

Tinúm

🛣️261

Hopelchén

🛣️180

Punta Seybaplaya

Edzná
🟡**26**

Q

Champotón

La Joya

C A M P E C H E

Sabancuy

Río Champotón

🛣️180

Francisco
Escárcega

🛣️186

Xpujil

🛣️186

🛣️186

RIO LAGARTOS
NATIONAL PARK

Santa Teresa
Sinaí Cabo Catoche
San Felipe Río Lagartos El Cuyo Isla Holbox
SAN FELIPE
TIONAL PARK
295 Chiquilá
Yucatán Punta Sam **Isla Mujeres**
Puerto Juárez 5
176 **Cancún** 1
Sucilá Kantunilkin
Tizimin 180
X-Can **Puerto Morelos** 22
Tunkas
Punta Bete
180 Pisté **Valladolid** 21 **Playa del Carmen** 23
20 Balancanchén Chemax Xcaret Molas
nichén Itzá **Cobá** 6 **Cozumel** 7
N Paamul Santa Pilar
Palancar Reef
Chemuyil 2 **Akumal** Punta Sur
Tihosuco Xcacel 3 **Xel-Há**
Parque 4 **Tulum**
Natural de Boca Paila
nta Rosa Quintana Roo
295 Punta Allen

Punta Pájaros

184 Tupak
Polyuc Felipe Carrillo Caribbean Sea
Puerto
NTANA ROO SIAN KA'AN Punta Herrero
293 307 BIOSPHERE
RESERVE
Limones

KEY
----- Ferry Lines

Laguna de
Bacalar
Bahía de
Bacalar Chetumal Majahual
307
El Cocal Cayo
ondito Centro Banco
Chetumal Chinchorro N
24
Bahía de
Corozal
Nicolás
ravo Santa Cecilia 0 40 miles
BELIZE 0 60 km

dent in the tourist trade—after a frenzy of rebuilding. But the natural assets of beaches and reefs will take longer to recover.

Cancún's beauty is beyond question. A 22.5-kilometer (14-mile), elbow-shape sandbar sheltering two inland lagoons on one side and the sea on the other, Cancún offers the best of the Caribbean, lightly spiced by Mexico. But its enviable success is also due to one other factor: the proximity of the Mayan ruins, which enables tourists to throw in some "culture" with their sun worship. The superiority of the clear Caribbean waters and beaches over those of Mexico's Pacific resorts, the spanking newness and unabashedly luxurious amenities of its hotels, and the absence of any ruins or other sights of cultural interest on the Pacific set Cancún apart from other Mexican sun-and-sand destinations.

There are actually two Cancúns. The hotel zone occupies the full length of the sandbar, which is spanned by a central boulevard, Paseo Kukulcán. Both halves of the sandbar are joined to the mainland by inconspicuous causeways: To the west, on the mainland, lies the "other" Cancún, called Cancún City or "downtown Cancún," where the workers live. Sixteen kilometers (9 miles) south of downtown is the airport.

The hotel zone reeks of elegance and luxury. Strict regulations control building size and style; neon is forbidden; and the hotels, while allowing for some range in prices, generally cater to affluent foreigners, who account for 75% of Cancún's guests. Budget travelers tend to stay in the more modest properties downtown, relying on public buses to get them to the beaches.

With the sea on one side and the lagoon on the other, virtually every hotel on the island looks out on the water. Building continues at a furious pace, so that Paseo Kukulcán is beginning to look like a resurrected Miami: condos, time-shares, shopping malls, restaurants, and discos vie for space with hotels, and empty stretches of beach are becoming a rare sight. There are very few reminders that one is actually in Mexico.

Out toward the airport, one catches a glimpse of Cancún the way it once was—scraggly, ragged, far from charming. Although the mangrove forests and swamplands have been razed and filled in, brilliantly colored tropical birds and fish still coexist with the waterskiers and snorkelers.

Like the hotel zone, Cancún City was built according to a master plan. Unlike the hotel zone, ugliness was not banned. The city looks like the boomtown it is: raffish and roaring, home for the busboys and chambermaids, the porters and taxi drivers who make the hotel zone work. (While many of the native Maya who first built Cancún have since left as demand for their unskilled labor ceased, the 200,000 workers from all over the country who replaced them have a higher standard of living than do many Mexican laborers.)

Shopping and dining are the only reasons many visitors staying in the hotel zone venture into Cancún City, where there is plenty of both. Avenida Tulum is the main drag, with many good restaurants along the side streets running into it.

A couple of miles north of the city is Puerto Juárez, once the only settlement in these parts and remarkably unchanged for all that has gone on around it. The passenger ferry to Isla

Mujeres departs from Puerto Juárez; the passenger-and-car ferry leaves from Punta Sam, farther north.

In the opposite direction is Route 307, the highway that leads to the Mayan ruins at Tulum, 129 kilometers (80 miles) south. Numerous tour operators conduct day trips to Tulum and Isla Mujeres. Dedicated Mayan buffs can also go out to the more spectacular ruins at Chichén Itzá and be back in a day, but this is a long trip, and it makes more sense to stay overnight at the site or visit it from Mérida, which is much closer.

Arriving and Departing by Plane

Airport and Airlines The Cancún International Airport is 16 kilometers (9 miles) southwest of the heart of Cancún City. **Aeroméxico** (tel. 800/237–6639) flies nonstop from Houston and New York. **American** (tel. 800/433–7300) has nonstop service from Dallas and Miami. **Continental** (tel. 800/231–0856) has daily service from both Houston and New York. **Mexicana's** (tel. 800/531–7921) nonstops are from Chicago, Dallas, Denver, Los Angeles, Miami, New York, Orlando, San Antonio, and San Francisco. **Northwest** (tel. 800/225–2525) flies direct from Tampa. **Pan Am** (tel. 800/221–1111) flies in from Miami. **United** (tel. 800/241–6522) flies direct from Chicago and Washington. **Aerocancún** (tel. 212/679–0360) and **LaTur** (tel. 800/32–LATUR), New York-based charter companies, run charters from New York, Orlando, Los Angeles, and other gateways. **Avioteca** (tel. 800/327–9832) has flights from Mexico City to Mérida, Flores, and Guatemala City. Flight times: from New York, four hours; from Houston, one hour, from Los Angeles, five hours. In Cancún, Mexicana subsidiaries **Aerocaribe** (tel. 98/86–0083) and **Aerocozumel** (tel. 98/86–0162) offer flights to Cozumel, the ruins at Chichén Itzá, Mérida, and other Mexican destinations.

Between the Airport and Center City You can either take a regular taxi or share a *combi* (an airport taxi Volkswagen minibus) for about $5 per person. Individual taxis, whether to downtown or the hotel zone, will run you about $25. Rates vary with the destination. Many car rental firms have desks in the departures building.

Arriving and Departing by Car, Bus, and Boat

By Car Cancún is at the end of Route 180, which goes from Matamoros on the Texas border to Campeche, Mérida, and Valladolid. The road trip from Texas to Cancún can take up to three days. Cancún can also be reached from the south via Route 307, which passes through Chetumal and Belize. Gas stations on these roads are infrequent, so try to keep your tank filled.

By Bus The bus terminal is in downtown Cancún at the corner of Avenidas Tulum and Uxmal. First-class buses make the trip from Mexico City, and first- and second-class buses serve Cancún from Puerto Morelos, Playa del Carmen, Tulum, Chetumal, Cobá, Valladolid, Chichén Itzá, and Mérida. Public buses (Route 8) make the trip out to Puerto Juárez and Punta Sam for the ferries to Isla Mujeres.

By Boat Boats leave Puerto Juárez and Punta Sam (both north of Cancún City) for Isla Mujeres every couple of hours, but schedules are flexible; the fare is about $2. A motorized catamaran (jetfoil) departs for Cozumel from Playa del Carmen every two hours or so from 5:30 AM to 7:30 PM; a one-way ticket costs about $4. A $12 shuttle service departs for Isla Mujeres from the Playa Linda dock near the Hotel Calinda three times a day (tel. 98/84–6433).

Getting Around

Motorized transport of some sort is necessary, as both island and Cancún City attractions are fairly spread out. Bus service is good and taxis are inexpensive.

By Bus Buses run from outlying hotels all along Paseo Kukulcán past the Convention Center and into Cancún City. Though not luxurious, they are fun and cheap (about 60¢).

By Taxi Taxis line up outside most hotels or can be hailed on the street for significantly less. Rates are posted at hotel entrances, and can fluctuate according to gasoline taxes and the drivers' whims. Note: Word has it that Cancún cabbies aren't as honest as they used to be, so confirm the price with the driver before you set out.

By Rental Car and Moped Driving here can be harrowing when you don't know your way around. Both Paseo Kukulcán and the downtown streets can get extremely crowded, and there are only a few traffic lights. Another hazard is added to driving when it rains and the streets flood, especially those in downtown. The speed limit on Paseo Kukulcán is 60 kilometers (36 miles) per hour, and it is enforced. There are many accidents on this overcrowded road, so watch out. Following is a list of the major car rental firms. In addition to regular compact cars, some also rent novelty vehicles and a variety of four-wheel-drive vehicles. **Avis** (airport, tel. 98/86–0147), **Budget** (airport, tel. 98/84–2126 or downtown main office, tel. 98/84–0730), **Econo-Rent** (airport, tel. 98/84–2147 or downtown, tel. 98/84–1826), **Hertz** (Reno 35, tel. 98/84–1326), and **Thrifty** (airport, tel. 98/84–3626 or Hotel Krystal, tel. 98/83–0373).

Many hotels and stores in the hotel zone rent mopeds. The moped path that parallels Paseo Kukulcán is nonexistent in the densest section of the hotel zone, so you'll have to brave the road. Downtown is considered too congested for novice moped users.

Important Addresses and Numbers

Tourist Information The state tourism office is located at Av. Tulum 29, S.M. 5, tel. 98/84–8073 (open daily 9 AM to 9 PM). They also maintain a small information booth outside the office on Avenida Tulum.

Cancún Tips, a pocket-size booklet, is distributed free at the airport and in most hotels. A handy guide, it does, however, limit listing to advertisers. The publishers also maintain information offices by the Convention Center (El Parián), open 9–1 and 4–8 except Wed. afternoons and Sun., tel. 98/83–0447), and at the Plaza Caracol II mall, open daily 10–10, tel. 98/84–4609.

Embassies **U.S. Consulate** (Av. Nader 40, S.M. 2A, Edificio Marruecos 31, tel. 98/84–2411). **Canadian Consulate** (Plaza México Local 312, tel. 98/84–3716).

Emergencies **Police** (tel. 98/84–1913); **Fire** (tel. 98/84–1202); **Red Cross** ambulance (tel. 98/84–1616); **Social Security Hospital** (tel. 98/84–1818); **Total Assist** (Claveles 5, tel. 98/84–1092 or 98/84–1058).

Bookstores **Fama** (Av. Tulum 105), **La Surtidora** (Av. Tulum 17).

Late-night **Farmacia Paris** (Av. Yaxchilán in the Marrufo Bldg., tel. 98/8
Pharmacies 4–0164). **Farmacia Turística** (tel. 98/83–1894) and **Farmacia Extra** (tel. 98/83–2827), both in Plaza Caracol, will deliver to hotels between 9 AM–10 PM.

Guided Tours

Every hotel along the beach—and most of them in town—has a travel agency that will set you up with a tour. The most popular destinations are the ancient and picturesque ruined Mayan cities around Yucatán. Among them, in order of proximity to Cancún, are Tulum, Cobá, Chichén Itzá, and Uxmal. Tulum tours cost about $40, and most include a stop for snorkeling at Xel-Há lagoon; Chichén Itzá tours start at about $50, depending on whether you travel by bus or van. Air tours are available through **Aerocaribe,** starting at $69 round-trip. Other excursions follow the coast of Quintana Roo south to beaches where you can snorkel, bird-watch, or just enjoy the sun. Travel agencies run tours (also in order of proximity) to Isla Mujeres, Contoy Island, Cozumel, and the Xel-Há Lagoon. There are also daily boat trips to Isla Mujeres ($12) from the Playa Linda dock (Turismo Aviomar, tel. 98/84–6433 or 4–5385). Tour operators can also arrange trips to Mérida and tickets for the Wednesday afternoon bullfights. Cancún's major tour and travel agencies include: **Intermar Caribe,** Calle Cereza 37 at Av. Bonampak S.M. 2A, tel. 98/84–4684, 98/84–2909, or 98/84–4568; and **Turismo Aviomar,** Calle Venado 30, S.M. 20, tel. 98/84–6742.

Exploring

The beaches, of course, are the big attraction, or at least they were. Hurricane Gilbert washed away all but a few meters of the sand on the Caribbean side of the island, while the beach on the leeward side increased in size. (Nature and the efforts of the Mexicans have restored most of Cancún's beaches.) Those busing in from the city can choose any beach they like; the seashore in Mexico is federal property and available to anyone who wants to use it. Lonesome stretches, however, should be avoided when it comes to swimming. Although most hotels have lifeguards on duty, the undertow in Cancún can be dangerous.

The sun, naturally, is another major attraction, and it, too, should be treated with caution. Cancún boasts more sunny days than almost any other Caribbean destination, but there is always the temptation to get started on a tan too quickly for fear it may be cloudy tomorrow.

The big beach sport is parasailing, soaring in a parachute pulled by a speedboat. It is thrilling and not quite as dangerous as it looks, but accidents do happen. Sailing, windsurfing, waterskiing, jet skiing, snorkeling, and scuba diving can be arranged at most beachfront hotel sports centers or at any of the many marinas that dot the island. Instructors are available.

The tranquil waters of the lagoon are ideal for mastering these skills.

There are five small Mayan ruins in Cancún. Though not particularly impressive, they may appeal to those who want to say they've seen a Mayan ruin and then get back to the beach. The largest site, **El Rey**, is just west of Paseo Kukulcán, about midway between the Sheraton and the turnoff for the Club Med, overlooking the Laguna de Nichupté (Nichupte Lagoon). As skeletons were found there, it may have been a royal burial ground; now all that remains is a pyramid. *Admission: $2.50. Open daily 8–5.*

Shopping

Resort wear and handicrafts are the best buys in Cancún, but the prices are among the highest and the selection quite predictable, so if you are traveling elsewhere in Mexico—particularly Mérida—you'd do best to wait. Handicrafts include a tremendous range of goods, everything from blown glass and handwoven textiles to leather and jewelry, much of it made of black coral and tortoiseshell. (Note that since they come from protected endangered species, black coral and tortoiseshell products cannot be imported into the United States and most other countries.)

Stores on master-planned Cancún Island are in either hotels or shopping malls. In Cancún City, they are along the streets. Rents being lower in the city, prices should be, too, but that is not always the case. You are advised to shop carefully and favor reputable-looking establishments; "Let the buyer beware" is a good philosophy to follow with some sleazy merchants.

Hotel Zone Heading toward the hotel zone from downtown Cancún, the first mall along Paseo Kukulcán is **Plaza Nautilus**, across from the Hotel Carrousel, with crafts, jewelry, sportswear shops, a bookstore, and restaurants. Just beyond the Hotel Presidente is a line of malls strung together so you can easily walk from one to another in a half-mile-long shopping spree; **Mayfair Galleries, Terramar, Plaza Lagunas, Plaza Caracol, Costa Blanca, Coral Negro, El Parián, Plaza La Fiesta,** and **Plaza Flamingo** sell buyables and edibles that run the gamut from Gucci to guacamole. Plaza Caracol is the flagship of Cancún shopping malls: It houses dozens of shops, among them some internationally known boutiques (such as Gucci and Ralph Lauren), as well as elegant restaurants and high-tech pizzerias.

Cancún City Serious shoppers and bargain-hunters should not miss the stores and markets of Cancún City. The main shopping streets are Avenida Cobá between Avenidas Bonampak and Tulum and Avenida Tulum between Avenidas Cobá and Uxmal. As you come off of Paseo Kukulcán onto Avenida Cobá, you will see on the left the **Plaza América,** which has dozens of inexpensive crafts (straw, leather, and jewelry) shops. On the right hand side of Avenida Tulum between Avenidas Cobá and Uxmal are a number of interesting stores. For sterling-silver jewelry try **Margarita's** (Av. Tulum 10). Next door is the **Ki-Huic crafts market,** with dozens of small folk-art and jewelry stores. Down the block is the large **San Francisco de Asis Supermarket** (Av. Tulum 18). On the other side of Avenida Tulum are shops such as **Omega** (Av. Tulum 103), which sells a variety of photo equipment and can develop film in one hour. Good craft shops are also concentrated in the **Plaza México** (Av. Tulum 200).

Participant Sports

Fishing Deep-sea fishing off Cancún may not be as spectacular as off Baja California, but in many ways it can be more fun. The crews, for instance, can arrange excursions to Contoy or one of the other small islands and fry up the catch for a picnic.

Deep-sea fishing boats and other gear may be chartered from the **Wild Goat Marina** (tel. 98/83–0062) for about $385 per day. Prices vary with the season, demand, and the size and make of the boat. Boats are also available for four hours ($200) and for six hours ($300). **Aqua Tours** (tel. 98/83–0400) arranges diving ($50 an hour) and fishing trips ($415) and also has a full-service marina. Open tickets are available for $65.

Golf Cancún's main golf course, 18-hole **Pok-Ta-Pok** (tel. 98/83–0871), is located between the Maya Caribe and the Stouffer Presidente hotels. Greens fees are $27, an electric golf cart rents for $20, and rental clubs are available. The Robert Trent Jones–designed links are open daily from 6 AM to 4 PM. There are also 18- and 5-hole golf courses at the **Hotel Melia Cancún** (Paseo Kukulcan, km 12, tel. 98/85–1160) and a 9-hole course at the **Oasis Hotel** (Paseo Kukulcan km 20, tel. 98/85–0867).

Jogging A jogging path runs parallel to Paseo Kukulcán from the Punta Cancún area into Cancún City, a distance of about 14 kilometers (8.7 miles).

Tennis Many of the larger hotels have tennis courts, some of which are open to nonguests. Courts cost $7–$12 per hour, rackets (if available) are $2.75–$3.50. A few hotels offer classes as well.

Water Sports Scuba diving is at its best along the Mexican Caribbean. The waters are both warm and astoundingly clear (in many areas of the world divers must don rubber suits to keep from freezing and, once below the surface, consider themselves lucky if they can see 6 meters or 20 feet in front of them). Novices can take a resort course or spend a few more days and get certified. Experienced divers are better off going to Cozumel to dive the famous Palancar Reef.

Marinas that rent powerboats and sailboats and organize glass-bottom boat tours, sailing voyages, and fishing trips line Paseo Kukulcán between Punta Cancún and downtown. **Marina Jet Ski** (tel. 98/83–0766), next to the Mauna Loa restaurant, is open from 9 to 5. **Club Lagoon** (tel. 98/83–1111) has sailboards, jet skis, sailboats, broncos, waverunners, and waterskiing. For diving, try **SCUBA Cancún** (tel. 98/83–1011); it runs daily dive and snorkeling tours and also gives lessons. Also try **Barracuda** (tel. 98/84–4551), which runs four-hour snorkeling tours of the reef around Punta Mizuc, including refreshments and equipment, for $30 per person. Trips leave at 10 AM from the Marina Punta del Este, opposite the Hyatt Cancún Caribe. Many resorts have small marinas that rent Hobie Cats, Sunfish, jet skis, and Windsurfers and also arrange for waterskiing in the Nichupte Lagoon.

Spectator Sports

Bullfights are held year-round at the ring outside Cancún City (tel. 98/84–5465 or 98/84–8284) on most Wednesday afternoons starting at 3:30. Tickets, available at hotel travel desks, cost $27 to see three bulls (compared with the usual six). **Charro rodeos** are held periodically. Again, hotels have full details.

Dining

After the sun, the sand, and the sea, dining out is a top Cancún activity. Hotels make a big push to keep guests on the premises, but there is an equal number of nonhotel establishments worth visiting, both in the Hotel Zone and in Cancún City. Dinner, the big meal of the day, is usually served from 7 to 10 PM, perhaps later. Fish caught from the waters around the island, then grilled and seasoned with lime juice, is a sure bet. Grilled pork and chicken prepared with spices used in Mayan cooking, like *achiote*, are other specialties. Service at most Cancún restaurants is attentive and friendly. Reservations are recommended, especially at the very expensive and expensive restaurants. Remember that imported liquor will add considerably to your tab. At about $7, brunches can be a great value—eat on the late side, and you won't be hungry until dinner. Highly recommended restaurants are indicated by a star ★.

Category	Cost*
Very Expensive	over $35
Expensive	$25–$35
Moderate	$15–$24
Inexpensive	under $15

per person, excluding drinks, service, and sales tax (10%)

Hotel Zone
Very Expensive

Bogart's. Cancún's premier fantasy restaurant is based on *Casablanca*, the movie, not the Moroccan seaport. The menu lists richly prepared steak, seafood, and sweet and creamy desserts. It is one of Cancún's most expensive restaurants. *Hotel Krystal, Punta Cancún, tel. 98/83–1133. Reservations required. Jackets suggested. AE, MC, V.*

Casa Rolandi. The flagship of the Rolandi's Pizza chain (purveyors of fine pizzas around the peninsula) serves Italian-Swiss nouvelle cuisine: fine steaks, seafood, pasta, and a generous self-service salad bar. The desserts are excellent, and the pale gray and earth-toned decor could be termed Mediterranean modern. *Plaza Caracol, Paseo Kukulcán, tel. 98/83–1817. Reservations suggested. Dress: casual. MC, V.*

El Mexicano. Here the emphasis is on classic regional dishes from around Mexico, such as *filete à la Tampiqueña* (grilled beef with a variety of accompaniments) or a stew of lobster, shrimp, and fish. The setting is a traditional covered courtyard inside the Costa Blanca shopping center. Diners are entertained by folkloric dancers and mariachis. *Costa Blanca Shopping Center, Paseo Kukulcán, tel. 98/83–2220. Reservations suggested. Dress: casual. AE, MC, V. No lunch.*

Maxime. Management has changed again here, but the French chef and 19th-century French country house decor remain in all its ornate grandeur. Lunch is served on an outdoor terrace dur-

Cancún Dining and Lodging

Dining

Bogart's, **21**

Carlos 'n Charlie's, **14**

Casa Rolandi, **19**

Du Mexique, **8**

El Mexicano, **16**

La Habichuela, **4**

Lorenzillos, **23**

Los Almendros, **9**

Maxime, **13**

100% Natural, **2**

Pop, **6**

Lodging

Albergue Crea, **10**

Calinda Viva Cancún, **17**

Camino Real, **20**

Caribe Internacional, **3**

Fiesta Americana
Cancún, **18**

Margarita Cancún, **7**

María Lourdes, **1**

Marriott
CasaMagna, **24**

Melía Cancún, **25**

Plaza del Sol, **5**

Plaza Las Glorias, **12**

Puerta al Sol, **26**

Radisson Sierra Plaza, **22**

San Marino, **11**

Stouffer
Presidente, **15**

ing May, June, and July. The upstairs bar has a pool table and separate exit. In high season, piano and classical guitar accompany dining. *Pez Volador 8 (next to the Casa Maya), Hotel Zone, tel. 98/83–0438. Reservations suggested. Dress: casual but neat. AE, MC, V.*

Moderate **Carlos 'n' Charlie's.** Get here early, because this branch of the popular chain attracts hordes of people who want to eat a lot of American and Mexican food, down pitchers of margaritas, play drinking games, listen to loud Motown music, and shout a lot. Photographs, sombreros, and bird cages clutter the walls and ceilings. *Paseo Kukulcán Km. 5.5, tel. 98/83–0846. No reservations. AE, MC, V.*

Lorenzillos. Perched on its own peninsula in the lagoon, this nautical spot provides a pleasant way to watch the sunset, sip a drink on the outdoor patio, or sample excellent seafood. Specialties include grilled or broiled lobster (you pick your own) and whole fish Veracruz-style. The seafaring theme extends to the names of both the dishes (like Jean Lafitte beef) and the restaurant itself (Lorenzillo was a 17th-century pirate). *Paseo Kukulkán Km 10.5, Hotel Zone, tel. 98/83–1254. Dress: Casual. AE, MC, V.*

Downtown **Du Mexique.** The white stucco walls of this restaurant and art *Expensive* gallery are covered with paintings. The cuisine is a combination of nouvelle French, Mexican, and Yucatecan. Some of the French chef/owner's inventions may seem a bit strange to unaccustomed palates. The seafood dishes are the specialty. For dessert try the chocolate tortilla, a sort of chocolate crepe folded over sweet cream and strawberries. *Av. Cobá 44, tel. 98/84–1077. Reservations suggested. Dress: casual. AE, MC, V. No lunch.*

La Habichuela. The name means "stringbean," and after a meal here you'll be anything but one. You can sit either out in the garden or under an enormous thatched Mayan-style roof in this converted mansion. Yucatecan and Mexican dishes are the focus, but also popular are the steaks and grilled seafood. Try *cocobichuela*—lobster and shrimp drenched in an Indian sauce served on rice inside a coconut shell. *Calle Margaritas 25 (near Av. Yaxchilán), tel. 98/84–3158. Reservations suggested. Dress: casual. MC, V.*

Inexpensive **Los Almendros.** This is the local branch of the Yucatán restau-★ rant chain, and one of the best restaurants in Cancún. Try the classic *poc chuc* (marinated grilled pork) or the *cochinita pibil* (piglet wrapped in banana leaves and baked in a special oven). The condiments—super-spicy *habanero* salsa and pickled purple onions—are almost as good as the main courses. The large octagonal dining room has colorful Mayan frescoes on the walls. *Avs. Bonampak and Sayil, tel. 98/84–0807. Dress: casual. AE, MC, V.*

100% Natural. These downtown veggie restaurants double as jazz clubs in the evening. They attract many young locals and European budget travelers. Try the fresh juices, yogurt drinks, and meatless Mexican dishes. Excellent breakfasts are also served. *Three locations: Av. Sunyaxchén 6, tel. 98/84–3617; Calle Tulipanes 26, tel. 98/84–2437; and Hotel Zone, tel. 98/83–1180. No reservations. MC, V.*

Pop. Next to City Hall, Pop is a big hangout for *políticos*. Try the American breakfasts and the Mexican specialties, such as tacos and quesadillas. *Av. Tulum 26, tel. 98/84–1991. Dress: casual. MC, V.*

Lodging

"New" is a relative term in Cancún, which didn't exist before 1974. All hotels in Cancún are "new"; most were built within the past 10 years. Properties in the hotel zone are the most expensive (and luxurious), but reasonably priced rooms are available on the mainland in Cancún City. Prices given are for the peak winter season, approximately mid-November through April; prices drop by at least a third after May 1. All hotels listed have private baths. Highly recommended lodgings are indicated by a star ★.

Category	Cost*
Very Expensive	over $200
Expensive	$100–$200
Moderate	$65–$100
Inexpensive	under $65

*All prices are for a standard double room, excluding 10% tax.

Hotel Zone
Very Expensive

Camino Real. The Camino Real has everything, even its own little Mayan temple. A shopping arcade has just been added, and many of the rooms and common areas have been renovated. All the rooms are large and luxurious and come with balcony and a view of the water, and the place is just a short walk to the convention center and many shopping malls. A new tower has 18 floors and 69 Royal Beach Club rooms, each with its own balcony. *Box 14, Punta Cancún 77500, tel. 98/83–0100 or 800/228–3000; fax 98/83–1730. 381 rooms, including Royal Beach Club. Facilities: pool, restaurants, bars, satellite TV, disco, 2 beaches, shopping arcade. AE, DC, MC, V.*

★ **Fiesta Americana Cancún.** The look here is of an overblown colonial hacienda. The rooms are spacious, with terraces and rattan furniture. The wings of the main building enclose an enormous free-form pool. The hotel is right across the street from the Mayfair Galleria and near lots more shopping. *Km 9.5, Paseo Kukulcán, Box 696, 77500, tel. 98/83–1400 or 800/FIESTA–1, fax 98/83–2502. 266 rooms and 15 suites. Facilities: 3 restaurants, 3 bars, color TV, minibars, pool. AE, DC, MC, V.*

Marriott CasaMagna. One of Cancún's newest luxury-properties, the Marriott is an absolutely palatial six-story hotel, designed with graceful Moorish domes and arches and a handsome pool area with moats, miniature waterfalls, and palm trees. Rooms are done in contemporary Mexican, with tiled floors, ceiling fans, and soft rose, mauve, and earth colors. *Paseo Kukulcán 77500, tel. 98/85–2000 or 800/228–9290; fax 98/85–1385. 450 rooms and 38 suites. Facilities: 4 restaurants, 4 bars, cable TV, in-room safes, hair dryers, minibars, pool, whirlpool, lighted tennis courts, health club, shop, rental car, beauty salon, parking. AE, DC, MC, V.*

★ **Meliá Cancún.** The stunning new Meliá Cancún dares to differ from its neighbors: instead of the nearly ubiquitous "neo-Maya" decor and colonial furnishings, it is boldly modern, with a waterfall rushing down a sheer, black marble wall at the entrance, a spacious and airy atrium lobby centered around a lush tropical garden, and a steel and glass triangle overhead. Public spaces are elegant and varied, with loving attention to detail. Rooms—all with private balconies—are painted in soft pastels; furniture is white acrylic, with wall-to-wall carpeting. Service is unusually courteous and efficient. *Paseo Kukulcán Km. 12, 77500, tel. 98/85–1160 or 800/336–3542; fax 98/85–1085. 450 rooms and 29 suites. Facilities: 2 pools, 5 restaurants, bars, satellite TV, in-room safes, hair dryers, minibars, shopping arcade, beauty salon, car rental, travel agency, 18-hole and 5-hole (executive) golf courses, health center, tennis courts. AE, DC, MC, V.*

★ **Puerto al Sol.** The water pressure in the showerheads is fantastic, and in case you have trouble figuring out how to turn on the Jacuzzi, it's the little white button behind you in the bathtub. Puerta al Sol opened its restorative doors in December 1990. Its marble-floored suites, delicate desert pastel appointments, and the spare, cool, tranquilizing feel to the furnishings are a virtual massage to the senses the minute you unload your bags and get used to the idea that you've really jumped the rat-race-ridden, squalid, mean streets back home. Every single suite overlooks the Caribbean's deep, aquamarine water. All-inclusive means convenience—what with unlimited food and beverages, day-and-night activities and entertainments, tours to Mayan ruins and Isla Mujeres—but why does it mean the food just doesn't cut it? *Paseo Kukulcán Km 20, tel. 98/851555 or 800/346–8225. 150 suites. Facilities: 3 restaurants, above-ground diving tank, outdoor whirlpool, indoor pool, outdoor pool, tennis, fitness center, game room with billiard tables, 75-seat theater. MC, V.*

Radisson Sierra Plaza. The former Inter-Continental has the advantage of being closer to town than the hotels on the southern end, while still seeming to be away from it all. Pastel-decorated rooms with light wood furnishings and tile floors are airy and comfortable. All rooms have a sunken lanai or private balcony. The poolside palapa restaurant is a serene spot for lunch. At press time, plans were under way to renovate the spacious lobby. *Paseo Kukulcán, Km 10, tel. 98/832444 or 800/333–3333, fax 98/833486. 261 rooms. Facilities: 3 restaurants, 3 bars, meeting facilities, beauty salon, travel agency, shopping, car rental. AE, DC, MC, V.*

Stouffer Presidente. This sand-colored, multistory monolith on the north side of Cancún Island, has well-designed rooms with recessed lighting, stone-topped tables, and large, firm beds. Extensively remodeled after the 1988 hurricane, the Stouffer won the AAA 4-Diamond award in 1990. *Blvd. Cancún 7, 77500, tel. 98/83–0202, 3–0218, or 800/HOTELS–1; fax 98/83–2602 or 3–2515. 294 rooms, including 15 suites, an all-suite Club Floor, handicapped rooms, and a nonsmoking floor. Facilities: 4 restaurants, bars, satellite TV, direct-dial phones, in-room safes, nightclub, fitness center, 2 pools, beach, Jacuzzis, lighted tennis court, travel agency, car rental, beauty parlor, shops. AE, MC, V.*

Moderate **Plaza del Sol.** Popular with students, Europeans, and Canadi-
★ ans, this 3-story colonial-style hotel is situated on a relatively quiet side street downtown. A pleasant bar welcomes visitors in the hotel lobby, and free shuttle service to the beach is offered. Rooms are "nondescript functional," smallish but carpeted, but the bathrooms are large. Ask for a view of the pool. *Av. Yaxchilán 31, 77500, tel. 98/84–3888. 87 rooms. Facilities:*

pool, bars, restaurant, satellite TV, rental car, shop, travel agency, parking. AE, DC, MC, V.

Plaza Las Glorias. This north beach hotel has been around since 1973. The three-story modern hotel certainly doesn't look its age; timely renovations have done their job. Water sports are a specialty, and you can rent a Windsurfer or sailboat at the onsite marina. *Km 3.5, Paseo Kukulcán, Box 227, 77500, tel. 98/83–0811. 110 rooms. Facilities: restaurants, bars, pool, beach. AE, DC, MC, V.*

Calinda Viva Cancún. This pink stucco, 10-story building is on the north beach near many malls. The rooms have marble floors; some have kitchenettes and/or balconies. On the wide beach there are windsurfing, snorkeling, and pedal and sailboats. *Km 8, Paseo Kukulcán, Box 673, 77500, tel. 98/83–0800. 210 rooms. Facilities: 3 restaurants, 3 bars, pools, tennis courts, shops, beach. AE, DC, MC, V.*

Inexpensive **Albergue Crea.** This modern, glass-walled youth hostel is the cheapest lodging on Cancún Island. Men and women sleep in separate dormitories, and on the ground level are a cafeteria and a lounge for mingling. Plenty of water-sports equipment is available. *Km 3, Paseo Kukulcán, 77500, tel. 98/83–1337. 100 rooms (350 beds) with shared baths. Facilities: cafeteria, basketball, volleyball, and ping pong. MC, V.*

Margarita Cancún. The 5-story Margarita is one of the newer downtown hotels (opened late 1989), and tastefully decorated in marble: marble bath walls, marble tiled floors. The vivid turquoise and gray tones in the rooms is a bit outspoken for the '90s, and the hotel looks nicer on the outside (Mission-style, white adobe walls with red tile trim). Ask for a room with a pool view. *Av. Yaxchilán S.M. 22, tel. 98/84–9333 or 800/223–9815. 100 rooms, all with satellite TV. Facilities: restaurant, snack bar, lounge, pool, shops, car rental, travel agency, parking. AE, DC, MC, V.*

San Marino. The San Marino has lovely hand-blown, blue-glass windows in the lobby. This two-year-old Moroccan hacienda-style hotel is one of the few on the lagoon side of the island, and is right next to the Plaza Nautilus. *Km 3.5, Paseo Kukulcán, 77500, tel. 98/83–0815. 56 rooms. Facilities: restaurant, bars, pool, travel agency, car rental, gift shop. AE, DC, MC, V.*

Downtown **María del Lourdes.** The María del Lourdes is a popular resting
Moderate spot for travelers from around the world. They like the nightclub, the pool, and the casual, friendly atmosphere. The rooms are designed in colonial Mexican style. *Av. Yaxchilán 80, 77500, tel. 98/84–4744, fax 98/84–1242. 51 rooms. Facilities: phones, TV, restaurant, pool, game room. AE, DC, MC, V.*

Inexpensive **Caribe Internacional.** This dramatically designed all-suite hotel features brightly colored junior and master suites and a patio with trees and flowers. In the back there's a garden restaurant and a pool with a sun deck. *Av. Yaxchilán at Sunyaxchén 36, 77500, tel. 98/84–3999 or 800/223–6510, fax 98/84–1993. 80 rooms. Facilities: restaurant, cafeteria, pool, cable TV, shop, travel agency, parking. MC, V.*

The Arts and Nightlife

In Cancún City and the hotel zone there are dozens of bars, discos, and dinner shows, but high art is nonexistent. Every night at least a couple of folkloric ballet and live Mexican music shows are performed at various hotels, including the **Club Verano Beat,** the **Sheraton,** the **Stouffer Presidente,** and the **Hyatt Regency. Mauna Loa** has two Polynesian shows nightly, and **Gypsy's Pampered Pirate** has two flamenco shows. For a different kind of dinner show, take the "Pirate's Night Adventure" (tel. 98/83–1488) to the stagey pirate-style show restaurant on Isla Mujeres. While the convention center is under construction, the Cortijo Flamingo hosts a more official **ballet folklórico** (tel. 98/83–0527 or 98/83–0921). Evening performances run from Tuesday through Sunday at about $40 a shot. The **Cancún Jazz Festival** began in 1991 and is expected to become an annual week-long event in April or May with nightly hotel performances by top musicians.

Discos are extremely popular in both the hotel zone and downtown. Try **Aquarius** in the Camino Real, **Christine** at the Hotel Krystal, **La Boom** on Paseo Kukulcán, or **Dady'o,** at Paseo Kukulcán Km. 9.5. In town there is **Risky Business** on Avenida Tulum. Local cinemas showing American and Mexican films are **Espectáculos del Caribe** (Av. Tulum 44) and **Cines Cancún** 1 and 2 (Av. Cobá 112).

Excursions from Cancún

Akumal, Xel-Há, and Tulum

2 **Akumal,** 35 kilometers (22 miles) south of Playa del Carmen, means "Place of the Turtle," and before it became a major resort the beach was littered with thousands of turtle eggs. Rich in history, the area is said to be the burial site of the famed pirate Jean Lafitte. It first attracted attention in 1926 when explorers discovered the *Mantanceros,* a Spanish galleon that sank in 1741. Soon after, Akumal became headquarters for the Mexican Underwater Explorers Club and a resort for wealthy underwater adventurers who flew into the area on small private planes and searched the waters for sunken treasures. A resort building boom of sorts has taken place in the past few years, and now there are a number of large time shares, condominiums, and hotel resorts, all ever-expanding.

The long curved bay and beach is rarely empty; most of the time it resembles the beaches along Cancún, with rows of glamorous sunbathers and swimmers. There is a small marine museum on the grounds of the Akumal Club Caribe, with exhibits of treasures from the sunken galleons just off the coast. Another underwater museum gives snorkelers and divers the chance to examine the wreckage.

Akumal can get crowded, especially when the tour buses to Tulum stop here for lunch, and it is most popular with those who want a resort with all the comforts of Cancún without the high rises.

3 A natural aquarium cut out of the limestone shoreline 6 kilometers (4 miles) south of Akumal, **Xel-Há** (Shel-ha) is a natural park and breeding center for countless species of tropical fish. Several lagoons are connected to one another by underwater currents; the rocky coastline curves into bays and coves where enormous parrotfish cluster around an underwater Mayan shrine. Another shrine marks the entrance to the park; gift shops and food stands line the parking lot. As you enter the grounds, you pass a large underwater preserve where swimming is prohibited. When the water is perfectly clear, it is possible to see stingrays and nurse sharks swimming about. A good restaurant sits at water's edge, and numerous rental shops carry diving and snorkeling gear and underwater cameras. Glass-bottom boats traverse the water's edge.

Xel-Há can get incredibly crowded at the peak of the tourist season, when buses unload hundreds of tourists from Cancún. Many sightseers prefer to watch the action from the rocky shoreline. Fortunately, the lagoons are very large, and it is possible to swim far enough out to snorkel alone and stare back at the lineup of oglers on the shore. Though the waters here are not as clear as they once were, Xel-Há is still an excellent snorkeling spot, as the fish are free to breed and survive, protected against fishing lines, spears, and nets. *Small entrance fee. Open daily 9–5.*

About 130 kilometers (80 miles) south of Cancún is one of the most beautifully situated of Yucatán's many ancient Mayan sites. **Tulum** is the only Mayan city built on the coast, the only one protected by a wall, and the only one known to have been inhabited when the conquistadors arrived.

Although there is evidence that Tulum was settled 1,500 years ago, most of the present buildings are no more than 800 years old. They belong to the late postclassic period when the Mayan civilization was in its decline. Certain artistic refinements found elsewhere are missing here, but the excellent state of preservation more than makes up for that. Tulum is dominated by the impressive **Castillo** (castle). It has now been identified as a temple to Kukulcán, the feathered serpent deity introduced by the Toltecs, an Indian horde that swept in from central Mexico and conquered the Maya only to be absorbed by them.

Believers in unidentified flying objects and others convinced that the earth was once visited by tiny aliens from some other planet have made Tulum a shrine of their own. They hold in greatest reverence the **Temple of the Descending God.** Over the doorway is a carved figure that does indeed appear to be tumbling from the heavens. More prosaic theories claim this represents either the setting sun or a bee (the Maya were and are great producers of honey). Visitors are no longer allowed to climb the temple's stairs for a closer look at the carvings.

Mayan myth maintains that Tulum was first built by prodigious dwarfs. Many of the lesser temples are tiny, and entranceways seem designed to accommodate short people. Archaeologists, however, insist that the doorways were designed to be low so that those who entered would be forced to bow if not crawl, this being only proper when approaching a god.

In its final days, Tulum was believed to have been a seaside trading center. It may have been a haven for the Chontal, a Mayan group from the Campeche side of the peninsula who operated a merchant fleet of canoes that made regular trips to Central America. Or it may have been a satellite of Cobá, once a city of 50,000 about 40 kilometers (25 miles) inland.

There are four main structures at Tulum, which can be seen in their entirety in about one hour. The **Temple of the Frescoes,** a two-story building fronted by four columns and a portico with bas-reliefs of the Descending God, contains some faintly col-

Tulum

Wall

Altars

Platforms

Temple
of the
Frescoes

Gran
Palacio

Temple of the
Descending God

Main
Gate

Inner
Courtyard

Castillo

Temple of the
Initial Series

Parking

Caribbean Sea

N

0   100 meters

0   100 yards

ored but well-preserved frescoes depicting the three worlds of
the ancient Maya and their major deities. East, toward the sea,
is a small complex housing two smaller temples and the tall
Castillo. While most of this lordly structure has been reconstructed, there are still carved traces of the ubiquitous Descending God and of the plumed serpent, evidence of the Toltec
influence over this Postclassic site. From the top of the Castillo,
you can look down 12 meters (40 feet) to the sea. The sanctity of
the place was honored as recently as 40 years ago, when modern-day Maya still came to burn copal incense within its somber
walls.

North of the Castillo, a path down to the sea has been carved
out of the cliff, if you care to swim. More empty beaches and
some inexpensive cabana hotels are located about 5 kilometers
(3 miles) farther south along Route 307.

Lodging

For price categories, consult the price chart in Cancún lodging.

Expensive **Hotel Akumal Cancún.** This large, multistory modern resort
has all the services of a Cancún property. The main building is
right on the water, and all rooms have a sea view, terrace, and
rattan furniture. Tennis and many water sports are available.
*For reservations write: Av. Bonampak y Cobá, Suites Atlan-
tis, Local 10, Cancún, Quintana Roo 77500, tel. 98/84–2272. 81
rooms and 11 villas. Facilities: beach, pool, restaurant, disco,*

> *tennis court, horseback riding, game room, lounge, dive shop, rental cars, shops. AE, MC, V.*

Moderate– Expensive **Hotel Club Akumal Caribe and Villas Maya.** Accommodations at this resort range from rustic but comfortable bungalows with red-tile roofs and garden views, to beachfront rooms in a modern 3-story hotel building (all with air-conditioning, ceiling fans, and refrigerators) and more secluded condominiums half a mile from the beach. Bungalows and rooms are furnished in rattan and dark wood with tiled floors, while the high-domed Mediterranean-style condos have kitchens and balconies or terraces overlooking the pool and beach. The club was originally built for CEDAM, the Mexican divers organization. Diving is still emphasized, but the properties also offer snorkeling, windsurfing, kayaking, and deep-sea fishing. *Reservations: Akutrame, Box 13326, El Paso, TX 79913, tel. 915/584–3552 or 800/351–1622. 40 bungalows, 21 rooms, 4 villas, and 3 condos. Facilities: beach, pool, restaurants, bar, dive shop, boutique, grocery. 3-night minimum stay. AE, DC, MC, V.*

Isla Mujeres

5 There's nothing to **Isla Mujeres.** That's the beauty of it. A wisp of an island with fine sand, palm trees and thatched huts, and the mesmerizing blue-green sea, Isla Mujeres is where sun-reddened gringos sit shooting the breeze with bartenders clad only in swim trunks, and local fishermen take foreigners out on their boats—no charge—just for the company.

The Isle of Women—as the Spaniards so beguilingly dubbed it because of the stone female figurines they found there in 1517—has much the same history and geography as Mexico's other Caribbean islands. After the Maya came the pirates and the fishermen; their descendants still harvest shrimp and lobster.

But change is coming to Isla Mujeres. Cancún has of course made a difference: "Isla" now hosts day-tripping picnic cruises from its opulent fellow island just 10 kilometers (6 miles) southwest across the bay. Isla Mujeres was hit badly by Hurricane Gilbert, and along with the immense labor of clean-up and rehabilitation came a wave of condo developers. Still, the island has funky hotels (mostly of the ceiling-fan variety), along with one first-class establishment; plenty of seafood restaurants; just enough shops hawking beach attire and hammocks; and a fair amount of action after dark. The bottom line is—it's cheap.

Come to Isla Mujeres if you don't care for the glitter of Cancún, or need a change of pace; if you like interacting with unpretentious Mexicans; if you don't mind humidity, sand, and mosquitoes; and especially if all you want is the great outdoors. Isla Mujeres offers excellent snorkeling at El Garrafón (an underwater national park, home to obliging parrotfish, blueheads, sergeant majors, and their buddies). The bird-watching—pelicans, flamingos, and cormorants—is fabulous at the nearby bird sanctuary on Contoy Island. The island's only Mayan temple succumbed to the record winds of Gilbert, and no trace remains. Similarly, very little is left of a 19th-century pirate's estate, but the island boasts some of the finest handicrafts for sale anywhere in Yucatán. The beaches are heavenly, ditto the shrimp and lobster, and you can also take a jaunt on a bike or moped (there are no rental cars available on the island) or charter a yacht for deep-sea fishing.

Important Addresses and Numbers

Tourist Information
Town Hall Tourist Office, Calle Guerrero 8, tel. 987/7–0317. Open weekdays 9–2:30 and 6–9.

Emergencies
Police (tel. 987/7–0082), **Medical Service** (tel. 987/7–0195), **health center,** on the main plaza at Guerrero N. 2 (tel. 98/82–0117).

Pharmacy
Farmacia Lily (Avs. Madero and Hidalgo).

Arriving and Departing

By Ferry
From the Cancún airport, take a minibus to downtown and then a taxi north to the ferry docks. Regular ferry service from the mainland to Isla Mujeres is available from Puerto Juárez (passengers only; just north of Cancún) and Punta Sam (cars, trucks, and passengers; 5 kilometers [3 miles] north of Puerto Juárez). Both ferries dock at the main pier in the center of town on Isla Mujeres. The trips take 45 minutes. The ferry from Puerto Juárez to Isla Mujeres runs from 6:30 AM to 7:30 PM; return trips are made from 6:30 AM to 5:30 PM, but the schedule varies seasonally. The Punta Sam ferry runs to the island from 7 AM to 10 PM and back from 6 AM to 9 PM. Another alternative is the water taxi between Punta Sam and Isla Mujeres, which is run by the Isla Mujeres **Cooperativa** from 7:30 AM to 8 PM for $18. You can also take the Shuttle from the Playa Linda dock in Cancún's hotel zone ($12 round-trip).

Getting Around

Since no rental cars are available on Isla Mujeres, getting around means taking a taxi or renting a moped. Cars can be brought over on the car ferry that departs from Punta Sam, but this scarcely seems worth the effort.

By Moped and Bike
Mopeds cost about $5 per hour or $25 per day. Credit cards are taken for deposit, but payment must usually be made in cash. Among the moped concessions are **Motorent Ciros** (Av. Guerrero N. 11, tel. 987/7–0351) and **Pepe's Motorenta** (Hidalgo 19, tel. 987/7–0019). Take the time to learn how to ride them, as lighting is poor and many of the streets are quite narrow. **Rent Me Sport Bike** on Av. Juárez at Morelos rents bicycles.

Guided Tours
The island's travel agencies can arrange fishing and snorkeling trips and tours of the Contoy Island park (snorkeling and birdwatching), Xel-Há (snorkeling in a beautiful, fish-filled lagoon), Cancún, and the ruins of Chichén Itzá and Tulum.

Exploring

The village has about all the amenities that Isla Mujeres has to offer. At the **malecón,** for instance, you can charter a fishing boat or arrange a scuba-diving trip. All the hotels, shops, and most of the restaurants are nearby. Isla Mujeres's main street is the Avenida Rueda Medina, which runs the length of the island along the western shore. When you step off the ferry, this is the street between the narrow beach and the town.

Isla Mujeres

TO ISLA CONTOY

Costa Club

Cave of the Sleeping Sharks

Cocos Beach

Bahía de Mujeres

Caribbean Sea

Tortoises Park

Ariel Magaña Baseball Park

Bahía de Mujeres

Makax Lagoon

Av. Gustavo Rueda Medina

N

| 0 | 1 mile |
| 0 | 1 km |

Playa Lancheros

Maria's Kan Kin Restaurant

El Garrafón

Lighthouse

TO CANCUN

Cocos Beach is at the far end of the malecón, just beyond the village near the northern tip of the island. The other beach up at this end is Pancholo, which faces the open Caribbean. Lovely to look at, this is no place to swim; the current is rough and dangerous.

Time Out   Try to get to Cocos in the late afternoon, just before sunset, and stop in for a beer at **Rutilio's y Chimbo's,** twin palapa restaurant-bars right on the beach, where locals come to drink beer, play dice, and chat. You can sit on the high stools and watch sailboarders or children playing until the sun sinks below the horizon. A glorious setting at the end of the day, Cocos is a great place to talk to isleños, who are clearly happy to share the beauty of this place.

Return to Avenida Rueda Medina for a trip to the south end of the island at Garrafón, where the finest snorkeling beach and other landmarks, such as they are, are located. Head south out of town (there is only one road) for about 2 kilometers (1.2 miles) until you see the small sign for Lancheros Beach. Just across the road is a small footpath leading through the brush to what remains of the **Casa de Mundaca,** once the home of Mundaca the Pirate.

Fermín Mundaca was the island's most notorious resident in the early 19th century. More of a slave trader than a buccaneer, Mundaca built this palatial home for a scrupulous young woman who repulsed his advances. She ran off with someone else, and the brokenhearted miscreant lived out his days in Mérida. All that's left of the estate after Hurricane Gilbert is a guard-house, an arch, a pediment, and a well.

Past Mundaca's estate, the road joins the leeward highway that runs to the lighthouse at the southern tip of the island. The re-mains of the lone Mayan temple to the goddess Ixchel were completely leveled by Hurricane Gilbert.

Double back along the same road to El Garrafón (the Jug), the beach where the picnic cruise boats from Cancún put in. El Garrafón is a national park, most of it underwater; while a beautiful spot, most of the marine life, and much of the reef it-self, has been destroyed by tourists. The crowds are thickest between 11 and 2 where the sand eases off into a reef, home to what remains of tropical fish—parrotfish, angelfish, blue-heads, sergeant majors, and any number of other colorful sea creatures. Snorkeling is the best way to see them, and gear is available for rent. There are a number of restaurants out this way, too.

Less than a mile up the coast toward town is **Lancheros Beach,** with its turtle and nurse shark pens. A little farther along is a turnoff to the bridge that leads across the Makax Lagoon. **Treasure Island,** a small theme park visited mostly by Cancún daytrippers, is on the other side of the bridge.

The main road runs along the shore of the lagoon, where, it is said, long before poor Mundaca, swashbuckling corsairs an-chored their ships or lay in wait for victims along the Spanish Main. From here the road runs back through town and all the way out to the Oasis International Hotel (formerly the Del Prado), which stands apart on its own little island and is one of the two first-class hostelries on Isla Mujeres. The Oasis is a couple of minutes' walk east of Cocos Beach.

Exploring, for most vacationers, includes a few boat trips. One of the most popular is to **Contoy,** an island bird sanctuary, home of cranes, ducks, pelicans, and countless other species. The voyage (45 minutes by speedboat) includes a picnic on the unin-habited island.

Shopping

The main commodities sold on Isla Mujeres are beachwear, cor-al jewelry, T-shirts, liquor, and a few arts and crafts. Most shops are concentrated downtown, along the streets near the main plaza. **Artesanías Alondra** (Av. Hidalgo 4) has a wide vari-ety of beach garb. **Casa del Arte México** (Av. Hidalgo 6) specia-lizes in well-made reproductions of Mayan figurines and reliefs, batik clothing, and silver jewelry. The usual inane T-shirts are available, along with shells, at **El Isleño II** (Av. Guerrero 3–A). **La Loma** (Av. Guerrero 6, second floor), on the east side of the main square, excels in interesting Mexican masks and other crafts from Mexico and Guatemala. The same owners run a similar shop on the main square, **La Sirena.** For beachwear, suntan lotion, hats, and so on, go to the **Caribbean Tropic Boutique** (Avs. Juárez and Morelos); they also rent snor-kel equipment and bicycles. **Alice** (Av. Juárez 7) sells duty-free liquor, Cuban cigars, and various munchables.

Sports

Diving and Snorkeling Sporting activities center on the water. The more expensive hotels, such as El Dorado and the Na Balam, have Windsurfers, Hobie Cats, and other water toys available to their guests for rent. There is excellent snorkeling at the eastern end of Playa Cocoteros and at El Garrafón. Even though there is widespread concern over loss of reef, ocean lovers will still be impressed by the underwater spectacle here. For scuba aficionados, there are good deeper reefs offshore, and there is one great novelty dive attraction: the Cave of the Sleeping Sharks. This is a cave 21 meters (70 feet) below the surface in which a number of large sharks "sleep," and you can supposedly approach them without being attacked. A number of reefs in the area, including La Bandera, which is between Isla Mujeres and Cancún, offer good diving. On the way to Contoy Island, divers can visit the remains of some Spanish galleons. **Mexico Divers** (Av. Rueda Medina just north of the ferry docks, tel. 98/82–0131) and the **Sociedad Cooperativa** (tel. 987/7–0274) next door rent scuba equipment and operate dive tours. An all-day dive with a complete outfit is $80 per person for a 2-tank trip, $350 for PADI certification.

Fishing Fishing charters are available from the **Cooperative Isla Mujeres** office (Av. Rueda Medina next to the ferry). The cost depends on the size of the boat and whether or not they provide the tackle, but averages at least $220. Spring is the season for catching deep-sea billfish, while the rest of the year there is good reef fishing for grouper, barracuda, and tuna.

Sailing Sailing enthusiasts come to Mujeres each April for the sailing regattas run by the **Club de Yates** (tel. 987/7–0211 or 2–0086).

Dining

Many people visit Isla Mujeres simply to have lunch. For those staying on the island, dinner often is the high point of the day. Expect to dine on some of the freshest fish you may ever have tasted. For price ranges, consult the price chart in Cancún dining.

Moderate
★ **Chez Magaly.** A very elegant restaurant on North Beach, Chez Magaly is tastefully furnished with wood floors, plants, leather chairs, Chinese blinds, and handsome place settings. Seafood grills, lobster quiche, *jambalaya* (Caribbean paella), and tequila-flambéed mangos are among the specialties; the wine list is extensive. *Av. Rueda Medina, Playa Norte, tel. 987/7–0259. Reservations advised. Dress: casual but neat. MC, V. Closed 2 weeks in June.*

María's KanKin. An extremely pleasant *palapa* (beach shack) overlooking the water, María's is also an island landmark, serving French cuisine with tropical ingredients ("landmark" means, alas, that they've jacked up their prices and gotten lazy about service). The specialty is lobster, but you can get baked fish or sole meunière for around $10. For starters, try the lobster bisque and finish with the coconut mousse. *Next to El Garrafón Park, tel. 987/7–0015. Reservations advised. AE, MC, V.*

La Flor de Mayo. Cheap sandwiches and various tortilla-based snacks are served. Try the juices and shakes, too. *Av. Hidalgo between Avs. Morelos and Madero.*

The Roof. Also known as "99% Natural," The Roof distinguishes itself as the only restaurant in town that offers a free medical visit (to Dr. Antonio Salas, the owner). This eatery serves health-conscious specialties like "good earth" and "jungle" salads. Dishes include crepes, sandwiches, and shakes made with fresh fruits as well as more exotic ingredients like *achiote*, an herb often used in Mayan cooking. Most tables are outside on a patio overlooking one of the town's main drags. *Av. Hidalgo 12, upstairs. No phone. No reservations. No credit cards.*

Inexpensive **Lonchería El Poc Chuc.** This tiny restaurant is named after the famous Yucatecan pork dish, which it serves. Try breakfast. *Av. Juárez between Avs. Madero and Morelos.*

Mirtita's, Tropicana, and **Villa del Mar.** Next to each other on Av. Rueda Medina across from the ferry dock, are local hangouts. All serve fresh seafood and Yucatecan specialties. *Av. Rueda Medina. No phones. No credit cards.*

Lodging

For prices, consult the price chart in Cancún lodging.

Expensive **Costa Club.** This seven-story hotel occupies the best spot on the island—its own private island barely nudging Playa Cocos and a short walk via plank bridge from town. In a perpetual state of being about to open for the past several years, the hotel has seen days as a Del Prado, Presidente, and Bojórquez. By spring of '93, it's scheduled to operate as an all-inclusive Costa Club resort. *Islote el Yungue/Punta Norte, tel. 987/7-0148 and 987/7-0153. 100 rooms. Facilities: 2 restaurants, 3 bars, game room, water sports, outdoor theater. AE, DC, MC, V.*

Moderate **Cabañas María del Mar.** This old beachfront property has been
★ recently renovated and expanded, and it shows. The rooms are on the small side and the decor slightly garish, but the hotel has a good location on Cocos Beach. There are 3 sections; you have your choice of air-conditioning or ceiling fan, sea view or no view (prices vary accordingly). All units come with fridges. Deluxe rooms in the newest building with its Moorish arcades have handmade touches, pine furniture, tiled floors and sinks, and custom-made ceramic lampshades; all rooms in this section have sea views. A tiny pool, a moped rental agency, and a good restaurant, Buhos, are on the premises; a disco was just completed in 1990. Price includes Continental breakfast. *Carlos Lazos 1, tel. 987/7-0213 or 2-0179, 800/826-6842, fax 987/7-0173 or 305/531-7616. 54 rooms, 12 of them deluxe "castle suites", and 12 cabañas. Facilities: pool, moped rental, restaurant/bar, travel agency, car and boat service. MC, V.*

★ **Na-Balam.** One of Isla's newest hotels, this is a small, lovely and informal place with palapas everywhere, right on Cocos Beach near the Oasis International. All rooms have dining rooms and patios facing the beach, fridges, and interesting photographs and colonial furniture. The three rooms with balconies are slightly more expensive, but worth it. *Calle Zazil Ha 118, tel. 98/82-0446 or 2-0279, fax 987/7-0011. 12 suites. Facilities: cafeteria. AE, MC, V.*

Inexpensive **Posada del Mar.** The Posada del Mar has a motelish look—modern, blue and white, two stories, and a large pool out front. It's on the north end of town across from the beach. *Av. Rueda Medina 15, 77400, tel. 987/7-0300, 987/7-0044, or 800/451-8891;*

fax 987/7–0266. 42 rooms. Facilities: pool, restaurant, bar, air-conditioning. AE, MC, V.

María's KanKin. This guest house and restaurant perches on a steep slope at the south end of the island. The nine rooms include doubles and large suites. The architecture is an attractive mix of orange stucco and thatched palm roofs. The restaurant serves gourmet French seafood (*see* Dining, *above*). *Box 69, 77400, tel. 98/83–1420. 9 rooms. Facilities: restaurant, bar, dock. AE, MC, V.*

The Arts and Nightlife

Nightlife on Isla Mujeres often consists of sitting on the beach and watching the sun go down, though it can be a trifle more exciting than that. People often eat late and linger over their dinner. Also, the municipal government occasionally stages dance and music performances in the **Casa de la Cultura,** on Avenida Guerrero. The liveliest bars and discos are **Buho's Disco Bar** (in the hotel Cabañas Maria del Mar), **Calypso Disco Bar** (at the north end of Av. Rueda Medina), **Tequila** (Avs. Hidalgo and Matamoros), and **Bronco's Grill** ("hangovers cured here"; Av. Bravo between Avs. Hidalgo and Juárez). **La Peña** (Calle Guerrero 5, tel. 987/7–0321) has salsa and reggae music and dancing on its open-air terrace overlooking the sea.

Cobá

6 A trip to **Cobá,** with the possibility of spending the night there, has much to recommend it. The towering pyramids, soaring above the rain forest, are among the most majestic in Mexico. The setting of what was once a great city on the shores of five lakes is ghostly in its beauty.

Not long ago, one had to drive east to Cancún, then south to Tulum, to reach the road running west again to Cobá. Now there are two paved roads running from Route 180 to the ruins, one at Chemax 29 kilometers (18 miles) east of Valladolid, and another at Nuevo X-Can, just inside the Quintana Roo border. The condition of both roads is unpredictable. At press time, the Chemax road was closed for repairs, but the other road cut a clear swath through the jungle. There are no gas stations or settlements of any type along this road; be sure to check your gas, water, and oil before heading through the jungle to Cobá.

Cobá was inhabited by about 400 BC, but seems to have developed its status as a city in the eighth century. The Spaniards never discovered it; thus the ruins are in better shape than those that were destroyed to make way for Christianity. The remains of 16 *sacbeob* (causeways)—they must have been more impressive than today's highways, although they were used only by human bearers (the Maya had no beasts of burden)—indicate that this was a great center of commerce. There was considerable trade, apparently, with the Maya of Tikal, in what is now Guatemala, and Tikal's architectural influence is strongly felt at Cobá, with its towering temple-pyramids.

Cobá is an enormous archaeological zone (admission: $3.50; open daily 8–5) with clusters of ceremonial centers built on the lake shores. It behooves the traveler to carry a map of the ruins, a canteen, and bug repellent. The jungle paths running through this zone that once held 40,000 inhabitants are confus-

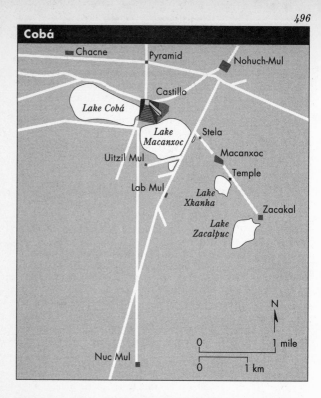

Cobá

Chacne · Pyramid · Nohuch-Mul

Lake Cobá · Castillo

Lake Macanxoc · Stela

Uitzil Mul · Macanxoc

Lab Mul · Temple

Lake Xkanha

Lake Zacalpuc · Zacakal

N

0 _____ 1 mile

0 _____ 1 km

Nuc Mul

ing at best. You are probably best off hiring one of the locals as an unofficial guide.

A 2.5-kilometer (1.5-mile) walk through the sweltering jungle leads to the tallest pyramid at Cobá. **Nohoch Mul** towers 45 meters (140 feet) over the jungle and contains at its top a temple honoring that mysterious figure found at Tulum, the Descending God. The climb up the 120 steps is a difficult one. There is another pyramid nearby, this one with a now empty tomb. All about are remnants of temples. About 30 carved stelae have been found at Cobá, some with intricate hieroglyphs depicting the city's history. They show some rather tyrannical rulers standing imperiously on the backs of either captives, subjects, or slaves.

Cobá is quite extensive. Each group of ruins is separated by about 3 to 5 kilometers (2 to 3 miles). Excavation of the site began in 1972, and seven groups of dwellings and temples have been uncovered. It is estimated that there are some 6,500 structures in the area, evidence that this was one of the greatest Mayan city-states. All told, it once covered an astounding 210 square kilometers (81 square miles).

A car is advised for a visit to Cobá; there is a bus that runs from Tulum, 42 kilometers (26 miles) east on the coast, to Cobá, but it is not reliable. Some small restaurants and shops are clustered at the entrance to the ruins.

Lodging The only recommendable hotel in the area is the **Villa Arqueológica Cobá**, a Club Med property on the banks of Lake Cobá and a mere 3 minutes' walk from the ruins. The two-story inn surrounds a patio filled with tropical plants, bird cages, and a large pool. The 40 air-conditioned rooms are white stucco with tile floors and are decorated with handicrafts of the region. A library houses reading material on the ruins in English, Spanish, and French. Villa Arqueológica Cobá is approximately 30 minutes by car from Tulum. *Tel. 800/CLUB-MED. 40 rooms. Facilities: restaurant, bar, pool, tennis court, library, and gift shop. AE, MC, V. Moderate.*

Cozumel

❼ Sun-saturated **Cozumel,** its ivory beaches fringed with coral reefs where angelfish and barracuda spawn, fulfills the tourist's visions of a tropical Caribbean island. More Mexican than Cancún and far less developed, Cozumel surpasses its better-known, fancier neighbor to the north in several ways. It has more—and lovelier—secluded beaches, superior diving and snorkeling spots, more authentically Mexican cuisine, more Mexican tourists, and even a greater diversity of handicrafts sold at better prices.

Cancún's top-of-the-line accommodations and nightlife are better than those in Cozumel. But for travelers who need less pampering and don't mind exploring on their own (renting a moped or Jeep is almost indispensable for getting around the island), Cozumel wins hands down.

Cozumel was once a shrine to the Mayan moon goddess, Ixchel, to whom women flocked in search of fertility. Cortés landed there briefly in 1519, en route to his conquest of Mexico. Henry Morgan, the English buccaneer, used it as a base for piracy, and then for 300 years the island was barely inhabited. Subdued echoes of its past emerge in the many crumbling Mayan ruins—none of them substantial enough to be worth visiting—and in the more spectacular sunken ships whose hulls slumber near the reefs.

Cozumel was rediscovered during World War II by American military diving teams in training for the Pacific arena. It was well chosen: the Palancar Reef is the fifth longest in the world, the second longest outside of Australasia. The divers' enthusiasm reached Jacques Cousteau, and after his visit and subsequent blessing, Cozumel and the entire eastern shore of Quintana Roo and Belize began attracting scuba divers from around the world. The tourist industry got going in the '60s, and today Cozumel has dozens of hotels, restaurants, boutiques, and dive shops.

Life on this flat jungle island—some 48 kilometers (30 miles) long by 18 kilometers (11 miles) wide—centers on **San Miguel** (also called *el pueblo,* or "the town"). San Miguel is on the western, leeward side of Cozumel, where the waters are calmer. Scuba divers, who make up the bulk of the island's visitors, congregate here, as do hundreds of cruise passengers in town for a day of shopping. Duty-free shops line the malecón; prices are marked in dollars, and the salespeople speak English. Jewelry made of shells, black coral, and tortoiseshell (the latter two are endangered species) abounds, as does an ample assortment of crafts from all over Mexico, particularly silver and pottery.

Resort hotels are slowly being built both north and south of town; the eastern, or windward, side of the island is almost deserted, and the strong currents and heavy waves there make swimming a risky pursuit at best. All the major hotels have excellent facilities for sunbathing and equipment for snorkeling and windsurfing. Most of the resort properties have dive shops, although better deals can often be found in town.

Many people set aside a few hours for a snorkeling tour on the *Zorro*, a 45-foot catamaran, or a glass-bottom boat tour. When catching endangered species was prohibited, these tours took over where the former "Robinson Crusoe" picnic trips left off. Participants visit a beach on the southern shore, with shallow reefs for snorkeling (optional), and enjoy fried fish caught at Playa del Carmen. Larger motorboats tour the more distant reefs. The Cozumel Museum also offers visitors the opportunity to participate in saving the prized sea turtle.

The ruins of Tulum, accessible by hydroplane, small plane, and ferry, are another popular day outing. An overnight excursion is best to see Chichén Itzá, which is farther afield. Sightseeing on Cozumel itself is rather limited, but there is a captivating underwater park in the lagoon at Chankanaab Park, 9 kilometers (5.6 miles) south of San Miguel, filled with dazzling tropical flora and fauna. (Unfortunately, one reef here was badly damaged by the 1988 hurricane.)

The atmosphere in Cozumel is easygoing: This is the T-shirt and shorts crowd, even at dinner. San Miguel has the usual disco or two, but many people are content just to get high on booze, the easy island amiability, and the elements.

Important Addresses and Numbers

Tourist Information There is an information booth on the main pier next to the Plaza del Sol (open daily 8 AM–1 PM). The main tourism office is on the second floor of the crafts mall on the east end of the plaza (tel. 987/2–0218 or 987/2–1915, open weekdays 9–2).

Emergencies **Police** (tel. 987/2–0092), **Red Cross** (tel. 987/2–1058), **Ambulance** (tel. 987/2–0639), **Hospital** (tel. 987/2–0140), **Fire** (tel. 987/2–0800), **Recompression chamber** (tel. 987/2–2387).

Arriving and Departing by Plane

Airports and Airlines The Cozumel Airport is in the north end of the small town of San Miguel. **Continental** (tel. 231–0856) has nonstop service from Houston. **Mexicana** (tel. 800/531–7921) flies nonstop from Dallas-Fort Worth, Los Angeles, Miami, and Mérida. **Aerocaribe** and **Aerocozumel** (tel. 987/2–0877 or 987/20928), both Mexicana subsidiaries, fly to Cancún and other destinations in Mexico, including Chichén Itzá, Chetumal, Mérida, and Playa del Carmen.

Between the Airport and Center City Numerous taxis are available, and the rates are fixed and reasonable. There are many car-rental offices in the airport terminal.

By Ferry The ferry from **Puerto Morelos** transports people and vehicles. It is inexpensive, currently about $30 for automobiles, $42 for RVs, and $4 per person. The schedule changes frequently, and ferries are often late. It is fairly safe to assume that the ferry makes one round-trip four days a week and two round-trips twice a week. Ferries leave from the international pier in front of the Hotel Sol Caribe to the south of town. The trip takes about three to four hours and should not be undertaken on an empty stomach. For exact departure times, call Maritima Chankanaab, tel. 987/2–0827. Tickets can be bought up to a day in advance.

The passenger-only ferry from **Playa del Carmen** costs about $6 per person. It leaves from the dock at Playa del Carmen (on the beach just south of the Plaza del Sol) approximately every two hours between 5:30 AM and 9 PM and takes 40 minutes to an hour (verify the schedule—it changes frequently).

By Jetfoil Two water-jet trimarans connect Cozumel (downtown pier) with Playa del Carmen. Like the ferry, the trip takes 40 minutes and costs about $6. Tickets go on sale at the main pier one hour before departure. To confirm the schedule, call 987/2–2915 or 987/2–0477; fax 987/2–1728.

Getting Around

The most efficient way to get around San Miguel is on foot. If you want to see the rest of the island—the beaches and the ruins—you need wheels. Taxis are ubiquitous. There are stands in front of all the major hotels and on Avenida Melgar just north of the main pier. An inexpensive but inconsistent bus service runs out to the north and south beach resort zones. Rentals—car, Jeep, or moped—are the most popular way to see the island. Mopeds are great fun, and you can circumnavigate the island on one tank of gas. Exercise great caution when riding them, however, and wear a helmet (Mexican law requires it); accidents are frequent and can be fatal. The only gas station on Cozumel is at the corner of Avenida Juárez and Avenida 30 (open daily 7 AM–midnight). Following is a list of rental firms that handle all types of two- and four-wheel vehicles (all the major hotels have rental offices): **Avis** (Calle 20 between R. Salas and 3 Sur, tel. 987/2–1923), **Budget** (5a Av. and Calle 2 N, tel. 987/2–0903), **Fiesta Cozumel** (Hotel Mesón San Miguel, tel. 987/2–0233), and **Hertz** (Av. Juárez and Calle 10, tel. 987/2–2136).

Guided Tours

General Tours Cozumel travel agencies run tours of the island that include the Chankanaab Park tropical garden and lagoon, the rugged east coast, and the San Gervasio ruins, a Mayan site with a number of small temples; the cost is about $30. You can also take a trip on Fiesta Cozumel's 45-foot catamaran, the *Zorro*, for sunbathing, snorkeling, and a picnic, or a glass-bottom boat trip around the island. Off-island tours are run to the ruins of Tulum and the nearby Xel-Há Lagoon, the magnificent Mayan city of Chichén Itzá, and the more modern pleasures of Cancún. A list of some island tour operators follows: **Aviomar** (5a Av. N, #8A between Calles 2 and 4, tel. 987/2–0588), **American Express** (Av. Melgar 27 between Calles 8 N and 10 N, tel. 987/2–0522), **Intermar Caribe** (Calle 2 N #101-B, between 5a and 10a Avs., tel. 987/2–0895), and **Viajes y Deportes del Caribe** (Hotel Presidente, tel. 987/2–0923).

Special-interest Tours If you're into birding, bring your binoculars, especially if your island vacation is in the spring or fall, when North American migrants fill the woodlands of the interior and feast on seeds in the fields. As in most climes, the best time to birdwatch is at dawn, when the birds are feeding; they quiet down considerably by 9 in the morning. Among the birds you'll see are the frigate, the Yucatán woodpecker, the tropical pewee, the Caribbean elaenia, the black catbird, the stripe-headed tanager, and the rose-throated tanager.

Aviomar charters 3-seater Cessnas for half-hour flights over the island at about $150; there are flights to Chichén Itzá as well.

Glass-bottom boats are a thrilling way to explore coral formations, teeming with sea life, without even getting your feet wet. Tours are available through **Viajes y Deportes del Caribe** (*see* General Tours, *above*) as well as many beachfront hotels.

Viajes y Deportes del Caribe agency also runs horseback tours. Snorkeling tours are offered by all the tour operators, and go for anywhere from $18 to $35, taking in the shallow reefs of Palancar or the Colombia lagoon. The **Cozumel Museum** offers visitors the chance to participate in the nationwide save-the-turtle campaign between May and September: participants seek out, mark, and collect the eggs, and then hear a lecture by biologists.

The 32 ruins on the island are insignificant when compared with those on the mainland, but you may want to visit **El Cedral,** once the island's population center (turn left onto the dirt road just past San Francisco Beach). The temple is small and dilapidated, but somewhat interesting. Next to the temple is a small modern church in which rows of small crosses are draped with intricately embroidered mantles, following a tradition that probably dates to the War of the Castes.

To get to the **Tumba del Caracol,** a small site where the Maya once worshiped, take the road to the windward side of the island and go down the dirt road toward the lighthouse at Punta Celerain.

Exploring

A good place to begin orienting yourself in San Miguel, an otherwise nondescript little town best known for its laid-back eateries and well-stocked shops, is at the **Museo de la Isla de Cozumel.** Exhibit halls on the first floor are devoted to the island environment and to the ecosystem of the surrounding reefs and water. Among the displays are large dioramas of local forests and reefs, and well-organized descriptions of the island's geology, flora, and fauna. The second floor has exhibits on Mayan and colonial life and history and on modern-day Cozumel. *Av. Melgar and Calle 4 N. Small admission fee. Open Sun.–Fri. 9–1 and 4–8.*

Time Out On the terrace off the second floor of the museum is **Restaurante del Museo** (Av. Melgar and Calle 4 N, tel. 987/2–0838), which sells drinks, beer, and full meals of *fajitas* (thin strips of grilled beef), barbecued meat, or grilled red snapper. It has a great view of the waterfront.

Head south out of town on Avenida Melgar (a car is required from this point on); your first stop, after 10.5 kilometers (6.5

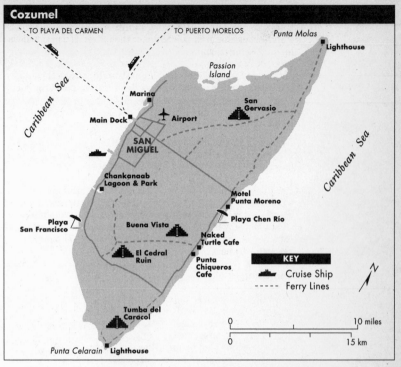

Cozumel

TO PLAYA DEL CARMEN   TO PUERTO MORELOS   *Punta Molas*

Lighthouse

Caribbean Sea

Passion Island

Marina

San Gervasio

Main Dock ■   Airport

SAN MIGUEL

Caribbean Sea

Chankanaab Lagoon & Park

Motel Punta Moreno

Playa Chen Río

Playa San Francisco

Buena Vista

Naked Turtle Cafe

El Cedral Ruin

Punta Chiqueros Cafe

KEY

Cruise Ship

– – – Ferry Lines

Tumba del Caracol

| 0 | | 10 miles |
| 0 | | 15 km |

Punta Celarain   Lighthouse

miles), will be the **Chankanaab Lagoon and Park** ("small sea" in Mayan). The natural aquarium has been designated an underwater preserve for the more than 50 species of tropical fish, as well as crustaceans and coral, that make it their home. Snorkeling and scuba equipment can be rented, and instruction and professional guides are available, as are courses for diving certification. There are also gift shops, snack bars, and a restaurant (open daily 10–4) serving fresh seafood dishes. *Carretera Sur, Km 9, no phone. Admission: $3. Open daily 9–5.*

The main road now skirts thick forest until it hits the east coast. When the road first meets the dunes, there is a turnoff to the right down a sandy road that passes the **Tumba del Caracol,** another small Maya temple, a little over 1.6 kilometers (1 mile), then ends at the **Southern Lighthouse** at Punta Celerain. (Note: This road is only for Jeeps and other four-wheel-drive vehicles.) From here the road runs north along the shore; the vegetation en route is sparse as the plants are stunted by the constant wind.

Time Out   The only human outpost on this windswept shore is the **Naked Turtle** (East Coast Rd.), a very casual restaurant and bar serving beer, soda, and a few simple seafood dishes.

About halfway up the island the road turns west back to San Miguel. However, if you are keen to explore, the east coast of Cozumel is a splendid succession of rocky coves and powdery beaches, most of them deserted. Swimming can be treacherous here, but there is nothing to prevent deliciously solitary sunbathing; camping is also possible. (Very few of the beaches on this side, however, offer any facilities.) Good bets include **Punta Chiqueros,** a moon-shaped cove sheltered from the sea by an offshore reef, and part of a longer stretch of beach most locals call **Playa Bonita** (it's sometimes also known as Playa San Martín or *Tortuga Desnuda* [Naked Turtle]); **Chen Río,** where the waters are clear and the surf not too strong; and the rocky beach at **Punta Morena,** which is also the site of the eastern coast's only hotel, and where the turtles come to lay their eggs on June nights when the moon is full.

Archaeology buffs may want to detour inland at this point to the jungle, and view the ruins of **San Gervasio.** The largest and most important Mayan site on Cozumel, it is in relatively good condition and has been recently restored. The northern tip of Cozumel terminates at the **Punta Molas Lighthouse.** This entire area is maneuverable only in 4-wheel drives, but the view—of a jagged shoreline and the open sea—is magnificent. Punta Molas, with its dense jungles and lagoons, is also an excellent spot for sunbathing, bird-watching, or camping, and is reachable by boat.

Shopping

San Miguel's biggest industry—even larger than diving—is selling souvenirs and crafts to cruise-ship passengers. The primary items are ceramics, onyx, brass, wood carvings, reproductions of Mayan artifacts, shells, silver, gold, sportswear, T-shirts, perfume, and liquor. Almost all stores take U.S. dollars as readily as pesos, and prices are marked in both currencies. San Miguel's shopping district centers on the Plaza del Sol and extends out from it along Avenida Melgar and Avenida 5 S and N. The east side of the plaza is occupied by the **Plaza del Sol mall,** two floors of jewelry and crafts. One of the finest crafts stores is **La Piñata;** there's also Cozumel's high-fashion store, the **Emma B. Boutique,** and a branch of the island's classiest jeweler, **Van Cleef.** The main **Van Cleef** store is a block away on Avenida Melgar between Avenida Juárez and Calle 2 N. Next door is **Santa Cruz-Casablanca,** a jeweler specializing in all types of gems, precious and semiprecious, as well as expensive crafts. The silver earrings at **Alexandra,** near Calle 4, are especially original in design; gold and gemstones are also for sale. At **Los Cinco Soles,** which occupies nearly an entire block, there is a wide choice of silver jewelry, soapstone earrings and beads, blue-rim glassware, talavera pottery, brass and tin animals from Jalisco, tablecloths and placemats, cotton gauze and embroidered clothing, onyx, T-shirts, and papier-mâché fruit. Farther north on Avenida Melgar, at the corner of Calle 6 N, is an outlet for Express, Guess?, and Esprit designer sportswear. The most bizarre store on the island is the **Cozumel Flea Market,** on Avenida 5 N between Calles 2 and 4, which sells reproductions of erotic Mayan figurines, Cuban cigars, antique masks, rare coins, and Xtabentún, the local anise and honey liqueur. Down the street at Avenida 5 N 148, **Arte Na Balam** sells high-quality Mayan reproductions, jewelry, and batik clothing. A number of shops can also be found at the cruise-ship passenger terminal south of town. Larger and less expensive souvenir department stores are the **Bazar del Angel,** at Avenida Melgar and Calle 3, and the **Orbi** store, right across the street. For fresh fruit and other foods, go to the **Municipal Market** (25a Av.

S and Calle Salas). Film is developed at **Omega** (5a Av. N between Av. Juárez and Calle 2), and out-of-town newspapers and American magazines are sold at the small bookstore on the east side of the plaza. The liquor store nearest to the plaza is **Bodegas del Caribe** (5a Av. S near Calle Salas). Many stores in town sell diving and snorkeling gear (*see* Sports, *below*).

Sports

Diving and Snorkeling

The water is warm and as clear as gin, and the reefs are large and teeming with marine life. So it's no surprise that most visitors to Cozumel are divers. A dip into the water around the offshore reefs reveals myriad life forms: three-story pillars of coral; lobsters and conch; huge schools of silvery fingerlings; sea urchins and sand dollars; and, yes, a few sharks. It is illegal to spearfish or touch the coral on Cozumel's reef. If you've never been diving before or need a refresher course, many schools on the island can certify you.

Be aware that a number of American diving fatalities have occurred on Cozumel, in part because most of the divers here are neophytes, and also because many people are diving while intoxicated. A Cozumel Association of Dive Operators has been formed, however, and is trying to establish minimum operational standards to ensure safety.

The most accessible reefs are those just off the **Chankanaab Lagoon and Park.** You can either dive in a protected lagoon filled with half-tame fish or venture out into open water through an underwater tunnel cut through the rock. The other great dive site near shore is **La Ceiba Reef,** in the waters off La Ceiba and Sol Caribe hotels. Here lies the wreckage of the **sunken airplane,** a twin-engine propeller plane that was blown up for a Mexican disaster movie. Farther offshore are the **Paraíso Reefs North and South.** These 11- to 15-meter- (35- to 50-foot) deep reefs are ridges of coral heads where divers often practice before heading to the deeper drop-offs. From these two reefs it is possible to swim out to the drop-offs called **La Ceiba** and **Villa Blanca.** For more advanced divers there are many deeper dives, which involve drifting along coral walls that drop off into the black, bottomless depths. The most famous of these is the **Palancar Reef.** Among the reef's many attractions are huge columns of coral that rise dozens of feet from the sea floor.

Many people both in Cozumel and abroad feared that Hurricane Gilbert had destroyed the great reefs offshore. Explorations after Gilbert showed that most of the reefs lived through the storm, and divers are now returning to Cozumel's reefs.

Cozumel's reputable dive shops include the following: **Aqua Safari** (Av. Melgar 39A, tel. 987/2–0101), **Blue Angel** (Hotel Villablanca, tel. 987/2–1631), **Fantasia Divers** (Av. 25, enter at Adolfo Rosado Salas and Av. 35, tel. 987/2–2840, fax 987/2–1210) and **Discover Cozumel** (Av. Rafael Melgar and Calle 5 Sur, tel. 987/2–0280). For further information, contact the **Cozumel Association of Dive Operators** (CADO), tel. 987/2–1842, fax 987/2–1842.

Deep-sea Fishing

Although there's no fishing around the protected reefs, Cozumel offers some excellent deep-water, big-game fishing and shallow flats fishing. Spring is the season to hook sailfish, blue marlin, and swordfish. On the flats you can catch bonefish, permit, snook, and the awesome tarpon. As part of a growing conservation movement, it's forbidden to kill certain species, including billfish, so be prepared to return prize catches to the sea. Contact **Yucab Reef Diving and Fishing Center** (Box 316, Cozumel, 77600, tel. 987/2–1842) or **Club Naútico Cozumel** (Box 341, Cozumel, 77600, tel. 987/2–0118 or 800/253–9701).

Dining

"Casual" is the word that best describes Cozumel dining. Many water-sports enthusiasts get up early and are ready for a hearty evening meal by 7 PM, which is early by Mexican standards but perfectly acceptable on Cozumel. The resort hotels on the north and south beaches have their own dining rooms, but it's sometimes fun to search out new dining experiences. For price ranges, consult the price chart in Cancún dining. Highly recommended restaurants are indicated by a star ★.

Expensive **Donatello's.** Very elegant, with pale pink walls, pink marble floors, dim lighting, and garish paintings on the walls, Donatello's is owned by one of Cozumel's leading tourism families, and they know how to lay on fine service. While not yet world-class, it is still the classiest place in town (less formal dining is available in the back garden). The accent is Italian; specialties are scampi, lobster, veal, and pasta, including macaroni with salmon. Desserts like coconut ice cream and bananas flambées are exquisite. *Av. Rafael Melgar S. 131, tel. 987/2–0090 or 987/2–2586. Reservations advised. AE, MC, V. Dinner only.*

Morgan's. Morgan's is all dark wood and varnish. At night the interior is lit up by the brandy-fueled flames of fancy seafood dishes. Lobster is the specialty. While no longer the "big night out" it used to be, this restaurant still offers impeccable service and international cuisine. *The plaza at Avs. Juárez and 5 N, tel. 987/2–0584. Reservations suggested. AE, DC, MC, V. Closed Sun. lunch.*

★ **Pepe's Grill.** This elegant waterfront restaurant serves steak, seafood, and Mexican dishes, all expertly prepared and served by tuxedoed waiters. *Av. Melgar and Calle Salas, tel. 987/2–0213. Reservations advised. Dress: casual but neat. AE, V. No lunch.*

Moderate **Carlos 'n' Charlies.** The local branch of the Mexican chain, this second-floor waterfront restaurant is decorated with oddball T-shirts and even has its own volleyball court. The food is the chain's own interpretation of Mexican and American dishes, such as hamburgers and fajitas. *Av. Melgar and Calle 2 N, tel. 987/2–0191. MC, V.*

★ **El Capi Navegante.** Locals say this is the best seafood place in town; it serves Caribbean specialties, such as oysters, grouper, lobster, shrimp, and fish filet. Highly recommended are the conch ceviche, deep-fried whole snapper, and stuffed squid. The decor is nautical with a blue-and-white color scheme, and life buoys on the walls. *10a Av. S. 312 at Calle 3, next to Discover Cozumel; tel. 987/2–1730.*

Las Palmeras. This open-air restaurant is across from the downtown pier. The extensive menu specializes in seafood. The food is less of a draw than the waterfront views. *West end of the plaza, tel. 987/2–0532. AE, MC, V.*

★ **Rincón Maya.** This is the top place on the island for Yucatecan cuisine. Píbil-style chicken, suckling pig, and poc chuc (marinated grilled pork) are among the excellent dishes. The decor is Maya style, and the restaurant is very popular with locals. *Av. 5 S and Calle 3 S. No phone. No reservations. No credit cards. Dinner only.*

Inexpensive **El Foco.** A *taqueria* serving pork, *chorizo* (spicy Mexican sau-
★ sage), and cheese soft tacos, this eatery also does ribs and steak. Graffitied walls and plain wood make it a casual, fun spot to grab a bite and a *cerveza*. *Av. 5 S and 13. No phone. No reservations. Dress: casual. MC, V.*

El Moro. Until recently undiscovered, this family-run restaurant with Yucatecan baskets on the walls has become a favorite of divers. It serves local cuisine, particularly seafood, chicken, and meat, at great prices and offers daily specials for lunch and dinner. Ask the taxi driver how to get there; it's on the eastern edge of town. *No phone. No credit cards. Closed Thurs.*

Lodging

San Miguel de Cozumel, the only town on the island, is the center of the action. Budget hotels are, for the most part, located in town; the resort properties are to the north and south. The resorts are on some of Cozumel's most beautiful beaches—particularly San Juan and Santa Pilar beaches, on the northern hotel strip. Most of the resort hotels provide water-sports equipment and can arrange excursions. Scuba divers and snorkelers frequent the hotels on the beaches to the south, closer to the reefs they've come to explore. Sailors and anglers favor the resorts to the north. For price ranges, consult the price chart in Cancún lodging. Highly recommended lodgings are indicated by a star ★.

Very Expensive **Fiesta Americana Sol Caribe.** This is an enormous 10-story hotel south of town, just across the street from its own vast beach. Architecturally "neo-Mayan", it is built of large white coral stones assembled under a wooden roof. A glass-encased elevator looks out on the huge and sinuous pool, with a breezy lobby bar, waterfall, and swim-up bar at pool level. There is always lots of bustle. Rooms are spiffily decorated in black and white with wicker furniture. Those in the main building lack balconies, but the new tower has them. Along with live music nightly in the lobby bar, the Mexican fiesta on Wednesday and Saturday nights is a big draw for Americans. *Box 259, Playa Paraíso Km. 3.5, tel. 987/2–0700 or 800/FIESTA–1, fax 987/2–1301. 321 rooms. Facilities: restaurants, bars, satellite TV, minibars, pool, tennis courts, water sports, travel agency, motorcycle and car rental, dive shop, boutiques, beauty salon. AE, DC, MC, V.*

★ **Holiday Inn Cozumel Reef.** Opened in summer of 1991, this property is ideally located for snorkeling and scuba diving. Occupying the undeveloped southern end of the island, near the Stouffer Presidente and Chankanaab, the beach here offers easy access to spectacular underwater scenery. Tiles in the lobby and beach and pool areas echo the soft corals, blues, and greens of the lobby and room furnishings. The beachside restaurant serves a delicious chicken taco salad for lunch. Ask for a room on the upper floors. *Carretera a Chankanaab Km 7.5, tel. 987/2–2622 or 800/HOLIDAY, fax 987/2–2666. 164 rooms. Facilities: 2 tennis courts, gym, pool, 2 restaurants, 2 bars, dive shop, water sports, meeting facilities. AE, DC, MC, V.*

★ **Stouffer Presidente.** This hotel has been dramatically refurbished since the 1988 hurricane. Service is unusually courteous, prompt, and efficient; the epithet "luxury hotel" is well-deserved. Located on its own beach at the southern extreme of the hotel zone, the Stouffer also has the best gourmet restaurant on the island and a very active water sports center. Deluxe rooms are handsomely decorated with pine trim, white walls, and pink, blue, and purple touches, and have their own private terraces fronting on the pool or beach—well worth the extra money. *Carretera a Chankanaab Km. 6.5, tel. 987/2–0322, 2–1520, or 800/HOTELS–1, fax 987/2–1360. 259 rooms. Facilities: restaurants, bar, pool, tennis courts, dive shop, water sports, boutique, car and motorcycle rental, travel agency. AE, DC, MC, V.*

Expensive **Villablanca.** This classy-looking motel-style lodging is in the south hotel zone. Its glitzy restaurant/nightclub, Amadeus, was gutted by Gilbert and has been reconstructed. There's a pool and sun deck if the tiny beach doesn't attract you. *Km 3.5, Carretera a Chankanaab, 77600, tel. 987/2–0730. 50 rooms with bath. Facilities: restaurant, tennis court, dive shop. DC, MC, V.*

Moderate **Melia Mayan Cozumel.** Located to the north of town, the picturesque Melia is small, quiet, and uncluttered. A handsome, ★ dark red tiled walkway leads to a pleasant lobby, done all in ivory. Because of its extensive water sports and dive center, Melia is popular especially with European and Canadian divers. The main pool isn't large, but the hotel is right on the beach, complete with palapas and snackbar. Superior rooms have their own balconies over the beach; standard rooms are smaller and the decor more rustic. The 170 rooms with sea views are preferable to those with a "garden view," which are in a separate building and look out over a swamp. *Box 9, Carretera a Sta. Pilar 6, tel. 987/2–0072, 2–0411, or 800/336–3542, fax 987/2–1599. 200 rooms, including 8 suites. Facilities: beach, pools, water sports center, tennis courts, satellite TV, minibars, in-room safety deposit boxes, restaurants, café, bars, shops, tour desk. AE, MC, V.*

★ **Villas Las Anclas.** Rated as a three-star hotel, the villas are actually furnished apartments for rent by the day, week, or month. The convenient location on 5a Av. S. is parallel to the malecón. Well-appointed two-level units feature a kitchenette and sitting room downstairs, while up the spiral staircase you find a small bedroom with a large desk, water purifier, and inset shelves over the double bed. Decor is spanking white and modern, but there are no phones. Fresh-ground coffee is sold at the front desk. *5a Av. S. 325, Box 25, tel. and fax 987/2–1403. No credit cards.*

Inexpensive **Bazar Colonial.** An attractive and modern hotel located over a small cluster of shops and prettified by bougainvillea, the Colonial has three stories and an elevator. There are red tile floors, natural wood furniture, kitchenettes, bookshelves, and sofa-beds, but no restaurant or pool. *5a Av. S. 9, tel. 987/2–0506, fax 987/3–0309 or 2–1387. 28 rooms. AE, MC, V.*

Mesón San Miguel. Situated right on the square where its large public bar and outdoor café are frequently filled with locals, the architecturally eclectic San Miguel (four stories and an elevator) has such flourishes as brown, black, and white art-deco floor tiles and thick, art-deco glass blocks set in the walls. The remodeled rooms are clean and functional, with balconies overlooking the zócalo. A good bet for your money. *Av. Juárez 2 bis, tel. 987/2–0323 or 2–0233, fax 987/2–1820. 97 rooms. Facilities: small pool, bar, café, game room. AE, MC, V.*

The Arts and Nightlife

After a full day in or on the water, many people retire early. But for those who want to play at night, mingle with other travelers, show off their tans, dance, and celebrate their vacations, there are places to go and people to see.

The **Museo de Cozumel** has regular theater and dance performances and lectures; check the bulletin board in the lobby or call 987/2–1545. Folkloric shows for tourists, with dancing and mariachis, are presented at the Fiesta Americana Sol Caribe, the Stouffer Presidente, the Melia Mayan Cozumel, and the Cabañas del Caribe hotels. The big discos on Cozumel are **Scaramouche** (Av. Melgar and Calle Salas), and **Neptuno** (Av. Melgar and Calle 11 S). Among the more popular bars is **Carlos 'n Charlies** (also a restaurant), on the waterfront north of the plaza. The island's two movie theaters, **Cine Cozumel** (Av. Melgar, between Calles 2 N and 4 N) and **Cine Cecillo Borgues** (Av. Júarez between Av. 30 and 35, tel. 987/2–0402), both show American and Mexican movies nightly at 9:15.

Mérida

Mérida is a subtle city, its character not easily discernible. Aging elegance pervades the stately colonial mansions on its broad boulevard, Paseo de Montejo, and the fading whitewash on its squatly built side streets gives it a frowzy, somewhat crumpled look. Yet it is a lovable city, one of the most lovable in Mexico, in the way one loves the tired, sagging air of New Orleans.

Most visitors hurry through this capital of Yucatán, which is understandable since its charm is so elusive. It is best appreciated in comparison with other Mexican cities, which are either indistinguishably modern or suffocatingly colonial. Both aspects are in Mérida, but there is another dimension—its Mayan nature. One definitely feels that the Meridanos are Yucatecos first, Mexicanos second. Generally they are friendlier than other urban dwellers, and the machismo of the Mexican male is absent. The style of dress adds to the incongruous, anachronistic impression of an Indian metropolis: the men almost all sport guayaberas—pale, pleated shirts worn beltless over the pants waist—while many Mayan women still pad around in *huipiles*, the sacklike, white cotton dresses trimmed with the gaily colored floral embroidery of their ancestors.

In typical colonial fashion, Mérida revolves around a zócalo, on the town's south side of which still stands the palace of the Montejos, the leading family of conquistadores. The square is shaded by ancient laurel trees manicured into geometric shapes, themselves falling under the shadow of the twin-spired, yellow cathedral. On the northeast side of the plaza is the Palacio de Gobierno (Governor's Palace), which fronts the streets leading to the Paseo de Montejo. Fine architectural details, including iron grillwork, carved wood doors, and Moorish archways, attest as much to the city's late-19th-century heyday as to its colonial heritage. Low-lying stucco edifices conceal marble tiles and exuberant gardens.

Mérida survived the turmoil during the indescribably bloody War of the Castes in the 1840s, which coincided with a short-lived Yucatecan separatist movement. Wealthy landowners, fearing an American invasion during the Mexican-American War, armed their virtually enslaved Mayan workers who, not surprisingly, turned against their masters. The Ladinos fled to Mérida and Campeche, begging Texas, Spain, and Britain to annex the province. It took years of fighting and the death of half the Mayan population to restore order.

The city returned to prosperity during the 1880s with the demand for henequen, a fiber produced from the sisal cactus and used to make rope and twine. Millionaires turned Mérida into the wealthiest capital in Mexico; they vacationed in New Orleans, and from Europe brought back art and *calesas*, the horse-drawn carriages that still ply the city streets. Hundreds of Lebanese families came to Yucatán at this time, and their descendants are among the contemporary elite running some of the city's finest restaurants. (Native Yucatecan cuisine—a most delicious and original blend of tastes and ingredients—was further enhanced by the addition of Middle Eastern flavors.)

The Museum of Anthropology and History has some good samples of Mayan handicrafts, mostly jade and sculpture, along with a modern art gallery. But it is the market that receives most of the kudos: here are huaraches, hammocks, huipiles, filigree jewelry (although good quality is becoming hard to find), piñatas, and the aroma of overripe produce that makes all Mexican markets so intoxicating.

Mérida possesses a number of pleasant, moderately priced hotels, many in former mansions with beautiful interior courtyards and pools. Many visitors use these accommodations as a base for visiting the ancient Mayan sites, returning exhausted to town in the evenings; however, we recommend dedicating at least two days to Mérida before heading to the ruins for an overnight stay. North American–style nightlife is limited; an inexpensive and less touristy alternative is to take in one of the folkloric events presented in the city's plazas.

Arriving and Departing by Plane

Airport and Airlines The Mérida airport is 7 kilometers (4 miles) west of the city's central square. The following airlines serve Mérida: **Aeroméxico** (tel. 99/279000 or 800/237–6639) has nonstop service from Cancún, Mexico City, Miami, and Villahermosa. **Mexicana** (tel. 99/24178 or 800/531–7921) flies nonstop from Cozumel, Havana, and Mexico City. Regional carriers serving Mérida include **Aerocozumel** (tel. 99/249559), **Aerocaribe** (tel. 99/230002), **Litoral, Aerovias,** and **Avioteca** (tel. 99/249477).

Between the Airport and Center City An airport taxi (usually a Volkswagen minibus) to your hotel costs about $3 for up to four passengers; private service is about $5. Pay the taxi ticket-vendor at the airport, not the driver. If you're driving into town, take the airport exit road, make a right at the four-lane Avenida Itzaes (also known as Route 180), and follow it until you reach Calle 59, just past El Centenario Zoo. Take a right on Calle 59 and go straight until

Calle 62, where you again turn right and drive one block to the main square.

Arriving and Departing by Car, Train, and Bus

By Car Mérida is on Route 180, the main road on the Gulf Coast that runs from the Texas border to Cancún. Mexico City is 1,550 kilometers (970 miles) to the west; Cancún is 320 kilometers (200 miles) due east.

If you rent a car in Cancún, it's a direct drive west along Route 180 to Mérida. You'll pass through Valladolid, Chichén Itzá, and lots of tiny towns along the way. From Campeche, it's about a two-hour drive to Mérida up Route 180. Or take Route 261 from Campeche, which goes past the ruins of Uxmal as well as other interesting Mayan sites; it is about a 3-hour drive. From Chetumal it's probably most efficient to take Route 307 to Felipe Carrillo Puerto, then Route 184 to Muna, continuing north on Route 261. These paved highways are all fairly new and still in good shape.

By Train Mérida's train station is on Calle 55 between Calles 48 and 46, nine blocks northeast of the main square. Train service (only second class) is available to Mexico City, Valladolid, and Campeche (with additional stops along these routes). However, because the service is inadequate and uncomfortable, and robberies a frequent occurrence, not even the tourist office recommends taking trains in Yucatán.

By Bus The main bus station is at the corner of Calles 69 and 70, six blocks southwest of the main square (tel. 99/24–90–55). First-class buses (all reserved seats) leave regularly for Mexico City and Campeche, less frequently for Villahermosa, Veracruz, and Puebla. Frequent first- and second-class service (second class means unreserved seats, older buses, and the possibility of sharing the space with live animals) is also available to many peninsular locations and beyond, including Cancún, Chetumal, Chichén Itzá, Tulum, Palenque, Uxmal, Valladolid, Celestún, and Sisal. One bus a day stops throughout the Puuc region, with 20-minute stops at Uxmal, Kabah, Sayil, and Labná. Buses leave for the nearby beaches of Progreso and the Mayan site of Dzibilchaltún every 20 minutes from the station at Calle 62 between Calles 65 and 67, tel. 99/24–89–91.

Getting Around

By Bus City buses run from 5 AM to midnight every day; they don't run on every street, though, and travel to specific destinations or neighborhoods. In the downtown area, buses run east on Calle 59 and west on Calle 61, north on Calle 60 and south along Calle 62. You can catch a bus to Progreso heading north on Calle 56.

By Taxi Taxis do not cruise the streets looking for passengers; instead they are available at 12 taxi stands around the city; among them, the airport, the zócalo, Paseo de Montejo, and by Parques Hidalgo and Santa Lucía. Call for one from your hotel or restaurant, or call the main taxi office at tel. 99/21–43–47. The fare should be established in advance because taxis aren't metered, but the minimum price is generally about $4.

By Carriage Horse-drawn carriages, or calesas, are found around the zócalo and surrounding streets; about $10 is the standard asking price, but if you're into bargaining, you may get the price down a bit. The standard tour, which will last between 60 and 90 minutes, is around the zócalo, up Paseo de Montejo, and back. Or ask to be taken to a specific destination if you have one in mind. If you're lucky, the driver will speak English and be able to point out some places of interest.

By Rental Car The major international rental agencies have booths at the airport as well as downtown offices, most of which are on the north side of the zócalo. If possible, reserve your car in advance from one of the large international companies, especially if you want air-conditioning or a larger car. A car is more of a hassle than a help in Mérida itself, but it is a great way to see the ruins and the villages surrounding Mérida. Rental agencies include the following: **Avis** (Calle 57 No. 507-A, tel. 99/28–20–96, or at the airport, tel. 99/24–79–91), **Budget** (Paseo Montejo 497, tel. 99/255453), or at the airport, tel. 99/24–97–91), **Dollar** (airport, tel. 99/24–02–80), **Hertz** (Calle 55 No. 479, tel. 99/249333) or at the airport, tel. 99/24–88–63), and **Arrendadora de Mexico** (Calle 60 No. 495, tel. 99/274916).

Important Addresses and Numbers

Tourist Information The **Tourist Information Center** is located at the Peón Contreras Theater (corner of Calles 60 and 57, tel. 99/24–92–90 or 24–93–89) and is open daily 8–8. Tourist information kiosks can be found at the airport and the main bus station.

Embassies **U.S. Consulate** (Paseo de Montejo 453, tel. 99/25–50–11). The **British Embassy** (Calle 58 No. 450, tel. 99/21–67–99). The **Canadian Embassy** (In Mexico City, tel. 254–3288).

Emergencies **Police** (tel. 99/25–21–33), **Fire** (tel. 99/24–92–42), **Red Cross** ambulance (tel. 99/21–24–45), **Hospital O'Horan** (tel. 99/23–87–11).

English-language Bookstores **Librería Dante** (Calle 59 No. 540, Calle 59 at Calle 68, and in the Peón Contreras Theater at the corner of Calles 60 and 57). **Mesoamerica** (Calle 59 No. 520).

24-hour Pharmacy **Farmacia Yza** (Calle 71 and Av. Aviación, tel. 99/23–8116).

Guided Tours

General Tours There are well over 50 tour operators in Mérida, and they generally all offer the same destinations. What differs is whether you go in a private car, a van, or a bus, and whether it's air-conditioned. A 2½-hour tour of Mérida and its museums, parks, public buildings, and monuments will cost between $7 and $20. A trip to the ruins of Chichén Itzá, with guide, entrance fee, and lunch, runs approximately $20–$30. For about the same price you can see the ruins of Uxmal and Kabah down in the Puuc region, and for a few more dollars you can add on the sites of Sayil, Labná, and the Loltún Caves. Many travel agencies run tours to Uxmal that leave in the afternoon and allow you to see the light-and-sound show at Uxmal, have dinner, and return by 10:30 PM, for $20–$30. If you want to combine archaeology and the seaside worlds, take a six-hour tour of the ruins of Dzibilchaltún and the nearby beach town of Progreso, which includes an excellent seafood meal. Some operators offer trips that will take you to Chichén Itzá and then drop you off in Cancún (about $35–$40). Most tour operators take credit cards. The following is a partial list of Mérida tour operators: **Mayaland Tours** (Av. Colón No. 502, tel. 99/25–21–33), **Ceiba Tours** (Calle 60 No. 495, tel. 99/24–44–77), **Molica Tours** (Hotel Caribe, Calle 11 No. 114, tel. 99/24–87–33), **Turismo Planeta** (Calle 59 No. 501, tel. 99/28–15–60).

Special-interest Tours There are sinkholes, or cenotes, in Timul, Chichén Itzá, Uxmal, Loltún, Dzibilchaltún, and other places easily accessible to Mérida. Cenote Dzitnup is a subterranean sinkhole where at midday the light enters from an orifice in the ceiling, creating a strange spectacle. In some places, scuba diving is permitted for certified divers only; in other cenotes you can swim.

Tours of the Ruta Maya, including sites in Mexico, Guatemala, and Belize, are offered by **VN Travel** (Calle 58 No. 488, tel. 99/245996) and **Vagabonder Tours** (tel. 303/674–9615 or 800/538–6802).

Exploring

Streets in Mérida are numbered, not named; most of them are one-way. For those with a sense of direction, this seems the essence of logic; for anyone else, it's a bit unnerving. North-south streets have even numbers, which increase from east to west. East-west streets have odd numbers, which increase from north to south. The zócalo is an important point of reference. It is bordered on two sides by Calles 60 and 62, and on opposite sides by Calles 61 and 63. Take the time to study a map, locating the zócalo and the streets immediately surrounding it. This will save you a lot of frustration later on, and will accustom you to the hub of the city.

Street addresses are confusing because they don't go according to blocks; for example, the 600s may occupy two or more blocks. A particular location is therefore usually referred to by indicating the street on which it is located and the nearest cross street: Calle 64 × 61, or Calle 64 between 61 and 63.

Numbers in the margin correspond to points of interest on the Mérida map.

8 Start at the **plaza grande** (officially **Plaza de la Independencia**), which was the heart of the Mayan city of T'hó, one of the last Mayan strongholds against the Spaniards. After the defeat of the Maya, the powerful Montejo family renamed the ruined city Mérida, after the city in southern Spain.

The Montejo family palace (1550) still stands on the south side of the zócalo, a monument to the family who literally made Mérida. The bas-relief on the facade depicts Francisco de Montejo (the younger), his wife and daughter, and, in addition, Spanish soldiers standing on the heads of the vanquished Maya. This arrangement is interesting since it parallels the Mayas' own habit of depicting themselves standing on the heads of defeated foes. The house is now a bank, Banamex, and you can visit the large interior courtyard during banking hours. *Admission free. Open weekdays 9–1:30.*

Stand in the zócalo and note the *S*-shape *confidenciales* (benches designed to facilitate "confidential" chats) and geometrically pruned laurel trees. From here you can see the twin spires of the yellow cathedral—impressive for its size if not for its architectural splendor. Built in 1561, the cathedral was indeed designed for defense, and it looks more like an impenetrable fort than anything else. Without, it is stark and unadorned, with gunnery slits instead of windows; inside, it is rather bleak, having been ransacked during the days of the Mexican Revolution and never restored. The looters, however, did not touch the Christ of the Blisters (el Cristo de las Ampollas). Legend has it that a peasant saw a tree burning all night, yet in the morning, it was untouched by the effects of fire. A statue of Christ was carved from the wood of that tree and placed in a church in the town of Ichmul. Later the church burned down, but the statue survived, although burned and covered with blisters. It was relocated to Mérida's cathedral.

9 On the northeast side of the zócalo is the **Palacio de Gobierno** (Governor's Palace), which takes up the eastern half of Calle 61. It is notable for the murals depicting the history of Yucatán, painted by the well-known artist Fernando Castro Pacheco. *Admission free. Open daily 9–9.*

Time Out Just to the left of the Palacio Municipal is **Jugos California**, a popular juice bar and hangout for locals and travelers where you can get delicious tropical fruit concoctions. **Pan Montejo**, next door, is one of the best bakeries in town. *Calle 61 between Calles 60 and 62. Open 10–10.*

10 The arcaded **Palacio Municipal** (City Hall), across from the cathedral, dates from the Montejo era. It originally functioned as a jail as well as a city hall; it was reconstructed along colonial lines in 1928.

Continue 1½ blocks south from the cathedral along Calle 60 to Calle 65. This is Mérida's main shopping street and the bustling heart of the commercial quarter. Turn left to the **García Rejón Market,** where local handicrafts and souvenirs are sold. Continue east on Calle 65, where both sides of the street are lined with shops selling dry goods, straw hats, and hammocks. A block farther, between Calles 56 and 58, are the **main post office** and **telegraph buildings,** two picturesque 19th-century edifices. Behind them sprawls the massive and pungent **Municipal Market.** This mazelike conglomeration of buildings draws city dwellers and rural Indians alike. Almost every spare patch of ground is taken up by Indian women selling chiles, herbs, and fruit. On the second floor of the main building is the **Bazar de Artesanías Municipales,** the official handicrafts market, where you can buy jewelry, pottery, clothes, scarves, T-shirts, hammocks, and straw bags for reasonable prices.

Calle 60 north of the zócalo features many noteworthy parks and historical buildings. Half a block from the main square is the small and pleasant **Parque Hidalgo** (Hidalgo Park), which is the scene of a marimba concert by a group playing regional instruments every Sunday at 11:30 AM.

Just north of the cathedral on Calle 60 is the **Teatro Peón Contreras** (Peón Contreras Theater). This theater of neoclassic design was completed in 1908 by Italian artists imported for the task by Mérida's wealthy land barons. The first Meridanos to exploit the area's resources successfully were exporters of dyewood (also called logwood), which was prized in Europe at the time. After interest in dyewood waned, henequen (or sisal), from which twine and rope are made, as well as chicle, the natural base of chewing gum, became the sources of local wealth. With their profits the rich landowners built the lovely mansions that line Paseo de Montejo, as well as the theater and other public works.

Imported goods were shipped to Mérida from Europe, filling fashionable homes with Italian tile, Carrara marble, and the antique furniture that can still be seen in many Mexican mansions. Other holdovers from the town's financial zenith include the calesas. During World War II, henequen was largely replaced by synthetics on the world market, and chicle has since suffered the same fate. Land barons lost the base of their wealth, and the decline is evident in the once-stunning mansions, some of which have been remodeled to fill other functions. These mansions are still stately and impressive, however, and give Mérida an Old World appearance, at least along the Paseo de Montejo.

Nowadays, drama, ballet, and opera are staged in the theater, and the State Folkloric Ballet performs regional dances there on Tuesday nights. To the right of the lobby is the main **Tourist Information Center.**

A visit to Mérida should include a stroll down Paseo de Montejo, rather wistfully known as Mérida's Champs-Elysées. This broad, tree-lined avenue can be reached by walking seven blocks north from the zócalo on Calle 60 and taking a right on Calle 47 just before the **Plaza Santa Ana** (where the church of the same name is worth a quick visit). Then walk two blocks

east to Paseo de Montejo, which for the next few miles abounds
with old mansions, restaurants, and hotels. The first great
 sight is the **Palacio Cantón,** two blocks north, at the corner of
Calle 43. This Italian Renaissance-style building was the official residence of the governors of Yucatán.

Time Out | **Soberanis Montejo** is the uptown branch of a seafood restaurant
chain. The fish, conch, lobster, and shrimp are moderately
priced, and the setting more modern and attractive than the
downtown version. *Paseo de Montejo 468 between Calles 39 and
37.*

Museums

The **Anthropology and History Museum,** which first opened in
1895, is housed in Palacio Cantón, a splendid mansion that at
one time served as the official residence of the governors of Yucatán. There are plans to relocate the museum to the old Juárez
Penitentiary, so check with the tourist office or at your local hotel before starting out. Rooms are devoted to exhibits of Chichén Itzá relics—*chac mools,* or rain gods, and artifacts
retrieved from the sacred cenote—as well as exhibits on henequen production and colonial religious art. *Calle 43 at Paseo de
Montejo. Admission: P$15,000; Sun. free. Open Tues.–Sat.
8–8, Sun. 8–2.*

The ground floor of the **Museum of Popular Art,** housed in a fine
old mansion, is devoted to Yucatecan arts and crafts. There are
exhibitions on huipil manufacture, weaving, beautifully carved
conch shells, straw baskets, and the like. The popular art of the
rest of Mexico is the focus on the second floor. *Calle 59 between
Calles 50 and 48. Admission free. Open Tues.–Sat. 8–8.*

History lovers should stop in at the small but informative **City
Museum,** on Calle 61 between Calles 60 and 58. Once a hospital
chapel for the only convent in the entire bishopric, it is now
crammed with prints, drawings, photographs, and other displays that recount the history of Mérida through the centuries.
*Calle 61 between Calles 60 and 58. Admission: $3.35; Sun. free.
Open Tues.–Sun. 8–8.*

Parks and Gardens

Mérida's squares and parks are among its most charming features. There are small parks; large parks; parks where bands
play; parks with zoos and arboretums; parks dedicated to the
nation, the saints, and even maternity. The **zócalo** is located on
the site of an ancient Mayan temple. It is a charming place to
stroll under centuries-old laurel trees and watch Meridanos at
play. Surrounding the zócalo are the governor's palace, the cathedral, the Casa de Montejo, and the municipal palace, as well
as outdoor cafés, banks, *dulcerías* and *sorbeterías* (candy and
ice-cream shops).

The square whose official name is Cepeda Peraza is known uni-
versally as **Parque Hidalgo.** It is located one block northeast of
the zócalo on Calle 60 and is almost as popular. There are several restaurants on the square, one of which has tables outside,
and there are always plenty of people about. One block farther
west you'll come to the tiny plaza popularly called **Plaza de la**

Madre because of the beautiful white statue of *La Maternidad* (Motherhood) located there.

Plaza Santa Lucía, on Calle 60 three blocks north of the zócalo, is built on the side of the diminutive church of the same name erected in 1585. The plaza hosts the Thursday night *serenatas* (serenades), as well as other celebrations during the year. On the Day of the Dead, one finds tables here showing typical *ofrendas*, tables artistically arranged with all the departed's favorite things. The park is rather plain, and its main draw are the frequent cultural offerings.

On a larger scale, **Parque de las Américas** is a great expanse of green, taking up four square blocks surrounding Paseo Colón, with trees from all the countries of the American continents. It is a nice place for a picnic, and to look at the trees, but it doesn't have a lot in the way of *movimiento* (action), as do the squares in town. The public library is here; there's also a children's playground, a band shell, and a large fountain.

El Parque del Centenario (the Park of the Centennial) is stuffed full of amusements, especially for children. Sunday afternoon is the best time to people-watch; weekdays you'll have the park more to yourself, especially during the off-season. There is a tiny sky ride and a little train. Ponies jog along tree-shaded paths with their small customers. There are boats to row around the green lake, a playground, and a zoo.

Churches

La Iglesia de Santa Lucía is a small church at the edge of the plaza of the same name, three blocks north of the zócalo on Calle 60. Built in 1575, it became the church assigned to the local black population—slaves and servants of Mérida's wealthy class.

The Church of the Third Order, across from Parque Hidalgo at Calles 60 and 59, was built by the Jesuits in the 17th century. The facade is one of the church's most interesting features, having been constructed with stone blocks taken from the great pyramid at T'hó, on which traces of Mayan bas-relief are still visible (these designs are most evident on the Calle 59 side of the church).

La Ermita de Santa Isabel, at Calles 63 and 64, is part of a Jesuit hermitage, built in 1743. A resting place for travelers in colonial days, the restored chapel is a pretty place to visit at sunset and perhaps a good final destination for a ride in a horse-drawn carriage. Next door there's a little garden with a waterfall.

Mérida for Free

Nearly every day of the week the state government sponsors free regional music and dance shows in the local parks. The shows are held Sundays at 11 AM and 1 PM in front of the Municipal Palace in the main square; 11 AM in the Santa Lucía Park (Calles 60 and 55); 11:30 AM in the Hidalgo Park (Calles 60 and 59); Mondays at 9 PM in front of the Municipal Palace; Tuesdays at 9 PM at the Santiago Park (Calles 59 and 72); Wednesday at 9 PM at the Casa Cultural Mayab (Calles 63 and 64); Thursdays at 9 PM in the Santa Lucía Park (Calles 60 and 55); and Fridays at 9

PM on the patio of the University of Yucatán building (Calles 60 and 57).

What to See and Do with Children

El Centenario Zoo and Park is Mérida's great children's attraction—a large, somewhat tacky amusement complex. It consists of playgrounds; rides; candy stands; and cages full of marvelous native monkeys, birds, and other animals, as well as pleasant wooded paths. *Av. Itzaes between Calles 59 and 65 (entrances on Calles 59 and 65). Admission free. Open daily 9–6.*

Shopping

Mérida is the best place in Yucatán to buy local handicrafts at reasonable prices. The main products are hammocks, hats, huipiles, guayaberas, henequen or palm baskets, and silver jewelry. The principal shopping areas are around the central market and Calle 65 between Calles 62 and 64, and along Calle 60 north of the main square. Yucatecan craftspeople weave some of the finest hammocks in the world. They come in individual, medium, "matrimonial," and family sizes. Matrimonial is a good size for one or two people; anything less is pretty small. The largest hammock store is **Hamacas El Aguacate** (Calle 58 No. 492). The huipil and the guayabera are two local styles of clothing. The **municipal artisans market** on the second floor of the main market building has many stalls selling a wide variety of huipiles. Most Mérida men wear guayaberas, a cool, cotton, short-sleeve shirt that is *never* tucked in. Among the guayabera shops are **Camisería Canul** (Calle 59 No. 496), **Guayaberas Lol Tun** (Calle 59 No. 523), **Jack** (Calle 59 No. 507-A), and **Genuina Yucateca** (Calle 58 No. 520).

A hat is a necessity in Yucatán. The best are known as *jipijapas* or just *jipis* (pronounced "hippies"), and you can buy them at two stores near the market: **Sombrería El Becaleno** (Calle 65 No. 483) and **La Casa de los Jipis** (Calle 56 No. 526). The streets north of the zócalo, especially Calle 60, contain craft and jewelry stores. The widest selection of local crafts is at the **Casa de las Artesanías** (Calle 63 No. 503). **La Canasta** (Calle 60 No. 500) sells an ample selection of good-quality crafts, including original local art, batik dresses, and masks. **Las Palomas** (Calle 60 between Calles 55 and 53) has a wide assortment of cheaper crafts. Fernando Huertas' two shops (one at Calle 62 No. 492, and the other, called **Marie Soleil**, at Calle 59 No. 511) feature women's clothing made from brightly colored local fabrics cut to "French-inspired" designs. Excellent silver jewelry is also sold at **Sonrisa del Sol**, Calle 62 No. 500. For newspapers and magazines from Mexico City and the United States, go to **Discolibros Hollywood** (Calle 60 No. 496). **Mericolor** (at Calle 59 No. 511 and Calle 62 at Calle 43) offers two-hour film developing.

Participant Sports

Golf   There is an 18-hole championship course at Club Campestre de Mérida (Calle 30, No. 500, tel. 99/71100 or 71700), 16 kilometers (10 miles) north of Mérida on the road to Progreso. The course has a clubhouse, bar, and restaurant.

Hunting As more and more species appear on the endangered list, this sport is practiced less than it once was. It is traditionally popular in Yucatán, however, especially on the northwest coast around Sisal, only 51 kilometers (32 miles) northwest of Mérida. November through March are the best months for hunting duck and other waterfowl; other prizes include the small jungle deer, quail, and wild boar. Importation of firearms and other arrangements can be complicated. It's best to go through a specialist; **Ceiba Tours** (Holiday Inn, tel. 99/25–63–89) is well versed at cutting through red tape and setting up expeditions, as is **Maya Tours** (Calle 60 No. 425, tel. 99/24–28–81 or 24–30–22). This tour operator can also arrange fishing tours and trips (overnight or longer) to Cozumel, Isla Mujeres, Playa del Carmen, and other seaside locations.

Spectator Sports

Baseball The sport is played with enthusiasm throughout Mexico; the season runs from March to July. The stadium is in the Kukulcán Sports Center at Calle 14 No. 17, next to the Carta Clara brewery.

Bullfights Events are most often scheduled from December through March, or to coincide with holidays, though there is no set schedule. Contact the travel desk at your hotel or one of the tourist information centers.

Dining

Yucatecan cuisine is distinctive, foreign even to most Mexicans. Although Yucatán is surrounded on three sides by the sea, Yucatecan dishes do not highlight seafood, but it is widely available. Traditional dishes are cooked with pork, chicken, venison, and turkey. Succulent *cochinita* (pork) or *pollo* (chicken) *píbil* is baked in banana leaves with a sauce of sour orange juice, *achiote* (annatto), and *cilantro* (coriander leaves). *Sopa de lima* (lime soup) contains bits of chicken and fried tortillas flavored with lime juice and condiments. The area specialty, *poc chuc*, is broiled pork flavored with sour oranges and served with marinated and grilled onions, cilantro, and black beans. *Huevos motuleños* constitute a hearty breakfast of fried eggs topped with ham, peas, beans, and cheese, served on a corn tortilla.

The local habanero chile is perhaps the most fiery in all of Mexico. Luckily, food is usually prepared with small amounts of the pepper, which is then served as a salsa (sauce) alongside the meal. If you like liqueurs, try the Mayas' own *iztabentún*, a mixture of fermented honey and anise—best drunk in small sips between bites of fresh lime, which gives a sweet-and-sour effect. The local brews are good but strangely hard to find in peninsular restaurants. They include the dark bock León Negra and the light Carta Clara and Montejo. A favorite all over Mexico, Yucatecan *horchata* is made from milled rice and water, flavored with vanilla. Try the *licuados*, either milk- or water-based, made with the delicious tropical fruits of the area. For prices, consult the price chart in Cancún dining. Highly recommended restaurants are indicated with a star ★.

Expensive **La Bella Epoca.** For a truly special dinner, nothing matches the elegance and style of this second-story dining room, with its tiny balcony tables overlooking Parque Cepeda Peraza. Crystal chandeliers enchant this ballroom of an old mansion that has been restored well beyond its former grandeur. An ambitious menu includes French, Mexican, Middle Eastern, Yucatecan, and vegetarian selections. Unusual Mayan dishes are good selections—try the *sikil-pak*, a dip with ground pumpkin seeds, and charcoal-broiled tomatoes and onions, or the succulent *pollo píbil* (chicken baked in banana leaves). *Calle 60, between Calles 57 and 59, tel. 99/281928. AE, MC, V. Open daily 6 PM–1 AM.*

Moderate **Alberto's Continental Patio.** Housed in a hacienda built in 1727,
★ this charming Lebanese, Italian, and Yucatecan regional restaurant figures in every guidebook, and well deserves to. Oil paintings hang from the lamp-blackened walls, which also enclose a small but lush patio. Pricey multicourse Arab meals, meat dishes, and sandwiches are served at Alberto's. *Calle 64 No. 482 at Calle 57, tel. 99/21–22–98. Reservations recommended Nov.–Jan. Dress: Casual. AE, MC, V.*

El Patio de las Fajitas. The aroma of chicken, pork, and shrimp on the open grill by the courtyard tables is enough to stimulate any appetite. If you are ravenous, order the cheese-stuffed baked potatoes along with your fajitas and you'll have a rib-sticking meal. *Calle 60 No. 467 at Calle 53, tel. 99/283782. MC, V. Open Mon.–Sat. 1–11 PM.*

Pancho's. The waiters wear Pancho Villa costumes in this steak and seafood restaurant, and they delight in serving flaming dishes and drinks. The bar attracts the international singles set, and there is dancing on the patio. *Calle 59 No. 509 between Calles 60 and 62, tel. 99/23–09–42. AE, MC, V. No lunch.*

Yannig. Attractive and reasonably priced, Yannig serves the best French food in Mérida. The onion soup, crepes, red snapper amandine, beef bourguignon, and other dishes are authentic. Yannig has a good wine list and, for dessert, an array of ice-cream sundaes, including one topped with local honey and a generous shot of tequila. *Av. Pérez Ponce No. 105, between Calles 21 and 21A, tel. 99/27–03–39. MC, V.*

Inexpensive **Café Pop.** Local university students come here to drink coffee, but you can also dine inexpensively on regional dishes, and it's a great place for breakfast. *Calle 57 between Calles 60 and 62 No. 50, tel. 99/21–68–44. MC, V.*

Express. Express is a much-frequented hangout overlooking Parque Hidalgo. Locals and tourists nurse coffee or beer and watch the passing scene all day and evening. The menu offers an assortment of sandwiches, local dishes, tacos, and breakfasts at reasonable prices. *Calle 60 N. 502 between Calles 59 and 61, tel. 99/281691. No credit cards.*

★ **Los Almendros.** Pleasant, family-style Los Almendros (The Almond Trees) is a must for anyone interested in Yucatecan cuisine. Although overrated, it does cater well to tourists. The specialty is its version of poc chuc. The Spanish/English/French menu features photographs and descriptions of the various pork, turkey, chicken, and beef dishes. Servings come with delicious corn tortillas. *Calle 50A No. 493 between Calles 57 and 59, tel. 99/21–28–51. AE.*

Lodging

Hotels in Mérida reflect the essence of the city itself: charming and charismatic, with an air of making the modern world fit into an old-fashioned setting. Most hotels are built around a central courtyard or garden where a profusion of tropical plants grow together in ordered chaos. As is true all over Mexico, the facade of the building rarely reveals the character of the hotel behind it, so check out the courtyard of a hotel before turning away unimpressed or disgruntled. Most hotels are located either downtown or on or near Paseo de Montejo, which is lined with slightly dilapidated but beautiful mansions. Downtown is more convenient for those given to spontaneous ramblings. All hotels listed as moderate, expensive, or very expensive have air-conditioned rooms, and all have private baths. For prices, consult the price chart in Cancún lodging. Highly recommended lodgings are indicated by a star ★.

Very Expensive **Holiday Inn.** Mérida's elite meet at this deluxe, modern hotel at the fashionable north end of Paseo de Montejo. Everything you could possibly need is here, including stores selling clothing, jewelry, crafts, and tobacco and a beauty salon. The rooms have satellite TVs and minibars. It's a long walk to the center of the city; you need a car here. *Av. Colón 498 at Calle 60, 97000, tel. 99/25–68–77 or 800/465–4329. 214 rooms. Facilities: restaurants, bars, disco, pool, tennis court, shops, parking. AE, DC, MC, V.*

Expensive **Calinda Panamericana Quality Inn.** The lobby of this large hotel four blocks east of the main plaza is built into an elegant old mansion; guest rooms, situated in a less attractive multistory wing, are large and clean but spartan. Folk dancers perform in the Tropical Bar Monday–Thursday and Sunday. There's also an expensive Yucatecan and international restaurant on the premises. *Calle 59 No. 455, 97000, tel. 99/23–91–11 or 800/228–5152, fax 99/286–5679. 110 rooms. Facilities: cable TV, restaurant, bar, disco, pool, shops, parking. AE, DC, MC, V.*

★ **Casa Mexilio.** One would never know that behind the drab exterior of this guest house sits the loveliest, most exquisitely decorated bed-and-breakfast in all Mérida, if not of the entire country. Middle Eastern wall hangings, French tapestries, colorful tile floors, tiled sinks, black pottery, rustic furniture, loft beds, and white walls make up the eclectic decor. Price includes breakfast. Casa Mexilio is affiliated with the Turquoise Reef Group. *Reservations: tel. 800/538–6802 or 303/674–9615; fax 303/674–8735. Calle 68 No. 495, tel. 99/21–40–32. 5 rooms. Facilities: pool, restaurant. AE, MC, V.*

Montejo Palace. The rooms of this hotel have balconies, TVs, and air-conditioning. Unfortunately, many of the colonial-style rooms are in need of renovation, particularly on the upper floors, and overall, the hotel is on the faded, characterless side. The Montejo Palace has a good Yucatecan/Mexican restaurant and is located 12 long blocks west of the main square. *Paseo de Montejo No. 483-C, 97000, tel. 99/24–76–44 or 800/221–6509. Facilities: satellite TV, restaurant, coffee shop, bar, nightclub, shops, travel agency, pool, parking. AE, DC, MC, V.*

Moderate **Caribe.** The Caribe is popular with international budget travelers. Set on the Parque Hidalgo a block from the main square, the hotel is built around a tiled interior patio. There is a small pool and sun deck on the third floor. Rooms are being renovated. *Calle 60, tel. 99/24–90–22, fax 99/24–87–33. 56 rooms with air-conditioning or fan. Facilities: restaurant, cafeteria, pool, travel agency, car rental, parking. AE, DC, MC, V.*

Casa del Balam. The Casa del Balam is a pleasant hotel two blocks from the main square with a tree-filled interior court-yard. The rooms are decorated with comfortable colonial furni-ture. Avoid the noisy lower-story rooms on Calle 57. The street-level restaurant serves local dishes. *Calle 60 No. 488, 97000, tel. 99/24–88–44 or 800/624–8451, fax 99/24–50–11. 54 rooms. Facilities: satellite TV, minibars, pool, restaurant, bar, sunroof, travel agency, car rental, gift shop. AE, DC, MC, V.*

★ **Gran Hotel.** Elegant and crammed with antiques, the Gran Ho-tel (one block from the main square) is a relic of Mérida's 19th-century opulence. The patio is surrounded by five stories of columns holding up the porches. There is a hint of decay to the tall-ceilinged rooms. At street level there's a very good, inex-pensive restaurant. *Calle 60 No. 496, 97000, tel. 99/24–76–22, fax 99/24–77–30. 24 rooms with fan or air-conditioning. Facilities: restaurant. MC, V.*

The Arts and Nightlife

Aside from the almost daily music and dance performances in the parks (*see* Mérida for Free, *above*), you can see dance, folk-loric, concert, and theater performances at the **Teatro Peón Contreras** (Calle 60 at Calle 57) and the **Teatro Daniel Ayala**, just down the street (Calle 60 between Calles 59 and 61). For information on performances, consult the tourist office or the local papers. The cinemas nearest to downtown are **Cine Aladino** (Calle 60 No. 514), **Cine Apolo** (Calle 60 No. 487), **Cine Fantasio** (Calles 59 and 60), **Cine Mérida** (Calle 62, and **Cine Rex** (Calle 57 No. 553). The **Calinda Panamericana** stages folkloric dances. **Tulipanes**, a restaurant and nightclub at Calle 46 No. 462-A, is built over a cenote and every night at 8:30 it stages a folkloric ballet and "Mayan ritual" performance that ends with the "sacrifice" of a shapely victim. A number of restaurants feature live music and dancing, including **El Tucho** (Calle 60 be-tween Calles 55 and 57), **La Prosperidad** (Calles 53 and 56), and **Pancho's** (Calle 59 between Calles 60 and 62). Discos appealing to a mix of locals and tourists are located at the **Holiday Inn, Calinda Panamericana** and **Montejo Palace** hotels. **Bim Bon Bao** has the reputation for being the hottest disco in town, al-though it's actually in Montecristo, a town 20 minutes by car/taxi from downtown Mérida. **Excess,** Mérida's newest and most exclusive disco, is in that how-can-you-miss-it lavender build-ing on Prolongación Paseo de Montejo.

Excursions from Mérida

Numbers in the margin correspond to points of interest on the Yucatán Peninsula map.

⓱ The trip to **Progreso** (about 35 kilometers—21 miles—north of Mérida) or the beaches to the north is a worthwhile venture and can be combined with a stop at the archaeological ruins at Dzibilchaltún. Progreso has been the chief port of entry for the peninsula since 1872, when the port at Sisal proved inadequate for handling large ships transporting henequen. The port is now being expanded to accommodate even larger vessels. But the only reason to visit Progreso is to go to the beach. Many Meridanos have summer homes here, and the palm-lined beach is reminiscent of those in Florida. The town, however, is posi-tively deserted on weekdays most of the year—Meridanos generally vacation in July and August. There are also nice beaches and new hotels in the town of **Yucalpetén,** about 3 kilometers (2 miles) west of Progreso, **Chicxulub Puerto,** about 4 kilometers (2.5 miles) to the east, and in the new development of **Nuevo Yucatán,** otherwise known as Telchac Puerto, 43 kilometers (27 miles) east. In Progreso there are a few restaurants along Calle 19, which runs along the beach, notably Restaurant Las Velas, Carabela's, and Capitán Marisco. On the square, Soberanis and Cordobés have reasonably good food at slightly lower prices. Since the bus runs to and from Mérida every 15 minutes 5 AM– 9 PM (leaving Mérida from Calle 62 between 65 and 67), and the trip takes only about 45 minutes, there's no reason to stay in Progreso unless you want to get away from all of humanity. If so, you might try the brand-new Hotel Progreso (in town, on Calle 29) or the Sian Ka'an (bungalows on the beach in Chelem, just west of Yucalpetén). For North American–style luxury (and prices), go to the Fiesta Inn Mérida Beach in Yucalpetén, or the new Paradíso Maya in Telchac Puerto.

⑱ Dzibilchaltún (literally, "the place where there is writing on flat stones"), which occupies more than 65 square kilometers (25 square miles) of land north of Mérida, is thought to have been the capital of the Mayan states at one time. Founded around 2000 BC, it appears to be the oldest continuously occupied Mayan ceremonial and administrative center. The site is generally more impressive to archaeologists and historians than to tourists, and much of it remains to be explored and excavated. The **Temple of the Seven Dolls** has been restored—the only Mayan temple with windows discovered thus far.

Located on the site of the ruins is the **Xlacah cenote,** which was apparently a supply of drinking water as well as a ceremonial font. Divers from the National Geographic Society have concluded that victims were sacrificed in the well, based on the number of bones and ceremonial objects found in it. Swimming is permitted on days when research teams are not at work.

A small museum at the entrance to the site displays the seven "dolls" found in the temple, thought to represent different deformities or illnesses, as well as figures and bones from the cenote. There is a small refreshment stand. *Small admission fee. Open daily 8–8*.

Buses to Dzibilchaltún leave seven times a day from Mérida (Calle 62 between Calles 65 and 67) and from the Progreso bus station. Those taking the 5:45 or 7:45 AM buses cannot be assured of a bus returning to Mérida, however. Buses between Mérida and Progreso leave every 15 minutes but leave you about 4 kilometers (2.5 miles) from the site on Route 273.

Celestún is a sleepy little fishing town at the end of a spit of land separating the Celestún estuary from the Gulf. Popular with Mexican tourists, the beach is pleasant during the day, but it tends to get windy in the afternoon, making the gulf choppy and the sand blow. Bright pink flamingos make the large estuary north of the town their home. The area between Sisal and Celestún is a favorite hunting ground (*see* Participant Sports in Mérida, *above*). There are several seafood restaurants on the beach strip. Restaurant Lupita, Calle 10 at Calle 7, can be recommended. Buses leave Mérida for Celestún from Autotransportes del Sur, Calle 77 No. 541-C, every hour or two; the trip takes about 1½ hours.

The state of Yucatán remains very Maya. The Mayan heritage endures in the hundreds of small towns outside Mérida in the dress, traditional thatched huts, delicious cuisine, and religious festivals (Catholic mixed with Mayan practices). These towns generally look much as they did during the colonial period, with a huge Spanish church in the center built, more often than not, from the stones of a Mayan temple. The most noteworthy ones are mentioned in the corresponding sections of this chapter.

But the Mayan past is most dramatically visible in the ruined cities. Chichén Itzá, the best-known, was a huge city whose massive, angular architecture reflected the warlike influence of the Toltecs, a tribe that conquered the Maya at the end of the classic period (AD 10th century). The site includes imperious pyramids, the shaved dome of an astronomical observatory, a ball court, and a sacred well into which the remains of sacrificial victims were flung. Uxmal, on the other hand, harks back to an earlier age: Its buildings are simpler and more elegant. The soft, feminine curves of the Temple of the Magicians contrast wonderfully with the lacy, geometrically whimsical mosaics adorning the Nunnery. The place shimmers in cool gray, amber, and oyster-shell white.

Both Chichén Itzá and Uxmal are within a couple of hours' drive from Mérida, and many tour operators run day trips. But an overnight stay at either or both sites is highly recommended, both to avoid being rushed through and to arrive early enough to bypass the crowds of sightseers.

Uxmal

Driving south from Mérida on Route 261 (turn left at Umán), you pass through flatland until you hit the town of Muna, on the side of a long ridge of hills. These hills are known as the Puuc (pronounced "pook"); they give their name to a style of Mayan architecture that began in this region and spread throughout the peninsula. **Uxmal** (Oosh-**mahl**), the first site along this road, 80 kilometers (50 miles) from Mérida, is a showpiece of Mayan architecture. The ruins have been expertly restored, and they're built close together, so it's easy to see all of them. There are three very good hotels near the site.

Uxmal, as tour guides will tell you, means "thrice built," though actually it was rebuilt at least five times. The center of the town first flourished sometime in the 7th century, about the era when Palenque (*see* Chapter 11) was reaching its peak. It was abandoned and reoccupied on a few occasions, and was built in several stages during the late classic period, then abandoned again. No one can say with any certainty why this happened. In the 10th century, the invading Toltecs seized what may well have been little more than a ghost town, held on there for a while, and then evacuated. Finally Uxmal became a Mayan ceremonial center of the post-classic era. The town was deserted for the last time some 90 years before the Spanish conquest.

The architecture is what sets Uxmal apart. Lines are clean and uncluttered, and the buildings themselves in excellent repair. It would seem that the successive waves of groups that made Uxmal theirs chose to honor the designs. In some cases efforts

Uxmal

0 ____ 200 meters
0 ____ 200 yards
N

(261) TO MERIDA

TO CAMPECHE →

North Group

Nunnery

Cemetery Group

Pyramid of the Magician

Ball Court

House of the Turtle

House of the Pigeons

Palace of the Governor

Great Pyramid

Pyramid of the Old Woman

were made to improve upon them, but seldom were they radically changed.

Worshiped here with great fervor was Chac, the elephant-snouted rain god whose face appears throughout Yucatán. The people of Uxmal had good reason to revere him, for water in these parts is scarce. There are no cenotes. The Maya dug cisterns, called *chultunes*, for collecting rainwater when it came. Drought may be the reason Uxmal was abandoned so often.

A sound-and-light show centers upon the dependence of the people on rain. The best thing about the show is the way the artificial light brings out details of carvings and mosaics that are so easy to miss when the sun is shining. There are, for example, replicas of Mayan huts reproduced in stone on one facade in the quadrangle. They resemble almost identically the huts seen in many Mayan villages today. The light-and-sound show is performed nightly in Spanish and English, and is one of the better such productions. Travel agencies from Mérida offer afternoon and evening tours to Uxmal, with dinner at a nearby restaurant before the show. At night, Uxmal has a sense of mystery. And the rounded Pyramid of the Magician, said to have been built overnight by a magical dwarf, takes on added beauty in the moonlight. *Sound-and-light show in Spanish, P$10,000, 7 PM; in English, P$15,000, 9 PM.*

The **Pyramid of the Magician,** which faces west toward the sun, has an unusual oval shape and stands about 30 meters (100 feet) high. The western stairway slopes at a 60° angle—once you reach the top, the view of the city of Uxmal and the surrounding hillsides is impressive. The **Nunnery** (named by the Spaniards) is a group of four buildings, decorated with latticework, masks, geometric patterns, and animal carvings; one wall is covered with red handprints. The **Palace of the Governor** is considered by some to be the finest example of pre-Hispanic art in Mesoamerica. Its 98-meter (320-foot) length is separated by three corbeled arches, creating narrow passageways or sanctuaries. The friezes along the uppermost section of the palace are as intricate as any in Mayan architecture, with carvings of geometric patterns overlaid with plumed serpents and Chac masks. These mosaics are said to have required over 20,000 individually cut stones. *Site and museum admission fee: P$13,000. Parking: P$2,000. Open daily 8–5.*

Kabah, another Puuc city, is located 23 kilometers (14 miles) south of Uxmal on Route 261. Five kilometers (3 miles) to the south there's a turnoff to Sayil, Xlapak, and Labná, three smaller Puuc sites also worth a visit. The road curves through beautiful jungled hills. Just before it hits Oxkutzcab the road passes the entrance to the **Loltún Caves,** an amazing series of caverns with Mayan and neolithic remains. If all this sightseeing has made you hungry, have lunch at the small restaurant at the caves. Or you can drive to **Ticul** and go to the Los Almendros restaurant, one of the best Yucatecan regional restaurants anywhere. Ticul is noted for its fine pottery, *huipiles,* and shoes.

Dining For price categories, see price chart in Cancún dining.

Los Almendros. The Ticul branch of this restaurant chain is the best. Ticul is a small city 28 kilometers (17 miles) east of Uxmal (turn left at Santa Elena) that specializes in pottery. Behind the restaurant, old Mayan women in their huipiles and baseball hats pat the corn tortillas by hand to order. The menu and the prices are the same as in the other branches—poc chuc, *cochinita píbil* (baked suckling pig), and so on—but the food is fresher and juicier here. The interior is simple and clean, with whitewashed walls. *Calle 23 No. 196, no phone. MC, V. Moderate.*

Lodging For prices, see price chart in Cancún lodging.

Villa Arqueológica Uxmal. The closest hotel to the ruins is a two-story Club Med property built around a large pool. The functional rooms are filled with niches for the beds and lighting and have powerful air conditioners. The restaurant offers well-prepared French cuisine served by Mayan women in traditional dress. Large cages located around the property house all kinds of tropical birds and monkeys. Day-trippers can eat at the restaurant and use the pool (for a fee). *Within walking distance of the ruins, tel. 99/24–70–53; in the U.S., 800/CLUB–MED. 44 rooms. Facilities: restaurant, bar, pool, tennis court, gift shop. AE, MC, V. Expensive.*

Hacienda Uxmal. Owned and operated by the powerful Barbachano family, Hacienda Uxmal is the oldest (1955) hotel at the site. The ruins are across the main road and about 100 yards south of this pleasant colonial-style building. The rooms are tiled and decorated with worn, yet comfortable, furniture. Inside a large courtyard there is a garden and a pool. *Uxmal, tel. 99/24–71–42; in Mérida, Mayaland Tours, tel. 99/25–21–33, fax 99/25–70–22. 80 rooms. Facilities: restaurant, bar, pool, gift shop. AE, DC, MC, V. Moderate.*

Chichén Itzá

20 **Chichén Itzá** is about 119 kilometers (74 miles) east of Mérida
on Route 180. A more leisurely and scenic way is to take Route
80 east from Mérida and pass through Tixkokob, a Mayan community famous for its hammock weavers. By cutting south at
Tekanto and east again at Citilcúm (the road has no number and
there are precious few road signs), you reach **Izamal.** This city
is interesting for its uniformity—every building is painted an
earth-toned yellow that gives the city the nickname Ciudad
Amarilla (Yellow City). A huge 16th-century Franciscan monastery sits atop a sacred cenote in the center of town. Bishop de
Landa supervised the completion of the monastery, begun by
Fray Juan de Mérida in 1553 to supplant the heathen temple
that once stood there. The church, with its rows of yellow
arches and gigantic atrium, is one of the largest and oldest religious structures in Mexico. A few blocks northeast of the main
plaza is a partially excavated Mayan site atop a high hill. The
pyramid, called Kinich Kakmó, is difficult to climb because of
the crumbling steps, but has a wonderful view of the surrounding countryside—flat fields of maguey cactus and henequen
broken only by an occasional clump of trees. On clear days it is
possible to spot Chichén Itzá, some 48 kilometers (30 miles)
southeast.

The town of **Pisté,** about 1 kilometer (.6 mile) west of Chichén
Itzá, has a few hotels, motels, and campgrounds. The hotels by
the ruins are delightful, restful resorts, and the archaeological
zone is the most extensively restored and, in some respects, the
most extraordinary of the pre-Hispanic centers.

Chichén is divided into two parts: old, and new. In fact, this is a
misnomer, because architectural motifs from the classic period
are found in both sections. A more convenient distinction is top-
ographical, as there are two major complexes of buildings separated by a dirt path.

Chichén Itzá is known best as a Mayan-Toltec center. The Toltec invaders from the mainland made this their religious capital, and the ruins are a monument both to their warlike ways
and to the genius of the Maya. Nowhere is this better seen than
at the pyramid called **El Castillo** (The Castle), which dominates
the site and is visible above all the other buildings.

El Castillo is topped by a temple to Kukulcán (known as Quetzalcóatl in mainland Mexico), the deity represented by a feathered serpent that led the Toltecs on their migration to Yucatán.
A climb of 91 steps reaches the top temple; those fearful of
heights can hold on to a rusted chain running down the center of
the steps. El Castillo is fraught with symbolism, with the four
stairways facing the cardinal directions and the steps totaling
365, representing the days of the year. Fifty-two panels on the
sides stand for the 52 years of the secular Mayan calendar,
while the 18 terraces symbolize the 18 months of the year. By
the base of one balustrade a great serpent head is carved. At
the spring and fall equinox, March 21 and September 21, the
afternoon lights and shadows strike the balustrade in such a
way as to form a shadow picture representing Kukulcán undu-
lating out of his temple and descending the pyramid to bless the
fertile earth. The engineering skill that went into this amazing
project boggles the mind. Thousands of people travel to Chichén to witness this sight, particularly in the spring since there

Chichén Itzá

Cenote
(Sacred Well)

N

Ball Court

TO
MERIDA

Platform of
The Skulls

Main
Plaza

Temple of
the Jaguars

Venus
Platform

Ball Court

Platform of
the Eagles

Tourist
Office

El Castillo

West
Colonnade
Court of the
Thousand
Columns

Ball Court

High Priests
Grave

Ball Court

Steam Bath

House of
the Deer

House
of the Corn
Grinders

The Market

Xtoloc
Cenote

Caracol
Observatory

The Snail
(El Caracol)

Hotel
Mayaland

180

Temple of the
Wall Panels

0   200 meters

Nunnery

0   200 yards

is always the chance that the fall rains will spoil the spectacle.
It is advisable to make hotel reservations well in advance—a
year ahead is not unreasonable.

In 1937, archaeologists discovered a more ancient temple inside
the Castillo, where a wet, slippery stairway leads upward to an
altar holding two statues—a Chac Mool and a bejeweled red tiger. Upon discovery, the tiger wore a mosaic disc of jade and
turquoise, now in the National Anthropology Museum in Mexico City. The inner temple is open to the public only during a few
hours in the morning and again for a few hours in the afternoon.
Those prone to claustrophobia should take heed—the stairs are
narrow, dark, and winding, and often there is a line of tourists
going both ways, making the trip somewhat frightening.

Nearby is a ball court, similar to those found at other ancient
centers in Mexico but bigger and more elaborate. The game
played was something like soccer (no hands were to be used),
and it fascinated the Europeans; indeed it might be said that
one of Mexico's gifts to the Old World was team sports and rubber balls. Ball games apparently had religious significance to
the Maya and their neighbors. A carving at the court shows
what appears to be a player being sacrificed by decapitation,
blood spurting from his severed neck to fertilize the earth. The
acoustics are so good that someone standing at one end of the
128-meter (140-yard) court can clearly hear the whispers of another person standing at the other end.

More sacrifices took place at the **Sacred Well,** a cenote about a
half mile from the main ceremonial area. Once it was believed

that virgins were hurled into these waters to appease the rain gods, but diving archaeologists have since discovered skeletons belonging to individuals of all ages. The story goes that men, women, and children were all thrown into the well to appease the gods in the early morning. The slippery walls were impossible to climb, and most could not swim well enough to survive until noon, when those who did hang on were fished out to relate the stories of what they had learned from the spirits in the water. Thousands of gold and jade artifacts, items highly precious to the Maya, have also been found in the murky depths of the cenote, which undoubtedly holds more treasures. Trees and shrubs have been washed into the well over the centuries, and their remains have prevented divers from getting to the bottom. Since the pool is fed by a network of underground rivers, it cannot be drained.

New Chichén is enormous—it can take days to explore fully the many buildings, most significant of which are the Group of the Thousand Columns, and the temples of the Warriors, Jaguars, and the Bearded Man. The less visited part of the site—across the main road, down a foot path to the south—is equally intriguing to the Mayan enthusiast, with its ancient buildings overgrown by flowering vines. El Caracol (the snail) is a famous Mayan astronomical observatory, built in several stages with additions of skull-shape incense burners from the Toltecs. The Nunnery (named by the Spaniards) has long, intricately carved panels. Mayan guides will willingly lead you down the path by an old narrow-gauge railroad track to even more ruins, barely unearthed.

The sound-and-light show in the evening is not as well done as the one at Uxmal, but it provides a form of after-dark entertainment as the colored lights enhance the carvings on El Castillo's walls. A fairly good restaurant and great ice-cream stand are located in the entrance building, and there are refreshment stands by the cenote and on the pathway near El Caracol. *Sound-and-light show in Spanish, P$10,000, 7 PM; in English, P$15,000, 9 PM. Site and museum open daily 8–5.*

Just a few kilometers east of Chichén Itzá is the **Cave of Balancanchén,** a Mayan shrine discovered in 1959. It was virtually undisturbed since the time of the conquest. Within it is the largest collection of artifacts yet found in Yucatán, mostly vases and jars once filled with offerings. An altar to the rain god rises above a small underground lake in which blind fish swim. Guided tours, which depart on the hour (noon and 1 PM are skipped; the last tour leaves at 4 PM), are mandatory for visitors to the cave. Even then one must be in fairly good physical shape, for considerable crawling is required. Claustrophobics should avoid Balancanchén.

The town of Pisté serves mostly as a base camp for travelers to Chichén Itzá. The hotels, restaurants, and handicraft shops are normally more expensive than elsewhere, but cheaper than those south of the ruins. There is a PEMEX station at the west end of town and a bank that will not exchange traveler's checks for pesos.

Lodging For prices, see price chart in Cancún lodging. All hotels mentioned have private baths.

Mayaland. The nearest hotel to the ruins is this charming, 62-year-old property with a hotel wing and a number of bungalows set in a large garden. The colonial-style rooms have decorative tiles, ceiling fans, and mosquito netting. Air-conditioning should be installed soon. At night musicians accompany dinner, poolside. *Tel. 985/6–2777; in Mérida, Mayaland Tours, tel. 99/25–21–33, fax 99/25–70–22. 62 rooms. Facilities: restaurant, bar, pool. AE, MC, V. Moderate.*

Dolores Alba. The best low-budget choice near the ruins is this family-run hotel, a long-time favorite in the country south of Piste. The motel rooms are simple, clean, and comfortable; some have air-conditioning. Hammocks hang by the small pool, and breakfast and dinner are served family-style in the main building. Free transportation to the ruins is provided for those without cars. *Carretera Piste-Cancún, 1.5 miles south of Chichén Itzá, tel. 99/213745. 28 rooms. Facilities: dining room, pool. MC, V. Inexpensive.*

Valladolid

From Chichén Itzá east toward the Caribbean, the highway winds 40 kilometers (25 miles) through **Valladolid.** Second-largest city in the state of Yucatán, Valladolid is picturesque, pleasant, and provincial, and enjoying growing popularity among travelers harried by more touristy towns. It has a couple of inexpensive hotels and passable eateries. A turnoff here leads north to **Río Lagartos** (Alligator River, although the alligators have long since been hunted into extinction). Flamingos in grand flocks make this neighborhood home. Seeing these long-necked pink birds soaring above the water and watching them settle in great red clouds makes the detour worthwhile. Río Lagartos, with its palmy beaches, will one day supposedly be developed into a seaside resort. Yucatán authorities have been talking about that for years. More likely it will be promoted among sportsmen. Tarpon fishing and hunting for deer and boar are excellent here. In the meantime, Río Lagartos is a national park harboring egrets, peregrine falcons, green turtles, and other wildlife.

From Río Lagartos motorists can either take a short cut back to Mérida or return to Valladolid and head east into Quintana Roo. Cancún and the Mexican Caribbean are no more than two hours away. The center of Valladolid, a city of 50,000 that was founded in 1543 by Francisco de Montejo, the conqueror of Yucatán, is almost exclusively colonial, although there are many 19th-century structures painted a mustard yellow. The main sights are the colonial churches, principally the large cathedral of the central square and the 16th-century San Bernardino church and convent of Sisal, three blocks southwest. Valladolid is also known as a center of Yucatecan cuisine. Try one of the restaurants within a block of the main square, which also has two very good and reasonably priced hotels. Good buys for sandals, baskets, and the local liqueur, xtabentún, can be had.

Lodging **El Mesón del Marqués.** This building on the north side of the main square is a well-preserved, very old hacienda built around a charming courtyard. The rooms—all air-conditioned—are furnished in an attractive old-fashioned style. On the premises are a pool and a shop with many local crafts items. The restaurant serves local specialties. *Calle 39 No. 203, tel. 985/6–2073.*

Facilities: restaurant, bar, gift shop, pool. MC, V. Inexpensive.

Quintana Roo

Introduction

While Cancún and Cozumel are Mexico's Caribbean resorts, the coastline of mainland Quintana Roo is Mexico's Caribbean wilderness, with a few luxurious lagoons, even fewer tourist traps, and an endless dose of paradise. Though most people refer to the Caribbean coast as Yucatán, it is officially part of the state of Quintana Roo.

The northern section of the state, including Cancún, is heavily influenced by its proximity to the state of Yucatán. The music, food, and cultural traditions are Yucatecan. The transformation of Cancún into a world-class resort has brought an international flair to the region, where Continental restaurants and exotic boutiques flourish a short distance from small Mayan villages. The rest of the state is more purely Mayan, with small seaside fishing collectives and jungle, and coastal neighborhoods where the close-knit Mayan residents carry on ancient traditions. The south, particularly Chetumal, is influenced by its status as a port area adjacent to Guatemala and Belize. The ethnic mix—Mayans, other Central Americans, Middle Easterners, and blacks—is reflected in the exotic cuisine and calypso and reggae music.

Though buses do connect these regions and are popular with backpackers, a rental car or four-wheel-drive vehicle allows you to explore more thoroughly and creatively without ending up alone in the jungle after dark or in the rain. Huge Mayarama tour buses from resort hotels in Cancún appear regularly at the ruins, parks, and beaches with their loads of sightseers who bolster local economies.

Route 307 is the only paved road running north–south along coastal Quintana Roo. The 350-kilometer (215-mile) route from Cancún to Chetumal hugs the coast up to the ruins at Tulum (*see* Excursions from Cancún, *above*); then it swings inward to Felipe Carrillo Puerto, once called Chan Santa Cruz; finally it cuts through the jungle to the bays and lagoons at Chetumal. The entrances to ruins, resorts, beaches, and campgrounds are marked with an assortment of road signs, ranging from billboards to painted tires hanging from wooden posts. Each year there are more picture-coded tourist signs, pointing the way to restaurants, gas stations, and hotels. Roads and paths, some seemingly impassable, branch off Route 307 through the short, dense jungle, leading to adventures 5 or 10 kilometers (3 to 6 miles) away.

Along the more civilized routes wild pigs, occellated turkeys, monkeys, iguanas, lizards, and snakes (including the notoriously poisonous, four-nosed nahuyaca) appear in the clearings. *Balam* (jaguar), *ceh* (stag), armadillos, tapir, wild boar, peccaries, ocelots, raccoons, and badgers all inhabit the dense, uncivilized jungle. Alligators, giant turtles, sharks, barracuda, and manatees, or sea cows, inhabit the reefs, lagoons, cenotes, and caves along the Caribbean and down the Hondo River, which runs along the borders between Mexico, Belize, and Guatemala. During July and August, tourists along the mainland coast witness the annual spectacle of sea turtles laying thousands of eggs on the beach. Many of those leathery eggs are harvested and sold as delicacies in Cancún and Mérida. Those that remain hatch in the night, and the sight of tiny turtle hatchlings fleeing to the sea is an unusual delight.

Coastal Quintana Roo attracts scuba divers and snorkelers to transparent turquoise and emerald waters strewn with rose, black, and red coral reefs, and sunken pirate ships. Schools of black, gray, and gold angelfish, sparkling green and purple parrotfish, earth-toned manta rays, and scores of other jeweled-toned tropical species seem oblivious to the clicking underwater cameras. The visibility in these waters is often 30 meters (100 feet); it's not unusual to get a sampling of the underwater scene without even getting wet.

Bird-watchers stare into the jungle for a rare glimpse of parrots, toucans, and the long red-and-green feathers of the sacred quetzal. Amateurs are entertained by yellow, blue, and scarlet butterflies, singing cicadas and orioles, sparkling dragonflies, kitelike frigates, and night owls nesting in the trees. Colorless crabs scuttle sideways toward the coconut groves over pale, white limestone and sand that never burns the soles of your feet. Tiny mosquitoes and gnats, impervious to mild repellents, bore through the smallest rips in window screens, tents, and mosquito nets and crave the blood of tourists. Always carry and use strong repellent if you react to such bites. Some say the bugs won't bother you if you take large doses of Vitamin B$_1$ for a few weeks or months before your trip.

The Caribbean coast is Mayan country. Spanish is frequently spoken and understood, but most of the towns, ranches, and coastal settlements have Mayan names, which the residents pronounce with the clicks and slurs of the Mayan language. Many of the maps handed out by rental and tourist agencies list towns and lagoons with a variety of spellings and have a tendency to misplace bays and lagoons. The 100-kilometer (60-mile) stretch between Cancún and Tulum boasts more and more signs with kilometer readings that help dispel the confusion. Wrong turns are no problem—they may lead you to private beaches and coves or barely discernible ruins that add to the adventure.

Puerto Morelos, Playa del Carmen, Felipe Carrillo Puerto, and Chetumal are the only major stops along the way where you can find groceries, sundries, banks, telephone offices, and auto supplies. Electricity and telephones are the exception rather than the rule, but most resorts have radio communication with the outside world. Incongruities such as the sound of Ozzie and Harriet Nelson beamed in by satellite to a hotel TV add to the magical charm of this remote region on the verge of discovery. Quintana Roo became a state only in 1974. For hundreds of years previously it was the frontier: wild, frequently rebellious, and relatively unpopulated. When the Spaniards first came in 1518, they saw a number of thriving Mayan cities along the coast, such as Tulum, some of which had thousands of inhabitants. After the conquest, the Mayan population was decimated by the dual foes of brutal Spanish marauders and the European diseases they brought with them. By the late-16th century, the land was left to a few Spanish settlers, a fitfully submissive Indian population, and a few settlements of pirates, including Jean Lafitte. In 1847 the Spanish-descent landowners of the Yucatán Peninsula armed their Mayan workers with rifles to counter the threatened U.S. invasion of the area. Instead, the Maya turned their guns on the Ladinos (Spanish Mexicans) and massacred them. After three years of skirmishes, the Mexican Army defeated the Maya in the area around Mérida and Valladolid. The Indians retreated to the wilds of Quintana Roo, where they held off the Mexicans for 50 years. They set up their own government and trade system based on traditional beliefs and prospered away from Mexican rule. In 1898, the Mexican Navy sailed down the coast of Quintana Roo and set up a city, Chetumal, that was to be their base for recapturing the territory. The Mexican forces overwhelmed the Maya and captured their capital of Chan Santa Cruz (now Felipe Carrillo Puerto). Over the next few decades the Mayan culture was further diluted by new roads and schools, which brought Mexican settlers and modern ideas. Quintana Roo entered the modern era in the 1960s, when the Mexican government decided to develop the area for tourism. In the late-1980s, huge resort and time-share complexes became an increasingly common sight, and future development is inevitable.

Important Addresses and Numbers

Tourist Information The **Government Tourist Office** in Chetumal is in the Palacio Municipal (City Hall) (tel. 983/2–0266). The office is open weekdays 10–2 and 5–8.

Arriving and Departing by Plane

Airports and Airlines From Playa del Carmen, **Aerocozumel** (no phone) runs 20-minute flights to both Cancún and Cozumel. Chetumal's international airport, just west of town, is served by **Aerocozumel** (tel. 983/2–6675), which has flights three times a week to Mérida, Cozumel, Mexico City, Guatemala City, and Flores, Guatemala, near the ruins at Tikal. Chetumal's sole car rental agency is **Avis** (tel. 983/2–0544), in the lobby of the Hotel del Prado (Avs. Héroes and Chapultepec).

By Car The state of Quintana Roo can be reached by road via Route 180 or 184 from Mérida and Route 186 from Campeche or Villahermosa. Quintana Roo's main road is the two-lane Route 307, which runs along the coast from Cancún south to Chetumal and the Belize border. You can also fly to Cancún, Cozumel, Chetumal, Playa del Carmen, Tulum, Belize City, and Flores, Guatemala (*see* these sections for more information). Smaller airports at Tulum and Playa del Carmen handle mainly charter flights.

By Bus Both Playa del Carmen and Chetumal can be reached from Mexico City, Veracruz, and Villahermosa.

Getting Around

The best way to travel is by car. Paved two-lane roads lead to almost every attraction. You can rent cars in Cancún and Chetumal. Another popular way to travel in this region is by bus: There is frequent first- and second-class service along Route 307 from Cancún to Chetumal, with stations at Puerto Morelos, Playa del Carmen, Tulum, Felipe Carrillo Puerto, and Bacalar.

Taxis can also be hired in Cancún or Playa del Carmen for trips along the Cancún-Tulum corridor.

Exploring

The itinerary described here assumes that your starting point is Cancún. Akumal, Xel-Há, and Tulum are treated separately in "Excursions from Cancún," above.

㉒ **Puerto Morelos,** a small coastal town that sports a few more streets, hotels, and homes each year, is 36 kilometers (22 miles) south of Cancún on Route 307. A PEMEX station and tourist signs mark the crossroads, and most shops, banks, and businesses are clustered around the central square and playground. Large cruise ships, buses, and small planes stop in town regularly. The car-and-passenger ferries sail to Cozumel from a long pier south of the square. Large trucks, RVs, Jeeps, and Volkswagen bugs line up hours before the ferry departs, supposedly twice a day. The fare is $4 per person, $25 for autos; there is a PEMEX station by the pier. Thus far, there are no major car-rental offices in Puerto Morelos. This creates a bit of a problem because you cannot take your rental car to the island on the ferry and leave it there. Cars must be returned in Cancún or Chetumal.

The two mainstay resorts, La Ceiba and Playa Ojo de Agua are still recovering from Hurricane Gilbert, but normally they cater to dive groups, offering dive shops, tours, equipment, and classes. The restaurants are quite good. Three lighthouses from different historical periods break up the long stretch of beach, which rarely feels crowded.

A 6-kilometer-long (3.7-mile) white, sandy beach, **Punta Bete,** between rocky lagoons, just 457 meters (500 yards) from Lafitte Reef, provides the setting for two unusual resorts created by an enterprising American named Arnold Bilgore. The bungalow lifestyle of Capitán Lafitte and the luxury camping at Kailuum draw a steady clientele of returnees and friends who discover their brand of paradise by word of mouth. Bilgore's resort empire has spread to the adjacent Shangri-La, a slightly more upscale version of Lafitte, which has since been copycatted by a new neighbor, Las Palapas. Water sports, gourmet dining, congenial conversation, and hammock relaxation are Bilgore's version of vacationing; the concept is carried on by his daughter Kassie, who manages Kailiuum. The cabins are about 2.3 kilometers (1.4 miles) down a dirt road; taxis bring travelers from the buses, ferries, and planes in Playa del Carmen. Other hotels and campgrounds occupy the Punta Bete beach less than 5 kilometers (3 miles) south. Except for the lights from the cruise ships and the shoreline of Cozumel, there is no sign of outer civilization.

㉓ **Playa del Carmen** is the busiest and most tourist-oriented town between Cancún and Chetumal, and has become the preferred destination of hip young Europeans who want to see the archaeological sites of Yucatán but can do without Cancún. Cruise ships and tour buses regularly discharge passengers to the strip of crafts stands leading to the pier, where the passenger ferry (no cars) to Cozumel departs every hour. Planes to Cozumel leave hourly during daylight from the airstrip just off Route 307. The bus depot is a large fenced parking lot in the middle of town; buses depart regularly for Cancún, Chetumal, and spots in between. Boys with bicycle carts patrol the route between the various transportation points, carrying travelers' luggage and purchases.

The town itself is not especially charming, nor is it overly commercialized (yet). Instead, it has a slew of funky, inexpensive bungalow-type properties and equally eccentric, latter-day hippie-style eateries. Condominiums are increasingly common.

The beaches at Playa del Carmen are crystalline white, despite all the boat and people traffic, and the water is a brilliant shade of blue that photographs beautifully. Windsurfers, snorkelers, swimmers, and sunbathers dot the long waterfront. Transportation to ruins, parks, and other beaches is readily available. There are plenty of doctors, ambulances, and pharmacies; shops carry most necessary items, including fan belts, batteries, and mosquito repellent. The long-distance telephone is located in a storefront just off the main plaza, under the orange-and-white tower. Because Playa is steadily acquiring the confident veneer (and clientele, along with expatriate hotel and restaurant managers) of an up-and-coming beach destination, prices for meals and rooms are a bit higher than on the rest of the coast, but the location is ideal for day trips to ruins and parks. **Playacar** is a first-class lavish hotel that has brought a sense of luxury and style to Playa del Carmen. Playacar was hosting its first guests at press time, though construction was still under way on some rooms and the adjoining shopping complex.

Xcaret has been transformed from a tranquil cove into a waterside amusement park. A mind-boggling combination of construction and destruction has changed an idyllic hidden cove with a few small ruins into an expanse of winding jungle trails leading to man-made *caletas,* or inlets, with white-sand beaches and waters that are still a bit clouded from the disturbances of bulldozers and trucks. The main feature at the new Xcaret park is an underground river ride, included in the admission price. Swimmers don life jackets (snorkels, masks, and fins come in handy as well) and float with the cool waters' currents through a series of caves. Holes were blasted and carved into the roofs of the caves to bring in sunlight and fresh air. Other attractions include a large palapa restaurant (expensive) overlooking the sea, several small saltwater ponds filled with tropical fish, and water sports equipment on the beach. Lockers, showers, and changing rooms are available. *Admission: $10. Open daily 9–6.*

The crescent-shape **Paamul** lagoon has choice snorkeling because a coral reef protects its mouth, leaving the waters placid and clear. The reef is easily reached by the average swimmer. A jungle path to the north leads to a lagoon four times the size of the first, and even more private. Trailer camps, cabanas, and tent camps are scattered along the beach, with one major restaurant selling cold beer and fresh fish. The beaches are better than most for beachcombers, who find shells, sand dollars, and even glass beads washed to the shore from the sunken pirate ships at Akumal. Paamul is a good spot for watching the seaturtle hatchlings in the late summer. There is a small fishing community called Xpuhá 9 kilometers (6 miles) south on a narrow path where residents weave hammocks and harvest coconuts. There are a few small overgrown ruins in the area with traces of painting on the inside walls. Just south of Paamul are Akumal, Xel-Há lagoon, and Puerto Aventuras, a megaresort presently under development.

The sign at the intersection on Route 307 calls **Chemuyil** "The Most Beautiful Beach in the World." The enthusiasm is understandable: Chemuyil is one of those idyllic settings that would delight an adventurous couple on their honeymoon. There isn't a tour bus in sight. Just a long white beach and coconut grove with a few dome tents hiding behind the tree trunks and colorful hammocks swinging in the shade. The bar/restaurant is a round palapa with a choice of seats—bar stools or hammocks. A small shop stocks bathing suits and T-shirts. Private palapas with mosquito netting for walls, a table, and two hammocks can be rented for overnight or just as a shady resting spot during a day at the beach. Some say the snorkeling here is the best on the coast; the series of coves are like private aquariums.

Chemuyil is gaining attention as a resort site. So far there is one luxurious white villa on the northernmost cove, but plans for luxury homes and condos in the area are in the works, and the first hotel opened in 1990.

The restaurant at the **Xcacel Lagoon** sits up on a sandy ridge overlooking yet another long white beach. There is a usage fee, and camping is allowed, but the restaurant is closed on Sundays. Some Mayarama buses stop here in the afternoon, and the showers and dressing rooms get crowded as the day ends.

From Xcacel it is only a 10-minute drive to Tulum and the end of the Cancún-Tulum corridor. From here you have several options: you can venture inland for 35 minutes to Cobá; spend a day or two at one of the beach bungalow properties just south of the ruins; or you can continue along a very bad road to the secluded and beautiful **Boca Paila peninsula,** part of the 1.3-million-acre **Sian Ka'an biosphere reserve.** Fresh water and coastal lagoons, mangrove swamps, watery cays, tropical jungle, a barrier reef, and hundreds of exotic species of animal life make this one of the last undeveloped stretches of coastline in North America. Boca Paila also hosts several luxury fishing resorts.

Route 307 intersects with Route 184 at **Felipe Carrillo Puerto**. The trip on Route 184 to Mérida is about 300 kilometers (175 miles) through jungle, ranches, and small settlements. Felipe Carrillo Puerto's main claim to fame is the role it played in the 1850s during the War of the Castes. The Maya at that time believed in "talking idols," so those living in Chan Santa Cruz, as it was then called, were not surprised when voices rose from the mahogany cross in the main church. The voices urged the people to create a new religion and go to war. Government troops arrived and killed the ventriloquist who spoke through the cross from a curtained chamber. The cross was destroyed during a battle. In the 1860s, the Indians began building a monumental temple of stone and mortar, which was never completed. The base of this temple still sits in Carrillo Puerto as a monument to the War of the Castes. There isn't much else to explore in this town, except the branch office of the Instituto Nacional Indigenista, a federal agency that helps Indians living in small jungle settlements adapt to modern times. Route 307 south from there travels through jungle inhabited by jaguars, boar, deer, and a few Indians.

The last Mexican town on the southern Caribbean is 400 kilometers (245 miles) southeast of Mérida and 380 kilometers (235 miles) south of Cancún. Devastated by a hurricane in 1955, **④ Chetumal** was rebuilt into a modern port city and appears newer and cleaner than most ports. The city was once a center of religious power. Now it is the capital of the state of Quintana Roo. Chetumal is visited by Mexican and Belizean travelers because of its status as a free port and major center for imported goods. There is an airport with flights to Mérida, Chichén Itzá, and Cozumel. Buses depart to other points in Mexico and Belize. Small local agencies rent cars and four-wheel-drive vehicles, but there are few major agencies. If you are renting a car elsewhere and plan to drop it off in Chetumal, be sure your agency has a branch there.

Chetumal is sometimes called "The City of the Red Soul"; in the Mayan tongue its name was *Chactemal*, meaning "where the red-woods (or dye sticks) grow," referring to the *chacte* tree, from which a red pigment is extracted. The port, located on Bahía Chetumal (Chetumal Bay), is a major shipping center for the hardwoods, such as mahogany, grown in the jungles. Many of the buildings and homes are built with red-hued mahogany, cedar, and yellow sapodilla, and have red tin roofs that glow in the light of the rising and setting sun. Most buildings are one story, with a few modern three-story government buildings and hotels. The wide Bahía Boulevard, lined with monuments and an old lighthouse, runs along the waterfront. The boulevard is a popular gathering spot at night.

The city is a free port and a haven for smugglers. For years there was no practical way to ship Mexican goods into Quintana Roo, and imports were exempted from taxes. Many items are still sold tax-free, and travelers heading into Yucatán or other parts of Mexico must first clear Customs. The shops along Avenida Héroes continue to sell goods that cannot be found elsewhere in Mexico, and the intrigue of the old days still hangs in the air. Smuggling thrives despite attempts to squelch it.

Chetumal is Maya, but has a mixed population with Caribbean influences. The music tends more toward calypso than mariachi, and there are communities of blacks and Middle Easterners who add an exotic flare to the city life. The food is also a mix of Yucatecan, Mexican, and Middle Eastern, and the most common dish is beans and rice with chicken, vegetables, and coconut milk. The traditional dish, *tikinchic*, includes grilled fish, rice seasoned with sour orange juice, and achiote sauce, made from a local red spice.

Chetumal's proximity to Belize (formerly British Honduras) adds to its mystique. The cities in Belize are not nearly as clean and orderly as those in Mexico, and the country is still young and unexplored enough to be considered a true "adventure travel" destination. Travelers to Belize must pass through Customs at the border, and leave their rental cars in Chetumal. Rickety buses with wooden benches depart from the border for Corozal and Orange Walk. Day visitors should stick with Corozal, only 16 kilometers (10 miles) inside the border, where they can get a good shrimp lunch at Tony's Motel and a fair sense of the wildness of Belize.

Chetumal's bayfront beaches are as clean and white as those along the coast. Calderitas, 8 kilometers (5 miles) north of town, has the best swimming, and divers frequent Banco Chinchorro, a 42-kilometer-long (26-mile-long) coral atoll and national park two hours offshore that is littered with shipwrecks. To those so inclined, fishing is prohibited at Chinchorro. Chetumal's major water attractions, however, sit farther inland. The Hondo River runs alongside the borders of Mexico, Belize, and Guatemala. In its wildest parts alligators roam the riverbeds, and manatees breed. The Palmar and Obregón springs by the river just outside Chetumal have rustic resorts. Cenote Azul, a huge sinkhole 200 meters (219 yards) in diameter, is on the edge of Bacalar Lagoon. It gets its name from its clear blue waters, with visibility of 80 meters (87 yards) or more. The cenote is surrounded by lush vegetation; the underwater caves are popular with divers. Laguna Milagros, 14 kilometers (9 miles) west of Chetumal, is a lovely lagoon with a center island and a shoreline graced by palms and blooming bougainvillea, but most travelers prefer to go 22 kilometers (14 miles) north to **Laguna de Bacalar.**

Bacalar is known as the lagoon of seven colors. As the sea and fresh waters mix, the shades of green and blue intensify, and the border of dark jungle growth contrasts starkly with the clear waters. Water sports of all sorts are popular here. There are a few rustic hotels and campgrounds in the villages of Bacalar and Xel-Há on the southern tip of the lagoon. Restaurants and rental shops line the shores of the lagoon. Fuerte de Bacalar, a Spanish fort built in 1733 to ward off pirates, became a Mayan stronghold during the War of the Castes, and it now holds some government offices and a museum. It is a pretty place for a picnic lunch among the colorful flower gardens.

Sixty-eight kilometers (42 miles) west of Chetumal off Route 186 lies **Kohunlich,** one of the more recently discovered ruins, with its Pyramid of the Masks portraying the Mayan sun god, and one of the oldest ball courts in Quintana Roo. The pyramid is thought to contain the tomb of a Mayan ruler, but no investigations have been made. Archaeologists believe **Kohunlich** was built and occupied during the early classic period, from about AD 300–600. *Admission: $3.50. Open daily 8–5.*

Lodging

For prices, see price chart in Cancún lodging.

Very Expensive **Sol Pez Maya.** An absolutely idyllic fishing resort smack in the
★ middle of the Boca Paila peninsula and the Sian Ka'an biosphere reserve, the Pez Maya—now managed by Melia Hotels/ Grupo Sol of Spain—consists of only 7 cabañas and a small restaurant. The simply furnished bungalows, with small patios, are set back slightly from the endless expanse of white beach, palm trees, and sea pines. Management can arrange for superb boat trips for fishing, birding, or exploring the lagoons. The price is steep, but includes all meals, daily fishing, and transfers to and from Cancún or Playa del Carmen. *Reservations: Box 9, Cozumel, Quintana Roo 77600, tel. 987/2–0072 or 800/ 336–3542, fax 987/2–1599. Facilities: 7 bungalows, restaurant, beach, fishing boats. No children allowed. No credit cards.*

Expensive **Continental.** Nice modern architecture sets the tone at this downtown Chetumal property, conveniently located across the street from the market. A small fountain gushes from the multi-angled pool, which is next to the restaurant (offering a bargain on breakfasts). Room decor tends to be on the eclectic side, with yellows and oranges predominating; at least the floors are carpeted. *Av. Héroes 171, Box 1, Chetumal, tel. 983/2–1100. 64 air-conditioned rooms and 10 suites. Facilities: color TV, minibars, restaurant, bar, disco, cafeteria, travel agency. AE, MC, V.*

Moderate **Las Molcas.** At the ripe old age of 14, this is the grande dame of Playa del Carmen hotels. The rooms are large, colonial-style, and air-conditioned. The restaurant has an excellent view of the ferry dock and serves passable but pricey Mexican and seafood dishes. *Box 79, Playa del Carmen, Quintana Roo, 77710, tel. 987/21–100 or 2–1200, ext. 109–111; reservations in Mérida, tel. 99/25–69–90 or 305/534–3716. 35 air-conditioned rooms. Facilities: restaurant, bar, pool, gift shop. AE, MC, V.*

★ **Posada del Capitán Lafitte.** The Fuentes family has run this hotel at Punta Bete, 10 kilometers (6 miles) north of Playa del Carmen, for almost 20 years. Guests stay in 2-unit cabañas with ceiling fans. On the premises are a pool, game room, and restaurant. Sailboats and Windsurfers are available for rent, or you can equip yourself at the dive shop and go out to the great reefs offshore. If you prefer a more rustic environment, stay in one of the "luxury tents" next door at the American-managed Kai Luum Camptel, with which the Lafitte is affiliated (prices are about $20 less). *Turquoise Reef Group, Box 2664, Evergreen, CO 80439, tel. 800/538–6802 or 303/674–9615; fax 303/674–8735. 39 rooms plus 2-bedroom duplex cabin. Facilities: restaurant, bar, beach, pool, dive shop, car rental. Land/air, scuba, honeymoon packages available. All reservations (minimum 3 nights) must be pre-paid. No credit cards. Closed approx. Sept. 1–Nov. 1.*

Inexpensive **Albatros.** Owned and managed by Americans Bill and Sam, the Albatros (opened late 1989) is a homey set of 18 thatched-roof cabañas right on the beach, with hammocks hanging on the patios. The 1-, 2-, and 3-bedroom cabañas are gaily painted in pastel colors and have hot water and ceiling fans; purified water is available from large demijohns, and extra care is taken to keep the premises free of insects. *6 blocks north of ferry pier; Box 31, Playa del Carmen, Quintana Roo, 77710; no phone. 18 cabañas. Facilities: private boat, safe, restaurant, bar. MC, V.*

Campeche

The state of Campeche, which occupies the southwestern part of the Yucatán Peninsula, is visited primarily as a point of transit between Yucatán and Villahermosa, capital of Tabasco. Campeche City is a large port with the laid-back ambience of a backwater. Maya enthusiasts may want to detour to the ruins of Edzná, about an hour's drive east. Otherwise, there is little to detain you.

Campeche City

㉕ The old part of downtown **Campeche** is decorated with extensive and well-preserved colonial fortifications. The culinary specialty of Campeche is fresh shrimp, and the city's seafood is known throughout Mexico. In Mayan times Campeche was a village called Ah Kin Pech, from which the Spaniards took the name Campeche. The Spaniards got their first permanent foothold on the peninsula in 1540, when Francisco de Montejo the Younger established a city there. In 1668, five years after Campeche was burned to the ground by buccaneers, the Spaniards began building an extensive network of fortifications to protect the city. Most of Campeche's sights are within the old walled city in the center of town. The wall surrounded a section of the city seven blocks by nine blocks that contained the main square and the cathedral. At the west side of the wall is the **Regional Museum,** which has a small collection of Mayan sculptures, masks, and stelae from around Campeche. *Open daily 8–5.*

At each corner of the walled city stand small *baluartes* (fortresses), which have been converted into museums, arts and crafts shops, and gardens. On the pleasant main square sits the imposing **Cathedral of the Conception,** the oldest church on the peninsula, constructed between 1540 and 1850. Other worthwhile attractions include the colonial mansions on Calle 59, Mansión Carvajal, and the Church of San Román.

Although Campeche is known for its fresh seafood, it's very hard to find a passable restaurant in the old town. Your best bet is to try one of the modern hotels on Avenida 16 de Septiembre.

Lodging   For prices, see the price chart in Cancún lodging.

Inexpensive   **López.** The Hotel López is straight out of a 1940s version of *Miami Vice.* It's built around a long rectangular courtyard above which are two stories of wildly curving balconies. The rooms (all with fans or air-conditioning) have yellow- or blue-tiled floors and walls and are outfitted with matching furniture that looks like it's from a *noir* movie. *Calle 12 No. 189, tel. 981/6–3344. Facilities: restaurant.*

Ramada Inn Campeche. The four-story Ramada Inn is the largest and most luxurious hotel in the city and is situated between the Gulf of Mexico and the old city. The restaurant is among the city's best. The rooms boast wall-to-wall carpeting, modern furniture, and terraces with a great view over the Gulf. *Av. Ruíz Cortines 51, tel. 981/6–2233 or 800/228–2828. 119 rooms. Facilities: restaurant, bar, disco, pool, shops, car rental, travel agency, parking. AE, DC, MC, V.*

Edzná

Sixty-two kilometers (38 miles) east of Campeche is the large Mayan site of **Edzná.** There is evidence of a settlement here as early as 300 BC, but the city really flowered in the classic era (AD 250–900). By the year 900 it had been abandoned, like many other cities on the peninsula. The main attraction is the **Temple of the Five Stories.** Situated on a large plaza, this structure is an early example of the Puuc style of architecture. The four lower stories have doors, some with columns, and many interior rooms. The temple on the top story is capped with a 6-meter-tall (20-foot) roof comb, once decorated with ornate carvings. Archaeologists have found the remains of an extensive drainage and irrigation system running through Edzná. This sophisticated network was capable of serving hundreds of acres of cultivated fields.

Of late Edzná has been attracting attention as possibly the place where the Mayan calendar—actually more accurate than the one the world uses today—may have been devised. The fact that the sun reaches its zenith over Edzná on what would be

Mayan New Year's Day has led to this theory. In other respects, the ruins, largely undisturbed since they were discovered, will impress only archaeology buffs. Edzná's restoration by Guatemalan refugees is presently on hold due to lack of funding. *Admission: $3.50. Open daily 8–5.*

Off the Beaten Track

The so-called short route to Mérida takes you past several villages and minor archaeological sites. **Hecelchakán,** 57 kilometers (35 miles) north of Campeche on Rte. 180, is known primarily for the **Museo Arqueológico del Camino Real,** an impressive collection of clay figurines from the Island of Jaina and stelae from the Puuc region. However, this pretty 15th-century town also boasts a lovely 17th-century church and ex-convent.

The Jaina figurines must be seen in Hecelchakán because it is not presently possible to visit the island itself, and in any case virtually all of these artful, highly realistic and intricate sculptures have left Jaina—most of them now located in Hecelchakán, and others scattered around the country's museums.

Spanish Vocabulary

Note: *Mexican Spanish differs from Castilian Spanish.*

Words and Phrases

	English	*Spanish*	*Pronunciation*
Basics	Yes/no	Sí/no	see/no
	Please	Por favor	pore fah-**vore**
	May I?	¿Me permite?	may pair-**mee**-tay
	Thank you (very much)	(Muchas) gracias	(**moo**-chas) **grah**-see-as
	You're welcome	De nada	day **nah**-dah
	Excuse me	Con permiso	con pair-**mee**-so
	Pardon me/what did you say?	¿Como?/Mánde?	pair-**doan**/**mahn**-dey
	Could you tell me?	¿Podría decirme?	po-**dree**-ah deh-**seer**-meh
	I'm sorry	Lo siento	lo see-**en**-toe
	Good morning!	¡Buenos días!	**bway**-nohs **dee**-ahs
	Good afternoon!	¡Buenas tardes!	**bway**-nahs **tar**-dess
	Good evening!	¡Buenas noches!	**bway**-nahs **no**-chess
	Goodbye!	¡Adiós!/¡Hasta luego!	ah-dee-**ohss**/**ah**-stah-**lwe**-go
	Mr./Mrs.	Señor/Señora	sen-**yor**/sen-**yore**-ah
	Miss	Señorita	sen-yo-**ree**-tah
	Pleased to meet you	Mucho gusto	**moo**-cho **goose**-to
	How are you?	¿Cómo está usted?	ko-mo es-**tah** oo-**sted**
	Very well, thank you.	Muy bien, gracias.	**moo**-ee bee-**en**, **grah**-see-as
	And you?	¿Y usted?	ee oos-**ted**?
	Hello (on the telephone)	Bueno	**bwen**-oh
Numbers	1	un, uno	oon, **oo**-no
	2	dos	dos
	3	tres	trace
	4	cuatro	**kwah**-tro
	5	cinco	**sink**-oh
	6	seis	sace
	7	siete	see-**et**-ey
	8	ocho	**o**-cho
	9	nueve	new-**ev**-ay
	10	diez	dee-**es**
	11	once	**own**-sey
	12	doce	**doe**-sey
	13	trece	**tray**-sey
	14	catorce	kah-**tor**-sey
	15	quince	**keen**-sey
	16	dieciséis	dee-es-ee-**sace**
	17	diecisiete	dee-**es**-ee-see-**et**-ay
	18	dieciocho	dee-**es**-ee-**o**-cho
	19	diecinueve	**dee**-es-ee-new-**ev**-ay
	20	veinte	**vain**-tay
	21	veinte y uno/veintiuno	**vain**-te-oo-no

30	treinta	**train**-tah
32	treinta y dos	train-tay-**dose**
40	cuarenta	kwah-**ren**-tah
43	cuarenta y tres	kwah-**ren**-tay-**trace**
50	cincuenta	seen-**kwen**-tah
54	cincuenta y cuatro	seen-**kwen**-tay **kwah**-tro
60	sesenta	sess-**en**-tah
65	sesenta y cinco	sess-**en**-tay **seen**-ko
70	setenta	set-**en**-tah
76	setenta y seis	set-**en**-tay **sace**
80	ochenta	oh-**chen**-tah
87	ochenta y siete	oh-**chen**-tay see-**yet**-ay
90	noventa	no-**ven**-tah
98	noventa y ocho	no-**ven**-tah **o**-cho
100	cien	see-**en**
101	ciento uno	see-en-toe **oo**-no
200	doscientos	doe-see-**en**-tohss
500	quinientos	keen-**yen**-tohss
700	setecientos	set-eh-see-**en**-tohss
900	novecientos	no-veh-see-**en**-tohss
1,000	mil	meel
2,000	dos mil	dose meel
1,000,000	un millón	oon meel-**yohn**

Colors	black	negro	**neh**-grow
	blue	azul	ah-**sool**
	brown	café	kah-**feh**
	green	verde	**vair**-day
	pink	rosa	**ro**-sah
	purple	morado	mo-**rah**-doe
	orange	naranja	na-**rahn**-hah
	red	rojo	**roe**-hoe
	white	blanco	**blahn**-koh
	yellow	amarillo	ah-mah-**ree**-yoh

Days of the Week	Sunday	domingo	doe-**meen**-goh
	Monday	lunes	**loo**-ness
	Tuesday	martes	**mahr**-tess
	Wednesday	miércoles	me-**air**-koh-less
	Thursday	jueves	who-**ev**-ess
	Friday	viernes	vee-**air**-ness
	Saturday	sábado	**sah**-bah-doe

Months	January	enero	eh-**neh**-ro
	February	febrero	feh-**brair**-oh
	March	marzo	**mahr**-so
	April	abril	ah-**breel**
	May	mayo	**my**-oh
	June	junio	**hoo**-nee-oh
	July	julio	**who**-lee-yoh
	August	agosto	ah-**ghost**-toe
	September	septiembre	sep-tee-**em**-breh
	October	octubre	oak-**too**-breh
	November	noviembre	no-vee-**em**-breh
	December	diciembre	dee-see-**em**-breh

| Useful phrases | Do you speak English? | ¿Habla usted inglés? | **ah**-blah oos-**ted** in-**glehs**? |

I don't speak Spanish	No hablo español	no **ah**-blow es-pahn-**yol**
I don't understand (you)	No entiendo	no en-tee-**en**-doe
I understand (you)	Entiendo	en-tee-**en**-doe
I don't know	No sé	no **say**
I am American/ British	Soy americano(a)/ inglés(a)	soy ah-meh-ree-**kah**-no(ah)/ in-**glace**(ah)
What's your name? My name is . . .	¿Cómo se llama usted? Me llamo . . .	**koh**-mo say **yah**-mah oos-**ted**? may **yah**-moh
What time is it?	¿Qué hora es?	keh **o**-rah es?
It is one, two, three . . . o'clock.	Es la una; son las dos, tres	es la **oo**-nah/sone lahs dose, trace
Yes, please/No, thank you	Sí, por favor/No, gracias	**see** pore fah-**vor**/no **grah**-see-us
How?	¿Cómo?	**koh**-mo?
When?	¿Cuándo?	**kwahn**-doe?
This/Next week	Esta semana/ la semana que entra	**es**-tah seh-**mah**-nah/lah say-**mah**-nah keh en-trah
This/Next month	Este mes/el próximo mes	**es**-tay mehs/el **proke**-see-mo mehs
This/Next year	Este año/el año que viene	**es**-tay **ahn**-yo/el **ahn**-yo keh vee-**yen**-ay
Yesterday/today/ tomorrow	Ayer/hoy/mañana	ah-**yair**/oy/mahn-**yah**-nah
This morning/ afternoon	Esta mañana/tarde	**es**-tah mahn-**yah**-nah/**tar**-day
Tonight	Esta noche	**es**-tah **no**-cheh
What?	¿Qué?	keh?
What is it?	¿Qué es esto?	keh es **es**-toe
Why?	¿Por qué?	pore **keh**
Who?	¿Quién?	kee-**yen**
Where is . . . ? the train station? the subway station? the bus stop? the post office? the bank? the . . . hotel? the store?	¿Dónde está . . . ? la estación del tren? la estación del Metro? la parada del autobús? la oficina de correos? el banco? el hotel . . . ? la tienda . . . ?	**dohn**-day es-**tah** la es-tah-see-**on** del **train** la es-ta-see-**on** del **meh**-tro la pah-**rah**-dah del oh-toe-**boos** la oh-fee-**see**-nah day koh-**reh**-os el **bahn**-koh el oh-**tel** la tee-**en**-dah

the cashier?	la caja?	la **kah**-hah
the . . . museum?	el museo . . . ?	el moo-**seh**-oh
the hospital?	el hospital?	el ohss-pea-**tal**
the elevator?	el ascensor?	el ah-**sen**-sore
the bathroom?	el baño?	el **bahn**-yoh

Here/there	Aquí/allá	ah-**key**/ah-**yah**

Open/closed	Abierto/cerrado	ah-be-**er**-toe/ ser-**ah**-doe

Left/right	Izquierda/derecha	iss-key-**er**-dah/ dare-**eh**-chah

Straight ahead	Derecho	der-**eh**-choh

Is it near/far?	¿Está cerca/lejos?	es-**tah** sair-kah/ **leh**-hoss

I'd like . . .	Quisiera . . .	kee-see-air-ah
a room	un cuarto/una habitación	oon **kwahr**-toe/ oo-nah ah-bee- tah-see-**on**
the key	la llave	lah **yah**-vay
a newspaper	un periódico	oon pear-ee-**oh**- dee-koh
a stamp	un timbre de correo	oon **team**-bray day koh-**reh**-oh

I'd like to buy . . .	Quisiera comprar . . .	kee-see-**air**-ah kohm-**prahr**
cigarettes	cigarrillo	ce-gar-**reel**-oh
matches	cerillos	ser-ee-ohs
a dictionary	un diccionario	oon deek-see-oh- **nah**-ree-oh
soap	jabón	hah-**bone**
a map	un mapa	oon **mah**-pah
a magazine	una revista	**oon**-ah reh-**veess**-tah
paper	papel	pah-**pel**
envelopes	sobres	so-**brace**
a postcard	una tarjeta postal	**oon**-ah tar-**het**-ah post-**ahl**

How much is it?	¿Cuánto cuesta?	**kwahn**-toe **kwes**-tah

It's expensive/ cheap	Está caro/barato	es-**tah** kah-roh/ bah-**rah**-toe

A little/a lot	Un poquito/ mucho . . .	oon poh-**kee**-toe/ **moo**-choh

More/less	Más/menos	mahss/**men**-ohss

Enough/too much/too little	Suficiente/de- masiado/muy poco	soo-fee-see-**en**-tay/ day-mah-see-**ah**- doe/**moo**-ee **poh**-koh

Telephone	Teléfono	tel-**ef**-oh-no

Telegram	Telegrama	teh-leh-**grah**-mah

I am ill/sick	Estoy enfermo(a)	es-**toy** en-**fair**-moh(ah)

Please call a doctor	Por favor llame un médico	pore fa-**vor** ya-may oon **med**-ee-koh
Help!	¡Auxilio! ¡Ayuda!	owk-**see**-lee-oh/ ah-**yoo**-dah
Fire!	¡Encendio!	en-**sen**-dee-oo
Caution!/Look out!	¡Cuidado!	kwee-**dah**-doh

On the Road

Highway	Carretera	car-ray-**ter**-ah
Causeway, paved highway	Calzada	cal-**za**-dah
Route	Ruta	**roo**-tah
Road	Camino	cah-**mee**-no
Street	Calle	**cah**-yeh
Avenue	Avenida	ah-ven-**ee**-dah
Broad, tree-lined boulevard	Paseo	pah-**seh**-oh
Waterfront promenade	Malecón	mal-lay-**cone**
Wharf	Embarcadero	em-bar-cah-**day**-ro

In Town

Church	Templo/Iglesia	**tem**-plo/e-**gles**-se-ah
Cathedral	Catedral	cah-tay-**dral**
Neighborhood	Barrio	**bar**-re-o
Foreign Exchange Shop	Casa de Cambio	**cas**-sah day **cam**-be-o
City Hall	Ayuntamiento	ah-yoon-tah-mee **en**-toe
Main Square	Zócalo	**zo**-cal-o
Traffic Circle	Glorieta	glor-e-**ay**-tah
Market	Mercado (Spanish)/ Tianguis (Indian)	mer-**cah**-doe/ tee-**an**-geese
Inn	Posada	pos-**sah**-dah
Group taxi	Colectivo	co-lec-**tee**-vo
Group taxi along fixed route	Pesero	pi-**seh**-ro

Items of Clothing

| Embroidered white smock | Huipil | whee-**peel** |
| Pleated man's shirt worn outside the pants | Guayabera | gwah-ya-**beh**-ra |

Leather sandals	Huarache	wah-**ra**-chays
Shawl	Rebozo	ray-**bozh**-o
Pancho or blanket	Serape	seh-**ra**-peh

Dining Out

A bottle of . . .	Una botella de . . .	**oo**-nah bo-**tay**-yah deh
A cup of . . .	Una taza de . . .	**oo**-nah **tah**-sah deh
A glass of . . .	Un vaso de . . .	oon **vah**-so deh
Ashtray	Un cenicero	oon sen-ee-**seh**-roh
Bill/check	La cuenta	lah **kwen**-tah
Bread	El pan	el pahn
Breakfast	El desayuno	el day-sigh-**oon**-oh
Butter	La mantequilla	lah mahn-tay-**key**-yah
Cheers!	¡Salud!	sah-**lood**
Cocktail	Un aperitivo	oon ah-pair-ee-**tee**-voh
Dinner	La cena	lah **seh**-nah
Dish	Un plato	oon **plah**-toe
Dish of the day	El platillo de hoy	el plah-**tee**-yo day oy
Enjoy!	¡Buen provecho!	bwen pro-**veh**-cho
Fixed-price menu	La comida corrida	lah koh-**me**-dah co-**ree**-dah
Fork	El tenedor	el ten-eh-**door**
Is the tip included?	¿Está incluida la propina?	es-**tah** in-clue-**ee**-dah lah pro-**pea**-nah
Knife	El cuchillo	el koo-**chee**-yo
Lunch	La comida	lah koh-**me**-dah
Menu	La carta	lah **cart**-ah
Napkin	La servilleta	lah sair-vee-**yet**-uh
Pepper	La pimienta	lah pea-me-**en**-tah
Please give me	Por favor déme	pore fah-**vor** **day**-may
Salt	La sal	lah sahl
Spoon	Una cuchara	**oo**-nah koo-**chah**-rah
Sugar	El azúcar	el ah-**sue**-car
Waiter!/Waitress!	¡Por favor Señor/Señorita!	pore fah-**vor** sen-**yor**/sen-yor-ee-tah

Index

WHEREVER YOU TRAVEL, *H*ELP IS NEVER FAR AWAY.

From planning your trip to replacing
lost Cards, American Express® Travel Service
Offices* are always there to help.

MEXICO

ACAPULCO
Costera Miguel Aleman 709-4
748-4.55.50

CANCUN
Av. Tulum and Brisas, Suite A
988-4.19.99

COZUMEL
Fiesta Cozumel
Ave. Rafael Melgar, #27
987-2.09.74

GUADALAJARA
Plaza Los Arcos
Vallarta 2440
36-15.89.10

MANZANILLO
Agencia de Viajes
Bahias Gemelas
333-3.21.00

MAZATLAN
Plaza Balboa
Cameron Sabalo S/N
69-83.04.66

MERIDA
Paseo de Montejo #494
Por La 43 Y 45
99-28.42.22

MEXICO CITY
Paseo de Reforma #234
5-533.03.80

MONTERREY
Padre Mier 1424. Pte. Esq. Bravo
83-43.09.10

OAXACA
Viajes Mexico Itso Y Caribe
Dr. Aurelio Valdiviesco, No. 2
951-6.65.22

SAN JOSE DEL CABO
Tourcabos
Plaza de los Cabos Local B
684-2.09.82

Personal Itinerary

Departure *Date*

Time

Transportation

Arrival *Date*   *Time*

Departure *Date*   *Time*

Transportation

Accommodations

Arrival *Date*   *Time*

Departure *Date*   *Time*

Transportation

Accommodations

Arrival *Date*   *Time*

Departure *Date*   *Time*

Transportation

Accommodations

A GREAT TRIP STARTS HERE

Mexico. See it before you really see it.

Take a front row seat for your own Fodor's Video preview of the most intriguing sights, scenic landscapes, famous landmarks, and undiscovered treasures in Mexico. Plan out your route in detail as you watch and replay scenes of the places where you'd like to linger during your trip.

Your Fodor's Video also includes these useful travel resources:

• Travel Planner segment, designed to make you feel at home. Local experts serve as your guide and reveal cultural insights, logistical information and timely tips. Find out what courtesies to observe, and where to find the best dining, hotels and shopping... and more.

• Traveler's Handbook, a powerhouse of information that fits into your pocket for quick reference while you're in Mexico. It includes essentials like local maps, language glossary money matters, how to get around, and more.

Only $29.95. Approx. 80 minutes; Full color, VHS, Hi-Fi Stereo.

Order Today! **Call 1-800-669-4486, ext. 401.**

Or send check or money order for $29.95, plus $4.00 shipping and handling (CA & TN residents add applicable sales tax) to:

International Video Network
2242 Camino Ramon
San Ramon, CA 94583

INTERNATIONAL VIDEO NETWORK

You can also take a Fodor's Video tour of these exciting destinations for just $29.95 each

• Great Britain	• Singapore	• Hungary	• Bangkok
• Hawaii	• Germany	• Italy	• France
• Spain	• Australia		

Fodor's Travel Guides

U.S. Guides

Alaska

Arizona

Boston

California

Cape Cod, Martha's
Vineyard, Nantucket

The Carolinas & the
Georgia Coast

Chicago

Disney World & the
Orlando Area

Florida

Hawaii

Las Vegas, Reno,
Tahoe

Los Angeles

Maine, Vermont,
New Hampshire

Maui

Miami & the Keys

New England

New Orleans

New York City

Pacific North Coast

Philadelphia & the
Pennsylvania Dutch
Country

San Diego

San Francisco

Santa Fe, Taos,
Albuquerque

Seattle & Vancouver

The South

The U.S. & British
Virgin Islands

The Upper Great
Lakes Region

USA

Vacations in New York
State

Vacations on the
Jersey Shore

Virginia & Maryland

Waikiki

Washington, D.C.

Foreign Guides

Acapulco, Ixtapa,
Zihuatanejo

Australia & New
Zealand

Austria

The Bahamas

Baja & Mexico's
Pacific Coast Resorts

Barbados

Berlin

Bermuda

Brazil

Budapest

Budget Europe

Canada

Cancun, Cozumel,
Yucatan Penisula

Caribbean

Central America

China

Costa Rica, Belize,
Guatemala

Czechoslovakia

Eastern Europe

Egypt

Euro Disney

Europe

Europe's Great Cities

France

Germany

Great Britain

Greece

The Himalayan
Countries

Hong Kong

India

Ireland

Israel

Italy

Italy's Great Cities

Japan

Kenya & Tanzania

Korea

London

Madrid & Barcelona

Mexico

Montreal &
Quebec City

Morocco

The Netherlands
Belgium &
Luxembourg

New Zealand

Norway

Nova Scotia, Prince
Edward Island &
New Brunswick

Paris

Portugal

Rome

Russia & the Baltic
Countries

Scandinavia

Scotland

Singapore

South America

Southeast Asia

South Pacific

Spain

Sweden

Switzerland

Thailand

Tokyo

Toronto

Turkey

Vienna & the Danube
Valley

Yugoslavia